RULES FOR
WHISTLEBLOWERS

Also by Stephen M. Kohn

Protecting Environmental & Nuclear Whistleblowers: A Litigation Manual

Jailed for Peace: The History of American Draft Law Violators, 1658–1985

The Labor Lawyer's Guide to the Rights and Responsibilities of Employee Whistleblowers
(with Michael D. Kohn)

The Whistleblower Litigation Handbook: Environmental, Health, and Safety Claims

American Political Prisoners: Prosecutions under the Espionage and Sedition Acts

Concepts and Procedures in Whistleblower Law

Whistleblower Law: A Guide to Protections for Corporate Employees
(with Michael D. Kohn and David K. Colapinto)

*The Whistleblower's Handbook: A Step-by-Step Guide to Doing What's Right
and Protecting Yourself*

RULES FOR
WHISTLEBLOWERS

A HANDBOOK
FOR DOING
WHAT'S RIGHT

STEPHEN M. KOHN

Essex, Connecticut

An imprint of Globe Pequot, the trade division of
The Rowman & Littlefield Publishing Group, Inc.
4501 Forbes Blvd., Ste. 200
Lanham, MD 20706
www.rowman.com

Distributed by NATIONAL BOOK NETWORK

Copyright © 2023 Stephen M. Kohn

British Library Cataloguing in Publication Information available

Library of Congress Cataloging-in-Publication Data
Names: Kohn, Stephen M. (Stephen Martin), author.
Title: Rules for whistleblowers : a handbook for doing what's right /
  Stephen M. Kohn.
Other titles: Whistleblower's handbook
Description: Essex, Connecticut : Lyons Press, [2023] | Includes
  bibliographical references and index. | Summary: "An updated edition of
  the first-ever consumer guide to whistleblowing by the nation's leading
  whistleblower attorney"— Provided by publisher.
Identifiers: LCCN 2022034617 (print) | LCCN 2022034618 (ebook) | ISBN
  9781493072804 (hardback) | ISBN 9781493059263 (paperback) | ISBN
  9781493059256 (epub)
Subjects: LCSH: Whistle blowing—Law and legislation—United States.
Classification: LCC KF3471 .K646 2023 (print) | LCC KF3471 (ebook) | DDC
  344.7301/2596—dc23/eng/20230105
LC record available at https://lccn.loc.gov/2022034617
LC ebook record available at https://lccn.loc.gov/2022034618

♾️™ The paper used in this publication meets the minimum requirements of American National Standard for Information Sciences—Permanence of Paper for Printed Library Materials, ANSI/ NISO Z39.48-1992.

This book is not a substitute for obtaining advice from an attorney. Every effort has been taken to ensure that the information in this book is accurate as of the date of publication, but legislatures can (and do) change the scope of legal protections, and courts often differ when interpreting legal rights. The circumstances surrounding every person's individual case are unique. If you have a legal issue, you should contact an attorney.

To my wife, Leslie M. Rose

He who exercises no forethought but makes light of his opponents is sure to be captured by them.

—Sun Tzu, Art of War

Contents

Acknowledgments, ix

Foreword by Sherron Watkins, xi

Introduction: The Revolutionary Roots of Modern Whistleblowing, xv

PART I: THE NEW RULES FOR WHISTLEBLOWERS, 1

Rule 1: In with the New—Out with the Old! 3

Rule 2: Be Confidential, 7

Rule 3: Don't Leave Money on the Table, 13

Rule 4: "It Takes a Rogue to Catch a Rogue," 21

Rule 5: Avoid the Traps, 25

Trap #1: Doing the "Right Thing" Is Not Enough, 25

Trap #2: Thinking Whistleblowing Is an Employment Dispute, 27

Trap #3: Ignoring Powerful Tools, 28

Trap #4: Delay, 32

Trap #5: Denial, 34

Rule 6: Think Globally, 37

PART II: TACTICS YOU NEED TO KNOW, 49

Rule 7: Protect Yourself, 51

Rule 8: Document, Document, Document, 57

Rule 9: Should You Tape?, 61

Rule 10: Know the Limits of "Hotlines," 65

Rule 11: Don't Let the Lawyers Throw You Under the Bus, 71

Rule 12: Don't Tip Off the Crooks, 77

Rule 13: Special Rules for Directors, Partners, or Auditors, 81

Rule 14: Don't Fear NDAs, 89

Rule 15: Talking to the Press, 95

PART III: REWARDS—THE LAWS, 103

Rule 16: Follow the Money, 105

Rule 17: The False Claims Act Reborn—With a Vengeance, 113

Rule 18: Tax Evasion and Underpayments: Report to the IRS, 127

Rule 19: Dodd-Frank (Securities and Commodities): Report to the SEC/CFTC, 137

Rule 20: Foreign Corruption and Bribery: Report to the SEC/CFTC, 155

Rule 21: Money Laundering and Sanctions-Busting: Report to FinCEN/Treasury, 167

Rule 22: Auto Safety: Report to the DOT, 177

Rule 23: Whistleblowing on the High Seas: Report to the Coast Guard, 183

Rule 24: Wildlife Trafficking, IUU Fishing, and Deforestation: Report to FWS, 189

Rule 25: Don't Think Small, 193

PART IV: RETALIATION—FIGHTING BACK, 197

Rule 26: Find the Federal Law That Works, 199

Rule 27: Don't Forget State Laws, 215

Rule 28: Government Retaliation: Use the First Amendment, 221

Rule 29: Federal Employees Are Special, 225

Rule 30: The Danger Zone: National Security Whistleblowing, 233

Rule 31: Winning a Case, 239

Rule 32: Your Disclosures Must Be Protected under Law, 247

Rule 33: Make Discovery Your Best Friend, 255

Rule 34: Prove Motive and Pretext, 259

Rule 35: Truth Is Power, 265

Rule 36: The Boss Must Make You Whole, 269

Rule 37: How to Afford a Lawyer, 273

CONCLUSION: CAN WHISTLEBLOWERS DRIVE A SPIKE THROUGH THE HEART OF CORRUPTION? 277

PART V: CHECKLISTS, 293

Checklist 1: Whistleblower Reward Laws (*Qui Tam*), 293

Checklist 2: Whistleblower Protections under Federal Law, 297

Checklist 3: Proof of Retaliation, 309

Checklist 4: Discovery, 321

Checklist 5: Violations Actionable under Dodd-Frank, 329

Annotated Chapter Sources, 331
Contacts for Whistleblowers, 397
Index, 399

Acknowledgments

Special thanks are owed to the founding partners of my law firm and the founding directors of the National Whistleblower Center, Michael D. Kohn and David K. Colapinto, who have courageously worked with me for many years fighting for whistleblowers. Additional thanks to my law partners Mary Jane Wilmoth and Todd Yoder, and the directors, fellows, and staff of the National Whistleblower Center and Whistleblower Network News—Siri Nelson, Jane Turner, Frederic Whitehurst, Cheryl Whitehurst, Mark Toney, and Gina Green. Special recognition to Grace Schepis, who worked with me to design the figures used in the book and proofread the manuscript, to Joseph Orr for assisting in the online law library for whistleblowers, and to my numerous law clerks and students who contributed to the content of this book through their research and assistance over the years.

Without the love, support, and inspiration from my entire family—Leslie Rose, Nataleigh Kohn, Max Kohn, Arthur A. Kohn, Michael Rose, Tom Lehman, Kaitlyn Conway, Louisa Rose Lehman, and Ana Maria Ramos Kohn—this book would not have been written. My late father, mother, and sister, Arthur H. Kohn, Corinne M. Kohn, and Estelle Kohn, taught me with the values necessary to fight for whistleblowers. My father's sacrifices for his country during World War II, and my mother's commitment to equal justice, guide my efforts every single day.

I would be remiss not to acknowledge the teachers, lawyers, and judges, some who are alive and others who have passed, who were my mentors: Howard Zinn, William Worthy, Hon. A. Leon Higginbotham Jr., Hon. Frederic Brown, Mary Jo Buhle, David Niblack, and many others. Finally, thanks to my agent, Rita Rosenkranz, and Lyons Press editors Rick Rinehart, Meredith Dias, and Brittany Stoner for doing all they do to make a book come to life. Thanks also to copy editor Ann Seifert, proofreaders Ashley Benning and Susan Higgins, layout artist Sue Murray, and indexer Jay Kreider for their hard work.

—*Stephen M. Kohn*
Washington, DC

Foreword

Stephen Kohn has been a committed champion and defender of whistleblowers for over four decades. He sees each whistleblower in all their humanity, their courage, their integrity, their fears, their grief, loss, and betrayal, and he fights for them to regain some semblance of their former life. Sometimes that includes a monetary reward through whistleblower programs, but it always includes emotional support and the sense of relief that comes when a wise, hardworking, and knowledgeable expert is now on their side.

His new book, *Rules for Whistleblowers*, is a fantastic resource for whistleblowers and supporters, whether that be family, friends, and attorneys to those on Capitol Hill and within the government and regulatory organizations tasked with protecting the public.

Whistleblowers are a check on abuse of power. They speak truth to power and to those who have the ability to hold power accountable. Too often, truth-tellers are quashed by powerful organizations behaving badly. Whistleblowers are too often ignored by media and even the regulators or authorities to whom they report problems.

Rules for Whistleblowers includes heartbreaking stories of truth-tellers who were not ready for the retaliation, the attacks on their character, or the lies and misinformation produced against them. Education and preparation are critical, and Kohn provides both in *Rules for Whistleblowers*; it is the go-to for anyone facing an ethical dilemma in their workplace.

Just over twenty years ago, in August 2001, I reported my fears that Enron would implode in a wave of accounting scandals to CEO Ken Lay. Although my warnings seemed to fall on deaf ears, Enron did "get rid of" the fraudulent accounting structures I was worried about—just not in an acceptable way. Enron announced that "a previously disclosed set of related party transactions" was being reversed and unwound, which would reduce earnings by hundreds of millions—but not to worry, this was a non-cash write off. This oddly worded announcement was made at the very end of the third quarter earnings call on October 16, 2001. Less than two months after the announcement, Enron did implode, as I feared, from accounting scandals. My memos and evidence that I had provided to Ken Lay were discovered in a box of subpoenaed documents by one of the several U.S. congressional committees investigating Enron's demise, and I was called to testify in early 2002.

During this same turbulent time for Enron and me, our country was attacked on 9/11. By December 2001, those responsible for orchestrating the terrorist attacks on the World Trade Center and the Pentagon had not been found or held to account. With Enron's demise, followed quickly by the bankruptcy of WorldCom and scandals at HealthSouth, Adelphia, Tyco, and many others, the hunt for corporate wrongdoers (who were easier to locate than Osama bin Laden) became somewhat of a source of comfort for the country. Going after white-collar criminals was a focused and successful endeavor in the early 2000s. There are two dozen felony convictions of Enron executives and over a dozen more from other corporate scandals from that time period. The Sarbanes-Oxley Act of 2002 (SOX) strengthened the ability to hold corporate executives accountable and also introduced anti-retaliation protections for whistleblowers, both internal and external. However, the new legislation and efforts were not enough to prevent the Wall Street collapse of 2008, and as Congress investigated the whys and hows of that financial disaster, they actually researched the rejected SOX whistleblower cases and found that the Department of Labor (put in charge of administering the whistleblower complaints of retaliation), had ruled in favor of whistleblowers in only 17 cases out of 1,273 complaints filed from 2002 to late 2008. (See Jennifer Levitz, "Whistleblowers Are Left Dangling," *Wall Street Journal*, September 4, 2008.)

By 2008, Wall Street firms and large banks had created a quagmire in the subprime mortgage world, impacting the viability of our whole financial system, and they had successfully silenced dissenting voices by firing whistleblowers, smearing their reputations, and destroying careers. There had been no balance of power accomplished by the whistleblower protections put in place through SOX.

Congress's response was to include robust protections and a monetary reward program in the Dodd-Frank Act passed in 2010. These new protections are modeled somewhat after the False Claims Act, which has successfully identified and stopped fraud against our government for decades.

Rules for Whistleblowers goes into great detail about all the laws and regulations protecting whistleblowers, but key, in my opinion, is that "under the new laws, if the whistleblower decides to be a confidential or anonymous source to the government (her choice), she can avoid being stigmatized with the label of 'whistleblower.'"

This is a huge victory for whistleblowers; the ability to remain anonymous, combined with the ability to hire talented legal expertise (the monetary awards provide whistleblowers with an ability to hire legal skills), have finally leveled the playing field just enough to offer whistleblowers a chance to survive speaking truth to power.

Rules for Whistleblowers not only provides resources and helpful advice on the subject matter, but it also serves as a historical record of the success of whistleblower protection programs in the United States and throughout the world, pointing out that corporate and complex white-collar crimes are nearly impossible for outsiders to detect. Without inside connections to whistleblowers who understand what's been done and by whom and how, the perpetrators would never be held to account or face just consequences.

After I testified in Congress on what I understood to be accounting problems and leadership failures at Enron, the media response was very positive. One of my husband's favorite articles was by Art Buchwald. Writing for the *Washington Post* on February 21, 2002, "Whistle While You Work," Buchwald described dinner with good friends whose sixteen-year-old daughter exclaimed that she wanted to be a whistleblower. Buchwald replied, "That's an honorable profession, but you have to work hard to catch a person who is up to no good." The dinner table banter about the matter continued, with the father remarking, "You will have fifteen minutes of glory, and then you can't find a job," which was followed by the sixteen-year-old replying that "Sherron Watkins of Enron is my role model. All the girls at school think she's fantastic." The back-and-forth continues in a humorous vein both well-known and beloved of Buchwald. There was mention of TV cameras on the lawn day and night, *Today* show and *Good Morning America* interviews, but most telling were the comments about whistleblowing being a lonely business: No one will want to speak to you at the water cooler, folks will call you a tattletale, and you probably will lose your job and health insurance. A wise observation about the thousands of whistleblowers you've never heard of, and then the wisest of all observations from the younger brother chiming in that he would "rather be a crooked accountant. You make more money." In under five hundred words, Buchwald had captured a whistleblower's life—it's a risky endeavor with the uncomfortable truth that quite often the white-collar perpetrator gets away with it.

Stephen Kohn has dedicated his life to supporting whistleblowers and uncovering wrongdoers. I admire his tireless efforts to ensure that our laws and regulations and support programs to protect whistleblowers are as robust as possible. *Rules for Whistleblowers* is written for the truth-tellers who more than likely are not lawyers and have little to no knowledge of the dangerous waters they have waded (or often jumped) into; it is a resource that is accessible to all, and I highly recommend this book.

—Sherron Watkins, Enron whistleblower,
Time *Person of the Year 2002*

INTRODUCTION

The Revolutionary Roots of Modern Whistleblowing

We are friends to constitutional liberty; we love America; we are willing to give up every thing that is dear, and, if necessary, Sacrifice life itself in our ravish'd, bleeding, injur'd country's cause; but Sr. we are very unwilling that our own lives, and that the continental Ships, which might be of Service to the independent States of America, Should be, either ignorantly, or designedly betray'd.
—Letter from America's First Whistleblowers to Robert Treat Paine, signer of the Declaration of Independence
February 11, 1777

In the pages that follow, you will learn how whistleblowing has dramatically evolved into a cornerstone for enforcing anti-corruption laws. Examples will be given where the leading law enforcement officials effusively praise the contributions, sacrifices, and courage of whistleblowers. Likewise, rules will be spelled out on how whistleblowers can safely file complaints without committing professional suicide. Under many of these laws, whistleblowers can obtain compensation that was previously unimaginable, including multimillion-dollar rewards for providing information resulting in high-profile enforcement actions.

But before the modern rules governing whistleblowers came into play, it is essential to step back in time to the origins of whistleblowing in the United States. It is a remarkable story of how three signers of the Declaration of Independence, including one of America's most important Founders, worked together to ensure that whistleblowing would become part of the American ethic. It all began in Providence harbor, just six months after the Declaration of Independence was signed. By way of background, it brought into conflict Founders of the United States who believed in the "common law constitution" that guaranteed the rights of citizens to participate in their government, against the first head of the U.S. Navy, who had previously served as the commander of the slave ship *Sally*. During its voyage to Africa, Hopkins was responsible for brutally suppressing an uprising aboard that ship among the kidnapped slaves.

During the winter of 1777, the warship *Warren* was anchored outside Providence, Rhode Island. On board, ten sailors and marines who had joined the U.S. Navy to fight for independence from Great Britain met, not to plot a battle against the king's armies, but rather to vet their concerns about the incompetence and lack of moral integrity of the commander in chief of the Continental Navy, Commodore Esek Hopkins. Their boss not only held the top Navy job but also came from a powerful family; his brother, Stephen Hopkins, had served as a colonial governor of Rhode Island and was one of the signers of the Declaration of Independence.

These sailors were devoted to fighting and winning the War for Independence. They were revolutionaries, risking their lives to build a free and independent America; they wanted nothing more than to fight and defeat their British foes. However, they feared that their commander could not successfully lead any such effort and that his morality and ethics foreshadowed doom for the new American Navy.

On February 11, 1777, the ten whistleblowers wrote a letter pleading for help to Robert Treat Paine. Paine, a member of the Continental Congress from Massachusetts and a signer of the Declaration of Independence, was a well-known attorney and Patriot who had been called on by Samuel Adams seven years earlier to prosecute the British soldiers who shot innocent civilians in the Boston Massacre.

In their letter the whistleblowers reported numerous instances of maleficence and crimes by the naval commander, including an allegation that he "treated prisoners in the most inhuman and barbarous manner." But their most significant charge concerned his vision of human nature, which was predicated on greed and self-interest. They wrote:

> [H]e is a man, if possessed of any principles at all, possessed of the most dangerous principles conceivable, especially when we consider his Station, for he positively declares that all mankind are exactly alike: that no man yet ever existed who could not be bought with money; who could not be hired with money to do any action whatsoever.

Paine suggested that they submit a formal petition to the Continental Congress. Eight days later they did.

The American Republic was not yet one year old. There was no First Amendment protection for freedom of speech. There were no legal protections for any whistleblowers, let alone sailors and marines who intended to expose misconduct by the top commodore of the U.S. Navy in the middle of a war. Yet these ten men petitioned Congress in order to expose crimes by the navy's highest officer. They became the first whistleblowers of the newly independent United States of America. Their names were Captain of the Marines John Grannis, First Lieutenant of the Marines George Stillman, Second Lieutenant of the Marines Barnabas Lothrop, First Lieutenant Roger Haddock, Second Lieutenant James Sellers, Third Lieutenant Richard Marven, Chaplain John Reed, midshipman Samuel Shaw, ship's gunner John Truman, and ship's carpenter James Brewer.

Their petition was straightforward and written from their hearts:

On Board the Ship 'Warren'
Feb 19, 1777
Much Respected Gentlemen: "We who present this petition engaged on board the ship *'Warren' with an earnest desire and fixed expectation of doing our country some service. . . . We are ready to hazard every thing that is dear & if necessary, sacrifice our lives for the welfare of our country, we are desirous of being active in the defense of our constitutional liberties and privileges against the unjust cruel claims of tyranny & oppression; but as things are now circumstanced on board this frigate, there seems to be no prospect of our being serviceable in our present situation. . . . We are personally well acquainted with the real character & conduct of our commander, commodore Hopkins & we take this method not having a more convenient opportunity of sincerely & humbly petitioning, the honorable Marine Committee that they would inquire into his character & conduct, for we suppose that his character is such & that he has been guilty of such crimes as render him quite unfit for the public department he now occupies, which crimes, we the subscribers can sufficiently attest.*

Each sailor also signed personal affidavits to Congress setting forth specific instances of misconduct committed by the commander in chief that they had witnessed. These included allegations that Commodore Hopkins mistreated prisoners, failed to attack a British frigate that had run aground (thereby permitting the enemy to escape), and stated that he would "not obey the Congress" of the United States.

Captain John Grannis agreed to secretly jump ship and travel from Providence to Philadelphia and present the whistleblowers' information to the Continental Congress. On March 24, 1777, he testified before a special subcommittee of the Congress Marine Committee appointed to hear the whistleblowers' concerns:

Q: Are you the man who signed the petition against Esek Hopkins, Esq. by the name of John Grannis?

A: Yes . . .

Q: Commodore Hopkins is charged with being a hindrance to the proper manning of the fleet, what circumstances do you know relative to this charge?

A: For my part his conduct and conversation are such that I am not willing to be under his command. I think him unfit to command . . . his conversation is at times so wild & orders so unsteady that I have sometimes thought he was not in his senses & I have heard others say the same . . .

Q: Had you liberty from Commodore Hopkins . . . to leave the frigate you belong to?

A: No. I came to Philadelphia at the request of the officers who signed the petition against Commodore Hopkins & from a Zeal for the American cause.

Q: Have you, or to your knowledge either of the signers aforesaid any difference or dispute with Commodore Hopkins since you or their entering into service?

A: I never had, nor do I believe that either of them ever had. I have been moved to do & say what I have done & said from love to my country . . .

On March 26, 1777, the Marine Committee concluded its investigation and presented the matter to the full Continental Congress, including all the papers signed by the officers of the *Warren*. After considering the matter, Congress stood behind its whistleblowing sailors and passed the following resolution: "Resolved, That Esek Hopkins, be immediately and he is hereby, suspended from his command in the American Navy."

Congress listened to the voices of the whistleblowers and suspended the country's highest-ranking naval officer. John Hancock, the president of the Continental Congress and the most famous signer of the Declaration of Independence, certified the resolution and ordered that it be served on Hopkins. Hopkins remained under suspension for over nine months. He never appeared before Congress to refute the allegations. On January 2, 1778, Congress voted to fully terminate Hopkins's service, and he was subsequently removed from the U.S. Navy.

Unfortunately, the incident did not end with the commodore's removal. Hopkins sought revenge against the whistleblowers—both during his short remaining stint as commodore and after he was stripped of his command. Upon learning of the letters signed by the ten sailors and the fact that the information was being delivered to the Continental Congress, Hopkins sprang into action during his last days as commander. He used his authority to pressure the sailors to change their testimony, and he organized a rump military prosecution for one of the petitioners, Lieutenant Marven. Marven, a follower of Thomas Paine, was accused of being the "prime mover in circulating" the petition. Hopkins ordered Marven arrested and tried by a court-martial.

The military court consisted only of Hopkins's supporters, including his own son. Hopkins was permitted to personally question the accused. If found guilty, Marven's only appeal would be to Hopkins himself. Marven's sole crime: having "signed" "scurrilous papers" "against his Commander in Chief."

At his court-martial Marven stood strong. He did not plead for mercy or back down from his actions. Indeed, he readily admitted to his crime of signing the petition against Hopkins. He told the prosecutors that the accusations brought forth against the commander "were of such a nature that we thought it was our duty to our Country to lay them before Congress."

Hopkins grilled Marven as to who else had signed the petition and what specific information was provided to Congress. Marven would not turn in his fellow sailors or tip off Hopkins as to the allegations provided to Congress. Instead, he stated, "I refuse answering to that until such time as I appear before Congress or a Committee authorized by them to inquire into the affair."

It was no surprise when Marven was found guilty of treating the commander with the "greatest indignity" by "signing and sending to the Honorable Continental Congress several unjust and false complaints." Commodore Hopkins immediately affirmed the findings of the court-martial and ordered Marven expelled from the navy. America's first whistleblower was fired from his job.

It did not stop there. Hopkins was not satisfied with merely firing the ringleader of the whistleblowers. On January 13, 1778, the former commodore sued the ten whistleblowers for conspiracy and criminal libel. Hopkins demanded ten thousand pounds in retribution, and the whistleblowers could be jailed if found guilty. Hopkins hired a well-known Rhode Island attorney, Rouse J. Helme, and filed his "writ of attachment" in the Rhode Island Inferior Court of Common Pleas. Only two of the ten sailors, Shaw and Marven, were actually served with the complaint. The others resided outside the jurisdiction of the Rhode Island court and thus escaped the retaliatory lawsuit.

Even though the United States was still in the middle of its War for Independence, Hopkins used his resources and connections in an attempt to destroy the lives of two sailors who had had the courage to file allegations of serious wrongdoing with the Continental Congress. Shaw and Marven were both arrested, held in jail, and forced to post an "enormous bail."

Shaw and Marven were not "men of means." They had nowhere to turn, except to plead for help from the Continental Congress. On July 8, 1778, while being held in a Providence jail, the two whistleblowers wrote an impassioned letter to the Congress:

> *Your petitioners, not being persons of affluent fortunes but young men who have spent*
> *most of their time in the service of their country in arms against its cruel enemies since the*

commencement of the present war, finding themselves arrested for doing what they then believed and still believe was nothing but their duty, held to bail in a state where they were strangers, without connections that can assist them in defending themselves . . . against a powerful as well as artful person who by the advantages of his officers and of the present war hath amassed great wealth—do most humbly implore the interposition of Congress in their behalf in such way and manner as the wisdom of that most august body shall direct and order . . .

The petition was read to Congress on July 23, 1778. A special "Committee of Three" was appointed to review the matter. After seven days, the committee reported back to the Continental Congress. History was made.

On July 30, 1778, the Continental Congress came to the defense of Marven and Shaw. The Congress, without any recorded dissent, passed a resolution that encouraged all citizens to blow the whistle on official misconduct. Perhaps for the first time in world history—and unquestionably for the first time in the history of the United States—a government recognized the importance of whistleblowers in exposing official misconduct of high-ranking officials working for the government itself. The act of Congress could have been written today:

That it is the duty of all persons in the service of the United States, as well as all other inhabitants thereof, to give the earliest information to Congress or any other proper authority of any misconduct, frauds or misdemeanors committed by any persons in the service of these states, which may come to their knowledge.

The Continental Congress was also sympathetic to the personal plight of Shaw and Marven. The Founders of the United States understood that finding whistleblowers guilty of criminal libel was counter to the framework of the new republic. Congress authorized the government to pay the legal costs and attorney fees for Shaw and Marven, enabling the two men to hire the best counsel available to fully defend themselves in the Rhode Island courts.

Moreover, Congress did not hide behind government secrecy edicts, even during time of war. Instead, the Congress authorized the full release of government records related to the appointment and removal of Hopkins as commander in chief, as well as the various papers of the Marine Committee as related to the information provided by the ten sailors. No "state secret" privilege was invoked, and Marven and Shaw did not even need to use a Freedom of Information Act to obtain documents necessary to vindicate their whistleblowing.

Just like in modern whistleblowing, documentary evidence can make or break a case. The Founders of the United States understood this simple fact and made sure that Marven and Shaw had the necessary evidence to defend their actions before a jury of their peers. But the Congress went beyond passing a law endorsing whistleblowers. They spent scarce federal monies to defend and protect the sailors who had had the courage to blow the whistle to them.

With the help of the Congress, Shaw and Marven retained top-notch legal assistance. Their main lawyer at the trial was William Channing—a distinguished Rhode Island attorney who had been recently elected as the attorney general for the state. His father-in-law was William Ellery, one of the signers of the Declaration of Independence.

Ellery had attended the initial examination of Grannis when he testified before the Marine Committee and was the member of the Congress responsible for transcribing Grannis's testimony. After the Revolution Ellery, a staunch abolitionist, attempted to aggressively enforce the laws against the slave trade. His grandson, William Ellery Channing (the son of William Channing) became the most famous anti-slavery theologian in the United States.

The criminal libel trial lasted five days. Shaw and Marven "relied almost entirely for their case upon" the information provided to them by the Congress, including "copies of letters from President John Hancock and others" to Commodore Hopkins, along with the "depositions of the officers and men on the *Warren* who had signed the petition to Congress against Hopkins."

The jury ruled in favor of the whistleblowers. Shaw and Marven were vindicated, and Hopkins was ordered to pay their court costs.

In May 1779 the Congress "examined the accounts of Samuel Shaw and Richard Marven for expenses incurred in defending an action at law brought against them by Esek Hopkins" and authorized the payment of "fourteen hundred and eighteen dollars and 7/90 to be paid to Mr. Sam. Adams," of which $500 was set aside for William Channing. Samuel Adams, among the most important revolutionary leaders, and a strong advocate of the "Common Law Constitution" designed to protect the liberties of all persons, played an instrumental role in the whistleblower case. Although his support for the whistleblowers was in the background, Congress compensated him for his efforts. The philosophy espoused by Samuel Adams justifying the American Revolution was fully articulated in the Declaration of Independence and the Bill of Rights and vindicated by Congress's treatment of Marven and Shaw.

Despite his so-called court-martial, Marven also received his full sailor's pension for his service during the Revolutionary War.

That it is the duty of all persons in the service of the United States, as well as all other inhabitants thereof, to give the earliest information to Congress or any other proper authority of any misconduct, frauds or misdemeanors committed by any persons in the service of these states, which may come to their knowledge.
—Resolution of the U.S. Continental Congress unanimously passed on the 30th day of July, 1778

Whistleblowers and the Founders of the United States

It was not by accident that the revolutionary leaders who founded the United States and who voted to defend the *Warren* whistleblowers would enshrine "freedom of speech" as the first governing principle of the Bill of Rights. The First Amendment to the U.S. Constitution established this rule: "Congress shall make no law . . . abridging the freedom of speech . . . or the right of the people . . . to petition the government for a redress of grievances." But this constitutional right was not the only law encompassing whistleblowing enacted in the First Congress of the United States.

On July 31, 1789, the First Congress passed the first of eighteen *qui tam* laws mandating that whistleblowers (informants) whose information resulted in a successful prosecution obtain a percentage of the fines obtained from the fraudsters. These original *qui tam* laws are the precise laws that Abraham Lincoln and the Civil War Republican Party used as the basis for the False Claims Act. They are premised on the principle of empowering the people to enforce the law, and rewarding them when they do. Today the *qui tam* model is the basis for all of the most successful whistleblower laws.

The Founders of the United States looked toward the people to be a full partner in enforcement of law—and included *qui tam* provisions in the major revenue-producing laws enacted by the First Congress. Among the eighteen were reward laws targeting customs violations (still covered under the False Claims Act), bribery, illegal conflicts of interest, criminal larceny, and reporting improper lending by the Bank of the United States. These rewards generally were set between 25 to 50 percent of the monies collected from the wrongdoer.

Over two hundred years later the U.S. Supreme Court heard a challenge to the constitutionality of the False Claims Act's *qui tam* reward provisions. *Qui tam* was under attack by a host of powerful special interests, including the U.S. Chamber of Commerce, American Petroleum Institute, and various government contractors fighting whistleblower-initiated fraud cases. In an opinion written by Justice Antonin Scalia, the Court unanimously upheld the law's constitutionality, citing the *qui tam* laws enacted by the First Congress.

Qui tam puts teeth into the right of the people to expose fraud and misconduct. It is the modern framework for protecting people who courageously step forward and report corruption. Although modern whistleblowing is deeply rooted in the finest traditions of American law, the rules governing their use today are strictly twenty-first-century smart.

PART I

The New Rules for Whistleblowers

There have always been mixed feelings about whistleblowers and many companies toler-ate, at best, their existence . . . it is past time to stop wringing our hands about whistleblow-ers. They provide an invaluable public service, and they should be supported. And, we at the SEC increasingly see ourselves as the whistleblower's advocate.
—Mary Jo White, Chair of the Securities and Exchange Commission,
"The SEC as the Whistleblower's Advocate," speech given at the
Ray Garrett, Jr. Corporate and Securities Law Institute,
Northwestern University School of Law, Chicago

RULE 1

In with the New—Out with the Old!

The Old

Vera English worked as a technician at General Electric's nuclear fuel production facility in Wilmington, North Carolina. In 1984 she discovered dangerous radioactive contamination at her workplace. She marked off contaminated areas and reported it to her bosses. She also reported it to the Nuclear Regulatory Commission. The NRC confirmed her fears and issued a Notice of Violation to GE.

To her face, the bosses reassured her that she could always report safety issues. But behind her back they conspired to get rid of her. With the help of the corporate lawyers they decided to take advantage of the very short statute of limitations for filing a nuclear whistleblower retaliation case (which at the time was thirty days). Their scheme was simple but effective: Instead of firing her straight out, she was told that reporting the contaminated area had made her unpopular, and she was given thirty days to find a new position at the GE facility. The trick worked. She diligently looked for a new posting, but no one offered her a new job during the thirty days. She was thereafter fired. According to the company she was not fired for raising safety concerns, but simply because she could not get along with her coworkers and could not locate a new position in the company. English then filed a nuclear whistleblower case, well within the thirty days of being fired.

But GE had a plan. They asked the judge to throw out her case. They said that her thirty-day time period for filing a claim commenced when she was told to relocate, *not* when she was actually fired. The trial judge saw through this pretext, held a hearing on the merits, ruled that English had been illegally fired, and ordered her reinstated, with back pay and an additional $77,000 for emotional distress. He also ordered GE to pay all her legal fees at "market rates," which were far higher than any fee English could have afforded.

Don't celebrate too soon. GE held an ace in the hole. They appealed the case. They claimed that the thirty-day statute of limitations should start when she was told to find a new position in the company, *not* when she was actually fired. On appeal GE won. The fact that they misled her about a new position, and tricked her into missing the short statute of limitations, did not matter. After years of fighting, English was left with nothing. No compensation, no job, no career.

The New

Times have changed since Vera English was fired in the mid-1980s. The gross mistreatment regularly faced by whistleblowers led to increased protections. Slowly, Congress recognized the critical role whistleblowers play as insiders who witness corporate crimes that are extremely hard for outsiders to detect. One by one Congress enacted laws designed to reward and incentivize employees who take the risks inherent in becoming a whistleblower. Slowly, most of the worldwide publicly traded economy became covered by modernized laws designed to protect, incentivize, and reward whistleblowers.

Here's how the new laws work if you are fortunate enough to be covered. Imagine a corporate insider who witnesses fraud. She decides not to report the violations to her managers (whom she suspects may be involved in the crimes) and alternatively files a whistleblower claim anonymously and confidentially with the federal government. She avoids butting heads with her bosses and instead helps the investigators fully document the criminal violations. Her bosses never know she blew the whistle and don't know she is a cooperating witness with the Feds. Her evidence plays a critical role in holding the corporate crooks accountable. Her employer is found guilty and pays a $100 million sanction. Under the new whistleblower laws, she is fully protected and also entitled to a big fat reward. For example, under one such law (the Dodd-Frank Act) she would be entitled to a minimum award of $10 million (which could be as large as $30 million). She avoids retaliation by her employer because the company never knows she was a whistleblower. Although she could continue working for her bosses, she cashes her multi-million-dollar government check and opts for early retirement.

This is not a wishful hypothetical.

Under the new laws, if the whistleblower decides to be a confidential source to the government (her choice), she can avoid being stigmatized with the label of "whistleblower." The crooks can be held accountable. The whistleblower never has to file a formal lawsuit and fight the company's lawyers. The government runs the enforcement action against the fraudsters. If the enforcement proceedings are successful, the victims of the crimes can obtain restitution, the taxpayers profit big, and the whistleblower is entitled to compensation directly tied to the quality of her evidence and her willingness to cooperate with prosecutors. The decision to remain confidential is hers, and hers alone. Although there is nothing to stop her from disclosing the issues to her bosses or going public, the overwhelming majority of whistleblowers who use the new laws remain confidential. She is rewarded for taking the risk to become a whistleblower and for doing the right thing. If the laws work properly, she does not have to sabotage her career to obtain compensation and justice.

The success of these new whistleblower laws is stunning and almost unbelievable. Since the first modern whistleblower reward law was passed in October 1986, well over $100 billion in sanctions have been collected from corporate crooks triggered by whistleblower disclosures and paid back to taxpayers and the victims of the crimes. But that is just the beginning of the benefits. Experts estimate that the deterrent effect caused by the fear that whistleblowers will use these new laws to expose wrongdoing is well over $1 trillion in savings. Of the thousands of whistleblowers who used these programs, many were protected and compensated. Since 1987, the government has paid over $10 billion in awards to whistleblowers.

Today, tens of thousands of employees are taking advantage of modernized whistleblower laws. These cases bear little resemblance to Hollywood stereotypes or the sensational stories that dominate the headlines. Instead, a silent army of whistleblowers are changing the very landscape of corporate crime. The most powerful institutions have been caught red-handed and held accountable, all thanks to whistleblowers. These include such diverse household names as Boeing, Novartis, Cisco, CVS, University of Phoenix, Bank of America, Shell Oil, Pfizer, Goldman Sachs, Mayo Clinic, Lockheed Martin, The Scooter Store, Office Depot, Citigroup, Merck, Walgreens, Harvard University, OfficeMax, Princeton Review, Chevron, JP Morgan, UBS, Northrop Grumman, and Deutsche Bank. They have all paid the price for violating the law and ignoring their whistleblowers.

Know Your Rights Before You Blow the Whistle

The law and common sense are not joined at the hip. Whistleblowers face many traps. But there are strategies they can use to win big cases. Figuring out how to blow the whistle, protect your job, hold wrongdoers accountable, and qualify for a reward should be the first rule governing every case. The fact that thousands of whistleblowers have successfully used the modernized whistleblower laws, and that they have collectively obtained billions in recoveries, speaks for itself. The stakes are high and the bumps along the road can be devastating. Whistleblowers should not to be caught up on old stereotypes. They need to understand how the new laws completely changed the rules of the game.

•

RULE 2

Be Confidential

[T]he most effective protection from retaliation is the anonymity of the informer . . . the shield of anonymity is preferable to the sword of punishment.
—Chief Judge Elbert Tuttle, U.S. Court of Appeals for the Fifth Circuit
Wirtz v. Continental, 326 F.2d 562 (1964)

It is very simple. If the boss does not know who blew the whistle, they do not know whom to fire. Proceeding anonymously or confidentially is the safest way to report wrongdoing. This marks a radical change from the high-profile public disclosures that popularized whistleblowing over the previous five decades, often with disastrous personal consequences. You cannot terminate, blacklist, harass, imprison, or retaliate against a person whose identity you do not know.

But that is not the only advantage to remaining confidential. If your goal is to stop the violations you witnessed, or hold those responsible accountable for their misconduct, the best place for you to be during a government investigation is on the job. While working for a company engaged in fraud, you can act as a confidential informant reporting white collar crime. If you remain employed, you can continue to gather information and alert the authorities to any potential cover-up. Moreover, you do not need to "set your hair on fire" trying to get the company to mend its ways. Let government investigators do their job while you remain out of harm's way, collecting your usual paychecks or executive bonuses.

Even if you have left employment with the targeted company, remaining confidential lets you move on with your life without being branded a whistleblower. You do not have to upend your career or social ties simply to do the right thing. If the investigation is a flop and there are no sanctions issued, you are not blamed for being the "skunk at the picnic."

The Dodd-Frank and Anti-Money Laundering Acts, covering securities and commodities trading, foreign bribery, violations of the Bank Secrecy Act, sanctions-busting, and money laundering, all permit anonymous filings, as does the auto safety whistleblower law. This statutory right to file anonymously has proven extremely effective. After monitoring its whistleblower program for years, the SEC described the law permitting anonymous filing as "critically" important, "[encouraging] company insiders and others to come forward by lessening their fear of potential exposure."

Although the IRS does not allow for anonymous reporting, it has strict confidentiality requirements and a workplace culture that provides some of the strongest protections against revealing the identity of a whistleblower. In 2022 the U.S. Court of Appeals for the District of Columbia Circuit upheld a decision by the IRS to refuse to even confirm whether a whistleblower claim had ever been filed, even when the requestor did not directly seek to learn the identity of the whistleblower. The court ruled that even acknowledging the existence of a whistleblower filing could trigger a witch hunt and enable wrongdoers to learn the identity of the informant.

All of these laws also permit whistleblowers to obtain financial rewards without ever having to reveal their identity to the targets of their disclosures. Award decisions are issued without any public disclosure of the whistleblower's identity or the company that paid the sanctions. Details that could expose the whistleblower to harm are not revealed in publicly available court cases.

Confidentiality Expanded

The move toward protecting confidentiality started in 1986 with the False Claims Act. Under that law the initial whistleblower disclosure is filed in federal court under "seal." This means the complaint remains secret and is neither placed on the public docket nor served on the defendant. Instead, the complaint and a "disclosure" statement are provided confidentially to the U.S. Attorney's Office and the attorney general. They permit the government to conduct an investigation without the wrongdoer knowing the identity of the whistleblower or the evidence being submitted against them. These provisions encourage reluctant whistleblowers to step forward, knowing that their bosses will not *initially* know they filed a charge against the company.

The only problem with the False Claims Act's confidentiality provision is that it is not permanent. Once the government decides whether or not to prosecute the company, the whistleblower's complaint, under most circumstances, is taken out of seal and becomes a matter of public record. A whistleblower can ask the court to continue the confidentiality requirements, but that is not mandated by law and rarely occurs. In practice, cases are often taken out of seal as a matter of course, making the complaint and the whistleblower's identity open to public inspection.

Despite this weakness, the ability to initially file cases secretly enhanced the willingness of thousands of employees to take the risk of becoming whistleblowers. Over time the positive impact of the sealing provisions could not be disputed. The False Claims Act was soon recognized even by its critics as the most effective anti-fraud law. Given the success of the FCA's limited confidentiality provisions, when a new generation of whistleblower reward laws was born as a result of the 2008–2010 economic crash, the need for enhanced confidentiality was recognized by all those interested in creating effective anti-fraud programs.

The big change came with the Dodd-Frank Act, signed into law on July 21, 2010. Dodd-Frank created the strong confidentiality provisions covering whistleblower disclosures. It closed the confidentiality loophole in the False Claims Act, recognizing that secrecy serves the interests of government investigators, the public, and the whistleblowers, who often face harsh retribution. Under Dodd-Frank, any individual can *anonymously* report securities or commodities violations (or violations of the Foreign Corrupt Practices Act) to the Securities and Exchange Commission or the Commodity Futures Trading Commission and *remain* anonymous. The government not only has to keep confidential any information that could identify the whistleblower, but the whistleblower also maintains the right to shield their identity from the government itself. In this way employees on Wall Street could be assured that their identity would be protected to the maximum extent permitted under law if they lawfully reported corruption through the proper channels.

Confidentiality Explained

The procedure for filing anonymous complaints under Dodd-Frank and the Anti-Money Laundering laws is very logical. It protects the identity of the whistleblower, but also requires that steps be taken to prevent frivolous or abusive filings. A whistleblower who wants to keep their identity secret has to hire an attorney. The attorney has to confirm the whistleblower's identity and make a good-faith effort to ensure that the complaint filed has a sound basis in law and fact. The lawyer has to personally sign the charge filed with the SEC (or the CFTC) and affirm under oath that the whistleblower in fact exists and that the information filed with the government is the same information provided by the whistleblower. The lawyer is also required to have the whistleblower sign a copy of the complaint under oath, prior to the attorney filing the complaint with the SEC or the CFTC, and to obtain a copy of a photo ID confirming the whistleblower's identity. The signed complaint, along with a copy of the whistleblower's photo ID, is kept confidential by the lawyer but may have to be produced to the government at the time the whistleblower files for an award.

A complaint filed under Dodd-Frank or the AML and tax whistleblower laws are *not* similar to the typical complaints filed in federal or state courts. Both the SEC and CFTC have created a special form, available online, known as Form TCR. One word of caution: The TCR form is very easy to fill out and file online. However, if the whistleblower, without an attorney, files it on-line, the case is not covered under the anonymity provisions of the law. Another important tip: In order to qualify for a reward, you must file a TCR complaint. There are strict time requirements on filing these complaints, so the best practice is to file the TCR complaint *before* you directly communicate with any government office or the news media. Additionally, the TCR complaint process is the formal mechanism to request and obtain confidentiality.

Once a claim is filed anonymously or confidentially, the SEC and CFTC are required to honor the secrecy of the whistleblower throughout the entire process, including the investigation and the proceedings initiated to qualify for and obtain a reward. But there are some exceptions.

First, if a whistleblower's allegations result in a successful enforcement action and the whistleblower thereafter wants to apply for a reward, they most likely will be required to reveal their identity as part of the award-granting process. The reason for this limited disclosure is well justified. The government must make sure that the award applicant is qualified to obtain payment. For example, it has to make sure that the whistleblower does not work for the SEC or that the whistleblower was not convicted of the very crimes they reported.

Second, the U.S. Constitution permits persons charged with crimes to discover evidence that may be used against them in court or evidence that may help prove their innocence. The Dodd-Frank Act cannot override constitutional protections. Constitutionally required disclosures have rarely ever been used, as most cases settle before trial or the government designed its case without needing to call the whistleblower as a witness.

Since Dodd-Frank was passed, Congress has used its confidentiality and anonymity provisions as a model for other laws. These include both the auto safety and the money laundering whistleblower laws.

The IRS Joins In

The tax whistleblower law does not provide for anonymous filing. The tax whistleblower must sign a Form 211 under oath in order to qualify for a reward. But once that form is filed, the IRS is required to keep the whistleblower's identity strictly confidential. As mandated in the *Internal Revenue Manual*, the IRS must aggressively protect the confidentiality of its whistleblowers. This includes:

- "Personnel are required to treat the identity of the whistleblower and the whistleblower's information as highly confidential and to exercise the appropriate security precautions."

- "The identity of the whistleblower must not be disclosed to any other Service officials or employees except on a 'need to know' basis in the performance of their official duties.

The IRS treats whistleblower information under the same legal standards they use to handle other taxpayer information. These rules are among the strictest secrecy requirements governing any federal agency. In a landmark case upholding the confidentiality of tax whistleblowers, the U.S. Court of Appeals ruled that under the Freedom of Information Act the IRS was not required to release information that could identity a whistleblower. They were also granted the authority to refuse to provide any information about a whistleblower case, including whether or not there was ever a whistleblower associated with a finding of a tax law violation.

The confidentiality provisions available under Dodd-Frank and the IRS law make it far easier for employees to blow the whistle. The number of whistleblowers willing to file confidential or anonymous claims with the government speaks for itself. As of the end of fiscal year 2011, the IRS had 27,017 open whistleblower cases. The SEC received 12,300 complaints in fiscal year 2022 and, as of September 30, 2022, had registered a total of 64,700 Dodd-Frank Act whistleblower claims reporting securities fraud or foreign bribery. Of these, over 5,000 came from overseas. These numbers are staggering, and far greater than the number of employees who exposed wrongdoing under the older, more traditional laws that do not facilitate confidential filings.

Cases recognizing the need for whistleblowers to remain confidential:

- *Management Information Technologies v. Alyeska Pipeline*, 151 F.R.D. 478 (D.D.C. 1993) (hardships faced by whistleblowers whose identities are revealed).

- *Whistleblower 14106-10W v. Commissioner*, 137 Tax Court No. 15 (2011) (standard for proceeding anonymously in Tax Court).

- *Montgomery v. IRS*, 40 F.4th 702 (D.C. Cir. 2022) (case finding that IRS is not required to disclose any information about a tax whistleblower under the Freedom of Information Act).

Administrative procedures for filing anonymous or confidential reward claims:

- Securities and Exchange Commission, 17 C.F.R. § 240.21F-7 and 21F-9(a).

- Commodity Futures Trading Commission, 17 C.F.R. 165.3(c), 165.4, and 165.7(c).

- Internal Revenue Service, *Internal Revenue Manual*, Section 25.2.1.5.4.

Keeping Up with the Changes

To keep up to date on changes in the laws, whistleblowers should access the free online law library created by the author, located at www.kkc.com/law-library. The administrative regulations and legislative histories of these laws are posted there.

RULE 3

Don't Leave Money on the Table

We must ensure that whistleblowers are empowered to come forward when they see misbehavior; that they are appropriately compensated according to the framework established by Congress . . .

—Gary Gensler, Chairman of the SEC
Speech on National Whistleblower Day (2022)

No one becomes a whistleblower to advance their career. So why are most whistleblower cases litigated as employment cases? Why not view your case differently? Why not use laws that will hold the wrongdoer accountable and permit you to avoid the pain of suffering from discrimination and retaliation? Why not prevent the bosses from putting your performance on trial, and instead put their frauds and misconduct in the hot seat?

Under traditional employment discrimination laws, whistleblowers are compensated if they suffer retaliation. Damages are based on a "make whole" theory (putting the employee back into the position they had before blowing the whistle), and include items such as reinstatement, back pay, and damages for pain and suffering. In other words, the amount you are paid is based on how much you suffer. If the best you can do if you win a traditional whistleblower case is being put back in the position you held prior to blowing the whistle, ultimately the whistleblower always loses. You may get your job back, but good luck ever having your career fully restored.

The reward-based laws constitute an entirely new way to view whistleblowing. They are *not* employment discrimination cases. The reward laws permit whistleblowers to obtain compensation completely untethered to their employment status. Compensation is not based on how much the whistleblower is harmed, but instead on the quality of evidence the whistleblower can provide to the government. The premium is on a whistleblower coming forward with good evidence. There is no need to suffer for doing what is right, nor should you put yourself in a position where you can be subjected to retaliation. It is better to smile at the fraudster and say, "Yes, boss," while simultaneously serving as a confidential source of information to law enforcement.

In a reward case compensation is based on a percentage of the fines and penalties paid by the wrongdoer. The better the evidence, the higher the penalties. The higher the penalties, the bigger the reward. A whistleblower never needs to suffer.

For example, under the False Claims Act, if a whistleblower's evidence was used to successfully prosecute a case, the government is required to pay the whistleblower 15 to 30 percent of the monies collected in fines and penalties. In a Medicare fraud case, for instance, if the government collects a $10 million fine, under the False Claims Act the whistleblower *must* be paid between $1.5 million and $3 million in compensation. This is true even if the company never knew who the whistleblower was and the whistleblower kept their job. These mandatory minimum and maximum reward percentages are reflected in other modernized whistleblower laws: Tax (15-30 percent);

Securities (10–30 percent); Commodities (10–30 percent); Motor Vehicle Safety (10–30 percent);money laundering (10–30 percent); Foreign Corrupt Practices (10–30 percent).

The government pays: Whistleblowers are rightfully skeptical as to whether the government will live up to its share of the bargain when whistleblowers are incentivized to report crimes. Will they honestly investigate? Will they hold powerful corporate interests accountable? Will they pay whistleblowers?

We now have over thirty-five years of experience with reward laws. Based on the empirical data, the answer to all three questions is yes! A review of the corporations held accountable (many of which are the most powerful in the world), the amount of sanctions paid (sometimes in the high millions or even billions), and the awards actually paid to whistleblowers demonstrate that the government is honoring its side of the bargain. These laws are working better than ever imagined. The numbers speak for themselves:

- Since 1987, under the False Claims Act, the government has collected over $72.578 billion in sanctions from fraudsters and paid whistleblowers $8.619 billion.

- Since 2011 the SEC has ordered fraudsters to pay over $6.3 billion in sanctions and awarded over $1.3 billion in awards.

- Since 2011 the IRS has ordered fraudsters to pay over $6.39 billion in back taxes and sanctions, and paid whistleblowers over $1 billion.

- Since 2014 the CFTC has collected over $3 billion in sanctions from fraudsters and paid over $300 million in awards.

Figure 1 shows the growth in the SEC's whistleblower program. As the number of whistleblower-triggered enforcement actions expand and additional billions in sanctions are obtained by successfully protecting investors from fraud, the payout to whistleblowers also grows.

Figure 1

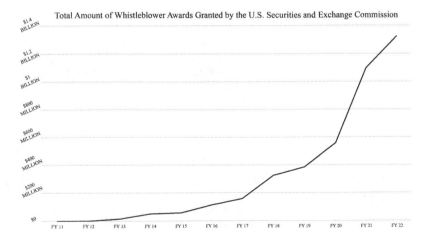

Total Amount of Whistleblower Awards Granted by the U.S. Securities and Exchange Commission

These new laws successfully align the interests of the whistleblower, the prosecutor, and the public, all of whom want to bring fraudsters to justice. The prosecutor needs the evidence the whistleblower has, and the public needs the prosecutor to hold the fraudsters accountable—a perfect alliance for achieving accountability.

Emphasis on being right: The next fundamental change in whistleblowing relates to the core concept of a protected disclosure. The original whistleblower cases created a firm rule: Whistleblowers were protected from *retaliation* even if the issue they disclosed turned out to be harmless or incorrect. A whistleblower's complaint only needed to be objectively "reasonable" or made in "good faith"; it did not have to be proved true. This legal principle, followed by every court, was based on the fact that employees would be very reluctant to ever report fraud or safety violations if they also had to prove their concerns were correct. The retaliation laws protect the act of disclosing information to the government, regardless of whether or not there is ever a successful enforcement action.

Reward laws are based on a completely different premise. The heart of the claim is the validity of the whistleblower's allegations. In a reward case, if the suspected violation turns out to be harmless or incorrect, the whistleblower gets nothing. Rewards are based on the usefulness of the information. Whistleblowers can obtain compensation if their allegations prove correct and support a government prosecution resulting in collection of sanctions from the wrongdoer. This is one of the reasons why the reward laws place a premium on confidential reporting—an anonymous whistleblower can remain an employee and continue to gather useful evidence during the government's investigation.

The massive amount of fines and penalties collected in whistleblower-reward cases demonstrates both the effectiveness of incentivizing insiders to report white-collar crimes and the fact that whistleblowers are among the best sources of information necessary to hold fraudsters accountable. Congress finally recognized that without whistleblowers, corporate crimes are almost impossible to detect and punish. Congress also recognized that the best whistleblowers can be those who never suffer retaliation, but instead remain imbedded within the corrupt enterprise, able to collect evidence for the Big Kill. Confidential informants bring fear into the heart of every would-be fraudster, as they never know if their coworker, co-conspirator, or "friend" may be looking for a payday from the government by turning them in.

Public reports issued by the Department of Justice (DOJ), SEC, CFTC, IRS, and other government agencies document how U.S. taxpayers and the victims of frauds have recovered at least $100 billion from whistleblower cases under the modernized reward laws. These massive payouts do not include the collateral benefits derived from successful whistleblower-triggered prosecutions, where the bad apples go to jail and their companies go bankrupt. In such cases there is often little or no financial recovery, but the public interest is served when crooks are held accountable and driven from the market. Likewise, in almost every whistleblower case where a corporation is sanctioned, the company is required to implement enhanced compliance programs designed to prevent future wrongdoing. Although the deterrent effect of such laws is not subject to scientific proof, various studies indicate that for every dollar collected as a sanction in a whistleblower case the long-term deterrent effects can be as high as ten or twenty dollars.

Crimes vs. Jobs: Under the old laws, whistleblower cases became hotly contested employment disputes. Employees allege that they were fired for making a protected disclosure. The company argues that the worker was fired for just cause, such as insubordination or poor work performance. Whether or not the underlying whistleblower allegation was proved correct is not even a required element of the case. A retaliation case is an employment case. The company's fraud is not on trial. Instead, the whistleblower is. The case places the employee on the defensive and centers on whether the whistleblower was incompetent or disgruntled and thus their termination was justified. Given the inequality of resources (i.e., the company usually has unlimited resources and highly competent attorneys hired to grind the whistleblower into the dirt), most employment cases are lost or settled on the cheap.

The reward laws change this narrative. The focus shifts. It is the company's misconduct that is on trial, not the employee's work record. This change helps the whistleblower. Instead of facing an embarrassing employment dispute, where the employer has an interest in digging up every piece of dirt against the employee, the goal in a reward case is to provide the government with enough evidence to prosecute the criminals and hold the company accountable for its violations of law. In an employment case the worker is never confidential. This is not true in reward cases, where keeping the identity of the whistleblower secret can aid in the successful prosecution of the crimes.

Impact: What happens when whistleblowers are empowered, protected, and rewarded? They become the single most important source for all fraud detection.

Why? Corruption is designed to be hidden. Unlike murder or robbery, a successful fraud, such as bribery, is hidden from public view. White-collar crime is accomplished in secret, with the goal that no one ever knows the crime occurred. There is no dead body, there is no outraged victim demanding justice. Without insiders who know the details about a bribe or a fraud, how can the government ever detect these crimes?

Figure 2 shows how an effective whistleblower program radically increases the number of reports. Two years after the Dodd-Frank Act was passed and the program was well-publicized, the SEC obtained 3,001 whistleblower tips (fiscal year 2012). By FY 2022 the SEC had obtained 12,300 whistleblower tips, and a grand total of over 65,000 tips as of January 2023.

Recognizing the significant contributions whistleblowers play in helping the government enforce anti-fraud laws, the government officials who manage the new whistleblower reward programs universally praise their effectiveness. In their own words:

- **Chair of the Securities and Exchange Commission:** The "whistleblower program . . . has rapidly become a tremendously effective force-multiplier, generating high quality tips, and in some cases virtual blueprints laying out an entire enterprise, directing us to the heart of the alleged fraud."

- **Attorney General of the United States:** The "impact" of the reward laws "has been nothing short of profound. Some of these [cases] may have saved lives. All of them saved money."

Figure 2

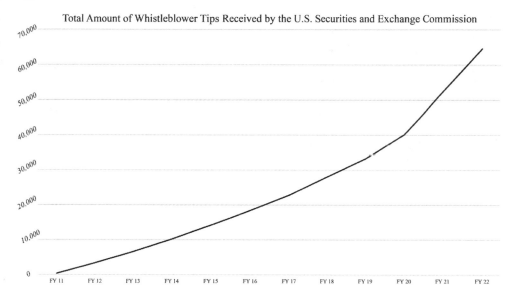

Total Amount of Whistleblower Tips Received by the U.S. Securities and Exchange Commission

- **Associate Attorney General** (responsible for civil fraud prosecutions): "The False Claims Act and its [whistleblower] provisions remain the government's most effective civil tool in protecting vital government programs from fraud. . . . The dollars involved are staggering."

- **U.S. Attorney,** in *U.S. v. Sun Ace Shipping*: "An award to these witnesses . . . encourage[s] those with information about unlawful conduct to come forward and disclose that information to authorities—information otherwise difficult, if not virtually impossible, to obtain."

- **Chairman of the Senate Judiciary Committee:** "One of the smartest things Congress has ever done is to empower whistleblowers to help the government combat fraud. They get results. . . . This is not rhetoric. . . . The False Claims Act is, hands down, the most effective tool the government has to fight fraud against the taxpayers."

Even the most notorious anti-whistleblower business-lobbying group, the U.S. Chamber of Commerce Institute for Legal Reform, in a 2015 report, lauded the False Claims Act as "the government's most important tool to uncover and punish fraud against the United States."

The reward-based approach to whistleblowing unlocks a powerful force critical to fighting corruption. It creates procedures that both promote insiders coming forward with high-quality evidence and provide the best protection possible for the whistleblower—compensation for doing the right thing.

Dos and Don'ts for Getting an Award

Once you have decided to participate in a whistleblower reward program, you should be guided by two principles: (1) Do not engage in conduct that will get you disqualified, and (2) do engage in conduct that will maximize the amount of your compensation. Because your case may take years to complete, a whistleblower cannot let frustration with the process undermine their eligibility for obtaining justice and the appropriate award. The IRS, CFTC, and SEC have published nearly identical information telling whistleblowers what they are looking for. These should be your guide in all reward cases.

FACTORS THAT WILL INCREASE THE AMOUNT OF AN AWARD:

- Timeliness of providing information

- Significance of the information provided

- Assistance provided to the government

- Reliability and completeness of information

- Saving the government time and money

- Providing "ongoing, extensive, and timely cooperation and assistance"

- Identifying other witnesses and encouraging others to assist in the investigation

- Letting the government know if you have suffered a hardship due to your whistleblowing

- Explaining why the government should have a heightened law enforcement interest in the issues you raise

- If you are able to take any steps to remediate the harm caused by the frauds or violations you reported

- If you help the government recover any of the fruits of the violations

- If paying the maximum award will enhance the ability of the government to enforce the laws, protect victims, or encourage others to come forward

- If you are disclosing an industry-wide practice

- The severity of the violations

- Whether the crimes you reported were isolated or ongoing

- Who was committing the violations and how high up the fraudsters are

- The amount of harm caused by the underlying violations

- Reporting concerns through a company's compliance program (The SEC and CFTC give credit to whistleblowers who have made internal reports.)

FACTORS THAT WILL DECREASE THE AMOUNT OF AN AWARD OR RESULT IN A DENIAL OF A REWARD:

- Your culpability or involvement in the violations you report

- If applicable, your background and experience when you engaged in the wrongdoing, such as your education, training, and position of responsibility at the time the violations occurred

- If applicable, whether you acted with "scienter"—someone with the knowledge that what you were doing was wrong—when you participated in the violations

- Whether you financially benefited from the crimes or were a repeat violator

- If applicable, the egregiousness of the underlying fraud committed by the whistleblower

- Whether you interfered with the government's investigation or enforcement actions

- If you have caused any delays in the investigation

- If you have unreasonably delayed in making the initial reports to the government

- Whether you failed to take reasonable steps to stop the violations or report them to internal or external authorities who could have stopped the violations

- If you have interfered with an internal corporate, legal, or audit process or otherwise delayed the detection of the violations

- If you have made any "material false, fictitious, or fraudulent statements or representations that hindered an entity's efforts to detect, investigate, or remediate the reported violations"

- If you have hindered efforts to detect, investigate, or remediate the reported violations

- If you have provided any "false writing or document knowing the writing or document contained any false, fictitious or fraudulent statements or entries"

- If you are convicted of a crime related to violations you have reported

As these lists indicate, eligibility to obtain a reward and the amount of compensation have little to do with your performance as an employee but everything to do with your cooperation with the government, the significance of your information, and whether you were culpable for the underlying violations. The laws are designed to help the government detect and prosecute crimes. It is your truthfulness and assistance that will be assessed in determining if you receive an award and in what amount.

PRACTICE TIPS

Part III of this guide covers the specific laws and procedures governing all the major reward laws. The criteria for judging the amount of an award is located at 17 C.F.R. § 240.21F-6 (SEC) and 17 C.F.R. § 165.9 (CFTC).

Keeping Up with the Changes

To keep up to date on changes in the laws, whistleblowers should access the free online law library created by the author, located at www.kkc.com/law-library. The administrative regulations and legislative histories of these laws are posted there.

RULE 4

"It Takes a Rogue to Catch a Rogue"

The bill offers a reward to the informer who comes into court and betrays his co-conspirator, but is not confined to that class. . . . In short, sir, I have based the [False Claims Act] on the old-fashioned idea of holding out a temptation, and "setting a rogue to catch a rogue," which is the safest and most expeditious way I have ever discovered of bringing rogues to justice.

With these words Senator Jacob M. Howard (R-Michigan) introduced the original False Claims Act on the floor of the Senate on February 14, 1863. Sixteen days later Senator Howard's bill was signed into law by President Abraham Lincoln. The seeds for all future whistleblower reward laws were planted. The basic premise of these laws, that it can take a "rogue" to catch a "rogue" has remained their centerpiece, critical for incentivizing real insiders to step forward and report.

Senator Howard's vision of empowering people to defend democracy was not unique to his support of *qui tam* laws. He worked closely with President Lincoln on drafting the Thirteenth Amendment abolishing slavery, and also served on the Joint Committee on Reconstruction that drafted the Fourteenth Amendment, guaranteeing all Americans due process and equal protection under law. Senator Howard was tired of contaminated food being fed to soldiers, sawdust sold as gunpowder, and blind horses being fitted for battle. He wanted to stop fraud in defense contracting so that the Union armies could win the war and his vision of a democratic America "of the people" and "by the people" could take hold. *Qui tam* was the tool.

Although the term "whistleblower" was unknown, the concept of using "insiders" to enforce the law was not. The False Claims Act used an old-fashioned law enforcement device known as *qui tam* to penetrate criminal conspiracies. The tactic had been used in Europe, colonial America, and by the first Congress of the United States to aid in the enforcement of laws by paying bounties. At the time of the Civil War, *qui tam* actions were widely used to enforce the payment of customs duties. Senator Howard designed a *qui tam* law to target fraud in government contracting. The newly minted FCA increased the penalties for fraud committed against the government (double damages), mandated that whistleblowers obtain 50 percent of any sanction obtained, and permitted "relators" (an early term for whistleblowers) to file their lawsuits directly in federal court on behalf of the United States. Whistleblowers could act as private attorneys generals and prosecute claims as if they were working on behalf of the government.

Critically, the law permits coconspirators to file cases. It recognizes that participants in the frauds often would have the best evidence needed to convict. Senator Howard lamented the fact that under the existing laws obtaining convictions were "entirely hopeless." But with *qui tam* incentives, the "rogues" could be brought to justice.

The clear intent of the original False Claims Act—permitting participants in fraud to become whistleblowers—has been incorporated into all modern *qui tam* laws. Just as Senator Howard understood, Congress continues to recognize that the best sources of information on white-collar and corporate crimes are insiders who can penetrate the otherwise secret conspiracies necessary for bribery, insider trading, kickbacks, illegal offshore banking, and fraud to thrive. The best insiders often have had a role in the wrongdoing, from a secretary who typed out a fraudulent invoice to a consultant who delivered a cash bribe. Any person involved in the entire chain of criminality, except those found guilty of the crimes or in most cases the "king pin," could file a whistleblower lawsuit. Inducing exceptionally well-placed informants to step forward remains one of the most important goals of *qui tam* reward laws.

Perpetrators of fraud usually need the assistance of others to accomplish their plans. This is an inherent weakness within white-collar crime conspiracies. Corporate crimes are unlike murder or robbery, which could easily be committed by a sole individual. Instead, corporate crimes almost always require a group of willing participants to cover each of the bases. Bribery, for example, always takes two to play. Money laundering requires someone who wants to hide their money and a bank willing to take the deposit. The reward laws seek to exploit this inherent weakness in large-scale corporate crime. Participants in frauds often know the inner workings of extremely complex and well-hidden crimes. If they can be induced to flip sides they can become an anonymous whistleblower and provide the government with the blueprints exposing the misconduct.

Permitting participants to obtain rewards is also the key to effective deterrence. When potential perpetrators contemplate committing a fraud, they need to fear the participant clauses of the *qui tam* laws. They need to understand that any of their cohorts might turn state's evidence against them in order to profit or protect themselves from a potential prosecution. Just think about it: If everyone sitting around a corporate board table knows that any one of their fellow executives can anonymously report a corporate fraud and potentially make millions, how likely is it that these officials will break the law? What better way to create a chilling effect on criminal activity than by making every participant in a fraud fearful that their coconspirators will turn them in and become rich.

The U.S. Securities and Exchange Commission considered enacting a rule to potentially exclude culpable persons (i.e., persons who participated in the criminal misconduct) from obtaining a reward. That suggestion was flatly rejected as being inconsistent with the statutory language of the Dodd-Frank Act and sound law enforcement tactics. The SEC relied on Senator Howard's 1863 explanation of the *qui tam* laws when it adopted its final Dodd-Frank requirements in 2011:

> [T]he original federal whistleblower statute—the False Claims Act—was premised on the notion that one effective way to bring about justice is to use a rogue to catch a rogue. This basic law enforcement principle is especially true for sophisticated securities fraud schemes which can be difficult for law enforcement authorities to detect and prosecute without insider information and assistance from participants in the scheme or their coconspirators. Insiders regularly provide law enforcement authorities with early and invaluable assistance in identifying the scope, participants, victims, and ill-gotten gains from these fraudulent schemes. Accordingly, culpable whistleblowers can enhance the Commission's ability to detect violations of the federal securities laws, increase the effectiveness and efficiency of the Commission's investigations, and provide important evidence for the Commission's enforcement actions.

But rewarding participants is not a black-and-white matter. There are gray areas, and all whistleblower laws contain various provisions either prohibiting rewards to whistleblowers convicted of the crimes they report or reducing rewards paid to "culpable" whistleblowers. Each reward law addresses whether or not the mastermind of a fraud can obtain protection, and no kingpin has ever been granted an award. One way criminal masterminds are discouraged from ever becoming a whistleblower is that persons who file Dodd-Frank or False Claims Act cases are not automatically granted immunity from prosecution. Without immunity, the risk of prosecution is just too great for true criminal kingpins.

Fear of prosecution can motivate some potential sources to step forward with highly valuable information. The government has little interest in prosecuting its *voluntary* sources, and rarely does. However, if the government learns about your involvement and requests to interview you (with or without a formal subpoena) *before* you file your whistleblower case, you will most likely be disqualified from obtaining any reward. Also, the risk of being prosecuted goes up if the government learns of your role in a criminal fraud before you blow the whistle on it. Being the first to step forward and expose a fraud simultaneously increases your change of obtaining a reward and decreases the risk of being prosecuted.

PRACTICE TIPS

- Senator Jacob M. Howard's statement discussing the intent behind the False Claims Act: *Congressional Globe*, 37th Cong., 3rd Sess., pp. 955–56 (Feb. 14, 1863).

- SEC discussion on culpable whistleblowers: 76 *Federal Register* 34300, pp. 34349–51 (June 13, 2011).

- False Claims Act authority to reduce rewards to whistleblowers who "planned and initiated" and exclude whistleblowers convicted of criminal conduct: 31 U.S.C. § 3730(d)(3); *Schroeder v. U.S.*, 793 F.3d 1080 (9th Cir. 2015).

Keeping Up with the Changes

To keep up to date on changes in the laws, whistleblowers should access the free online law library created by the author, located at www.kkc.com/law-library.

RULE 5

Avoid the Traps

[W]hen groups can select their members, individuals who report lies are generally shunned, even by groups where lying is absent. This facilitates the formation of dishonest groups where lying is prevalent and reporting is nonexistent.
—Ernesto Reuben and Matthew Stephenson, "Nobody Likes a Rat: On the Willingness to Report Lies and the Consequences Thereof," *The Journal of Economic Behavior & Organization*, Columbia University Business School

---

Trap #1: Doing the "Right Thing" Is Not Enough

Bosses who cheat for profit do not admit to their crimes. They cover them up. But if you think reporting misconduct at work will automatically win you a grand prize, think again.

One of the biggest mistakes shared by most whistleblowers is a belief that somehow doing the "right thing" will be rewarded. In fact, if what you are reporting is a real crime, those who stand to be found guilty have a strong motive to undermine your credibility, destroy your reputation, and remove you from your position.

Many whistleblowers find themselves in trouble before they ever suspect that the axe may fall. But if you realize the potential for retaliation before blowing the whistle and take steps to protect yourself, you stand a fighting chance to end up on top. Whenever you are thinking about reporting wrongdoing, first ask the following questions:

- What laws will protect me? Are they weak or strong? Do I meet their requirements?

- How strong is my evidence of wrongdoing?

- Can I report my concerns confidentially or anonymously?

- If I cannot be confidential, how good is my employment record? Could I win a wrongful discharge suit or are there enough past problems to make my case questionable to a judge or jury?

- Am I prepared to be treated poorly? Whistleblowers whose identities are known to the bosses should not think they will be treated like other employees or like they were treated in the past.

- Do I have documentary evidence to support my case? E-mails, tapes, reports, internal audit findings?

- Can I obtain a monetary reward?

- Can I obtain confidential expert advice from an attorney before I stick my neck out?

One of the tragedies for whistleblower attorneys is having to tell a client who "did the right thing," who saved lives or saved consumers millions of dollars, that they have already lost their case before it even started. This can happen for various reasons, such as missing a deadline, not reporting the wrongdoing to the proper office, or thinking that blowing the whistle to the boss or your compliance program is protected.

Just as bad is having to tell a whistleblower who has been fired and had their reputation smeared that they could have reported all their concerns safely and confidentially and avoided the wrath of the wrongdoers. But even worse is having to tell a whistleblower that they could have qualified for a large, multi-million-dollar award, but due to legal technicalities, they won't get one red cent.

Being right is not enough. Doing the right thing is not enough. Whistleblowers must take the time to ensure that their disclosures are fully protected and that the pitfalls existing in complex laws and regulations are avoided. Whistleblowers are now entitled to better protections against retaliation and have an opportunity to qualify for financial rewards if they disclose their evidence in a timely and lawful manner to the appropriate authorities. Due diligence is the new name of the game.

The ostrich approach of sticking one's head in the sand and hoping for the best does not work when reputations, careers, money, and jobs are on the line. Know your rights. Follow the law. Do not lie. Be prepared.

--------- PRACTICE TIPS ---------

- Ernesto Reuben and Matt Stephenson, "Nobody Likes a Rat: On the Willingness to Report Lies and the Consequences Thereof," 93 *Journal of Economic Behavior & Organization* 384 (Sept. 2013).

- An excellent book discussing what employees face after they blow the whistle is by Myron and Penina Glazer, *The Whistleblowers: Exposing Corruption in Government and Industry* (New York: Basic Books, 1989).

- Aaron Kesselheim et al., "Whistle-Blowers' Experiences in Fraud Litigation against Pharmaceutical Companies," *N. Engl. J. Med.* 362:19 (May 13, 2010).

Trap #2: Thinking Whistleblowing Is an Employment Dispute

Forget every preconceived notion you have about whistleblowers and their behavior. To understand how whistleblowing has evolved over the past forty years, you must rethink old assumptions and stereotypes. Even the term "whistleblower" now fails to capture the nature of modern-day whistleblowing.

In the past, whistleblowing came to mean high-profile public exposés calculated to call public attention to major scandals. But the new whistleblowing permits anonymous and confidential filings. Many whistleblowers still make sensational public exposures, but the majority of today's whistleblowers follow a radically different path. The new laws promote anonymous disclosures to shield whistleblowers from retaliation and permit law enforcement to conduct investigations without revealing their sources. Thousands of whistleblowers are taking advantage of confidentiality protections, and as a consequence, their cases never make the press, and their contributions are not publicly known.

Two very different systems governing whistleblowing coexist. One system is made up of old whistleblower laws based on an anti-retaliation model. The whistleblower raises a concern. The boss knows who the whistleblower is. The whistleblower is fired. The anti-retaliation law kicks in, and the whistleblower can challenge the termination in court or before an agency like the Department of Labor. The whistleblower is entitled to compensation commensurate with the damages suffered. These cases are often widely publicized. Most whistleblowers lose, as they are up against well-financed corporations that are able to hire top attorneys and use every trick in the book to smash the informant. Under the older laws a whistleblower case was usually synonymous with an employment case.

The new whistleblower laws defy the popular preconceived notions about who a whistleblower is and what they do. The focus is on using a whistleblower's insider status to uncover hidden frauds and misconduct. By protecting a whistleblower's identity the whistleblower can remain on the job and continue to assist in investigations. Compensation is based on being right, not on the amount of harm you suffer.

A growing number of the new laws, including those covering securities and commodities frauds, money laundering, and foreign bribery, permit whistleblowers to anonymously and confidentially alert the government to violations. The right to be confidential has created a new class of whistleblowers. Employees and other insiders can report wrongdoing, but the targets of their allegations do know who filed a claim. This permits whistleblowers to remain employed while at the same time cooperating with government investigators.

Thus, a whistleblower can be transformed into one of the most powerful and effective law enforcement tools available to uncover crimes in otherwise highly secretive conspiracies. The tactic, known as utilizing a "recruitment-in-place," is considered one of the most prized procedures available to law enforcement, if investigators are sufficiently skilled in cultivating such informants. In various law enforcement contexts, including counterespionage and counterterrorism, a recruitment-in-place acts as a super-confidential informant, potentially providing intelligence on the entire criminal conspiracy. These are considered the gems of any undercover operation.

A prized recruitment-in-place is an individual who is in a position close to leadership within a criminal conspiracy before they start cooperating with the government. They become informants while still holding a position of trust among the wrongdoers. Historically, they are a high-value resource used to undermine major criminal conspiracies, including organized crime, spy rings, and terrorism. A recruitment-in-place does not need to infiltrate the criminal ring. They are already a key member. All that has to happen is for the RIP to secretly switch sides.

For example, instead of trying to infiltrate a Mob ring, the RIP tactic recruits existing members who are already trusted by the criminal kingpin and convinces them to work with law enforcement. From their unique insider position the RIP can inform the government of all of the major details of the criminal conspiracy, and ultimately provide the evidence necessary to stop the crimes, often before they are completed. Being an RIP is no easy task. It can be highly stressful, and there is always a risk that the crooks will figure out who is leaking to the government.

Is this tactic being employed in the context of corporate whistleblower laws? You betcha. A hint of this procedure was revealed by Mary Jo White, the former chair of the SEC. She explained that "in some cases" the whistleblower can provide evidence of the *"virtual blueprints laying out an entire enterprise, directing us to the heart of the alleged fraud."* This is the precise type of evidence government investigators can obtain from RIPs. Former chair White was sending a message to Wall Street: Beware. There are new cops on the block and they may be sitting in the C-Suite with you.

Whistleblowing is no longer limited to fighting employment battles. Although many whistleblowers find themselves embroiled in an employment dispute, it is a mistake to view whistleblowing through the lens of such controversies. Instead, whistleblowers now can try to avoid employment issues and remain fully "loyal" to their bosses, while at the same time working confidentially to fight corruption, stop environmental crimes, and ultimately hold corporate crooks accountable.

PRACTICE TIPS

- Chairman Mary Jo White, Securities and Exchange Commission, Remarks at the Securities Enforcement Forum, Washington, DC (October 2013).

- Decisions of the SEC discussing rewards paid in anonymous and confidential cases can be found on the website of the SEC's Office of the Whistleblower, www.sec.gov/whistleblower. The Commodity Futures Trading Commission's rulings are located at www.whistleblower.gov.

Trap #3: Ignoring Powerful Tools

Changes in the law have created a web of protections that can make whistleblowing work. The change started in 1986 when Congress modernized the False Claims Act. The FCA contained a *qui tam* provision that permitted whistleblowers to file lawsuits alleging that a government contractor had ripped off taxpayers. If the whistleblower's allegations were proven, the whistleblower would obtain a reward of 15 to 30 percent of the monies collected on behalf of the government. The lawsuits were filed under seal, and the government would have time to investigate the case. During the investigation the company would not know about the lawsuit or the identity of the whistleblower.

No one knew if this law would work, but an experiment was underway. Were whistleblowers simply disgruntled employees, or were they the key to fraud detection in major corporations? For the first time, the effectiveness of whistleblowers could be objectively quantified. Because whistleblowers were entitled to a reward, the government would have to evaluate each fraud case, determine whether the whistleblower's information was the reason the case was successfully prosecuted, and allocate an award based on the whistleblower's contribution. In this manner, the benefits whistleblowers bring to the table could be calculated to the penny.

The results of this experiment surprised even the strongest whistleblower advocates. They were phenomenal. When the FCA was initially modernized, the government was having a very difficult time detecting fraud. In 1987 the government collected a total of $86 million in civil penalties from fraudsters nationwide. The amount attributed to whistleblowers was $0. Within six years the total recoveries obtained by the United States dramatically increased. In 1993 the government recovered $372 million from corrupt government contractors. Whistleblowers were *directly responsible* for more than half of those recoveries. The increases continued year after year, and the percentage of recoveries directly attributed to the high quality of whistleblower disclosures skyrocketed and is currently 70 percent of the civil fraud recoveries from corrupt contractors. **Figure 3** tracks the total sanctions obtained by the U.S. government under the False Claims Act thanks to whistleblowers from 1987 to 2021, broken down in ten-year blocks.

Figure 3

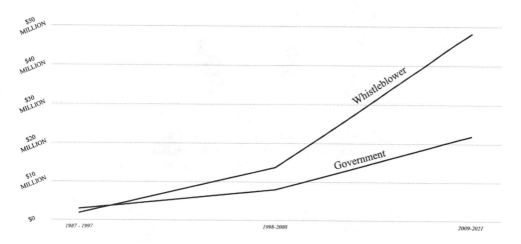

Amount Recovered by DOJ:
Comparing Whistleblower Cases to Non-Whistleblower Cases *(1987-2021)*

While the FCA was demonstrating, in dollars and cents, the effectiveness of reward-based whistleblowing in government contracting cases, the stock market was being rocked by scandal. In 2002, corporate giants Enron and WorldCom went bankrupt, caused by fraud committed by top executives. Thousands of investors lost their retirements and life savings. Consequently, academics and private trade associations started to study the science of fraud detection. They wanted to learn how corporations could prevent meltdowns, as well as protect themselves from misconduct.

These studies all came to the same conclusion: The largest source of all fraud detections were tips from whistleblowers. **Figure 4** is a chart of how companies detect fraud. It is based on comprehensive surveys conducted by the Association of Certified Fraud Examiners (ACFE) in 2022. As can be seen, tips (i.e., whistleblowers) are the largest source of all fraud detection and constitute 42 percent of frauds detected within corporations. Law enforcement was able to identify only 2 percent of the frauds. Thus, a fraud detection program dependent on government agents or regulators to uncover fraud is destined to fail. But if whistleblowers can be encouraged to report, the ability to detect fraud will radically increase.

Figure 4

The first comprehensive study on whistleblower reward laws came out of the University of Chicago Booth School of Business. In the wake of the collapse of Enron, leading economists from the University of Chicago and University of Toronto published a groundbreaking article, "Who Blows the Whistle on Corporate Fraud?" Their goal was to "identify the most effective mechanisms for detecting corporate fraud," and their study was based on an in-depth analysis of "all reported fraud cases in large U.S. companies between 1996 and 2004." Here is what they found:

- "A strong monetary incentive to blow the whistle does motivate people with information to come forward."

- "[T]here is no evidence that having stronger monetary incentives to blow the whistle leads to more frivolous suits."

- "Monetary incentives seem to work well, without the negative side effects often attributed to them."

Their conclusion was groundbreaking: Whistleblowers were the key to fraud detection, but within existing corporate cultures, whistleblowers were punished. "Not only is the honest behavior not rewarded by the market, but it is penalized. . . . Given these costs, however, the surprising part is not that most employees do not talk; it is that some talk at all."

Fifteen years later researchers at the Harvard School of Business confirmed the utility of paying whistleblower rewards as a fraud-fighting tactic. In the most comprehensive study ever conducted on the effectiveness of the *qui tam* reward provisions of the False Claims Act, the Harvard professors concluded: "In sum, these findings support the view that cash-for-information programs help to expose misconduct. Specifically, our findings show that whistleblowers respond to financial incentives by filing additional lawsuits, which the DOJ investigates for a longer period and that are more likely to result in a settlement."

Just as the economists at the Universities of Chicago and Toronto dismissed the slanderous allegations that whistleblower claims are meritless, the 2021 Harvard Business School study, after looking at over five thousand cases, came to the same conclusion: "We do not find support for critics' views that stronger financial incentives for whistleblowing primarily trigger additional meritless lawsuits."

Whistleblower reward laws work. The U.S. government has compensated whistleblowers to the tune of $10 billion as a direct result of their providing the government with "original information" that was strong enough to provide the basis for holding corporate fraudsters accountable. Every dime of their compensation came from the corporate crooks they exposed—not a penny from the taxpayer. The awards serve a fundamentally important public interest: They incentivize others to come forward and to deter wrongdoing. Nothing prevents corporate executives from engaging in fraud like the fear of detection based on the fact that one of their compatriots may confidentially turn them in and reap the benefits Congress has set.

Welcome to the new world of whistleblowing.

<hr>

PRACTICE TIPS

The most important new whistleblower laws are:

- False Claims Act, 31 U.S.C. § 3729-32.

- Tax Evasion and Underpayments (IRS), 26 U.S.C. § 7623.

- Dodd-Frank Act (Commodities Frauds and Market Manipulation), 15 U.S.C. § 78u-6.

- Dodd-Frank Act (Securities and Foreign Corruption), 7 U.S.C. § 26.

- Motor Vehicle Safety Act, 49 U.S.C. § 30172.

- Anti-Money Laundering Act, 31 U.S.C. § 5323.

The University of Chicago study was initially published as: Alexander Dyck et al., "Who Blows the Whistle On Corporate Fraud?" *The Initiative on Global Market's Working Paper No. 3*, Chicago Booth School (October 2008).

The Harvard Business School professors paper is available at Aiyesha Dey et al., "Cash-for-Information Whistleblower Programs: Effects on Whistleblowing and Consequences for Whistleblowers," *Harvard Law School Forum on Corporate Governance* (June 10, 2021).

> **Keeping Up with the Changes**
>
> To keep up to date on changes in the laws, whistleblowers should access the free online law library created by the author, located at www.kkc.com/law-library. The administrative regulations and legislative histories of these laws are posted there.

Trap #4: Delay

Whistleblowers should not delay in alerting the appropriate authorities to fraud, misconduct, or criminal violations. Two legal rules govern the timing of a whistleblower case. First is the traditional statute of limitations. Most laws set a deadline for filing claims, including the anti-retaliation discrimination laws. If you do not meet these mandatory deadlines, you will automatically lose your case. Exceptions to these deadlines are extremely narrow.

The second timing requirement relates, in one way or another, to all of the reward laws. The False Claims Act only permits the first person to file a False Claims Act lawsuit to obtain a reward. All of the reward laws incorporate a "first to file" concept that permits whistleblowers who are the first to alert the government to a fraud to qualify for a reward, while those who delay in filing are either automatically barred from a reward or will obtain a reward at a lower level (depending on the statute). The first to file concept encourages quick reporting and is not tied to a mandatory statute of limitations.

Bottom line: Delay is deadly. If you miss a deadline, you may lose your case, regardless of merits or hardship.

The third timing issue involves the "voluntary" requirement applicable to reward laws. Essentially these laws require the whistleblower to contact the government before the government contacts the whistleblower. There are many reasons for this rule, but if the government already knows about the scandal and wants to talk to you about it, your status as an original source is questionable, and you risk being implicated as a "bad guy." You do not want the government to come calling for you. This point was driven home by Eugene Ross's case. Ross worked as an investment advisor for the disgraced firm of Bear Stearns. He discovered that money was being stolen from one of his client's accounts. He reported the theft to his client, who thereafter reported the crimes to the Justice Department and the SEC. Ross's client told the government officials that Ross had discovered the frauds and urged them to contact him for the proof. The government called Ross, who thereafter fully cooperated with the SEC and DOJ. He was the star witness in the criminal trial against the corporate crooks. Guilty verdicts were rendered, the thieves went to jail, all of the harmed investors obtained restitution, and fines of over $50 million were issued. But Ross, who did everything right, was denied a reward. One of the reasons given by the SEC for rejecting his claim was the timing of his contacts with the government. Under the SEC regulations, Ross was required to contact the government investigators *before* the government investigators contacted him. In other words, because his client was the first to contact the government and provide the government with Ross's information, Ross was disqualified. He was disqualified because the government investigators contacted him before he contacted the government. There was no statute to limitations issue. All of the charges were timely filed. But by waiting to talk to the government agents until after his client alerted them to the frauds, Ross was out of luck.

If you suspect the government may contact you for information, you need to contact them first. If you think someone else may file a reward claim, you need to beat them to the courthouse or the commission. If you have been fired, you need to immediately look up the statutory deadline for filing a case and make sure you comply. Delay is deadly.

─────────── PRACTICE TIPS ───────────

- U.S. Supreme Court decision explaining the False Claims Act's "first to file" rule. *Kellogg Brown & Root et al., v. U.S. ex rel Carter*, 575 U.S. 650 (2015).

- The SEC and CFTC regulations narrowly defining the timing necessary to be considered a voluntary whistleblower. The rules are codified at 17 C.F.R. § 240.21F-4(a) (SEC) and 17 C.F.R. § 165.2(o) (CFTC).

- Eugene Ross's SEC decision is located on the commission's Office of the Whistleblower website as decision Whistleblower Award Proceeding File No. 2021-67 (July 9, 2021).

Keeping Up with the Changes

To keep up to date on changes in the laws, whistleblowers should access the free online law library created by the author, located at www.kkc.com/law-library.

Trap #5: Denial

"I am not a whistleblower! I was only doing my job!" These are the famous last words of whistleblower after whistleblower. Picking a career-ending fight with one's boss is never the goal of employees with legitimate concerns. No one starts out cherishing the idea of being a whistleblower. No one courts that label.

In almost every instance, employees tagged as whistleblowers started out simply doing their jobs. A truck driver tells a dispatcher that his brakes need maintenance, a teacher questions why new textbooks never arrived, an engineer refuses to certify that bolts can stand up to reasonable stress—the list is nearly endless. Before employees ever think they are whistleblowers, they often believe they are merely doing a good job help-ing their employer follow the rules. But as one judge described it, perhaps they were doing their job "too well." They think telling the company's lawyers about a fraud they witnessed will win them a prize. In most cases it won't. But it can be the first step in being shown the door.

When should an employee begin to suspect that they may be a whistleblower? The answer is simple: as soon as possible. Without accepting this change of status, employ-ees cannot begin to take the crucial steps to protect their careers. In the infamous 2002 Enron corporate meltdown, the whistleblower Sherron Watkins sent a heads-up memo to her boss Kenneth Lay. Watkins believed she was doing the right thing by alerting her boss to accounting problems, which just so happened to be the same problems that would land Enron officials in jail and cause the company to collapse. Her boss did not appreciate these disclosures and asked the corporate attorneys what whistleblower rights Watkins enjoyed. At the time, publicly traded companies were not covered under federal whistleblower laws. She also was not covered under Texas law.

Given the lack of protection, Enron's president was given a green light to fire the whistleblower. Before Watkins even knew she was a whistleblower, the company had already labeled her as such, reviewed its legal options, and commenced a strategy to "shoot the messenger."

This scenario is not unique.

It is important to see yourself as a whistleblower, even you have no intention of ever dropping the dime on your employer. The majority of whistleblower wrongful dis-charge cases start with a report to a boss.

The fact remains that many employees naively expect their chain of command to be appreciative when they are being told how badly they have screwed up. Under this assumption employees believe their concerns will be taken seriously and investigated accordingly. If wrongdoing is proven, they believe that their company will fix the problem.

Despite employee hopefulness, the reaction of managers with something to hide is typically not to sing the employees' praise. No one likes to be told that they have a mistake, let alone from a subordinate. No one likes to be told that they may have vio-lated a law. Corporate or political loyalty is often synonymous with a culture that warns employees to "mind their own business," and in doing so not to question upper-level decisions. No one likes a rat.

- Every statute has its own definition of a protected disclosure—choose carefully.

- *Phillips v. Interior Bd. Mine Op.*, 500 F.2d 772 (D.C. Cir. 1974) (broad definition of internal protected activity).

- The latest Supreme Court wisdom on reporting internally is *Digital Realty Trust v. Somers*, 138 S.Ct. 767 (2018). Read this case before you report a violation of law internally or to corporate compliance.

- Links to cases interpreting the scope of protected disclosures can be accessed at the free whistleblower law library, located at www.kkc.com/law-library.

RULE 6

Think Globally

Corruption is an insidious plague that has a wide range of corrosive effects on societies. It undermines democracy and the rule of law, leads to violations of human rights, distorts markets, erodes the quality of life and allows organized crime, terrorism, and other threats to human security to flourish.

So wrote the UN secretary-general in the official introduction to the United Nations Convention against Corruption. Since the convention's approval by the UN General Assembly in 2004, it has been ratified by more than 140 countries, including the United States. It mandates that each signatory take steps to combat corruption and recognizes the importance of protecting whistleblowers as a tool in fighting corruption. Yet most of the signatories have no effective whistleblower laws, and many are among the most notorious human rights violators.

The European Union approved a directive requiring whistleblower protections. However, it lacks clout. The directive did not include strong mandatory protections for whistleblowers, but instead left it up to each nation-state how to devise its own unique whistleblower laws within the directive's often vague guidelines. Left out of the directive were such details as the types of damages a whistleblower who prevailed in their case is entitled to, how whistleblowers can afford to hire attorneys, whether whistleblowers have a right to go to court to defend their rights, and what (if any) restrictions are needed to protect whistleblowers from libel lawsuits or other legal forms of harassment. Needless to say, the directive made no mention of paying rewards to whistleblowers.

Very few other countries have any track record of prosecuting deliberate . . . violations, let alone a legal process that would protect witnesses from obstruction of justice . . .
—U.S. Department of Justice, in *United States v. Efploia*

Although international protections for whistleblowers, if they exist at all, are weak, the story is very different in the United States. The Dodd-Frank Act's powerful whistleblower laws have transnational application. Non-U.S. citizens can use Dodd-Frank and other laws to report, anonymously and confidentially, violations of the Foreign Corrupt Practices Act, market manipulation, money laundering and other crimes that originate outside the United States. Since Dodd-Frank was passed well over 5,000 non-U.S. citizens have reported fraud and corruption taking place in over 130 countries, See **Figure 5.**

Regardless of where they live, employee-insiders are the best source of information on corporate and government corruption. In 2022 the Association of Certified Fraud Examiners conducted a massive international survey on how frauds are detected

Figure 5

Countries Where Whistleblowers Have Submitted Tips Under U.S. Law

(2011-2021)

5,911 international
tips received by the
SEC since 2011.

worldwide. Tips from insiders were by far the number one source for uncovering frauds. When compared to the ability of law enforcement to uncover frauds without the help of whistleblowers, the need for employees to have access to U.S.-style whistleblower programs is apparent.

Figure 6 is a chart based on the statistics assembled by the ACFE regarding fraud reporting outside the United States. As can be seen from the chart, whistleblowers are far more effective at detecting the hidden crimes of corruption and fraud than any other group, including law enforcement.

What effective options are available to international whistleblowers who want to expose fraud or corruption?

The United States Takes Leadership in the Fight Against International Corruption

In December 2021 the United States declared war on international corruption. Fighting corruption was identified by the White House and every major U.S. agency involved in foreign policy as a "core interest" necessary to defend U.S. national security. "Establishing the Fight Against Corruption as a Core United States Security Interest," became official U.S. policy:

> *Corruption robs citizens of equal access to vital services, denying the right to quality healthcare, public safety, and education. It degrades the business environment, subverts economic opportunity, and exacerbates inequality. It often contributes to human rights violations and abuses, and can drive migration. As a fundamental threat to the rule of law, corruption hollows out institutions, corrodes public trust, and fuels popular cynicism toward effective, accountable governance.*

Figure 6

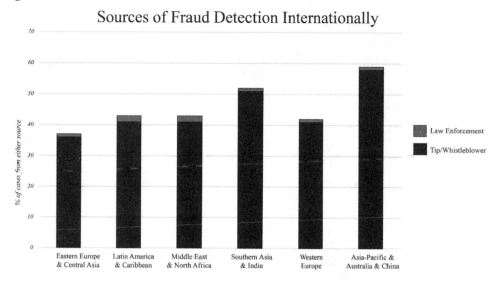

Sources of Fraud Detection Internationally

The United States' new international strategy contends that corruption has been an economic engine fueling dictatorial regimes, ripping off billions in much-needed international aid dollars, permitting worldwide tax evasion, and facilitating untold horrors of systemic human rights abuses. But there was a new twist to America's transnational fight against corruption. The agencies that drafted the anti-corruption strategy (including the Departments of Defense, Justice, Treasury, and State) recognized whistleblowers as key nongovernmental actors who can help bring "aggressive enforcement action" on issues such as tax enforcement and money laundering. The strategy pledged to increase protection for anti-corruption actors, including whistleblowers, and declared that it was U.S. policy to "stand in solidarity" with whistleblowers who "challenge corrupt power structures."

The United States wasted no time in becoming the worldwide leader in supporting whistleblowers who report international corruption. In a comprehensive peer-reviewed study of the United States' implementation of the international treaty against foreign bribery, the Organization for Economic Co-operation and Development (OECD) strongly praised the United States' efforts to combat foreign corruption. The OECD's lead examiners "commend[ed] the United States for its sustained and demonstrable commitment to enforcing its foreign bribery offence[s]" and highlighted the "prominent role that the United States plays globally in combating foreign bribery."

Among the programs highlighted by the OECD was the "Dodd-Frank Act's multifaceted protections" available to whistleblowers, including the ability to file confidential reports and the "powerful incentives for qualified whistleblowers to report foreign bribery allegations." The OECD examiners welcomed the strong incentives offered under the Dodd-Frank Act that provide practical help to Foreign Corrupt Practices Act whistleblowers, including "confidentiality guarantees, financial incentives, as well as remedies, including double back pay, to compensate whistleblowers who suffer retaliation." These provisions provide "a powerful framework to encourage whistle-blowing concerning potential foreign bribery violations."

The OECD concluded its report in clear and unequivocal terms: "The Working Group congratulates the United States for its sustained and outstanding commitment to enforcing its foreign bribery offence.... Enforcement has increased remarkably ... confirming that the United States plays a leading role in combating foreign bribery." Whistleblowers are now a critical component in the United States' fight against foreign bribery, money laundering, bank secrecy, and corruption.

Transnational Reward Laws on a Worldwide Stage

On September 22, 2014, the U.S. Securities and Exchange Commission, the top cop on Wall Street, issued a historic ruling in a case under the Foreign Corrupt Practices Act. The commission awarded a non-U.S. citizen $30 million for turning in a corporation that paid bribes to foreign government officials. In making this award, it sent a message to whistleblowers worldwide: The rewards program was open to anyone.

In issuing the $30 million award, the SEC stated:

In our view, there is a sufficient U.S. territorial nexus whenever a claimant's information leads to the successful enforcement of a covered action brought in the United States. . . . When these key territorial connections exist, it makes no difference whether, for example, the claimant was a foreign national, the claimant resides overseas, the information was submitted from overseas, or the misconduct comprising the U.S. securities law violation occurred entirely overseas.

The SEC's payment had its intended impact. Between 2011 and September 2021, 5,908 non-U.S. persons in over 130 different countries filed corruption claims in the United States to the SEC alone (see **Figure 5**). Although the Commodity Futures Trading Commission does not publish statistics as to the country of origin of their complainants, it also commenced paying non-U.S. citizens who report corruption.

After making its first payment to a foreign national, the SEC continued paying rewards to other non-U.S. citizens, including paying an Australian whistleblower $3.75 million for reporting illegal payments made to Chinese officials by an Australian company. Australians took notice. One local senator told the *Sydney Morning Herald*: "Whistleblowers in the United States get rewarded and protected, but here they get punished and ruined." In 2021, one in five persons who obtained a reward from the SEC was a foreign national.

Rule 20 details how the FCPA works and how international companies are covered under the law. **Figure 7** is a map of the countries whose companies paid bribes to foreign officials and were held liable under the FCPA. As can be seen, most of the large international bribes were paid by wealthy nations in order to obtain business advantages in the developing world or resource-rich nations. This map illustrates the importance of the SEC's ability to investigate and prosecute corporations traded on international stock exchanges.

Figure 7

Countries Where Corporations Paid Foreign Bribes, Confirmed in FCPA Prosecutions
(2010-2021)

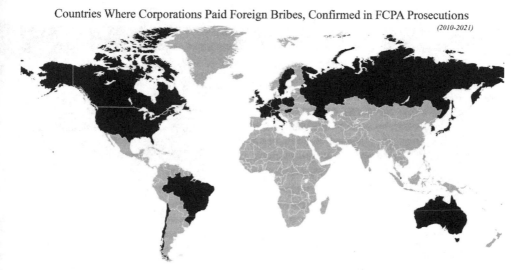

Figure 7 also identifies the countries whose government officials took the bribes in cases successfully prosecuted under the FCPA. The U.S. government has jurisdiction to prosecute companies that pay bribes. FCPA whistleblower cases target the bribe-payers, not those who accept the bribes. By targeting the bribe-payers the United States plays a vital role in fighting corruption. Similarly, the two major CFTC enforcement actions targeting foreign corruption sanctioned Dutch and Swiss corporations that engaged in corrupt activities in numerous developing nations. These two commodity cases alone resulted in over $1.3 billion in collected proceeds.

The Foreign Corrupt Practices Act is not the only U.S. law with transnational application. As explained below, other U.S. laws that have transnational application include the Anti-Money Laundering Whistleblower Improvement Act, the Act to Prevent Pollution from Ships, the False Claims Act, the Lacey Act/Endangered Species Act, the Internal Revenue Act, the Securities Exchange Act, and the Commodity Exchange Act.

The bottom line is simple: The best bet for whistleblowers worldwide is to try to find a U.S. whistleblower law under which the misconduct they have witnessed may be covered.

FOREIGN CORRUPT PRACTICES ACT (FCPA)

The Foreign Corrupt Practices Act targets bribery of foreign government officials by publicly traded corporations or U.S. persons. The FCPA has significant transnational application. It covers companies that trade in the U.S. stock exchanges, but also foreign companies that permit U.S. persons to invest in their companies through an instrument known as American Depository Receipts, or ADRs. Companies that trade in ADRs are covered under the FCPA, whether they are based in Paris, London, Hong Kong, or the cities of any other country. Consequently, over the past ten years the majority of corporations sanctioned under the FCPA were non-U.S. based.

Figure 8

Top Ten International Corruption Cases ₍₂₀₁₄₋₂₀₂₂₎

YEAR	COMPANY	REGISTERED COUNTRY	PENALTY
2020	GOLDMAN SACHS GROUP INC.	UNITED STATES	$3.3 BILLION
2020	AIRBUS SE	NETHERLANDS/FRANCE	$2.09 BILLION
2022	DANSKE BANK	DENMARK	$2.059 BILLION
2018	PETRÓLEO BRASILEIRO S.A. - PETROBRAS	BRAZIL	$1.78 BILLION
2022	GLENCORE	SWITZERLAND	$1.18 BILLION
2019	TELEFONAKTIEBOLAGET LM ERICSON	SWEDEN	$1.06 BILLION
2017	TELIA COMPANY AB	SWEDEN	$1.01 BILLION
2019	MTS	RUSSIA	$850 MILLION
2016	VIMPELCOM	NETHERLANDS	$795 MILLION
2015	ALSTROM	FRANCE	$772 MILLION

Figure 8 is a chart of some international corporations registered on foreign stock exchanges that were held liable under the FCPA. As can be seen, some of the largest FCPA cases concerned non-U.S.-based companies.

As a result of its broad international jurisdiction, the FCPA is a powerful and effective transnational anti-corruption law. In 2010, when Congress passed the Dodd-Frank Act's securities reward law, whistleblowers from around the world became eligible for a reward if they provided original information about bribery or other violations of the FCPA. Whistleblowers filing allegations of bribery or corruption under the FCPA are also permitted to file confidential and anonymous complaints. The filing procedures under Dodd-Frank are explained in Rule 19.

But the FCPA is not the only law in the SEC's Dodd-Frank toolbox. On December 13, 2022, the SEC sanctioned the Danish bank, Danske Bank, over $400 million for failing to have an adequate anti–money laundering program. Although Danske had few contacts with the United States it was smacked with a large fine in part because it permitted dirty money to flow into the U.S. financial system. On the same day the Justice Department forced Danske to plead guilty to conspiracy to commit bank fraud, and sanctioned the bank another $2 billion. The United States was getting serious about policing international corruption, especially when its dirty impact hits U.S. shores.

COMMODITY FRAUD WHISTLEBLOWERS

The Commodity Exchange Act's (CEA) whistleblower reward law has the potential to become the most significant international anti-corruption law worldwide. Administered by the U.S. Commodity Futures Trading Commission (CFTC), the whistleblower law was passed as part of Dodd-Frank and covers the national and international commodities trading markets. Unlike the SEC, whose primary jurisdiction is limited to publicly traded companies, the CFTC can sanction both public and privately held companies that engage in unlawful market manipulation in the commodities markets. The CFTC exercised its broad authority to ensure that commodity trading in the developing world is not tainted by corruption by sanctioning two of the largest commodity trading companies—a total of $1.316 billion.

The size of the markets regulated by the CFTC is astronomical. At the time the Dodd-Frank Act became law, then-CFTC chairman Gary Gensler explained the massive scope of the commission's new authorities: "The law gave the Commodity Futures Trading Commission oversight of the *$300 trillion swaps market*. . . . At such size and complexity, it is essential that these markets work for the benefit of the American public; that they are transparent, open and competitive."

The CFTC has publicly urged whistleblowers to come forward and help with its international enforcement efforts. The commission publishes "Whistleblower Alerts" urging employees and other "insiders" to come forward with information on numerous violations outside the traditional FCPA case, including the Bank Secrecy Act, insider trading, spoofing, swaps, money laundering, fraud in the derivative, futures and options trading, market manipulation, benchmark manipulation, and frauds associated with foreign currency exchanges and cryptocurrencies.

In December 2020 the CFTC took action on its first international corruption case. The commission sanctioned the Dutch oil trading company Vitol, Inc. $130 million for engaging in foreign corrupt practices. The commission explained that bribery and other forms of corruption would be actionable under the CEA as forms of "market manipulation." Using its authority to police manipulation of international commodities markets was recognized by the leading law firms representing white-collar criminals as a game changer for using the commodities laws as a tool for combating international corruption. Gibson and Dunn, a mega-corporate law firm that represents multinational corporations and corrupt officials worldwide, warned of a coming enforcement storm:

> This is the first public action coming out of the CFTC's initiative to pursue violations of the Commodity Exchange Act ("CEA") involving foreign corruption. The CFTC's action rests on an aggressive theory that seeks to approach allegations of corruption through its historic ability to pursue fraud and manipulation. . . . It is an enforcement area we expect will continue to be a priority for the CFTC.

How true their warning was. In May 2022 the CFTC sanctioned another huge commodity trading company, Glencore. The sanction against Glencore, over $1.18 billion, made the Vitol fines look like chump change. Moreover, the CFTC signaled its willingness to work with numerous foreign regulatory and law enforcement authorities in policing the commodities markets. In the Glencore case the CFTC officially acknowledged the assistance provided to the U.S. government by the United Kingdom's Serious Fraud Office, the Brazilian Securities Market Commission, the Bermuda Monetary Authority, the Hong Kong Securities and Futures Commission, the Luxembourg Commission de Surveillance du Secteur Financier, the Mexico Comisión Nacional Bancaria y de Valores, the UK Financial Conduct Authority, and the Banco Central del Uruguay.

> "[A]s the growing number of multi-jurisdictional and agency anti-corruption resolutions suggest, the FCPA units of the DOJ and SEC are not the only cops on the beat, and they have not been for quite some time."
>
> —Gibson and Dunn

The lawyers at Gibson Dunn had a warning for companies engaged in international commerce:

> "whistleblowing is likely to increase. . . . Just as the Dodd-Frank whistleblowing award program has significantly increased FCPA tips to the SEC (and DOJ), we expect the CFTC's whistleblowing push could significantly increase the amount of information the CFTC receives and, in turn, the CFTC's ability to bring enforcement actions relating to foreign corruption."

The CFTC's transnational jurisdiction also includes money laundering, bank secrecy, foreign exchange, and cyber currency. **Figure 9** is a list of some of the banks located in the United Kingdom and Canada that were subjected to recent CFTC enforcement actions.

Like the SEC, the leadership of the CFTC has publicly committed to paying generous awards to non-U.S. citizens: "The Whistleblower Program has become an integral component in the agency's enforcement arsenal. . . . We hope that an award of this magnitude will incentivize whistleblowers to come forward with valuable information

Figure 9

Examples of Banks in the United Kingdom and Canada Sanctioned by the CFTC

YEAR	BANK	REGISTERED COUNTRY	PENALTY
2020	THE BANK OF NOVA SCOTIA	CANADA	$127,400,000
2017	THE ROYAL BANK OF SCOTLAND PLC	UNITED KINGDOM	$85,000,000
2015	BARCLAYS PLC, BARCLAYS BANK PLC, AND BANK CAPITAL INC.	UNITED KINGDOM, UNITED STATES	$115,000,000
2015	BARCLAYS BANK PLC	UNITED KINGDOM	$400,000,000
2015	THE ROYAL BANK OF CANADA	CANADA	$35,000,000
2015	CITIBANK, N.A. HSBC BANK PLC, JPMORGAN CHASE BANK N.A., THE ROYAL BANK OF SCOTLAND PLC, UBS AG	UNITED STATES, UNITED KINGDOM, SWITZERLAND	$1,400,000,000
2014	LLOYDS BANKING GROUP PLC, LLOYDS BANK PLC	UNITED KINGDOM	$105,000,000
2013	THE ROYAL BANK OF SCOTLAND	UNITED KINGDOM	$325,000,000
2012	BARCLAYS PLC, BARCLAYS BANK PLC, AND BARCLAYS CAPITAL INC,	UNITED STATES, UNITED KINGDOM	$200,000,000

and provide notice to market participants that individuals are reporting quality information about violations of the Commodity Exchange Act [CEA]."

The Commodity Exchange Act's whistleblower law is explained in Rule 19.

OFFSHORE BANKING, MONEY LAUNDERING, OR TAX FRAUD

Bankers from any nation in the world can now turn in their U.S. clients who hold illegal offshore bank accounts or are evading taxes and qualify for large rewards. Under the Internal Revenue Service program, whistleblowers can confidentially disclose any violation of U.S. tax laws, including violations perpetrated by foreign banks. The IRS law also covers any illegal activity investigated by the IRS criminal division, including money laundering and asset forfeiture. Likewise, on January 1, 2021, the U.S. Department of the Treasury was granted authority to pay rewards to whistleblowers who disclose violations of anti-money laundering (or AML) requirements. Money laundering is quintessentially transnational in nature.

The role of the IRS whistleblower law in aiding in the prosecution of international banks was driven home by the Bradley Birkenfeld case. Birkenfeld was a Swiss banker with inside information as to how the then-largest bank in the world, the Zurich-based UBS, had an illegal program serving nineteen thousand Americans. All of these clients held nondisclosed, secret accounts in Switzerland for which they did not pay U.S. taxes. Although Birkenfeld was a U.S. citizen, there is nothing in the law that requires whistleblowers to be U.S. citizens. Any individual can provide information to the IRS, regardless of their country of citizenship.

Birkenfeld's disclosures triggered the largest successful tax fraud prosecutions in world history. After the UBS case was resolved, fifteen other Swiss banks were indicted for tax fraud. The prosecutions are ongoing, but as of 2016 Credit Suisse pled guilty to criminal conspiracy and paid $2.811 billion in fines and penalties, Bank Leumin group had paid $270 million in fines, and the Julius Baer Group Ltd. had paid $547 million in fines and penalties. Moreover, another whistleblower turned in the oldest bank in Switzerland, Wegelin & Co., which pled guilty to tax fraud, paid $74 million in fines, and was forced into bankruptcy. Wegelin's bankruptcy sent additional shock waves throughout the Swiss banking system, and, for the most part, all known illegal U.S. accounts were closed.

After indicting the fifteen banks, the DOJ cut deals with 80 smaller Swiss banks, which agreed to pay a total of $1.36 billion in penalties. In addition, these banks were forced to "make a complete disclosure of their cross-border activities; [and] provide detailed information on an account-by-account basis for accounts in which U.S. taxpayers have a direct or indirect interest." They also agreed to close all illegally held U.S. accounts and "provide detailed information as to other banks" that hold illegal U.S. accounts.

Hundreds of U.S. taxpayers who held illegal offshore accounts were successfully prosecuted, and over $13.7 billion had been collected from the Swiss banks and their U.S. account holders.

Employees who work for international banks and want to file a confidential whistleblower reward claim must follow the rules governing IRS tax whistleblowers, as set forth in Rule 18, or the AML whistleblower law explained in Rule 21.

WILDLIFE TRAFFICKING, PROTECTION OF ENDANGERED SPECIES, AND ILLEGAL LOGGING

The U.S. Congress enacted whistleblower reward provisions in key laws prohibiting wildlife trafficking and protecting endangered species. Whistleblowers can obtain rewards under the Lacey Act, the Endangered Species Act, and the Fish and Wildlife Improvement Act when they disclose violations of laws protecting plants, fish, and animals under the major international treaty banning trade in endangered species (the CITES Convention). These laws cover illegal logging, which destroys the habitat for many critically threatened species.

The laws are explained in Rule 24.

FALSE CLAIMS ACT

The oldest whistleblower reward law, the False Claims Act, also has extraterritorial application. Many schemes that are hatched by foreign companies are covered under the FCA, and whistleblowers who are non-U.S. citizens are fully qualified to file claims under the law and collect rewards. Because the False Claims Act is such a powerful law (allowing treble damages and recovery of attorney fees, and including a private right of action and mandatory rewards for qualified whistleblowers), employees who work outside the United States should be fully aware of the types of misconduct covered under this law. Following are some examples of the misconduct for which foreign companies have been held liable:

- Toyo, Inc., from Japan and CMAI from China were sanctioned for failure to pay customs or "anti-dumping" duties and violation of tariff obligations.

- The India-based Infosys Technologies was sanctioned for improperly relocating employees in the United States (B-1 visa violations).

- Three international companies involved in making or importing defective body armor—Lincoln Fabrics (Canada), Barrday (Canada), Itochu (Japan)—paid millions in sanctions because their defective products were sold to the United States.

- International drug companies Valeant Pharmaceuticals (Canada), Serono (Switzerland), Organon International (Netherlands), and B. Braun Melsungen AG (Germany) were sanctioned for making kickbacks or engaging in the illegal marketing of drugs paid for by Medicaid, Medicare, and the Veterans Administration.

- Louis Dreyfus Group (France) and Royal Dutch Shell (Netherlands) had to pay millions for related to their leases to drill oil.

- Sanctions for fraud in providing food and water to U.S. troops in Afghanistan: Supreme Foodservice FZE (United Arab Emirates)

- Phony claims submitted to the U.S. government for payment: BNP Paribas (France)

- Violation of terms in fixed price contract: Hesco Bastion Limited (UK)

- Using misleading testing certificates in selling products to the U.S. Army: Alcatel-Lucent (France)

- Improper billing of defense contracts: Securitas GmbH Werkschutz (Germany)

- Selling adulterated drugs: Ranbaxy Laboratories (India)

Employees working for foreign companies are often unaware of whistleblower rewards available under U.S. law. Employees who work for companies that import products to the United States, sell goods or services to the American government (including state governments), or obtain U.S. government contracts are all potentially eligible for whistleblower rewards.

The False Claims Act law is fully explained in Rule 17.

PREVENTING OCEAN POLLUTION: THE ACT TO PREVENT POLLUTION FROM SHIPS/MARPOL

The Act to Prevent Pollution from Ships (APPS) permits whistleblowers from any country in the world to report ocean pollution committed on the high seas and obtain a financial reward. This whistleblower provision has proven, over time, to be the key to the successful prosecution of shipowners who dump oil and other waste into the oceans in violation of the International Convention for the Prevention of Pollution from Ships, as modified by the protocol of 1978, better known simply as the MARPOL Protocol. The APPS law has enabled the United States to use whistleblower information as the basis for successfully prosecuting ships registered outside the United States, including those whose flagship nation is Turkey, Jordan, Portugal, South Korea, Denmark, Liberia, Germany, Cyprus, Greece, Panama, Italy, Japan, the Bahamas, Malta, Egypt, Bermuda, Singapore, China, Spain, Norway, New Zealand, Sweden, and the Philippines, among others.

The APPS whistleblower law is explained in Rule 23.

MOTOR VEHICLE SAFETY

As set forth in Rule 22, in December 2015 the U.S. Congress passed a reward law covering motor vehicle safety. This law has transnational application, as numerous automobiles and their parts (such as airbags) are manufactured outside the United States. In fact, in 2021 the Department of Transportation rewarded a whistleblower who raised safety concerns related to Kia and Hyundai automobiles. Whistleblowers from countries such as Korea, Japan, Mexico, and Germany who report safety concerns in accordance with this law should fully qualify for rewards.

For whistleblowers outside the United States, the bottom line is clear. Until other nations implement effective whistleblower programs, U.S. laws offer the best opportunity to effectively expose fraud and corruption and obtain fair compensation.

- The OECD Phase IV Report on the U.S. FCPA program is available at www.justice.gov/criminal-fraud/file/1337591/download.

- The United States Strategy on Countering Corruption is available online at www.whitehouse.gov/wp-content/uploads/2021/12/United-States-Strategy -on-Countering-Corruption.pdf.

Keeping Up with the Changes

To keep up to date on changes in the laws, whistleblowers should access the free online law library created by the author, located at www.kkc.com/law-library.

PART II

Tactics You Need to Know

Our President has gone on a rampage about news leaks on Watergate. He told the appropriate people, "go to any length to stop them"... Internal investigations, plus he wants to use the courts... Nixon was wild, shouting and hollering that "we can't have it and we're going to stop it, I don't care how much it costs...

—Bob Woodward, quoting the whistleblower "Deep Throat"

RULE 7

Protect Yourself

Unfortunately, companies with a corporate culture that punishes whistleblowers for being "dis-loyal" and "litigation risks" often transcend state lines, and most corporate employers, with help from their lawyers, know exactly what they can do to a whistleblowing employee under the law.
—Senator Patrick Leahy, Senate floor speech in support of passage
of the Sarbanes-Oxley Act

W histleblowers have no choice but to engage in self-help tactics. They have to obtain evidence to prove their cases. But this can be tricky. There are privacy requirements, trade secret restrictions, rules governing the use of company computers, telephones, e-mail accounts, and even the use of copying machines. How does an employee balance the need to collect supporting information with various rules that limit or prohibit evidence gathering?

When engaging in self-help tactics, whistleblowers have to be extremely careful. Judges will not sympathize with your plight simply because it is difficult for whistleblowers to obtain supporting witnesses or because the company has an overwhelming advantage regarding access to documents. No matter how hard it is to obtain evidence of wrongdoing, courts continuously warn employees "not to engage in dubious self-help tactics . . . in order to gather evidence." In the context of employment, the law is clear on this issue: Engaging in protected activity does not immunize employees from being accused of "inappropriate workplace activities," even if their engagement in that conduct is intended to document corporate wrongdoing.

To further complicate the matter, there are no bright-line rules that set clearly defined standards for how employees can document wrongdoing or protect themselves against retaliation. The leading cases all apply a "balancing test" for determining whether an employee's evidence-gathering tactics are protected. In one case widely followed by other courts, the U.S. Court of Appeals for the Fifth Circuit explained: "Courts have required that the employee conduct be reasonable in light of the circumstances, and have held that the employer's right to run his business must be balanced against the rights of the employee to . . . promote his own welfare."

Using the confidential reward laws, and avoiding direct litigation with an employer in court, can help shield an employee from the potential adverse consequences of some controversial self-help tactics, such as removing documents from work. Employees who provide evidence of potential criminal activity directly to the government for use by the government in an investigation minimize the risk that they will be questioned about their conduct in court proceedings. However, whistleblowers who file discrimination cases are often aggressively questioned about all their self-help tactics and accused of misbehavior because they tried to obtain evidence to prove their cases.

DON'T BREAK THE LAW

Do not break the law. This is a basic rule that should be followed. If a court determines that an employee broke a criminal law in order to obtain evidence, the employee most likely will suffer a sanction, including having their employment case dismissed, their credibility attacked, and in extreme circumstances, a referral for criminal prosecution. Even if dismissal is not imposed, the employee's ability to introduce illegally obtained evidence in court may be blocked, and the defendants will capitalize on this conduct at every phase of the case.

In reward-based cases where the whistleblower provides information confidentially to the government, the basic rule of thumb centers on admissibility. Can the prosecutors use your evidence in their investigation or in a civil or criminal prosecution? If they can, you are good shape. But if the evidence is tainted in a manner that would permit a judge to block its use at a trial, your entitlement to a reward may be compromised. You are entitled to a reward only if your evidence triggered an investigation or contributed to a final sanction. If the government cannot rely on your information due to misconduct, it is hard to argue that you should obtain compensation.

BEWARE: THE BOSS WILL MONITOR E-MAILS AND COMPUTERS

Do not think work e-mails or text messages are private. Do not think that any computer or cell phone owned by the company (including laptops they let you bring home) is safe from a complete search of the hard drive, including searches for deleted documents. It is now standard operating procedure for a company to seize a whistleblower's computer, especially when the employee is about to be fired. It is also becoming standard for the company to aggressively search hard drives and e-mails for any document it can use to impeach the whistleblower.

The open season on employee's e-mails and hard drives was made easier in 2010 by the Supreme Court's decision in *City of Ontario v. Quon*. The case concerned the search of an employee's text messages, which were sent on a cell phone owned by the city. Because the government conducted the search, the employee challenged it on the basis of the U.S. Constitution's restrictions on warrantless searches. The Supreme Court held that government agencies can, under certain conditions, search the computer files of its employees without a warrant. The holding was broad: "[W]hen conducted . . . for the investigation of work-related misconduct, a government employer's warrantless search is reasonable if it is justified at its inception and if the measures adopted are reasonably related to the objectives of the search and not excessively intrusive . . ."

The authority of private-sector employers to search company-owned computers is even broader. In warning employees of this management power, the Privacy Rights Clearinghouse summarized the current state of the law as follows:

> *New technologies make it possible for employers to monitor many aspects of their employees' jobs, especially on telephones, computer terminals, through electronic and voice mail, and when employees are using the Internet. Such monitoring is virtually unregulated. Therefore, unless company policy specifically states otherwise (and even this is not assured), your employer may listen, watch, and read most of your workplace communications.*

The ability of employers to search company-owned computers is extremely significant in whistleblower cases. First, courts have held that evidence of an employee's misconduct obtained during the search of an employee's computer can be used against that employee in a subsequent discrimination case. Second, employees sometimes include private information on their company-owned computers, including legal documents, communications with counsel and personally sensitive information. At a minimum, placing these types of materials on company computers can provide the company with a treasure trove of information that would be otherwise unavailable. At worst, the employee will be accused of doing personal business on company time, some of which may be very embarrassing.

Bottom line: An employee should not use company property to blow the whistle. They need to keep protected activities private. Do not give the company the rope it will need for the hanging.

DO NOT DESTROY EVIDENCE

An employee should not destroy evidence. Evidence cannot be destroyed simply because it does not support their claim or may be embarrassing. For example, if an employee uses a company-owned computer, they cannot simply wipe out the hard drive, especially if the employee is afraid that the computer contains files that the company may use against them in an upcoming legal case. The rule is fairly clear: "A litigant or potential litigant is under a duty to preserve evidence in his possession that he knows or should have known is relevant to the litigation or which might lead to the discovery of admissible evidence." Stated another way: "Willful spoliation occurs when a party has clear notice of an obligation to preserve evidence and proceeds to intentionally destroy evidence in spite of its obligation not to."

In one unfortunate case filed under the False Claims and Sarbanes-Oxley Acts, the employee used a wiping program to erase data from the hard drive of his company-issued computer. When trying to justify the destruction of evidence, the employee's explanations only made matters worse. He admitted to having highly embarrassing personal materials on the computer. This did nothing to further his claims, except to undercut his credibility even more. The issues of retaliation and corporate wrongdoing were lost in the dispute over the computer files, what he wiped off the hard drive, and how those materials may have helped the company. Because the documents were gone forever, the company was able to speculate as to what might have been located in the employee's personal directories and what could have been used by the company to bolster its case. As a direct result of the spoliation of evidence, the employee lost his case and had to pay the company a sanction.

Given the Supreme Court precedent permitting management access to employee information stored on company-owned computers (including e-mails, text messages, and documents stored on hard drives), it is extremely important that employees be aware that they lack basic rights of privacy when using company equipment—even company equipment that they are permitted to take home and use on their own time.

On the other hand, spoliation cuts both ways. There are far more examples of companies destroying evidence than there are of employees doing so. Corporations must maintain accurate records under audit, tax, and government contracting rules. The laws prohibiting spoliation of evidence have been successfully used by employees and have likewise resulted in judgments in favor of employees.

DO NOT LET THE BOSS ABUSE "AFTER-ACQUIRED EVIDENCE"

What happens in a case where the reasons given for a termination were retaliatory, but during discovery the bosses learn of other misconduct that *would have* resulted in a termination regardless of any protected whistleblower activity? For example, what happens if during the course of the employee's deposition they admit to lying on the job application and did not have the professional licensing required for their position. It is under these circumstances that the "after-acquired evidence" rule applies.

The rule is simple. If the termination was illegal, the employee can still win the case. But damages are cut off, effective the date on which the company learned of the offensive conduct and can show that it would have fired the employee, even if they had not engaged in protected activity.

Requiring the reinstatement of a worker who should have been fired would be rather odd, and the law simply does not require it. Furthermore, under the after-acquired evidence rule, damages are cut off from the date the company learned of the disqualifying misconduct. Thus, if an employee is fired, but thirty days later the company learns of the disqualifying conduct, the employee is only entitled to thirty days' back pay.

When debating the merits of the after-acquired evidence defense, there was a three-hundred-pound gorilla in the room. Could an employer use pretrial discovery to snoop around an employee's background in order to obtain information about misconduct that would have justified a termination? The potential for abusing this practice was evident. If companies could use the fact that an employee filed a whistleblower case to engage in extensive discovery to try to dig up dirt, these tactics would have a strong chilling effect on the willingness of anyone to blow the whistle or file retaliation claims. No one wants to invite such a wide-ranging review of their past conduct.

In permitting the use of after-acquired evidence, the U.S. Supreme Court, in *McKennon v. Nashville Banner Publishing*, warned against this type of discovery and prohibited its use: "The concern that employers might as a routine matter undertake extensive discovery into an employee's background or performance on the job to resist claims under the Act is not an insubstantial one, but we think the authority of courts to [sanction discovery abuses] will deter most abuses."

This warning to company attorneys in *McKennon* is of critical importance to employees. Assuming that an employee did engage in some workplace misconduct that the company does not know about, the employee should not freely *admit* to engaging in such violations. It is up to the company to learn these facts through legitimate and relevant discovery. Questions by employers such as "Did you rummage through your supervisor's office?" or "Did you improperly remove company documents before you were fired?" should be objected to, and if necessary should be the focus of a motion for protective order or sanctions.

SELF-HELP CAN MAKE OR BREAK A CASE

Gunther v. Deltek: Case Study in Taping and Removing Documents

Dinah Gunther worked as a financial analyst for the technology company Deltek, Inc. She was fired after reporting suspected financial fraud to her bosses and the SEC. She fought Deltek for years and eventually prevailed in a showdown at the U.S. Court of Appeals for the Fourth Circuit. Gunther's case is textbook on why employees have to tape conversations and obtain documents to win their cases.

The central dispute concerned a meeting between Gunther, the company's director of human resources, and a high-ranking supervisor. Deltek accused Gunther of being "confrontational," "demanding," and "challenging" toward the director at the meeting and used her so-called unprofessional conduct as the main justification for firing her. Thus, what happened at that meeting was the key to whether Gunther's termination would be sustained.

The company had the word of its HR director and a management witness who attested to her aggressive and inappropriate behavior. Two against one; alone, Gunther did not stand a chance. But Gunther had a secret weapon. She had surreptitiously taped the meeting (which is legal in the state of Virginia, where she was employed).

The judge listened to the tape and could determine what actually happened during that meeting. In ruling in favor of Gunther the judge explained: "Based upon my listening to the recording, I find there was no basis for asserting that [Gunther] was confrontational. . . . Having listened to the tape more than once, I do not agree with [the HR director's] characterization of [Gunther's] actions. . . . At all times [Gunther] was calm, quiet, and polite."

The judge also explained that Gunther's taping was reasonable in the context of her employment. The taping "was done in furtherance of [Gunther's] case, and it was these tapes which revealed that [Deltek's] reasons for terminating [Gunther] were pretext. . . . [Gunther's] recordings were all made in furtherance of her whistleblower claims and therefore constitute protected activity."

Without that tape, it is almost certain Gunther would have lost. But with the tape she could demonstrate that the company lacked credibility, was doctoring testimony, that a witness apparently lied on the stand, and that the reasons given for her termination were a pretext. The tape ensured that Gunther would eventually win her case and obtain more than $500,000 in back pay, front pay, and damages.

The company also attacked Gunther for removing company documents (i.e., sending company information to her home e-mail account) in contravention of her confidentiality agreement and company policy. They sought to use the after-acquired evidence defense to deny damages to Gunther. Under that defense, Deltek argued that once it learned Gunther had removed documents in violation of company policy, it had the right to deny her reinstatement and cut off her ability to collect damages. Deltek cited cases holding that "Sarbanes-Oxley is not a license to steal documents or break contracts."

The Department of Labor judge carefully reviewed the law on document removal, recognizing "the inherent tension between a company's legitimate business policies that protect confidential information and the whistleblower programs created by Congress." The cases cited by Deltek were not black and white. None of them prohibited the removal of documents under all circumstances. An employee's conduct had to be reviewed on a case-by-case basis. The judge concluded that Gunther "forwarded these documents in an effort to support her Sarbanes-Oxley Act [SOX] allegations." She also noted that Gunther "only took documents relevant to her SOX complaint and did so for fear that they would be shredded," and that there were "strong policy reasons for permitting whistleblowers in SOX cases to take necessary actions to protect relevant documents from being destroyed, as long as the employee's actions are necessary, reasonable, and not overbroad."

The judge also understood that the legality of an employee's removal of confidential business documents in violation of company policy "would depend on the facts of each case," and that the "indiscriminate misappropriation of proprietary documents would not be protected." But in this case, Gunther "took these documents for the sole purpose of preserving evidence relevant to her whistleblower complaint and alleged violations under SOX." Thus Gunther's actions were not only permitted but also constituted protected activity.

Gunther's case is a lesson learned. If you are careful using self-help tactics, you can prevail. But if you engage in unjustified unprofessional activity or destroy evidence, you may find yourself out of luck.

PRACTICE TIPS

- The Supreme Court decision on the after-acquired evidence rule: *McKennon v. Nashville Banner Publishing*, 513 U.S. 352 (1995).

- Senator Leahy Senate Speech on Sarbanes-Oxley, Vol. 148, *Congressional Record*, p. 7358 (July 25, 2002).

- The Department of Labor case of *Gunther v. Deltek, Inc.*, 2010-SOX-49, affirmed *Deltek v. Department of Labor*, 2016 U.S. App. LEXIS 9274 (4th Cir. 2016), provides analysis of both document removal and one-party taping.

- *Webb v. Government for the District of Columbia*, 175 F.R.D. 128 (D.D.C. 1997) (default judgment against employer for destroying documents).

- *City of Ontario v. Quan*, 560 U.S. 746 (2010) (company access to employee's cell phone records).

- Links to cases discussing the after-acquired evidence rule, workplace taping, and removal of documents can be accessed at the free whistleblower law library, located at www.kkc.com/law-library.

RULE 8

Document, Document, Document

[The] wholesale destruction of documents . . . extended beyond paper records and included efforts to "purge the computer hard drives and E-mail system of Enron related files."
—Senate Report Discussing the Cover-Up Surrounding the ENRON scandal

---

Whistleblowers need documentation. Access to financial records, emails and internal reports are of obvious importance, whether you are trying to demonstrate a securities fraud or trying to save your job. In most cases the ability to of a whistleblower to back-up their allegations is the difference between winning and losing. How to legally and effectively obtain documentary evidence is of critical importance in whistleblower cases.

Judges decide document-removal cases on a case-by-case basis. But this analysis will depend on whether or not the case concerns an employment dispute, or whether your evidence is being used by the government to prove illegality in a reward case.

Removing Company Documents in Employment Cases

In retaliation cases employers will attack whistleblowers if they learn company documents were stolen or removed in violation of a corporate policy. Sometimes they use the removal issue as a justification for firing a whistleblower, other times they use it as "after-acquired evidence" as a basis for cutting off back-pay liability and blocking reinstatement. In extreme cases they file counterclaims or lawsuits demanding that all of the documents be returned. Once a company learns that you removed documents in violation of company policy you should anticipate a corporate counterattack on your credibility.

Some judges are hostile to employees who remove documents in violation of policy. For example, One judge from the U.S. district court for the Eastern District of Virginia used the document issue as a means to slam the whistleblower, calling him a "disgruntled employee" who "pilfer[ed] a wheelbarrow full of an employer's proprietary documents." Other judges understand the whistleblowers need for documentation and uphold the legality of the removals. In a case out of California the judge pointed to the "the strong public policy in favor of protecting whistleblowers who report fraud against the government," and refused to sanction the employee for removing the materials from the job and giving them to the Feds.

Today most courts apply a six-part balancing test when deciding whether an employee's removal of documents was justified. The factors are:

1. How were the documents obtained? Did the employee have proper access to the documents? Did the employee rifle through company files and surreptitiously copy the material?

2. To whom did the employee show the documents? Were they shown to coworkers and friends, or were the documents just provided to government investigators?

3. What was in the documents? Was the information the type that should be kept strictly confidential and clearly not have been copied?

4. Why were the documents obtained?

5. What was the employer's privacy or confidentiality policy?

6. Could the employee have obtained the material in a manner that did not violate company policy?

In addition to these factors other issues often come into play. For example, it is a very bad idea to sneak into a supervisor's office and steal documents. That will all but guarantee that the whistleblower will lose in court.

Removing Company Documents to Demonstrate Fraud or Misconduct in Reward Cases

In False Claims Act cases, where the document-taking was limited to materials that could demonstrate fraud, and the documents were only provided to whistleblower's attorney and the government, courts have upheld the legality of the removals In *Ruhe v. Masimo Corp.* a district court judge in California explained: "[The whistleblower] sought to expose a fraud against the government and limited their taking to documents relevant to the alleged fraud. Thus, this taking and publication was not wrongful, even in light of nondisclosure agreements, given 'the strong public policy in favor of protecting whistleblowers who report fraud against the government.'"

A similar holding was reached in *Erhart v. BOFI Holding, Inc.,* where the court noted that a whistleblower who provided documents to the Securities and Exchange Commission in violation of a nondisclosure agreement was protected: "[A]ny attempt to enforce the agreement as to this conduct would violate the SEC's rule prohibiting [the bank] from 'enforcing, or threatening to enforce, a confidentiality agreement' to impede Erhart from communicating with the SEC."

Alternatively, under some circumstances the company never needs to know that an employee removed documents. Under laws such as Dodd-Frank whistleblowers can confidentially and anonymously file allegations (backed up by company documents obtained from a whistleblower's workplace) directly to the government. Under the rules governing Dodd-Frank the government is required to keep the whistleblower's identity shielded throughout the investigation. If the company never learns who "leaked" information, they cannot sue the whistleblower for theft. In such cases the government can "back source" access to the documents by requesting the company produce these files directly, and therefore avoiding the need to reveal that the documents were already provided by the whistleblower. In this manner the government can honor its obligation to protect the identity of confidential sources.

Can the government use documents provided by a confidential whistleblower, even if those documents were removed from the company in violation of policy? The short answer is YES. Years ago the federal courts concluded that if a private citizen illegally obtains evidence, and provides that evidence to the government, the government can use it in court. In such cases the private citizen must voluntarily provided the documents to the government, without the government being behind the "search." This waives any obligation the government had to obtain the evidence through a search warrant.

This doctrine was explained in the 1899 case of n Bacon v. United States, 97 F. 35, 40 (8th Cir. 1899): "[I]f an individual by an illegal search or seizure obtains possession of an article or document, the state may nevertheless make use of the same as evidence against the person from whom they were wrongfully obtained to convict him of a crime; and that the inhibition found in article 4 of the amendments to the federal constitution . . . has no reference to unauthorized acts of individuals." This doctrine was upheld by the U.S. Supreme Court in 1921, and in numerous decisions thereafter.

In a 1968 case the Supreme Court looked at this doctrine in light of an individual's right to privacy. They held that if "private information" is voluntarily revealed to a confidential informant, the right to privacy no longer shields the information. A person engaged in a crime must "assume" that his or her "confident" may "reveal" "private information to another," and thus takes the "risk that his confident will reveal that information to the authorities."

This case is instructive in understanding the difference between an employee obtaining access to incriminating information while performing his or her job, as opposed to "rummaging through a supervisors desk." If an employee obtains evidence while at work doing his or her job, that is fair play. But violating the supervisor's right to privacy by sneaking into an office and stealing documents would be a bridge to far.

A whistleblower with access to "smoking gun" documents demonstrating a violation of law should carefully weigh the benefits of confidentially providing that document to the government under laws such as Dodd-Frank. Regardless providing those documents to persons outside of legal counsel or the government is highly risky and could easily backfire.

─────────────── PRACTICE TIPS ───────────────

- *Niswander v. Cincinnati*, 529 F.3d 714 (6th Cir. 2008) (setting forth the six-factor test for removing documents from work in an employment case).

- Employment cases permitting document removal: *Deltek v. Department of Labor*, No. 14-2415 (4th Cir. 2015); *Erhart v. BOFI Holding, Inc.*, Case No. 15-cv-02287-BAS-NLS (S.D. Cal. Feb. 14, 2017).

- *Ruhe v. Masimo Corp.*, 929 F. Supp. 2d 1033, 1038-39 (C.D. Cal. 2012) (permitting document removal in False Claims Act case).

- Cases permitting the government to use information illegally obtained by a private citizen: *Bacon v. United States*, 97 F. 35, 40 (8th Cir. 1899); *United States v. Jacobsen*, 466 U.S. 109 (1984); *United States v. Gianatasio*, 578 F. Supp. 3d 105 (D. Mass. 2021).

- *O'Day v. McDonnell Douglas*, 79 F.3d 756 (9th Cir. 1996) (warning against "rummaging through" the "supervisor's office").

RULE 9

Should You Tape?

Georgia Power's president admitted that he suspended and discharged Mosbaugh solely because of his tape recording. Therefore, the company admittedly fired Mosbaugh for engaging in activity that was legal and in furtherance of protected activity. Thus, Georgia Power has admitted to a violation of the [nuclear safety] employee protection provision.
—Secretary of Labor Robert Reich in ruling that the termination of Allen Mosbaugh violated the nuclear whistleblower law (91-ERA-1)(1995)

Whistleblowers tape. In numerous cases, employees have testified regarding their fear that no one will believe their story and that they need to document the oral admissions of witnesses in order to prove their case. Without a doubt, these fears are well-founded. Taped conversations have often proven to be key evidence in a whistleblower's case, as they can be the difference between winning and losing.

Tape-recorded conversations can also be powerful evidence proving wrongdoing. When Linda Tripp taped Monica Lewinsky, her coworker at the Pentagon, she obtained admissions that directly led to unprecedented sanctions against a sitting president of the United States, including a contempt citation, disbarment, an adverse finding in a sexual harassment case, and a vote by the House of Representatives for impeachment. The tapes provided irrefutable evidence. They documented oral admissions that would have been denied under oath by all the other witnesses.

The Tripp case is not without precedent. Many other whistleblowers have successfully used taped conversations to document serious wrongdoing. But is taping legal or ethical?

The rule on one-party taping traces back to a 1961 incident where IRS agent Roger S. Davis interviewed German Lopez, the owner of Clauson's Inn in North Falmouth, Massachusetts. Lopez paid Davis a bribe. Davis promptly reported the payoff to his supervisors and returned to Clauson's Inn to collect more evidence. But when he returned to the inn, he had a pocket tape recorder and another taping device on his body. This time he taped the conversation with the inn's owner, and the tape was key evidence in convicting Lopez. However, there was one major pitfall: Davis never obtained a search warrant and did not inform Lopez that he was recording his every word.

Davis's taping would become the landmark federal decision on the legality of "one-party" taping (i.e., when one party to a conversation tapes the conversation without telling the other party), whether done by federal agents or private persons. When the case of *Lopez v. United States* wound its way up to the Supreme Court three years later, Justice John Harlan upheld the legality of one-party taping. He reasoned that the "electronic device" was not used to document "conversations" the IRS agent "could not otherwise have heard. Instead, the device was used only to obtain the most reliable evidence possible of a conversation" in which the person using the hidden tape recorder "was a participant" and was "fully entitled to disclose."

The IRS agent was a party to the conversation, and the person making the criminal admissions knew that the agent could hear him. The court drew a strict distinction between using a tape recorder when you are a party to a conversation and planting a listening device (which would have been illegal if a search warrant for the device had not been obtained).

Chief Justice Earl Warren, one of the Supreme Court's most vocal supporters of a right to privacy, supported the decision. To ensure that there was no misunderstanding as to why he joined in the ruling, Chief Justice Warren wrote a separate concurring opinion. For Chief Justice Warren, permitting one-party taping was a simple matter of fairness. It would be wrong for the court to render Davis "defenseless" against attacks on his own "credibility." How else could someone defend themselves against countercharges that during the conversation they attempted to obtain a bribe or they acted to illegally entrap a defendant? Chief Justice Warren understood that no matter what the outcome of the court trial may be, the IRS agent had his reputation to defend. As he explained:

> [When] faced with situations where proof of an attempted bribe will be a matter of their word against that of the tax evader and perhaps some of his associates [IRS agents such as Mr. Davis] should not be defenseless against outright denials or claims of entrapment, claims which, if not open to conclusive refutation, will undermine the reputation of the individual agent for honesty and the public's confidence in his work. Where confronted with such a situation, it is only fair that an agent be permitted to support his credibility with a recording as Agent Davis did in this case.

In 1968, five years after the *Lopez* decision, Congress enacted the federal wiretapping law governing citizen one-party taping. The law memorialized the rules set forth in Justice Harlan's and Chief Justice Warren's opinions. One-party taping by both private citizens and government agents was explicitly permitted under the federal act, but surreptitious taping was outlawed unless a search warrant was obtained. Thus, under federal law, if you personally tape a conversation for which you are a party, your actions are legal. But if you plant the tape recorder in a room and tape a conversation for which you are not a party, that conduct is strictly prohibited. This is the critical distinction in the law governing taping of conversations.

The fact that your taping may be permitted under federal law does not end the issue. States are also permitted to regulate privacy matters and the legality of one-party taping. Although most states follow the federal model, a number of states specifically limit or prohibit one-party taping and require that all persons participating in a private conversation consent before any one person is permitted to tape. Specifically, twelve states (listed below) either do not permit one-party taping or place restrictions on its use. If an employee's taping of a conversation violates state law, they may be fired and even referred to state prosecutors to face possible criminal charges.

The Reporters Committee for Freedom of the Press published a highly useful booklet online titled *A Journalist's Guide to Taping Phone Calls and In-Person Conversations in the 50 States and D.C.* (2008, printed at www.rcfp.org). The committee conducted a careful state-by-state analysis of the law governing one-party taping, and summarized the current status of the law as follows:

Federal law allows recording of phone calls and other electronic communications with the consent of at least one party to the call. A majority of the states and territories have adopted wiretapping statutes based on the federal law. . . . Thirty-eight states and the District of Columbia permit individuals to record conversations to which they are a party without informing the other parties that they are doing so. . . . Twelve states require, under most circumstances, the consent of all parties to a conversation. Those jurisdictions are California, Connecticut, Florida, Illinois, Maryland, Massachusetts, Michigan, Montana, Nevada, New Hampshire, Pennsylvania and Washington. . . . Regardless of the state, it is almost always illegal to record a conversation to which you are not a party, do not have consent to tape, and could not naturally overhear. Federal law and most state laws also make it illegal to disclose the contents of an illegally intercepted call or communication.

Ensuring that taping is legal is just the first step in weighing whether or not to surreptitiously record a conversation. Even if a taping is legal, an employee still must be concerned with a variety of questions that could impact the taping, such as:

- Does the company have a rule that prohibits such conduct?

- Will a decision to tape appear credible? In the *Lopez* case no one could doubt the reasonableness of the agent's decision to tape. He had been offered a bribe, and he wanted to document the next offer, which he reasonably expected would occur during the meeting he taped.

- What if the taped conversation contains no evidence that is helpful to the employee's case? If the taped conversation contains a "smoking gun," the decision to tape the conversation will most likely appear reasonable to an objective observer (such as a judge or juror). But what if the supervisor suspects the employee may be "documenting" the conversation and decides to make statements that make the employee look bad? Taping carries risks. Once a record of the conversation is created, for better or worse, that record will have an impact on the outcome of a case.

- Will the company learn of the taping? Most likely, yes. In civil discovery the company's attorneys can ask whether or not the employee taped any conversations and can require that the employee produce copies of the tape(s).

- If an employee tapes conversations, can they destroy tapes that do not help the case? No. The failure to preserve evidence (for example, erasing the contents of the tapes) can be considered a serious discovery abuse and result in sanctions. Even if the tapes prove of no value, destroying them will be used against you in court. You may be asked if you taped a conversation. If you answer the question, but state that the tape was innocently erased, you will be accused of destroying evidence, and sanctions may follow.

- What if a government official asks an employee to tape? In such circumstances the taping will almost always be found reasonable. If the government wants the whistleblower to tape, it usually means there is strong evidence of misconduct, which can significantly support the employee's case.

- How can an employee demonstrate that a taping was reasonable? In a decision by the U.S. Court of Appeals for the Second Circuit, the court recognized that "a range of factors" could justify taping, including an employee's "belief that he was gathering evidence" to support a discrimination claim.

But there is no better way to demonstrate the reasonableness of taping than the contents of the tapes themselves. For example, in a case filed under the Clean Water Act's whistleblower provision, the employee's one-party recording of the Eastern Ohio Regional Wastewater Authority revealed that the violations committed at the plant could harm the political career of a key manager. When the court rendered its decision, this taped admission was critical: "The best indication that [the employee's] dismissal was motivated by his protected activity is contained in the tape recorded comments of the Board members . . . [who were] obviously aghast at [the employee's] whistleblower letter and were fearful of the effect the disclosure of environmental violations would have on their reputations and careers."

One-party taping has been instrumental in exposing fraud and misconduct, protecting the public's health and safety, and enabling whistleblowers to win their cases. But whether or not to tape always raises complex questions that should be carefully weighed before an employee decides to put a recorder in their pocket and have at it.

PRACTICE TIPS

- Do not violate the federal or state wiretap laws when taping. You cannot lawfully plant a bugging devise or tape a conversation that you are not a party of.

- The best one-party taping case is *Mosbaugh v. Georgia Power Co.*, 91-ERA-1/11 (Nov. 20, 1995), where the secretary of labor decided that one-party taping constituted a protected activity for which an employee could not be fired. See www.oalj.dol.gov (DOL whistleblower cases are published on this site)

- *Heller v. Champion International*, 891 F.2d 432 (2nd Cir. 1989) (one-party taping permitted for gathering evidence of discrimination).

RULE 10

Know the Limits of "Hotlines"

The court held that . . . Complainant's internal safety and quality complaints "were not protected by the statute." Accordingly, the complaint in this case is DISMISSED.
—Final order of the secretary of labor dismissing the whistleblower case of Ronald Goldstein

---

D o not blindly trust corporate-sponsored hotlines or compliance programs. Every major employer must deal with a basic fact: Love them or hate them, employee whistleblowers are the single most important source of information uncovering fraud and abuse in the workplace. If you want to know what is really going on in your company, you need reasonable and effective channels for information to be disclosed and investigated.

As a consequence, there has been a worldwide proliferation of internal reporting programs. They usually start with a hotline—for example, a toll-free phone number, publicized on a poster, that urges employees who witness misconduct to place a confidential phone call to a responsible company agent. Thereafter, a compliance department supposedly independently investigates the concern.

There's just one hitch. Is the hotline truly independent? Can it really keep callers' identities confidential? Will there be a proper investigation? Is contacting the internal compliance group really the right thing to do? As explained in Rule 11, corporate compliance programs that are managed by attorneys working for the company are completely compromised and can lawfully throw whistleblowers under the bus. But there are other problems inherent whenever a corporation tries to police itself. Some are obvious, but others are extremely legalistic and can land an honest employee, who's simply trying to do the right thing, in hot water.

Don't Be Tricked

Before you use a company's internal compliance program, make sure that any such contacts are protected under law. Regardless of company propaganda, corporations regularly go into court and argue that internal reporting is not a protected activity and that employees who raise concerns to their managers can be fired.

Case in point: Houston Lighting and Power Company and its subcontractor, EBASCO Constructors, Inc. In the 1980s, Houston Lighting was investing millions in the construction of two nuclear power plants known as the South Texas Project. One of the main companies hired to actually build the plant was EBASCO. The South Texas Project was plagued by regulatory violations, building delays, and cost overruns all while under heightened regulatory scrutiny. In response to these pressures, Houston Lighting established an "independent" internal compliance program known as SAFETEAM. SAFETEAM was given the authority to receive and investigate safety complaints filed by employees. Houston Lighting and EBASCO heavily promoted the program. As a Department of Labor review concluded, "[P]ostings about SAFETEAM" were "quite visible" throughout the plant, and employees were strongly encouraged to contact this safety program.

On its face, the SAFETEAM program was very reasonable. It offered employees a safe haven to raise concerns while promising a full and objective investigation into safety violations. What company would not want to promote safety and compliance with regulatory requirements? What company would want its nuclear power plant to have an accident?

Just ask Ronald J. Goldstein. He would know. Goldstein was hired by EBASCO as a craft supervisor at the South Texas Project. In the summer of 1985 he identified serious safety problems on-site, including the failure of project managers to follow correct safety inspection procedure(s), the falsification of documents, the failure of employees to issue non-conformance reports on safety problems, and serious quality control violations that impacted systems critical for the safe construction of the plant. Consistent with company policy, Goldstein reported his concerns to SAFETEAM.

But what Houston Lighting and EBASCO did not tell their employees was that the company did not believe that reports to its SAFETEAM program were legally protected. In other words, they believed they could fire employees who raised safety concerns with SAFETEAM. Goldstein learned that the hard way. After raising his concerns with SAFETEAM, he was fired.

In the beginning, everything went according to plan. He filed a whistleblower complaint under federal law with the U.S. Department of Labor. After a hearing the DOL found that Goldstein's termination was illegal. The DOL found that Goldstein's reports to SAFETEAM were protected activities. How could they not be? He raised safety concerns to a responsible, independent organization designed to investigate and fix problems in order to ensure that the nuclear plant was safe. The judge ordered that Goldstein be reinstated with full back pay. He also awarded compensatory damages for emotional distress and attorney fees and costs. His employment record was cleared up, and references to his termination were expunged.

Lynn Martin, President George W. Bush's secretary of the DOL, affirmed the judge's ruling. She ruled that SAFETEAM was "an organization established by Houston Lighting and Power Company to receive and investigate allegations of safety and quality violations" and that reporting violations to SAFETEAM was therefore protected activity.

The company appealed to the U.S. Court of Appeals for the Fifth Circuit, arguing that SAFETEAM was simply an internal management program and that in order to be legally protected, employees had to contact government regulators. According to the company, Goldstein's case had to be dismissed because his complaints to SAFETEAM were not covered under the federal nuclear whistleblower law. Obviously this limitation was not presented in any of the literature or posters that encouraged employees to report safety concerns to SAFETEAM. Who would contact a hotline program if the propaganda encouraging such contacts also told employees they could be fired simply for making a hotline disclosure? Indeed, reading the company propaganda, one would readily expect that employees who filed such allegations would be rewarded, not punished.

Incredibly, the appeals court agreed with the company. The court reversed Secretary Martin's ruling and concluded that the federal nuclear safety whistleblower law did *not* protect employees who made disclosures to SAFETEAM. According to the court, whistleblowers had to contact a government agency to be protected, and SAFETEAM, although marketed to employees as an independent safety program designed to investigate complaints, was, legally speaking, a sham. Contact with SAFETEAM offered no protection whatsoever, and companies were free to use these programs to identify whistleblowers and fire them.

Goldstein lost his right to back pay, compensatory damages, and attorney fees. He lost his right to work at the South Texas Project. His termination was upheld.

In the wake of the Goldstein decision, and other similar rulings stripping protection from employees who raised nuclear safety concerns with corporate-run programs, Congress amended the nuclear whistleblower law to explicitly protect such internal reports. But the precedent was set, and even today it is still uncertain whether reports to internal hotlines or compliance programs are fully protected. Where a statute explicitly protects such disclosures, the law is clear. But in the absence of such rules, contacting an internal hotline may result in retaliation that is outside the law's protection.

In a sense, Houston Lighting and its contractor EBASCO won the legal battle. But ultimately they lost the war. Corporations that undermine their own internal compliance programs are simply inviting employees to keep their whistleblower status completely confidential and to report concerns directly to the government.

Should Employees Avoid Hotlines?

Question: Are corporate compliance and ethics programs just window-dressing?
Answer: In many companies, probably yes.
—Donna Boehme, former Chief Compliance Officer, BP

Before contacting a corporate compliance program employees should carefully consider whether the program is independent or whether it can act as a Trojan Horse and be used to undermine your rights. Employees should consider taking the following ten steps to evaluate the costs and benefits of making an internal disclosure:

STEP 1: ENSURE THE CONTACT IS PROTECTED UNDER LAW

Are the internal reports you want to make protected under law? If not, find another way to raise your concerns.

STEP 2: RESEARCH THE IN-HOUSE PROGRAM

Before using an in-house program, employees should quietly try to obtain information about the program's reputation. This could include talking to an attorney who has experience handling employment cases against your employer. If the company has a history of retaliating against whistleblowers, contact the program at your own risk.

STEP 3: DOCUMENT EVERYTHING

Whistleblowers need to create a detailed paper trail. If a lawsuit were to develop, contacts with the hotline program will be very relevant. Employees can also conduct civil discovery into the company's hotline and compliance records after a lawsuit is filed. These records can be extremely helpful in demonstrating protected activity, employer knowledge, retaliation, or pretext.

STEP 4: DON'T REST ON LAURELS

Whistleblowers cannot assume the system will work. The contact with a compliance program often is just the first step in a series of disclosures. It is common for workers to first raise a concern with a supervisor, then elevate the concern to an internal compliance department, and finally file a concern with a government agency. But simply relying on a hotline investigation to fix a problem or provide protection is naive.

STEP 5: DON'T TAKE LEGAL ADVICE FROM A COMPLIANCE OFFICER

Compliance officers and hotline investigators work for the company; they do not work for the employees. They are under no obligation to provide employees with complete or accurate advice. They are under no obligation to inform employees of their rights or the laws that may protect them.

STEP 6: BE SKEPTICAL ABOUT CONFIDENTIALITY

Many hotline programs promise confidentiality. Under the Sarbanes-Oxley Act and the Federal Acquisition Regulations, companies are required to grant confidentiality to employees. However, it is well-known that the very nature of an employee's complaint can act to identify the worker. Often, only a small group of workers are aware of the details concerning a regulatory violation. When the hotline investigator commences their review of the complaint, it may be easy for the employer to figure out the identity of the whistleblower.

STEP 7: AVOID PROGRAMS MANAGED BY CORPORATE ATTORNEYS

Whistleblowers should investigate who manages the compliance program. Some compliance programs report directly to a company's chief executive officer or to an independent audit committee. These programs tend to have more integrity than compliance programs that report to, or are managed by, the company's general counsel. Not surprisingly, company attorneys focus on protecting employers from lawsuits, not fixing problems. Programs that report to the office of general counsel or other company attorneys should be avoided or approached with extreme caution.

STEP 8: DON'T TAKE ADVICE FROM THE COMPANY ATTORNEY

Company lawyers work for the company and owe a duty to act in the company's best interest, not yours. They can use your disclosures to "throw you under the bus."

STEP 9: GIVE THEM THE ROPE TO HANG THEMSELVES

The failure of a corporation to properly investigate a hotline/compliance concern can constitute evidence of a cover-up and evidence that a company was hostile to the whistleblower. Often hotline records can be obtained as part of pretrial discovery. These files may contain significant information that could help prove retaliation, including statements by various managers and factual findings related to the underlying allegations of misconduct. Even when a company tries to use its hotline investigation to demonstrate that an employee's concern had no basis, an employee can still muster additional facts that the compliance officers failed to consider and impeach the company's conduct.

STEP 10: BLOW THE WHISTLE ON THE LACK OF PROPER INTERNAL CONTROLS

A publicly traded company that lacks effective internal controls necessary to detect securities fraud, ensure accurate corporate disclosures, and detect improper payments (such as paying bribes) may be in violation of securities laws. These failures can result in sanctions and undermine the credibility of a company.

PRACTICE TIPS

- The Sarbanes-Oxley Act requirement mandating that audit committees include a confidential employee concerns program is codified at 15 U.S.C. § 78j-1(m)(4). On June 30, 2008, the Close the Contractor Fraud Loophole Act became law. This law requires federal contractors to protect internal whistleblower disclosures. See Federal Acquisition Regulations 48 C.F.R. Chapter 1 and Subpart 3.900.

- In 2011 the Securities and Exchange Commission and the Commodity Futures Trading Commission implemented whistleblower reward rules that create incentives for employees to report potential violations to corporate compliance programs, but explicitly do *not* require employees to report in-house. These new incentives are codified at SEC Final Rules 17 C.F.R. §§ 240.21F-4(b)(7) and F-6(a)(4) and CFTC Final Rules 17 C.F.R. §§ 165.2(i)(3) and 165.9(b)(4).

- In the case of *Digital Realty Trust v. Somers*, 138 S.Ct. 767 (2018), the U.S. Supreme Court unanimously held that the Dodd-Frank Act whistleblower reward law was designed to encourage, reward, and protect employees who directly reported violations to the SEC, *not to* internal compliance programs. Under SEC and CFTC regulations, to ensure that you can qualify for a reward, you must file a complaint with these agencies within 120 days of making an internal report.

- *Halliburton v. ARB*, 771 F.3d 254 (5th Cir. 2014) (violating the confidentiality of a whistleblower who reported concerns internally can be an adverse).

- Ronald Goldstein's case is cited as *Goldstein v. EBASCO*, 86-ERA-36 (April 7, 1992), *reversed*, 986 F.2d 1419 (5th Cir. 1993).

RULE 11

Don't Let the Lawyers Throw You Under the Bus

---

*I am a lawyer for the Company. I represent only the Company and do not represent you
personally. If you would like legal advice, you should consult your own attorney.*
—Joshua B. Simon, Esq. and John Song, Esq., Kirkland & Ellis LLP

The above quote, from the law firm of Kirkland & Ellis, tells the entire story. Kirkland &
Ellis is a leading law firm that specializes in representing major corporations accused
of violating the law. When you talk to an attorney for the company, that lawyer *does
not represent you*. They are not your friend. They work for the boss—and the boss may want
to throw you under the bus.

Corporate lawyers will try to convince you to help the company, even if the company ultimately decides to blame you for a violation or turn you in to the government
for prosecution. They will not advise you of your whistleblower rights.

Corporate counsel's role in compliance investigations can be downright devious.
The lessons learned by Harry Barko when he tried to hold KBR accountable for ripping
off the government is a case in point. At the height of the war in Iraq, employees from the defense contractor Kellogg Brown & Root, Inc. (better known as KBR)
provided highly credible evidence to KBR's compliance program that subcontractors
were involved in bribery and "presented inflated and fraudulent bills" for terrible
work. At the time they did not know that the compliance program was managed by
the company's general counsel, whose primary goal was to protect the company, not
combat corruption. The compliance investigators (none of whom were attorneys)
sent their investigatory reports that confirmed the fraud up the chain of command
and, ultimately, to the company lawyers in Houston, Texas. None of the information
disclosed by the whistleblowers was ever provided to the government.

Some years later, Harry Barko, one of the KBR employees frustrated that the
company had gotten away with fraud, filed a complaint under the False Claims
Act. As part of his case he requested the release of the compliance interviews.
KBR objected, claiming the documents were protected under corporate attorney-
client privilege. The basis for objecting was simple: KBR's compliance program
ultimately reported to the company's general counsel; therefore, all its documents,
including direct evidence of fraud provided to the company via internal whistleblowers, was confidential.

The trial judge reviewed the contested documents in camera (privately) without
giving a copy to Barko's counsel. After looking at the materials, he ordered KBR to
produce them for Barko's review. The judge noted that the documents contained no
legal advice, were not written by lawyers, and the employees who were interviewed were
never directly advised that their interviews were covered under an attorney-client or

attorney–work product privilege. In his order the judge described the materials as "eye-openers," and explained that they included evidence of:

- Preferential treatment to a favored subcontractor

- KBR employees accepting payoffs to illegally steer business to an unqualified subcontractor

- Permitting the less-qualified subcontractor to improperly undercut bids submitted by companies that were not paying bribes by giving them inside information

- Approving contracts that were more expensive to the United States, with "terrible completion performance" and "regular attempts to double bill"

- Awarding a contract despite the "bid being twice [as expensive as] another bid from a competent contractor"

- Paying the full bills from a favored subcontractor (which had given payoffs to KBR employees), despite the work being incomplete, late, and substandard

- Paying ballooned costs (three times the contract price) for work, even when performance was terrible

KBR, with strong support from the U.S. Chamber of Commerce, filed an emergency appeal to the U.S. Court of Appeals District of Columbia Circuit. The basis of their appeal was simple: KBR's compliance program was ultimately managed by the company's legal department. Thus, all of the investigatory files and interview notes were protected from disclosure under attorney-client or work-product privilege.

The U.S. Court of Appeals, in an opinion authored by now–Supreme Court Justice Brett Kavanaugh, sided with KBR. The documents would remain secret, despite the fact that they proved that taxpayers had been robbed. Nor did it matter that none of the persons interviewed at KBR were directly told that the interviews were covered under the company's attorney-client privilege.

The Court of Appeals justified its holding by reasoning that "[t]he attorney-client privilege protects confidential employee communications made during a business's internal investigation led by company lawyers." Because the privilege applied not only to the lawyers themselves but also to agents and subordinates working under the direction or control of the lawyer, everyone working within compliance can fall under the privilege. In the case of KBR, this included its entire compliance program. In this way a company can choose to hide the results of an internal investigation (if the results are harmful), release the results (if they do not vindicate the whistleblower), or use some (or all) of the investigatory materials to build a defense against a government sanction or a whistleblower case.

The incriminating KBR documents remained secret. Barko, the U.S. government, and the American public were denied access to these materials and Barko's case was dismissed.

It doesn't take a pig farmer from Iowa to smell the stench of conflict in that arrangement.
—Senator Charles Grassley on general counsel
running compliance programs

The ability for companies like KBR to twist compliance programs to serve their self-interest is far greater than simply hiding information. KBR, as the corporate client, can always decide to waive the privilege and release the attorney-client information any time it is to their advantage. If the documents had been critical of Barko, KBR could have used them to attack his credibility. If the reports demonstrated that the company was a good corporate citizen, they could be released to impeach the good faith of the whistleblower or to demonstrate to a court how thorough and objective its program is. Under the KBR precedent, the purported goals of a lawyer-run compliance program can be twisted and, instead of promoting ethical corporate behavior, become a prime enabler for corporate crime.

New York Ethics Opinion 650

Should there be any doubt as to where a lawyer-run compliance program's loyalties lie, the cautions approved by Opinion 650 of the New York State Bar Association Committee on Professional Ethics settle the issue. These warnings, which are almost never given, are designed to ensure that an employee who contacts an attorney-managed program clearly knows that the program is designed to protect the company, not the worker or whistleblower.

In its opinion, the committee addressed the question of whether a corporate attorney could participate in a compliance program under which employees are required to report illegal or unethical behavior. The committee determined that lawyers, as well as those individuals operating under the attorneys (such as paralegals or investigators), could participate in such programs but certain precautionary measures should be taken. The committee approved an adverse-interest script, drafted by the company seeking the ethics opinion. The company mandated that this script be read to all persons who called the company's compliance program:

> When it appears that a caller's interests may differ from or there is a reasonable possibility that such interests may be "in conflict" with the Company's interests:
>
> 1. Determine whether the caller is represented by counsel. If so, make the following statement: "The Company's policy requires that you report non-compliance with the law or other unethical behavior. However, as you are represented by counsel, I can only

talk to you through your counsel. Please have him/her call me or give me his/her name and I would be happy to call him/him."

2. *If the caller is unrepresented by counsel, please make the following statement: "I want to caution you that I am an attorney for the Company and not for you or other employees. Therefore, while I can record your complaint, I cannot and will not give you legal advice, and you should not understand our conversation to consist of such advice. I do advise you to seek your own counsel, however, as your interests and the Company's may differ. Having said this, I would be happy to listen to your complaint," etc.*

The committee also noted that although the Code of Professional Conduct is addressed to lawyers, lawyers are required to diligently supervise *non-lawyers* to ensure that these subordinates do not violate the Code of Professional Responsibility. Thus, non-lawyers supervised by lawyers may also be required to provide these warnings to employees who call the compliance hotline. The New York rule is consistent with the general ABA rules governing attorney conduct.

What to Do If the Company's Attorneys Knock on Your Door

The key advice for any potential whistleblowers who may find themselves in the middle of a corporate investigation is to confidentially contact your own attorney before you make any disclosures. Whether or not to meet with or provide information to a company lawyer or compliance personnel who works for the lawyer must be made on a case-by-case basis. You must understand that the company lawyer does not represent you and may use any information you provide or don't provide against you.

A frequent issue arises when the company informs you that you are a witness in an investigation and then offers to pay for an attorney to represent you personally. This is very common, especially in Foreign Corrupt Practices Act cases, where individuals can be held personally accountable, along with the company itself. Don't be fooled by this offer. You get what you pay for. When companies hire outside attorneys to represent their employees, these outside lawyers are almost always beholden to the company that pays their fee. In most every case these attorneys will work hand in hand with the company lawyers, share your information with the company, and will give you bad advice. Moreover, it is a leap of faith to ever imagine that the company-sponsored lawyers will advise you to become a confidential informant against the company and file for a reward.

The decision whether to let the company hire a lawyer for you and what you say to that lawyer is another strategic move. If all the other company witnesses are letting the company hire and pay for their attorneys, you will stick out like a sore thumb if you refuse.

One option every whistleblower should consider if the company offers to hire an attorney to represent you is to simply say yes, but confidentially hire your own private attorney to give you advice. The company and its hired gun never need to learn of this decision. Your own private attorney can give you the advice you need to protect your interests, regardless of what a company-sponsored attorney may say.

If you decide to hire your own counsel (which you should do!), you do not have to tell the company lawyer of your plans. You can work with your own private counsel and develop your own strategy that protects you, not the company. You can use your own attorney to confidentially and anonymously file a whistleblower reward claim, even while you are working with the company-controlled internal investigation. Don't wait until you have prejudiced your own ability to obtain a reward. Don't wait until the company throws you under the bus and tries to blame you for the violations it sponsored, planned, or turned its back on.

———————————— PRACTICE TIPS ————————————

- *Upjohn Co. v. United States*, 449 U.S. 383 (1981) (Supreme Court decision discussing when attorney-client privilege applies to a compliance investigation).

- *In re: KBR*, 756 F.3d 754 (D.C. Cir. 2014) (broadly defining corporate attorney-client privilege in the context of compliance investigations).

- *In re Grand Jury*, 23 F.4th 1088 (9th Cir. 2021) (modified view of *In re KBR*).

- *U.S. ex rel. Barko v. Halliburton Co.*, No. 1:05-cv-2276, Opinion and Order dated March 6, 2014 (D.D.C.) (district court docket in the *KBR* cases).

- New York State Bar Association Committee on Professional Ethics Opinion 650, July 30, 1993; available at https://archive.nysba.org/CustomTemplates/Content.aspx?id=7336.

- Here is how corporate attorneys discuss these issues: Sara Kropf, "Upjohn Warnings from Both Sides of the Table," Kropf Moseley (Mar. 30, 2017); Simon and Song, "Upjohn and the 'Corporate Miranda Warnings' During Government Investigations," Kirkland & Ellis.

RULE 12

Don't Tip Off the Crooks

Are you required to disclose fraud or criminal activity to your boss before going to the government? The answer is no. No such requirement exists under powerful whistleblower laws such as Dodd-Frank, Sarbanes-Oxley, False Claims, Foreign Corruption, Anti-Money Laundering, and the Internal Revenue Acts. Requiring a whistleblower to tip off the bosses is in direct conflict with the right of employees to remain confidential or anonymous. Any such requirement could also expose the employee to retaliation or alert criminals as to the witness(es) who may land them in jail.

Under Dodd-Frank, AML, Foreign Corrupt Practices, IRS, and False Claims, the choice to report a concern directly to the government or internally is yours and yours alone. No code of conduct, handbook, or employment agreement can negate this right.

Writing for a unanimous Supreme Court, Justice Ruth Bader Ginsberg explained the core purpose of the Dodd-Frank Act, and described that an individual could *only* obtain whistleblower status under Dodd-Frank if they directly contacted the government:

> The "core objective" of Dodd-Frank's robust whistleblower program . . . is "to motivate people who know of securities law violations to tell the SEC." By enlisting whistleblowers to "assist the Government [in] identify[ing] and prosecut[ing] persons who have violated securities laws," Congress undertook to improve SEC enforcement and facilitate the Commission's "recover[y] [of] money for victims of financial fraud." To that end, [Dodd-Frank] provides substantial monetary rewards to whistleblowers who furnish actionable information to the SEC. . . . Dodd-Frank's award program and anti-retaliation provision thus work synchronously to motivate individuals with knowledge of illegal activity to "tell the SEC."

But the mere fact that you can go directly to the government does not mean you should. Once again, the timing of any disclosure, and to whom you report, is a strategic decision made on a case-by-case basis. Both the SEC and the CFTC understood this when they approved regulations implementing Dodd-Frank. Although whistleblowers always have the right to report directly to the government, these two commissions created unique rules that also encouraged employees to make internal reports at their own discretion.

The procedure is somewhat ingenious. If an employee decides to make an internal disclosure to the company, they can do this and still fully qualify for a reward. This is true even if the company itself makes a voluntary disclosure of the misconduct to the government. Here is how it works:

- The commissions established a grace period in which a whistleblower who reported frauds to their supervisor or a compliance program could still qualify for a reward, provided that they also submit the same allegations to the SEC within a 120-day time period or the CFTC within the 180-day time period

- Thus a whistleblower would not be prejudiced by initially reporting frauds to their employer if they also complied with the grace period, even if another whistleblower filed an identical claim during the grace period, and even if the company self-reported the violation to the government during the grace period. The individual whistleblower would still be considered voluntary and the first to file, provided they eventually filed their case within the grace period.

The chair of the commission, when approving the SEC's final whistleblower regulations, explained the policy behind creating the grace period:

I believe that the final [rule] strikes the correct balance—a balance between encouraging whistleblowers to pursue the route of internal compliance when appropriate—while providing them the option of heading directly to the SEC. This makes sense as well, because it is the whistleblower who is in the best position to know which route is best to pursue. . . . I believe that incentivizing—rather than requiring—internal reporting is more likely to encourage a strong internal compliance culture. Our rules create incentives for people to report misconduct to their employers, but only if those companies have created an environment where employees feel comfortable that management will take them seriously—and where they are free from possible retaliation.

The key benefit of the grace period is that it permits whistleblowers to have it both ways. They can work internally with their compliance officials or auditors and try to get the company to do the right thing. Doing so will not impact their rights under the reward provisions *if they file their official TCR complaint within the grace period.* These procedures are unique to Dodd-Frank. They do not apply to cases filed under other reward laws, such as the False Claims Act or the IRS whistleblower law. Those laws require a direct report to the government, and no credit is given for internal disclosures.

Keeping Up with the Changes

To keep up to date on changes in the laws, whistleblowers should access the free online law library created by the author, located at www.kkc.com/law-library.

- The SEC 120-day rule for providing information to a compliance officer before contacting the SEC is set forth at 17 C.F.R. § 240.21F-4(b)(7).

- The Commodity Futures Trading Commission's 180-day rule for providing information to a compliance officer before contacting the CFTC is set forth at 17 C.F.R. § 165.2(i)(3).

- Best practice: If you report a fraud internally, file your reward claim within 120 days of the initial report to the SEC or 180 days of the report to the CFTC.

- The whistleblower obstruction of justice law is found at 18 U.S.C. § 1513e).

RULE 13

Special Rules for Directors, Partners, or Auditors

It is no secret that top-level directors, executives, and auditors are often under tremendous pressure to "go along to get along." They are also often in the best position to learn about misconduct, fraud, and violations of law. All but one of major award laws permit executives, directors, attorneys, and anyone with compliance responsibilities to qualify for whistleblower rewards. If you are the chairman of a company's Audit Committee, you can become a whistleblower. The same is true for every executive vice president, every chief compliance officer, every director, and every partner. However, based on your status, different rules may apply as to procedures you must follow to ensure that you will qualify for a reward and the maximum legal protections affordable under law.

Two changes in the laws have opened the doors to top corporate officials becoming whistleblowers. First is the right to be anonymous and confidential under Dodd-Frank and the money laundering/sanctions whistleblower laws (and to a lesser extent, the tax whistleblower law). Thus, you can hold a top-level position and your peers may never learn that you blew the whistle. Second, the prospect of getting a reward provides a safe harbor for highly compensated employees.

The rules governing top executives can be divided into three classes. The first class consists of most whistleblower laws, including the False Claims and Internal Revenue Acts. These laws have no restrictions on the rights of directors, auditors, or compliance officials to blow the whistle. Attorneys can also blow the whistle, but must be careful not to violate valid bar rules governing the attorney-client and work-product privilege.

The second class consists of the Dodd-Frank Act. The Securities and Exchange Commission and Commodity Futures Trading Commission approved special rules that apply to persons who perform compliance functions and directors, partners, and attorneys. These rules do not block these top-level executives and compliance officials from blowing the whistle and qualifying for a reward. But they place procedural restrictions on these rights that must be complied with. These procedural requirements are explained below.

The third class consists of employees under the AML/Sanctions whistleblower law. This law covers directors and partners. However, if your "official duties" include enforcing laws prohibiting money laundering, you may be excluded from obtaining a reward.

Auditors under Fire and the Regulators Respond

Compliance professionals and management officials have traditionally been subjected to tremendous pressure to commit or cover up frauds. As reflected in **Figure 10**, the pressure comes from the C-Suite. In 2015 the Institute of Internal Auditors, a trade

Figure 10

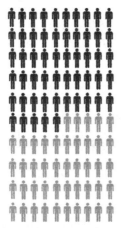

55% of chief audit executives were directed to omit important findings from their audit reports.

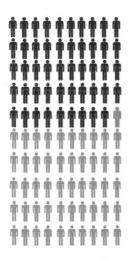

49% of chief audit executives were directed "not to perform audit work in high-risk areas".

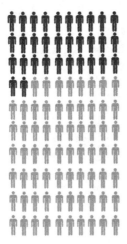

32% of chief audit executives were instructed to audit "low-risk" areas, in part so that executives could "retaliate against another individual".

association of more than 180,000 members in 170 countries, published the *Politics of Internal Auditing*. Five hundred North American chief audit executives (CAEs) were questioned concerning the pressures they faced when trying to do their jobs. A stunning 55 percent of all CAEs were directed to omit material findings from their reports.

Likewise, these executives reported tremendous pressure to suppress negative audit findings:

- 55 percent of the CAEs were directed to omit important findings from their audit reports.

- 49 percent were directed "not to perform audit work in high-risk areas."

- 32 percent were instructed to audit "low-risk" areas, in part so that executives could "retaliate against another individual."

The pressure to change audit reports came from the top (see **Figure 11**). When asked who directed them to suppress or significantly modify a valid internal audit finding, the CAEs reported that 38 percent of these requests came from a company's chief executive officer, 24 percent came from a chief financial officer, and 12 percent came from the board of directors. Significantly, 18 percent of the requests came from persons with significant oversight responsibility (the chief compliance officer, legal or general counsel, the chief risk officer, or the company's audit committee).

Consistent with these findings, a survey of 14,518 auditors from 166 countries reported vicious retaliation when the auditors refused to change their findings. Retaliation tactics included pay cuts, transfers to other positions, terminations, forced ease into retirement, budget cuts, exclusion from important meetings, ostracization, audit department

Figure 11

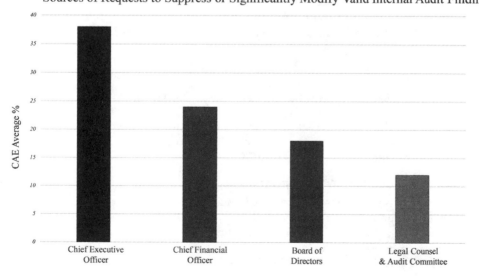

Sources of Requests to Suppress or Significantly Modify Valid Internal Audit Findings

outsourcing, and hostile working conditions. Without a doubt, compliance professionals are positioned to identify frauds, but are often subjected to retaliation simply for doing their job. Instead of keeping companies honest, these professionals are an easy target to coerce into aiding in a cover-up or simply to hide any bad news.

It is little wonder that after Dodd-Frank was signed into law the U.S. Chamber of Commerce worked overtime to block directors, auditors, and compliance officials from coverage. The chamber, with the full support of hundreds of public companies and their trade associations, vigorously argued that employees paid by the company to uncover, report, or correct problems should not be covered under Dodd-Frank. They lobbied for a strict prohibition barring corporate directors and all workers who had oversight duties from collecting rewards. The list of special interests that lobbied to quash the rights of corporate directors and compliance professionals is a who's who of Wall Street, along with the criminal defense attorneys who represent corporate crooks. They included the National Association of Corporate Directors, Cardinal Health, Verizon, Honeywell, Merck, Microsoft, Wells Fargo, Deloitte, the Business Roundtable, National Association of Criminal Defense Attorneys, Vinson & Elkins law firm, PricewaterhouseCoopers, Gibson and Dunn law firm, United Technologies, Citigroup, Johnson & Johnson, Intel, Target, AT&T, JP Morgan Chase, Pfizer, Prudential Insurance, Google, General Electric, Ernst & Young, Association of Corporate Counsel, Boeing, and Goodyear. Not surprisingly, many of the corporations involved in this massive lobbying campaign had been sanctioned in the past based on evidence reported by whistleblowers.

Wall Street lost this fight. In a 3–2 vote the SEC approved a creative approach that promoted honest and independent compliance programs, while at the same time recognizing that directors, attorneys, and auditors can qualify for rewards. Shortly thereafter, the Commodity Futures Trading Commission adopted an identical regulation.

The final rules are tricky. The bottom line is that in almost every case directors, partners, and employees with compliance responsibilities who learn about violations of law as part of their official duties can qualify for rewards. However, they must pay careful attention to the finely tuned technical procedural details governing the SEC and CFTC's approach to this issue. But keep in mind these rules only apply in the context of the Dodd-Frank Act, and do not apply when filing claims with the IRS or under the False Claims Act. The same cannot be said for whistleblowers under the AML/Sanctions whistleblower law.

Five Steps Directors and Auditors Must Follow Under Dodd-Frank

The following are the five steps that directors, partners, lawyers, and persons working in auditing or compliance functions must take to qualify for rewards under Dodd-Frank (i.e., when filing claims with the SEC or CFTC).

STEP 1: DON'T BE FOOLED BY THE BROAD EXEMPTION

At first glance, directors, partners, and other employees "whose principal duties involve compliance or internal audit responsibilities" appear to be disqualified from obtaining a reward under SEC and CFTC regulations. Additionally, any employee who has learned of the violations "in connection with the entity's processes for identifying, reporting, and addressing possible violations of law" is also exempt from a reward. This exemption also applies to employees from any outside firm "retained to perform compliance or internal audit functions."

Based on these prohibitions, it would appear that Wall Street won the day and that thousands of employees were excluded from the rewards available under the Dodd-Frank Act. But that isn't the whole story. *The exceptions are the rule.*

STEP 2: THE 120-DAY HOLD

The exceptions contained in the SEC and CFTC regulations permit directors, attorneys, partners, auditors, and compliance officials to file claims and obtain awards in cases where the company does not timely and accurately inform the government that it may have violated the law. These rules are designed to also protect the rights of the original whistleblower who reported the underlying violations to their supervisor or compliance program and to encourage corporations to institute effective internal controls to police fraud.

The processes approved by the SEC and CFTC are ingenious. They take into consideration the numerous issues raised by permitting persons who have an official responsibility to report or investigate violations internally to qualify for Dodd-Frank protections and awards.

First, the original source whistleblower is fully protected. The employee who actually first reported the violation to a compliance official, a company attorney, or a director can immediately file a case with the SEC as the original source or can wait up to 120 days and still qualify as an original source (or 180 days under the CFTC rules). In such cases the original source whistleblower is the individual who uncovered the violation and internally reported it to compliance or a supervisor. Thus the first employee-whistleblower who discovered the violation is protected—but only for a limited period of time.

Second, under the SEC regulations a company is given 120 days to investigate the original allegation and self-report any violation to the government. Corporations are rewarded for having competent and independent compliance programs that can effectively respond to a whistleblower complaint in a timely manner. If the company in fact fully and completely self-reports, the original whistleblower still can fully qualify for a reward, but the compliance officials responsible for the internal investigation cannot. But if the company delays in confessing to the government, or covers up all or part of the crimes, it's game on. After the 120-day hold, the executives, directors, and compliance officials who are aware that the company was not fully honest with the government, or who believe that the company failed to self-report the violations within the 120-day time period, can confidentially file claims and fully qualify for rewards.

STEP 3: READ THE FINE PRINT

After 120 days from the first internal disclosure, everything changes. Any company that attempts to hide violations from the SEC or simply fails to timely self-report the violations during the 120-day hold period stands to face a regulatory nightmare. Why? After 120 days from the first internal report, *every* director, partner, auditor, and compliance official—including outside consultants—can file a claim and obtain a mandatory whistleblower reward. This would include everyone from the chair of the company's audit committee to the chief compliance officer to the hotline operator who answered the original call placed by the employee-whistleblower. The floodgates are opened.

STEP 4: COVER-UPS ARE NOT TOLERATED

The 120-day hold creates a clear deadline permitting directors and auditors to file claims once that time period expires. But there are other exceptions that also can be relevant. The army of auditors, directors, and compliance officials can immediately file with the SEC and qualify for rewards under two additional circumstances: First, if the underlying violation is large and could immediately harm investors. And second, if the company is engaging in a cover-up. The SEC describes these two exceptions as follows:

- If "you [the compliance officer, director, attorney, auditor, etc.] have a reasonable basis to believe that disclosure of the information to the Commission is necessary to prevent the relevant entity from engaging in conduct that is likely to cause substantial injury to the financial interest or property of the entity or investors," you can immediately report your concerns to the SEC and qualify for a reward.

- If "you have a reasonable basis to believe that the relevant entity is engaging in conduct that will impede an investigation of the misconduct," you can immediately report your concerns to the SEC and qualify for a reward.

STEP 5: THE ORIGINAL TIPSTER REMAINS PROTECTED

The commission's regulations also protect the employees who raised the original concerns with a supervisor, compliance official, company attorney, or director. These original sources are given 120 days to file their claim with the SEC (or 180 days with the CFTC) and will still be considered the first to file, even if the company self-reports the violation. Those who are the first to file are in the best position to qualify for a reward, if they file a formal TCR complaint within the 120-day (or 180-day) grace period. But after this grace period, all bets are off.

Thus, in most circumstances auditors and directors will qualify for a reward. This is true because these executives and compliance officials can qualify for a reward even if they simply contribute to an ongoing investigation. Based on their positions in the company, it is evident that a compliance official or director who has responsibility for investigating an original whistleblower's concerns may have significant additional information that can help to achieve a successful enforcement action. These directors and compliance personnel simply have to wait 120 days before they file their TCR with the SEC. The Commodity Futures Trading Commission has a nearly identical rule.

After approving these procedures, the SEC wasted no time in granting monetary rewards to compliance professionals. One of the first whistleblowers to receive a financial reward from the SEC worked in compliance. The SEC issued a press release to publicize the $1.5 million awarded to this auditor: "Individuals who perform internal audit, compliance, and legal functions for companies are on the front lines in the battle against fraud and corruption. They often are privy to the very kinds of specific, timely, and credible information that can prevent an imminent fraud or stop an ongoing one." The commission's message was clear: The goal of the whistleblower reward program is to protect investors, not to prevent employees from becoming whistleblowers simply because they work as auditors, attorneys, compliance professionals or even sit as members of the company's board of directors.

AML/Sanctions Whistleblower Act

The Anti-Money Laundering (AML) Whistleblower Act, which became law on January 1, 2021, has an exemption for whistleblowers whose "job duties" include working in a financial institution's anti-money laundering department. The law states: "No award" "may be made" to a whistleblower who "acquired the original information" while acting in the "normal course" of their "job duties." The precise contours of this exclusion will be defined by the Department of Treasury when they issue rules on the AML whistleblower law. But if you work within an anti-money laundering program you should consider filing claims under other laws, such as Dodd-Frank and the IRS whistleblower laws, which do not contain such an exemption. For example, numerous banks have been sanctioned under Dodd-Frank, including billion dollar sanctions against Goldman Sachs Group and Danske Bank, for money laundering.

PRACTICE TIPS

- The SEC regulation on auditor, compliance, and director eligibility for rewards is set forth at 17 C.F.R. § 240.21F-4(b)(4)(iii) and (v).

- The Commodity Futures Trading Commission's regulation on auditor, compliance, and director eligibility is set forth at 17 C.F.R. § 165.2(g)(4), (5), and (7).

- Best practice: If you are a compliance official, director, attorney, or auditor, file your reward claim 120 days after the company was alerted to the violation.

Keeping Up with the Changes

To keep up to date on changes in the laws, whistleblowers should access the free online law library created by the author, located at www.kkc.com/law-library.

RULE 14

Don't Fear NDAs

This corporate code of silence . . . creates a climate where ongoing wrongdoing can occur with virtual impunity.

—Senate Report, Sarbanes-Oxley Whistleblower Act

The law on nondisclosure agreements has radically changed since whistleblowing exploded in the workplace. Corporations historically used their economic power to have employees sign highly restrictive nondisclosure agreements, or NDAs. NDAs are regularly included in employment, severance, or settlement agreements. Although corporations have the right to protect confidential information, they cannot interfere with an employee's right to report crimes to law enforcement or regulatory authorities.

The battle to ensure that NDAs cannot be used to suppress whistleblowers from reporting violations was first fought in the late 1980s by a journeyman electrician, Joseph J. Macktal Jr., who worked for the multinational construction company Halliburton/Brown & Root. He was fired from his job at the Comanche Peak nuclear power plant after he raised safety concerns. He filed a whistleblower case.

Brown & Root wanted his silence and was willing to pay. Macktal's attorneys strongly urged him to accept the company's offer. Macktal felt trapped. He documented his opposition to the settlement and even recorded his lawyers delivering a threat from Brown & Root: If you do not remain silent, Brown & Root will "follow you to the ends of the earth." Macktal thought he had no choice. He signed the deal.

As part of the settlement, he agreed not to testify about any of his nuclear safety concerns. If subpoenaed, he would do his best to resist service. He agreed to keep the entire deal strictly confidential, and if he ever told anyone about the secret settlement, Brown & Root could sue him, retrieve all of their settlement money, and force Macktal to pay all the company's attorney fees and costs. Disclosure meant bankruptcy.

The settlement ate at Macktal's conscience. In September 1988 Macktal did something that no other whistleblower had ever done. He publicly released his strictly confidential agreement and requested that the Department of Labor and Nuclear Regulatory Commission strike it down as void against public policy. Macktal placed everything at risk to do the right thing. If the agreement's legality was sustained, he all but admitted to massive liability, risking a Brown & Root counter-lawsuit for breach of contract.

Macktal's actions were unprecedented. No one knew how the NRC or DOL would decide the case. The NRC acted first, and blew it. It issued a decision finding that paying witnesses *not* to provide testimony to the NRC was *not* a safety violation. The NRC refused to take action against Brown & Root. The ruling set Macktal up for a counterclaim and financial ruin.

Backed against the wall, Macktal and his attorneys went to Congress and found a sympathetic ear with the staff of the U.S. Senate Subcommittee on Nuclear Regulation.

The committee staff (and their bosses) were outraged by the agreement. They understood the insidiousness of the agreement and how paying witnesses not to testify could threaten the integrity of the entire nuclear regulatory regime. The subcommittee took action. They subpoenaed Brown & Root and their high-priced corporate attorneys, demanding documents related to the Macktal agreement and other hush money deals the nuclear power industry had demanded from its workers. They called the NRC officials on the carpet and grilled them.

The chair of the subcommittee, Senator John Breaux from Louisiana, did not hold back: "It is shocking to me that we should even have to hold a hearing on such questions. It seems self-evident that it is wrong to pay witnesses not to testify, regardless of context. Yet we find that in the area of nuclear regulation the practice may be common."

Senator Alan K. Simpson from Wyoming was slightly more blunt: "This stinks!"

Under pressure, the NRC reversed its ruling. It issued a new decision finding that such agreements violated public policy. The NRC then went even further and sent a letter to every nuclear utility in the United States demanding that every such hush money settlement be turned over and that all the workers who signed these agreements be informed that the restrictions on blowing the whistle were unenforceable. Numerous Macktal-style agreements became public, and the nuclear industry was given a big black eye.

The DOL issued a series of decisions ultimately completely outlawing restrictive settlements. The first *Macktal* decision held that the specific clause in the agreement restricting Macktal's right to blow the whistle to government agencies was void. Macktal challenged that ruling in the U.S. Court of Appeals for the Fifth Circuit. He demanded that the DOL void the entire deal and reinstitute his labor case.

Fifth Circuit Judge John Minor Wisdom agreed with Macktal and held that it was all or nothing—the DOL could not effectively rewrite the agreement by striking one clause. The case was sent back to the DOL. Following the Fifth Circuit's decision, the Department of Labor issued a series of orders setting the future precedent outlawing restrictive NDAs:

- If a settlement contained restrictions on an employee's right to blow the whistle, testify, provide information to government regulators, or engage in any statutorily protected activity, the *entire agreement* was void.

- If the settlement was voided, the employee had the right to continue their labor case, as if no settlement had ever been issued.

- If the company had paid money to the worker, the employee could *keep the settlement money* and still pursue their case.

Based on the *Macktal* precedent, the DOL held that inserting gag provisions in a settlement was an adverse action, permitting an employee to sue their employer for retaliation and obtain damages and attorney fees. The U.S. Court of Appeals upheld that ruling. On August 23, 2016, the director of the Department of Labor's Whistleblower Protection Program issued policy guidelines instructing the Occupational Safety and Health Administration (OSHA) to reject any settlement agreement that contained restrictions on employee whistleblower rights. OSHA investigators were asked to keep an eye out for any settlement agreements that contained a provision that:

- Restricts an employee's "ability to provide information to the government, participate in investigations, file a complaint, or testify in proceedings."

- Requires an employee "to notify his or her employer before filing a complaint or voluntarily communicating with the government."

- Requires an employee "to affirm that he or she has not previously provided information to the government or engaged in other protected activity, or to disclaim any knowledge that the employer has violated the law."

- Requires an employee "to waive his or her right to receive a monetary award from a government-administered whistleblower award program for providing information to a government agency."

The SEC Follows Macktal

On August 12, 2010, just weeks after the president signed the Dodd-Frank Act, representatives of the Securities and Exchange Commission met with the National Whistleblower Center (NWC) to discuss the Dodd-Frank regulations being drafted by the commission. The NWC explained that the commission had the legal authority to ban retaliation against whistleblowers and prohibit restrictive nondisclosure agreements. At the heart of the NWC's argument was legal precedent that treated retaliation not simply as an employment matter, but also as a major regulatory concern. If companies could restrict or intimidate employees from providing information to regulatory authorities like the SEC, the government would not be able to do its job of protecting the public.

The SEC agreed. The commission approved regulations prohibiting restrictive nondisclosure agreements: "No person may take any action to impede an individual from communicating directly with the Commission staff about a possible securities law violation, including enforcing, or threatening to enforce, a confidentiality agreement." Thereafter, the commission commenced striking down restrictive NDAs.

In a paradox of history, the first SEC-NDA case was filed against Kellogg Brown & Root (or KBR), the same company that had forced Macktal to sign a restrictive settlement agreement back in the 1980s. KBR had once again resorted to using illegal nondisclosure agreements. This time the company compelled employees who had information that KBR was cheating on its Iraq war contracts to sign restrictive nondisclosure agreements, prohibiting employees from discussing their concerns about bribery and fraud in the company's lucrative war contracts with anyone without the approval of corporate attorneys. When a whistleblower challenged this NDA, the SEC did not hesitate to strike it down. The commission not only decided that the agreement was illegal but also fined KBR $130,000 for making an employee sign it. KBR paid the fine. This precedent triggered numerous companies to change their severance and settlement agreement terms or risk being sanctioned.

The *Macktal* rulings remain good law, and based on the actions of the SEC, and other government agencies, this is now widely accepted.

Restrictive Settlements and Public Policy

Under state law courts have also struck down the enforceability of overly broad non-disclosure or non-disparagement agreements, even when the offending terms were not limited to restricting the right of employees to inform the government of potential violations of law. For example, Jessica Denson, a former employee of Donald Trump for President, Inc., signed extremely broad nondisclosure and non-disparagement agreements. The challenged contractual terms were not limited to restricting her right to blow the whistle to the government. Instead, she agreed not to disparage Donald Trump and his family and to keep almost anything about the Trump presidential campaign confidential.

The U.S. District Court for the Southern District of New York, applying state contract law, found the employment agreement completely void and unenforceable. The court found that the restrictive provisions of Denson's employment agreement were vague and overbroad. Moreover, the court held that the agreement created a chill on speech concerning matters of public interest. According to the court, the Trump for President's NDA was harmful not only to the workers who signed the agreement, but also to the general public.

Under the False Claims Act, a number of courts have prevented (or limited) companies from using private agreements to interfere with the ability of the government to learn about contracting fraud. As one court explained:

> *It is in the Government's best interest to gain full information from the relator. To enforce the release . . . would ignore the public policy objectives spelled out by Congress in the FCA and would provide disincentives to future relators. . . . [E]nforcing the release and indemnification clauses would encourage individuals guilty of defrauding the United States to insulate themselves from the reach of the FCA by simply forcing potential relators to sign general agreements invoking release and indemnification from future suit.*

But in the context of the FCA, some courts have upheld releases that prohibit employees from filing *qui tam* cases. These courts have held that if the government had knowledge of the fraud before the employee agreed to a general release of claims against their employer, that release could prevent the filing of a False Claims Act case. These cases do not uphold hush money terms, but do permit companies to have False Claims Act cases filed by whistleblowers dismissed on the basis of a contractual waiver.

Keeping Up with the Changes

To keep up to date on changes in the laws, whistleblowers should access the free online law library created by the author, located at www.kkc.com/law-library.

The following are key statutes, regulations, and court cases on enforcement of NDAs:

- Federal Obstruction of Justice statute, 18 U.S.C. § 1513(e).

- Dodd-Frank Act regulations restricting NDAs, 17 C.F.R. § 240.21F-17 (SEC) and 17 C.F.R. § 165.19 (CFTC).

- Defend Trade Secrets Act, 18 U.S.C. § 1833(b) (permitting disclosure of trade secrets under specific conditions).

- *CL&P v. SOL*, 85 F.3d 89 (2nd Cir. 1996) (restrictive agreement as adverse action)

- *U.S. v. Purdue Pharma*, 600 F.3d 319 (2010) (releases under False Claims Act).

- *In the Matter of KBR, Inc.*, SEC File No. 3-16466 (Apr. 1, 2015) (decision sanctioning company for restrictive NDA).

- *Denson v. Donald J. Trump for President, Inc.*, 530 F. Supp. 3d 412 (S.D.N.Y. 2021).

RULE 15

Talking to the Press

The people shall not be deprived or abridged of their right to speak, to write, or to publish their sentiments, and the freedom of the press, as one of the great bulwarks of liberty, shall be inviolable.
—James Madison speech in Congress introducing the Bill of Rights, 1789

Roger Wensil worked as a pipe fitter at the massive Savannah River Site nuclear weapons complex in Aiken, South Carolina. He witnessed numerous safety violations, including the buying and selling of illegal drugs on-site. He reported these crimes up the chain of command. For his good efforts he was fired, along with his wife and a star witness. He filed a claim under the nuclear safety whistleblower law. But every branch of the federal government shut him down. The Labor Department, the Department of Energy, and the courts all found that the nuclear whistleblower law did not apply to atomic weapons facilities. He was left jobless.

But the *Washington Post* caught wind of the story. They investigated the facts and determined that Wensil had indeed been fired for raising safety concerns. They also found an internal Labor Department report that fully backed up Wensil but had never been issued and was secreted from the public. The *Post* started to run stories on the case, some landing on page one. After the Secretary of Energy was questioned about the case, the department decided that they needed to put a lid on the embarrassing facts surrounding the case and their initial failure to act properly. The DOE decided to hold a hearing on Wensil's termination, despite his lack of any legal rights.

Remarkably, Wensil won his case and was ordered back to work with full back pay. Wensil literally won his case in the newspapers. The bad press, combined with the outrageous facts highlighted by the *Post*, forced the government to rule in Wensil's favor despite the fact that no law existed granting him whistleblower protections. After the case was over Congress amended the nuclear whistleblower law to cover companies working at the numerous nuclear weapons facilities. It was an amazing outcome obtained solely from the willingness of Wensil to work with the press.

From the day "Deep Throat" secretly met with *Washington Post* reporter Bob Woodward in a Washington, DC parking garage, the potential impact of whistleblowing was seared into the American psyche. Whistleblowers have successfully worked with the press for years and accomplished incredible reforms. "Deep Throat" played an instrumental role in exposing the impeachable offenses committed by President Richard Nixon. Daniel Ellsberg's leaks to the press helped end the Vietnam War and taught the American people incredible lessons about their government. More recently, the media exposés by Christopher Wylie in the *Guardian* and *New York Times* regarding

Facebook and Cambridge Analytica's privacy abuses led to $5.1 billion in sanctions against Facebook and critical reforms protecting election integrity.

But whistleblowers have also suffered immensely by talking to the press. Edward Snowden released information regarding illegal government spying on citizens and now lives in exile in Russia. Reality Winner spent four years in a federal prison after releasing a report documenting Russian interference in the 2016 presidential election. Linda Tripp had her identity and information publicly revealed, in part after a journalist decided she no longer should be considered a confidential source. Her reputation was dragged through the mud in historical proportions.

Obtaining protection for going to the news media can be tricky, difficult, and sometimes highly risky. It can also be the key to alerting the public to major disasters, saving lives, and forcing the government to do its job. Many government agencies acknowledge the positive role disclosures published in the news media can have on protecting the public interest. For example, in a policy statement concerning freedom of the press the U.S. Securities and Exchange Commission praised the role of the media in exposing wrongdoing and helping the SEC learn about threats to investors:

> *Freedom of the press is of vital importance to the mission of the Securities and Exchange Commission. Effective journalism complements the Commission's efforts to ensure that investors receive the full and fair disclosure that the law requires, and that they deserve. Diligent reporting is an essential means of bringing securities law violations to light and ultimately helps to deter illegal conduct. In this Policy Statement the Commission sets forth guidelines for the agency's professional staff to ensure that vigorous enforcement of the federal securities laws is conducted completely consistently with the principles of the First Amendment's guarantee of freedom of the press. . . .*

Regardless of the constitutional protections afforded citizens who disclose wrongdoing to the news media, whistleblowers must be very careful when talking to the press. As a threshold matter, the confidentiality reporters often offer to their sources is difficult to enforce in court. There is no federal shield law protecting these rights. Reporters can be subpoenaed and compelled to reveal their informants or risk jail-time. But even riskier than a subpoena to a journalist are the incredible means the government or corporations have in tracking down a confidential source even if the journalist refuses to breach their professional obligations.

Moreover, a whistleblower may be compelled to reveal, under oath, whether or not they were a source to the news media. In such circumstances the whistleblower's options are very limited, as they should *never* lie under oath.

QUI TAM REWARD LAWS AND DISCLOSURES TO THE PRESS

Can a whistleblower obtain a monetary reward if they report wrongdoing to the news media? When Congress passed the first modern whistleblower law (i.e., the False Claims Act amendments of 1986), it was well aware that employees often blow the whistle to the news media and that such disclosures often serve the public interest. As a result, Congress carved out a special dispensation for False Claims Act whistleblowers who report corporate rip-offs of taxpayer dollars to the press. Under the False Claims Act, whistleblowers can collect a reward under a variety of circumstances, including when the government learns about a fraud from the news media. But the whistleblower must be the original source of the information published in the press in order to make sure that they can qualify.

Similar procedures were adopted in the other major reward laws, including the IRS whistleblower law, the Dodd-Frank Act, and the auto safety and money laundering whistleblower reward laws. In each, whistleblowers can qualify for a reward even when the government learns about the violations from news media accounts, *if the whistleblower was the original source to the news media and they can prove it.*

Although under the *qui tam* laws communications with the press are recognized as a valid means to alert the government to a scandal, whistleblowers still must comply with all the other technical requirements required under these statutes in order to qualify. Going to the news media is not enough. Media reports are simply the very beginning of the disclosure process. There are numerous other requirements that must be met in order to obtain a reward. This includes compliance with the technical filing requirements, the need to demonstrate that all disclosures are voluntary, and proof that you were the original source to the press. If a whistleblower makes an initial disclosure to the press, they should, as quickly as possible, determine what additional steps must be made to comply with an agency's administrative requirements and qualify for a reward. Delay can be deadly in these circumstances, as some agencies have strict deadlines for filing formal reward applications after they learn of the allegations from third parties such as the news media, even if the whistleblower was indeed the original source of the information.

For example, going to the press does not exempt a whistleblower from the False Claims Act's first to file rule. You may be the first to publicly report a violation, but if someone else beats you to the courthouse and files a False Claims Act lawsuit before you do, you may be completely out of luck. Similar timing issues can arise under other reward laws. Unfortunately, most agencies do not have clear rules concerning the interplay between media disclosures and the mandatory technical filing procedures required for obtaining a reward. If you are aware of your ability to seek an award, it is a best practice to file a reward claim before speaking to the press. If you learn about your rights to obtain a reward after the news media has blasted your allegations to the public, it is best to file your claims as quickly as possible before someone beats you to the starting line or agencies take action that could disqualify you from a reward.

The bottom line is very simple. Just because a whistleblower can use the news media to provide original information to the government, that does not mean that a whistleblower *should* engage in this tactic. There are significant benefits to be obtained if an employer has no idea that a whistleblower exists. Talking to the press can blow your cover.

- False Claims Act provision on providing original information through the press: 31 U.S.C. § 3730(e)(4)(A).

- Whistleblower reward laws covering information originally provided to the press: 15 U.S.C. § 78u-6(a)(3) (Securities Exchange and Foreign Corrupt Practices Acts); 26 U.S.C. § 7623(b)(2)(B) (Tax); 7 U.S.C. § 26(a)(4) (Commodity Exchange Act); 49 U.S.C. § 30172(a)(3) (Motor Vehicle Safety Act); 31 U.S.C. § 5323(a)(3) (Anti-Money Laundering Act).

- SEC Policy Statement supporting freedom of the press: 17 C.F.R. § 202.10.

PUBLIC EMPLOYEES AND THE FIRST AMENDMENT RIGHT TO REPORT CONCERNS TO THE PRESS

The U.S. Constitution protects the right of public employees to report matters of public concern to the news media. See Rules 28–30 But securing these rights can be tricky. Ask Michael Andrew.

After thirty-one years on the Baltimore Police Department, Michael Andrew was troubled. He witnessed a police shooting where officers had killed an old man who had barricaded himself in his apartment. Thereafter he wrote an internal memorandum expressing concerns over the misuse of deadly force. When upper management tried to cover up misconduct surrounding the killing, Andrew took his concerns to the *Baltimore Sun*. For that, he was fired. As in most whistleblower cases, loyalty trumps truth—even if someone was wrongfully shot to death.

Was providing his memorandum to the newspaper protected? The district court said no, leaving Andrew out on the bricks. The U.S. Court of Appeals for the Fourth Circuit disagreed, affirming Andrew's right to talk to the press. Judge J. Harvie Wilkinson, in a concurring opinion, eloquently explained why such protections were necessary: To throw out a case because an employee "took his concerns to the press" would have "profound adverse effects on accountability in government." Without such protection, "scrutiny of the inner workings of massive public bureaucracies charged with major public responsibilities" would be "in deep trouble." The "First Amendment should never countenance the gamble that informed scrutiny of the workings of government will be left to wither on the vine. That scrutiny is impossible without some assistance from inside sources such as Michael Andrew."

In cases of public employment, lawful and reasonable contacts with the press are constitutionally protected under the First Amendment. State and local government employees who suffer retaliation for blowing the whistle to the news media can file a case in federal court using the Civil Rights Act of 1871 (42 U.S.C. § 1983). Under this law public employees are entitled to a jury trial, injunctive relief (including reinstatement), punitive and compensatory damages, back pay and attorney fees.

FEDERAL EMPLOYEES AND DISCLOSURES TO THE NEWS MEDIA

In 2015 the U.S. Supreme Court decided the case of Robert J. MacLean, a federal air marshal who was fired by the Department of Homeland Security (DHS) after warning that Al-Qaeda may be planning suicide hijackings with the intent to "destroy aircraft in flight, as well as to strike ground targets." Before he spoke to the press, MacLean was personally informed by his managers that terrorists planned to "smuggle weapons in camera equipment or children's toys through foreign security," and then "fly into the United States . . . overpower the crew or the Air Marshals and . . . fly the planes into East Coast targets."

Just days after this briefing, MacLean learned that air marshals were being *removed* from airplanes despite the real terrorist threat. MacLean was shocked, and "believed that cancelling those missions during a hijacking alert was dangerous." MacLean went to his bosses to try to change the policy, but they refused and told him that the air marshals were grounded "to save money on hotel costs because there was no more money in the budget."

Frustrated, MacLean leaked the story to an MSNBC reporter, and NBC ran a story titled "Air Marshals pulled from key flights." After the press exposed the scandal, the Department of Homeland Security/TSA reversed its decision and placed marshals back on the planes. MacLean's disclosures served the public interest, but DHS was embarrassed and wanted to take revenge on the whistleblower. DHS investigated the press leaks and after MacLean admitted he was the source. He was fired.

MacLean sued the agency under the Whistleblower Protection Act, arguing that leaks to NBC were protected disclosures. Significantly, in MacLean's case there was *no specific law that prohibited his communications with the press.* Instead, he had violated regulations issued by his employer. The case dragged on in the courts and administrative agencies for over ten years and eventually landed in the U.S. Supreme Court. In *Department of Homeland Security v. MacLean*, Chief Justice John Roberts ruled that MacLean was illegally fired. Because MacLean's disclosures to NBC were not specifically prohibited by law, he had the right to expose the threat to public safety caused by the government's irresponsible decision to withdraw air marshals from transnational flights during a major terrorist alert. Justice Roberts did not buy the agency's argument that its internal rule should have the force of law, writing, "Congress passed the whistleblower statute precisely because it did not trust agencies to regulate whistleblowers within their ranks."

The MacLean case did not concern disclosures to the news media in the context of classified information, which are covered under other, more restrictive laws. Rules concerning the disclosure of information by employees working for intelligence agencies or who have access to classified and top-secret information are discussed in Rule 30.

PRIVATE SECTOR EMPLOYEE DISCLOSURES TO THE NEWS MEDIA

The U.S. Department of Labor has long-standing case precedent that protects private sector whistleblower disclosures to the press. In cases arising under the Occupational Safety and Health Act and the environmental and nuclear whistleblower laws, the DOL has consistently upheld an employee's right to communicate concerns to the press as a first step in alerting the government to potential safety problems. These precedents have been upheld in various judicial decisions.

However, in a private-sector case that was filed in federal court, the U.S. Court of Appeals for the Ninth Circuit found that communications to the press were not covered under the Sarbanes-Oxley Act. In that case the court left open the possibility that press contacts could be protected under provisions of the law not relied upon by the employees who filed the lawsuit. Precedents under Title VII of the Civil Rights Act (prohibiting discrimination on the basis of sex, race, religion, and other protected categories) have also upheld the right of employees to report concerns directly to the news media.

WHISTLEBLOWER WEBSITES/WIKILEAKS

Various organizations sponsor websites or other online services that solicit whistle-blowers to disclose confidential information. Some promise anonymity. These sites often claim that they can protect the identify of their sources, but leaking informa-tion through these services is extremely risky and can be counterproductive. There are numerous reasons why whistleblowers should be very wary of these sites. Here are a few:

First, there is no legal privilege associated with communications to websites such as Wikileaks. They are not covered under attorney-client or law enforcement privilege. A website that sponsors the whistleblowing service can be subjected to subpoena, civil discovery, or various high-tech searches conducted under the U.S. Patriot Act and other legal authorities. If a whistleblower is questioned under oath (such as in a deposition) as to whether they were a source to the website, their choices are to admit to the leak, plead the Fifth Amendment against self-incrimination, or commit perjury. It puts the whistleblower in a lose-lose-lose situation. *Never commit perjury.*

Second, the Chelsea Manning case should be a lesson to any whistleblower think-ing of doing an online document dump. Manning leaked information to Wikileaks. She was discovered and sentenced to thirty-five years in prison. Her mistreatment resulted in two suicide attempts while in military jails. Although Manning wanted to expose wrongdoing, the method she used to disclose her information stripped her of the rights she potentially had as a whistleblower under the military whistleblower law and opened her to criminal prosecution.

Or take the case of Reality Winner. She served four years in prison for leaking con-fidential information concerning Russian interference with the 2016 election to *The Intercept*, an online news organization. In her first post-prison interview, Winner gave a stark warning to others who might be thinking of using online publications such as *The Intercept*: "I wasn't the first source that they burned and I definitely wasn't the last."

Third, you may be harming legitimate law enforcement investigations. An online document dump could tip off the company about the evidence that could be used against it as part of a criminal investigation and permit the company to create a strong defense. The company could also claim that any investigation was tainted by the improper theft of its documents.

Fourth, courts have been unkind to whistleblowers who "steal" information from the government or their employer and then have it published online.

Fifth, you could be jeopardizing an otherwise strong reward case under the False Claims Act and other related laws.

Finally, the online site is under no legal obligation to protect you. They can profit from your information, even if you go to jail. The law views publishers of information differently from those who leak information. It is rare for a news organization to be prosecuted for publishing classified information, whereas sources of classified information have been investigated, fired, and prosecuted.

Contact an attorney before using an online whistleblower website to make a disclosure. Learn the risks associated with such a document-dump, how you may release materials lawfully, and alternatives that may exist to using these services.

PRACTICE TIPS

- *Pickering v. Board of Education*, 391 U.S. 563 (1968) (landmark case protecting the right of government employees to blow the whistle to the press); *Sanjour v. EPA*, 56 F.3d 85 (1995) (right of government whistleblowers to engage in outside speaking, writing, and teaching); *Dep't of Homeland Sec. v. MacLean*, 574 U.S. 383 (2015) (right of federal employees to lawfully disclose misconduct to the news media).

- Department of Labor decisions protecting disclosures to the media: *Diaz-Robainas v. Florida Power & Light Co.*, 92-ERA-10, Order of Secretary of Labor, 1996 DOL Sec. Labor LEXIS 6 (Jan. 10, 1996); *Donovan v. R.D. Andersen Constr. Co.*, 552 F. Supp. 249 (D. Kan. 1982).

- Title VII decision protecting disclosures to the news media: *Wrighten v. Metro. Hosps., Inc.*, 726 F.2d 1346 (9th Cir. 1984).

- *Huffman v. Office of Personnel Management*, 263 F.3d 1341, 1351 (Fed. Cir. 2001) (holding that media disclosures are an indirect way of disclosing information of wrongdoing to a person in a position to provide a remedy) (Whistleblower Protection Act case).

- *Tides v. Boeing*, 644F.3d 809 (9th Cir. 2011), holding that employee contacts with the press were not protected under 18 U.S.C. section 1514A(a)(1) of the Sarbanes-Oxley Act. However, the court left open the issue as to whether contacts with the press were protected under another clause of the act, section 1514A(a)(2).

- *Pacheco v. Waldrop*, 84 F.3d 606 (W.D. Ky. 2015) (media disclosure not protected under state whistleblower statute).

PART III

Rewards—The Laws

These rules are as old as law. They rise out of the very elements of law. It is to protect human rights, and promote human welfare. Law is in its nature opposed to wrong, and must everywhere be presumed to be in favor of the right. The pound of flesh, but not one drop of blood, is a sound rule of legal interpretation.
—Frederick Douglass, "The Dred Scott Decision" speech before the American Anti-Slavery Society (May 11, 1857)

RULE 16

Follow the Money

Complex economic wrongdoing cannot be detected or deterred effectively without the help of those who are intimately familiar with it. Law enforcement will always be outsiders to organizations where fraud is occurring. They will not find out about such fraud until it is too late, if at all. . . . Given these facts, insiders who are willing to blow the whistle are the only effective way to learn that wrongdoing has occurred.
—University of Alabama Professor Pamela Bucy, testimony before the Senate
Judiciary Committee (2008)

Greed. This is what drives corruption and fraud. People don't pollute because they like the smell of garbage. Playing by the rules has a price. In one of the first federal whistle-blower cases, U.S. Court of Appeals Judge Malcolm Wilkey got it right. His basis for ordering the reinstatement of Franklin Phillips, a miner who was fired for complaining about dangerous coal dust, can be summarized in three words that highlighted his decision: "Safety costs money."

Judge Wilkey went on to explain how the drive for profits underscores whistleblowing: "The temptation to minimize compliance . . . and thus shave costs is always present . . . competitors who get away with cutting costs . . . are really engaged in unfair competition." His words are equally applicable to a stockbroker who engages in insider trading, a banker who fails to report the money laundering of a rich client, or an oil executive who authorizes a bribe to obtain an oil lease in a poor African country.

Corruption can be very profitable. Those who do not cheat can be driven from the markets by those who are willing to violate the law. Ultimately, unless corruption can be readily detected and effectively policed, it can never be made unprofitable. This is where the whistleblower reward laws come into play. They target the greed that drives fraud.

How does a whistleblower "follow the money"? Carefully evaluate the profit motive behind a violation of law. Sometimes the fraud is obvious, such as a direct violation of material terms in a federal contract. But other times the frauds are far less obvious, such as the illegal marketing of a drug that is later purchased by a patient but paid for with Medicare or Medicaid funds. An oil spill may look like an environmental disaster, but it can also be evidence of a violation of a federal lease requirement covered under the False Claims Act. Illegal deforestation in Southeast Asia may be predicated on the violation of laws against foreign bribery. The use of slave labor in China may be a violation of U.S. import and customs regulations.

How We Got Here: The Birth of Modern Whistleblower Protections

Understanding how whistleblower reward laws work begins with following the twists and turns of the False Claims Act, from its birth on March 2, 1863, when President Abraham Lincoln signed the bill into law, through a series of amendments, and finally to its final form as the most effective tool in combating fraud against taxpayers. Its history has not always been pretty, but the lessons learned from its numerous amendments laid the foundation for all future reward laws.

During the Civil War President Lincoln and his supporters in Congress were disgusted with government contractors, some of whom were selling sawdust as gunpowder and profiting from the terrible costs of the war. Congressional investigations uncovered "waste and squandering" of public funds. Overcharging was common, and war contracts were given, without any advertising, at exorbitant rates above market value.

When Congress investigated these frauds, it discovered that the cases were not only widespread, but also that insider employees had blown the whistle and were subjected to retaliation. In one case, the architect at the Benton barracks in Missouri reported that he was "cursed and abused, terrified," and threatened with imprisonment for blowing the whistle on bribes paid to obtain construction contracts for the barracks.

To encourage citizens to disclose frauds, Michigan senator Jacob Howard introduced Senate Bill 467, what is today referred to as the False Claims Act. As Senator Howard explained, a key provision in the law was a *qui tam* clause based on the "old-fashioned idea of holding out a temptation" for persons to step forward and turn in thieves. Howard understood that this *qui tam* mechanism would empower citizens to sue wrongdoers in the name of the U.S. government (i.e., "in the name of the king") in order to ensure compliance with the law. Senator Howard strongly defended the bill as, in his words, the "safest and most expeditious way I have ever discovered of bringing rogues to justice."

Under the law, any person who had knowledge of the fraud—referred to today as whistleblowers—was authorized to file a lawsuit on behalf of the United States. If frauds were proven, the wrongdoer had to pay up to twice the amount of the fraud, plus a large fine of $2,000. The whistleblower, known in the law as the "relator," would get half the money, and the United States would collect the other half.

On March 2, 1863, President Lincoln signed S. 467 into law. The FCA was visionary legislation. It was passed before the rise of modern industry and before the federal government became a multitrillion-dollar enterprise. Like other visionary civil rights legislation signed during the Civil War and Reconstruction eras, it was progressive, years ahead of its time; its use would remain dormant until the New Deal and the outbreak of World War II, when government procurement would reach a previously unimaginable amount.

In the late 1930s and early 1940s, in the wake of large New Deal and war-related federal spending, the FCA was dusted off and a handful of *qui tam* suits were filed. By 1943 a mere twenty-eight FCA cases were pending in all the courts in the United States. Although small in number, they targeted some of the most powerful corporations and political machines in the country, including Carnegie–Illinois Steel Corporation (for selling "substandard" steel to the U.S. Navy), the Anaconda Wire & Cable Company (for selling "defective wire and cable"), contracts awarded to Hague Machine (led by Frank

Hague, Jersey City mayor and the co-chair of the Democratic National Committee), and corrupt contracts awarded to a company owned by Tom Prendergast, the notorious "boss" from Kansas City.

These suits caused panic within the powerful government-contractor community. Before the law was ever really tested, though, Congress voted to gut the heart of the FCA. On April 1, 1943, Congressman Frances Walter took to the floor of the House of Representatives and obtained, without any real debate, "unanimous consent" to repeal the *qui tam* provision in the FCA. The whistleblower law would have been repealed, except that William Langer, the controversial populist Republican senator from North Dakota, rose to defend it.

On July 8, 1943, Senator Langer commenced a filibuster. He recounted President Lincoln's concern that "persons who were willing to make money out of the blood and sufferings of our soldiers" threatened the "very life of our Nation" and "induced" his supporters in the Civil War Congress to take action to stop the abuses. After mentioning this history, Langer concluded: "These far-seeing Senators realized that the most potent weapon to deter these plunderers of our National Treasury, was to make such cheating and defrauding unprofitable."

Senator Langer then warned that the effort to repeal citizen rights under the FCA (i.e., the *qui tam* powers) was an effort to "destroy the most formidable weapon in the hands of the Government" to fight the "fraud practices" that were "inflicted upon our nation." The senator warned that frauds were concocted "in every way" that "human ingenuity could devise." It was the *qui tam* provision of the law, "as old as the common law itself," that "provide[d] the safeguard" and the most "potent weapon to deter" the "plunderers of our National Treasury."

But Senator Langer could not hold off his political foes. His filibuster did succeed in blocking the outright repeal of the FCA, but the law was radically weakened. Under the 1943 amendments, whistleblowers were stripped of their practical ability to file *qui tam* claims. The amendments had razor-sharp targets. Among the main attacks on the law were radically reducing the amount of awards (reduced from a mandatory 50 percent to a maximum award of 10 percent); making payment of rewards discretionary (the government could simply refuse to pay an award); and creating procedural hurdles to qualify for any compensation whatsoever (done by changing the type of information that could qualify for a reward). (Note: Without jumping ahead of the story, these are the same three targets that contemporary enemies of effective whistleblowing focus their attacks on.)

After 1943, attempts by whistleblowers to use the FCA were fruitless. *Qui tam* relators or whistleblowers could not get around the numerous procedural or substantive roadblocks that prevented them from filing claims or collecting recoveries. Consequently, over one hundred attempts to use the law to hold contractors accountable failed in the courts. The law was down and out, but not dead.

Resurrection and the False Claims Reform Act

At the height of the "Reagan Revolution," and its gargantuan increases in defense spending, a freshman senator from Iowa, Chuck Grassley, led the charge to increase oversight and accountability for federal spending by resurrecting the False Claims Act.

On August 1, 1985, he, along with Congressman Howard Berman from California, introduced the False Claims Reform Act. The target of the reforms was the irresponsible 1943 amendments that had gutted President Lincoln's law. Senator Grassley clearly explained the history behind his proposals:

> In 1863, Abraham Lincoln recognized both the danger of government contractor profiteering and the need for private persons to become involved in its prevention when he signed into law the Federal False Claims Act. That act came in response to Civil War era horror stories that sound all too familiar, contractors selling boxes of sawdust in place of boxes of muskets, and reselling horses to the cavalry two and three times.
>
> The False Claims Act allows an individual knowing of fraudulent practices to bring suit on behalf of the government and receive a portion of the recovery if the action is successful. Unfortunately, the teeth of President Lincoln's law were removed during World War II, and the provision has been little used since.

The Senate Judiciary Committee's hearings on the Reform Act revealed the troubling fact that since 1943 contractor abuses had gotten completely out of control. Things were so bad that the General Accounting Office reached the following conclusion: "The sad truth is that crime against the Government often *does* pay."

While Congress debated the False Claims Reform Act, scandals and tragedy pushed the law across the finish line.

America watched in horror when on January 28, 1986, just five months after the Reform Act was introduced into Congress, as the space shuttle *Challenger* exploded on national television. Among the seven dead astronauts was Christa McAuliffe, a high school teacher and the first civilian passenger permitted on a space mission.

After the explosion, NASA's top manager for the shuttle program quickly proclaimed that there was no pressure to launch the *Challenger* and that flight safety was the program's top priority. Neither was true. The public soon learned that employees for one of NASA's private contractors, Morton-Thiokol, had raised specific safety concerns over the design defects that ultimately caused the explosion. Their internal safety warnings were ignored. Before the launch high-ranking NASA officials intimidated these engineers, who kept their concerns from the astronauts who boarded that doomed flight. When the *Challenger* launched, the whistleblower-engineers actually prayed that the spacecraft would not explode.

The *Challenger* disaster occurred at the very same time that weaknesses in existing whistleblower laws were becoming obvious. Whistleblowers were exposing corruption in government contracting and widespread environmental violations and regularly reporting absurd cost overruns ripping off taxpayers. Newspapers were filled with stories on how contractors had billed the Department of Defense $7,622 for a coffeepot, $435 for a hammer, and $640 for a toilet seat. The public was outraged. The pressure on Congress to act was overwhelming.

Change would come. As 1986 came to an end, Congress became serious about protecting whistleblowers. First up was the False Claims Act, the weakened and ignored Civil War–era statute originally designed to protect employees, such as the Morton-Thiokol federal contractors who were silenced.

The 1986 False Claims Act Amendments

The False Claims Reform Act of 1986 reversed the most vicious anti-whistleblower provisions of the 1943 amendments, modernized the law, restored the rights of whistleblowers to file claims, and set mandatory reward levels regardless of the amount of money collected from the corrupt or abusive contractor.

The 1986 amendments reestablished the ability of whistleblowers to file *qui tam* lawsuits and set the standard that would permit these fraud-fighters to prevail in court. They permitted whistleblowers to directly litigate their cases against contractors, whether or not the United States joined in the action. If the United States decided not to file any claim against the contractor, the whistleblower had the right to continue the lawsuit, conduct discovery, participate in a trial, and attempt to prove that the contractor had stolen from the taxpayer. If the United States decided to join the lawsuit, the whistleblower was still guaranteed the right to participate in the case, protect their rights, and present the case against the contractor.

The 1986 amendments also set mandatory guidelines for monetarily rewarding whistleblowers. If a whistleblower filed an FCA suit and the United States used this information to collect damages from the contractor, the whistleblower was guaranteed between 15 and 25 percent of the total monies collected. If the government refused to hold the contractor accountable, the whistleblower could pursue the case "in the name of the United States," even without the intervention or support of the Justice Department. If the whistleblower won the claim, they would be entitled to between 25 and 30 percent of the amount of money collected by the United States. The Justice Department did not have the authority or discretion to reduce whistleblower rewards below the statutory minimums.

Other provisions of the law were substantially improved as well. First, Congress no longer simply doubled the amount of money owed by the contractor. The law called for treble damages—the contractor would have to pay three times the amount of the fraud. Second, the amount of the per-violation fine was increased from $2,000 to between $5,000 and $10,000. (Note: The amount of the per-violation fine is tied to inflation. As of 2022, the minimum sanction is $12,537 per false claim, and the maximum sanction per submission is $25,076.) The contractor would have to pay the attorney fees and costs incurred by the whistleblower in pursuing the claim. An anti-retaliation provision was also included in the law. Companies were prohibited from firing or discriminating against employees who filed FCA lawsuits. If fired, the employee was entitled to reinstatement and double back pay, along with traditional special damages, attorney fees and costs.

The New *Qui Tams*: Taxes, Securities, Commodities, and More

The reformed False Claims Act worked. Between October 1986 and September 2021, more than $70 billion was paid back into the U.S. Treasury, and whistleblowers obtained over $8 billion in rewards. Countless billions of dollars were saved through better regulations, deterrence, and internal corporate oversight sparked by the fear of FCA cases. Thousands of wrongdoers have been prosecuted, and many have been thrown into jail.

The tremendous success of the False Claims Act is demonstrated by looking at the recoveries obtained in whistleblower cases. **Figure 12** sets forth the amount of sanctions recovered in Justice Department–initiated cases, as compared with cases triggered by a whistleblower's complaint in the area of healthcare fraud. As can be seen, in the years since the False Claims Act was amended, whistleblower-triggered cases recovered over $48 billion for the taxpayers, and whistleblowers were compensated to the tune of $8 billion for the risks they took in providing invaluable insider information and initiating lawsuits against corrupt Medicaid and Medicare providers and greedy pharmaceutical companies that illegally billed billions to the taxpayers. Approximately 76 percent of all civil fraud recoveries for health care frauds came directly from the insider information provided by whistleblowers.

Figure 12

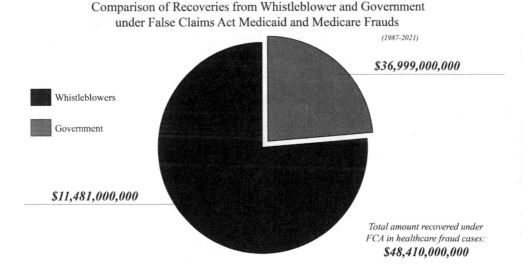

Comparison of Recoveries from Whistleblower and Government
under False Claims Act Medicaid and Medicare Frauds

(1987-2021)

$36,999,000,000

Whistleblowers

Government

$11,481,000,000

*Total amount recovered under
FCA in healthcare fraud cases:*
$48,410,000,000

Based on these successes, Congress enacted new *qui tam* laws, covering taxes (2006), securities fraud and violations of the Foreign Corrupt Practices Act (2010), fraud in the commodities futures and swaps markets (2010), auto safety (2015), and money laundering (2021–22). Each of the laws is somewhat different, but given the breadth of coverage, numerous whistleblowers will be reached by their provisions. Taxpayers, honest investors, banks, and contractors who play by the rules will be the big winners.

The first test of these new whistleblower laws came in the area of taxes. It was a home run for accountability and oversight as well as for whistleblowers. The ink was hardly dry on the federal tax whistleblower law before billions of dollars in claims were filed with the IRS. Most famous of these were allegations submitted by Bradley Birkenfeld, a banker who had worked for UBS bank in Switzerland. When Birkenfeld blew the whistle, UBS was the largest bank in the world. UBS had created a "major wealth" section that catered to offshore North American accounts. Over eighteen thousand Americans had stashed their wealth in this UBS program, where their income was hidden and taxes were evaded. Because the accounts were secret, the stock trades conducted on behalf of these millionaires and billionaires by the UBS bankers were all illegal. The North American program had $20 billion in assets, all in secret nondisclosed accounts that violated numerous U.S. tax laws.

Within months of the passage of the new IRS whistleblower law, Birkenfeld walked into the offices of the Department of Justice with thousands of pages of evidence fully documenting the UBS tax scheme. He provided all the details of the accounts, including the fact that UBS bankers regularly traveled to the United States with encrypted laptops to transact illegal business with their American clients. The scandal that followed shook UBS and Swiss banking to its core.

When the Justice Department and IRS confronted UBS with Birkenfeld's information, the bank immediately folded its hand and paid up. In 2008, UBS agreed to a $780 million settlement with the United States. Moreover, UBS agreed, for the first time in Swiss history, to turn over the names of more than four thousand U.S. citizens who held illegal accounts with the bank.

The False Claims Act has provided ordinary Americans with essential tools to combat fraud, to help recover damages, and to bring accountability to those who would take advantage of the United States government—and of American taxpayers.
—Then-Attorney General Eric Holder

Thousands of Americans with Swiss accounts feared being exposed to public shame, heavy fines, and criminal prosecutions. The IRS capitalized on these fears and initiated a one-time amnesty program, in which U.S. citizens with illegal offshore accounts could confidentially turn themselves in, pay reasonable penalties, and escape criminal prosecution. Over one hundred thousand Americans took advantage of this program and paid the U.S. Treasury fines and penalties in the billions of dollars. As of 2022, the United States has recovered more than $24 billion in sanctions directly attributable to or triggered by the IRS tax whistleblower law.

What was the role of the whistleblower in the largest ever tax fraud case? That was the very question asked by the federal judge to the prosecutor in the Birkenfeld case:

The Court: *Now, you said something that has great significance . . . but for Mr. Birkenfeld this scheme would still be ongoing?*

The Prosecutor: *I have no reason to believe that we would have had any other means to have disclosed what was going on but for an insider in that scheme providing detailed information, which Mr. Birkenfeld did.*

The legendary system of Swiss bank secrecy was cracked wide open by *one* former employee turned whistleblower. *One* whistleblower forced the largest Swiss bank to shut down a multi-billion-dollar, highly profitable program and pay the U.S. Treasury a large fine. *One* whistleblower's disclosure triggered widespread voluntary compliance with the tax laws, resulting in additional billions of dollars pouring into the U.S. Treasury. The first publicly known case under the 2006 IRS whistleblower law resulted in the largest tax fraud recoveries in U.S. history.

On August 6, 2012, Birkenfeld's disclosures also led to what was at that time the largest single payment to a whistleblower under a *qui tam* law ($104 million). Is it any wonder that Congress looked toward the IRS whistleblower law when passing two new *qui tam* laws as part of the Dodd-Frank Act? Just as the FCA and IRS laws produced spectacular results, the Wall Street reward laws have been likewise highly successful. In its short history the SEC has already granted over $1.3 billion in awards, while the Commodity Futures Trading Commission broke all records and awarded a whistleblower $200 million for his role in exposing a billion-dollar bank fraud.

In light of these successes, Congress passed the Anti-Money Laundering Improvement Act in December 2022, creating Dodd-Frank-styled protections and rewards for persons reporting money laundering, violations of the Bank Secrecy Act, and sanctions-busting. The War in Ukraine fueled support for the bill, as Congress recognized how whistleblower reward laws will play a central role in detecting the wealth of sanctioned Russian oligarchs. Whistleblowers were viewed as a weapon for fighting Russian corruption and aggression, although the AML whistleblower law will have far greater reach than just Russian crooks and thugs. For the first time in history, whistleblowers have been the clear winners when exposing frauds at high risk to themselves.

———————————— PRACTICE TIPS ————————————

- Checklist 1 offers a list of federal, state, and local *qui tam* laws, along with their official legal citation.

- Reward laws are complex. They have very specific filing requirements. You must pay careful attention to the rules governing each law, as a minor mistake can cost a whistleblower millions. How to use these laws is explained in Rules 17–25, along with the tools and warnings explicated in Rules 2–15.

Keeping Up with the Changes

To keep up to date on changes in the laws, whistleblowers should access the free online law library created by the author, located at www.kkc.com/law-library.

RULE 17

The False Claims Act Reborn—With a Vengeance

Going after waste, fraud, and abuse without whistleblowers is about as useful as harvesting acres of corn with a pair of rusty old scissors.
—Senator Chuck Grassley, Chairman of Senate Judiciary Committee,
speech given on National Whistleblower Day (July 30, 2018)

Always ask: Is the taxpayer, directly or indirectly, on the hook for any of the costs associated with your disclosure? Do your concerns touch on federal spending, procurement, or contracting? If you answer yes, you may be protected under the most effective whistleblower law in the United States: the False Claims Act (FCA).

The False Claims Act is a law that is simply too good to miss. If a whistleblower prevails in an FCA case, the company must pay treble damages based on the contract or procurement fraud. It also has to pay a fine for each false claim, adjusted annually for inflation. As of May 2022, the minimum fine for each false claim was $12,537, and the maximum fine was $25,076. The whistleblower reward is between 15 and 30 percent of the amount recovered by the government, in addition to attorney fees and costs. Employers cannot retaliate against any employee who takes any action under the FCA or who undertakes any effort to stop one or more violations of the act. The *qui tam* provision can result in large rewards, and, if fired, the employee is entitled to double back pay, special damages, and fees.

What Is a False Claim?

The reach of government spending is vast, and so is the scope for the FCA. The U.S. government is the largest landowner and the largest employer in the United States. Billions upon billions of federal taxpayer dollars are spent on hiring contractors, allocating grants to state and local governments, buying goods and services, healthcare, and handing payouts to massive government programs. Federal monies are spent on everything from highway construction to social services to our nation's defense. Federal money is spent in every state, in nearly every nation on earth, and has even been spent on the moon and Mars, not to mention billions in government spending for Medicare and Medicaid. The FCA prohibits fraud in the spending of every penny of taxpayer money.

The FCA also reaches into other programs that do not directly implicate government spending, such as the payment of royalties on government leases (e.g., oil and gas leases), false statements to obtain benefits from the government, false customs declarations, or statements made to avoid having to pay fines or fees to the United States.

The ways in which government money can be ripped off are as diverse as the imagination. Some examples include misrepresentations in grant applications, billing for services not rendered, billing for services not needed, billing for services not properly performed, selling defective merchandise, failure to ensure quality standards, kickbacks to obtain grants or sell products, failure to meet grant requirements, improperly using government property, overcharging for services, billing to the wrong accounts, underpaying on obligations or leases, improper marketing to increase the demand on goods and services paid for by the government, improper denial of required coverage, upcoding (false diagnosis to increase payments), obtaining early payments, failure to pay mandatory penalties, fees, or customs duties, violation of contracting rules, conflicts of interest, and bill padding (including unnecessary items on a bill). The list is only limited by the creativity of those looking to improperly profit at the taxpayer's expense.

In 2009 and 2010 Congress expanded the scope of the FCA, broadening the definition of *claim* and *obligation*, increasing the reach of the law's conspiracy provisions, and ensuring that subcontractors and government-sponsored corporations or programs were covered under the act. In closing various loopholes in the law, Congress explicitly demanded that the law be interpreted to "protect all Federal funds." Every dime is covered, regardless of who submits the bill or who commits the underlying fraud:

> *[FCA liability] attaches whenever a person knowingly makes a false claim to obtain money or property, any part of which is provided by the Government without regard to whether the wrongdoer deals directly with the Federal Government; with an agent acting on the Government's behalf; or with a third-party contractor. . . . The FCA reaches all false claims submitted to State-administered programs.*

On the floor of the House of Representatives, Congressman Howard Berman of California, one of the principal sponsors of the 1986 FCA amendments, explained the scope and reach of "our Nation's most effective fraud-fighting tool, the federal False Claims Act." Congressman Berman outlined the following as conduct that clearly violates the False Claims Act:

- Charging the government for more than was provided

- Seeking payment when the applicant was not eligible

- Demanding payment for goods or services that do not conform to contractual or regulatory requirements

- Attempting to pay the government less than is owed for any goods, services, concession, or other benefits provided by the government

- Fraudulently seeking to obtain a government contract

- Submitting a fraudulent application for a grant of government funds

- Submitting a false application for a government loan

- Requesting payment for goods or services that are defective or of lesser quality than those for which the government contracted

- Submitting a claim that falsely certifies that the defendant has complied with a law, contact term, or regulation

- Submitting a claim for payment if the applicant was violating conditions material to the contract or the conditions of participation

For years corporations argued for a narrow interpretation of what qualifies as a false claim. They urged courts to ignore common sense and strictly apply the terms explicitly set forth in the four corners of a contract. If a requirement was not set forth in a formal contract or a billing statement, there would be no liability. They wanted to convert a law designed to target fraud into a simple breach of contract case.

This dispute came to a head in a case over the death of Yarushka Rivera, who was being treated in a mental health facility owned by Universal Health Services, Inc. Her care was paid for by taxpayers under the Medicaid program. Rivera was prescribed medication by a "doctor." She had an adverse reaction, suffered seizures, and died. She was seventeen years old.

An employee of Universal told Rivera's parents the truth about her treatment. The psychologist who diagnosed Rivera's condition did not have a medical license. Instead, the PhD she did have was awarded by an unaccredited internet college, and her application for a state license had been rejected. The individual who prescribed the medication purported to be a psychiatrist but was actually a nurse who lacked authority to prescribe medications.

The case filed by Rivera's parents alleged that Universal had ripped off taxpayers by billing for services of unlicensed staff. Universal argued that the billing statements did not explicitly require the persons treating Rivera to be licensed or even qualified. They argued that the FCA did not permit claims to be filed for implied requirements. Universal was joined by the most powerful healthcare and corporate lobbyists, including the U.S. Chamber of Commerce and the American Health Care Association. These special-interest groups forcefully argued that no matter how despicable the treatment, if it was not explicitly prohibited in a contract, there could be no FCA case.

In 2016 the U.S. Supreme Court unanimously rejected these arguments. The Court upheld the theory of implied certification. If a defendant "knowingly fails to disclose . . . noncompliance" with a material "statutory, regulatory, or contractual requirement," the company can be guilty of violating the law even if that requirement is not explicitly set forth in the agreement entered into between the defendant and the government.

Government contractors can be liable even if their noncompliance was "not expressly designated as conditions of payment." A condition of payment can be implied if it was material to the services provided: "What matters is not the label the Government attaches to a requirement, but whether the defendant knowingly violated a requirement that the defendant knows is material to the Government's payment decision."

The Court explained that during the Civil War, when the FCA was passed, Congress was concerned about the United States being "billed for nonexistent or worthless goods, charged exorbitant prices for goods delivered, and generally robbed in purchasing the necessities of war." It is not the terms of a contract that are controlling, but whether the goods being sold are "worthless."

"Materiality" was defined as "having a natural tendency to influence, or be capable of influencing, the payment or receipt of money." The Court warned that minor or insubstantial noncompliance is not material. But material terms do not need to be spelled out in every contract, and can indeed be implied.

Rivera's case could go forward.

How the Law Works

The False Claims Act permits whistleblowers to file claims on behalf of the United States and demand that companies *that have ripped off the taxpayer* be held fully accountable. The whistleblower can obtain a reward for this public service. The FCA permits whistleblowers to go to court and show that the government was financially taken advantage of. If the whistleblower's claims are proven to be correct, the whistleblower is entitled to a percentage of the monies recovered for the United States, plus all attorney fees and costs.

The amounts of these rewards can be staggering, sometimes in the multiple millions of dollars. In 2005 the General Accounting Office determined that the average whistleblower reward under the FCA was $1.7 million. In some instances the whistleblowers were able to collect well over $50 million in rewards for a single FCA case, and in 2022 a whistleblower obtained a court-ordered reward of over $200 million. Between 1987 and 2022, whistleblowers were paid *$8.619 billion* in rewards. There is no upper limit or cap on the amount of an award.

As explained in **Figure 13,** since the FCA was modernized in 1986, whistleblowers account for almost 70 percent of all civil fraud recoveries. Between 1987 and 2021 the United States recovered a total of $70.148 billion under the False Claims Act. Of this amount, whistleblowers were able to force fraudsters to pay directly to the federal treasury over $48.221 billion. This number does not include the deterrent effect caused

Figure 13

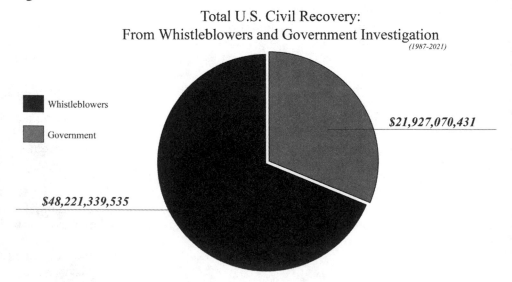

Total U.S. Civil Recovery:
From Whistleblowers and Government Investigation
(1987-2021)

Whistleblowers

Government

$21,927,070,431

$48,221,339,535

by the fear of detection triggered by the law or the benefits obtained under collateral criminal prosecutions.

In remarks given on June 9, 2016, before the American Bar Association, acting Associate Attorney General Bill Baer (who has responsibility over the federal government's efforts to hold federal contractors accountable) confirmed what the statistics prove. The False Claims Act's whistleblower provision "remains the government's most effective civil tool in protecting vital government programs from fraud schemes." The amounts involved are "staggering."

The law does not only result in monetary recoveries. Defense attorney John T. Boese, who has extensively written about and testified in support of corporate positions on the FCA, noted that the Justice Department uses the law to encourage adoption of best practices so companies can police themselves. This includes requiring companies to enter into "corporate integrity agreements" when they settle an FCA case.

Given the success of the FCA, a majority of states and a handful of major municipalities have now enacted local versions. Furthermore, the federal government has established incentives that strongly encourage states to enact FCAs protecting the use of state tax revenue.

Even without a local FCA, state spending is often covered under the federal law. All states and most local governments supply services and sponsor projects in whole or in part through the use of federal monies. If a contractor defrauds a state agency, but federal money is involved, the FCA applies. If a state or local government fails to properly use federal monies, the FCA applies and can be used to hold these local governments accountable.

The FCA is complex. But in considering a case under this law, always keep in mind Congress's intent to enact a highly effective fraud-fighting tool. One of the first cases ever decided under the FCA contains perhaps the best statement of that original intent. Although decided in 1885 by a district court in Oregon, the decision is far from outdated:

> The statute is a remedial one. It is intended to protect the Treasury against the hungry and unscrupulous host that encompasses it on every side and should be construed accordingly. It was passed upon the theory, based on experience as old as modern civilization, that one of the least expensive and most effective means of preventing frauds on the Treasury is to make the perpetrators of them liable to actions by private persons acting, if you please, under the strong stimulus of personal ill will or the hope of gain.

Every employee who works for government contractors or who has any knowledge of how government monies are acquired or spent is a potential relator under the act. The law is designed to encourage, protect, and reward employees who risk their careers to do the right thing.

Should an employee with information about false claims against federal or state governments blow the whistle? Given the amounts at stake for the whistleblower, the benefits obtained by the taxpayers, and the public interest in holding government contractors fully accountable, the question is rhetorical. Any employee who believes that they have information that the government is being ripped off—that contracts were illegally bid, that kickbacks were paid, that defective products were sold, or that the government was overcharged—should, at a minimum, obtain expert advice as to whether or not there may be an FCA case. There is too much at stake to ignore the benefits of this powerful law.

Twelve Steps to Filing a Successful False Claims Act Case

A number of critical requirements are unique to the False Claims Act. It is very easy for whistleblowers to make simple but costly mistakes. Despite Congress's clear intent, given the high stakes in FCA cases, it is imperative that anyone filing a claim strives to conform to a narrow reading of the law. Otherwise they risk giving crooked contractors an excuse to throw the case out of court before a jury can hear the facts.

STEP 1: THINK TWICE BEFORE GOING PUBLIC

The FCA does not encourage whistleblowers to publicly disclose their allegations. The opposite is true. When an employee learns that an employer is ripping off the government, going to the press may actually prejudice the case. The FCA processes whistleblower claims in two categories. The first is made up of cases for which there has been no public disclosure. That is the best category for employees. If there has been no public disclosure, almost any person can file a claim and qualify as a relator, as the term is used under the FCA. Relators do not have to be traditional whistleblowers; they only have to be persons who have knowledge of the underlying fraud and report the fraud to the United States pursuant to the procedures set forth in the FCA. Corporations (including nonprofit public interest groups) have qualified for relator status under the FCA.

However, if there has been a public disclosure, the class of persons who can qualify for obtaining a reward under the FCA is limited. The rationale is simple: If the allegations of fraud are publicly available, anyone could simply read about the fraud in the newspaper and then file an FCA *qui tam* case. But the "original source" of the public disclosure can usually qualify for a reward, as long as they still are the "first to file." Thus, even if some or all of the allegations are publicly available, the government still wants to encourage true insiders to step forward and provide the United States with firsthand knowledge about the frauds unknown to the government. In this manner, whistleblowers who engage in old-fashioned whistleblowing to the news media or Congress can still qualify for a reward. But this is an exception to the rule.

Ultimately, the government wants to know what the whistleblower knows before the wrongdoers have an opportunity to hide their crime. If the targets of a fraud investigation learn that there is a whistleblower on the jobsite, they can take steps to discredit the source and cover up the crime. The government not only loses the element of surprise, but it can also lose access to its most important source of information: the whistleblower. Moreover, any information publicly circulated may aid wrongdoers in coaching or intimidating witnesses, hiding information, spinning the problem in a misleading manner, or engaging in an outright cover-up. If there has been no public disclosure, there is a stronger possibility that the whistleblower's existence will remain confidential, permitting the government to conduct a more thorough investigation. The whistleblower can serve as an undercover informant while still working for the company and provide information on white-collar crimes that is often impossible to detect without the assistance of employees willing to risk their careers to do the right thing. In fact, it is not uncommon for government agents to ask the whistleblower to wear a wire and secretly record conversations with those involved in the fraud.

That said, Congress was fully aware that many whistleblowers expose wrongdoing in the press and that these disclosures can serve the public interest and even be the catalyst for initiating government investigations. Consequently, in defining the term "original source" in the False Claims Act, Congress was careful to include whistleblowers whose disclosures to the news media or Congress that caused the government to open an investigation. Whistleblowers who go to the news media before contacting the Justice Department can fully qualify for a reward, provided that other requirements of the law are strictly followed. Additionally, the federal courts have held that whistleblowers have a First Amendment right to disclose their fraud allegations to the public.

STEP 2: TRY TO QUALIFY AS AN ORIGINAL SOURCE

As explained in step one, if the basis of an FCA claim was not publicly disclosed, almost every potential whistleblower will have standing to file an FCA claim and qualify for a reward. But if the basis for a claim was publicly disclosed, you will most likely have to demonstrate that you were an original source of the allegations that form the foundation of the FCA case.

Never assume that there was no public disclosure. Companies have become infamous for scouring the public record in an attempt to find any release of information that could possibly qualify as a public disclosure of the transactions or allegations that form the basis of an FCA case. Even if you are not aware of any public disclosure, it is best to prepare for such a defense. When drafting the initial complaint in the case, if possible, set forth the basis for your argument that you are an original source of the allegations.

STEP 3: CONFIDENTIALLY FILE ALLEGATIONS WITH THE GOVERNMENT

It is best practice to disclose allegations to government regulators *prior* to filing a formal False Claims Act case. Voluntarily providing information to the government before filing the formal complaint can satisfy one of the requirements for qualifying as an original source whistleblower.

Providing information to the government before filing a formal FCA complaint is very easy. Many whistleblowers, without even understanding the law, contact government agencies before filing a *qui tam*. Employees often initiate contact with government contracting officials or provide information on government-sponsored hotlines. Every major government agency has an office of inspector general. That office has jurisdiction to accept and investigate allegations of contractor fraud and/or any form of procurement abuse.

STEP 4: FILE FIRST

Another unique provision in the law is the "first to file" rule. Only the person who files the claim first has the right to pursue the case and collect the reward. If an employee has information on potential false claims, it is imperative that they assemble the evidence and file their claim as quickly as possible. An informal disclosure to the government does not count. Additionally, if the government files a claim against the contractor before the whistleblower files their claim, the right to file the *qui tam* may also be barred. Whistleblowers cannot delay. Procrastination is fatal.

The False Claims Act works. It works because it is an effective tool to fight fraud across the full spectrum of federal programs and initiatives. The FCA works because it provides powerful incentives for companies to do business the right way.
—Stuart Delery, Assistant U.S. Attorney General

STEP 5: CHOOSE THE VENUE

One of the most useful features of the False Claims Act is a very liberal venue requirement. A party can file a lawsuit in any jurisdiction in which any of the named defendants "can be found, resides, transacts business, or in which any [false claim] occurred." This often gives a whistleblower a choice of districts in which they can file a claim. A claim should be filed in the venue that is most favorable for pursuing the case, not necessarily in the judicial district where the company and/or the whistleblower resides.

STEP 6: PREPARE A DETAILED DISCLOSURE STATEMENT

Most civil suits are initiated with the filing of a short, concise complaint that is processed in the local court. Not so with the FCA. The FCA requires that the whistleblower/relator file a detailed disclosure statement with the United States at the same time a complaint is served on the government. The rule is fairly simple: "A copy of the complaint *and written disclosure of substantially all material evidence and information the person possesses* shall be served on the Government pursuant to Rule 4(d)(4) of the Rules of Civil Procedure" [emphasis added]. The disclosure statement is *only* filed with the U.S. government. It is *not* filed with the court and it is *not* served on the defendants. The statement should be kept strictly confidential.

The disclosure statement requirement is consistent with other aspects of the FCA. Essentially all the evidence the whistleblower has to back up their allegations of misconduct should be contained in the statement. All documentary evidence that supports the claim should be copied and submitted along with the written statement. This requirement compels the whistleblower to surrender the evidence of wrongdoing to the government as quickly as possible. It also permits the United States to commence its investigation in a timely manner.

Put your best foot forward when filing a disclosure statement. The statement constitutes a documentary record of the nature of your allegations and establishes the scope of your claims. The information set forth in the disclosure can and will play a critical role in determining whether the United States joins in your lawsuit.

STEP 7: FILE THE COMPLAINT UNDER SEAL AND KEEP IT CONFIDENTIAL

Unlike a normal lawsuit filed in court, a False Claims Act case must be filed under seal. Everything about the filing of the complaint is strictly confidential. The defendant is not informed that a lawsuit has been filed. The complaint is kept confidential and only provided to the Justice Department and the court. The whistleblower cannot tell anyone that they filed a complaint. The complaint is not served on any party, except the United States.

Until the court issues an order lifting the seal, no one else is provided with a copy of the complaint. When a case is initially filed, secrecy is key. If you tell the news media, the defendants, or anyone else for that matter that you filed the claim, you may lose your case and be subject to sanctions for violating a court-ordered confidentiality requirement.

The specific rule for filing a complaint consists of a two-part process: First, the complaint is filed with the court. Second, the complaint and the disclosure statement are formally served on the United States.

As for the court filing: "The complaint shall be filed *in camera*, shall remain under seal for at least 60 days, and shall not be served on the defendant until the court so orders." In other words, inform the clerk of the court that the complaint must be filed confidentially and *never* serve the complaint on the defendant until the court officially lifts the seal and orders that service be completed.

As for the United States, as explained above, both a copy of the complaint and the written disclosure statement must be served on the government pursuant to Rule 4(d)(4) of the Rules of Civil Procedure. This rule of procedure mandates that the complaint and disclosure statement be served both upon the attorney general of the United States in Washington, DC, and upon the U.S. attorney for the judicial district in which the complaint is filed.

Eventually the complaint will be taken out of seal, and the parties can proceed in a manner consistent with other traditional lawsuits, but the initial complaint must be filed confidentially.

Once the government concludes its investigation and determines whether or not to intervene, the court will take the case out of seal; the proceedings will become public; and if the case is to go forward, the complaint must be served upon the defendants. But before this happens, you *must* honor and follow the sealing order requiring that FCA complaints be kept strictly confidential.

STEP 8: THE COMPLAINT FILED IN COURT MUST BE DETAILED

The FCA complaint should contain detailed factual statements setting forth the basis for the complaint. Courts view FCA cases in a manner similar to other fraud cases. Under Federal Rule of Civil Procedure 9(b), fraud cases are subjected to a "heightened pleading" standard. As one court explained, this rule requires plaintiffs to "place the defendants on notice of the precise misconduct with which they are charged" in order to "safeguard defendants against spurious charges of immoral or fraudulent behavior."

Courts uniformly have applied this 9(b) standard to FCA cases. Thus, unlike other federal court complaints, which merely require a plain statement of the factual basis for the case, FCA cases must contain specific information setting forth the grounds for the claim, including precise information on which the FCA violations are based.

Beyond satisfying the technical procedural pleading requirements for fraud cases, there are other good reasons for making sure the complaint (and the disclosure statement that is required to be filed with the government) is very detailed. First, because of the first to file rule, what happens if your complaint is vague on a key issue of fraud, but another whistleblower files a similar complaint, which provides specific detail of the wrongdoing? Whose complaint meets the first to file rule? This is a question every *qui tam* relator should seek to avoid ever having to answer. A properly detailed complaint should go a long way toward resolving such a dispute.

Second, under the Supreme Court's ruling in the *Rockwell International* case, whistleblowers are only entitled to a reward for those frauds properly included within the scope of their complaint. If allegations are vaguely worded and if the complaint lacks specificity on key issues, the *qui tam* relator risks having their claim denied under *Rockwell*.

Third, the more specificity contained in the complaint (and disclosure statement), the more credibility the whistleblower will have with government investigators. This will also increase the chance that the government will intervene in the case.

Finally, there is always tension between filing a detailed complaint and disclosure statement and adhering to the first to file rule. These issues should be considered on a case-by-case basis.

STEP 9: KEEP INVESTIGATING THE CLAIM AFTER THE COMPLAINT IS FILED

After the FCA complaint is filed and the disclosure statement served, do not rest on your laurels. Whistleblowers can and should continue to investigate and collect additional information that backs up their claims. Sometimes this can be done by the employee working on their own (without ever disclosing the existence of the FCA claim to anyone), and sometimes this occurs in conjunction with the government investigation. For example, it is common for government investigators to obtain assistance from the relator after a case is filed. This can include anything from providing additional documents to government investigators all the way to wearing a wire while meeting at work with the managers responsible for the fraud. When determining award amounts, the depth of assistance to the government is considered and may land you a major award increase.

STEP 10: DETERMINE WHETHER STATE FUNDS ARE INVOLVED

A growing number of states and municipalities now have local versions of the False Claims Act. They include California, the City of Chicago, Colorado, Connecticut, Delaware, the District of Columbia, Florida, Georgia, Hawaii, Illinois, Indiana, Louisiana, Maryland, Massachusetts, Michigan, Montana, Nevada, New Hampshire, New Mexico, New Jersey, New York City, New York State, North Carolina, Oklahoma, Philadelphia and Allegheny County, Pennsylvania (not the Commonwealth of Pennsylvania), Rhode Island, Tennessee, Texas, Vermont, Virginia, and Washington. Some of these laws are mirror images of the federal FCA, while others contain significant differences. Some of these states restrict the scope of their local FCA to fraud in Medicaid spending.

When federal and state monies are jointly involved, it is very common to include state claims in the federal complaint. The federal FCA has a special provision that establishes federal jurisdiction "over any action brought under the laws of any State for the recovery of funds paid by a State or local government if the action arises from the same transaction or occurrence as an action brought under [the federal False Claims Act]."

The state FCAs are very similar to the federal law, but most have some statutory differences. Just as with the federal law, if you are using a state FCA, meticulous care must be undertaken to comply with the law's rules and procedures. When including pendent state claims in the federal FCA, it is typical to include any separate count(s) within the complaint for each state and to use this part of the complaint to ensure that any special terms required under state law are met, and that additional causes of action are included for states that have more liberal liability or standing procedures than the federal law.

State recoveries can be very large, especially if the defrauded program was a joint federal and state enterprise. A prime example of this was the settlement in the Eli Lilly case, where $362 million of the $800 million set aside to compensate for the losses to the Medicare and Medicaid programs was allocated for paying state claims. Joint federal and state settlements are common in FCA cases, especially in the area of healthcare.

State False Claims Act cases can be filed even if there is no federal money involved. These lawsuits focus on frauds related to local or state taxpayer dollars. For example, in March 2021 the New York attorney general announced a $105 million settlement of a New York FCA case. Previously, New York prevailed in an FCA case against Sprint, collecting $330 million in sanctions and paying the whistleblower a $62.7 million award.

STEP 11: PREPARE FOR A RETALIATION CASE

If a whistleblower is discriminated against or fired for raising allegations of fraud, they have the right to include retaliation claims as part of the False Claims Act lawsuit (or as a stand-alone retaliation case). Subsection (h) of the act prohibits retaliation against employees who engage in protected activities designed to further an FCA lawsuit or who engage in "other efforts to stop one or more violations" of the procurement/contracting violations outlawed by the FCA. This law provides for double back pay, reinstatement, special damages, and attorney fees and costs. The statute of limitations for the retaliation claim is three years.

Often subsection (h) retaliation cases are included in the FCA complaint as a placeholder. The retaliation case is filed and preserved along with the *qui tam* rewards-based claim, but a formal decision whether to actually pursue such a case is left for a later date.

The retaliation claim is handled separately from the contractor-fraud case. These cases can be pursued regardless of the outcome of an FCA award claim. Even if the United States declines to intervene in the fraud case, and even if upon further investigation the fraud claims appear to have no merit, an employee still has the right to pursue retaliation claims based on discrimination in the workplace.

STEP 12: DECIDE WHETHER TO PROCEED WITH A CIVIL CASE

After the government completes its investigation into the confidential complaint, the United States will inform the court whether or not it will intervene in some or all of the claims filed by the relator. This can be the most important decision in an FCA case. Based on raw statistics, if the United States intervenes in a case, the odds of prevailing are extremely high. But if the United States declines to intervene, the vast majority of cases are dismissed.

If the United States intervenes in the case, as a matter of law the government takes over primary control of the litigation. Once this happens, the relator plays a secondary role to the government, and courts often defer to the judgment of the United States. After all, it is the government's money that was defrauded. The FCA defines the role of the government and relator in intervened cases as follows: "If the Government proceeds with the action, it shall have the primary responsibility for prosecuting the action, and shall not be bound by an act of the person bringing the action"; however, the relator "shall have the right to continue as a party to the action."

This provision does not leave the whistleblower out in the cold. The whistleblower has the right to fully participate in the civil proceeding, conduct discovery, file briefs and motions, question witnesses at trial, and otherwise be fully included in every aspect of the case. The relator also must be informed of any settlement agreement and has an opportunity to oppose court approval of a settlement. By actively participating in an intervened case, the whistleblower can help the government prevail on the merits and at the same time protect their interests as the relator. Additionally, the relator is also entitled to a payment of attorney fees and costs from the defendant. Thus, even in cases in which the final recovery may be modest, the relator's counsel can still be paid by the defendant pursuant to the statutory attorney fee provision contained in the FCA.

If the United States declines to intervene in the case, the whistleblower must make the major decision of either dropping the case or moving forward with it. Under the *qui tam* provision, the whistleblower is empowered to pursue the case "on behalf of the king." So even if the United States decides that it will not prosecute the claim, a whistleblower can still go forward and prove the merits of the case. If they prevail, the United States still collects the lion's share of the award, but the whistleblower is entitled to a minimum 25 percent and maximum 30 percent relator's share of any money recovered by the United States, along with a statutory attorney fee.

The FCA contains a section that permits a defendant to seek reverse attorney fees from the whistleblower if the United States declines to intervene and the employee-relator continues with the claim. These reverse fees can be awarded only under narrow circumstances: "If the Government does not proceed . . . and the person bringing the action conducts the action, the court may award to the defendant its reasonable attorneys' fees and expenses if the defendant prevails in the action and the court finds that the claim . . . was clearly frivolous, clearly vexatious, or brought primarily for purposes of harassment."

The government's decision not to intervene should not be held against the whistleblower in subsequent litigation. Despite this, courts are unfortunately more skeptical of the merits of a case for which the United States did not join.

No matter how strong you may think your case is, if the United States declines to intervene, it is absolutely imperative that you stop and take a hard look at your claim. You must evaluate why the United States declined to intervene and assess the costs and risks of going forward. The False Claims Act remains the taxpayer's primary civil remedy in stopping fraud in government programs.

- State and local FCAs signed into law as of 2022 are listed in Checklist 1.

- The False Claims Act is codified at 31 U.S.C. §§ 3729-32. Its legislative history is contained in Senate Report No. 99-345 (July 28, 1986) and S. Rep. No. 110-507 (Sept. 17, 2008).

- Recent Supreme Court cases interpreting the FCA are *KBR v. U.S. ex rel. Carter*, 135 S.Ct. 1970 (2015) (clarifying first to file rule and statute of limitations); *U.S. ex rel. Escobar v. Universal Health Services*, 136 S.Ct. 1989 (2016) (recognizing implied certification claims); and *State Farm v. U.S. ex rel. Rigsby*, 137 S.Ct 436 (2016) (sanctions for violating seal); *U.S. ex rel. Polansky v. Executive Health*, No. 21-1052 (Supreme Court 2023) (dismissal of claims of United States); *U.S. ex rel. Schutte v. SuperValu*, No. 21-1326 (Supreme Court 2023) (definition of "knowingly violated" the FCA).

Keeping Up with the Changes

To keep up to date on changes in the laws, whistleblowers should access the free online law library created by the author, located at www.kkc.com/law-library.

RULE 18

Tax Evasion and Underpayments: Report to the IRS

The IRS' serious efforts to combat offshore tax evasion, which had long been a problem, began in 2008 with our efforts to address specific situations brought to our attention in part by whistleblowers.

—John Koskinen, Commissioner, IRS

At a breakfast meeting of 100 senior wealth management leaders held on September 12, 2012, top Swiss bankers and their consultants discussed changes in the infamous secret Swiss banking system—a system that had permitted thousands of millionaires and billionaires to hide their wealth in Swiss banks, escaping taxation and detection from their local governments. The exclusive gathering, held at the Hotel President Wilson in Geneva, Switzerland, occurred just one day after former Swiss banker Bradley Birkenfeld sponsored an international press conference at the National Press Club in Washington, DC, publicly revealing that the U.S. Internal Revenue Service had ruled in his favor and awarded him $104 million as a result of his having blown the whistle on the Swiss banking giant UBS.

According to a report from an *Agence France-Presse* reporter who was able to attend, there was a doomsday mood during this elite meeting. The attendees were seething at Birkenfeld and attacking the whistleblower's "total lack of morality" for having the audacity to blow the whistle on over 19,000 secret bank accounts held by wealthy Americans, resulting in numerous criminal prosecutions and the payment of billions in back taxes, fines, and penalties.

Beyond the hatred directed at the whistleblower, the "scandals" he triggered had "driven a nail into the heart of the once seemingly invincible Swiss bank secrecy" system. The head of the Swiss banking group Reyl & Co, Francois Reyl, described the new reality: "The storm has swept everything away." A respected banking consultant was reported as saying that "Banking secrecy is no longer there. That's gone. It is over."

Whistleblower Bradley Birkenfeld, a former international banker employed at UBS (at the time, the world's largest bank), had blown the lid off the entire Swiss banking empire. As described by the Internal Revenue Service in its ruling awarding Birkenfeld the largest single payment ever given to one whistleblower under U.S. laws, Birkenfeld had provided information that "formed the basis for unprecedented actions against UBS, with collateral impact on other enforcement activities."

The reward given to Birkenfeld sent shock waves throughout the international banking community. The effective use of a tax whistleblower law had changed "everything" with the illegal offshore secret banking systems that were estimated to hold trillions of dollars in U.S. assets. The reason was simple. Under a U.S. tax whistleblower law, anyone with original information on tax law violations or underpayments could disclose their evidence to the IRS and, if proven true, could qualify for a large cash reward equaling 15 to 30 percent of the proceeds collected by the IRS as a result of the whistleblower's disclosure.

Based on this law, every international banker who turns in American clients holding illegal offshore accounts could potentially qualify for a multimillion-dollar reward. When Birkenfeld first stepped forward, the IRS reward law was brand-new. In the beginning of his case, he met with disaster. Instead of blowing the whistle to the IRS Whistleblower Office (the office designated with the responsibility of receiving whistleblower claims), Birkenfeld walked into the office of a Justice Department prosecutor and, with no immunity, dumped his documents at their doorstep. The Justice Department, completely ignoring the new whistleblower law, prosecuted Birkenfeld. The international banking community watched with glee at what first appeared to be the destruction of a whistleblower's career. They were convinced the IRS law was broken and would not work. But when it became public that Birkenfeld, despite having gone to jail, was still able to successfully litigate his claim before the IRS and prevail in his request for a $104 million reward, everything changed.

The reality that whistleblowers could effectively report tax fraud and that the U.S. government would follow the law and award whistleblowers (even if the law required payments in the hundreds of millions of dollars) sank in rather quickly for an audience of bankers and private wealth managers. They recognized that any of their colleagues could turn in their institutions and clients and become multimillionaire heroes overnight. They also realized that Birkenfeld's rather simple mistake (i.e., giving information to a prosecutor without immunity, as opposed to the lawfully designated IRS Whistleblower Office) could be easily fixed. They recognized the impact whistleblowers could have on their banks and clients under the new IRS whistleblower law. They lamented that their highly profitable secret banking programs for U.S. taxpayers had been "swept away."

One of the smartest things Congress has ever done is to empower whistleblowers to help the government combat fraud. They get results. Without whistleblowers, the government simply does not have the capability to identify and prosecute the ever-expanding and creative schemes to bilk the taxpayers. That is not rhetoric. That is history.
—Senator Chuck Grassley, House Judiciary Subcommittee
on the Constitution and Civil Justice Hearing on
"Oversight of the False Claims Act" (2016)

How We Got Here

In March 1867 Congress passed a reward law for people who reported tax crimes. The law was enacted years before there was a federal income tax, and unlike the False Claims Act, there was no *qui tam* provision. Rewards paid to informants were strictly discretionary. The law did not work. Because the IRS was not required to do anything to help would-be whistleblowers, they didn't. The rewards provision remained mostly unused and ignored for years.

One hundred forty years later, Iowa Senator Chuck Grassley used his position as chairman of the powerful Senate Finance Committee to rectify this problem. The FCA had proven to be the most successful fraud-detection law in U.S. history, but it *excluded* false claims related to tax payments.

In 2006 the inability of the government to detect massive violations of the tax code was reminiscent of the government's inability to police its contracts twenty years before. Tax fraud was rampant. For example, in illegal offshore accounts alone, it was estimated that over $5 trillion was stashed. For years, millionaires and billionaires had devised sophisticated tax-avoidance schemes, and there was no incentive whatsoever for bankers, accountants, and insiders to blow the whistle. In fact, the reality was far from it—if an accountant blew the whistle on a client, that accountant would be ostracized from the industry.

On December 20, 2006, Congress passed the Grassley-sponsored amendment to the archaic IRS informants law. Following the lead of the FCA, a *qui tam* law was enacted *requiring* the IRS to pay rewards to whistleblowers who exposed major tax underpayments, violations of internal revenue laws, or any actions of persons "conniving" to cheat on their taxes. The IRS was required to establish a Whistleblower Office, and if a claim was denied, the employee could appeal that decision to the Tax Court.

The law is *not* limited to tax fraud or evasion. It also covers non-fraudulent underpayments of tax. Moreover, the scope of the law was significantly enlarged in 2018, when Congress included all criminal tax cases, violations of the Foreign Bank and Financial Accounts (FBAR) requirements, and all matters investigated by the IRS. Thereafter, in 2019 Congress prohibited job-related retaliation against tax whistleblowers.

Since the 2006 amendments the IRS has paid over 2,500 whistleblowers a total of $1.05 billion, and collected over $6.4 billion in sanctions. However, due to the long backlog in calculating whistleblower awards, these numbers are actually ten years behind. The actual amount of sanctions obtained from whistleblower disclosures is radically higher.

Factors Used by the IRS to Judge Awards

When putting together a reward filing, it is important to know the factors applied by the IRS when it evaluates a claim to determine at what percentage to set the award.

The "positive factors" set forth in the IRS's *Internal Revenue Manual* (Part 25, Chapter 2) are as follows:

- Did the whistleblower act "promptly to inform the IRS or the taxpayer of the tax noncompliance"?

- Did the information provided identify an "issue or transaction of a type previously unknown to the IRS"?

- Was the information provided "particularly difficult to detect through the IRS's exercise of reasonable diligence"?

- Did the whistleblower present information thoroughly and with "factual details of tax noncompliance in a clear and organized manner"?

- Did the whistleblower's information save "IRS work and resources"?

- Did the whistleblower provide "exceptional cooperation and assistance during the pendency of the action(s)"?

- Did the information provided identify "assets of the taxpayer that could be used to pay liabilities, particularly if the assets were not otherwise known to the IRS"?

- Did the information provided identify "connections between transactions, or parties to transactions, that enabled the IRS to understand tax implications that might not otherwise have been understood by the IRS"?

- Did the information provided have "an impact on the behavior of the taxpayer, for example by causing the taxpayer to promptly correct a previously-reported improper position"?

The following factors will be used by the IRS to reduce (but not deny) a reward:

- Whether the whistleblower "delayed" reporting the violations

- Whether the whistleblower's actions "contributed to the underpayment" of taxes

- Whether the whistleblower interfered or harmed the IRS investigation

- Whether the whistleblower violated instructions given by the IRS or violated a confidentiality agreement or other contract entered into with the IRS

Another ground for reducing an award is whether the whistleblower "profited from the underpayment of tax or tax noncompliance identified." Profiting from the underlying violations is not grounds for denying a reward, but if the whistleblower is found criminally guilty of planning and initiating the violations, there may be grounds for an outright denial.

How the Law Works

The basic rules that govern the IRS whistleblower law are as follows:

1. **Violations Covered.** The tax whistleblower law is not limited to tax fraud. It covers any underpayment of taxes, fraudulent or not. As a result of a 2018 amendment, it now covers criminal tax fraud prosecuted by the Justice Department and all violations investigated by the IRS, including some

money laundering and asset forfeiture cases. The law also covers those who conspire to violate the laws. The monetary basis for which a reward is paid includes not just the back taxes, but any "penalties, interest, additions to tax, and additional amounts" obtained by the U.S. government on the basis of the whistleblower's information.

2. **Proceedings Covered.** The whistleblower is eligible for a reward if monies are recovered by the United States based on the whistleblower's information, regardless of if the money is obtained from an administrative proceeding, a judicial proceeding, a settlement, or "any related action." However, unlike the False Claims Act, the whistleblower does not have the right to initiate legal proceedings against the taxpayer. It is up to the IRS and/or the U.S. government to file the lawsuit, or reach a settlement with the taxpayer. Once the United States collects the back taxes, interest, penalties, and so on, the whistleblower then becomes entitled to their percentage share from the monies recovered by the United States. If the United States does not initiate legal or administrative action against the taxpayer, the whistleblower cannot file their own lawsuit against the taxpayer.

3. **Who Can File.** The applicant for the reward does not have to be an employee of the targeted company. They can be an outside contractor, a compliance official, a banker, a business partner, or any other person who is able to obtain credible information of a major tax fraud or underpayment.

4. **Procedure for Filing.** IRS whistleblower claims are filed directly with the IRS. There is no lawsuit. There is no public filing. Nothing is officially served on the employer or the individual who violated the tax laws. You do not have to tell your boss about the tax fraud or file an internal complaint. Doing so could result in your boss retaliating, especially if the IRS were to open an investigation on the very issues you tried to get fixed.

5. **IRS Form 211.** The IRS has created a form that must be used for filing a whistleblower claim. The form, titled "Application for Award for Original Information," is better known simply as "Form 211," named after its official IRS number. Under IRS rules, Form 211 must be completed in its entirety, dated, signed personally by the whistleblower, and filed by the applicant or their attorney.

Although not required, whistleblowers should first file Form 211, and thereafter commence working with investigators.

6. **Information Wanted by the IRS.** In the IRS's own words: "The IRS is looking for solid information, not an 'educated guess' or unsupported speculation. We are looking for a significant Federal tax issue—this is not a program for resolving personal problems or disputes about a business relationship." If the whistleblower's allegations cannot be independently corroborated, a claim will be denied.

7. **Lawful Disclosures/Obtaining Documents.** A whistleblower should not violate the law in order to obtain information about tax frauds. The IRS's guidance on filing claims states: "Under no circumstances do we expect or condone illegal actions taken to secure documents or supporting evidence." If the whistleblower knows about the existence of supporting evidence, but cannot lawfully obtain that information, the IRS suggests that the whistleblower "should describe these documents and identify their location to the best of his or her ability." In other words, do not steal information. Instead, carefully describe where the documents are hidden so that the IRS can lawfully obtain it through a subpoena or other legal means. In these circumstances, sometimes the whistleblower carefully places supporting documents in a specific location at work and then notifies the government where the document(s) can be found.

8. **Confidentiality.** The IRS Form 211 cannot be filed anonymously. However, the IRS has strong confidentiality protections. The *IRS Manual* requires the Service to protect the identity of any person seeking the whistleblower reward "to the fullest extent permitted by law." But under some circumstances the whistleblower's identity may have to be disclosed, such as if the whistleblower "is needed as a witness in a judicial proceeding." The IRS states that the circumstances where such a disclosure is needed are rare, and that the "Service will make every effort to notify the whistleblower before deciding whether to proceed in such a case."

9. **No Anonymous Submissions.** The statute requires that all claims be filed "under penalty of perjury." The whistleblower making the claim must personally sign Form 211/written submission, swear that they have examined the application and any accompanying statement and supporting documentation, and affirm that the "application is true, correct and complete, to the best of" their knowledge.

   Because the application *must* be filed under the penalty of perjury, the IRS guidance states that claims *cannot* be submitted "anonymously or under an alias." Furthermore, the whistleblower's lawyer cannot simply sign the submission. The whistleblower must personally sign the form. If a joint claim is being filed, all the claimants must personally sign the form and swear to the truthfulness of the information. However, under IRS rules whistleblowers can obtain confidential informant status in order to protect their identity.

10. **Where to File/The Whistleblower Office.** The IRS has a special Whistleblower Office. The office is required to analyze information received from whistleblowers and has the statutory authority to issue an award to the whistleblower. The decision to make a payment to a whistleblower belongs to the director of the Whistleblower Office, not the secretary of the treasury or the head of the IRS. Form 211 is filed with the Whistleblower Office.

11. **Acknowledgment of Claim.** The Whistleblower Office will acknowledge receiving a claim in writing. Each claim is given a formal claim number. The whistleblower has to be sure that this acknowledgment letter is received, as it is their proof that a claim was filed and documents the date the claim was formally received by the Whistleblower Office.

12. **Amount of Reward.** The reward provision is modeled on the FCA. If the IRS collects sanctions based on information provided by the whistleblower, the whistleblower is entitled to a reward of between 15 percent and 30 percent of any amount recovered by the IRS. These are the same percentages permitted under the FCA. The law also permits the whistleblower to obtain a reward based on monies collected from "related actions."

13. **Judicial Review.** The whistleblower has the right to appeal award-determination decisions of the Whistleblower Office to the U.S. Tax Court. Appeals must be filed within thirty days of the Whistleblower Office's ruling. The Tax Court has published rules for these appeals (Rule 340-344). They require that the whistleblower file a petition with the Tax Court, setting forth the date the Whistleblower Office made its determination and an explanation as to why the whistleblower "disagrees with the determination" of the Whistleblower Office, a statement of facts that supports the whistleblower's appeal, and a specific petition for relief, along with other information.

14. **When Payments Are Due.** Under the law, the IRS will not pay the whistleblower until the IRS actually obtains the money from the delinquent taxpayer and the deadline for appealing the payments or obtaining a refund expire. This has resulted in large delays in payment. If the delinquent taxpayer challenges the IRS's actions administratively or in court, the payment to the whistleblower will be "delayed until that litigation has been concluded with finality." Given the number of claims being filed by whistleblowers, the small number of employees currently staffing the IRS Whistleblower Office, and the necessity to await final payment to the IRS before any monies are paid to the whistleblower, payments to whistleblowers are taking years to adjudicate and resolve.

15. **Financial Threshold.** The Grassley Amendment targets large taxpayers. Consequently, the IRS reward program now has two parts. The first part is based on the 1867 law. It covers small tax frauds and underpayments (under $2 million). The amount of any reward paid to informants under this program is strictly discretionary, and there is no appeal of an IRS denial.

The second part of the IRS program, created by the 2006 Grassley Amendment, mandates that the IRS pay rewards, sets the percentage amounts for such rewards, and provides a judicial review. However, the mandatory reward provisions only apply to large tax cases.

The IRS Whistleblower Office describes these thresholds as follows: "To be eligible for an award under [the Grassley Amendment], the tax, penalties, interest, additions to tax, and additional amounts in dispute must exceed in the aggregate $2 million and, if the allegedly noncompliant person is an individual, the individual's gross income must exceed $200,000 for any taxable year at issue in a claim."

16. **No Bar to Recovery If You Participated in the Fraud.** Whistleblowers who participated in the fraud are entitled to a full reward. This aspect of the law dates back to the original False Claims Act signed by President Lincoln. The Civil War Congress that drafted the original FCA was very clear that the law was designed to encourage "rogues" to step forward and turn in other "rogues."

17. **Planning and Initiating Tax Frauds.** Congress drew a distinction between persons who simply participate in tax frauds and those who actually "plan and initiate" the fraud. This makes sense. For example, if an accountant plans and initiates a tax fraud on behalf of a client and then turns in the very fraud planned and put into effect, should that accountant be able to profit from the illegal scheme they devised?

    Because of this possibility, Congress permits the IRS Office of the Whistleblower to reduce the amount of an award to a whistleblower who "planned and initiated the actions that led to the underpayment of tax" or who planned and initiated the tax fraud. The *IRS Manual* explains that "if the whistleblower participated substantially in the actions that resulted in the underpayment of tax, the Whistleblower Office may deny an award."

18. **Criminal Convictions.** If the whistleblower is criminally convicted of a crime related to their role in planning and initiating the tax violations, the whistleblower is disqualified from any reward. This is a very narrow exception. A word of caution: Although the IRS Office of the Whistleblower has been very supportive of whistleblowers who may have engaged in wrongdoing, the Justice Department Tax Division has taken a different (and highly counterproductive) approach. It has filed charges against tax whistleblowers, including the most famous tax whistleblower of all time, Bradley Birkenfeld. Thus, when approaching the IRS, it is important to be sensitive to the Justice Department Tax Division's differing view of whistleblowing.

19. **Persons Not Qualified to File a Claim.** The class of excluded persons is very limited. According to IRS regulations, the IRS will not process whistleblower claims filed by employees of the Department of the Treasury; persons working for federal, state, or local governments if they are "acting within the scope of his/her duties as an employee" of the government; persons "required by Federal law or regulation to disclose the information"; and persons precluded from disclosing the information under other federal laws.

20. **Power of Attorney.** A whistleblower who wants to be represented by counsel must sign and file a Power of Attorney, IRS Form 2848. Without this form the IRS will not talk to your attorney or send your attorney any information.

─────────────── PRACTICE TIPS ───────────────

- The IRS *qui tam* law is codified at 26 U.S.C. § 7623. The internal IRS rules governing the rewards provision are located in Part 25 of the *IRS Manual*, available at www.irs.gov. Rules for filing claims are also codified at 26 C.F.R. Part 301.7623-1. The whistleblower law was amended in 2018 to cover criminal tax frauds, among other crimes. See Section 41108 of Public Law 115-123 (Feb. 9, 2018). An anti-retaliation provision was added in 2019 in Section 1405 of Public Law 116-25 (July 1, 2019).

- The IRS has taken a strong position in federal court protecting the identity of whistleblowers. *Montgomery v. IRS*, 40 F.4th 702 (D.C. Cir. 2022).

- *Whistleblower 14106-10W v. Commissioner of the IRS*, 137 Tax Court No. 15 (Dec. 8, 2011) (decision of the Tax Court setting standards for a whistleblower to remain confidential in Tax Court proceedings).

- *Whistleblower 13412-12W v. Commissioner*, T.C. Memo. 2014-93 (May 20, 2014) (setting forth procedures for requesting anonymity in Tax Court proceedings).

- *Whistleblower 21276-13W v. Commissioner*, 147 Tax Court No. 4 (Aug. 3, 2016) (broad interpretation of "related action" rule permitting whistleblowers to obtain rewards based on tax-related criminal proceedings). This decision was approved by Congress in 2017 and codified into law.

- *Whistleblower 21276-13W v. Commissioner*, 144 Tax Court No. 15 (June 2, 2015) (whistleblower can qualify for a reward if initially provides information to other government agencies instead of the IRS Whistleblower Office).

Keeping Up with the Changes

To keep up to date on changes in the laws, whistleblowers should access the free online law library created by the author, located at www.kkc.com/law-library.

RULE 19

Dodd-Frank (Securities and Commodities): Report to the SEC/CFTC

[T]he whistleblower program has been a critical component of the Commission's efforts to detect wrongdoing . . . particularly where fraud is well-hidden or difficult to detect.
—Then-Chair of the SEC Jay Clayton (September 2020)

The Dodd-Frank Act is quickly becoming the most popular whistleblower law. The Securities and Exchange Commission (SEC) and the Commodity Futures Trading Commission (CFTC) have paid out huge awards, including multiple payments topping $100 million. The SEC Office of the Whistleblower's 2022 Annual Report remarked on the program's remarkably short yet successful history, confirming that whistleblower cases recovered more than $6.3 billion in sanctions from fraudsters, of which over $1.5 billion was returned to harmed investors and another $3.1 billion was paid up by huge corporations in "disgorgement" of "ill-gotten gains." Payments to whistleblowers surpassed the billion-dollar mark.

The commission's view of whistleblowers was a far cry from the bad old days when employee disclosures were ignored by the SEC and corporate whistleblowers were fired at will. Instead of repeating the slander that whistleblowers are simply disgruntled employees, the head of the SEC office "applaud[ed]" their "courage and commitment," recognizing that they often submit valuable and "high-quality information regarding possible securities laws violations to the Commission."

How We Got Here

In the summer of 2010, Congress enacted the Dodd-Frank Wall Street Reform and Consumer Protection Act. The nation was still reeling from the devastating impact of the Great Recession of 2008, in which millions of Americans lost their jobs, their homes, and their retirement. In large part, the recession was fueled by misconduct on Wall Street, including outright fraud, the most notorious instance of which was the Bernard Madoff Ponzi scheme that resulted in over $20 billion in losses to thousands of innocent investors, many of whom lost their life savings.

But as with so many other scandals, it turned out there were whistleblowers with inside information who either tried to call attention to the frauds and were ignored or were too afraid to step forward. The Senate Banking Committee, in devising a long-term fix to the obviously broken Wall Street regulatory system, heard extensive testimony on the role of whistleblowers in detecting and preventing frauds.

When the final 2,000-page Dodd-Frank Act was finally passed, a whistleblower incentive program was at the heart of a new enforcement regime. Two new *qui tam* provisions were signed into law.

The Nuts and Bolts

The two laws cover trillions of dollars in market transactions. One law established a *qui tam* reward law under the Commodity Exchange Act (CEA). The second *qui tam* reward law was attached to the Securities Exchange Act (SEA). In addition, the laws also cover violations of the Foreign Corrupt Practices Act, along with other anti-corruption laws that the Security Exchange Commission and Commodity Futures Trading Commission have regulatory authority to enforce. Furthermore, both laws have liberal "related action" provisions that let whistleblowers obtain rewards when other agencies prosecute crimes related to Dodd-Frank violations. This can include Justice Department criminal prosecutions. The new *qui tam* provisions are sweeping in scope and cover a significant portion of the world economy.

The Securities Exchange Act is the signature law regulating finances in the United States, including all trades conducted on various stock exchanges, such as the New York Stock Exchange and the NASDAQ, and all securities sold in the United States, including stocks, bonds, American Depository Receipts, and debentures.

The Commodity Exchange Act is similar to the securities law, but instead of covering the sale of securities, it covers the sale of commodities—the futures trading of fungible goods and assets, such as agricultural products (grain, animal products, fruits, coffee, sugar); energy (crude oil, coal, electricity); cryptocurrency, market manipulation, and insider trading of commodities; natural resources (gold, precious gems, plutonium, water); commoditized goods (generic pharmaceuticals); and financial commodities (foreign currencies and securities). The CEA also covers the $300 trillion "swaps" markets. In other words, the scope of the CEA is massive and transnational. The law is not limited to regulating public companies in the United States, but also covers the worldwide commodities markets, regardless of whether those traders are regulated by the SEC or not.

By incorporating *qui tam* incentive provisions into the fabric of these two extremely broad regulatory statutes, Congress sent a clear message: Employees were expected to play a critical role in protecting investors and consumers from financial fraud.

As the program has grown, not only have we received more tips, but we also continue to receive higher quality tips that are of tremendous help to the Commission in stopping ongoing and imminent fraud, and lead to significant enforcement actions. . . . The program has also created a powerful incentive for companies to self-report wrongdoing to the SEC—companies now know that if they do not, we may hear about the conduct from someone else.

—Mary Jo White, Then-Chair, Securities and Exchange Commission

---

The two Dodd-Frank *qui tam* laws are substantially identical. They are modeled on the federal False Claims Act and the 2006 IRS whistleblower reward law. Under Dodd-Frank, qualified whistleblowers are entitled to rewards of "not less than 10 percent" and "not more than 30 percent" of the total amount of money collected by the government as a "monetary sanction" against companies or individuals who violate either of the two laws (and numerous other federal laws that are incorporated by reference into these two laws). Like the IRS *qui tam* provision, the laws only cover major frauds, and the incentives are paid only if the total amount of sanctions exceed $1 million.

The monetary sanctions on which the reward is based include direct fines paid to the commissions, interest, penalties, and monies paid as part of a "disgorgement." The disgorgement payments can be massive, as they are the mechanism by which the commissions require a wrongdoer to release its "fraudulent enrichment." Disgorgement is measured by the amount of ill-gotten gains, and amounts often are many times larger than actual fines or penalties. Sanctions also include monies placed in the SEC-administered "fair funds"—the funds set aside to benefit investors who were harmed by the violations.

Both *qui tam* laws contain anti-retaliation provisions, prohibiting employers from firing employees who file *qui tam* actions or contact the commissions concerning potential violations of law. Employees must file their retaliation claims directly in federal court. Under the SEA anti-retaliation provision, wrongfully discharged workers are entitled to double back pay.

Anonymous Whistleblowing

Dodd-Frank added a new feature unique to American whistleblower law: Whistleblowers are permitted to file their *qui tam* claims to the government anonymously. This is a major breakthrough and provides extra protection to whistleblowers heretofore unknown under any other reward law.

To be anonymous whistleblowers must act through an attorney intermediary. In this manner the attorneys sign the complaints and the whistleblowers' names are not revealed, even to the government. This reduces the risk that the government will inadvertently disclose the identity of whistleblowers. Whistleblowers can consciously, carefully, and intelligently figure out, in advance, how to disclose the fraud in a manner that will reduce the risk that their employer will identify the "skunk at the picnic," or even know that there is a whistleblower.

Anonymous whistleblowing not only benefits the employee who fears retaliation, but can be exploited by the commissions as an investigative tool. If the whistleblower remains undetected by management, they are in an invaluable position to obtain further information about a possible cover-up, or even information that could result in a criminal obstruction of justice charge.

Although the whistleblower can remain anonymous throughout the investigatory process, when a whistleblower applies for a reward the SEC requires the whistleblower's identity to be revealed. This disclosure is kept strictly confidential and never released. It is necessary so that the government can verify the whistleblower's eligibility as an original source before the check is placed in the mail.

Steps to Filing a Wall Street *Qui Tam*

Congress enacted two separate Dodd-Frank *qui tam* laws: one for securities and the other for commodities. Except for the office where a particular *qui tam* is filed, these laws were drafted by Congress in a virtually identical manner. Below are the basic rules governing the SEC and CFTC award programs. However, before you decide to enter these programs you need to be aware that once becoming a government witness certain rules apply, including the expectation that you will fully cooperate with the government investigators, and that you will never provide the government investigators with any false, misleading, or incomplete information. If you do not want to answer specific questions, that is your right. But once you provide information, the failure to be fully truthful can result in the disqualification for a reward. Providing false information to the government is a serious crime.

1. **Who Can File.** Any individual or two or more individuals acting jointly can file. In addition to the stereotypical whistleblower (i.e., a company insider), the Dodd-Frank Act also permits analysts to file reward claims. An analyst is not a traditional original source, but rather a person who puts together public or secondary information in a manner that permits the commissions to learn that a violation has occurred.

2. **Where to File.** Claims under the Commodity Exchange Act must be filed with the Commodity Futures Trading Commission. Claims under the Securities Exchange Act must be filed with the Securities and Exchange Commission. Under both, claims must be filed "in a manner established by rule or regulation" by the respective commission. The mandatory filing procedures of the SEC and CFTC are published on the websites of each. There is a very specific form, known as Form TCR, that must be timely completed in order to qualify for a reward. The best practice is to *first* file your information with the SEC or CFTC's Office of the Whistleblower using the mandatory Form TCR, and only then communicate with any other agency or employee of the commissions. Failure to timely file a Form TCR can result in being disqualified from a reward, even if you have provided your information to the SEC or CFTC through other formal or informal contacts. The commissions require reward applicants to use the Form TCR, and any delay in filing the form can result in the denial of a reward.

3. **Anonymous Filings.** One of the critical advances in the two Wall Street *qui tam* laws was authorizing whistleblowers to make anonymous filings. If you decide to file anonymously, you must hire an attorney to act as your intermediary with the SEC and/or the CFTC. Thus, the whistleblower can vet the insider information confidentially with counsel of their own choosing and decide what information should be provided to the commissions. In weighing what information and how to present it, you can seek to establish the strongest case of fraud (in order to increase the chance that the government investigators will aggressively pursue the claim), while at the same time masking the identity of the source of information. The statute permits a whistleblower to have maximum confidentiality with maximum impact.

4. **Strictly Follow the Commissions' Rules.** The commissions have the authority to deny whistleblower rewards simply because the applicants failed to file the claim in the manner prescribed by the commissions. The laws contain the following reward disqualification: No award shall be made "to any whistleblower who fails to submit information to the Commissions in such form as the Commissions may, by rule or regulation, require." Both commissions have published extremely detailed rules of procedure governing the whistleblower rewards program. They are published on the commission websites and codified at 17 C.F.R. Parts 240 and 249 (SEC) and 17 C.F.R. Part 165 (CFTC). Any person seeking to obtain a reward under the SEA or CEA *must* review the most recent version of the whistleblower rules published by the SEC or the CFTC. Whistleblowers *must* ensure strict compliance with these rules. Even if you believe that the rule is inconsistent with the substantive or procedural rights contained in the Dodd-Frank Act, whistleblowers should still file claims as mandated in the commission rules, and if a claim is denied, challenge the rules in court.

   Among the most important rules that must be followed is the use of the official TCR form to file a reward claim. Both the SEC and CFTC require that these forms be used when *first* contacting the respective agency.

5. **Basis for Qualifying for a Reward.** Rewards are permitted if the individual voluntarily provides original information to the respective commission that leads to the successful enforcement of the SEA or CEA in a "covered judicial or administrative action" or a related action (including a settlement). The enforcement action (or settlement) must result in "monetary sanctions exceeding $1 million." Monetary sanctions include all monies ordered to be paid to the commissions, including fines, penalties, interest, and monies collected as part of a "disgorgement" of ill-gotten profits. Once this monetary threshold has been reached, whistleblowers are also entitled to compensation from sanctions issued by other agencies (such as the Justice Department or Federal Trade Commission), state law enforcement criminal prosecutions, and fines and penalties obtained by self-regulatory organizations (SROs) approved by the SEC or CFTC, such as FINRA (Financial Industry Regulatory Authority) or the New York Stock Exchange. Whistleblowers who provide information directly to SROs can qualify for a reward.

6. **Disclosures Must Be "Voluntary."** To qualify, whistleblowers must voluntarily provide their information to the proper commission or to another government agency (or other qualifying third-party) before the government contacts them about the violations. If you are compelled to provide the information—for example, if you are subpoenaed to testify before a grand jury—the commission will argue that the disclosure was not voluntary and consequently deny the application for a reward. It is in the best interest of any person who seeks a reward to file Form TCR *before* any government agent requests to interview the whistleblower. Under current regulations, if the government first requests an interview, even a voluntary interview, the SEC or CFTC can use that fact to allege that the

disclosures were not voluntary. It is important for any person seeking to obtain whistleblower protection under the Dodd-Frank Act to be the first person to provide the information to the SEC or CFTC, before their identity is revealed by a third party, their employer, other government entities, Congress, or the news media, and before they are subject to a request for an interview by any federal government entity.

7. **The Whistleblower's Information Must Be "Original."** To qualify for a reward, the information provided to the commission by the whistleblower must meet the definition of "original information." For information to be considered original, it must be "derived from the independent knowledge or analysis" of the whistleblower. Also, you have to be the first person to provide the information to either the SEC or CFTC. If another whistleblower provides the information to the government first, you are at risk of being denied a reward because the government already knew of your allegations from another source.

8. **Public Disclosure Bar.** Like the FCA, the securities and commodities *qui tam* statutes are intended to encourage the disclosure of information to the government that is not already known to the government. The laws consequently prohibit whistleblowers from obtaining a reward under two circumstances. First, rewards are denied if the commission is already aware of the information provided by the whistleblower, "unless the whistleblower is the original source of the information"; and second, if the whistleblower "exclusively" derives their information from an "allegation made in a judicial or administrative hearing, in a government report, hearing, audit, or investigation, or from the news media," *unless* the whistleblower is a source of the information. The *qui tam* law is designed to encourage employees or other individuals who have inside information or original analytical skills to step forward and blow the whistle to the commissions. If information is already known to the government or is already in the public domain, what is the purpose of paying a reward for information that the government knows or can obtain from a Google search?

9. **Third-Party Disclosures.** If you first provide your original information to qualifying third parties, both the SEC and CFTC will give you full credit for that information, provided that you also provide the information to the SEC or CFTC in a timely manner. Both agencies have a grace period for submitting information to them that was originally provided to qualifying third parties, such as other government agencies or Congress. The grace period under the SEC for filing a Form TCR rules is 120 days. The grace period under the CFTC rules is 180 days.

Under the CEA, third-party disclosures can be made to the following entities: internal compliance programs; Congress; any other federal, state, or local authority; a foreign futures authority; a registered entity; a registered futures association; and a self-regulatory organization (like FINRA).

Under the SEA third-party disclosures can be made to internal compliance programs, Congress, any other authority of the federal government, a state attorney general or securities regulatory authority, or any self-regulatory organization (such as FINRA).

The Dodd-Frank Act also permits whistleblowers to first disclose their original information to the news media. However, neither the SEC nor CFTC have approved regulations implementing this important right.

10. **Amount of Reward.** If the whistleblower's disclosure qualifies for a reward, the individual who filed the claim must file a second application, known as a WB-APP, in order to have the commissions determine their eligibility. This payment is required under regulations, and the failure to timely file the WB-APP will result in the denial of a reward even if you were otherwise qualified. The range of the reward is set by statute. The whistleblower (either individually or, if more than one, collectively) must receive "not less than 10 percent" and "not more than 30 percent" of the total amount of monetary sanctions actually collected by the government as a result of the covered administrative or judicial actions, any monies obtained from related actions, and any money recovered as a result of a settlement. Awards can be based not only on sanctions obtained by the SEC or CFTC enforcement actions, but also on related actions (i.e., fines and penalties obtained from other agencies and securities or commodities self-regulatory agencies, such as the Justice Department or FINRA).

11. **Determination of Amount of Reward.** The commissions have wide discretion on determining the amount of the reward (i.e., whether to grant the whistleblower 10 percent, 30 percent, or some percentage in between). In setting the percentage award, Congress required the commissions to weigh the following factors: (a) the "significance of the information provided," (b) the "degree of assistance provided by the whistleblower" or their attorney, (c) the "programmatic interest" of the commissions in "deterring violations" of law by "making awards to whistleblower," and (d) other factors that the commissions may establish by "rule or regulation." Some of the "other factors" the commissions have established by regulation are discussed below.

To obtain a reward, a whistleblower must file the WB-APP form within ninety days of the SEC's posting a notice on its website that the offending corporation or individual has been sanctioned for at least $1 million. This posting is known as a "Notice of Covered Action" and is available on the SEC's Office of the Whistleblower website, to which you can subscribe for e-mail alerts of new postings. Failure to meet the filing deadline for submitting the award application can and will result in the denial of a reward. The CFTC also requires the filing of a timely WB-APP.

Persons who file the Form TCR should monitor the commissions' websites where the Notices of Covered Action are posted. The commissions are under no obligation to inform a whistleblower that there was a successful enforcement action. Consequently, if there is a successful enforcement action, but you fail to file the WB-APP form within 90 days of the notice, you will lose your right to obtain a reward. The websites for the notices are: SEC: https://www.sec.gov/whistleblower/claim-award. CFTC: https://www.whistleblower.gov/notices. Neither commission posts notices of related actions. It is up to the whistleblower to monitor enforcement actions considered related actions and file an WB-APP form seeking compensation on those claims within the 90-day time period.

12. **First to File.** Similar to the FCA, the Dodd-Frank Act *qui tam* contains a modified first to file rule. Rewards are paid to the first whistleblowers who individually or jointly provide the commissions with original information. If a whistleblower is the second person to file an identical claim, their claim could be denied. Claims are considered related under this disqualification if they are "based on the facts underlying the covered action submitted previously by another whistleblower." In practice, the harsh results mandated by the first to file rule are sometimes avoided, and the SEC has paid numerous awards to multiple whistleblowers. This is because SEC and CFTC rules permit whistleblowers who contribute new information to an ongoing investigation to qualify for a reward. This exception is not contained in the False Claims Act. Bottom line: Don't miss the bus. File first.

Even if you are not the first to file, it is still to your advantage to fully cooperate with an ongoing investigation and provide the government with new information that the original whistleblower could not or did not contribute.

There are three important exceptions to the first to file rule. First, if you raise a concern internally to a corporate compliance program, you have a 120-day grace period for filing with the SEC and still being considered the first to file (even if the company self-reports the violation you disclosed). Second, if you first raise a concern with one of the third-party entities described above, you also have a 120-day grace period to file your case with the SEC and still be considered the first to file. Third, if you first report your allegations to the news media and the SEC learns of your allegations from the press, you can still be considered the first to file. However, the SEC has not yet published any rules regarding time deadlines or procedures for cases where the commission first learns of your allegations from the press.

The CFTC has identical filing requirements, but provides whistleblowers with a 180-day grace period for filing with the CFTC Whistleblower Office, instead of the 120 days permitted by the SEC.

Regardless of these exceptions, it is always to a whistleblower's advantage to be the first to file the official Form TCR with either the SEC or the CFTC, and to do so as quickly as possible. Failure to do so within 30 days of your initial contact with the SEC can result in disqualification from a reward.

13. **Limitations on Filing Anonymously.** Under very limited circumstances the commissions can also reveal the identity of a whistleblower if compelled by a court or if such a disclosure is required under the U.S. Constitution

or other legal authority. These circumstances have rarely, if ever, occurred, and the SEC and CFTC have been extremely careful about protecting a whistleblower's identity. However, when a case proceeds to court a defendant may have the right to discover the identity of witnesses (including confidential informants) or other information that could result in the discovery of the whistleblower's identity. Dodd-Frank does not override constitutional due process protections or the requirements of the Federal Rules of Criminal Procedure.

14. **Settlement Coverage.** The statute explicitly ensures that *qui tam* rewards are based not only on monies obtained as a result of judicial or administrative action, but also include monies obtained by the government as a result of settlement. The basis for rewards also includes actions taken by the commissions that are based upon the original information provided by the whistleblower, including indirect related actions. In its September 23, 2020, rulemaking, the SEC also confirmed that rewards are paid on non-prosecution or deferred prosecution agreements. Rewards can also be paid based on sanctions collected from SROs such as FINRA and other third-party entities discussed above.

15. **Disqualification of Certain Employees.** Various classes of employees are disqualified by statute from obtaining rewards. The disqualification is primarily applied to government employees whose job it is to detect fraud, such as employees of an "appropriate regulatory agency," employees of the Department of Justice, or "law enforcement organization(s)" employees of the SROs and the "registered futures association." Persons who work for foreign government agencies are prohibited from obtaining a reward. The CFTC prohibits rewards to persons employed by foreign regulatory or law enforcement agencies. The SEC prohibits awards paid to persons who at the time they acquired the original information were "a member, officer, or employee of a foreign government, any political subdivision, department, agency, or instrumentality of a foreign government, or any other foreign financial regulatory authority."

16. **Whistleblowers Disqualified from Obtaining Rewards.** Even if a whistleblower is completely eligible to obtain a reward, there are three grounds for disqualification. First, if the whistleblower is "convicted of a criminal violation related to the judicial or administrative action for which the whistleblower otherwise could receive an award." Second, if the whistleblower "knowingly and willfully makes any false, fictitious, or fraudulent statement" when filing their *qui tam*. Persons who knowingly file false statements in an attempt to obtain a reward or when providing information to the government can be criminally prosecuted. Third, the failure to file claims in accordance with the rules published by the commission can, standing alone, result in the denial of a claim. This is why it is extremely important to carefully follow the procedures mandated by

the SEC and CFTC. This includes filing the official Form TCR when first alerting the SEC or CFTC to a potential violation.

17. **Anti-Retaliation.** No employer can terminate or discriminate against any employee who files a *qui tam* claim, who testifies in a *qui tam* case, or who assists in a *qui tam*–related investigation. Under the CEA anti-retaliation provision, discrimination cases must be filed directly in federal court within two years of the retaliatory adverse action. Employees are entitled to reinstatement, back pay, special damages, and attorney fees and costs. The SEA's protections also require that claims be filed in federal court, but have a three-year statute of limitations (which can be lengthened up to ten years, depending on when the employee learns of the retaliation). The scope of damages under the two laws are somewhat different. Whereas the CEA directly permits an award of special damages, the SEA is silent on that provision. But the SEA mandates an award of double back pay, whereas the CEA only provides for a straight back pay award. There is no provision in the law for filing retaliation cases confidentially, and an employer will know who the plaintiff is in any such case.

The rewards "create powerful incentives" for informants "to come to the Commission with real evidence of wrongdoing . . . and meaningfully contributes to the efficiency and effectiveness of our enforcement efforts."
—Mary Jo White, Chair, Securities and Exchange Commission

The Sarbanes-Oxley corporate reform law also prohibits retaliation against whistleblowers who allege securities fraud. The SOX law has additional protections on which Dodd-Frank's SEA provisions are silent, including a prohibition on mandatory arbitration and protection for internal whistleblowers. Corporate whistleblowers can initially file claims under SOX and, if appropriate, join the CEA or SEA claims with the SOX case. The SOX law has a 180-day statute of limitations, and initial complaints must be filed with the Department of Labor.

In a major breakthrough for whistleblower protection, the commissions view retaliation as a securities or commodities law violation. The logic behind this rule is compelling. The anti-retaliation provisions of Dodd-Frank are both part of the SEA or CEA. Under the law, the commissions can sanction a person who violates *any part* of the SEA or CEA. Thus, as a matter of law, firing a whistleblower is a violation of the SEA/CEA, just as engaging in insider trading is also a violation. In December 2016 the SEC sanctioned SandRidge Energy Inc. $1.4 million for retaliatory actions.

Because the sanction in the SandRidge Energy retaliation case was over $1 million, the whistleblower who disclosed that violation to the SEC (most likely the victim of the retaliation) would be entitled to a reward of no less than $140,000 and no greater than $420,000.

18. **Confidentiality.** The commissions prohibit their employees from disclosing any information "which could reasonably be expected to reveal the identity of the whistleblower," except under very specific circumstances, such as during a grand jury proceeding, or if the commissions file a lawsuit against a corporation and the corporation is entitled to learn the identity of the informant. The commissions must also ensure that any information about the whistleblower shared with other law enforcement or regulatory agencies is held in confidence by those agencies.

19. **Access to Information.** The ability of corporations or the public to learn the identity of whistleblowers who provide information under the *qui tam* provisions is extremely limited. The statute ensures that the Freedom of Information Act cannot be used by third parties to obtain any information that may identify the whistleblower. However, these documents are not completely shielded from public view, especially if the government prosecutes the wrongdoer and information is used in administrative or court proceedings.

20. **Non-Preemption.** The SEA and CEA whistleblower protection provisions do not preempt states from enacting similar whistleblower laws and are not exclusive remedies. The Dodd-Frank Act contains an explicit savings clause that prevents the law from being interpreted so as to "diminish the rights, privileges, or remedies of any whistleblower under any Federal or State law, or under any collective bargaining agreement."

21. **Rights Cannot Be Waived.** The law prevents any employer from requiring employees to waive their rights to file whistleblower claims under the SEA and CEA. The SEC, by regulation, ensured that employers could not interfere with employee communications to the commission: "No person may take any action to impede an individual from communicating directly with the Commission staff about a possible violation, including enforcing, or threatening to enforce, a confidentiality agreement . . ." The Commodity Exchange Act has a similar rule, as does the amended version of the Sarbanes-Oxley Act.

    The SEC has put teeth into these provisions and has sanctioned companies that required employees to sign restrictive nondisclosure agreements, including imposing monetary fines and penalties.

    On October 24, 2016, the SEC's Office of Compliance Inspections and Examinations issued a "Risk Alert," carefully setting forth the commission's policy on restrictive NDAs. Corporations were advised to review their compliance manuals, codes of ethics, employment agreements, and severance agreements for any policies or rules that could restrict or create a chilling effect on an employee's willingness to contact law enforcement about potential violations or restrict an employee's right to apply for or obtain a reward.

22. **No Mandatory Arbitration.** Under the Commodity Exchange Act, whistleblowers cannot be required to have their employee discrimination cases subjected to mandatory arbitration. Even if an employee signs an arbitration agreement that, under federal or state law, would typically require a dispute to be arbitrated, these types of agreements are void under the CEA. The SEA does not contain a similar prohibition. To avoid mandatory arbitration in securities cases, whistleblowers have to file their retaliation case under the Sarbanes-Oxley Act. The SOX law prohibits mandatory arbitration. SOX has a 180-day statute of limitations and must be initially filed with the U.S. Department of Labor.

23. **Follow the Rules.** Both commissions were granted explicit rulemaking authority under the whistleblower provisions. Under the law, whistleblowers are required to follow these rules, and failure to file a claim in accordance with the specifications set forth by the SEC or CFTC constitutes grounds for denying a reward. Any person filing a *qui tam* should obtain the most recent version of any rules published by either commission and ensure strict compliance with those rules. The SEC also established a separate Whistleblower Office dedicated to administering the rewards program and ensuring SEC compliance with the Dodd-Frank Act. The SEC's whistleblower rules are published at 17 C.F.R. Parts 240 and 249. The CFTC's rules are published at 17 C.F.R. Part 165.

24. **File the Second Application.** The SEC's regulations governing whistle-blower rewards established a two-step process for qualification. Whistle-blowers must initially file a Form TCR ("Tip, Complaint, or Referral"). This form, available online from the SEC, initiates the reward process. The Form TCR can be amended or supplemented as many times as the whistleblower deems appropriate without leave from the commissions. If the SEC issues a sanction against a company where a reward could be paid, the SEC is required to post notice of this sanction on its website. These notices are for-mally known as a "Notice of Covered Action" and are published regularly on the SEC and CFTC Office of the Whistleblower websites. Thereafter, in order to obtain a reward, a whistleblower must file a second application— and complete a new form known as WB-APP. This new application must be filed within ninety days of the publication of the Notice of Covered Action. The CFTC follows a nearly identical process.

    When filing the Form WB-APP a whistleblower should address all of the factors applied by the commissions when determining the range of an award. These factors are fully explained in SEC Rule § 21F-6 and CFTC Rule 17 C.F.R. § 165.9. These two rules are substantially identical and provide a detailed discussion of the following factors used to increase or decrease an award.

25. **Appeals.** Whistleblowers can appeal the denial of their *qui tam* claims. The scope of appeal under the SEA and CEA differ in one material respect.

Under the CEA, any determination by the commission regarding the whistleblower's *qui tam* case is subject to appeal, "including whether, to whom, or in what amount" an award is made. The SEA *qui tam* also permits an appeal of any determination made by the SEC, *except* the "amount of an award." In other words, the SEC's discretion as to whether to pay the whistleblower 10 percent, 30 percent, or some amount in between is non-reviewable. Under both laws an appeal must be filed within thirty days "after the determination is issued by the Commission." Appeals are filed with the U.S. Court of Appeals, and the decision of the commission is reviewed under the Administrative Procedure Act, 5 U.S.C. § 706. Before an appeal can be filed in court, the whistleblower must fully comply with and exhaust the administrative procedures mandated under the SEC and CFTC rules. This includes filing an internal administrative appeal of any preliminary or proposed denial.

26. **Obtain an Exemption to the SEC Rules.** Section 36(a) of the Securities Exchange Act permits the SEC to waive any rule, regulation, or securities law if such a waiver is in the public interest and would benefit investors. Exercising this authority is within the discretion of the commission. In whistleblower cases the SEC has waived its rules on the timing of a TCR form and on applying its strict definition of "voluntary" when other circumstances demonstrated that a reward should be paid.

27. **No Amnesty.** Filing a whistleblower complaint does not give you amnesty from future prosecution. However, voluntary whistleblowers are rarely charged with a crime, provided they are truthful and fully cooperative. The government may offer you a "non-prosecution agreement." If so, you must fully comply with all of the terms of that agreement, or risk being charged with a crime.

The SEC and CFTC Implement the Law

As of February 2023, the U.S. Securities and Exchange Commission has paid whistle-blowers more than $1.4 billion in rewards based on their "unique and useful information" that, in many cases, has permitted the SEC to "move quickly and initiate enforcement action against wrongdoers before they could squander the money." **Figure 14** shows the top ten awards paid by the SEC.

Copies of award decisions are published on the SEC's Office of the Whistleblower website (www.sec.gov/whistleblower). To protect confidentiality, decisions usually do not identify either the company sanctioned or the whistleblower who obtained a reward.

The commission has given awards to employees who performed compliance functions, and awarded a foreign resident $30 million, noting that the Dodd-Frank Act's whistleblower reward program had extraterritorial reach, covering foreign nationals, persons who reside overseas, crimes committed outside the United States, and information submitted to the SEC or DOJ from outside the United States.

Figure 14

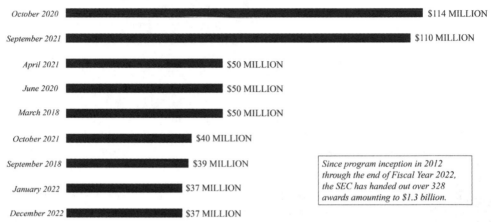

Top Ten SEC Awards to Whistleblowers

October 2020	$114 MILLION
September 2021	$110 MILLION
April 2021	$50 MILLION
June 2020	$50 MILLION
March 2018	$50 MILLION
October 2021	$40 MILLION
September 2018	$39 MILLION
January 2022	$37 MILLION
December 2022	$37 MILLION

> *Since program inception in 2012 through the end of Fiscal Year 2022, the SEC has handed out over 328 awards amounting to $1.3 billion.*

In a precedent-setting ruling (*In re KBR*), the commission sanctioned the multinational defense contracting firm $130,000 for requesting employees to sign restrictive confidentiality agreements concerning disclosures they made to company attorneys, who managed the internal compliance program. Although the confidentiality agreements did not specifically prohibit communications with the SEC, their restrictions were broad enough to cover communications with the commission: "KBR required witnesses in certain internal investigations interviews to sign confidentiality statements with language warning them that they could face discipline and even be fired if they discussed matters with outside parties without prior approval of KBR's legal department." The SEC found that these terms violated Rule 21F-17, which prohibits companies from taking any action to impede whistleblowers from reporting possible securities violations to the SEC.

Following up on the *KBR* precedent, the commission sanctioned Virginia-based communications company Neustar, Inc. $180,000 for requiring employees to sign restrictive severance agreements that prohibited communications with the SEC. In its investigation the commission determined that 246 employees had signed agreements that prohibited them from making any statement that "disparages, denigrates, maligns, or impugns" the company. The SEC has also voided agreements that require employees to waive their right to file for or collect rewards.

The CFTC Program: "The Little Engine That Could"

To many Wall Street observers, the biggest surprise is the unanticipated success of the Commodity Exchange Act's reward law. As of 2022 the CFTC has given out the largest individual whistleblower award in history, coming in at $200 million. Moreover, the CFTC has commenced tackling international corruption. In December 2020 the commission issued its first sanction in an international bribery case. Vitol, a Dutch oil trading company, paid $130 million in fines for corruptly manipulating international commodities markets by paying bribes in Brazil, Ecuador, and Mexico. In May 2021 the CFTC outdid itself and was the leading agency in sanctioning Swiss-based oil and energy trading company Glencore $1.186 billion. The sanctions were based on the company's manipulation of the price of oil and paying kickbacks and bribes in Brazil, Cameroon, Nigeria, and Venezuela.

Without question, manipulating oil markets can drive up the cost Americans pay at the pump or to heat their homes. And today my message to the markets is clear: the CFTC will continue to pursue even the slightest hint of manipulative, corrupt, or fraudulent behavior.
—CFTC Chairman Rostin Behnam

Perhaps most surprising is that the CFTC, a little-known regulatory agency with no criminal law enforcement authority, has done all this on a tiny budget. In fiscal year 2021, the agency's entire annual budget was approximately $300 million, and its Whistleblower Office operated on just $3 million. Despite this shoestring budget, the agency was able to issue over $3 billion in sanctions against corporate wrongdoers based on whistleblower disclosures. What U.S. government agency brings revenue to the federal treasury of over ten times its annual budget? Moreover, all the revenue comes from corporate wrongdoers who are being held accountable for their corrupt actions. All the rewards paid to whistleblowers come directly from the sanctions obtained from the white-collar crooks. Not one penny comes from the taxpayer.

When Congress passed the Commodity Exchange Act's whistleblower law, there were few, if any, known cases of whistleblowers in the commodity exchange markets. The Commodity Futures Trading Commission had no history of ever working with whistleblowers, had no whistleblower office, and had never paid a whistleblower reward. The Dodd-Frank Act required the CFTC to create a whistleblower program, which the commission did with flying colors. They funded and staffed their whistleblower office, approved regulations (modeled on those of the SEC), publicized the program, and issued public alerts explaining the types of frauds the CFTC was interested in prosecuting.

Eighteen months after Congress passed the commodities whistleblower law, only fifty-eight individuals had filed complaints with the CFTC. This number of complaints fell quite short in comparison to the SEC's whistleblower program, which had seen over three thousand complaints filed during the same period. Moreover, the CFTC did not pay its first whistleblower reward until May 19, 2014, nearly four years after the Dodd-Frank Act was signed into law. That first award, which totaled $240,000, was only a tiny fraction of what whistleblowers were obtaining under the whistleblower laws of the False Claims Act, IRS, and SEC.

But the CFTC whistleblower program has since seen phenomenal growth. As of 2022 the CFTC has paid $300 million in awards and collected over $3 billion in sanctions from fraudsters. The number of whistleblowers using the program has also radically grown. By 2022, five thousand whistleblowers had filed formal complaints with the CFTC, averaging one thousand per year since 2020. This was a far cry from the tiny amount of complaints (fifty-eight) filed in 2012, the first year the CFTC reported the number of annual Dodd-Frank Act whistleblower tips.

The growth in the CFTC's program, based on the statistics published annually by the CFTC's Office of the Whistleblower, is demonstrated in two charts. **Figure 15** tracks the number of rewards paid to whistleblowers since the program was established. This chart shows the rapid growth in high-quality reporting and the willingness of the government to pay awards.

Figure 15

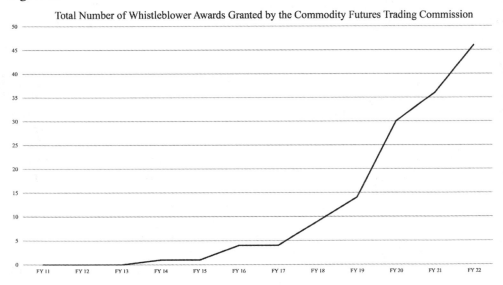

Total Number of Whistleblower Awards Granted by the Commodity Futures Trading Commission

Figure 16 demonstrates the radical increase in the number of whistleblower complaints filed with the CFTC. These complaints are the backbone of the program. They contain the information needed to effectively police commodity frauds.

In hindsight, the growth in commodities whistleblowing is not surprising. Similar *qui tam* laws designed to incentivize whistleblowers to report tax evasion, fraud in government contracting, and securities fraud have also been highly successful. Moreover, the size of the markets regulated by the CFTC is astronomical. At the time Dodd-Frank became law, then-CFTC chairman Gary Gensler explained the massive scope of the commission's new authorities: "The law gave the Commodity Futures Trading Commission oversight of the $300 trillion swaps market. . . . At such size and complexity, it is essential that these markets work for the benefit of the American public; that they are transparent, open and competitive." As further explained in the CFTC's 2020 Annual Report, "the U.S. derivatives markets are the most vibrant, developed, and influential in the world." These markets impact the prices of "countless goods and services" and are "vital to the real economy."

The types of fraud that corrupt the commodities markets are also vast and complex. They include "spoofing," swaps, fraud in the derivative, futures and options trading,

Figure 16

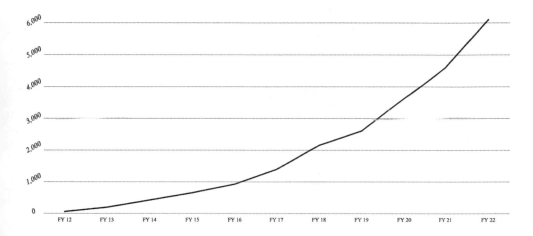

Total Amount of Whistleblower Tips Received by the Commodities Futures Trading Commission

foreign corruption, false reporting, market manipulation, insider trading, money laundering, forex trading, benchmark manipulation, and frauds associated with foreign currency exchanges and cryptocurrencies.

On a tiny budget, the CFTC has become "the little engine that could."

—————————————————— PRACTICE TIPS ——————————————————

- The sections of Dodd-Frank that relate to whistleblower rewards are Section 748 (Commodity Exchange Act) (7 U.S.C. § 26) and Sections 922-24 (Securities Exchange Act) (15 U.S.C. § 78u-6).

- On June 13 and August 25, 2011, the SEC and CFTC published final rules implementing the Dodd-Frank whistleblower reward program. These regulations have been subsequently amended. The SEC's Office of the Whistleblower publishes one of the best websites for whistleblowers: www .sec.gov/whistleblower. It posts all SEC award rulings and copies of the law and regulations. The CFTC also publishes a similar highly useful website at www.whistleblower.gov.

Keeping Up with the Changes

To keep up to date on changes in the laws, whistleblowers should access the free online law library created by the author, located at www.kkc.com/law-library.

RULE 20

Foreign Corruption and Bribery: Report to the SEC/CFTC

Corruption robs citizens of equal access to vital services, denying the right to quality healthcare, public safety, and education. It degrades the business environment, subverts economic opportunity, and exacerbates inequality. It often contributes to human rights violations and abuses, and can drive migration. As a fundamental threat to the rule of law, corruption hollows out institutions, corrodes public trust, and fuels popular cynicism toward effective, accountable governance.

—United States Strategy on Countering Corruption (December 2021)

Historically, the most important international anti-corruption law was the Foreign Corrupt Practices Act (FCPA), which targets bribery of foreign government officials in order to obtain a business advantage. Enacted by the U.S. Congress in 1977, its goal is to stop global corporate bribery. Although the FCPA remains the most significant transnational anti-corruption law, the Commodity Exchange Act (CEA) has started to rival it in scope and importance. Whereas the FCPA primarily targets publicly traded corporations that pay bribes, the CEA has no such limitations. Its jurisdiction is based on the international trade in commodities, regardless of whether a company is publicly traded.

Both the FCPA and CEA's ability to combat corruption were radically enhanced in 2010 as part of the Dodd-Frank Act, when whistleblowers from around the world were authorized to obtain monetary rewards for reporting FCPA and CEA violations. These two laws are the most important transnational anti-corruption laws ever enacted. They cover whistleblowers regardless of citizenship. Both U.S. and non-U.S. residents can file confidential and anonymous disclosures about corruption occurring outside the United States and still qualify for large monetary rewards. The laws target large corporations that illegally exploit resources in developing countries by paying bribes to government officials, or by corruptly manipulating markets in oil, minerals, and other commodities. Whistleblowers from the most undemocratic countries, with no effective rule of law, can use the enhanced rights under Dodd-Frank to combat corruption in their home countries.

Figure 17 documents the rise in whistleblower claims filed with the SEC by persons residing in the 50 most corrupt nations in the world, as defined by the respected corruption index published by Transparency International. Although most international whistleblowers come from Europe, employees from the poorest and most dangerous countries in the world are learning to take advantage of the confidential filing and reward provisions available to them under Dodd-Frank.

The importance of Dodd-Frank in policing foreign bribery was recognized by the Organization for Economic Cooperation and Development (OECD), a highly respected intergovernmental body with 38 full nation-state members, including the United States and every other major Western democracy. The OECD's 2022 audit of

Figure 17

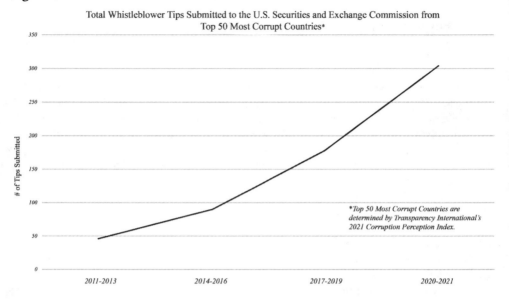

Total Whistleblower Tips Submitted to the U.S. Securities and Exchange Commission from Top 50 Most Corrupt Countries*

Top 50 Most Corrupt Countries are determined by Transparency International's 2021 Corruption Perception Index.

the U.S. anti-bribery program praised Dodd-Frank's "robust framework of protections and incentivizes for whistleblowers who report FCPA violations" and recommended enhancing the program. They also confirmed that whistleblowers were the largest source of information about corporate FCPA violations. All-in-all, the U.S. program was praised for its "leading enforcement role" in fighting international corruption.

The FCPA

The FCPA is extremely broad in scope. It targets both direct payments and payments made through intermediaries, and also prohibits the aiding and abetting of violations. Furthermore, it requires that all member states broadly assert territorial jurisdiction over these crimes so that "extensive physical connection to the bribery act is not required."

The FCPA permits the United States to exercise broad extraterritorial jurisdiction to target bribes paid by non-U.S. citizens to foreign officials in countries outside the United States. Historically, this has made the FCPA a highly effective transnational anti-corruption law.

The law also requires corporations that trade on U.S. stock exchanges to have strong internal controls, prohibiting off-the-books accounting. These record-keeping requirements are a key enforcement method; they mandate an accurate accounting of all assets, thereby forcing a company to admit on paper that it has paid a bribe or face harsh sanction.

Under the "books and records" provision, publicly traded companies (known in the law as "issuers") must maintain detailed "books, records and accounts" that "accurately and fairly reflect" the company's transactions and how it spends its money. Additionally, the law requires publicly traded companies to have a "system of internal accounting controls" capable of accounting for all corporate assets, spending money as intended by company management, and recorded in "conformity with generally accepted accounting principles," ensuring that monies are lawfully spent as intended.

Wharton School professor Philip M. Nichols aptly described the FCPA as a law designed to regulate transnational business firms that operate in the global market. He warned against viewing the FCPA as a law that applies only to U.S. businesses, instead explaining that "the reality of transnational business activity, often labeled globalization, consists of networks of relationships that take little notice of national borders and which cannot be siloed." He explained that Congress "intended the Act to be part of a global regime to control bribery. . . . [The] Act is concerned with bribery that occurs outside the United States or that relates to a transaction that extends beyond the United States." According to Professor Nichols, those responsible for passing the Foreign Corrupt Practices Act "viewed bribery as presenting an existential threat to international business."

Congress's official report discussing the purpose of the FCPA backed up this view:

> The payment of bribes to influence the acts or decisions of foreign officials, foreign political parties or candidates for foreign political office is unethical. It is counter to the moral expectations and values of the American public. But not only is it unethical, it is bad business as well. It erodes public confidence in the integrity of the free market system. It short-circuits the marketplace by directing business to those companies too inefficient to compete in terms of price, quality or service, or too lazy to engage in honest salesmanship, or too intent upon unloading marginal products. In short, it rewards corruption instead of efficiency and puts pressure on ethical enterprises to lower their standards or risk losing business.

Two agencies with direct responsibility for prosecuting Foreign Corrupt Practices Act cases are the Department of Justice and the SEC. In their jointly published guide to the FCPA, these agencies explained the important goals of the FCPA: "Corruption impedes economic growth . . . undermines democratic values . . . and weakens the rule of law . . . It threatens stability and security . . . and impedes U.S. efforts to promote freedom and democracy, end poverty, and combat crime and terrorism across the globe. Corruption is also bad for business. Corruption is anti-competitive, leading to distorted prices and disadvantaging honest businesses that do not pay bribes."

Although it does not have direct jurisdiction over FCPA cases, the Commodity Futures Trading Commission also investigates foreign corruption and violations of the FCPA based on its authority to sanction the manipulation of the commodities markets. The CFTC's role in combating foreign bribery is extremely significant, as that agency has authority over non-publicly traded companies that participate in the international commodities markets. Likewise, the Anti-Money Laundering Improvement Act, passed in December 2022, will also provide Dodd-Frank-style incentives for persons to report money laundering that often accompanies money laundering.

For thirty years the Foreign Corrupt Practices Act lacked a whistleblower rewards provision. That changed in 2010, when Congress passed the Dodd-Frank Act. Dodd-Frank required the SEC and the CFTC to establish whistleblower offices that can accept confidential and anonymous complaints and mandated that they pay whistleblowers monetary rewards if their original information resulted in sanctioning a corporation for over $1 million. Moreover, the law required that the commissions award any qualified whistleblower a minimum of 10 percent and a maximum of 30 percent of the sanctions obtained by the U.S. government as a result of the whistleblower's disclosures. The criteria used for setting the award amount under the FCPA is identical to that used by the SEC and CFTC in other securities or commodities fraud cases.

FCPA whistleblower cases are filed with either the SEC or CFTC, and all the laws, rules, and regulations that are applicable to other Dodd-Frank Act cases submitted to the SEC or CFTC are also applicable to FCPA cases. The ability to obtain a reward for violations of the FCPA is not limited to U.S. citizens. Both the SEC and CFTC welcome complaints from non-U.S. citizens alleging violations of the FCPA.

International Whistleblowing under the FCPA

The passage of the Dodd-Frank Act allowed, for the first time, whistleblowers from foreign countries to report bribes paid to their leaders by foreign corporations and obtain monetary rewards under a U.S. whistleblower law. In granting its first FCPA award, the SEC noted that "it makes no difference whether . . . [the whistleblower] was a foreign national, resides overseas, the information was submitted from overseas, or the misconduct comprising the U.S. securities violation occurred entirely overseas."

The director of the SEC's Division of Enforcement, Andrew Ceresney, explained the critical role international whistleblowers play in reporting foreign bribery:

> [I]nternational whistleblowers can add great value to our investigations. Recognizing the value of international whistleblowers, we have made . . . awards to whistleblowers living in foreign countries. In fact, our largest whistleblower award to date—$30 million—went to a foreign whistleblower who provided us with key original information about an ongoing fraud that would have been very difficult to detect. In making this award, the Commission staked out a clear position that the fact that a whistleblower is a foreign resident does not prevent an award when the whistleblower's information led to a successful Commission enforcement action brought in the United States concerning violations of the U.S. securities laws.

The ability of non-U.S. citizens to qualify for whistleblower rewards has triggered an avalanche of foreign bribery cases flooding into the SEC. As shown in Rule 5's **Figure 5,** 5,908 foreign nationals in over 130 countries have filed international corruption cases with the SEC.

Since the SEC paid the first international whistleblower a reward in 2014, the commission has paid numerous other non-U.S. citizens for providing original information regarding violations of the FCPA. As disclosed by the SEC's Office of the Whistleblower in its 2021 Annual Report, successful whistleblowers paid by the commission hailed from six continents and constituted 20 percent of the meritorious claimants.

In issuing [a $30 million USD] award, the Commission specifically noted that allowing foreign nationals to receive awards under the program best effectuates the clear Congressional purpose underlying the award program."

—Securities and Exchange Commission Report

The FCPA and whistleblowers are a near-perfect fit. How else could the U.S. government learn about these secret payments, especially when payments happen in foreign countries? Corporate insiders play a key role in enabling the government to obtain proof of a bribe, proof that a company's books are inaccurate, or proof that a company lacks internal controls over some of its business activities. This point was driven home in a joint publication authored by the DOJ and the SEC. In their *Resource Guide*, these agencies described whistleblowers as "among the most powerful weapons in the law enforcement arsenal." Whistleblower disclosures are used to "swiftly hold accountable those responsible for unlawful conduct."

FCPA cases can be big. The DOJ and SEC have pursued numerous high-profile FCPA cases that have resulted in billions of dollars in fines and disgorgement penalties. The list of companies prosecuted under the FCPA, and the amount of monies they paid in fines and penalties, is impressive. It includes corporate giants such as Alcatel-Lucent ($137 million), BAE Systems ($400 million), Chevron Corp. ($30 million), ENI, S.p.A./ Snamprogetti Netherlands ($125 million), Kellogg Brown & Root (now KBR) and three other companies (collectively paid $1.28 billion in fines and penalties), and Siemens ($800 million).

Because of the extraordinary transnational scope of the law, currently most of these sanctions obtained by the U.S were paid by international companies registered outside the United States. **Figure 18** shows judgments recorded between 2014 and 2020 under

Figure 18

Top Ten Penalties Under the Foreign Corrupt Practices Act

YEAR	COMPANY	REGISTERED COUNTRY	PENALTY
2020	GOLDMAN SACHS GROUP INC.	UNITED STATES	$3.3 BILLION
2020	AIRBUS SE	NETHERLANDS/FRANCE	$2.09 BILLION
2018	PETRÓLEO BRASILEIRO S.A. - PETROBRAS	BRAZIL	$1.78 BILLION
2019	TELEFONAKTIEBOLAGET LM ERICSSON	SWEDEN	$1.06 BILLION
2017	TELIA COMPANY AB	SWEDEN	$1.01 BILLION
2019	MTS	RUSSIA	$850 MILLION
2008	SIEMENS	GERMANY	$800 MILLION
2016	VIMPELCOM	NETHERLANDS	$795 MILLION
2014	ALSTOM S.A.	FRANCE	$772 MILLION
2018	SOCIÉTÉ GÉNÉRALE S.A	FRANCE	$585 MILLION

the FCPA or the Commodity Exchange Act. As can be seen, a whopping $14.222 billion has been collected, mostly from international corporations.

Overview of FCPA Jurisdiction

Here is an overview of the FCPA's major provisions:

Who is covered? First, "issuers" (companies that sell stock to U.S. citizens) and their officers, directors, employees, and agents are subject to prosecution under the FCPA. An issuer does not have to be a U.S. company. Issuers are broadly defined to include companies that trade on U.S. stock exchanges and foreign companies that trade in American Depository Receipts (ADRs). Foreign corporations that sell securities to U.S. investors using ADRs are covered under the statute. Persons acting on behalf of an issuer are also personally liable, including corporate officers, directors, employees, agents, or coconspirators. Between companies that trade on Wall Street and foreign companies that utilize ADRs, most major public corporations in the world are subject to the FCPA, and their employees are eligible for rewards under the Dodd-Frank Act.

Second, all "domestic concerns" are also covered. A domestic concern is defined as any citizen, national, or resident of the United States or any corporation, partnership, association, business trust, sole proprietorship, or other association organized under the laws of the United States. The law also covers foreign nationals who, directly or indirectly, commit "any act in furtherance of a corrupt payment" while in the United States.

Third, issuers or domestic concerns that work with foreign companies in joint ventures are also covered. Joint ventures can be particularly high risk. Daniel Grimm, an attorney with a major FCPA defense firm (Sullivan & Cromwell), explained that companies can be liable for FCPA violations under a "willful blindness, deliberate ignorance," or "conscious disregard" standard. Thus the failure to exercise due diligence over the actions of a non-U.S. joint venture partner can trigger liability, even if the U.S. partner did not pay or authorize any bribes.

Jurisdictional triggers. The FCPA covers conduct that occurs inside the United States or in a foreign country. The act broadly defines the interstate commerce necessary to trigger jurisdiction for foreign nationals or companies under the law. The DOJ/SEC *Resource Guide* puts it this way: "Placing a phone call or sending an e-mail, text message, or fax from, to, or through the United States involves interstate commerce—as does sending a wire transfer from or to a U.S. bank or otherwise using the U.S. banking system, or travelling across state borders or internationally to or from the United States." As for U.S. persons and corporations, the interstate commerce requirement was removed in 1998 amendments, and such persons are subject to the FCPA "even if they act outside the United States."

What is a prohibited bribe? The law covers payments intended to influence foreign officials to use their positions "in order to assist . . . in obtaining or retaining business for or with, or directing business to, any person." The FCPA prohibits paying a bribe to gain a business advantage. The DOJ/SEC *Resource Guide* lists the following actions as prime examples of when corporations are often induced to pay bribes to foreign officials: (1) "winning a contract," (2) "influencing the procurement process," (3) violating "rules for importation of products," (4) "gaining access to non-public tender information," (5) "obtaining exceptions to regulations," and (6) "avoiding contract termination."

What types of payments constitute a bribe? Paying "anything of value" to a foreign official in order to obtain a business advantage can constitute a bribe. The law is very broad and, as explained in the DOJ/SEC *Resource Guide*, "bribes come in many shapes and sizes." This would include any corrupt "offer, payment, promise to pay, or authorization of the payment of any money, or offer, gift, promise to give, or authorization of the giving of anything of value" to a foreign official, such as consulting fees, commissions, travel expenses, and expensive gifts.

These payments must be made with "corrupt intent" (i.e., the purpose behind the payment is to secure an improper business advantage or improperly influence foreign government officials in order to gain such an advantage). In determining what constitutes a bribe, whistleblowers need to apply common sense. Small gifts or paying something of nominal value, such as covering a taxi ride, will not be actionable. However, as the DOJ/SEC warns in their *Resource Guide*, "the larger or more extravagant the gift, . . . the more likely it was given with an improper purpose." DOJ and SEC enforcement cases have "involved single instances of large, extravagant gift-giving (such as sports cars, fur coats, and other luxury items)." But companies can pay "reasonable expenses associated with the promotion of their products" and can make payments to facilitate routine governmental action.

What is aiding and abetting? Persons or companies that aid or abet in a bribery scheme are guilty under the law to the same degree as those who pay a bribe. As explained in the DOC/SEC *Resource Guide*, "a foreign company or individual may be held liable for aiding and abetting an FCPA violation . . . even if the foreign company or individual did not take any act in furtherance of the corrupt payment while in the territory of the United States."

What is a business purpose? Like other provisions in the law, the "business purpose" test is very broad and includes payments to obtain or keep a contract or lease, influence the procurement process, eliminate customs duties, prevent competitors from entering the market, avoid permit requirements, circumvent importation laws, gain access to nonpublic information to help obtain a contract or government tender, evade taxes, or obtain exemptions for regulations.

Who is a public official? The foreign officials covered under the act include "any officer or employee of a foreign government, or any department, agency, or instrumentality." Instrumentalities include state-owned or state-controlled entities, including government healthcare programs. Foreign political parties are also included in the definition, as are candidates for foreign political office. In 1998 the FCPA was amended to include public international organizations within the definition of foreign officials, including entities such as the World Bank, International Monetary Fund, and the Organization of American States.

Books and records violations: The "books and records" provision prohibits off-the-books accounting. Companies can be prosecuted for books and records violations independent of a prosecution for paying a bribe. The law requires publicly traded companies to accurately account for all assets, and forms the backbone of most SEC and DOJ accounting fraud cases. In the context of the FCPA, its significance is obvious. Bribes are not accurately recorded in corporate books. When a company pays a bribe, it does not admit the purpose of the payment in its financial records.

Congress included the bookkeeping requirements in the FCPA, recognizing that "corporate bribery has been concealed by the falsification of corporate books and records." By mandating large civil and criminal penalties for falsifying financial records, Congress intended to "strengthen the accuracy of the corporate books and records and the reliability of the audit process, which constitute the foundations of our system of corporate disclosure."

The accounting provisions of the FCPA have two major requirements. The first mandates that issuers "keep books, records, and accounts that, in reasonable detail, accurately and fairly reflect an issuer's transactions and dispositions of an issuer's assets." The second provision requires that issuers "devise and maintain a system of internal accounting controls sufficient to assure management's control, authority, and responsibility over the firm's assets."

Although these requirements are not strictly tied to foreign bribery, it is evident how the accounting provisions can be used to prove violations of the FCPA. As explained in the DOJ/SEC *Resource Guide*, "Bribes, both foreign and domestic, are often mischaracterized in books and records. . . . Bribes are often concealed under the guise of legitimate payments, such as commissions or consulting fees." If, for a technical reason, the government cannot meet the standard to prove a bribe, companies can still be held liable under the books and records provision if the improper payments were not accurately recorded in the company's books. Given the large fines associated with an internal controls violation, this prosecutorial tool can be used to close potential loopholes in the bribery provisions.

In FCPA cases, companies have been found guilty of books and records violations when they recorded a bribe in the corporate books as a commission, a consulting fee, sales and marketing expenses, travel and entertainment expenses, rebates and discounts, service fees, miscellaneous expenses, petty cash payments, and write-offs, among other obfuscations.

The accounting provisions do not apply to privately held companies but do apply to all issuers, including companies that trade securities on the national securities exchanges in the United States and foreign issuers that trade in ADRs. The requirements also apply to subsidiaries of publicly traded companies.

Third-party liability: The FCPA prohibits the practice of using third parties or intermediaries to pay the bribes. Companies cannot deny knowledge that a bribe was paid simply by using intermediaries to make the payments. The fact that a company may hire a foreign agent or attorney to conduct its business affairs does not insulate the company from liability for the actions of these agents or intermediaries. In order to demonstrate that the company knew or should have known that the third party was paying bribes, the DOJ/SEC look at various red flags to determine third-party liability, such as (1) excessive commissions paid to agents or consultants, (2) unreasonably large discounts, (3) consulting agreements that include vaguely described services, (4) use of a third party who is "related to or closely associated with the foreign official," or (5) if a third party requests payment to offshore bank accounts.

Knowledge requirement: Corporations can be held liable under the FCPA under the "willful blindness" standard. As explained in the DOJ/SEC *Resource Guide*, "Because Congress anticipated the use of third-party agents in bribery schemes—for example, to avoid actual knowledge of a bribe—it defined the term 'knowing' in a way that prevents individuals and businesses from avoiding liability by putting 'any person' between themselves and foreign officials. . . . [I]t's meant to impose liability not only on those with actual knowledge of wrongdoing, but also on those who purposefully avoid actual knowledge." In its 1988 legislative history on the FCPA, Congress described the firm's knowledge requirements as prohibiting "the so-called 'head-in the sand'" defense, which would include willful blindness, deliberate ignorance, or other "unwarranted obliviousness" that should have alerted them to a high probability that the FCPA could be violated.

Red flags: According to the DOJ/SEC, the following red flags can trigger corporate liability for the actions of third parties, even if the corporation did not have any direct knowledge of a bribe: (1) excessive commissions to third-party agents or consultants, (2) unreasonably large discounts, (3) third-party consulting agreements that are vague, (4) close associations between consultants and foreign officials (especially if the consultant becomes part of the transaction at the request of the foreign official), (5) shell companies as third parties, and (6) payments made to the consultant or third party to offshore bank accounts.

Sanctions and fines: The amount of the sanction or fine paid under the FCPA is very important for whistleblowers, as the Dodd-Frank reward provisions only kick in if the government (or the SEC) obtains over $1 million in sanctions. The penalties for FCPA violations include fines up to $2 million for each violation committed by corporations or business entities and fines up to $100,000 for each violation committed by an individual.

The accounting laws have far higher penalty provisions. Corporations can be fined up to $25 million and individuals fined up to $5 million for these violations. Moreover, under the Alternative Fines Act, courts can impose "up to twice the benefit that the defendant sought to obtain by making the corrupt payment" as a penalty in an FCPA case. Even larger sanctions can be recovered under the accounting provisions of the act, which permit the SEC to obtain disgorgement penalties equal to "the gross amount of the pecuniary gain to the defendant as a result of the violations." There is no upper limit on a disgorgement penalty. The more profits a company made from paying a bribe, the higher the disgorgement penalty.

Other violations: An FCPA violation may also result in prosecution for other related crimes, including obstruction of justice, mail and wire fraud, tax violations based on how the bribes were reported to the IRS, securities violations related to the accuracy of corporate books, and the failure to disclose liabilities to shareholders. The AML Whistleblower Act can also be used to sanction persons who pay or take bribes. It is obvious that persons engaged in foreign bribery often will hide their ownership of the bank accounts where their ill-gotten gains are deposited, thus violating money laundering laws.

The Commodity Exchange Act

One of the most important developments in transnational whistleblowing occurred on December 3, 2020, when the Commodity Futures Trading Commission sanctioned the international energy and commodities trading firm, Vitol, Inc. Vitol, a non-public company headquartered in the Netherlands, was required to pay the CFTC fines and penalties of over $95 million for corrupt activities, including paying bribes that impacted global oil markets.

The mega-corporate law firm of Gibson and Dunn expressed alarm over CFTC's "aggressive approach to bringing enforcement actions involving foreign corruption."

They warned of "multi-agency targeting of conduct involving foreign corruption," which is precisely what happened in the Vitol case. Thus, in addition to the CFTC fines, the Justice Department also sanctioned Vitol $135 million for paying bribes and kickbacks in Brazil, Ecuador, and Mexico. In the end, Gibson and Dunn had a clear warning for their multinational corporate clients:

> [G]oing forward, we expect that foreign corruption allegations involving commodities-related business will continue to be investigated and pursued by multiple agencies, domestic and foreign, approaching the issue from different angles.

On May 24, 2022, Gibson and Dunn's warning to international commodity traders came true. The Commodity Futures Trading Commission issued its largest civil penalty in its history: $1.186 billion against the Swiss-based global oil and energy trading firm Glencore International A.G. and its subsidiaries. The sanctions were issued for manipulative and deceptive conduct based on foreign corruption in the U.S. and global oil markets. CFTC Chairman Rostin Behnam explained the importance of the Glencore case not only in protecting U.S. consumers from paying more for oil, but also in fighting worldwide corruption, especially in the commodity-rich developing world:

> Without question, manipulating oil markets can drive up the cost Americans pay at the pump or to heat their homes. And today my message to the markets is clear: the CFTC will continue to pursue even the slightest hint of manipulative, corrupt, or fraudulent behavior.
> Glencore is one of the world's largest commodity trading firms, and a major participant in the global oil markets. The deceptive and corrupt conduct was deliberate, long-standing, and egregious in that it involved a concerted effort by individuals at all levels within the oil trading group—including its most senior leadership—to undermine the pricing mechanism on which trillions of dollars of financial derivatives contracts, which the CFTC oversees, are based.

The CFTC order sanctioning Glencore predicated its enforcement action on evidence that the company's personnel engaged in this conduct with the "specific intent to manipulate the price of fuel oil products in interstate commerce and to create artificial prices." The illegal conduct included fraud, misappropriation of information, and corrupt payments (e.g., bribes and kickbacks) in numerous countries, including Brazil, Cameroon, Mexico, Nigeria, and Venezuela. By making multiple corrupt payments, Glencore obtained unlawful competitive advantages "to the detriment of its counterparties and market participants."

Another significant development in the Glencore case was the CFTC's cooperation with other international law enforcement agencies, including the United Kingdom's Serious Fraud Office, the Comissão de Valores Mobiliários (Brazilian Securities Market Commission), the Bermuda Monetary Authority, the Hong Kong Securities and Futures Commission, the Luxembourg Commission de Surveillance du Secteur Financier, the Mexico Comisión Nacional Bancaria y de Valores, the UK Financial Conduct Authority, and the Banco Central del Uruguay. Under the Commodity Exchange Act, whistleblower rewards can be based on sanctions paid not only to U.S. law enforcement agencies, but also to international commodity regulators.

As is evident by the international corruption cases filed by the CFTC, that agency has broad international jurisdiction over non-U.S. companies (including privately held companies) that pay bribes or engage in other corrupt activities in extracting, transporting, or selling commodities (i.e., most natural resources) on the international commodity markets. Given the fact that much of the foreign corruption concerns mineral extraction and the exploitation of natural resources from developing countries, the use of the Commodity Exchange Act to enforce anti-corruption laws is revolutionary.

Like the FCPA, international whistleblowers who report violations of the Commodity Exchange Act are fully eligible for monetary rewards under the CFTC's whistleblower program. As explained by the director of the CFTC's Division of Enforcement: "[W]histleblowers around the world with information about potential violations of the Commodity Exchange Act can participate in the CFTC's Whistleblower Program. The award also serves as another example of the increasing significance of whistleblowers in our enforcement program, a trend I expect to continue going forward."

Whistleblowers should heed the wisdom contained in the unanimous ruling of the Securities and Exchange Commission when in 2014 it paid a non-U.S. citizen a multi-million-dollar award, explaining that it did not matter if the whistleblower lived overseas, submitted their information from overseas, and the crimes they reported were witnessed overseas. Both U.S. citizens and non-citizens alike can take advantage of U.S. anti-corruption [break on hyphen] laws, and both have equal rights to confidentiality and awards under Dodd-Frank.

PRACTICE TIPS

- Under Dodd-Frank, non-U.S. whistleblowers can remain anonymous and confidential.

- The Foreign Corrupt Practices Act is codified at 15 U.S.C. § 78m and § 78dd-1, et seq.

- The Department of Justice resource page on the FCPA is located at www.justice.gov/criminal-fraud/foreign-corrupt-practices-act.

- The best source of information explaining the requirements of the FCPA is the 2020 version of the *Resource Guide to the U.S. Foreign Corrupt Practices Act*, available at www.justice.gov/criminal-fraud/fcpa-resource-guide.

- Information on the CFTC's enforcement action against Glencore is linked on the commission website at https://www.cftc.gov/PressRoom/PressReleases/8534-22.

Keeping Up with the Changes

To keep up to date on changes in the laws, whistleblowers should access the free online law library created by the author, located at www.kkc.com/law-library.

RULE 21

Money Laundering and Sanctions-Busting:
Report to FinCEN/Treasury

For too long, corrupt actors and their financial facilitators have taken advantage of vulnerabilities in the U.S. and international financial systems to launder their assets and obscure the proceeds of crime. . . . To counter corruption effectively around the globe, the U.S. Government must [use] . . . new information generated by whistleblower programs. . .
—United States Strategy on Countering Corruption (December 2021)

Financial markets were shaken when Danske Bank was found to be at the center of the largest money laundering scandal in history: Over $236 billion in "suspicious" or illegal monetary transactions had passed from Russia and former Soviet republics, through the Danish bank, and into major Western banks in New York, including Bank of America and JPMorgan Chase. Documents revealed that both the Russian FSB (their secret police) and members of President Vladimir Putin's family were part of the scheme. In a report issued in September 2018, Danske Bank's lawyers admitted that every safeguard designed to prevent money laundering in its Estonian branch had failed. Four years later they were finally held accountable by U.S. authorities.

On December 13, 2022, the U.S. Department of Justice (DOJ) and Securities and Exchange Commission (SEC) issued the first of what is expected to be numerous sanctions against the participants in the money laundering scheme. Danske pled guilty to "conspiracy to commit bank fraud" and agreed to pay $2.472 billion in penalties.

Danske's crimes were reported and ultimately stopped by a whistleblower named Howard Wilkinson. As explained in the SEC's complaint: "In December 2013, a senior-level employee at Danske Estonia [Wilkinson] reported to Danske management that a specific Danske Estonia non-resident customer [i.e., a major Russian customer] had engaged in transactions evidencing money laundering through the use of shell companies and had provided false filings with U.K. authorities." The whistleblower's report triggered a number of internal audits, and in early 2014 the auditors concluded that the Russian customers had "intentionally used corporate structures to conceal the identity of the account owners." The auditors also found that the bank's internal AML controls had failed. Despite the whistleblower's having informed Danske senior management of these failures, the money laundering scheme was covered up and continued for at least two additional years.

The criminal plea agreement entered into between the United States and Danske provided more detail:

- Danske's internal whistleblower had revealed Russian customers using false account documentation and shell companies to engage in what appeared on its face to be widespread and gross money laundering. The DOJ explained that the "Whistleblower concluded that Danske Bank 'may itself have committed a criminal offense, . . . likely breached numerous regulatory requirements[,] [and had] a near total process failure.'"

- The first audit into the whistleblower's allegations, which was covered up, "confirmed that some [Russian] customers were shell companies that had false or insufficient information in Danske Bank Estonia's customer files" and that Danske Bank Estonia "conducted almost no due diligence on the [Russian] customers." One auditor described the situation as a "fire raging." These conclusions were also affirmed in other bank follow-up audits.

- Danske Bank's response to the whistleblower allegations, the internal audit reports, were "deliberately insufficient and delayed."

- Bank executives "vetoed an independent investigation that could have identified and prevented further violations of law by Danske Bank Estonia employees and customers." Other recommendations to alert authorities to these crimes were ignored for years.

Danske's response to the internal whistleblower complaint was all too typical. The whistleblower resigned from the bank for "ethical reasons" and was forced to sign a nondisclosure agreement to obtain a severance payment. Thereafter the bank hid or watered-down audit reports, failed to report violations to regulators, and engaged in various cover-ups.

At the end of 2017, in response to media reports based on leaked information, Danish regulators requested information about Danske's AML procedures, and finally the bank started to report its crimes to proper authorities. But an additional $40 billion had been laundered through the bank after the whistleblower had made his reports.

Underpinning Danske's crimes and the failure of Danish regulators to learn of the massive money laundering schemes was the lack of any whistleblower protections in Estonia or Denmark coupled with strict bank secrecy laws that cover up most bank misconduct throughout Europe.

But the Danske case, along with other large banking and money laundering scandals, would start a change in this backward legal landscape.

The United States' first attempt to fix the problem became law on January 1, 2021. Congress upgraded its money laundering laws and, for the first time, included whistleblower protections for employees reporting AML violations. But the problems with this "reform" became evident when all of the major banks in the United States applauded it. *The American Banker* said it clearly: "Banks can Smell Victory on Key Anti-Laundering Measure." No wonder. The whistleblower law was not a glorious reform but was instead shot through with holes rendering it completely unworkable. For example, bankers employed in the United States (i.e., within credit unions or FDIC-insured institutions) were denied any protections against retaliation. A pseudo-reward law was established, though it was unfunded and could not pay any rewards whatsoever even if the Treasury or Justice Departments wanted to. The banks were happy. But even before the law was put into effect, whistleblower lawyers pointed out the defects and commenced a two-year effort to enact an effective AML whistleblower law.

On December 30, 2022, as a result of this grassroots campaign to fix the broken law, President Joe Biden signed the AML Whistleblower Improvement Act. Although not perfect, it did correct the two major deficiencies in the law and expanded its coverage to include sanctions-busting and conspiracies. Starting in 2023, whistleblowers who report violations of the Bank Secrecy Act, AML, or sanctions requirements will be entitled to mandatory rewards similar to those currently available under the Dodd-Frank securities and commodities laws. The Improvement Act created a fund to pay rewards and made these payments mandatory to any whistleblower who meets the qualifications.

The potential scope of crimes covered under the AML law, although untested in court, is mind-boggling. The Danske scandal alone covered $230 billion in illegal or suspicious activities. Who launders money? Everyone, from millionaires and billionaires trying to escape taxes or hide their wealth to drug cartels, cryptocurrency traders, foreign leaders stashing their profits from bribery, corporations hiding how they pay bribes to obtain business in developing countries, and terrorists and international rogue states needing to shield their financial transactions to obtain arms and engage in trade. Fines paid by banks caught laundering money can run into the hundreds of millions, and even billions, of dollars in penalties.

The Department of Treasury's Financial Crimes Enforcement Network (FinCEN) has primary jurisdiction for enforcing the Bank Secrecy Act, the major law covered under the new AML whistleblower law. Below is an outline of some of FinCEN's major enforcement actions in 2021 and 2022, along with an outline of the legal theories that triggered the payment of sanctions.

Coverage under the AML Whistleblower Law

The new whistleblower law covers a wide range of conduct related to money laundering and violations of sanctions. The entities involved include banks that operate in the United States or transfer money into the United States, money transmission services, money services businesses or MSBs, and cryptocurrency wallets. MSBs include (1) dealers in foreign exchange, (2) check cashers, (3) issuers or sellers of traveler's checks or money orders, (4) providers of prepaid access, (5) money transmitters, (6) U.S. Postal Service, or (7) sellers of prepaid access. Money transmission services include a person that either "provides money transmission services" or who is otherwise "engaged in the transfer of funds."

Money transmission includes "the acceptance of currency, funds, or other value that substitutes for currency from one person and the transmission of currency, funds, or other value that substitutes for currency to another location or person by any means," which can cover crypto or virtual currencies. In its enforcement action against the cryptocurrency trading company Bittrex, FinCEN warned that although "certain Anonymity-Enhanced Cryptocurrencies (AECs) present unique money laundering risks and challenges," companies engaged in this practice must still comply with Bank Secrecy Act requirements. According to FinCEN, companies using AECs need to be "aware of the risks and challenges presented by the AECs" that are exchanged on their platforms and be prepared to address those risks.

Only time will tell the scope of coverage courts and agencies will give to the Improvement Act, but FinCEN has recently (2021–22) taken enforcement actions on the following five types of violations.

Failure to Develop, Implement, and Maintain an Effective AML Program

Banks, other financial institutions, and even cryptocurrency wallets that are covered under the Bank Secrecy Act must establish effective anti-money laundering programs. These programs must be "reasonably designed to assure and monitor Bank Secrecy Act compliance." Their minimum requirements include: "(a) the development of internal policies, procedures, and controls; (b) an independent audit function to test programs; (c) designation of a compliance officer; (d) an ongoing employee training program; and (e) appropriate risk-based procedures for conducting ongoing customer due diligence."

Failure to File SARs

The Bank Secrecy Act requires all covered banks and financial institutions to file suspicious activity reports or SARs whenever a financial transaction occurs that is over $10,000. But that reporting threshold is lowered to $5,000 if a bank or covered service "knows, suspects, or has reason to suspect" the transaction "(a) involves funds derived from illegal activities, or is conducted to disguise funds derived from illegal activities; (b) is designed to evade the reporting or record-keeping requirements of the BSA or regulations under the Act; or (c) has no business or apparent lawful purpose or is not the sort in which the customer normally would be expected to engage, and the bank knows of no reasonable explanation for the transaction after examining the available facts, including background and possible purpose of the transaction."

Violation of "Know Your Customer" or KYC Requirements

The Bank Secrecy Act requires financial institutions to have "[a]ppropriate risk-based procedures for conducting ongoing customer due diligence" better known as a "know your customer" or KYC programs. Banks and other entities covered under the Bank Secrecy Act must understand the "nature and purpose" of their customers and develop a "customer risk profile." The KYC obligations include "policies, procedures, and processes for determining whether and when, on the basis of risk, to update customer information to ensure that customer information is current and accurate." Furthermore, KYC rules require covered entities to have "an understanding of the money laundering, terrorist financing, and other financial crime risks of its customers to develop the customer risk profile."

OFAC Sanctions Enforcement (Including Cryptocurrency Violations)

Even before the AML whistleblower law was amended to cover violations of sanctions requirements, FinCEN and the Department of the Treasury's Office of Foreign Assets Control (OFAC) have worked together to penalize financial institutions that violate sanctions requirements. For example, on October 11, 2022, FinCEN and OFAC jointly announced a $53 million sanction against virtual currency exchange Bittrex, Inc. The joint investigation was predicated on violations of multiple sanctions programs and willful violations of the Bank Secrecy Act, including the requirement to file SARs. The interrelationship between violating sanctions and AML rules is caused by the need for those violating sanctions to hide beneficial ownership and launder funds to accomplish their illegal goals. Virtual currency, such as Bitcoin, has been used to hide these types of crimes, and consequently FinCEN and OFAC have started policing financial services that deal in cryptocurrencies.

Cryptocurrencies/Virtual Currency Exchanges

In approving sanctions against the virtual currency exchange Bittrex, OFAC Director Andrea Gacki explained, "Virtual currency exchanges operating worldwide should understand both who—and where—their customers are. OFAC will continue to hold accountable firms, in the virtual currency industry and elsewhere, whose failure to implement appropriate controls leads to sanctions violations."

FinCEN's acting director further explained the basis for the sanctions: "Bittrex's AML program and SAR reporting failures unnecessarily exposed the U.S. financial system to threat actors" creating "exposure to high-risk counterparties including sanctioned jurisdictions, darknet markets, and ransomware attackers. Virtual asset service providers are on notice that they must implement robust risk-based compliance programs and meet their BSA reporting requirements. FinCEN will not hesitate to act when it identifies willful violations of the BSA."

Furthermore, virtual currency exchanges that operate outside the United States are also at risk for being sanctioned under the AML laws. For example, FinCEN sanctioned BitMEX $100 million, although BitMEX represented that "it only did business outside the U.S." and transactions within the United States were "prohibited." But BitMEX "actively ignored signs that U.S. customers traded on the platform" and overlooked data that some of its customers were located in the United States. Thus, even if a bitcoin trader is located offshore, there can still be jurisdiction under the AML whistleblower law if it has customers within the United States. Given the nature of these exchanges, the risk that U.S. customers may be accessing the platforms is significant.

FinCEN AML Cases 2021–22

The following cases were successfully prosecuted by FinCEN in 2021–22 and provide insight as to what crimes whistleblowers can report under the AML Whistleblower Improvement Act in order to qualify for mandatory rewards between 10 and 30 percent of the recovered sanction.

Bittrex, Inc.: Bittrex owns and operates a convertible virtual currency trading platform that hosts digital wallet services for storing and transferring cryptocurrencies such as bitcoin, ethereum, monero, zcash, and dash. This included over $17 billion worth of bitcoin transactions during the time period under investigation. Bittrex was required to pay fines and penalties of over $53 million based on the following violations:

(a) Failure to develop, implement, and maintain an effective AML program

(b) Engaging in prohibited OFAC-covered transactions (i.e., sanctions violations)

(c) The failure to implement "proper risk-based controls" for high-risk transactions

(d) The failure to file suspicious activity reports

All financial institutions subject to the Bank Secrecy Act and laws governing sanctions and money laundering are subject to investigations and sanctions for violating any of these four requirements. In regard to sanctions, the OFAC and FinCEN explained that "Bittrex had failed to prevent persons located in the Crimea region of Ukraine, Cuba, Iran, Sudan, and Syria from using its platform to engage in approximately $263,451,600.13 worth of virtual currency-related transactions between March 2014 and December 2017."

USAA Federal Savings Bank: USAA was sanctioned $140 million for failing to implement an adequate AML program, failure to train its employees on money laundering requirements, failure to implement a proper customer due diligence (i.e., a KYC) program, and failure to file suspicious activity reports.

BitMEX: As one of the oldest "convertible virtual currency" exchanges, BitMEX has consistently ranked among the largest by trade volume, having facilitated over a trillion U.S. dollars' worth of trades, accepted over $11 billion in convertible virtual currency deposits, and collected over $1 billion in fees. Examples of convertible virtual currencies include bitcoin, ethereum, zcash, monero, dash, ripple, and litecoin. BitMEX was sanctioned $100 million by FinCEN for "willfully failing to implement an Anti-Money Laundering Program," failure to conduct customer due diligence and transaction monitoring, "willfully failing to implement a Customer Identification Program," operating in "darknet and other illicit marketplaces," and engaging in transactions involving fraud and scams.

Capitol One Bank: Capital One's wallet was smacked to the tune of $390 million due to its check-cashing service's failure to implement and maintain an effective AML program guarding against money laundering and its failure to "accurately and timely" file SARs reports. These violations resulted in the failure of the bank "to accurately and timely report millions of dollars in suspicious transactions, including proceeds connected to organized crime, tax evasion, fraud, and other financial crimes laundered through the Bank into the U.S. financial system." For example, organized crime figure Domenick Pucillo, "was one of the largest check cashers in the New York-New Jersey area." Pucillo pled guilty to conspiring to commit money laundering in connection to loan sharking and illegal gambling proceeds that flowed through his Capital One accounts as an associate of the Genovese organized crime family.

In addition to the AML Whistleblower Improvement Act, other federal agencies with strong whistleblower reward laws have also sanctioned banks for money laundering.

This includes the historic sanctions against Danske Bank issued by the SEC for failure to inform investors of their AML crimes, even though FinCEN had taken no action.

The AML-Sanctions Whistleblower Law

The AML Whistleblower Improvement Act, signed into law on December 29, 2022, is modeled on the Dodd-Frank Act's highly successful SEC and CFTC programs. Like the other Dodd-Frank reward laws, the AML whistleblower law will only make payouts in large cases—that is, where either the Departments of Treasury (including FinCEN) or Justice individually or collectively issue a sanction of over $1 million. The law targets all actors in the money laundering chain, including banks, bankers, and cryptocurrency wallets, which often turn a blind eye toward large and questionable depositors. Those who engage in the money laundering face civil and criminal penalties and asset forfeiture. Whistleblower claims must be filed with either the Department of Treasury or Justice. Reward applications are filed only with Treasury, which is required to pay rewards between 10 and 30 percent to all qualified whistleblowers.

Some of the AML whistleblower law's highlights are that it:

- Requires the Treasury Department to pay rewards between 10 and 30 percent of sanctions obtained by qualified whistleblowers

- Permits whistleblowers to file claims with either the Justice or Treasury Departments anonymously and confidentially, under the same confidentiality requirements governing the SEC and CFTC whistleblower laws

- Covers "judicial or administrative actions" filed by either the Justice or Treasury Department concerning a wide variety of laws covering banks and monetary transactions, sanctions violations, cryptocurrencies, and violations of the Bank Secrecy Act

- To qualify for a reward the Treasury and/or Justice Departments must issue sanctions exceeding $1 million

- Is consistent with Dodd-Frank in that a whistleblower must voluntarily provide the government with original information "derived from the independent knowledge or analysis" of the whistleblower with the original information not known by the government, "unless the whistleblower is the original source of the information"

- Is consistent with Dodd-Frank in that the law contains a "related action" provision that permits a whistleblower to obtain a reward even if another agency sanctions the wrongdoer based on the original information provided by the whistleblower

- Permits anonymous filings in accordance with the procedures established under Dodd-Frank; that is, the whistleblower must hire a licensed U.S. attorney to act as their intermediary in filing the claim

- Covers reports initially made to the news media, Congress, or other federal agencies, provided a whistleblower is the original source of the information and follows the rules published by the Treasury Department

- Allows 30 days for the whistleblower to challenge the denial of a reward by filing an appeal with the appropriate U.S. Court of Appeals

- Guarantees the rights of whistleblowers under the AML law may not be waived by contract or corporate nondisclosure agreements

But the law still contains some of the loopholes contained in the weak January 1, 2021, version that were not fixed by the Improvement Act. The major drawbacks are:

- The law's anti-retaliation provision, requiring job-related complaints to be initially filed with the Department of Labor, follows best practices. However, employees working in credit unions or FDIC-insured financial institutions are excluded from protection. This exclusion makes no sense.

- Unlike Dodd-Frank, the scope of sanctions for which a reward can be based is limited and does not directly include proceeds collected as a forfeiture, restitution, or monies paid in victim compensation. These limitations may impact the size of an award. Consequently, whenever filing an AML case, whistleblowers should also consider separately filing under the IRS, FCPA, or Dodd-Frank laws, which can cover civil and criminal money laundering violations but also pay awards based on sanctions collected for forfeiture, restitution, and payments to victims. Don't miss out by viewing your case too narrowly.

- Employees whose official job duties are to work within a company's AML program are excluded from obtaining rewards. The precise scope of this exclusion, or how the Treasury Department will interpret it, are not known. But any employee whose official job duties include investigating or reporting AML violations should also consider filing claims under the other reward laws that have no such exclusion, such as Dodd-Frank and the IRS whistleblower law.

Whistleblowers who report money laundering or sanctions violations should always consider whether their disclosures may be covered under other reward laws. For example, the Danske Bank case included sanctions issued under the Securities Exchange Act, which are covered under Dodd-Frank. Likewise, FinCEN's sanctions against BitMEX also included sanctions issued by the CFTC, which would again be covered under Dodd-Frank. Likewise, the IRS whistleblower program directly covers money laundering and asset forfeiture within the jurisdiction of the IRS or subject to investigation by the IRS. The IRS was directly involved in the Bittrex case. These alternative laws broadly cover the activities of most banks, and also some of the underlying crimes that money launderers use to hide their criminal profits, such as bribes paid in violation of the Foreign Corrupt Practices Act.

Prior to filing a claim, whistleblowers should contact FinCEN, the DOJ, and/or the Treasury Department to inquire about the proper filing procedures.

PRACTICE TIPS

- The AML whistleblower law is codified at 31 U.S.C. § 5323. The legislative history of the AML Whistleblower Improvement Act is published as House Report 117-423 (July 20, 2022).

- The Improvement Act covers violations of the money laundering laws, the Bank Secrecy Act, and sanctions-busting.

- The IRS whistleblower law that covers crimes investigated by the IRS criminal division, which can include money laundering and asset forfeiture, is located at 26 U.S.C. § 7623(c)(2).

- FinCEN can take enforcement actions under the Bank Secrecy Act (BSA), 31 U.S.C. 5311 et seq., and its implementing regulations at 31 C.F.R. Chapter X. This includes actions based on record-keeping violations (31 C.F.R §1010.415); Currency Transaction Report violations (31 C.F.R. §1010.311); failure to file SARs, or Suspicious Activity Reports (31 C.F.R. § 1021.320), failure to report foreign bank accounts (i.e., FBAR violations) (31 C.F.R §1010.350); and failure to register money services businesses (31 C.F.R §1022.380).

- FinCEN publishes its enforcement actions online at https://www.fincen .gov/news-room/enforcement-actions.

Keeping Up with the Changes

To keep up to date on changes in the laws, whistleblowers should access the free online law library created by the author, located at www.kkc.com/law-library.

RULE 22

Auto Safety: Report to the DOT

On December 27, 1994, the Chrysler Corporation fired safety executive Paul Sheridan. His discharge commenced a twenty-one-year battle to pass whistleblower protections for autoworkers. It wasn't until 2012 that autoworkers obtained federal protections against being fired for simply raising safety concerns. Three years later, in the wake of some of the worst auto safety scandals in history, including deadly airbags and malfunctioning ignition switches, Congress passed the first whistleblower law designed to pay rewards when employees exposed safety hazards.

A quarter century after Sheridan's life was shattered, the U.S. Department of Transportation's National Highway Traffic Safety Administration (NHTSA) paid its first *qui tam* reward: $24 million to a whistleblower who reported Hyundai and Kia's untimely recall of over 1.6 million vehicles that had serious defects in their car's engines. The road from Sheridan's first disclosures to the NHTSA's first whistleblower reward was long, cruel, and bloody.

The Road to Protection

It all started when Paul Sheridan reported a defective liftgate latch used on Chrysler minivans, just as the vehicle was being introduced into the market. He raised concerns with management, who ignored his worries. He filed an anonymous tip with an auto safety public interest group, and ultimately some of his concerns were reported in an industry newspaper. Sheridan told his bosses that he was going to report the defect to the National Highway Traffic Safety Administration. Chrysler's reaction was brutal.

During the Christmas holiday season, Sheridan's office was raided. Shortly thereafter, he was fired. Chrysler went to court "without notice and obtained an *ex parte* 'muzzle order' which threatened him with arrest if he disclosed what he knew about Chrysler safety defects." Despite these attacks, Sheridan testified before the NHTSA, which investigated his concerns and found them to be true.

Sheridan's safety allegations were vindicated, but not in time to save some of the lives for which he risked his career. The liftgate latch defect was linked to thirty-seven deaths.

During the NHTSA investigation, Chrysler increased its pressure to shut Sheridan up. The company amended a lawsuit it had filed against him in state court, demanding financial damages in addition to simply gagging him. Under pressure from the company's lawsuit, Sheridan was forced to settle his own state whistleblower claims in exchange for Chrysler dropping its lawsuit. As the U.S. Senate investigation revealed, for trying to save lives, Sheridan "suffered untold sums in legal expenses and personal trauma."

Sheridan's mistreatment prompted Congress to pass the first whistleblower protections for autoworkers. In 2012 the Moving Ahead for Progress in the 21st Century Act, known simply as MAP-21, was signed into law. It should have been named "Sheridan's Law." Modeled on the Sarbanes-Oxley Act and the airline and trucker safety laws, it utilizes the DOL procedures that can be effective in fighting retaliation. It covers employees working for "motor vehicle manufacturer(s), part supplier(s) or dealership(s)" who are discriminated against for reporting motor vehicle defects or noncompliance with auto safety laws to their employer or the Department of Transportation. The process is as follows:

- MAP-21 has a 180-day statute of limitations. This means that employees filing a whistleblower retaliation complaint must file their charge with the U.S. Department of Labor within *180 days* of any discriminatory action.

- After a complaint is filed with the Occupational Safety and Health Administration, OSHA conducts an investigation and thereafter either the employee or employer can request a hearing. The case can be adjudicated within the Department of Labor. However, an employee is given the right to seek a trial in federal court if the Labor Department does not issue a final decision in 120 days. How these DOL laws are administered is explained in Rule 26.

Whistleblower Rewards

MAP-21 helped with retaliation, but it wasn't the solution to ending misconduct in the auto industry. Employees, like Sheridan, who suffered brutal retaliation could get some relief, but the law did nothing to incentivize workers to blow the whistle. Scandals continued to plague the industry. Who would want to suffer as Sheridan had, even if you could eventually prevail in a wrongful discharge lawsuit? The anti-retaliation law also had a major loophole: It did not cover employees who worked outside the United States, where many cars are designed and built. U.S. employment laws could not protect autoworkers in Mexico, Japan, Korea, or Germany.

The solution: Create a reward law. That is precisely what Congress did. Legislators took the language from the Dodd-Frank Act and the IRS reward law and crafted an auto safety reward law. Senator John Thune explained that his legislation was "modeled after existing statutory whistleblower protections that encourage individuals to share information with the Internal Revenue Service and the Securities and Exchange Commission."

In 2014, the year before the auto safety reward law was passed, the NHTSA recalled 63 million vehicles for safety problems, including GM cars that had faulty ignition switches and numerous models that used the deadly Takata air bags. Auto companies and suppliers paid $126 million in fines. Based on this record, which included "numerous injuries and deaths," Congress looked toward the highly effective reward laws as a model. As stated in the Senate Report, the law would incentivize workers to "provide information about defects, instances of noncompliance, and motor vehicle safety reporting violations as early as possible to help improve automobile safety."

The auto safety reward law tracks the Dodd-Frank Act but has some important differences. Here are the major provisions:

1. To qualify for the reward the whistleblower must be an employee or contractor in the auto industry, and the sanction obtained by the U.S. government must be at least $1 million. The reward range was set between 10 percent and 30 percent of the sanction.

2. Whistleblowers must voluntarily provide original information to the Department of Transportation. The definition of original information is the same as that contained in Dodd-Frank.

3. The information must relate to a "motor vehicle defect, noncompliance, or any violation" (including reporting violations) that is "likely to cause unreasonable risk of death or serious physical injury."

In determining the amount of a reward (if any) to give to a whistleblower, the Department of Transportation was mandated to consider the following factors:

- Factors that can *increase* a reward:
  - Reporting the safety concern internally first
  - Significance of the original information
  - High degree of assistance provided by the whistleblower (or their lawyer) in the government investigation
  - Other factors identified by the secretary of transportation when the final rule on this law is published. The Department of Transportation has not yet published these regulations.
- Factors that will result in a reward being *denied*:
  - Being convicted of a criminal violation related to the enforcement action triggered.
  - "Knowingly and intentionally makes any false, fictitious, or fraudulent statement" to the government
  - If the same information was previously filed with the secretary of transportation. This is similar to the False Claims Act's first to file rule
  - Failing to follow the procedures required by the secretary of transportation Until the regulations are published, whistleblowers can file claims and apply for a reward. Information is available at https://www.nhtsa.gov/laws-regulations/whistleblower-program

Internal Compliance Requirements

Unlike any other whistleblower reward law, the auto safety law requires that, under some circumstances, an employee first report their concerns *within* the company to be eligible for a reward. This provision conflicts with the right of whistleblowers to file confidential claims with the government, which is also protected under the law. It is very common for the boss to suspect that the employee who raised concerns internally became the person who later reported the company to the government. Additionally, the mandate could be highly problematic for whistleblowers outside the United States, where most countries lack any effective legal protections for whistleblowers.

The simple truth is that in whistleblowing, "no good deed goes unpunished." Employees who have to let their company know about problems often get fired before they have the time or wherewithal to report their concerns to the government. If they do eventually report to an authority outside the factory gates, they become the primary suspect for snitching on the company. This places employees in a difficult position: Risk being disqualified for a reward or potentially give up your confidentiality.

Under the reward law, with some important exceptions, if the auto company/supplier/dealership has "an internal reporting mechanism in place to protect employees from retaliation," a whistleblower must use that mechanism in order to qualify for a reward. The provision sets a dangerous precedent. Historically, many companies have used internal reporting programs as a trap for whistleblowers. For example, many corporations delegate responsibility for internal compliance with the company's general counsel. In doing so, the company can use attorney-client privilege to hide information from the government and pressure on the employee to keep quiet.

The exceptions to the internal reporting requirement demonstrate that Congress was aware that compliance programs can be problematic. Whistleblowers can bypass internal reporting requirements if:

- A whistleblower reasonably believes they would be subject to retaliation if the issues were reported internally through the company's mechanism.

- The whistleblower reasonably believes the safety concern was already reported internally, was the subject of a company investigation or inquiry, or was already known to the employer.

- The Department of Transportation has "good cause to waive" the requirement. This good cause will be defined in the rules the Department of Transportation is required to publish.

Confidentiality

The auto reward law has strong confidentiality protections. As a general matter, the Department of Transportation cannot disclose information that "could reasonably be expected to reveal the identity of a whistleblower." This statutorily mandated confidentiality requirement has a number of carefully defined exceptions.

The main exception to confidentiality is if the whistleblower's identity is "required to be disclosed to a defendant" in "connection with a public proceeding instituted" by the secretary of transportation. Most enforcement actions are resolved through a settlement. If there is a public proceeding, the benefits of a strong sanction can sometimes outweigh the costs of losing confidentiality.

Moreover, even when there is a public proceeding that could result in the disclosure of a whistleblower, the secretary of transportation must take "reasonable measures to not reveal the identity of the whistleblower."

If criminal proceedings are initiated, the statute also permits the secretary of transportation to share evidence obtained from the whistleblower with a grand jury or with witnesses or defendants in ongoing criminal investigations. Because of this exception, whistleblowers should consider obtaining confidential informant status from the Justice Department if federal prosecutors indicate an interest in using the whistleblower's information in a criminal case.

Appeals

A whistleblower can appeal a reward decision issued by the Department of Transportation to the U.S. Court of Appeals, pursuant to the Administrative Procedure Act, 5 U.S.C. § 706. Appeals must be filed within thirty days of the denial.

PRACTICE TIPS

- The autoworker's anti-retaliation law is codified at 49 U.S.C. § 30171, and its implementing regulations are located at 29 C.F.R. § 1988.

- The reward law is codified at 49 U.S.C. § 30172.

- Legislative history of the reward statute: Senate Report 114-13, "Motor Vehicle Safety Whistleblower Act, Report of the Committee on Commerce, Science, and Transportation on S. 304" (Apr. 13, 2015).

- Information on the auto safety reward law is posted on the NHTSA's whistleblower program's website, found at https://www.nhtsa.gov/laws -regulations/whistleblower-program.

Keeping Up with the Changes

To keep up to date on changes in the laws, whistleblowers should access the free online law library created by the author, located at www.kkc.com/law-library.

RULE 23

Whistleblowing on the High Seas: Report to the Coast Guard

The government's success in detecting the illegal activity and obtaining sufficient evidence to support investigations and prosecutions is dependent upon the willingness of a crew member to step forward.

— U.S. Department of Justice in *USA v. Noble Drilling*

How can the United States prosecute illegal pollution that is dumped into the high seas, outside U.S. waters? How can the United States hold foreign shipowners accountable? How can you blow the whistle on a ship in the middle of the Indian Ocean, where not a soul on the ship is an American citizen? By its very nature, pollution on the high seas occurs in waters outside U.S. jurisdiction. But despite all these impediments, the United States has become the number-one country enforcing the international convention prohibiting ocean pollution. Why? The answer is simple: whistleblowers.

To understand how a U.S. whistleblower law can be applied in such circumstances is to begin to understand the potential transnational scope of whistleblowing and its true law enforcement potential.

It starts with an international treaty: the International Convention for the Prevention of Pollution from Ships, better known simply as the MARPOL Protocol. This convention, signed by more than 150 countries including the United States, prohibits, among other things, dumping oil or garbage on the high seas. After signing on to the convention, the United States enacted the Act to Prevent Pollution from Ships (APPS) to enforce its requirements.

The second step is based on paperwork. The APPS law requires every ship entering U.S. territorial waters to have an accurate log of all discharges. If a ship from a foreign country, owned by a foreign company and staffed by a foreign crew, enters U.S. territorial waters, the U.S. Coast Guard can ask to inspect the discharge log. If the log does not record all discharges accurately, the ship is in violation of the APPS. *The basis for prosecution is not the dumping of oil or garbage on the high seas but the failure to record that dumping in the oil record book.* In this way, the United States can prosecute a crime that occurs within the United States: the crime of having inaccurate paperwork.

Most ship captains who illegally pollute the oceans do not accurately record their criminal actions in the discharge log. Catching a ship captain for failure to keep an accurate log is like catching Al Capone on tax evasion.

To prosecute a case under APPS, the U.S. government needs proof that an illegal discharge was not accurately recorded in the ship's log. Whistleblowers are the key to unlocking this door. Crewmembers are in a position to witness the discharges and gather evidence to prove that a ship illegally dumped. This evidence often consists of photos taken on crewmembers' cell phones and the ability of crewmembers to show Coast Guard inspectors where the equipment used to discharge oil is hidden onboard.

Why would crewmembers who reside outside the United States, and who would have little or no protection from retaliation in their native lands, risk their jobs to report ocean pollution? The answer is simple: large whistleblower rewards, paid by the United States regardless of country of citizenship.

APPS also has prosecutorial teeth. Sanctions and fines under the law are steep. Once the Coast Guard obtains credible evidence of an APPS violation, the ship can be impounded, the captain arrested, and the shipowners sanctioned millions of dollars.

The prosecution of the *Aquarosa* is a case in point. This ship was operated by a Marshall Islands corporation based in Greece, registered in Malta, and owned by a Danish company. The ship sailed from China, with stops in Singapore, Brazil, and the Netherlands, but eventually arrived in a Baltimore, Maryland, harbor. During the ship's travels, crewmember Salvador Lopez (a Philippine national) took photos of the illegal oil dumping with his cell phone. When the ship arrived in Baltimore, he handed Coast Guard inspectors a note that stated, "I have something to till [sic] you but secret." He met with the inspectors, provided more than 300 photographs depicting the discharges, drew diagrams for the government, showed them the location of tools and equipment used in the discharges, and provided them with a notebook.

The United States was able to use Lopez's information to successfully prosecute the ship's operator and owner, as well as the ship's chief engineer (who was sentenced to three months in prison), for having an inaccurate discharge log. A total of $1.85 million in fines and community service payments were awarded. The DOJ, with court approval, earmarked more than $500,000 of the collected penalties for projects to improve the Chesapeake Bay. Salvador Lopez, the whistleblower, was awarded $550,000.

The availability of the APPS award aptly reflects the realities of life at sea and the pollution of the oceans. A monetary award both rewards the crew member for taking that risk and may provide an incentive for other crew members on other vessels to alert inspectors and investigators regarding similar crimes.

—Department of Justice in *U.S. v. Odfjell*

When the plea agreement was approved, the DOJ reiterated its policy to vigorously prosecute APPS cases: "the intentional dumping of oil and plastic from ships . . . threaten our precious ocean resources." In approving the whistleblower reward, the court stated, "[T]he APPS whistleblower provision reflects a congressional intent to encourage seafarers to come forward with information regarding illegal pollution activities, which otherwise would be difficult to detect. . . . The Court finds it appropriate to render a total award that is sufficient to provide incentive for seamen to inform the United States of violations of the MARPOL protocol."

APPS permits a court to award whistleblowers up to 50 percent of the criminal penalties obtained by the government for APPS prosecutions. The government is also permitted to earmark a percentage of the fines and penalties to be used to address the environmental harms caused by ocean pollution. The DOJ regularly asks the courts to pay these international whistleblowers the maximum award, and consistently seeks restitution payments to benefit the environment. The result demonstrates again how whistleblower reward laws can have a transnational impact, by preventing pollution outside the United States, rewarding whistleblowers who are non-U.S. citizens, and generating funds to protect the environment.

As reflected in **Figure 19,** the track record under the APPS speaks for itself:

- **Fines collected.** Between 1993 and 2021 the U.S. government collected over $300 million in fines and penalties from APPS violators in whistleblower-originated cases.

- **Public interest.** From all fines and penalties collected, $53 million was paid directly to environmental organizations as part of community service or restitution payments. The monies were used to directly benefit the environment and oceans, such as the payments directed to the Chesapeake Bay in the *Aquarosa* prosecution.

- **Incentivizing and protecting whistleblowers.** From APPS fines collected, courts approved over $36 million in compensation to the whistleblowers. In 80 percent of the cases, the court approved a maximum whistleblower reward (50 percent of the fines collected). The largest reward paid to an individual whistleblower was $2,100,000 in *USA v. Omi Corporation.* The largest total compensation set aside in one case for payment to whistleblowers was $5,250,000, awarded to twelve whistleblowers from the Philippines in *USA v. Overseas Shipholding Group.* The average reward paid per whistleblower is in the $500,000 range.

Figure 19

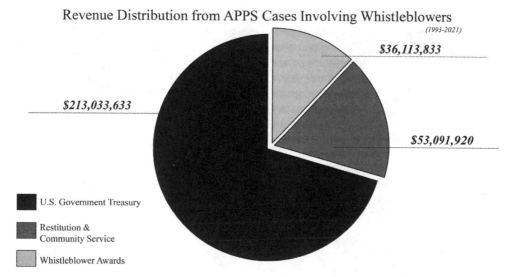

Revenue Distribution from APPS Cases Involving Whistleblowers
(1993-2021)

$36,113,833

$213,033,633

$53,091,920

■ U.S. Government Treasury

■ Restitution & Community Service

■ Whistleblower Awards

When the DOJ Environment and Natural Resources Division (the DOJ unit with jurisdiction over APPS) asks a court to approve rewards at the maximum 50 percent level, the DOJ carefully explains the importance of paying "significant whistleblower awards" as a matter of routine practice. DOJ's rationalization for paying maximum rewards says it all:

> *The APPS award provision serves a valuable law enforcement purpose by encouraging those most likely to know of the illegal conduct to report it and cooperate with law enforcement. Because the discharge of oily waste typically takes place in the middle of the ocean in international waters, the only persons likely to know about the conduct and the falsification of the ORB [the discharge log] are the crewmembers. Absent crewmembers with firsthand knowledge of the illegal conduct coming forward, APPS violations are otherwise extremely difficult to uncover. The government's success in detecting the illegal activity and obtaining sufficient evidence to support investigations and prosecutions is dependent upon the willingness of a crewmember to step forward. In turn, a crewmember must assess the risks associated with coming forward, such as the possibility that the crew member will lose relatively lucrative employment and be blacklisted and barred from working in the marine shipping industry in the future.*
>
> *A substantial monetary award, as provided by APPS, both rewards the crewmember for taking those risks and provides an incentive for other crewmembers to come forward and report illegal conduct on vessels in the future.*

Examples of how the fines and penalties collected in APPS cases are used to enhance the environment is reflected in **Figure 20**.

In regard to the transnational impact of the law, whistleblowers obtained rewards for triggering the successful prosecution of ships owned by or registered in Turkey,

Figure 20

Beneficial Purposes of Sanctions Obtained in APPS Cases with Whistleblowers

SAMPLES OF GROUPS WHO OBTAINED RESTITUTION	EXAMPLES OF PROJECTS FUNDED
Smithsonian Environmental Research	Restoring U.S. water ecosystems
Florida National Keys Marine Sanctuary	Conservation of wildlife resources for U.S. coastline
Alaska Sea Life Center	Protection of coral reefs
Puget Sound Marine Conversation Fund	Scientific research of marine habitats
National Fish and Wildlife Foundation	Projects and initiatives benefitting the maritime environment and marine and coastal natural resources
Abandoned Seafarers Fund	Financial support to seafarers in the U.S. currently aiding U.S. Coast Guard investigation
Oil Spill Liability Fund	Pay removal costs and damages from oil spills
National Marine Sanctuary of American Samoa	Abatement, cleanup, and remediation of pollution in American Samoa
Columbia River Conservation Fund	Education on protecting marine environments from pollution

Jordan, Portugal, South Korea, Denmark, Liberia, Germany, Cyprus, Greece, Panama, Italy, Japan, the Bahamas, Malta, Egypt, Bermuda, Singapore, China, Spain, Norway, New Zealand, Sweden, and the Philippines. Court records confirm that whistleblowers from the Philippines, Greece, Honduras, Venezuela, Korea, and the United States have all obtained payments.

The biggest problem with the APPS is the lack of enforcement. The federal government has dedicated insufficient resources to these cases and is unable to prosecute all but a tiny fraction of them. Moreover, the Coast Guard has not opened a designated whistleblower office and has no coordinated program to educate and protect its whistleblower sources, many of whom are international and already removed from mainstream whistleblower knowledge in the U.S. In addition, there is no provision for anonymous or confidential reporting of these crimes.

Even with its shortcomings, when used the APPS is impactful. For example, the Carnival Corporation was prosecuted under APPS for illegal discharges from one of its cruise ships. It paid an $18 million fine. Thereafter, Carnival made a public presentation to the American Association of Port Authorities. It's recommendation to other cruise lines was very clear:

> *What gets reported? Everything—when in doubt report even the slightest pollution. Don't shoot the messenger.*

PRACTICE TIPS

- The Act to Prevent Pollution from Ships whistleblower reward provision is codified at 33 U.S.C. § 1908(a).

- A detailed listing of APPS cases for which rewards were paid is posted at www.kkc.com/law-library.

- The Marine Defenders handbook, designed to help seamen involved in government investigations, is available at www.marinedefenders.com/commercial/rewards.php.

- Tips are supposed to be filed at the U.S. Coast Guard National Response Center, which offers a toll-free number (800-424-8802) and a web page that contains an online spill report form (www.nrc.uscg.mil).

- A major case explaining the reward provision is *U.S. v. Efploia Shipping Co. S.A.*, Case 1:11-cr-00652-MJG, Bench Decision *Re: Whistleblower Award* (ECF Doc. 80) (D. Maryland) (Apr. 25, 2016).

Keeping Up with the Changes

To keep up to date on changes in the laws, whistleblowers should access the free online law library created by the author, located at www.kkc.com/law-library.

RULE 24

Wildlife Trafficking, IUU Fishing, and Deforestation: Report to FWS

Powerful tools are needed to combat and control the massive illegal trade in wildlife which threatens the survival of numerous species, threatens the welfare of our agricultural and pet industries, and imposes untold costs upon the American taxpayers.
—The House Report No. 97-276

Five years before the False Claims Act would be modernized, with no fanfare, Congress enacted whistleblower reward laws covering two important wildlife protection laws: the Lacey Act and the Endangered Species Act. The problem the laws targeted was of exceptional public importance: stop the extinction of iconic and endangered species and protect their habitat worldwide. The strategy to be used was simple: incentivize informants to report violations of the laws protecting endangered species and prohibiting illegal wildlife trafficking by paying monetary rewards to whistleblowers. Unfortunately, these laws were based on archaic reward laws, which do not require any payments to whistleblowers and, to date, have uniformly failed.

The agencies responsible for their implementation, the U.S. Fish and Wildlife Service (FWS), the National Oceanic and Atmospheric Administration (NOAA), and the Department of Agriculture have not implemented effective whistleblower programs. The laws are unknown to most wildlife protection organizations, and none of the responsible federal agencies have established a whistleblower office. Over the next forty years, the Fish and Wildlife Service only paid a handful of awards, and these have all been in token amounts. NOAA has not paid any. In documents produced under the Freedom of Information Act, FWS referred to the payments as a form of Christmas gift for doing the right thing. They were completely oblivious to the incredible deterrent effect these laws could have and how incentivizing whistleblowers would result in a massive increase in credible reporting.

Illegal wildlife trafficking is big business. Extinctions continue, and the illegal trade has grown exponentially. Reports issued by the international police organization INTERPOL and the United Nations Environment Program estimate that total losses worldwide due to illegal trafficking in plants, fish, and animals and illegal logging ranges from $48 to $153 billion annually. Wildlife trafficking also promotes organized crime and undermines the rule of law in numerous countries. On April 22, 2015, John Cruden, the assistant attorney general responsible for the Environment and Natural Resources Division of the DOJ, described the problem in testimony before Congress: "Wildlife trafficking . . . has become one of the most profitable types of transnational organized crime. Illegal trade at this scale has devastating impacts: It threatens security, hinders sustainable economic development, and undermines the rule of law. The illicit trade in wildlife is decimating many species worldwide."

Whistleblower Rewards under the Lacey and Endangered Species Acts

The principal law for stopping wildlife trafficking is the Lacey Act. Originally passed in 1900, it has been amended over time to become the premier anti-trafficking law. Under the act, it is "unlawful for any person to import, export, transport, sell, receive, acquire, or purchase in interstate or foreign commerce" any fish, wildlife, or plant "taken, possessed, transported, or sold in violation of any law or regulation of any State or in violation of any foreign law." The Lacey Act's scope includes trafficking in violation of the Convention on International Trade in Endangered Species of Wild Fauna and Flora (CITES), the international convention designed to protect endangered species and forests.

In 1981 Congress amended the Lacey Act to include whistleblower rewards. Under these amendments the secretaries of the Commerce, Interior, and Treasury Departments were authorized to pay whistleblower rewards. The Department of Agriculture was also given authority to pay awards under the plants provision of the act, which includes illegal logging. These agencies have broad discretion to reward whistleblowers and, unlike most other whistleblower reward laws, there is no cap on the amount of award or percentage of collected proceeds that may be given to a whistleblower.

The 1981 Lacey Act amendments also contained a miscellaneous section that included an identical reward provision for whistleblowers who report violations of the Endangered Species Act.

On December 31, 1982, Congress went even further. A little-noticed appropriations act contained a provision "for other purposes," amending the Fish and Wildlife Improvement Act. One of these other purposes was the grant of sweeping authority to the Departments of Interior and Commerce to pay whistleblower rewards from appropriations. Unlike other whistleblower reward laws, payments would not have to be based on the amount of funds recovered in a specific enforcement action. Instead, these departments can use appropriated funds to compensate whistleblowers who report violations. Rewards can be paid even if no "collected proceeds" are ever obtained. The goal of the Fish and Wildlife Improvement Act's whistleblower provision was to incentivize the reporting of violations, regardless of whether or not the United States could ever successfully prosecute the case.

During the House floor debate on the amendment, Congress understood the importance of paying rewards in order to detect crimes. Then-congressman John Breaux (D-LA) explained that undercover activities, which implicitly included almost all whistleblower cases, were always "difficult and dangerous but highly successful." Additionally, the amendment was designed to draw out insiders who could help "apprehend large-scale commercial violators of wildlife laws."

But alas, all of these laws have been mostly ignored. In contrast to the SEC and CFTC, none of the agencies responsible for enforcing the Lacey or Endangered Species Acts have created whistleblower offices, and except for brief mentions on their websites (essentially forced on them as a result of a General Accounting Office audit), none have taken any effective steps to implement the laws. There are no publicly available regulations setting forth the procedures necessary to qualify for a reward and no rules setting forth the amount that should be paid.

Nonetheless, whistleblowers who report violations of wildlife trafficking laws, including IUU fishing violations and illegal logging, should demand their right to be fully and fairly rewarded be strictly enforced. Don't ignore these laws. Don't let the government avoid its responsibilities. Among the steps that should be taken are:

1. Carefully document the information provided to U.S. (or other) law enforcement officials that was used to trigger an investigation or contribute to a successful prosecution.

2. Monitor any civil or criminal prosecution that is triggered by the information or for which the information is used.

3. If any sanctions are obtained for any of the crimes you report, file a reward claim with the agencies of the federal government responsible for paying the rewards, including the Fish and Wildlife Service, which also operates a special "Lacey Act Reward Fund" that was designed to pay whistleblower rewards. Even if the government is ignoring these laws, you should not.

4. If applicable, also file your case under one of the modernized whistleblower reward laws, such as Dodd-Frank (covering publicly traded companies and corruption in the commodity markets) the AML money laundering laws, and the False Claims Act (customs violations). The new laws are light-years ahead of the rights whistleblowers have under the Lacey or Endangered Species Acts. Unfortunately, the victims of these crimes—forests, elephants, and tigers—do not have the political might that others enjoy.

Until the laws are updated, those struggling to prevent extinctions, protect the oceans, and stop deforestation will be fighting with one hand tied behind their backs. But the other hand can file a claim and demand that the government do its job.

Reforms on the Horizon?

The international community now recognizes the need to protect and reward whistle-blowers who report environmental violations, threats to fisheries, deforestation, and wildlife trafficking. At the 2021 worldwide conference of the International Union for the Conservation of Nature (IUCN) for the first time numerous resolutions were passed supporting whistleblowers. The IUCN is the premier transnational environmental/wildlife protection organization.

The vote on Resolution 39, that included numerous provisions supporting whistle-blowers, was lopsided. Of the 112 representatives from nation-states, 106 voted in support of the resolution. In regard to the nongovernmental members, 568 supported the resolution, and only 31 opposed.

At the 2021 World Conference the IUCN also approved its "Program for the Union 2021-24," which included an international call for enhancing whistleblower protection and reward laws:

"Realizing rights, obligations and principles inherent to the environmental rule of law and to justice requires strong legal frameworks . . . and fair enforcement of the law to protect and restore biodiversity on land, water and the oceans . . . [The] IUCN will promote whistleblower protection and reward laws. IUCN will fight illegal wildlife trafficking and other environmental crimes, stand by environmental defenders and ensure that their rights are properly respected."

The international community has recognized the connection between whistleblower protections and the ability of governments to enforce wildlife and environmental protection laws. Until reforms come, the best bet for wildlife trafficking whistleblowers are the state of the art anti-corruption reward laws, including False Claims, Dodd-Frank, IRS, and AML.

PRACTICE TIPS

- The three main wildlife whistleblower reward laws are Lacey Act, 16 U.S.C. § 3375(d); Endangered Species Act, 16 U.S.C. §1540(d); and Fish and Wildlife Improvement Act, 16 U.S.C. §7421(c)(3).

- The congressional history behind the original 1981 amendments to the Lacey Act and the 1982 Fish and Wildlife Improvement Act are located in House Report No. 97-276 (Oct. 19, 1981) (Lacey); 128 Cong. Rec. H10207 and H31972 (Dec. 17, 1982) (Improvement).

- The wildlife whistleblower laws and program are fully explained in Kohn, "Monetary Rewards for Wildlife Whistleblowers: A Game-Changer in Wildlife Trafficking Detection and Deterrence," 46 *Environmental Law Reporter* 10054 (Jan. 2016), available at www.whistleblowers.org/wildlife.

- Because of weaknesses in the wildlife whistleblower laws, Congress is considering significant amendments. Prior to filing a case, whistleblowers should check for updates.

Keeping Up with the Changes

To keep up to date on changes in the laws, whistleblowers should access the free online law library created by the author, located at www.kkc.com/law-library.

RULE 25

Don't Think Small

Imagine if the federal government could pay financial rewards in every case where a disclosure triggered a sanction—regardless of what law was violated. Imagine if a whistleblower could obtain a reward for disclosing violations for which *no* whistleblower law even existed. Take a deep breath. This is precisely what happened on September 16, 2021, when the Securities and Exchange Commission paid a whistleblower $70 million for reporting violations of a law that were *not* covered under the Securities Exchange Act, that was *not* investigated by the SEC, and whose penalties were *not* collected by the SEC. Moreover, the reward was paid based on a violation of law that had *no* provision authorizing the payment of any money to a whistleblower.

The new whistleblower laws include a little-understood tool that can radically change the game plan. Known simply as a "related action," this mechanism increases the impact, scope, and effectiveness of whistleblower disclosures. It permits the U.S. government to use a whistleblower's information to obtain full accountability for all laws violated by incentivizing a whistleblower to work with numerous federal agencies, not just the SEC, Justice, Treasury, FinCEN, or CFTC.

Related actions expand the scope of narrowly drafted reward laws. For example, Dodd-Frank encourages reporting to the two agencies with robust reward programs (the SEC and CFTC). But Congress did not stop there. The related action provision, if properly used, can also drive insiders with actionable intelligence into the arms of other law enforcement agencies. The related action provisions eliminate much of the guessing game as to what laws may be covered when a whistleblower steps forward, and instead provides powerful incentives to whistleblowers to fully cooperate in all investigations related to their initial reports.

The clearest definition of "related action" was used in the Dodd-Frank Act:

> The term "related action" . . . means any judicial or administrative action brought by . . . [the Attorney General of the United States, an appropriate regulatory authority, a self-regulatory organization, or a State attorney general in connection with any criminal investigation] . . . that is based upon the original information provided by a whistleblower . . . that led to the successful enforcement of the Commission action.

Translated into English, this simply means that if a whistleblower's original information resulted in a successful enforcement action by the SEC, the whistleblower can also qualify for rewards based on enforcement actions brought by other agencies. Related action payments are available if other federal regulatory or law enforcement agencies issue a sanction based on the information provided to the SEC or CFTC. Depending on the law, related action payments can also be obtained if sanctions are ordered by non-federal authorities, such as state prosecutors or Wall Street self-regulatory organizations, such as FINRA.

Under Dodd-Frank a successful enforcement action requires the SEC or CFTC to obtain over $1 million in sanctions from the fraudster. But once that threshold is reached, a whistleblower can collect rewards based on fines, penalties, and other sanctions obtained by these other agencies, even if those violations have nothing to do with the violation of securities laws. It is the $1 million-plus sanction under the securities laws that triggers the related action rule. Dodd-Frank clearly spells out the conditions that must be met in order for a whistleblower to qualify for a related action payment:

> *In any [enforcement action brought by the Commission that results in a sanctions of $1 million or more] . . . the Commission . . . shall pay an award or awards to 1 or more whistleblowers who voluntarily provided original information to the Commission that led to the successful enforcement of [a]* **related action,** *in an aggregate amount equal to— (A) not less than 10 percent, in total, of what has been collected of the monetary sanctions imposed in the [SEC enforcement] action or* **related actions;** *and (B) not more than 30 percent, in total, of what has been collected of the monetary sanctions imposed in the [SEC enforcement] action or* **related actions.**

Without either the SEC or CFTC issuing a sanction of over $1 million, no related action payments can be made. But once that requirement is met, prosecutions pursued by other agencies can also qualify for a reward. This procedure radically expands the scope of the Dodd-Frank Act (and other laws that also have a related action provision) and creates a *de facto* nationwide whistleblower reward law, if you can meet the related action requirements.

Here is how it works in practice. Say, for example, that a publicly traded mining company is accused of violating the Securities Exchange Act by failing to disclose environmental crimes to investors that could result in a billion-dollar clean-up. Although the case originates with the SEC as a Dodd-Frank claim, it is clear that these violations may also impact laws enforced by other agencies, such as the Environmental Protection Agency. Under Dodd-Frank, if the SEC sanctions the company $10 million for violating the Securities Exchange Act, the whistleblower would be entitled to a minimum reward of $1 million (10 percent) and a maximum reward of $3 million (30 percent) for the securities law violations.

But this is just the beginning of the potential impact. In this example, assume that the information the whistleblower gave to the SEC was also shared with the EPA, and the EPA thereafter fined the company $100 million for polluting the environment. Under the related action rule, the whistleblower would also be entitled to a reward based on the fines and penalties imposed by the EPA. This reward would be paid within the same statutory range as the direct SEC action. Because the EPA fine was significantly larger than the SEC penalties, the related action reward will be significantly larger than the reward paid for the securities law violations. In this hypothetical the minimum related action reward would be $10 million (10 percent of the EPA fine) and the maximum $30 million (30 percent of the EPA fine), triggered by the pollution-related crimes. Assuming that the SEC decided to make an award of 10 percent to this claimant, the total amount of compensation obtained by the whistleblower would be $11 million, $1 million paid as a result of the SEC sanction and $10 million paid because of the EPA fine.

This is what happened in the case decided by the SEC on September 16, 2021 (the case discussed at the beginning of this chapter). The SEC sanctioned the corporation $40 million for violations of the securities laws. Because another agency also sanctioned the company, the whistleblower was additionally entitled to a related action award. The fine issued by the other agency had to be extremely large, as the related action award was $70 million.

The whistleblower in that case obtained a total reward of $110 million: $40 million for the securities law violation and another $70 million for the related action sanction issued by another agency.

By incentivizing whistleblowers to fully cooperate in all the investigations related to their actionable evidence, Congress provided a mechanism to ensure that a whistleblower's insider information would benefit the public interest to the maximum extent possible, so all "rogues" could be brought to justice.

Currently, three laws have nearly identical related action provisions: the two enacted as part of the Dodd-Frank Act (covering commodities and securities law violations, along with violations of the Foreign Corrupt Practices Act), and the newly minted anti-money laundering (AML) whistleblower reward law. Although similar in almost all respects, each law has a slightly different definition of the agencies for which they will pay related action awards. All three laws cover related federal enforcement actions and state criminal prosecutions. The AML and commodities laws also cover state non-criminal cases, while the commodities law covers actions taken by international commodities regulators too.

The tax whistleblower law and False Claims Act also permit rewards to be paid for related actions. But the IRS and Justice Department have been far more reluctant to use those authorities. At one point, the IRS denied a reward based on a related criminal prosecution against a bank that was facilitating offshore tax evasion. The Tax Court rejected the IRS's narrow interpretation and ordered the whistleblower to be paid both on the direct tax case and on the related criminal prosecution conducted by the Justice Department. But despite the reluctance from some agencies, the SEC and CFTC are implementing the law, and Congress's intent to use whistleblowers in the most effective manner possible is being realized, much to the surprise of numerous white-collar criminals.

Keeping Up with the Changes

To keep up to date on changes in the laws, whistleblowers should access the free online law library created by the author, located at www.kkc.com/law-library.

- The Dodd-Frank Act related action provisions are codified at 15 U.S.C. § 78u-6(a)(5) (SEC) and 7 U.S.C. § 26(a)(5) (CFTC).

- The IRS related action provision is codified at 26 U.S.C. § 7623(b)(1).

- The Tax Court decision broadly apply "related" criminal actions: *Whistleblower 21276-13W v. Commissioner of IRS*, 147 Tax Court 4 (2015).

- The False Claims Act has a similar "alternative remedy" provision codified at 31 U.S.C. § 3730(c)(5).

- The AML whistleblower law's related action provision is codified at 31 U.S.C. § 5323(a)(4).

- *Whistleblower Award Proceeding* No. 2021-91 (decision of the SEC making a $70 million related action payment) is linked at https://www.sec.gov/news/press-release/2021-177.

PART IV

Retaliation—Fighting Back

It is the duty and right . . . of every citizen . . . to communicate to the executive officers any information which he has of the commission of an offense against those laws; and such information, given by a private citizen, is privileged.
—In re Quarles and Butler, 158 U.S. 532 (U.S. Supreme Court, 1895)

RULE 26

Find the Federal Law That Works

Whenever a whistleblower is facing retaliation, the first question to ask is what law should be relied on to protect your job? Any anti-retaliation law worthy of consideration must, at a minimum, reasonably define protected activity, cover your industry, ensure due process, and permit you to obtain a complete "make whole" remedy, including reinstatement to your job, back pay, attorney fees, and reasonable damages.

The second question is where to file the case. There are generally three possible choices: federal court, state court, or the U.S. Department of Labor. These laws may overlap and may offer a whistleblower a choice of forum.

How do you find the best federal law that will actually protect you? Carefully. There is no one general law protecting all whistleblowers. Instead, the laws cover specific industries and specific violations. Federal whistleblower protections were enacted on a scandal-by-scandal basis, and there is no uniformity in this web of legal remedies.

The procedures for filing retaliation cases are not the same as those required for filing a reward claim. For example, under the tax whistleblower law, reward claims are filed by submitting a Form 211 to the IRS. The retaliation case is filed with the Department of Labor. You cannot file your tax reward case with the DOL, nor can you file your retaliation case with the IRS. Confusing? You bet. The procedures for applying for a reward and the procedures for protecting your job follow completely different litigation lanes.

What follows is a summary of major federal whistleblower laws prohibiting retaliation in private corporations. A list of federal whistleblower laws, including proper citations and references to important cases decided under those laws are available online at the following website: www.kkc.com/law-library. State whistleblower laws and federal whistleblower laws governing government employees are outlined in Rules 27 (state laws), 28 (state and local government employees), 29 (federal employees), and 30 (national security).

Where to File a Retaliation Case under Federal Law

Federal whistleblower laws provide two different procedures for filing a complaint against a corporate employer. Some laws require a whistleblower to file an employment case directly in U.S. District Court. These include cases under the First Amendment and those filed under the Commodity Exchange Act. The second category requires that cases be filed with a federal administrative agency, such as the Department of Labor or the Equal Employment Opportunity Commission (EEOC). Each law clearly sets forth the mandatory filing requirements.

THE U.S. DEPARTMENT OF LABOR WHISTLEBLOWER LAWS

Most federal corporate whistleblower laws require filing a complaint with the U.S. Department of Labor (DOL). But after the initial filing some of the laws permit employees to remove their case to federal court and request a trial by jury. Other laws require you to have your case heard by DOL Administrative Law Judges. Either way, you have to file a timely complaint with the DOL Occupational Safety and Health Administration (OSHA). Complaints can be very informal and do not have to conform to the standards required under the Federal Rules of Civil Procedure.

Under these DOL laws, filing the complaint triggers an investigation by OSHA. OSHA will make a merits determination concerning the case. Either the employee or employer can appeal and request a hearing before a Department of Labor Administrative Law Judge (ALJ). Once the ALJ issues a final order, either side can appeal to the DOL Administrative Review Board (ARB). The ARB issues a final order that can thereafter be appealed to the U.S. Court of Appeals with jurisdiction over the proceeding.

Although the initial employment case *must* be filed with the DOL, some of the whistleblower laws permit the employee (*not* the employer) to opt out of the Labor Department forum and have their case heard in federal court (usually with the right to a jury trial). Under these laws an employee has a choice: Proceed with the case before a DOL judge or remove the case to federal court. This is a unique option that permits employees to decide which forum is better suited for their case. In all such cases a whistleblower must ask the following critical question: Should I have my case decided by a DOL judge or should it go before a federal judge and potentially a jury? This decision will dictate who will decide the merits of a case, but also what procedures will be applied and what legal precedents will control the outcome.

Even though many whistleblowers and their attorneys believe that federal court is always best, this can be a big mistake. Only the whistleblower has the right to move a case from the DOL to federal court. This gives the whistleblower a distinct advantage. The whistleblower can carefully consider numerous factors and select the best forum to obtain justice. Additionally, there is no rush to remove a case. The employee can conduct discovery and file various pretrial motions while the case is pending at the DOL, giving the whistleblower the ability to judge the fairness of the Labor Department remedy. The right to remove a case to federal court only terminates when the Labor Department issues a final decision, which can take years.

Among the factors that may be relevant in figuring out whether to remove a case from the DOL into federal court are:

- **Who the judge will be:** The removal decision can be made after a DOL judge is assigned. The reputation of the local federal judges who could hear the case should be well known to most practicing attorneys. Similarly, the decisions issued by DOL judges in whistleblower cases can all be accessed online at the DOL Office of Administrative Law Judges website.

- **Costs:** DOL proceedings are far less expensive than those in federal court. There are no filing fees, and if an employee loses a case, an employer cannot obtain cost reimbursements from the whistleblower.

- **Case law:** The legal precedents governing the Labor Department judges are sometimes better than those applied by federal judges. Whistleblowers can identify the tricky legal issues that may arise in their case and determine whether the DOL has better legal precedent on these issues then the federal courts.

- **Relaxed rules of evidence:** The DOL has relaxed rules of evidence, making it easier for employees to present their cases or admit hearsay evidence.

- **Effective procedures:** The rules of procedure for DOL cases are based on the same rules governing federal court proceedings. The DOL rules are published at 29 Code of Federal Regulations Part 18. The discovery rules in both federal court and the DOL are very similar, but those in the DOL do not have some of the procedural restrictions that are in the federal rules.

- **Worker-friendly venue:** DOL hearings are conducted close to the employee's home, and most issues related to the proper venue or jurisdiction of a court do not arise.

- **Sanctions:** The DOL prohibits, or severely limits, any sanctions that can be imposed on an employee, and the laws do not permit workers or their attorneys to be sanctioned under what is commonly known as "Rule 11." The few laws that do permit sanctions generally limit them to a token amount, such as $1,000. Taking away the threat of facing sanctions is a major plus for whistleblowers. But once a case is removed to federal court, there is nothing to stop an employer from seeking sanctions against a whistleblower.

- **Counterclaims:** Employers cannot file counterclaims against employees in the DOL.

- **Taping:** The DOL has good case law regarding whether or not taping is a protected disclosure or otherwise should be permitted and/or introduced into evidence.

- **Scope of protected activity and news media contact:** The DOL's precedent on the scope of protected activity is very whistleblower-friendly. The Labor Department has favorable case law on protecting communications with the news media. Federal courts have little or no precedent on this issue, with mixed holdings.

- **Third-party witness subpoenas:** This is one area where the federal courts have a distinct advantage. Employers generally must produce, for deposition or as trial witnesses, their own employees or managers. But persons who do not work for the employer may refuse to testify in DOL cases. Third-party subpoenas can be enforced in federal court, an option that is often not available in DOL cases.

- **Adding claims:** If a case is removed to federal court, a whistleblower can join the federal case with other potential federal or state law remedies. Thus, if the whistleblower wants to pursue a state common law claim, removal is the best option.

- **Jury trials:** Removal to federal court also permits the whistleblower to have their case heard by a jury.

The following laws permit the employee to remove their DOL case to federal court after exhausting administrative remedies:

Affordable Care Act

Anti-Money Laundering Act

Atomic Energy and Energy Reorganization Act

Auto Safety Act

Consumer Financial Protection Act

Consumer Product Safety Act

Criminal Anti-Trust Act

Food Safety Act

National Transit Security Act

Pipeline Safety Act

Railway Safety Act

Sarbanes-Oxley Act

Seaman's Protection Act

Surface Transportation Act

Taxpayer First Act

The following laws require the employee to adjudicate their case within the Department of Labor:

Airline Safety Act

Clean Air Act

Comprehensive Environmental Response, Compensation and Liability Act (better known simply as the "Superfund" law)

Water Pollution Control Act

Safe Drinking Water Act

Solid Waste Disposal Act

Toxic Substances Control Act

PRACTICE TIPS

- The rules of practice in adjudicating these cases before the DOL Office of Administrative Law Judges are located at 29 C.F.R. Part 18.

- DOL decisions in environmental whistleblower cases are all located online at https://www.dol.gov/agencies/oalj/topics/libraries/LIBWHIST.

- A comprehensive list of the DOL whistleblower protection laws, along with citations to major cases decided under these laws, is located on the free online law library created by the author, located at www.kkc.com/law-library.

Other Federal Whistleblower Anti-Retaliation Laws

BANKING AND FINANCIAL INSTITUTIONS

There is no single whistleblower law that covers banks. If you can obtain coverage, the best anti-retaliation laws available to bankers are the laws covering tax whistleblowers, the Sarbanes-Oxley Act, or the Dodd-Frank Act. Depending on the nature of the underlying violations, these three laws can be used effectively to protect bankers. The AML whistleblower law has a strong anti-retaliation provision. However, employees at FDIC-insured institutions and credit unions are currently unable to use that law.

If you do not fit within one of these laws, your default protections come from three older whistleblower laws that cover employees at credit unions, financial institutions, FDIC-insured institutions, federal banking agencies, and the Federal Reserve. All three laws are essentially identical in nature and protect employees who blow the whistle on "gross mismanagement," "gross waste of funds," an abuse of authority, possible violations of any law or regulation, or specific dangers to the public health or safety. Cases must be filed directly in federal court. Damages include reinstatement, compensatory damages, and other appropriate remedies. There is a two-year statute of limitations for filing a case. These laws do not provide for statutory attorney fees. Also, the definition of protected activity is completely deficient, and internal disclosures to management are not protected.

COMMODITY EXCHANGE ACT

See Rules 19 and 20.

CONTRACTOR AND GRANTEE WHISTLEBLOWER PROTECTION ACT

On December 14, 2016, Congress made permanent a law designed to protect persons who work for federal contractors or under a federal grant. The act contains a number of job-protection provisions that complement or expand on the anti-retaliation provisions of the False Claims Act. These include a broad definition of protected activity (including internal complaints), a pro-employee burden of proof, and the ability to have a claim investigated by the Office of Inspector General before having to decide whether or not to file a complaint in federal court. Section (c)(7) of the law should prohibit mandatory arbitration of disputes. The law does not cover contractors performing work on behalf of the intelligence community. The False Claims Act anti-retaliation provision contains no such exception.

Complaints must be filed within three years of an adverse action with the Office of Inspector General for the agency that awarded the grant or contract. Employees can file claims in federal court once administrative remedies are exhausted. Damages available under the act are consistent with other whistleblower laws, including reinstatement, back pay, compensatory damages, and attorney fees and costs.

This law complements the False Claims Act. See Rule 17.

DISCRIMINATION LAWS

Every major employment discrimination law contains an anti-retaliation provision. They prohibit retaliation against employees who oppose discriminatory practices or who blow the whistle on violations of equal employment opportunity laws, such as Title VII of the Civil Rights Act and the Age Discrimination Act.

The employment discrimination laws that have anti-retaliation provisions include Titles VII and IX of the Civil Rights Act of 1964, the Americans with Disabilities Act, the Age Discrimination Act, the Fair Labor Standards Act, the National Labor Relations Act, the Family and Medical Leave Act, the Employee Polygraph Protection Act, the Migrant and Seasonal Agricultural Workers Act, and the Employee Retirement Income Security Act.

DODD-FRANK WALL STREET REFORM AND CONSUMER PROTECTION ACT

The Dodd-Frank Act's whistleblower protections under the Securities Exchange Act, the Commodity Exchange Act, and the Foreign Corrupt Practices Act are explained in Rules 19 and 20.

EMPLOYMENT CONTRACTS/UNION GRIEVANCE PROCEDURES

Most union contracts protect employees (including government employees) from dismissal unless "good cause" exists. Obviously, firing a worker simply for making a lawful disclosure of misconduct to the appropriate authority would not constitute good cause. In these cases an employee has the option to seek protection through their labor union under contract, grievance, or arbitration procedures. However, utilizing these remedies may result in the waiver of an employee's right to obtain relief under other whistleblower protection laws, and damages available in grievance or arbitration proceedings may be limited.

FALSE CLAIMS ACT

The False Claims Act is explained in Rule 17.

FEDERAL EMPLOYEES

Protections for federal employees are explained in Rules 29 and 30.

FINANCIAL INSTITUTIONS REFORM, RECOVERY, AND ENFORCEMENT ACT

The Financial Institutions Reform, Recovery, and Enforcement Act (FIRREA) created civil liability for violations of fourteen underlying criminal laws, mostly as they relate to banks (or "federally insured financial institutions" as defined in the statute). These laws include mail and wire fraud, making false statements to government officials, and financial institution fraud. If someone makes a *criminal* false statement to a government official related to fraud in a bank, that person can be criminally indicted under criminal law. But that person can also be held civilly liable for money damages under FIRREA.

FIRREA contains a weak and ineffective reward law that offers no job protection. Rewards are paid at the discretion of the government. Whistleblowers have no enforceable rights. If a whistleblower is lucky enough to be granted an award (which rarely occurs), compensation is capped at a maximum of $1.6 million. Even the U.S. attorney general recognized that this maximum award would not properly incentivize employees to risk their careers to step forward and in many cases would not even compensate Wall Street bankers for their direct financial losses when they were fired for being whistleblowers. In 2014 the attorney general called for the law to be amended, consistent with the False Claims Act.

FIRREA has unique filing provisions that require a whistleblower to execute a detailed declaration and confidentially file it with the attorney general. These provisions are set forth in Title 12 U.S. Code, sections 4201–23. Declarations must be made under oath and explain the basis of the whistleblower's information. The factual assertion should be very specific and must contain "at least one new factual element necessary to establish a prima facie case" of a FIRREA violation that was unknown to the government.

While waiting for FIRREA to be fixed, whistleblowers do have a number of other options. The bank frauds that trigger FIRREA liability may also trigger liability under other federal laws with stronger whistleblower provisions, such as the Securities Exchange Act, the IRS reward law, the False Claims Act, and the Commodity Exchange Act. The AML Whistleblower Enhancement Act should always be considered as an option, as the law covers the Bank Secrecy Act.

The key in bank fraud cases is not to rely solely on FIRREA, but to think outside the box and determine whether the bank's misconduct also violated other civil or criminal laws that have real reward provisions.

FIRST AMENDMENT PROTECTIONS FOR PUBLIC EMPLOYEES

State and local employee-whistleblowers are covered under the First Amendment to the U.S. Constitution and the Civil Rights Act of 1871, 42 U.S.C. § 1983, which are discussed in Rule 28.

IMMIGRATION LAW: POLITICAL ASYLUM

Whistleblowers have been granted political asylum in the United States. The landmark case concerned Dionisio Grava, who worked for the Philippine government's Bureau of Customs where he witnessed corrupt supervisors profiting from smuggling schemes. He blew the whistle. At first he was falsely accused of work-related misconduct but was completely cleared of any wrongdoing. Failing that, his bosses transferred him to an outlying post in an attempt to shut him up. That did not work. In defiance of his direct supervisor's wishes, he filed charges and testified against a customs official in a corruption case. Unfortunately for Grava, the official had "family ties to the Philippine Congress and the National Bureau of Investigations." The retaliation got personal. His pet dog was poisoned; his car tires were slashed; and he received death threats. Fearing for his life, Grava fled to the United States. Upon arrival, he applied for political asylum.

The U.S. immigration authorities (the Immigration and Naturalization Service, or INS) initially ruled that he must be deported. The INS refused to recognize whistleblowers as a group that could qualify for asylum, but a landmark ruling from the U.S. Court of Appeals for the Ninth Circuit reversed the deportation order. The court noted that Grava's "tormentors" were not "mere criminals or guerrilla forces," but rather they were "instruments of the government itself."

Not every whistleblower can obtain asylum, though "where the whistle blows against corrupt government officials, it may constitute political activity sufficient to form the basis of persecution. . . . [O]fficial retaliation against those who expose and prosecute governmental corruption may, in appropriate circumstances, amount to persecution on account of political opinion."

The process for filing for asylum as a whistleblower is completely distinct from the legal remedies available under other whistleblower laws. Whistleblowers seeking asylum should contact attorneys with expertise in immigration law.

MEDICARE/MEDICAID AND HEALTHCARE FRAUD

There is no specific federal law covering whistleblowers who allege fraud in healthcare programs. However, the False Claims Act and its powerful *qui tam* whistleblower procedures cover all medical treatments paid for by Medicare and Medicaid. Thus, healthcare providers, pharmaceutical companies, pharmacists, doctors, dentists, hospitals, hospice centers, and nursing homes can all be found liable under the False Claims Act if they misuse federal monies.

The most common types of Medicare or Medicaid fraud include:

- Payments of kickbacks to induce providers to prescribe products or prescriptions

- Billing for unnecessary procedures or procedures not performed

- Billing for unnecessary medical tests or tests never performed

- Billing for unnecessary equipment

- Upcoding

- Mistreatment at nursing homes

- Overcharge for services or products

- Off-label marketing of prescriptions, devices, or equipment

The FCA's *qui tam* procedures are fully explained in Rule 17. A majority of states have similar laws that cover the use of state and local taxpayer funds.

MILITARY/ARMED SERVICES

The Military Whistleblower Protection Act permits members of the armed services to lawfully communicate with Congress, their chain of command, and military inspectors general. The act also permits members of the armed services to raise allegations of violations of law, discriminatory conduct, and "gross mismanagement, a gross waste of funds, an abuse of authority, or a substantial and specific danger to public health and safety."

Retaliation cases are filed with the Office of Inspector General. There is a sixty-day statute of limitations, but the IG can waive that deadline. Once filed, the IG must expeditiously review the claims and determine whether a full investigation is warranted. The IG's report of investigation is filed with the secretary for the division of the military for which the member served. Appeals of the IG actions can thereafter be filed with the Board for Correction of Military Records. The board can conduct a full evidentiary hearing. The board's ruling is then provided to the head of the relevant military department for a ruling. That decision is appealable to the secretary of defense. If a final decision is not rendered within 180 days, the service member is deemed to have exhausted their administrative remedies and should be able to appeal the rulings to court.

Under the law, members of the armed services who prevail in whistleblower cases are entitled to a wide range of relief, including correction of their military records, financial compensation, and remedies related to any courts-martial that may have been retaliatory.

In a time when heroes seem few and far between, [whistleblowers] stand as brave examples to our sons & daughters of what it means to live by our convictions. Thank god for you. Yours is preventative medicine; the thousands of lives you've saved as a result of your individual acts of courage can't be counted. But through your work you heal the future. The inspiration of your acts encourages others to take the same tough stand. You're not alone.
—Statement provided to the National Whistleblower Center from Academy Award–winning actress Meryl Streep, who played Karen Silkwood in the Hollywood movie *Silkwood*

MINE HEALTH AND SAFETY

Miners who raise health and safety complaints are protected under the Mine Health and Safety Act. Administered by the Department of Labor, the law protects complaints raised internally with mine management and those filed with government officials. There is a sixty-day statute of limitations. Employees are entitled to preliminary reinstatement pending the outcome of a hearing if the Mine Health and Safety Commission determines that a complaint was not "frivolously brought." Remedies under the act include reinstatement, back pay, and attorney fees.

Although the law contains some progressive features, the statute of limitations is short; damages are limited; and there is no right to a federal court trial. The Mine Health and Safety Commission publishes a very informative online booklet on miners' rights to report safety problems. The booklet is available at https://www.msha.gov/miners-rights-and-responsibilities.

OBSTRUCTION OF JUSTICE/RICO

What happens when a whistleblower is a witness in a federal law enforcement proceeding and is called a rat and a "snitch ass bitch" on Facebook? That Facebook bully risks getting busted. This happened in the case of *U.S. v. Edwards*, where the U.S. Court of Appeals for the Sixth Circuit upheld the conviction of a person who derided a witness on Facebook. The harasser was criminally prosecuted under the whistleblower protection provision of the obstruction of justice laws. The penalty—three months jail time and three and a half years of supervised release—was intended to send a clear message: Retaliating against a whistleblower can land you in jail. The defendant argued that her Facebook statements did not result in any concrete harm, but instead constituted "everyday activity on Facebook." But identifying the whistleblower, who was acting as a confidential informant, and instilling fear in her were enough for the court to uphold the guilty verdict.

The obstruction of justice statute sets forth a clear public policy outlawing discrimination against whistleblowers who provide truthful information to federal law enforcement:

> *Whoever knowingly, with the intent to retaliate, takes any action harmful to any person, including interference with the lawful employment or livelihood of any person, for providing to a law enforcement officer any truthful information relating to the commission or possible commission of any Federal offense, shall be fined under this title or imprisoned not more than 10 years, or both.*

The law does not permit whistleblowers to sue for damages. Instead, as a criminal law it is the responsibility of the U.S. Attorney's Office to file charges against a retaliator. Whistleblowers who suffer damages as a result of a violation of this law may be entitled to restitution under federal victim protection laws. However, violations of the obstruction of justice law can give rise to a civil cause of action for damages.

In 2011 the U.S. Court of Appeals for the Seventh Circuit considered whether retaliating against a whistleblower in violation of the obstruction of justice statute violated the Racketeer Influenced and Corrupt Organizations Act (better known as "Civil RICO"). Michael J. DeGuelle worked in the tax department of S.C. Johnson & Son, Inc. He was fired after reporting millions of dollars in alleged tax fraud schemes to federal law enforcement agencies. DeGuelle sought protection under the RICO statute because he contacted federal cops and suffered more than two acts of retaliation. The court ruled that whistleblowers who are retaliated against in violation of § 1513e) can sue their employer under the Civil RICO statute, provided they meet the other qualifications under that act. The RICO statute provides very strong remedies for victims who suffer a harm, including double damages. Civil RICO cases are filed directly in federal court, and a jury trial is available.

PRACTICE TIPS

- The federal obstruction of justice statute prohibiting retaliation against whistleblowers is codified at 18 U.S.C. § 1513(e).

- The U.S. Court of Appeals for the Seventh Circuit case upholding a RICO cause of action based on whistleblower retaliation is cited as *DeGuelle v. Camilli*, 664 F.3d 192 (7th Cir. 2011).

- Other criminal laws may also be implicated whenever a federal witness is threatened or harmed.

OSHA/WORKPLACE SAFETY

One of the first federal whistleblower protection laws was the Occupational Safety and Health Act of 1970, administered by the Occupational Safety and Health Administration, or OSHA. As is true with other older whistleblower laws, the protections offered under this law are weak and often ineffective. Whistleblowers should consider some of the alternative remedies outlined below.

The Department of Labor's OSHA division is responsible for investigating allegations of retaliation and filing lawsuits on behalf of whistleblowers who suffer discrimination based on reporting workplace hazards or refusing to perform life-threatening work. If victorious, the employee is entitled to "all appropriate relief," which includes reinstatement, back pay, and compensatory and punitive damages.

But as one of the first whistleblower laws passed by Congress, it has major flaws. First, a worker must file their discrimination claim within thirty days of the adverse action. This short statute of limitations results in numerous claims being automatically denied.

Second, there is no "private right of action." It is up to OSHA to protect the employee. An employee's complaint triggers an OSHA investigation, but not a lawsuit. Only OSHA can file a case in court against an employer. If OSHA does not prosecute on your behalf, you have *no federal remedy*. Even if OSHA does file a lawsuit on your behalf (which is very rare), OSHA controls the pace of the lawsuit and is responsible for any settlement.

OSHA's resources are limited, and it cannot file a lawsuit on behalf of every meritorious claim. The vast majority of employees obtain no relief whatsoever. The lucky few do not get rich. Indeed, when OSHA does act on behalf of a worker (which it does in just a minority of cases), the results are abysmal. According to the most recent statistics available, in 2007 OSHA settled 172 occupational safety cases. The average settlement was $5,288. Not one case settled for over $100,000. In other words, if an employer fires a worker who complains about safety, even if OSHA gets involved in the case, the penalty is token.

In 2021 OSHA adjudicated 2,263 cases, but only issued a merits decision in favor of twenty-one employees. OSHA reported that it was able to reach a settlement in 286 cases, and also reported that an additional 312 cases obtained an outcome described as "settled/other." Regardless of these statistics, the stories of employees abandoned by OSHA are indeed horrific. For example, Roger Wood reported serious worker safety problems at the Johnson Atoll Chemical Agent Disposal System, a worksite that processed highly toxic chemicals. After OSHA investigated his safety claims, it found that the company was guilty of two serious safety violations. But the fact that his employer violated the law and threatened the safety of its workers did not protect Wood from losing his job. Like thousands of others, Wood looked for help from OSHA.

OSHA investigators concluded he had a valid complaint and ordered relief. The company arrogantly ignored the findings and dared OSHA to file a lawsuit. After *ten years* of administrative delays, OSHA lawyers backed down. Wood challenged this decision in court and demanded either that OSHA protect his rights or that he be able to file a lawsuit on his own behalf. The courts threw out his case. They ruled that only OSHA can file a lawsuit on behalf of a fired worker and that there was no private right of action. Despite an administrative finding that he was illegally fired and despite having exposed two serious safety violations, Wood had no remedy, and his company got off scot-free. Wood was left with nothing.

What lesson should be learned from this hardship and delay? Employees fired for exposing safety hazards at work should not exclusively rely on OSHA for protection. It is best to look elsewhere.

In reaction to the defective federal Occupational Safety and Health Act, workers have sought relief under state whistleblower laws, often with great success. Most state courts that have addressed the issue recognize that the federal act is inadequate, and therefore they permit workers to pursue a case under state laws, regardless of any decision OSHA has made in a case. As explained by the Missouri Court of Appeals:

> *OSHA only allows an employee to file a complaint with the Secretary of Labor who then decides whether to bring an action . . . the employee's right to relief is further restricted in that the complaint must be filed within thirty days. . . . The decision to assert a cause of action is in the sole discretion of the Secretary of Labor and the statute affords the employee no appeal if the Secretary declines to file suit.*

Consistent with this ruling, the Kansas Supreme Court evaluated Occupational Safety and Health Act and also found it to be inadequate. The court permitted employees in Kansas to seek relief under the common law "public policy exception." Under this doctrine, whistleblowers were granted the right to file lawsuits based on state tort (i.e., personal injury) law. If they prevailed, they could request substantial relief from a jury, including back pay and other economic, compensatory, and punitive damages. Other state courts have followed these precedents, including Alaska, California, Illinois, Iowa, Minnesota, New Mexico, New Jersey, Nevada, Ohio, and Oklahoma.

In addition to common law remedies, a number of states have comprehensive whistleblower protection statutes that also protect OSHA-related whistleblowers from having their careers ruined for reporting safety problems at work. For example, the Maine Whistleblower Protection Act explicitly protects employees who raise concerns regarding "unsafe condition(s)" or practices that "put at risk the health or safety of that employee or any other individual."

Potential state law remedies for whistleblowers are further explained in Rule 27.

PUBLIC HEALTH/COVID-19

Congress has never passed a law directly covering employees who blow the whistle on threats to the public health and safety. Instead, a patchwork of laws can be used to protect these whistleblowers. The scope of coverage depends on where you work, for whom you work, and the violations you are reporting.

The first step is to determine if any of the violations implicate federal or state government money. If so, you may have a claim under the False Claims Act. This law may cover violations wherever government spending is at issue, such as healthcare paid for by Medicaid or Medicare.

Examples of the healthcare-related violations that could be covered by the False Claims Act were described in a March 3, 2020, public release by the Justice Department announcing a National Nursing Home Initiative. This release, unrelated to the outbreak of the coronavirus, explained that the Justice Department was targeting abuse at nursing homes that obtain Medicare funding for *qui tam* lawsuits. The types of violations included:

- Failure to provide adequate staff for residents

- Substandard hygiene and infection controls

- Inadequate nutrition for residents

- Improper use of physical or chemical restraints, including withholding of pain medication

- Inadequate facility cleanliness

The U.S. Supreme Court upheld such lawsuits. The Court held that the failure to provide required health services paid for by the government could trigger a False Claims Act *qui tam* case. In *Universal Health Services v. U.S. ex rel. Escobar*, the High Court held that a healthcare provider that did not use licensed physicians to treat patients could be liable in a case where a patient died at the hands of hired quacks. The *Escobar* case is instructive as to how a claim for federal or state government payments can result in a False Claims Act case based on the failure to provide proper medical services:

> *Specifically, liability can attach when the defendant submits a claim for payment that makes specific representations about the goods or services provided, but knowingly fails to disclose the defendant's noncompliance with a statutory, regulatory, or contractual requirement. In these circumstances, liability may attach if the omission renders those representations misleading.*

State and local government workers can seek protection under the First Amendment of the U.S. Constitution. Reporting threats to public health and safety would constitute speech of "public concern," permitting government workers to seek relief under the Constitution and its implementing statute, commonly referred to as 42 U.S.C. section 1983. This law, which provides strong remedial relief in federal court, is explained in Rule 28.

A third place to look is under state law and the doctrine known as the common law "public policy exception to the termination at-will doctrine" (explained in Rule 27).

Some states have also enacted specific laws covering nurses and/or disclosures of public health–related violations. The National Nurses Union (NNU) has published on its website an excellent survey of state laws covering health and safety issues, available at https://www.nationalnursesunited.org/whistleblower-protection-laws-for-healthcare-workers.

The Whistleblower Protection Act (WPA) is the primary law covering most federal employees. It has a specific provision protecting disclosures of "a substantial and specific danger to public health or safety." This provision does not apply to dangers that are speculative, but does cover credible threats to the public's safety. That law is explained in Rule 29.

Finally, employees within the federal Public Health Service are covered under the military whistleblower law. This law is explained below.

PUBLIC HEALTH SERVICE

Public Health Service (PHS) Commissioned Corps officers play a vital role within the Centers for Disease Control in protecting public health. The whistleblower regulations covering the PHS Commissioned Corps are rooted in the corps unique origin as part of the unarmed services (i.e., the doctors who treated wounded soldiers during the American Revolution). As a result of this unique history, PHS officers are covered under military law.

PHS officers may make protected disclosures to the following offices:

- A member of Congress

- An inspector general

- A member of a Department of Defense audit, inspection, investigation, or law enforcement organization

- Any person or organization in the chain of command

- Any other person or organization designated pursuant to regulations or other established administrative procedures for such communications

To be protected the whistleblower must "reasonably" believe that their disclosure "constitutes evidence of any of the following: (A) a violation of law or regulation. . . . Gross mismanagement, a gross waste of funds, an abuse of authority, or a substantial and specific danger to public health or safety." Whistleblowers have one year to file their retaliation complaints with the inspector general.

The PHS whistleblower law is weak. It does not guarantee a right to a hearing and has no provision for appealing decisions to federal court. Damages are not defined, and attorney fees are not included in the law. The PHS regulations implementing the military whistleblower law within the Public Health Service are outlined in Commissioned Corps Directive 121.06.

RACKETEER INFLUENCED AND CORRUPT ORGANIZATIONS ACT
See Obstruction of Justice/RICO.

SURFACE MINING ACT

The Surface Mining Act requires employees to file their whistleblower claim with the Department of the Interior within thirty days of an adverse action. The law is modeled on the Clean Air Act and permits the employee to have their case heard within the Interior Department. Few cases have been filed under this law, which has been virtually ignored by Interior.

TRADE SECRETS

The Defend Trade Secrets Act, 18 U.S.C. § 1833(b), established specific procedures by which employees can blow the whistle using information their employers classify as trade secrets, closing a major loophole in protection for whistleblowers.

Before this law was passed, corporations tried, often successfully, to silence whistleblowers by alleging that the concerns they raised included trade secrets and that their disclosure outside the company was prohibited by law. To close this loophole, Congress included a whistleblower immunity provision when it passed the Defend Trade Secrets Act in 2016. Employees who provide trade secret information to federal or state officials, pursuant to the procedures established in the law, are immunized from either civil or criminal liability under both federal and state law.

As explained in Senate Committee on the Judiciary Report 114-220, employees can disclose trade secret information to "a Federal, State, or local government official or to an attorney," if they do so "in confidence" and if the disclosure is "for the purpose of reporting or investigating a suspected violation of law."

Employees can also use trade secret information in a court proceeding, provided the lawsuit is filed "against an employer for retaliation for reporting a suspected violation of law." The litigation-disclosure rule permits trade secret information to be used in court as long as the whistleblower provides "any document containing the trade secret under seal and does not disclose the trade secret other than pursuant to a court order." Whistleblowers can confidentially show their attorneys trade secret information.

All employers are required to give their employees notice of this immunity provision. Failure to do so will prevent employers from obtaining exemplary damages or attorney fees from employees who disclose trade secrets in violation of the law. Under the law employees are still prohibited from releasing trade secret information to the public.

WITNESSES IN FEDERAL COURT PROCEEDINGS

As part of the Civil Rights Act of 1871, Title 42 of the United States Code section 1985, Congress prohibited all conspiracies to deter or harass witnesses who testified in U.S. court proceedings. The procedures and remedies under this law are identical to those afforded employees under the other portions of the CRA of 1871, and include the right to a trial by jury in federal court and the full array of damages. In the case of *Haddle v. Garrison*, 525 U.S. 121 (1998) the Supreme Court unanimously permitted an at-will employee to file a CRA claim after he was fired for obeying a federal grand jury subpoena for testimony.

- A comprehensive list of federal whistleblower protection laws, along with citations to major cases, is located on the free online law library created by the author, located at www.kkc.com/law-library.

- Employees can fully resolve employment disputes and still file a reward claim directly with federal authorities and in the Checklists at the end of the book.

Keeping Up with the Changes

To keep up to date on changes in the laws, whistleblowers should access the free online law library created by the author, located at www.kkc.com/law-library.

RULE 27

Don't Forget State Laws

Historically, employment relationships were controlled under the common law "at-will" doctrine. This doctrine, which was adopted by every state, gave employers a near-absolute right to fire workers for "any reason or no reason." It was a whistleblower who first put a fatal crack into this old laissez-faire rule.

In October 1955, Peter Petermann worked as a business agent for the Teamsters Union. He was called to testify before a California State Assembly committee looking into corruption. His supervisor demanded that Petermann falsely testify. Petermann refused and was consequently accused of disloyalty for embarrassing his union bosses when he "gave correct and truthful answers to all questions." He was summarily fired the very next day.

Petermann challenged his termination in state court. The lawyers representing his bosses argued that under the at-will doctrine companies could fire employees for any reason or no reason unless they had an employment contract. That was the standard rule governing employment in all fifty states. Breaking one hundred years of legal tradition, the California court rejected this argument. It held that the "right to discharge an employee" could be limited by public policy, even when there was no statute protecting the employee.

The court did not use the word *whistleblower*, as that term had not yet entered the vocabulary of employment law. But the court held that employees could not be fired for testifying about their company's wrongdoing: "It would be obnoxious to the interests of the state and contrary to public policy and sound morality to allow an employer to discharge any employee . . . who declined to commit perjury."

The court recognized Petermann's right to sue the Teamsters Union for damages, and awarded him $50,000.

This landmark decision upheld a cause of action for wrongful discharge based on a violation of public policy. A company could not use its economic might to punish an employee who simply wanted to follow the law and tell the truth in court. The whistle-blower revolution had started. Within twenty-five years the majority of states agreed with California, and today whistleblowers are protected under the common law in all but a few holdouts.

Under the public policy exception to the at-will doctrine, bosses can still fire employees for any reason or no reason; they just cannot fire workers for the wrong reason—for a reason that violates public policy. Most states consider this claim a tort, which means employees file their cases in court and have a right to a jury trial, and the juries can award economic damages (for example, lost wages and benefits), compensatory damages (loss of reputation and emotional distress), and, in egregious cases, punitive or exemplary damages.

Each state has its own definition of what type of conduct is protected under the public policy exception, but almost every state protects the following types of disclosures or conduct:

- Refusal to violate a law

- Performance of job duties required under law

- The exercising of a legally protected right (such as testifying in court or filing a workers' compensation claim)

- Reporting violations of law for the public benefit

If applicable, the public policy tort is a great fit for whistleblowers fighting retaliation, as it permits an employee to obtain punitive damages and have their case heard before a jury. But that is not the only common law remedy employees can use to protect their careers. Whistleblowers have also obtained coverage under more traditional causes of action, such as intentional infliction of emotional distress, defamation, breach of contract, and other similar remedies.

In addition to common law, a majority of states and a handful of municipalities have enacted their own versions of the False Claims Act, permitting whistleblowers to file *qui tam* reward cases when there is fraud in state and local government spending. The state FCAs are all modeled on the federal law, but each has its own unique features. These local FCAs also have anti-retaliation protections permitting employees to file retaliation claims for wrongful discharge and discrimination. New York and the District of Columbia have expanded their *qui tam* reward laws to cover tax frauds.

States are beginning to fully exploit the law enforcement potential unleashed under their False Claims Acts. Recent state law recoveries under the New York and California laws include:

- State of New York: $330 million settlement of New York FCA against Sprint; whistleblower obtained a $62.7 million award

- City of New York: $1.5 million settlement against Siemens Electrical, LLC

- State of New York: $105 million settlement of tax-related FCA case against the Hedge Fund of Thomas Sandell; whistleblower obtained a $22 million award

- State of California: $9.86 million recovery against Walgreens under California's Medicaid Program

- State of California: $241 million settlement against Quest Diagnostics

- State of California: $49.5 million settlement against Laboratory Corp. of America

- State of California: $102 million recovery against BP for overcharging schools and cities for natural gas

Specific State Laws

Listed here is a summary of where the states fall, but always check for changes in the state laws.

COMMON LAW PROTECTION

States that offer common law protections under the public policy exception are Alaska (limited to contract damages), Arizona (modified by statute), Arkansas (limited to contract damages), California, Colorado, Connecticut, Delaware, the District of Columbia, Florida (modified by statute), Hawaii, Idaho, Illinois, Indiana, Iowa, Kansas, Kentucky, Maryland, Massachusetts, Michigan (except if covered under a statutory remedy), Minnesota (except where displaced by statutory remedy), Mississippi, Missouri, Nebraska, Nevada, New Hampshire, New Jersey, New Mexico, North Carolina, North Dakota, Ohio (the legislature passed a weak whistleblower law, but the courts still permit common law public policy claims), Oklahoma, Oregon, Pennsylvania, Rhode Island, South Carolina, South Dakota (contract damages only), Tennessee, Texas, Utah, Vermont, Virginia, Washington, West Virginia, Wisconsin, and Wyoming (except if the employee is covered under another statute or a collective bargaining agreement). The exception is also recognized in Guam and the U.S. Virgin Islands.

STATES THAT HAVE REJECTED A COMMON LAW PUBLIC POLICY REMEDY FOR WHISTLEBLOWERS

Alabama, Georgia, Montana (the courts affirmed whistleblower rights under the public policy rule, but the state legislature enacted a law overturning that decision and implementing a very weak state law that provides no real protections for whistleblowers), and New York. Although these states have rejected common law remedies, Georgia, Montana, and New York enacted False Claims Act laws that cover numerous whistleblower disclosures. New York also amended its state whistleblower statute to broadly cover most whistleblowers. The trend to fully cover whistleblowers continues to expand, with Alabama being the only radical holdout.

STATES WITH A COMPREHENSIVE WHISTLEBLOWER PROTECTION ACT

Whistleblowers who reside in the following states should review their local Whistleblower Protection Acts: Arizona, Connecticut, Florida, Hawaii, Maine, Michigan, Minnesota, New Hampshire, New Jersey, New York, and Rhode Island.

OTHER STATE WHISTLEBLOWER PROTECTION STATUTES

In addition to state Whistleblower Protection Acts, almost every state has narrower whistleblower protection statutes that cover specific claims, such as occupational safety, protection for nurses and other specific professions, and special protections for state-employee whistleblowers. Many states have recognized whistleblowers' abilities to rely on traditional common law remedies, libel, breach of contract, or intentional interference torts.

STATES AND MAJOR CITIES WITH FALSE CLAIMS ACTS

Most states and some cities have passed False Claims Acts that protect the integrity of state and local taxpayer spending. Some are stronger than the federal law; others are weaker. The State of New York and the District of Columbia also permit whistleblowers to file a *qui tam* lawsuit for tax fraud under its state FCA. A number of states only cover fraud in state Medicaid programs. There is a strong trend for states to enact FCAs, so it is important to check your specific state to determine if a local FCA exists or if the laws have been amended.

The following states and major cities currently have FCAs: California, the City of Chicago, Colorado, Connecticut, Delaware, the District of Columbia, Florida, Georgia, Hawaii, Illinois, Indiana, Iowa, Louisiana, Maryland, Massachusetts, Michigan, Minnesota, Montana, Nevada, New Hampshire, New Jersey, New Mexico, New York, New York City, North Carolina, Oklahoma, Philadelphia and Allegheny County of Pennsylvania (the Commonwealth of Pennsylvania has not yet passed an FCA), Rhode Island, Tennessee, Texas, Vermont, Virginia, and Washington.

Preemption and Preclusion

Shortly after states commenced protecting whistleblowers, corporations went on a counterattack. The first phase was to use the federal preemption doctrine to have cases dismissed. Companies argued that federal whistleblower laws, which were weaker than state laws, should provide an exclusive remedy. In other words, states should be preempted from protecting whistleblowers because those protections would somehow interfere with the implementation of the federal whistleblower laws.

This issue came to a head in 1990 when nuclear whistleblower Vera English challenged the federal preemption doctrine before the U.S. Supreme Court. Her federal case was dismissed due to the thirty-day statute of limitations contained in the federal law. The Supreme Court unanimously sided with English, permitted her to file a new case under state common law, and put an end to the federal preemption defense in whistleblower cases.

One pitfall that must be carefully avoided is the preclusion defense. A number of states do not permit employees to pursue the common law public policy exception claim if a statutory remedy exists. These courts require an employee to use a statute, if one exists, arguing that the statute somehow precludes the use of a common law remedy. Although this doctrine is illogical, it does have its supporters.

One way to guard against having a case thrown out under the preclusion doctrine is to sue under both the common law and a federal or state whistleblower protection statute. If the common law remedy is precluded, the statutory remedy should still go forward. The reverse can also be true. For example, in one case decided by the U.S. Court of Appeals for the Ninth Circuit, the court threw out the federal Sarbanes-Oxley Act claim on technical grounds, but upheld a large jury verdict under California's common law.

Additionally, there is a judicial policy of requiring employees to include all claims in one lawsuit. Courts discourage parties from parceling out various causes of action and filing multiple lawsuits. Indeed, the failure to include all causes of action in one lawsuit can result in a waiver of non-included claims under arcane doctrines of law. If an employee files a claim in U.S. District Court, the Federal Rules of Civil Procedure permit the inclusion of state claims in the federal lawsuit under a doctrine known as "pendant jurisdiction."

PRACTICE TIPS

- Checklist 1 provides a summary list of states that have enacted False Claims Acts.

- Always consider filing a state retaliation lawsuit, even if your claims are also covered under a federal law.

- *Walder v. Bio-Rad Laboratories, Inc.*, 916 F.3d 1176 (9th Cir. Feb. 26, 2019) (dismissing federal claims, but upholding state common law cause of action).

Keeping Up with the Changes

To keep up to date on changes in the laws, whistleblowers should access the free online law library created by the author, located at www.kkc.com/law-library.

RULE 28

Government Retaliation: Use the First Amendment

The public interest in having free and unhindered debate on matters of public importance [is] the core value of the Free Speech Clause of the First Amendment . . . the threat of dismissal from public employment is [a] potent means of inhibiting speech.
—Justice Thurgood Marshall, *Pickering v. Board of Education*

For state and local government workers, the major breakthrough in whistleblower protection occurred in 1968, when the U.S. Supreme Court decided that the First Amendment guarantee of freedom of speech applied to public employees who blew the whistle on matters of public concern.

The case started after Marvin Pickering, a high school teacher from Will County, Illinois, wrote a letter to the local newspaper. He strongly criticized his school system for practicing "totalitarianism" and accused the school's administration of taking the taxpayers "to the cleaners" by mismanaging the high school. Pickering alleged that the school board was misleading voters in a hotly contested bond issue referendum and identified serious shortcomings at the school, including classrooms that lacked doors, the failure to have running water in the first-aid treatment room, and overcharging children in the cafeteria.

The board's reaction was typical. Pickering was accused of making false statements, impugning the "motives, honesty, integrity, truthfulness, responsibility and competence" of the board, and damaging the professional reputations of the school's administrators. His letter was labeled as "disruptive of faculty discipline." The board fired Pickering because the "publication of [his] letter was detrimental to the best interests of the school," and would foment "controversy, conflict and dissension" within the school system.

The Supreme Court decided the case in *Pickering v. Board of Education*. Writing for the Court Justice Thurgood Marshall held that the First Amendment prohibited government officials from using the power of the paycheck to cover up their own wrongdoing. Government workers who blew the whistle on matters of public concern were therefore protected from discrimination and wrongful discharge under the First Amendment's guarantee of freedom of speech.

The *Pickering* decision spelled out precisely why whistleblowers needed legal protections. Millions of government workers—from schoolteachers to police—could not afford to be fired from their jobs or lose their pensions simply for engaging in constitutionally protected speech. Without prohibiting retaliation, the underlying right to blow the whistle would be meaningless. Justice Marshall recognized that the threat of dismissal constitutes a "potent means of inhibiting speech."

The Supreme Court affirmed that public employees did not give up their constitutional rights when they took a job with the government. "[F]ree and unhindered debate on matters of public importance" is part of the "core value" standing behind the "Free

Speech Clauses of the First Amendment." Government workers were in a position to learn about official misconduct, and they often had specialized insider knowledge on matters of public concern that the people needed to know in order to make informed decisions within a democratic society.

However, these rights had limits. Whistleblowers were not immune from termination simply because they engaged in protected speech. The Supreme Court balanced the needs of employers to maintain discipline in their workplace with the right of free speech: "The problem in any case is to arrive at a balance between the interests of the teacher, as a citizen, in commenting upon matters of public concern and the interest of the State, as an employer, in promoting the efficiency of the public services it performs through its employees."

State and Local Government Workers and the Civil Rights Act of 1871

The Supreme Court ruling had teeth. It married an old Reconstruction-era civil rights law with the Constitutional right to freedom of speech. The Civil Rights Act of 1871, better known today simply as 42 U.S.C. section 1983, created a private cause of action for any person alleging that, under the "color of law," they were deprived of a right "secured by the Constitution and laws" of the United States. As a result of the *Pickering* decision, state and local government workers who were fired for blowing the whistle could collect damages under the 1871 act.

The Civil Rights Act permitted a tort-like remedy for whistleblowers. Employees can file lawsuits in federal court and obtain a trial by jury. Whistleblowers who prevail are entitled to a full range of damages and injunctive relief, including back pay, reinstatement, compensatory damages, punitive damages, and attorney fees and costs.

The Civil Rights Act of 1871 only covers violations committed by state and local government officials and does not apply to the federal government or private-sector jobs.

The law has a number of pitfalls, including a prohibition of directly suing a state government—the law permits lawsuits against persons, not the state. Thus, whenever a state government is responsible for the retaliation, it is imperative to name all the individual managers responsible for the termination, the governor of the state, and the head of the relevant state agency. Local governments can be directly sued.

The biggest setback to whistleblower protections under the First Amendment occurred in 2006 when the Supreme Court, in the case of *Garcetti v. Ceballos*, denied protection to public employees who reported wrongdoing through their chain of command. The Court ruled that employee disclosures made as part of their official duties were unprotected. According to the Supreme Court, public employees who exposed frauds to the news media, a state representative, or the city council could be protected, but alerting a supervisor to a fraud could get you fired with no federal remedy. Most whistleblowers initially report violations through their chain of command, and consequently the *Garcetti* case has blocked numerous public employees from coverage under the U.S. Constitution.

Injunctive Relief Under the First Amendment

State and federal government employees can also directly use the First Amendment to challenge workplace rules that harass, restrict, or prevent employee whistleblowing. For example, in 1992 the Environmental Protection Agency implemented "outside speaking" rules that restricted its employees from speaking publicly about problems with the agency. In *Sanjour v. EPA*, the rules were challenged under the First Amendment, resulting in a nationwide injunction preventing all federal agencies from using the rule to restrict whistleblowing speech. The whistleblower did not win damages, but rules that could have been used to discipline him were struck down as unconstitutional. The *Sanjour* precedent has been applied to state and local governments. In 2002, Justice Samuel Alito, while still an appeals court judge, applied *Sanjour* and other precedents to strike down an unconstitutional Philadelphia police department rule that limited the right of police officers to testify against their department.

PRACTICE TIPS

- *Pickering v. Board of Education*, 391 U.S. 563 (1968) (landmark case establishing First Amendment protection for public employee whistleblowers).

- *Garcetti v. Ceballos*, 547 U.S. 410 (2006) (affirming and explaining *Pickering*, but limiting protections for internal disclosures).

- Other important Supreme Court cases are *Lane v. Franks*, 573 U.S. 228 (2014) (explaining limits to *Garcetti*); *New York Times Co. v. Sullivan*, 376 U.S. 254 (1964) (protection against retaliatory libel lawsuit); *Carey v. Piphus*, 435 U.S. 247, 253 (1978) (§ 1983 creates tort-like liability); *Will v. Michigan*, 491 U.S. 58 (1989) (sovereign immunity issues).

- *Heck v. Humphrey*, 512 U.S. 477, 483 (1994) (no requirement to exhaust state administrative remedies).

Keeping Up with the Changes

To keep up to date on changes in the laws, whistleblowers should access the free online law library created by the author, located at www.kkc.com/law-library.

RULE 29

Federal Employees Are Special

In the vast federal bureaucracy it is not difficult to conceal wrongdoing provided that no one summons the courage to disclose the truth.
—Senate Report, Whistleblower Protection Enhancement Act (2012)

Federal employees often find themselves on the hot seat. They can witness abuses that are embarrassing to those who live in the White House. Their expertise is called on to address the hottest topics that divide the country, such as how to combat terrorism, protect the public from pandemics, or address climate change. They were the driving force in the three recent presidential impeachment proceedings ("Deep Throat" for Nixon, Linda Tripp for Clinton, and the anonymous "Ukraine whistleblower" for Trump). Given the sensitive nature of the work performed by civil servants, federal employees are regularly caught in the middle between special-interest lobbyists, political opportunists, and their obligation to simply do their jobs. They become whistleblowers, either by choice or just plain bad luck.

The Whistleblower Protection Act (WPA)

The Whistleblower Protection Act is the main law protecting federal employees. It covers applicants, employees, and former employees working in the federal civil service. Originally passed as part of the Civil Service Reform Act of 1978, the Senate Report accompanying that law spelled out the intent of the new whistleblower protections:

> *Often, the whistleblower's reward for dedication to the highest moral principles is harassment and abuse. Whistleblowers frequently encounter severe damage to their careers and substantial economic loss. Protecting employees who disclose government illegality, waste, and corruption is a major step toward a more effective civil service. In the vast federal bureaucracy, it is not difficult to conceal wrongdoing provided that no one summons the courage to disclose the truth. Whenever misdeeds take place in a federal agency, there are employees who know that it has occurred, and who are outraged by it. What is needed is a means to assure them that they will not suffer if they help uncover and correct administrative abuses.*

After its enactment in 1978, the law proved to be weak and ineffective. It was amended in 1989, but still did not function properly. Amended again in 1994, problems persisted. In 2012 it was amended once again. Although still plagued with continuing problems, some of its most glaring defects were fixed. But unlike the rights afforded to whistleblowers under most other laws, federal employees are required to have an administrative agency, the Merit Systems Protection Board (MSPB), decide their cases.

The board is supposed to act independently, but its composition undermines its independence. The board consists of three presidential appointees. Two of these members are required to be members of the political party that holds the White House, and one member is required to be a member of the opposition. Although Senate approval is needed for these appointments, there are no required judicial qualifications. The vast majority of federal employee cases are decided by this board.

PROTECTED ACTIVITY UNDER THE WPA

The Whistleblower Protection Act broadly describes what conduct is protected:

> *any disclosure of information by an employee or applicant which the employee or applicant reasonably believes evidences—(i) any violation of any law, rule, or regulation; or (ii) gross mismanagement, a gross waste of funds, an abuse of authority, or a substantial and specific danger to public health or safety, if such disclosure is not specifically prohibited by law . . . or Executive order [emphasis added].*

The WPA creates a safe haven by explicitly protecting disclosures to certain receiving offices such as the Office of Special Counsel or an inspector general. These disclosures may be made confidentially.

FILING A RETALIATION COMPLAINT

The WPA permits employees subjected to retaliatory discipline to seek protection from the Office of Special Counsel or the Merit Systems Protection Board, depending on the type of adverse action at issue. Employees can also choose to file a grievance under their union contract. These options are mutually exclusive.

Most federal employees file their initial whistleblower complaint with the Office of Special Counsel (OSC). Complaints can be confidentially filed, and the OSC is required to protect the whistleblower's privacy. Cases filed with the OSC trigger specific due process rights, culminating with the right to a hearing before an administrative judge and judicial review before the U.S. Court of Appeals. Parties to MSPB proceedings have the right to conduct discovery.

If an employee requests a hearing before the MSPB, the administrative judge must issue a written decision, which either party can appeal to the three-member board. The board then issues the final agency decision, which either party can appeal to the U.S. Court of Appeals. Judicial review is extremely narrow.

Some federal employees have the option to skip the OSC investigatory process and request an immediate hearing before an MSPB judge. There are two benefits to this option. First, the case will move very quickly, as the MSPB judges are required to expedite discovery and conduct the hearing on the merits in a fairly short time period. Second, the employee can demonstrate that the adverse action they are challenging violated other civil service rules, not just the prohibition against discriminating against whistleblowers. By filing a case directly with the MSPB, and bypassing the OSC, an employee can enjoy the full benefits of civil service protection.

Although confusing, it is important to remember that if you file your case directly to the OSC, the only issue that can be addressed is whether your adverse action violated the Whistleblower Protection Act. Even if the case is appealed to an MSPB judge, the only issue is the WPA issue. But if you are able to file directly with the MSPB judges, the MSPB and Court of Appeals also can decide whether your adverse action complied with the rules governing the civil service.

Another major distinction between filing your case with the OSC and filing it directly with an MSPB judge concerns the statute of limitations. The WPA has *no* statute of limitations; a complaint can be filed at any time with the OSC. However, if you are able to file a case directly with the MSPB, there is a thirty-day statute of limitations.

DISCOVERY

One of the major traps in the MSPB process concerns discovery. Discovery permits employees to question managers and obtain agency documents. Whistleblowers can learn all the justifications for the adverse action and try to obtain evidence that supports a finding that the discipline was not justified but motivated by retaliatory animus. But, as set forth in **Figure 21,** the MSPB's regulations concerning the timing of discovery requests are borderline bizarre:

- All initial discovery must be filed within thirty days of the administrative judge issuing the initial docketing order. In other words, it is best to have your discovery prepared and served at the time you file your request for a hearing.

- Responses to discovery must be served by the agency within twenty days. If the agency does not answer your discovery or if the answers are incomplete, you must file a motion to compel within ten days. Failure to file a motion

Figure 21

Discovery in Merit Systems Protection Board Employment Cases

Initial Disclosures	Filed within 10 days of the administrative judge's acknowledgement order.
Initial Discovery Requests (e.g., depositions, documents, interrogatories)	All initial disclosures filed within 25 days after the date the judge issues an order to the respondent agency to produce the agency file (which is usually contained in the acknowledgement order).
Response to Discovery Request	Filed within 20 days after the date of service of the request.
Additional Discovery Requests	Must be served within 10 days of the date of service of the prior response.
Motion to Compel	Must be filed within 10 days of the date of service of objections or, if no response is received, within 10 days after the time limit for the response has expired.
Motion to Dispose a Non-Party (third party discovery requests)	Submitted to the judge within 25 days after the date on which the judge issues an order to the respondent agency to produce the agency file.
Opposition to Motion to Compel	Filed with the judge within 10 days of the date of service of the motion.

to compel waives all your objections to the answers (or non-answers) of the agency. This procedure is the opposite of that used in federal court. Instead of trying to encourage parties to avoid filing discovery motions, the MSPB procedures force employees to file motions to compel.

- If you are intending to file a second round of discovery, it must be filed within ten days of the agency's responses to your initial discovery (or within ten days of the agency's failure to respond) or else discovery is considered completed. This rule is clearly designed to trap employees into waiving their discovery rights.

BURDEN OF PROOF AND REMEDIES

Congress created a pro-whistleblower standard of proof under the WPA. The first step to winning a WPA case is for the whistleblower to demonstrate that their protected disclosure was a contributing factor in the adverse personnel action. The proof necessary to demonstrate a contributing factor was intended to be very low. The WPA specifically authorized the use of circumstantial evidence alone to meet this burden and codified a timing test.

If the employee can meet the contributing factor threshold, the actual burden of proof shifts to the agency. Thereafter, the agency must demonstrate by "clear and convincing evidence that it would have taken the same personnel action in the absence" of the protected disclosures. These shifting burdens were designed by Congress to make it easier for whistleblowers to win their cases.

If the whistleblower prevails, the MSPB must order corrective action, which may include the following relief: (i) placing the whistleblower "as nearly as possible, in the position the individual would have been in had the prohibited personnel practice not occurred"; (ii) back pay and related benefits, medical costs incurred, travel expenses, any other reasonable and foreseeable consequential damages, and compensatory damages (including interest, reasonable expert witness fees, and costs); (iii) attorney fees and costs for the WPA case; and (iv) attorney fees and costs incurred as a result of any investigation conducted by the agency in retaliation for the protected disclosures.

Contacting Congress

In the early 1900s, Presidents Theodore Roosevelt and William Taft battled with Congress over whistleblower rights. Federal workers were providing information to Congress, and Roosevelt and Taft wished to silence them. They implemented gag rules restricting federal employees from communicating with Congress. This triggered a major dispute between Congress and the president. In 1912, after strenuous debate, Congress exercised its authority and passed the Lloyd-LaFollette Act. This law prohibits retaliation against federal employees who provide information to any member or committee of Congress. Communications with Congress are also protected under the WPA.

Communication with Congress is often a key to successful whistleblowing. A supportive member of Congress can exert significant pressure on the federal bureaucracy to stop retaliation.

The Alternative to Blowing the Whistle at Work: Outside Speaking and Writing (Including Talking to the Press)

One of the most effective avenues for public employees to expose wrongdoing is by speaking or writing outside of work. But like all constitutional rights, freedom of speech has its limits. Not all outside speech is protected.

The basic law governing the right of public employees, on their own time, to criticize their government agencies was established in the 1968 landmark case of *Pickering v. Board of Education*. The Supreme Court held: "Individuals do not automatically relinquish their rights under the First Amendment by accepting government employment" and consequently, it is essential that government employees "be able to speak out freely on [matters of public concern] without fear of retaliatory dismissal." This speech is protected even though the government employee is attacking his superiors: "Statements by public officials on matters of public concern must be accorded First Amendment protection despite the fact that the statements are directed at their nominal superiors."

Although *Pickering* concerned the rights of state and municipal government workers, the U.S. Supreme Court and D.C. Circuit Court of Appeals applied these principles to federal employees, too. In *United States v. National Treasury Employees Union*, the Supreme Court held that restricting the right of federal employees to engage in outside speaking and writing activities was unconstitutional. The *NTEU* decision was further clarified in the case of William Sanjour, a policy analyst for the Environmental Protection Agency, who sought permission to publicly criticize the agency's decision to permit toxic waste incinerators in poor and predominantly minority communities. In *Sanjour v. EPA*, the U.S. Court of Appeals for the D.C. Circuit held that government regulations that empower officials to restrict outside-employee speech based on the content or viewpoint of the speaker were unconstitutional:

> [A] law or policy permitting communication in a certain way for some but not for others raises the specter of content and viewpoint censorship. This danger is at its zenith when the determination of who may speak and who may not is left to the unbridled discretion of a government official. . . . [W]e have often and uniformly held that such statutes or policies impose censorship on the public or press, and hence are unconstitutional.

Both *NTEU* and *Sanjour* concerned challenges to government regulations that placed restrictions on outside speaking to, writing to, or teaching of federal employees. In each case the employees did not seek monetary damages. Instead, the cases requested broad injunctive relief, finding the challenged laws and regulations unconstitutional and unenforceable.

LIMITS ON OUTSIDE SPEAKING AND WRITING

The right of government employees to speak out on matters of public concern is broad, but not without limits. Federal employees should try to ensure that their outside disclosures are covered under the definition of a protected disclosure under the Whistleblower Protection Act. Other cautionary steps include:

- Make sure you clearly indicate that you are not representing the official position of the U.S. government. Employees have been sanctioned for not giving a disclaimer when speaking out on their own time.

- Do not release information that must be held in confidence as a matter of law, that is protected under the Privacy Act, or that is classified.

- Do not use government property, such as laptops or cell phones, or utilize government-owned servers when blowing the whistle or communicating with counsel.

- If your agency has a prepublication clearance policy, follow it.

- Exercise common sense. Be aware that your managers or those in higher positions may be listening/reading.

Options Outside a WPA Case: Mixed Cases

If an employee has both a whistleblower case and a discrimination case, the two causes of action can be consolidated into one lawsuit, and the employee has an option to file the merged case in U.S. District Court. This procedure is known as a "mixed case." The laws governing mixed cases are complex and are explained in detail in the case of *Bonds v. Leavitt* decided by the U.S. Court of Appeals for the Fourth Circuit.

Environmental Whistleblowers

The DOL environmental whistleblower laws outlined in Rule 26 have been successfully used by employees at the Environmental Protection Agency and other government departments as an alternative to the Whistleblower Protection Act. The DOL procedures are more employee-friendly then those used by the Merit Systems Protection Board. The decision to use environmental whistleblower laws to defend jobs and careers is a viable option for employees who may raise concerns over hot-button environmental issues such as climate change.

In *Erickson v. EPA*, the U.S. Office of Legal Counsel, an agency that provides binding guidance to administrative agencies on legal matters, informed the U.S. Department of Labor that federal employees could file cases under the Clean Air Act, Safe Drinking Water Act, Superfund, and the Solid Waste Disposal Act. These laws permit federal employees to have their cases heard pursuant to the standard Department of Labor procedures outlined in Rule 26.

- The major laws governing federal employees are the Whistleblower Protection Act, at 5 U.S.C. §§ 2302 (general law), 1214–15 (OSC procedures), and 1221; the Protection of Intelligence Community Whistleblowers Act, 50 U.S.C. § 3234; and the FBI Whistleblower Protection Act, 28 C.F.R. Part 27.

- Under 50 U.S.C. 33412(b)(7), whistleblowers have a limited right to challenge denial of a security clearance.

- The Merit Systems Protection Board website (www.mspb.gov) has special Q&As on the Whistleblower Protection Act and links to the regulations that govern discovery, hearings, filing requirements, and how to participate in MSPB proceedings.

- The website for the U.S. Office of Special Counsel (www.osc.gov) has detailed information on filing a whistleblower complaint and how to make a confidential whistleblower disclosure about government abuse.

- The Equal Employment Opportunity Commission (EEOC) has a comprehensive website that fully explains the rules governing federal employee discrimination or retaliation cases. See https://www.eeoc.gov.

Keeping Up with the Changes

To keep up to date on changes in the laws, whistleblowers should access the free online law library created by the author, located at www.kkc.com/law-library.

RULE 30

The Danger Zone: National Security Whistleblowing

Secrecy in government is fundamentally anti-democratic, perpetuating bureaucratic errors. Open debate and discussion of public issues are vital to our national health. On public questions, there should be "uninhibited, robust, and wide-open" debate.
—Justice William Douglas, *U.S. v. New York Times* (Pentagon Papers case)

On June 13, 1971 the controversy surrounding national security whistleblowers was plastered on the front pages of the *New York Times*. Daniel Ellsberg, who worked for a government contractor (the Rand Corporation), had access to top-secret government documents regarding the Vietnam War. After months of reflection over whether to release these highly explosive documents, he leaked the "secret history" of the Vietnam War to the press. He provided the *New York Times* and *Washington Post* more than seven thousand pages of classified documents known as the Pentagon Papers. Although these papers exposed systemic abuses of authority that surrounded the United States' involvement in the Vietnam War, Ellsberg was indicted for leaking confidential information and faced criminal charges that could have resulted in a 117-year prison sentence. In the middle of his trial, some of the worst abuses of the Watergate era surfaced, resulting in a dismissal of all criminal charges. Ellsberg was a free man.

Oddly enough, Ellsberg would become one of the first beneficiaries of the Watergate scandal. During Ellsberg's criminal case, the court learned that officials working for President Richard Nixon had engaged in gross misconduct in a covert campaign to discredit Ellsberg. The White House had established a clandestine "plumber's unit" designed to "plug leaks," and their first illegal operation was to break into Ellsberg's psychiatrist's office to obtain information that could discredit him in the eyes of the public. They wanted to find dirt, and they figured the best place to start was with his psychiatrist, where they might learn his most private and embarrassing secrets. Once the break-in was exposed, the government's case collapsed. It was this misconduct that would result in the dismissal of the criminal charges against him.

The Ellsberg case did not set legal precedent protecting future national security whistleblowers. In the Pentagon Papers case, which arose directly out of Ellsberg's disclosures, the Supreme Court weighed in on whether the Nixon administration could obtain an order halting two newspapers from publishing the classified documents Ellsberg had released. The Court sided with the newspapers, refused to halt the presses, and permitted the *New York Times* and *Washington Post* to print the classified material. However, a number of Supreme Court justices wrote concurring opinions addressing the potential liability of the leaker. These justices sent a clear warning that the United States could use criminal laws to prosecute anyone involved in releasing classified information. They warned that although the newspapers could publish the material, the person who leaked the information could be prosecuted.

Ellsberg escaped conviction only because of prosecutorial misconduct. Other whistleblowers have not been so lucky. More recently there have been indictments and convictions of intelligence agency employees who illegally released classified top-secret information, including Edward Snowden, who was indicted under the Espionage Act, and Thomas Drake, Reality Winner, and John Kiriakou, who were convicted of illegally releasing classified information when they tried to expose official misconduct.

Prepublication Review

After the Pentagon Papers rulings, the next major intelligence whistleblower case to come before the U.S. Supreme Court was *Snepp v. United States*. Frank W. Snepp III was a former CIA employee who published a book exposing problems within that agency. Even though Snepp's book did not contain classified information, the Court upheld the right of intelligence agencies to review, prior to publication, its employees' (and former employees') publications in order to ensure that no classified information was publicly revealed. In *Snepp* the Court affirmed the constitutionality of a prepublication clearance process utilized by various national security institutions, including the FBI and CIA.

Although the Court ruled against Snepp, it did affirm that the U.S. Constitution and the Bill of Rights applied to federal employees working at the CIA and other intelligence agencies, although those rights could be severely limited. The *Snepp* decision established procedures employees with access to classified information can use to make their whistleblower concerns public.

Under these clearance procedures, intelligence agents may publish nonclassified information about their agencies (including information concerning official misconduct), but first they must provide a copy of their publications to their employer and permit their employer reasonable time to ensure that classified information is not revealed. If an employee disagrees with the classification decision, they can obtain judicial review. The burden of proof is on the government, not the whistleblower. Both the executive agencies and the courts are required to expedite the adjudication of these cases. This procedure can be used by both current and former employees.

This process gives employees a "safe harbor" for making disclosures, and the right to challenge, in court, the government's attempt to keep its misconduct secret. Examples of how this procedure has been successfully used by employees with access to highly classified information are those of Frederic Whitehurst and Bassem Youssef, supervisory special agents with the FBI. Whitehurst, an explosives expert, was granted permission by the FBI to speak publicly about major problems at the FBI crime lab that impacted cases, including the first World Trade Center bombing and Oklahoma City bombing cases, and the O.J Simpson murder case. Similarly, Youssef, a highly decorated expert in the FBI's counterterrorism program, was granted permission to speak before the American Library Association and NBC national news and expose significant problems in the Bureau's war on terror. All of these appearances were approved by the FBI, even though the employees continued to work for the Bureau and continued to have top-secret security clearances.

Statutory Right to Blow the Whistle

In 1978 the national security establishment blew it. Congress was on the verge of passing a comprehensive whistleblower law covering all federal employees, but the intelligence agencies wanted out. They wanted to deny their employees the right to blow the whistle. These agencies had the power with Congress, and the final version of the Civil Service Reform Act, signed into law by President Jimmy Carter October 13, 1978, exempted national security and intelligence agency employees from protection.

This exemption had a terrible impact both on national security whistleblowers and the public's right to know about abuses within these excluded agencies. But abuses would continue, and national security employees would continue to blow the whistle, at great personal peril. These often "illegal" disclosures reached historic proportions when Edward Snowden released a massive amount of classified information on the National Security Agency's illegal domestic spying program. A national debate erupted as to whether his actions were justified. Some argued that he was a whistleblower, others labeled him a leaker, while some saw him as a traitor. But one part of this debate was clear: The legal protections afforded to employees like Snowden, who wanted to expose national security–related concerns, were grossly deficient. Without adequate legal protections, blowing the whistle could have catastrophic repercussions. Whistleblowers could lose their jobs, security clearances, and possibly even their freedom.

THE PROTECTION OF INTELLIGENCE COMMUNITY WHISTLEBLOWERS ACT OF 2014

In the wake of the Snowden case, Congress took basic steps to fix the problem. Tucked into the Intelligence Authorization Act for Fiscal Year 2014 was the first federal law providing a semblance of protection for national security whistleblowers. The law, titled Protection of Intelligence Community Whistleblowers, codified at 50 U.S.C. section 3234, is very simple (and very weak).

First, the law covers the intelligence community, including employees who work with such highly secretive agencies as the CIA and NSA.

Second, it contains a very narrow definition of protected activity. Employees are given the right to blow the whistle to specific offices, including: (1) the director of national intelligence, (2) the inspector general of the intelligence community, (3) the head of the employing agency (e.g., the director of the CIA), (4) the inspector general of the agency that employs the whistleblower, (5) a congressional intelligence committee, and (6) a member of a congressional intelligence committee.

The law prohibits retaliation if "the employee reasonably believes evidences (1) a violation of any Federal law, rule, or regulation; or (2) mismanagement, a gross waste of funds, an abuse of authority, or a substantial and specific danger to public health or safety."

This sounds pretty good but . . .

Unlike every other whistleblower law enacted over the past three decades, the intelligence agency law does not permit the employee to seek judicial review of an adverse determination. National security whistleblowers cannot get access to court in order to ensure that the minimum rights afforded them under the Protection of Intelligence Community Whistleblowers Act are enforced. The president of the United States is given the authority to approve the procedures that will be made available to whistleblowers. The law simply states: "The President shall provide for the enforcement of this section."

Another defect in the law is equally glaring. It does not stipulate the remedies available to the whistleblower. The relief available under this law is up to the president or the intelligence agencies delegated with authority to decide these cases. The lack of independent or judicial review permits the fox to guard the chickens.

The FBI WPA

The FBI also has a special law that covers its whistleblowers. This law is stronger than the Intelligence Community Whistleblower Protection Act, but it still has problems. Like NSA and CIA employees, FBI agents were also excluded from civil service protections under the 1978 Civil Service Reform Act. However, the FBI Whistleblower Protection Act, codified as 5 U.S.C. § 2303, required the president of the United States to ensure that FBI agents have rights consistent with those of other federal employees. This mandate ultimately resulted in much stronger remedies for FBI agents than their counterparts working in the CIA or NSA. The FBI WPA was amended in 2016 to permit disclosures to supervisors and Congress.

The FBI WPA was originally passed in 1978. Between 1978 and 1998, all presidents ignored the law until FBI Supervisory Special Agent Frederic Whitehurst sued President Clinton and demanded that it be implemented. Whitehurst had been removed from his position as the FBI's top explosives expert after he exposed widespread abuses in the Bureau's crime lab, including misconduct in the first World Trade Center and the Oklahoma City bombing cases. As a result of the lawsuit, President Bill Clinton issued a directive requiring the U.S. attorney general to implement the FBI WPA and publish administrative protections for FBI employees. These procedures, published as Title 28 C.F.R. Part 27, permit FBI employees to make disclosures to the Justice Department's inspector general or the Office of Professional Responsibility, the director of the FBI, their supervisor, Congress, and other designated offices. If they are retaliated against, the DOJ inspector general must investigate their claims, and they can request an administrative hearing. Remedies include reinstatement, back pay, and attorney fees and costs.

Coming Full Circle

Forty years after opposing protections for national security whistleblowers the intelligence establishment was transformed. Instead of squashing or deriding whistleblowers at every possible turn, the director of national intelligence, as the leader of the entire national security establishment, did a complete about-face at least on paper. He decided to celebrate whistleblowers and their contributions to the United States. The leadership of the intelligence community sponsored events praising whistleblowing and instructing their employees on how to legally and safety blow the whistle.

For example, in a press release issued by the Director of National Intelligence in 2019 members of the intelligence community were informed that the director of national intelligence would give a speech highlighting and commemorating "the contributions of whistleblowers throughout the United States Government . . . in providing the proper authorities with lawful disclosures to save the taxpayers billions of dollars each year and serving the public interest by ensuring that the United States remains an ethical and safe place."

One of the events highlighted by the DNI was a panel discussion on how to "get the 'right information' to the 'right people'" chaired by the inspector general of the entire intelligence community, Michael Atkinson. Approximately two months after publicly celebrating the role of whistleblowers in keeping the American government ethical Atkinson informed Congress of the allegations of a confidential intelligence community whistleblower known simply as the "Ukraine whistleblower." The allegations centered on President Donald Trump's attempt to improperly pressure the president of Ukraine to provide dirt on his political rival's son (i.e., Joseph Biden's son Hunter). The whistleblower's allegations eventually resulted in the first impeachment of President Trump. After those proceedings concluded Atkinson refused to reveal the identity of the Ukraine whistleblower. Because he was a presidential appointee Trump had the authority to fire Atkinson, which he did on April 3, 2020.

Atkinson's firing did not change the growing commitment within the national security establishment to support whistleblowers and maintain their confidentiality. For example, in July 2022 President Biden's inspector general for the intelligence community echoed Atkinson's praise for whistleblowers in a statement published throughout the intelligence communities: "Whistleblowers are vital to the Intelligence Community's mission . . . particularly the principles of Lawfulness, Integrity and Stewardship. Whistleblowing is consistent with Office of the Director of National Intelligence's Core Values, including Courage."

PRACTICE TIPS

- The Protection of Intelligence Community Whistleblowers Act is located at 50 U.S.C. § 3234.

- The regulations governing the FBI Whistleblower Protection Act are located at 28 C.F.R. Part 27.

- The Office of the Director of National Intelligence (DNI) publishes on its website a notice, "Making Lawful Disclosures," with information on how intelligence community whistleblowers can report violations of law. See https://www.dni.gov/index.php/who-we-are/organizations/icig/icig -related-menus/icig-related-links/making-lawful-disclosures.

- "DNI Coats and ODNI Leadership Will Celebrate National Whistleblower Appreciation Day on July 30, 2019," Press Statement Issued by DNI (July 2019).

Keeping Up with the Changes

To keep up to date on changes in the laws, whistleblowers should access the free online law library created by the author, located at www.kkc.com/law-library.

RULE 31

Winning a Case

What is the fundamental rule for winning a retaliation case? Every law sets forth a series of elements that must be met. If these requirements are not met, you will lose. However, if you prevail on each element, you should win your case.

Corporate lawyers are trained to find problems within one or more of these requirements. Whenever a whistleblower lawsuit is filed, the very first thing an employer does is pull out a checklist. The checklist begins with a set of mandatory elements needed for a valid case. One by one the skilled and highly paid company lawyer examines each element to find any technicality to have a court throw out the case. It will not matter if the whistleblower saved lives or saved money. To the company, winning is the sole objective from the start. If you do not meet the criteria for each element, the employer will file a motion to dismiss your case, and it is a sure bet that your case will be dismissed. You will lose your case before it even starts. It's trench warfare. Element by element you must engage the company's lawyers—and fight to win each and every requirement.

Know the Checklist of Mandatory Requirements Under Law

When facing retaliation, whistleblowers need to review the same checklist the company lawyers use. Make sure you cover all the bases before filing an employment case. Elements universally applicable to whistleblower retaliation cases include the following:

1. The whistleblower must be an employee covered under the law.

2. The company must be an employer covered under the law.

3. The employee must have engaged in protected activity.

4. The management must have known of the protected disclosures.

5. The whistleblower must have suffered an adverse action.

6. There must be some proof of a connection between the adverse action and the protected conduct (i.e., discriminatory motive).

7. Evidence is needed to demonstrate that the reasons given for the adverse action are not truthful or legitimate.

8. A case must be filed within the statute of limitations time period.

9. Administrative exhaustion requirements must be followed when required under a law.

THE EMPLOYEE AND EMPLOYER MUST BE SUBJECT TO THE LAW

This is usually not a major issue. However, some laws narrowly define whom they cover, and some employment situations are inherently problematic. For example, are employees who work in a foreign country for an American corporation protected? What happens if a person works for a subcontractor and the contractor retaliates? What liability does a parent corporation have for a subsidiary? These types of issues are complicated, and there are no simple answers. It is best for whistleblowers to find laws that explicitly cover their job and their employer.

ENSURE THAT YOUR DISCLOSURES ARE PROTECTED

This is an area where common sense does not apply. Each law defines to whom an employee can make a disclosure and what types of disclosures are protected. Beware: The laws are not consistent or logical. Thus, before blowing the whistle an employee needs to decipher what type of whistleblowing is protected. They should ask questions such as: Does the law protect disclosures to supervisors? Does the law protect disclosures to hotlines? Does the law protect disclosures to the news media? Are there specific government agencies identified in the law for which disclosures are encouraged or permitted?

Protected activity is defined within the text of the statute. But these definitions can be quite general, and often judicial decisions provide additional guidance. The risks are immense for employees who blow the whistle before knowing what disclosures are protected under law, because a good faith disclosure may result in a bad faith termination.

WHEN FILING A RETALIATION CASE, MAKE SURE THE BOSS KNOWS
WHO BLEW THE WHISTLE

For three reasons, the "knowledge" requirement in retaliation cases is extremely tricky. First, unquestionably, the best way to prevent retaliation is for the boss *never* to know who made a report. Employees who successfully blow the whistle confidentially or anonymously are the least likely to be fired.

Second, in some cases being confidential is not an option, even if an employee thinks it is. Before becoming a whistleblower, many employees complain about problems to their managers or company compliance programs. Thereafter, if a government investigator starts to look into problems raised by that employee, like it or not the employee has a target on their back—and is usually suspected of being the rat fink.

This leads to a paradox. In order to be protected under a retaliation law, the boss needs to know the employee is a whistleblower. But the best defense against retaliation is to be confidential. Consequently, the knowledge requirement can cause significant problems and must be strategically analyzed. The law is clear on this issue: The manager responsible for the adverse employment action must either know or suspect that the employee was a whistleblower. If the boss never knew who blew the whistle, how can an employee be fired for something the boss did not know they did?

Most courts permit employees to prove knowledge by direct or circumstantial evidence. In other words, if an employee was a confidential whistleblower, they can use circumstantial evidence, such as offhand comments, or the nature of the allegations themselves (for example, they were one of the few persons who spoke out against the violation) to demonstrate that the employer thought that employee was the informer.

Employees who reported the violations to their supervisor usually can meet the knowledge requirement. A boss will have great difficulty denying knowing that an employee engaged in protected activity when the disclosure was made directly to them. Moreover, once an employee complains internally about a violation, that employee is always the number-one suspect if a government regulatory agency becomes involved.

The modern reward laws create an alternative path for compensation and protection. Congress has created legally permitted procedures for filing confidential disclosures under laws such as the False Claims, Foreign Corrupt Practices, Motor Vehicle Safety, Dodd-Frank, Anti-Money Laundering, and the IRS tax whistleblower law. The confidential nature of these disclosures can benefit employees. Filing a claim is statutorily protected, so if the boss discovers that you were the claimant, you are protected under the whistleblower law. Moreover, if you become a witness to federal law enforcement, the obstruction of justice laws kick in and retaliation can be criminal, putting significant pressure on the bosses not to retaliate. Under the Dodd-Frank Act, employees can obtain whistleblower rewards if they file their claims anonymously with the government. The boss never has to know who blew the whistle, even if the informant walks away with a million-dollar reward paid by the government.

PROTECTED ACTIVITY MUST BE CONDUCTED IN GOOD FAITH

This is a confusing element applicable to retaliation cases. The "good faith" standard does not mean that an employee who blows the whistle must be an angel or must be strictly serving the public interest. Most laws, and nearly every court, understand that the subjective motive of an employee for blowing the whistle may be less than honorable (for example, an employee who is upset they did not get a promotion). The good faith element looks at whether an employee has a reasonably objective belief that what they are disclosing constitutes a violation of law, a threat to public safety, fraud, and so forth.

The good faith standard does not relate to an employee's subjective motivation for becoming a whistleblower. Take a case in which an engineer blows the whistle on defective welds. The engineer believes that the defect in the welds could cause a bridge to collapse and files a complaint with the Department of Transportation. The government investigates the complaint, and the welds are found to be in fine shape. Should the employee be protected under a whistleblower law?

Almost universally, courts addressing this issue have held that if an employee's safety concerns had a reasonable basis in fact, the whistleblower must be protected. Courts seek to determine whether a reasonable person could have a good faith belief that the welds could fail and cause harm. If the factual predicates for the claims are reasonable, courts will find that the whistleblowing was in good faith, and those disclosures will normally be fully protected. But in cases in which a reasonable person could not, in good faith, have suspected that the welds were faulty, the employee may lose protection. How much proof should an employee put forward to demonstrate to a court that their concerns were objectively reasonable? That is decided on a case-by-case basis, and different standards can be applied to different laws. Consequently, even though employees do not have to prove that their allegations were correct, it is important to ensure that they are based on objective facts.

No federal anti-retaliation law requires that the employee's allegations of misconduct be verified. For example, when Congress debated the Sarbanes-Oxley corporate whistleblower law, they cited with approval an environmental whistleblower case decided by the U.S. Court of Appeals for the Third Circuit that clearly set forth this rule:

> [A]n employee's non-frivolous complaint should not have to be guaranteed to withstand the scrutiny of in-house or external review in order to merit protection . . . for the obvious reason that such a standard would chill employee initiatives for bringing to light perceived discrepancies in the workings of their agency.

The key feature of whistleblower laws is to encourage employees to *report* suspected wrongdoing to the proper authorities. Employees are often motivated by a desire to serve the public good; however, angelic motives are not required in whistleblower law.

AN EMPLOYEE MUST SUFFER ADVERSE ACTION

Merely calling oneself a whistleblower does not mean a person can file a suit. In order to file a retaliation case an employee must suffer some form of adverse action. A termination is universally accepted as an adverse employment action. Conduct short of a firing, such as a demotion, a suspension, or placing an employee on probation may also be considered adverse actions. There are numerous court decisions evaluating nearly every type of potential adverse action, ranging from a hostile work environment to "constructive discharge" (i.e., when the working conditions become so intolerable that an employee is permitted to quit and then sue for being terminated).

What constitutes adverse action differs from state to state, law to law, and court to court. On the one hand, some states require an actual discharge in order to file a public policy tort. On the other hand, under federal law, a hostile work environment can constitute adverse action, even if no direct negative action was ever taken against the whistleblower. Adverse action can include transfer to a dead-end position, blacklisting, bad evaluations (that could impact pay or benefits) or bad references, denial of a promotion or benefits afforded other workers, retaliatory layoff, refusal to hire, a hostile work environment, reprimands or suspensions, and constructive discharge.

In *Burlington Northern & Santa Fe Railway Co. v. White* the Supreme Court wrestled with the issue of whether employer action that did not result in an employee losing money or benefits constituted adverse action. The Court held that an adverse action could be proven if harassment was "likely to deter" a reasonable employee from exercising protected whistleblower activities. This was a big win for whistleblowers, as it recognized the chilling effect employer conduct, short of a discharge, has on workers.

But it is equally well settled in law that "not everything that makes an employee unhappy is actionable adverse action." Although it is very important to document changes in working conditions that follow the whistleblowing (as these changes may constitute evidence of retaliation), an employee should not automatically file a lawsuit over every minor action taken by an employer. If the judge or jury does not think that the harmful conduct rose to the level of a true adverse action, the case will be thrown out.

Take-home message: Don't pick a fight over any minor slight. Wait until the fight is both winnable and worth the effort.

EMPLOYEES MUST DEMONSTRATE "CAUSATION" (DISCRIMINATORY ANIMUS) AND PRETEXT

The final elements needed to present a valid case are evidence of causation (i.e., linking an employer's animus toward whistleblowing to the adverse action) and pretext (i.e., the reasons given for the adverse action are not accurate or would not legitimately support the discipline). The act of whistleblowing must be the cause of the adverse action. If the boss has a legitimate reason for firing a whistleblower (for example, coming into work drunk), then the causal link is broken. Because proving discriminatory motive and pretext are often the hardest part of a case, this element is fully discussed in Rule 34. The types of evidence used to support a finding of causation and pretext are listed in Checklist 3.

DON'T MISS THE DEADLINE FOR FILING A COMPLAINT

Because there is no single comprehensive whistleblower law, there is no standard filing deadline. Figuring out when a case must be filed can be a nightmare. See Trap #4, which is explained in Rule 5.

Each of the more than fifty whistleblower retaliation laws have their own statute of limitations. Some old employment laws require claims to be filed within thirty days, while others permit years to pass before a case is filed. Once an employee identifies the best legal protections that apply to their case, compliance with each and every technical requirement of the law is absolutely required. The statute of limitations is the strictest of these requirements. Miss the deadline, lose the case. It is that simple.

Figure 22 is a summary of the filing deadlines for retaliation cases that must be originally filed in federal court. **Figure 23** summarizes the deadlines for filing complaints under major laws that must be initially filed with the Department of Labor.

In retaliation cases the deadlines start running on the day an employee is given notice of the termination or discipline will occur, not the last day of work. With very few exceptions, the failure to comply with these statutes of limitations spells doom.

Figuring out the filing deadlines for qualifying for a reward is somewhat tricky. All the reward laws place an emphasis on being the first to file. This means that whoever files a reward claim first may be the only person who qualifies to obtain compensation. The False Claims Act has a strict first to file rule. Whoever files the case first is the only person who has standing to pursue that claim. Thus, regardless of the actual statute of limitations for filing a case, you may lose your rights if you do not act quickly and secure your position as first to file.

Figure 22

Statute of Limitations for Retaliation Cases Filed in Federal Court		
Name of Law	**Citation**	**Amount of Time to File**
Banking Fraud (Credit Unions, FDIC-Insured Institutions, and Monetary Transactions)	12 U.S.C. § 1790b 12 U.S.C. § 1831j 31 U.S.C. § 5328	2 years
Commodity Exchange Act (Retaliation)	7 U.S.C. § 26 (h)(1)(B)(iii)	2 years
False Claims Act (Retaliation)	31 U.S.C. § 3730(h)(3)	3 years
First Amendment 42 U.S.C. § 1983 (State, Municipal, and County Employee Speech on Matters of Public Concern)	*Owens v. Okure*, 488 U.S. 235, 240-241 (1989)	Federal Court: No uniform statute of limitations. Follow relevant statute of limitations in state where claim is filed.
Securities Exchange Act (Retaliation)	15 U.S.C. § 78u-6(h)(1)(B)(iii)	6 years after the violation occurred or 3 years after the date when facts material to the right of action are known or reasonably should have been known by the employee. Required action within 10 years.

Figure 23

Statute of Limitations for Retaliation Claims Initially Filed with the Department of Labor		
Name of Law	**Citation**	**Amount of Time to File with the Department of Labor**
Airline Safety	29 Code of Federal Regulations § 1979	90 days
Consumer Financial Fraud	29 Code of Federal Regulations § 1985	180 days
Consumer Product Safety	16 Code of Federal Regulations § 1102	180 days
Environmental Safety (Clean Air, Superfund, Clean Water, Safe Drinking, Waste Disposal, and Toxic Substances)	29 Code of Federal Regulations § 24	30 days
Food Safety	29 Code of Federal Regulations § 1987	180 days

Nuclear Safety	29 Code of Federal Regulations § 24	180 days
Occupational Safety and Health Act (OSHA)	29 Code of Federal Regulations § 1977	30 days
Sarbanes Oxley Act (Securities Fraud)	18 U.S.C. § 1514A(b)(2)(D); 29 Code of Federal Regulations § 1980	180 days
Transportation Safety Laws (Railroad, Automobile, Transit, Maritime, and Trucks)	29 Code of Federal Regulations § 1982 & 1978	180 days

EXHAUST ADMINISTRATIVE REMEDIES OR PROCEDURES

The final technicality is the "exhaustion" doctrine. This doctrine applies to the numerous statutes that require employees to file a claim with a designated administrative agency before a case can be filed in court. For example, under the Sarbanes-Oxley Act, a complaint must be filed with the U.S. Department of Labor. Only after the case has been pending before the DOL for 180 days can the case be removed to federal court. Even if the DOL has taken no action, the employee must still wait until they have exhausted administrative remedies. If the claim was filed directly in federal court, the case would be dismissed due to the failure to exhaust.

Numerous employment laws require exhaustion of administrative remedies, including Title VII of the Civil Rights Act (sex- and race-based discrimination). Others, like the Clean Air Act or the Mine Health and Safety Act, only allow for administrative proceedings.

Regardless of whether you want to pursue your case in court or in an agency, it is absolutely imperative to carefully review the filing and appeal procedures to ensure that you fully run through all administrative requirements at each step of the game.

─────────── PRACTICE TIPS ───────────

- *NLRB v. Scrivener*, 405 U.S. 117 (1972) (premier case on broad scope of protected activity)

- *Passaic Valley Sewerage Commissioners v. U.S. Dept. of Labor*, 992 F.2d 474 (3rd. Cir. 1993) (premier case on "good faith")

- *Fraizer v. MSPB*, 672 F.2d 150 (D.C. Cir. 1982) (premier case on employer knowledge)

- *Burlington Northern & Santa Fe Railway Co. v. White*, 548 U.S. 53 (2006) (premier case defining adverse action)

- *Halliburton v. ARB*, 771 F.3d 254 (5th Cir. 2014) (applying *Burlington* to corporate whistleblower cases)

- *Nat'l R.R. Passenger Corp. v. Morgan*, 536 U.S. 101 (2003); *Lewis v. City of Chicago*, 130 S.Ct. 2191 (2010) (continuing violations) (must show present violation within statutory filing period)

- *Delaware State College v. Ricks*, 449 U.S. 250 (1982) (when the clock starts ticking on your filing deadline)

- *Bonham v. Dresser Indus.*, 569 F.2d 187 (3rd. Cir. 1977) (cases explaining potential equitable justifications for enlarging the statute of limitations)

- *KBR v. U.S. ex rel. Carter*, 135 S.Ct. 1970 (2015) (clarifying first to file rule and statute of limitations under the False Claims Act)

RULE 32

Your Disclosures Must Be Protected under Law

Liberty is meaningless where the right to utter one's thoughts and opinions has ceased to exist. That, of all rights, is the dread of tyrants. It is the right which they first of all strike down. They know its power.
  —Frederick Douglass, "Plea for Free Speech in Boston" (1860)

Freedom of speech is part of the American credo. The fundamental right to expose wrongdoing, criminality, or corruption was recognized by the Founders of the United States when they supported the first whistleblowers in 1777-78, and was later embedded into the heart of the Constitution as one of the foundations of the American Way.

On June 8, 1789, James Madison stood before the First Congress of the United States of America and proposed that the Constitution be amended to include a Bill of Rights. His words were clear, and the intent behind what would eventually be incorporated into the Constitution as the First Amendment was unmistakable:

The people shall not be deprived or abridged of their right to speak, to write, or to publish their sentiments; and freedom of the press, as one of the great bulwarks of liberty, shall be inviolable.

Although the right to expose wrongdoing is at the heart of free speech, courts and Congress do not always see it that way. Not every disclosure is protected. Far from it. The laws giving workers the right to report waste, fraud, and abuse at work are not absolute. Before you blow the whistle, make sure that what you are reporting and to whom you are reporting are protected. The schism between the whistleblowing celebrated in Hollywood movies and the reality of the legal protections for this speech is deep and wide.

Understanding Protected Disclosures

The starting point for being protected against retaliation is to make sure your disclosures are covered under law. If they are not, you may have already lost your case. Because there is no uniform definition of a protected disclosure, many employees are rightfully confused as to how to report wrongdoing. Each statute contains its own unique definition, and courts have not been consistent in applying these principles.

To ensure that disclosures are covered carefully, check the legal requirements set forth in the statute you will be relying on for protection. In practice, this is not so simple. Most employees engage in protected activities *first* and ask questions about the law only when they suspect retaliation. Whistleblowers should not be faulted when they use common sense in making a disclosure, but the law does not always conform to common sense and can be unforgiving to an employee who raised concerns to the wrong office.

Follow Mandatory Procedures

To obtain legal protection, some laws contain specific requirements on how to make a disclosure. This is particularly true for all the reward laws, which have carefully structured filing requirements designed to make sure that the proper law enforcement officials obtain the whistleblower's information. Six laws to pay particular attention to the mandatory filing procedures are the False Claims Act, the Motor Vehicle Safety Act, the Anti-Money Laundering (AML) Act, the Internal Revenue Code, the Securities Exchange Act (whose filing requirements also cover the Foreign Corrupt Practices Act), and the Commodity Exchange Act. Each of these laws, either by statute or regulation, contains specific rules on how to file a claim in order to qualify for a reward. These rules *must* be strictly followed if you want to qualify for a reward.

Reports to Federal Law Enforcement

Whistleblower laws protect reporting crimes and regulatory abuses to federal law enforcement agencies. Any doubt that existed on this matter was cleared up in 2002, when Congress amended the obstruction of justice statute and criminalized retaliation against any person who provided truthful information to federal law enforcement concerning the possible violation of any federal offense.

The terms of the 2002 amendment to the obstruction of justice law are clear, broad, and applicable to all Americans:

> *Whoever knowingly, with the intent to retaliate, takes any action harmful to any person, including interference with the lawful employment or livelihood of any person, for providing to a law enforcement officer any truthful information relating to the commission or possible commission of any Federal offense, shall be fined under this title or imprisoned for not more than 10 years, or both.*

The obstruction of justice law is criminal. That means it is up to a federal prosecutor to enforce its penalties. Despite this weakness, the obstruction law sets forth an immovable standard. No person can harm any other person's livelihood for making a truthful report about a possible crime to federal law enforcement. Employees can and should use this law as both a sword and a shield when blowing the whistle. It sets forth a federal public policy that can help whistleblowers in numerous contexts, including arguing that reports to federal authorities are protected or that severance agreements restricting such reports are void and unenforceable.

Dodd-Frank and SOX Corporate Disclosures

Based on the Supreme Court's decision in *Digital Realty Trust v. Somers*, to be protected against retaliation under the Commodity Exchange Act and the Securities Exchange Act, employees must directly contact the SEC and/or the CFTC. Similarly, to qualify for rewards, formal claims must be filed with these two agencies. The Sarbanes-Oxley Act has a much broader definition of protected activity, covering disclosures to Congress, supervisors, the SEC, and federal agencies, among others.

Reports to Congress

The right to petition Congress for a redress of grievances was recognized as a fundamental human right by the Founders of the United States, and it was explicitly incorporated into the First Amendment of the U.S. Constitution.

Some whistleblower laws explicitly reference an employee's right to provide information to Congress, such as the Sarbanes-Oxley Act, the Federal Railway Safety Act, and the Taxpayer First Act. Reward laws permit employees to make disclosures to Congress, but also require that these disclosures be timely made to the respective regulatory agency. However, even without these specific statutory references, there are no known modern cases under either federal or state whistleblower laws in which the firing of an employee for lawfully providing information to Congress (or to a state legislature) was upheld.

Disclosures to Congress can provide whistleblowers with a key ally. It is one thing for an employee to personally stand up for their rights; it is an entirely separate matter when a company learns of a formal congressional investigation or gets a letter from a member of Congress warning them against retaliation.

Disclosures to the U.S. Attorney General

The False Claims Act requires whistleblowers to make a formal disclosure of substantially all their allegations to the U.S. attorney general. These disclosures are protected. The FCA mandates that employees must make a disclosure to the attorney general at the time they file their lawsuit.

Under the Dodd-Frank Act reward provisions there is a twist to the right to report violations of law to the attorney general. The Securities and Exchange Commission approved a rule that can result in the denial of a reward if whistleblowers make their initial disclosure of a violation to the Justice Department or other federal agencies. In these circumstances whistleblowers must follow up and also file their claim with the SEC within 120 days of communicating with other government entities or risk being denied a reward. The Commodity Futures Trading Commission has a similar rule. Because Dodd-Frank requires that persons seeking a reward file their claim with the SEC or CFTC, simply reporting your concerns to the attorney general is not enough. You still must file with the SEC or CFTC in a timely manner.

The bottom line is clear. Reporting violations of law to the U.S. attorney general is always a safe bet, but you must read the fine print as to how to qualify for a monetary reward and also make sure you conform to those requirements.

Testifying in Court

During the post–Civil War Reconstruction period, Congress was concerned about the ability of citizens, especially those from the South, to protect their federal rights. This led to the passage of the Civil Rights Act of 1871. This law contained numerous provisions applicable to modern-day whistleblowing, including a provision codified as 42 U.S.C. § 1985. This clause prohibits conspiracies to retaliate against witnesses in federal court proceedings. In 1996 the U.S. Supreme Court applied this provision to whistle-blowers, permitting an employee to file a damages lawsuit for wrongful termination after being fired for testifying. Court testimony is also covered under most (if not all) other federal and state whistleblower laws, provided the testimony concerns the subject matters protected under the specific statute.

Refusing to Violate a Law

Almost every state recognizes the common law public policy exception to the "termination at will" doctrine that prohibits firing workers who reasonably refuse to violate a law. Similar protections are also found under the majority of federal whistleblower laws.

There is, however, one very important caveat regarding work refusals. Should management demonstrate that the requested conduct is legal or safe, the right to refuse to perform that work terminates, and an employee can thereafter be disciplined for failing to perform the task.

Disclosing a Violation of Law

Most, if not all, federal and state whistleblower laws protect employees who disclose violations of law to the proper authorities. The laws usually spell out which agencies are covered. All the reward laws require such disclosures to the government before an employee can qualify for a reward. The *qui tam* provisions of the False Claims Act, the Internal Revenue Code, Commodity Exchange Act, the Anti-Money Laundering Act, the Motor Vehicle Safety Act, and the Securities Exchange Act all require specific and detailed disclosures to specific government agencies to qualify for a reward.

Disclosures to Supervisors or Corporate Compliance Programs

In *Digital Realty Trust v. Somers*, the U.S. Supreme Court held that the Dodd-Frank Act's anti-retaliation provisions did not apply to internal disclosures by employees to supervisors or corporate compliance programs. In the context of state and local government employees, the Supreme Court reached a similar result. Consequently, if a law does not explicitly protect internal reporting, courts may deny protection to employees who make reports to their managers. Unless internal disclosures are unequivocally protected or required in the statutory definition, it is best to assume that internal disclosures will not be protected.

Disclosures to the News Media

See Rule 15.

Disclosures That Bypass the Chain of Command

It is common for whistleblowers to bypass their formal chain of command when they raise concerns within their company. If a supervisor is the perceived problem, employees may decide that this level of management should be ignored and they should inform higher-level officials of the concern. Likewise, some companies have established complaint processes that employees are either required or urged to follow, but these also can usually be bypassed.

When the U.S. Department of Labor reviewed this issue, it held that employees could not be disciplined simply for failing to follow the chain of command when making protected disclosures. Moreover, the DOL held that if an employer fired a worker for refusing to follow the chain of command when making a protected disclosure, that discharge was, per se, illegal.

Disclosures by Attorneys

Can attorneys blow the whistle? Under well-established legal precedents governing attorney-client privilege, lawyers must keep the secrets of their clients. But under whistleblower laws, all employees have the right to report violations of law to appropriate authorities. What happens when these two principles collide?

The U.S. Courts of Appeals have recognized that lawyers can sue for wrongful discharge if they are fired for blowing the whistle inside their companies. In one such case, Shawn and Lena Van Asdale worked as in-house counsel for a publicly traded company. They reported possible shareholder fraud in connection with a merger to the company's general counsel and were subsequently fired. They sued the company under the Sarbanes-Oxley Act, which explicitly protected internal disclosures. The company asked the court to throw out the lawsuit on the basis of their status as attorneys. This argument was completely rejected. Looking at the text of the Sarbanes-Oxley Act, the court held that attorneys could be protected under the law, reasoning that "Congress plainly considered the role attorneys might play in reporting possible securities fraud." The court further explained that procedures could be employed, such as issuing a protective order, to safeguard a company's legitimate interests if the case went to trial and confidential matters became relevant to the case.

In a second case, the U.S. Court of Appeals for the Fifth Circuit summed up the status of lawyers: "[T]he attorney-client privilege" is *not* a "per se bar to retaliation claims under the federal whistleblower statutes." In other words, being an attorney does not automatically forfeit your whistleblower rights.

Although the courts have been amenable to attorneys filing wrongful discharge lawsuits, the issue of when, how, and to whom an attorney can make a protected disclosure is complex and often contested. It is imperative that attorneys take special care to ensure that any disclosures they make conform to local bar association and state or federal laws. Put another way: Be cautious what you report and to whom so that you do not end up fired or disbarred for trying to do the right thing.

Federal and state courts have applied attorney ethics to attorney-whistleblower disclosures. In one such case, *Quest Diagnostics*, the U.S. Court of Appeals for the Second Circuit dismissed the whistleblower's case, even though the court recognized that the dismissal could result in the dismissal of a legitimate whistleblower claim. The court determined that protecting the attorney-client privilege may, in some cases, "impede the pursuit of meritorious litigation to the detriment of the justice system."

The U.S. Securities and Exchange Commission has special procedures on attorney conduct. Attorneys who appear or practice before the SEC can raise securities fraud issues to the client or to their supervisors at a law firm. Under federal law there are specific circumstances under which a corporate attorney can provide privileged information to the SEC. An article published by Latham & Watkins (a large corporate law firm that does *not* represent whistleblowers) explained the legal status of these confusing requirements. According to the article, if an attorney reasonably believes their SEC-regulated corporate client is continuing to commit a "material violation" of law, that attorney can disclose privileged information to the SEC.

According to the Latham firm, these reports are limited to three circumstances: (1) "to prevent a material violation" of law "that is likely to cause substantial injury to the financial interest" of the company or its investors; (2) to prevent the company from committing perjury, suborning perjury, or committing a fraud on the SEC; or (3) to "rectify the consequences of a material violation" caused by the company that is likely to cause a substantial injury to the financial interests of investors, if the "attorney's services were used." The law in this area is still developing.

Don't Be Insubordinate

Blowing the whistle does not give an employee license to be insubordinate. The courts recognize that emotions may run high in whistleblower cases, and acknowledge "some leeway for impulsive behavior." An issue in these cases is "whether an employee's actions are indefensible under the circumstances." This analysis is often conducted on a case-by-case basis and will be based on the type of work an employee performs and what type of "unduly disruptive" behavior is involved. It is always best for a whistleblower to be polite!

Read the Fine Print

Remember that each whistleblower protection law is different. The laws all have their own definitions of protected activity, and there is no judicial consensus defining even the most basic parameters of employee rights of speech. Often an employee blows the whistle first and then tries to figure out if the disclosures were protected. Before you sound the alarm, find out what law may protect you.

— PRACTICE TIPS —

- Checklist 2 lists federal whistleblower laws.

- An excellent critique of court decisions that narrowly define protected activity is contained in the Senate Report on the Whistleblower Protection Enhancement Act, S. Rep. 112-155, pp. 4–8.

- Every statute has its own definition of a protected disclosure—choose carefully. See the Annotated Sources section for numerous case citations.

- The latest Supreme Court wisdom on reporting internally is *Digital Realty Trust v. Somers*, 138 S.Ct. 767 (2018). Read this case before you report a violation of law internally or to corporate compliance.

- Links to cases interpreting the scope of protected disclosures can be accessed at the free whistleblower law library, located at www.kkc.com/law-library.

RULE 33

Make Discovery Your Best Friend

Don't be fooled—modern civil lawsuits have nothing in common with the courthouse dramas portrayed on television shows such as *Law & Order*. The case is not won as a result of a dramatic admission during a trial. There are no sobbing confessions, nor are there admissions of guilt. Friends forget, coworkers get scared, and witnesses lie. Jurors can be skeptical, and judges cynical. Whistleblowers' motives will be under scrutiny, and their actions will be aggressively challenged.

Whistleblowers do not win their employment cases because justice is on their side. Retaliation cases are won and lost on hard evidence, usually obtained through the extraordinary efforts of whistleblowers before they are fired or through their attorneys during the pretrial discovery process. Simply being right is not enough. Whistleblowers have to *prove* they are right.

Contemporaneous documentation is key. If a report was falsified, where is the original? If a quality assurance standard was not met, where are the test evaluations? If a concern is raised with a supervisor, where is the e-mail documenting these disclosures? Was a log kept? Were incriminating conversations lawfully taped? The hard and often tedious work of collecting evidence, saving documents, and engaging in extensive discovery is the foundation of a good case. There are no shortcuts.

Begin Discovery Ahead of Time and Be Thorough

The legal discovery process can and should start well before a lawsuit is filed, because documentary evidence makes or breaks a case. When someone is lying, a simple e-mail can prove a claim.

As important as collecting documentation is, be sure efforts at self-help do not cross the line. Don't sneak into your boss's office at night and steal company documents. Stealing confidential personnel files about other employees usually results in a severe sanction against the whistleblower. If an employee breaks the law to prove a case, they have probably already lost.

Documentary Evidence Is Vital

Examples of the critical role documents play in any employment case are endless. Performance records of the whistleblower are crucial in establishing the employee's credibility. E-mails can substantiate employer knowledge of protected activity and document animus against the whistleblower. Safety records can prove that the company lied. Applications for government contracts can demonstrate false statements used to illegally obtain a grant or contract, and financial records can prove tax fraud. The list goes on and on, and the need for the records is obvious.

There are effective ways to obtain documents and other information from your company through the legal process. If a case enters active litigation, the company must respond to discovery requests filed by the whistleblower. Under the rules of Federal Civil Procedure (which are consistent with the rules of practice under state laws and within the Department of Labor), a party to a lawsuit can engage in discovery, which permits a whistleblower to submit broad document requests for information to force the company to produce relevant documents, such as performance records, personnel records of other comparable employees, internal investigative reports and audits, e-mails, and records related to the whistleblower allegations. In addition to document requests, witnesses can be questioned, under oath, in pretrial depositions, and subpoenas can be served on persons who have information relevant to the case.

Discovery is the single most important part of the pretrial process. It creates the factual record necessary to defeat a motion for summary judgment (an attempt by the employer to have a case thrown out of court by a judge) and permits the whistleblower to test all the material evidence prior to trial. The following are the major tools at the disposal of a whistleblower during the discovery process.

DEPOSITIONS

Attorneys from each side can question relevant witnesses under oath prior to the trial. This gives an employee the opportunity to question all of the company employees identified as having participated in the adverse action. These employees may confirm that the whistleblower engaged in protected activity. They may have information about causation, hostility against the employee's whistleblowing, or pretext. Any witness with potentially relevant information should be able to be questioned about the case before trial. Depositions can be used at trial to impeach witnesses who try to change their story.

DOCUMENT REQUESTS

A company can be required to produce relevant documents, including e-mails, personnel files, and internal investigatory files. To prevent companies from destroying evidence, it is a good practice to compile a detailed list of materials that should be subpoenaed while still employed. If a company obtains a request for documents, it may suspect that you already have the materials and consequently will produce them, without a big argument, or you may be able to find evidence that it improperly destroyed documents and use these facts as a basis to seek sanctions.

You can also request that a company produce documents that you already possess. This can be important in two circumstances: First, if you removed documents from your workplace and are concerned about their admissibility, ask the company to produce them. If they do, use the documents the company produced at the trial. Second, if you are trying to maintain confidentiality regarding materials you provided to the government, requesting the same documents from the company may throw them off your track.

INTERROGATORIES AND REQUESTS FOR ADMISSIONS

Interrogatories are written questions that the company must answer under oath. Admissions are similar to interrogatories in that the company must admit or deny various facts under oath. These can be used to force a company to explain specific actions in order to eliminate any surprises at trial. For example, if an employee is fired, the company may be asked to explain the precise grounds for the termination and identify all persons responsible for the adverse action. In this manner an employee can conduct further discovery to disprove the justifications for the firing. Furthermore, the employee can act without the worry that the company will change its story at trial once the weaknesses in its case are documented.

THIRD-PARTY SUBPOENAS

If evidence is not in the control or possession of the employer, third-party subpoenas can be filed. These subpoenas permit a party to conduct discovery (such as depositions and requests for production of documents) on former employees, government investigators, and other nonparty witnesses.

What to Look for in Discovery

Discovery tends to be far more important for the employee than the employer. The company usually possesses most of the relevant records, such as the employment files of other employees (to determine whether the whistleblower was subjected to "disparate treatment") and documentation related to the underlying whistleblower allegations. However, the company can conduct discovery against the employee as well.

Common areas of company discovery include psychological records (if the employee is alleging emotional distress), an employee's prior work history (in an attempt to either argue that the employee engaged in résumé fraud to get their job or argue that the employee had a history of poor performance), and fishing expeditions in an attempt to find derogatory information to use in cross examination.

There are a number of important goals of discovery that an employee whistleblower needs to identify in planning their case:

- Learn precisely what the company's case is against the employee to prevent any surprises at trial.

- Start building a defense. Learn the company's case, along with its strengths and weaknesses. If the whistleblower doesn't know what the company witnesses are going to say, how can they prepare a solid impeachment?

- Prove that the underlying whistleblower allegations were true. This can bolster an employee's credibility while impeaching the company's motives. Although the company may argue that evidence of misconduct is irrelevant, this is simply not the case. If the company did in fact engage in misconduct, that misconduct is highly relevant to proving the true reason for retaliation and a potential cover-up.

- In a False Claims Act case, prove the fraud.

- Verify "disparate treatment." Disciplining a whistleblower for offenses for which other employees are regularly given a pass constitutes strong evidence of discrimination and pretext. Under a disparate treatment analysis, even if the whistleblower did have performance problems, the employee can prevail in the case if they experienced harsher treatment than other workers who never engaged in protected activity. That is the classic definition of discrimination: treating two similarly situated employees differently solely because one engaged in protected activities and the other did not. The primary method for proving disparate treatment is to engage in discovery concerning how other employees are treated, including obtaining access to disciplinary records and personnel files.

- Obtain e-mails and other computer-generated files. This type of contemporaneous documentation is often highly relevant to a case, as it contains confirmation that various managers knew or suspected that an employee was a whistleblower and often documents how these managers reacted to the protected activities of their subordinate.

- Obtain evidence of pretext. In order to demonstrate weaknesses in the company's case against the employee, each manager responsible for the adverse action can be questioned under oath. Did the company thoroughly investigate the allegations against the employee? Did the company give the employee a fair shot in disproving those allegations? Are there conflicts regarding the reasons given by the managers for taking the adverse action? Did anyone lie about the employee? Is the oral testimony of the managers consistent with the documentary evidence? Proving that a company lied about an employee is never an easy task, but without discovery it is usually an impossible one.

During the discovery process a whistleblower should gather all the evidence that may help prove their case or disprove the company's case. Discovery is an opportunity to find out the other team's weaknesses and adjust strategy accordingly.

─────────────── PRACTICE TIPS ───────────────

- Checklist 4 sets forth the common areas for which employees seek discovery in retaliation cases, along with supporting case authority.

- Samples of discovery requests commonly used in retaliation cases can be found at the free whistleblower law library, located at www.kkc.com/law-library.

- The discovery rules applicable in federal court are located at Federal Rules of Civil Procedure 26–37.

- The discovery rules applicable in U.S. Department of Labor proceedings are located at 29 C.F.R. §§ 18.50–57.

- The discovery rules applicable in Merit Systems Protection Board proceedings are located at 5 C.F.R. §§ 1201.25, .33, .71–75 and .81–85.

RULE 34
Prove Motive and Pretext

The penultimate question in every retaliation case is proving causation and pretext. Employers do not admit that they fired an employee because of whistleblowing. Regardless of how outrageously an employee was treated, a company will formulate a pretext, or a so-called legitimate justification for disciplining an employee. Otherwise, the company would have to admit it broke the law, which none of them ever do.

For example, a company may state that it simply "loved" the employee and greatly "appreciated" the fact that the employee's whistleblowing cost them millions of dollars, but unfortunately, the company had no alternative but to lay off the employee due to "lack of work."

Sometimes the justification for firing a whistleblower is malignant. A company uses allegations of serious performance failures to justify firing the worker. The employee is confronted with a choice: voluntarily resign and sign various releases (which will prevent the whistleblower from suing the company) and the company will keep the so-called performance-based reasons for the firing confidential and may even provide a reference for finding another job. The gun is put to the employee's head: Quit and drop any case, or the company will fire you for misconduct. Meanwhile the company is very aware of the fact that firing the employee for cause can make it difficult for the whistleblower to find another job.

The risks for whistleblowers attacked in this manner are enormous. Given the resources available to a company, including ready access to witnesses and documentation, how does an employee defeat a company's performance-based allegations?

In rare cases the company admits that the reason it fired the employee was retaliatory. This usually occurs when the company does not understand that the employee's conduct is protected, and thus its admission as to why the employee was fired becomes legally damning. For example, many laws protect employees who blow the whistle outside the chain of command. Under these laws, if management admits that the employee was fired because of violating the chain of command and going above the supervisor's head to raise a concern, the company indirectly admits to the wrongdoing. Direct evidence that an employer was angry with a worker who tipped off a government inspector or raised a concern to upper management without the courtesy of telling their immediate boss can be key to proving causation. But in most cases the proof of causation will be far subtler.

An Iowa federal court judge explained how difficult it can be for employees to prove that their protected activities caused their termination:

Employment discrimination and retaliation, except in the rarest cases, is difficult to prove. . . . Today's employers, even those with only a scintilla of sophistication, will neither admit discriminatory or retaliatory intent, nor leave a well-developed trail demonstrating it.

Because adverse employment actions almost always involve a high degree of discretion, and most plaintiffs in employment discrimination cases are at will, it is a simple task for employers to concoct plausible reasons for virtually any adverse employment action ranging from failure to hire to discharge.

One important method an employee can use to prove causation is by demonstrating that an employer's justification for an adverse action was not truthful. If a company lies about an employee's performance, that lie can constitute persuasive circumstantial evidence of intentional discrimination. Writing for the U.S. Supreme Court, Justice Sandra Day O'Connor put it this way:

The fact finder's disbelief of the reasons put forward by the defendant (particularly if disbelief is accompanied by a suspicion of mendacity) may, together with the elements of the prima facie case, suffice to show intentional discrimination. Thus, rejection of the defendant's proffered reasons will permit the trier of fact to infer the ultimate fact of intentional discrimination.

Disparate Treatment and Circumstantial Evidence

Because few employers will ever admit they fired an employee for an illegal reason, the U.S. Supreme Court has held that employees can rely solely on circumstantial evidence to prove causation. No "smoking gun" is necessary to win a case.

[E]vidence that a defendant's explanation for an employment practice is "unworthy of credence" is one form of circumstantial evidence that is probative of intentional discrimination.

—Justice Clarence Thomas, *Desert Palace v. Costa* (2003)

Although the types of circumstantial evidence an employee can use to prove causation are case-specific, the timing of an adverse action is often relied on in whistleblower cases. How did the boss view the employee before they became a whistleblower? How was the employee viewed after the whistleblower incident? Other than becoming a whistleblower, did anything else happen within the employment context that could rationally explain why there was a change in attitude toward the employee after the whistleblowing?

The following list is not exhaustive, but it sets forth some of the facts courts have considered to sustain a finding of causation or pretext:

- Excellent performance rating before the whistleblowing and performance problems after the protected disclosure

- The failure of an employer to follow routine procedures, such as adequately investigating the charges against the employee or failure to seek an employee's input prior to making a decision to downgrade or terminate the employee

- Absence of previous complaints against the employee

- Disparity between the way the whistleblower was treated and the manner in which other employees who did not blow the whistle were treated

- A determination that an employee was not guilty of the alleged violations

- Statements that an employee's protected activity was "disloyal" or somehow wrong

- Any remarks whatsoever that indicate that the employer was upset or displeased with an employee's protected activities, including statements indicating that the employee was a troublemaker or failed to follow the chain of command

- A pay increase shortly before the whistleblower disclosure was made and adverse action shortly after the disclosure

- Hostility or anger directed toward an employee's protected activities

- Shifting explanations for the reason(s) given for the adverse action

- Advising employees not to report safety problems or to talk with government inspectors

- Any dishonesty by an employer regarding facts material to a case, including knowledge of protected activity, reasons given for taking adverse action against an employee, or statements about the validity of the underlying whistleblower disclosure

In some cases, employers inadvertently admit to facts that prove causation, such as when managers testify that they are upset that employees went above them to raise a concern. Who would not be upset that a subordinate ignored them and went over their head to report a violation of law? Who would not be upset that a lower-level employee did not have the courtesy of pointing out errors and giving time to fix the problem before making a "federal case"? Who would not be embarrassed by such acts of disloyalty? These may appear to be honest feelings or reasonable reactions from a manager to a whistleblower. The only problem with these admissions is that they constitute direct evidence of guilt. An admission that a supervisor was upset or troubled by an employee's whistleblowing constitutes evidence of discriminatory motive.

The "Contributing Factor" Test

Under most state and federal laws, employees have the burden of demonstrating both causation and pretext. Employees must prove these two elements by a preponderance of evidence. However, starting in 1989, Congress came to understand that this burden was often difficult for employees to meet. Companies generally control information about employment practices. Likewise, witnesses are often under the control of the employer because of fear, a mistaken sense of loyalty, or concerns over their own jobs.

In the Whistleblower Protection Act of 1989 (the law covering most federal employees), Congress established a special standard applicable to whistleblower cases making it easier for employees to win their cases. Commonly referred to as the "contributing factor" test, Congress explained why it created this standard:

> *The bill makes it easier . . . to prove that a whistleblower reprisal has taken place. To establish a prima facie case, an individual must prove that whistleblowing was a factor in the personnel action. This supersedes the existing requirement that whistleblowing was a substantial, motivating or predominant factor in the personnel action. . . . . The bill establishes an affirmative defense for an agency. . . . [C]orrective action would not be ordered if the agency demonstrates by clear and convincing evidence that it would have taken the same personnel action in the absence of the disclosure.*

Instead of having to prove hostility toward the whistleblower as the main motivating factor in an adverse action, the employee need only prove that the hostility was a factor, regardless of how small. As explained by the U.S. Court of Appeals for the Federal Circuit, "contributing factor . . . mean(s) any factor which, alone or in connection with other facts, tends to affect in any way the outcome of the decision."

Just as the burden of proving causation was decreased for the employee, the burden for proving a legitimate business reason was significantly increased for management. Instead of the employee having the burden of proving pretext, the burden shifted to the employer. The employer had to demonstrate a legitimate reason for the discipline or discharge. This burden was increased from preponderance of evidence to clear and convincing evidence, a much higher standard.

Laws that apply the contributing factor test include the Consumer Product Safety Act, the Whistleblower Protection Act, the Motor Vehicle Safety Whistleblower Act, the Contractor Whistleblower Act, the Affordable Care Act, the Seamen Whistleblower Protection Act, the Sarbanes-Oxley Act, the Food Safety Modernization Act, the Atomic Energy Act, the Consumer Financial Protection Act, the Airline Safety Act, the IRS tax anti-retaliation law, the anti-trust whistleblower law, the Surface Transportation Act, the Railroad Safety Act, the AML Whistleblower Act, and the Pipeline Safety Improvement Act. Some states are also following this precedent, including the public employee whistleblower law enacted by the District of Columbia.

- Checklist 3 provides a list of factors used to demonstrate discriminatory motive and pretext in retaliation cases.

- *Desert Palace, Inc. v. Costa*, 539 U.S. 90 (2003) (key case regarding evidence needed to demonstrate discriminatory motive necessary to survive a motion for summary judgment).

- *Fordham v. Fannie Mae*, ARB No. 2021-0029, ALJ No. 2010-SOX-00051 (ARB July 19, 2021) (per curium) (Decision and Order) (explanation of contributing factor test by Labor Department).

Keeping Up with the Changes

To keep up to date on changes in the laws, whistleblowers should access the free online law library created by the author, located at www.kkc.com/law-library.

RULE 35

Truth Is Power

Whistleblowers should never lose sight of why they placed their job on the line. Although the "black letter" law holds that employees fighting retaliation are under no obligation to prove the accuracy of their whistleblower allegations, if in fact your allegations were correct, the bosses would have a powerful motive to attack your credibility and ultimately terminate your employment. If you accuse your boss of a crime and your allegations are true, what is the boss to do? Admit they committed fraud or undermine your credibility so as to mask wrongdoing? The stronger your evidence of wrongdoing, the greater a motive your boss may have to silence you, or, in the alternative, destroy your reputation.

Demonstrating that your boss had a strong motive to retaliate against you in order to cover up wrongdoing may be your best move to prove your case. An unbiased juror or judge will understand that a company would want to suppress an employee whose complaints were accurate. What better reason to retaliate against an employee than to gloss over a mistake or regulatory violation?

Getting the Facts Out: The Turner Trial

On a frozen February morning in 2007, ten Minnesota jurors returned from their deliberations to announce their verdict in a nine-year legal battle between Jane Turner and her former employer, the FBI. During the two weeks of trial, three government lawyers, two from the Justice Department and one from the FBI, called witness after witness to attack Turner. The witnesses included the top official from the FBI's powerful Criminal Division and the former special agent in charge of the FBI's Minneapolis division. A high-ranking former inspector, who led an "independent" review of Turner's performance, was one of the government's star witnesses. Turner, who had worked as an agent for twenty-five years, listened to these managers tear apart her career, and she was not at all surprised at what they had to say.

Turner had challenged one of the most tight-knit and insular agencies in the country—an employer with an authoritarian history and a motto proclaiming: "Thou Shall Not Embarrass the Bureau." Turner had directly taken on the FBI's "old boy network." She had accused respected and high-level G-men of incompetence and misconduct in handling horrendous child-crime cases. She had accused her bosses of ignoring the brutal rape of a five-year-old Native American. Shocking allegations.

As a technical matter, Turner was not obligated to prove that the FBI had botched child-crime cases. Like most retaliation cases, she only needed to demonstrate the reasonableness of her concerns, not their truth. At first blush, the issue at trial appeared similar to any employment case. Turner claimed she was an excellent agent with years of strong performance. Her FBI managers claimed her performance had radically dropped, that she botched cases, and that she no longer could perform her job. The scenario was typical. Like almost every company bent on retaliation, the FBI built a case against Turner—documenting every minor infraction, monitoring her every movement, and placing her on endless "performance improvement plans" whose essence was creating a mechanism to document performance failures.

Turner challenged the FBI head-on. She provided evidence documenting her main whistleblower concern: that the FBI had botched child-crime cases. If she was right, her managers would be discredited. If she was wrong, the performance failures would appear credible. The truth of her serious allegations of misconduct became the centerpiece of the trial.

Turner subpoenaed two assistant U.S. attorneys with whom she had worked during the five months her performance allegedly collapsed. She questioned them about a case she worked over the summer and fall of 1999. Turner was very lucky. Although they were still employed as prosecutors for the United States and regularly interacted with their FBI investigators, both told the truth without hesitation. They explained what happened in the controversial child-crime case Turner had worked, despite the objection from her immediate supervisor.

On the July 4 weekend in 1999, a five-year-old boy from the Turtle Mountain Indian Reservation was hospitalized. The child suffered from severe injuries consistent with having been brutally raped. Nurses in the emergency room were traumatized over the injury. The parents, who acted cold and detached while at the hospital, said that the injury resulted from a car accident. The treating emergency room doctor found the explanation absurd. However, the Bureau of Indian Affairs police officer accepted the story. The FBI agent responsible for the Turtle Mountain reservation reviewed the file and decided that no charges would be pursued. Case closed.

Turner visited the local hospital weeks later. The medical staff accosted her, including the doctor who had worked on the child in the emergency room. They were angry. Why were no charges filed? Why was the child sent back to the family—where the stepfather (the most likely suspect) would have access to him?

Turner reviewed the case file and immediately contacted the U.S. Attorney's Office. She relayed what had occurred. Just as management was hammering her over so-called performance issues, she now was confronted once again with another example of FBI mishaps, another example of the FBI turning its back on a child victim on an Indian reservation. She too could turn her back and support the decision of her fellow agent, or she could pursue the matter and potentially once again "embarrass the Bureau."

She reopened the case. It did not take long for Turner to demonstrate that the ridiculous story initially credited by the FBI was bunkum. The auto accident theory forensically fell apart, and the one witness who initially backed up the suspected rapist recanted his testimony. An objective review of the medical information left only one explanation for the injuries. Turner knew the profile well, as she had successfully cracked other cases and was a certified psychological profiler trained by the FBI's top experts.

Turner recommended that the stepfather be asked to undergo a voluntary polygraph and questioned about the incident. After significant delays, at the request of the federal prosecutors Turner's recommendation was followed. A confession was obtained. The stepfather pled guilty to the sexual assault.

Instead of greeting Turner's superb gumshoe work on the child-rape case with gratitude, her managers grew even more upset. How dare Turner second-guess a fellow agent? How dare she embarrass the FBI by reopening a closed case—after the FBI had made a determination that the child had not been raped? The FBI's reaction to Turner was typical of how mid-level and upper-level managers often react to whistleblowers. Circle the wagons; defend the line supervisor implicated in the retaliation; and "shoot the messenger." Turner was given another terrible performance review. She was a pariah—an agent to be avoided at all costs.

But Turner could prove she was right. A child had been brutally raped. The FBI had accepted a patently absurd alibi without any investigation. It had closed the case. As confirmed by the federal prosecutors who worked the case, but for Jane Turner's tenacity, a child rapist would have been walking the streets.

The managers who tried to justify the FBI's handling of the case lost their credibility before the court. How could a juror believe the testimony of FBI supervisors who attacked Turner's performance, when these same managers had backed up the agent who closed the child-rape case? The truth of Turner's allegations that the FBI botched child-crime cases at the Turtle Mountain Indian Reservation impeached every FBI witness who tried to smear her.

The *Minneapolis Star Tribune* reported on the jury's verdict:

> *Federal jurors hugged former FBI agent Jane Turner. "I think you were the very best FBI agent," juror Mashima Dickens told Turner, who investigated child sex-abuse crimes.*
>
> *"Looking at the way you were treated, I just said you were screwed left and right," Dickens said, tears rolling down her cheeks.*
>
> *"I just want to tell you I have nothing but the utmost respect for you," juror Renee Anderle said as she hugged Turner in the hallway outside Chief U.S. District Judge James Rosenbaum's courtroom in Minneapolis.*
>
> *"This is vindication," said Turner, 55, of St. Paul. "We spoke truth to power, and we won."*

The truth behind a whistleblower's cause can be the engine that drives a case, pushing it forward while placing the company on the defense, establishing strong credibility for the whistleblower, and eventually enabling an employee to triumph against a far stronger and well-funded foe.

The *Qui Tam* Alternative

Proving retaliation is not easy. However, under the reward laws the truth behind a whistleblower's disclosure is always the driving force behind a winning case. This is why many whistleblowers, when they can, shift the focus of their claim from a wrongful discharge to a whistleblower reward case. If an employee's whistleblowing concerns misuse of taxpayer monies, securities, commodities, money laundering, or tax frauds (among other covered crimes), they can shift the focus of the case from proving employment discrimination to proving a false claim or other frauds that can result in the payment of a financial reward. It is possible to pursue both a retaliation and a reward case at the same time. There is no bar to seeking a reward while at the same time fighting to get your job back.

In the end, the hardest part of a case is to make whistleblowing work. Sometimes this can be done using a reward law. Other times an employee must simply fight to save their job or reputation. If you are lucky, both types of law may be able to work in your favor.

PRACTICE TIPS

The U.S. Department of Labor's Administrative Review Board has issued a number of rulings explaining how proof of employer violations constitutes important evidence of retaliatory motive. Two to consider are:

- *Khandelwal v. Southern Cal. Ed.*, 97-ERA-6 (ARB, Mar. 31, 1998)

- *Seater v. Southern Cal. Ed.*, 95-ERA-13 (ARB, Sept. 27, 1996)

RULE 36

The Boss Must Make You Whole

Against many odds you win your employment case and are awarded damages. What happens next? It's time to make sure that a court or jury awards you every penny you deserve.

The basic rule in setting damages in employment cases is commonly referred to as the "make whole" remedy. Damages are designed to place the wrongfully discharged whistleblower in the precise place they would occupy if the discrimination never occurred. An 1867 U.S. Supreme Court case explained that compensation awarded to a victim must be "equal to the injury . . . the injured party is to be placed, as near as may be, in the situation he would have occupied if the wrong had not been committed."

Just as the scope of protected activity is different under every whistleblower law, so is the scope of relief. In deciding which law or laws a claim should be filed under, it is very important to carefully review the relief available and make sure you create a record justifying economic justice.

The major categories of damages relevant in whistleblower cases include the following:

- **Reinstatement.** Employees are entitled to reinstatement in their old job, or if not possible, a comparable job. This includes a position with the same status and promotional opportunities as the one they lost.

- **Front pay.** Front pay is an alternative to reinstatement. It can be available in cases when "irreparable animosity" exists between the company and the whistleblower. The amount of front pay is calculated to compensate employees for lost future earnings. However, employees are not automatically entitled to front pay, and the authority to award this form of relief is vested with a judge or jury.

- **Back pay and benefits.** All employment laws permit an award of back pay and lost benefits. However, employees need to be fully aware that companies can escape large back-pay awards by alleging that the employee failed to "mitigate" damages. This means that an employee cannot simply be fired and await the outcome of the legal case. They are under an obligation to look for new employment. If an employee does not look for work, the amount of damages to which they may be entitled can be reduced.

- **Compensatory damages.** Compensatory damages are awarded for pain and suffering, humiliation, emotional distress, and loss of reputation. Although not required, expert psychological testimony is often relied on to justify major emotional distress damages. Sometimes referred to as "special damages," compensatory damages are available under state public policy tort claims and most federal statutes. A request for compensatory or special damages should be pleaded in the initial complaint, as this is sometimes a requirement for obtaining a jury trial or qualifying for such relief.

- **Punitive or exemplary damages.** Punitive damages are available under state public policy tort claims and some federal statutes (including First Amendment or witness retaliation claims filed under the Civil Rights Act of 1871). Even if available, punitive damages are not automatically awarded. According to U.S. Supreme Court precedent, employees must demonstrate that the employer's conduct was "motivated by evil motive or intent" or that the employer acted with "reckless or callous indifference to the federally protected rights of others."

- **Other relief.** Apart from the big-ticket items listed above, the make whole remedy available under federal law can be aggressively and creatively applied in order to ensure that whistleblowers have true restitution.

When arguing for the maximum amount of relief, an important question to ask is how the make whole requirement can be molded to ensure that a whistleblower can get all they deserve. This includes relief related to the loss of status and career opportunities, which always flow from a termination or other adverse action. The types of relief awarded can include:

- Monetary compensation for lost overtime pay that an employee would have earned but for the discharge

- Restoration of vacation time

- Interest on all damages

- Restoration of seniority

- Restoration and/or compensation for all lost benefits, such as parking privileges and financial compensation for having lost access to a company car

- Positive recommendations from the employer

- Back-pay awards to take anticipated salary increases into consideration

- Compensation for forced sale of assets due to a prolonged unemployment

- All job search expenses (including the use of a headhunter)

- Removal of negative information from a personnel file

- Reinstatement of stock options and employee savings plans

- Restoration of lost retirement benefits

- Medical expenses (including future expenses)

- A letter of apology from the company president to all employees

- A notification from the company to all employees that it violated the law when it fired the whistleblower

- Company-wide training for managers about the rights of whistleblowers

- *Qui tam* damages. Proof of damages in a False Claims Act and other *qui tam* reward cases are totally different than the proof necessary in an employment retaliation case. Under the reward laws, damages are not tied to the harm suffered by an employee. Instead, they are set by the economic harm experienced by taxpayers or the sanctions permitted under laws such as the Securities Exchange Act. Under these laws a whistleblower is entitled to a percentage of the monies obtained by the government (generally between 10 and 30 percent).

—————————————— PRACTICE TIPS ——————————————

- Before filing a claim, review the relief available under each statute or under the common law.

- The reward laws permit whistleblowers to obtain significant compensation without having to suffer any adverse employment action. This is why a majority of whistleblowers are now using the reward laws both to protect themselves and to obtain compensation for the risks they take.

- *Hobby v. Georgia Power Co.*, 90-ERA-30 (ALJ, Sept. 17, 1998), affirmed DOL Administrative Review Board (Feb. 9, 2001) and U.S. Court of Appeals for the 11th Circuit (Sept. 30, 2002), carefully reviewed the full range of damages available to employees under Department of Labor–administered whistleblower laws.

RULE 37

How to Afford a Lawyer

One of the major problems encountered by whistleblowers fighting for their job is the ability to retain legal counsel. Employment cases are complex, hard fought, and the company will hire the best lawyers money can buy. To address this problem, most whistleblower laws have a "statutory fee" provision that requires a company to pay a whistleblower's attorney their fees if the employee wins his or her case. These provisions were designed to encourage high-quality lawyers to represent discrimination victims, almost all of whom cannot afford to pay lawyers at market rates.

Under the "American Rule," absent a statute, parties to civil lawsuits are responsible for paying their own attorney fees, regardless of who wins or loses a lawsuit. However, under most whistleblower retaliation laws Congress amended this rule. By statute Congress now permits workers who win whistleblower retaliation cases to have the company pay their legal fees at full market rates. Thus, an attorney can be incentivized to represent a whistleblower because if the whistleblower prevails at trial the lawyer can be paid by the company as part of the damages owed the victim of discrimination.

The reason for including the payment of fees as part of the damages in employment cases was explained by Congress in the Senate Report on the Civil Rights Attorney Fee Awards Act of 1976, codified as 42 U.S.C. § 1988: "If private citizens are able to assert their civil rights, and if those who violate the nation's fundamental laws are not to proceed with impunity, then citizens must have the opportunity to recover what it costs them to vindicate these rights in Court."

The Civil Rights Attorney Fee Awards Act permits employees who win to obtain fees in civil rights cases, including retaliation cases filed under Title VII of the Civil Rights Act of 1964 and First Amendment cases filed under the Civil Rights Act of 1871. After this law was passed in 1976, Congress included similar provisions in most employment discrimination laws, including nearly every whistleblower retaliation law (most reward laws do not include this provision because in those cases lawyers are expected to be compensated under a contingency fee arrangement).

The U.S. Supreme Court recognized that fee-shifting statutes were intended by Congress to "ensure effective access to the judicial process" by properly compensating attorneys in order to ensure that employees had the ability to "attract competent counsel" to represent their claims. As Justice Samuel Alito explained in *Perdue v. Kenny*, the statutory fee provisions are intended "to ensure that federal rights are adequately enforced."

Thus, under most whistleblower retaliation laws if the employee wins the case, the company must pay the employee's counsel at reasonable market rates. Attorneys can be paid fees in the hundreds of thousands of dollars (or even millions of dollars), and the payment of attorney fees is not directly tied to the amount of money awarded to the employee or the sum the employee was able to pay an attorney as part of a retainer agreement. As explained in *Perdue*, a "reasonable fee is a fee sufficient to induce a capable attorney to undertake the representation of a meritorious civil rights case . . . but that does not produce windfalls to attorneys."

The amount of attorney fees can and often does exceed the amount of damages awarded to the employee. This permits an attorney to spend the time necessary to carefully litigate a whistleblower case. It enables a whistleblower's counsel to compete with big firms, conduct aggressive discovery, and fight a case as hard as the most obstinate employer.

The following are the basic principles governing awarding attorney fees and costs to employees who win a whistleblower case:

- Properly document all costs incurred and the amount of time an attorney spends working on every aspect of the case. If the whistleblower wins, the attorney will be required to submit a detailed statement of all hours worked on the case and all costs incurred.

- In setting a reasonable fee, the court will apply a "lodestar" calculation in which the reasonable amount of time spent working on the case is multiplied by the reasonable market rate for the attorney's services. The market rate is not tied to the amount of fees actually charged by the attorney, but is established by the general market rates governing complex civil litigation. The market rate is governed by the rates charged by attorneys engaged in non–public interest work. Often the market rate is pegged to the amount of fees charged by large for-profit law firms that represent paying defendants. Attorneys should not be penalized because they choose to represent whistleblowers or other public interest clients at a reduced rate. To establish the prevailing market rates, sworn affidavits from other attorneys are most useful.

- There is no proportionality rule. The amount of attorney fees is not conditioned by the size of the judgment obtained. The Supreme Court confirmed this precedent in 1986, when it upheld an award of $245,456.26 in attorney fees in a case in which the damages awarded to the victim of the discrimination were limited to $33,350.00. If an employee obtains injunctive relief only (no monetary judgment), there is still no cap on attorney fees and costs.

- Prevailing employees can obtain compensation for expert witness costs only if the statute permits payment for expert witnesses.

- The attorney fee provisions also permit payment for paralegal and law clerk fees.

- Attorney fees are permitted for work performed during every phase of a case, including administrative proceedings.

- Applications for attorney fees and costs are generally submitted after the court issues a judgment for the employee.

- The rates of attorney fees are not determined by the fee agreement entered into between the attorney and the client, but are established by the controlling market rates.

- Attorney fees are permitted even if an employee is only partially successful in their case.

- Reasonable costs incurred by the client or the attorney are compensable, including travel costs, meals, hotel and airline expenses, deposition costs, arbitration costs, telephone fees, copy costs, subpoena fees, and filing fees.

Attorney Fees in Reward Cases

With the exception of the False Claims Act, whistleblower reward laws do not contain a statutory attorney fee provision. Many attorneys represent clients in reward cases on a contingency fee agreement and do not charge any up-front fees. Instead, the attorney is paid if a case has a successful outcome. A standard contingency fee is usually between 33 percent and 40 percent.

TAXATION OF ATTORNEY FEES

How are attorney fees taxed? On October 22, 2004, President George W. Bush signed the American Jobs Creation Act into law. Section 703 of that act contains the Civil Rights Tax Relief Act. This act prevents the double taxation of attorney fees obtained in employment discrimination, whistleblower, and False Claims Act lawsuits. Under this act a client does not pay any tax on fees paid to the attorney. The Tax Relief Act sets forth the method that the awards must be reported to taxing authorities in order to avoid double taxation.

The Commodity Exchange Act, Securities Exchange Act, and IRS whistleblower laws have specific provisions that prevent the double taxation of attorney fees. Congress has also exempted fees obtained in state False Claims Act cases from double taxation.

Each whistleblower anti-retaliation law must be checked to ensure that attorney fees are either covered explicitly under the law or eligibility for fees are included in the Civil Rights Attorney Fee Awards Act, 42 U.S.C. § 1988. Here are key Supreme Court decisions on how to calculate statutory fee awards:

- *Perdue v. Kenny*, 559 U.S. (2010) (fee enhancements)

- *Hensley v. Eckerhart*, 461 U.S. 429 (1983) (lodestar method)

- *Blum v. Stenson*, 465 U.S. 886 (1984) (determining fee rate)

- *Missouri v. Jenkins*, 491 U.S. 274 (1989) (use of current rates; paralegals)

- *City of Riverside v. Rivera*, 477 U.S. 561 (1986) (no proportionality)

- *Blanchard v. Bergeron*, 489 U.S. 87 (1989) (fee not controlled by agreement)

Keeping Up with the Changes

To keep up to date on changes in the laws, whistleblowers should access the free online law library created by the author, located at www.kkc.com/law-library.

CONCLUSION

Can Whistleblowers Drive a Spike through the Heart of Corruption?

White-collar criminaloids, however, are the most dangerous to society of any type of criminals . . .
                    —Professor Edwin H. Sutherland, *Principles of Criminology* (1939)

Why has whistleblowing been such an effective tool in the detection and prosecution of fraud and corruption?

To find the answer we need to go back in time to 1939, when the famous criminologist, Professor Edwin H. Sutherland, first coined the phrase "white-collar crime." Sutherland explained the sharp distinction between crimes committed by corporations or government officials and what he termed simply as "street crime." In so doing, he explained, for the first time, the types of violations modern-day whistleblowers would be best suited to expose and who was committing these crimes.

Shortly before the outbreak of World War II, the U.S. Armed Forces Institute published Professor Sutherland's book *Principles of Criminology*, in which he first explained the unique characteristics of white-collar corporate crimes:

> *The danger from robbery or kidnaping is clearly realized, for they involve direct sensory processes. . . . [But] theft by [fraud] . . . affects persons who may be thousands of miles away from the thief. . . . These white-collar criminaloids, however, are the most dangerous to society of any type of criminals from the point of view of the effects on private property and social institutions.*

Sutherland did not hold back on explaining who was behind white-collar crimes such as bribery and price fixing: They were committed by the "upper classes." To Sutherland, the stereotypes of poor "slum dweller(s)" committing crimes did not apply to the "the crimes of the business world." Corporate crimes are "indirect, devious, anonymous and impersonal." The difference between stealing from an individual by a personal theft and indirectly stealing from thousands of people by manipulating stock prices made white-collar crime unique. Sutherland observed that "persons practicing fraud have ordinarily felt no pangs of conscience, for the effects of fraudulent behavior have not become apparent in individual victims known to the defrauders but have been impersonal and diffuse."

Professor Sutherland warned that white-collar crime can undermine the social institutions necessary for people to trust their government in a democracy. His words of caution are ominous, even today, given the rise in authoritarian leaders within numerous democratic countries. Sutherland was extremely concerned that large-scale corruption would undermine the very fabric that holds society together:

> The financial loss from white-collar crime, as great as it is, is less important than the damage to social relations. White-collar crimes violate trust . . . lower social morale and produce social disorganization. Many of the white-collar crimes attack the fundamental principles of the American institutions. Ordinary crimes, on the other hand, produce little effect on social institutions or social organization.

Where do whistleblowers fit into this analysis? Sutherland understood that the largest problem in fighting corruption was *detection*. Since these crimes are committed in secret with no direct victim, "arrests were seldom made." He cautioned that "expert techniques of concealment have been developed . . . for the purpose of preventing" the detection of white-collar crime. Sutherland understood the problem, but it would take years before academia, or Congress, would recognize the most effective method to detect these crimes.

Sutherland took the first step in coming to grips with the cancer of big business corruption. The second step was taken by Professor Gary Becker, the University of Chicago Nobel Prize–winning economist. In order to develop a strategy for combatting white-collar crimes, it was imperative to also understand why top business leaders, wealthy individuals, and highly educated executives were willing to risk their positions and violate the law. Professor Becker's answer to that question was radical, but ultimately based on common sense: White-collar crime was good for business. Without a realistic risk of getting caught evading taxes, paying bribes, or defrauding the government was a *rational economic activity*. Only by understanding why committing white-collar crimes was a rational business decision would it be possible to develop tactics for fighting those crimes.

In his landmark 1968 paper, "Crime and Punishment: An Economic Approach," Becker explained that crime was best understood as a rational economic activity. If a business could be more profitable by breaking the law, why not break the rules for profit? Without the risk of being detected (and a sufficiently high sanction if you were caught), breaking the law was a rational business decision, increasing corporate profits and making its owners wealthy.

Becker postulated a straightforward formula for understanding white-collar crime and how to fight it: The risk of detection plus the amount of punishment would equal the rate of crime. Or, as Becker explained in economic terms: "If the aim" was "deterrence," by raising the "probability of conviction," corporate executives could be deterred from committing these crimes. Under this formula, once the act of committing white-collar crime is viewed as a rational decision often made by highly educated and well-paid executives, only then can the tactics necessary to combat this crime be understood. If the risk of detection was high and punishment was severe, the rate of crime would be low. No rational executive would engage in corrupt activities if they thought they would be caught. The greater the risk, the greater the punishment, the lower the rate of criminal activity.

The key was increasing the risk of detection so that committing a crime "exceed(ed) the gain" obtained from breaking the law. A realistic fear of detection, coupled with strong sanctions against those who got caught, would deter a rational economic actor from engaging in white-collar corrupt activities. Instead of crime being profitable (and fully justifiable on a cost-benefit approach), by increasing rates of detection and penalties, crime could become a detriment to business profits and an impediment to the private accumulation of wealth.

According to Becker, if his formula was followed, criminal offenses properly targeted "could be reduced almost at will," because "[f]or the individual to elect to engage in crime, the gain relative to its loss must exceed the odds of capture." At the heart of his crime-busting theory was a fundamental premise: The government would have to figure out a method to increase its ability to detect well-hidden white-collar crimes. The government needed to create laws where a rational executive, when "contemplating whether to commit a crime," is forced to take into "consideration not only the punishment they face if caught *but also their chances of being apprehended.*"

Without a realistic risk of detection and punishment, engaging in illegal corporate activities is a rational business decision. Those who are honest would be forced out of the market, forced to accept lower profits, or forced to join with their corrupt competitors in order to prosper. As will be shown, this is why whistleblowing is the cornerstone to ensuring fair competition, ensuring that all honest citizens and businesses can enjoy the benefits of a civil society, without being prejudiced by greedy corporate crooks.

The Detection Conundrum

Congress was not deaf to the problem of corporate corruption. In 1978 the U.S. House of Representatives Committee on the Judiciary, Subcommittee on Crime held a series of public hearings titled "White-Collar Crime." Congress wanted to know why law enforcement's efforts to tackle corruption were not working. Based on the testimony, it quickly became obvious that a principal impediment to enforcing laws governing corporate ethics was the inability to detect violations. Without detection there could be no cases to prosecute. The strictest laws protecting consumers, preventing fraud in government contracting, or punishing tax evaders would not work unless there was a method to find out who was breaking the law. Congress decided it was time to hear from the nation's top prosecutors and demand answers.

Benjamin Civiletti, the deputy attorney general, reported that government contractors were knowingly selling defective airplane parts to the Air Force and subjecting impoverished Medicaid patients to unnecessary medical tests simply to make more money. Like Professor Sutherland, Civiletti warned that public corruption creates a "deep sense of betrayal and disappointment" in the government, fueling widespread public cynicism. He was blunt:

> [T]he impact of white-collar illegality extends beyond simply pecuniary loss. Corruption of government officials can affect the quality of our food, and the safety of our homes. Such illegality also has invidious effect on the public's perception of the integrity of our political,

economic, and social and governmental institutions. Official corruption invariably involves breaches of trust, either in a legal or moral sense, and such offenses generate in the public a deep sense of betrayal and disappointment. . . . Such public perceptions are fertile ground for the development of widespread public cynicism and a conviction that the entire economic and political system is corrupt and lacks integrity. . . . [W]hite-collar offenses have the capacity to subvert the basic assumptions of our institutions and drain our national will . . .

Civiletti testified that methods to detect corporate crime must be improved. The "crime detection techniques developed in response to so-called street crimes" simply are not applicable when enforcing anti-corruption laws: "[I]nvestigators must look at not merely a single discrete act constituting the offense, but an entire course of conduct spanning months and even years. Relevant evidence may be spread out across the nation or around the world. Unlike street crimes where the crime is evident and the investigation focuses on establishing the identity of the culprit, an investigation of white-collar illegality centers primarily on determining if a crime actually occurred."

He further testified:

[White-]collar offenses are low visibility crimes. Victims may never be aware of the victimization . . . the covert nature of white-collar illegality requires us to move from a reactive enforcement posture [i.e., an investigation triggered when the victim of a crime makes a complaint] . . . to a enforcement posture in which we affirmatively seek out and pursue evidence of white-collar illegality even if no victim ever files a formal complaint. This would include using undercover techniques.

Other witnesses confirmed the hidden nature of criminal corruption, describing white-collar crime as invisible. For example, Herbert Edelhertz, former chief of the Fraud Section, DOJ Criminal Division, testified that a white-collar crime investigation is "an exercise which can only be compared to an archeological excavation—the tombs are carefully hidden and constructed with fake passages and antechambers to divert the search. The search itself is so laborious and complex an effort that it can easily destroy the trail it seeks to follow."

Congressional witnesses read directly from Gary Becker's playbook. They recognized that business executives would, consciously or not, engage in a rational cost-benefit analysis when considering whether to break the law for profit. Only if laws could be enacted that increased the risk of detection and increased the level of punishment could prosecutors successfully fight back. The U.S. attorney for the Southern District of New York testified that white-collar criminals were "smart enough to calculate the 'risks-to-benefits'" before engaging in corrupt activities. But under the current system there was simply *no effective deterrent*:

They are very smart. They are committing these crimes not out of need but out of greed, and they are smart enough to weigh the risks-to-benefits before they go into the crime. The profit from this kind of crime is enormous. They know the risk of detection, even with everything the Federal Government is trying to do now, is very slight. The cases are very difficult to investigate and very difficult to prosecute. And if, at the end of all that, after you have investigated and prosecuted successfully, a Federal judge is going to give somebody 2 months in jail or probation. . . . [T]here is nothing to deter the next person for engaging in that kind of criminal activity.

The U.S. attorney for New Jersey agreed with this assessment: White-collar crimes are of a "premeditated, calculated nature" and their motivation is greed. Thus, "if we can, through law enforcement, demonstrate to would-be white-collar offenders that not only will they run the risk of criminal prosecution and perhaps incarceration or like treatment, but in addition they will simply not be permitted to retain their ill-gotten gains which we will seek to recover through pursuit of civil remedies, I think the deterrent effect will be greatly heightened."

Eight years later Congress would approve a new technique for detecting white-collar crimes: incentivizing insider-whistleblowers to do the job.

Congress Wakes Up

There have always been whistleblowers willing to take massive personal risks to expose corruption. Some of these early whistleblowers, such as Daniel Ellsberg, are held up as heroes, while most others are forgotten. Regardless of their level of public recognition, all faced harsh personal consequences. In the early 1980s, Congress began to acknowledge that an effective anti-corruption detection system cannot be dependent on the one in a thousand whistleblower willing to place everything at risk and suffer severe retaliation. Not only was such reliance unrealistic, but the retaliation faced by these early whistleblowers created a massive chilling effect on other potential informants. Leading economists from the Universities of Chicago and Toronto, in their breakthrough study "Who Blows the Whistle on Corporate Fraud?" understood this problem well: "Honest behavior is not rewarded. . . . Given [the] costs [of whistleblowing], the surprising part is not that most employees do not talk, it is that some talk at all."

Congress started to look for a legal procedure that could break this corporate code of silence. They found it in an old Civil War law designed to combat fraud in defense contracting.

The original False Claims Act had been signed into law by President Abraham Lincoln on March 2, 1863. It was designed to empower the American people to help in the fight against defense contractor fraud that was undermining the Union army. Corrupt war profiteers were becoming rich and threatening the outcome of the war. Union soldiers were dying as a result of widespread frauds that impacted the quality of their food (contaminated meat), the strength of their horses (contractors sold the army blind horses), and the quality of their munitions (sawdust sold as gunpowder). The False Claims Act targeted these fraudsters by using a technique known as *qui tam*.

Qui tam whistleblower reward provisions are intended to incentivize insiders to turn on their coconspirators. *Qui tam*, a Latin phrase that roughly translates to "in the name of the king," empowering citizens to file lawsuits in order to enforce the law. The *qui tam* "relator" (the term used for whistleblowers in the 1863 law) could file a lawsuit in federal court against fraudsters who were ripping off the government by paying kickbacks to obtain government contracts (or engaging in other corrupt activities at the expense of the taxpayers). If they prevailed, they would collect a bounty.

On August 1, 1985, a freshman senator from Iowa, Charles Grassley, rose to the floor of the U.S. Senate and announced that he was introducing a bill to revitalize the Civil War False Claims Act and its *qui tam* whistleblower reward provisions. He was clear in purpose: Laws to prevent corruption were "in desperate need of reform." His goal was "expanding enforcement tools, by strengthening deterrence, and by encouraging disclosure of fraud by private individuals."

A year later, Grassley's vision was signed into law. Game on. The False Claims Act was modernized. The amendments created procedures that could incentivize whistle-blowers to provide the U.S. attorney general with their best evidence of fraud. Under the updated law the Justice Department was required to review the whistleblower's evidence and conduct an investigation. If the Justice Department agreed with the whistle-blower, the government could intervene in the lawsuit and prosecute the fraudster. The discretion of the government to deny otherwise qualified whistleblowers from obtaining a reward was ended. The law created a guaranteed minimum and maximum pay-out based on the amount of sanctions obtained from the fraudster and the quality of information provided by the whistleblower. Rewards for qualified whistleblowers were mandatory, and all the rights of a *qui tam* relator could be enforced in federal court.

Qui tam was back and modernized to target white-collar crime. Whistleblowers could obtain large financial rewards if their evidence was truthful and strong enough to find a fraudster guilty. So began a bold experiment in whistleblower advocacy. Time would tell if incentivizing insiders with large financial rewards based solely on the size of the sanction imposed on large-scale corporate crimes would solve the detection problem inherent in white-collar crime cases.

Whistleblowing Works

Thirty-five years after the False Claims Act amendments were signed into law by President Ronald Reagan, the proof is in the pudding. Congress had found a mechanism to incentivize insiders to report otherwise impossible-to-detect white-collar crimes. The first conundrum decried by Professor Sutherland was solved. Professor Becker's crime-fighting equation had found an answer. The thousands of successful prosecutions and the billions collected in fines under the FCA created a new era of corporate accountability. Whistleblowers were the shock troops in a war against corruption—a war that could be won.

The best starting point for evaluating the success of the *qui tam* whistleblower reward laws is to look at the 35-year history of the False Claims Act. Because the United States must pay whistleblowers who prevail in these claims a percentage of the monies *actually recovered* by the government from dishonest contractors, the U.S. Department of Justice keeps accurate statistics of *every FCA recovery*. The DOJ, down to the penny, has calculated the monies obtained as a direct result of whistleblower disclosures and compares those numbers to sanctions obtained in government-initiated cases. The results are stunning. Hard data exists that precisely quantifies the impact of whistleblowers.

Statistics published by the U.S. Department of Justice Civil Fraud Division speak for themselves. Between October 1, 1987, and September 30, 2022, the following recoveries have been obtained:

- By the DOJ Civil Fraud Division *without* the help of whistleblowers under the FCA: $22.1 billion

- By the DOJ Civil Fraud Division based on FCA cases *filed by whistleblowers*: $50.3 billion

- Rewards *actually paid* to whistleblowers under FCA: $8.619 billion

- Total amount of sanctions under the False Claims Act: $72.5 billion

- Since the False Claims Act was amended in 1986, whistleblowers are the direct source of approximately 70 percent of civil fraud recoveries obtained by the United States.

Most [civil fraud cases that result] in recoveries were brought to the government by whistleblowers under the False Claims Act.
                                                    —U.S. Assistant Attorney General

---

The following are examples of the amounts of money actually recovered by the taxpayer under the federal or state FCA due to the risks taken by employees who blew the whistle:

- Amerigroup Insurance: $225 million for illegally denying Medicaid coverage to pregnant women

- Archdiocese of New Orleans: $1 million for Hurricane Katrina-related frauds

- Armor Holdings, Inc. and Hexcel Corporation: $45 million for manufacturing and selling defective body armor

- Bank of America: $1 billion for banking/mortgage fraud

- Beverly Enterprises, Inc.: $170 million for charging to Medicare the salaries paid to nurses who worked on non-Medicare patients

- Bristol-Myers Squibb: $515 million for illegal pricing and marketing of over fifty different types of drugs

- Ciena Capital, LLC: $26.3 million for false certification of small business loan requirements

- Cisco Systems: $48 million for overcharging and defective pricing

- Citigroup: $158 million for mortgage fraud

- ConocoPhillips: $97.5 million for underpayment of natural gas royalties on public lands

- C.R. Laurence Co.: $2.3 million for evading customs duties

- CVS Corporation: $37 million for overcharging Medicaid

- Deutsche Bank: $202 million for defrauding HUD and the FHA

- Duke University: $112.5 million for submitting falsified research on NIH and EPA grants

- Eli Lilly & Co.: $1.415 billion for promoting drugs for uses not approved by the Food and Drug Administration

- Freedom Mortgage Corp.: $113 million for issuing HUD-backed mortgages that did not meet requirements

- GlaxoSmithKline: $750 million for selling adulterated drugs

- Hospital Corporation of America: $840 million for performing medically unnecessary tests, overbilling, "upcoding" (using false diagnosis codes to increase payments), and billing for non-reimbursable costs

- Lockheed Martin: $10.5 million for filing false invoices to obtain early payments

- Los Angeles Department of Water and Power: $160 million for overcharging customers

- Merck: $650 million for kickbacks and Medicaid Best Practice violations

- NetCracker Technology Corp.: $11.4 million for using individuals without security clearances on defense contracts

- Northrop Grumman: $191 million for fraudulent overcharging and selling defective equipment

- Oracle: $200 million for price-gouging on computers

- Pfizer, Inc.: $2.3 billion for illegal kickbacks and illegal marketing of numerous drugs, including Lipitor, Viagra, and Celebrex

- Pratt & Whitney: $52 million for defective turbines used in fighter jets

- Purdue Frederick Co.: $634.5 million for misbranding the painkiller Oxycontin

- Schering Plough: $435 million for illegal sales and marketing of brain tumor, cancer, and hepatitis drugs

- Science Applications International Corporation: $5.9 million for violations of conflict of interest requirements in contracts with the Nuclear Regulatory Commission

- Shell Oil Company: $110 million for underreporting and underpaying royalties

- Smithkline Beecham Clinical Laboratories: $325 million for charging the government for tests that were not performed, adding on unnecessary tests to increase billable costs, paying kickbacks to obtain a doctor's medical business, and double billing for dialysis tests

- Tenet Healthcare: $900 million for Medicare billing violations, kickbacks, and bill padding

- Toyobo Co. of Japan: $66 million for selling defective fiber used in bulletproof vests

- University of Phoenix: $67.5 million for violations of student loan regulations

- Walgreens: $120 million for improper drug switching

- Zoladz Construction Co.: $3 million for improperly obtaining set-aside contracts designated for disabled veteran–owned companies

The list goes on and on and on: Abbott Labs ($400 million recovery for taxpayers); Bank of America ($187 million recovery); Bayer Corporation ($257 million recovery); Boeing ($54 million recovery); BP/Amoco ($32 million recovery); Chevron ($95 million recovery); ConocoPhillips ($97 million recovery); General Electric ($59.5 million recovery); Harvard University ($31 million recovery); Hercules, Inc. ($26 million recovery); Ingersoll-Rand ($3 million recovery); MCI/WorldCom ($27 million recovery); Mellon Bank ($16.5 million recovery); Office Depot ($4.75 million recovery); OfficeMax ($9.8 million recovery); Princeton Review ($10 million recovery); Roche Biomedical Laboratories ($325 million recovery); Rockwell International ($27 million recovery); State of California ($73 million recovery); Texaco Oil ($43 million recovery); The Scooter Store ($4 million recovery); United Technologies ($150 million recovery); University of Pennsylvania ($30 million recovery).

But these successful prosecutions only tell half the story. The ability of the government to leverage reward laws to increase the ability to detect fraud has been remarkable. **Figure 3** in Rule 5 (Trap 2) shows the overall growth in fraud recoveries from when the False Claims Act was modernized in 1986 until 2021. Not only did the percentage of recoveries triggered by whistleblower disclosures increase, the overall amount of fraud recoveries also skyrocketed. As reflected in **Figure 24,** between 1987 and 2021 the United States recovered a total of $70.148 billion under the False Claims Act. Of this amount whistleblowers were able to force fraudsters to pay over $48.221 billion directly to the federal treasury. This number does not include the deterrent effect caused by the fear of detection triggered by the law, or the benefits obtained under collateral criminal prosecutions. In these cases the whistleblower obtained a total of $8.066 billion in awards.

Figure 24

Total Recoveries from Whistleblowers and Government under False Claims Act
(1987-2021)

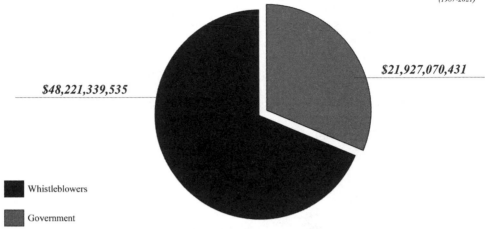

$48,221,339,535

$21,927,070,431

■ Whistleblowers

▨ Government

None of these rewards obtained by the whistleblowers were paid for by the taxpayer. The companies that fired or harassed the whistleblowers had to pay the bill. Although the average reward paid is approximately $1.5 million in FCA cases, a handful of astronomically large rewards have created a powerful incentive both for employees to blow the whistle and for companies to ensure that they are impeccably honest.

The remarkable success of the False Claims Act pushed Congress to enact a series of other laws aimed at paying rewards to whistleblowers to incentivize reporting of other white-collar crimes. The first new reward law, passed in 2006, covered tax evasion and underpayments. Almost immediately the law was used to crush illegal offshore Swiss banking. Next up were two powerful reward provisions included in the Dodd-Frank Act, one covering securities frauds and foreign bribery and the other covering commodities frauds. All of these laws included the same basic principles pioneered in the modernized False Claims Act: mandatory rewards, the ability to file confidential claims, and major incentives promoting insider disclosures. All of these laws have followed in the footsteps of the False Claims Act and have revolutionized the detection of white-collar crime. In December 2022 Congress expanded the reward laws to include money laundering, violations of the Bank Secrecy Act, and sanctions-busting. Thus, based on objective emperical data, and the strong support from law enforcement, whistleblower reward laws now cover most of the publicly traded U.S. economy and have broad transnational application.

The success of the post–False Claims Act reward laws can also be objectively demonstrated. Under the Dodd-Frank Act, the Commodity Futures Trading Commission reported that as of 2022 it has collected over $3 billion in sanctions from whistleblower cases and paid over $300 million in awards. This success is all the more remarkable given the small size of the CFTC, which operates on a tiny annual budget of approximately $300 million.

The program showed phenomenal growth. The CFTC did not issue its first award until 2014, and that was for only $240,000. As shown in **Figure 25,** since that date the amount of awards given to whistleblowers has exploded. Likewise, the number of

Figure 25

Total Amount of Whistleblower Awards Granted by the Commodity Futures Trading Commission

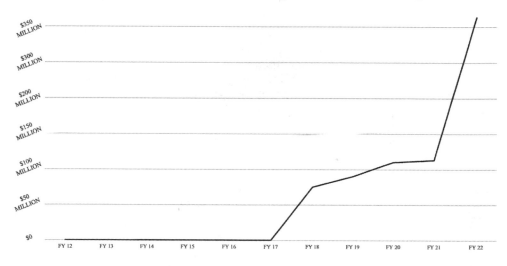

whistleblowers filing claims under the Commodity Exchange Act has risen from only 58 in 2012, to 1,506 in fiscal year 2022.

The SEC's program saw similar growth. In fiscal year 2012 (the first year a reward was paid), the total amount paid to whistleblowers was only $45,739.16. But in FY 2021 that number grew to $564 million. Overall, as of 2022 the SEC has paid $1.3 billion in awards and obtained over $6.3 billion in sanctions from fraudsters, of which over $3 billion was in disgorgement of ill-gotten gains. Over $1.5 billion was directly returned to harmed investors. In 2022 alone the SEC received over 12,300 tips from whistleblowers.

The whistleblower program . . . has rapidly become a tremendously effective force-multiplier, generating high quality tips, and in some cases virtual blueprints laying out an entire enterprise, directing us to the heart of the alleged fraud.
—Then-Chairman Mary Jo White, U.S. Securities and Exchange Commission

---

The size of judgments triggered by whistleblower disclosures sends the shock waves necessary for entrenched corporate traditions to change. These judgments create the most powerful incentive known under law for ensuring honesty in the marketplace. Large rewards grab headlines, advertise the existence of powerful whistleblower laws incentivizing disclosures of corporate crimes, and encourage an extremely reluctant workforce to come forward and report frauds and threats to the public safety.

The top government officials managing reward programs have publicly praised the contributions whistleblowers make in fighting corruption. In September 2020, all five SEC commissioners (three Republican members appointed by President Trump and two Democratic members) unanimously celebrated the SEC's whistleblower program and firmly rejected arguments that rewards should be limited in large cases. The

Trump-appointed chairman of the commission, Jay Clayton, expressed the views of the entire SEC when he stated: "Over the past ten years, the whistleblower program has been a critical component of the Commission's efforts to detect wrongdoing . . . particularly where fraud is well-hidden or difficult to detect."

After the 2020 elections these same sentiments were echoed by the Biden-appointed chairman of the SEC, Gary Gensler: "Whistleblowers provide a critical public service and duty to our nation. The tips, complaints, and referrals that whistleblowers provide are crucial to the Securities and Exchange Commission. . . . We must ensure that whistleblowers are empowered to come forward when they see misbehavior [and] that they are appropriately compensated."

Deterrence Is Documented

In September 2012 the world learned that a Swiss bank whistleblower, Bradley Birkenfeld, had just obtained the largest award ever given to an individual whistleblower. For turning in UBS's massive illegal offshore banking operation, Birkenfeld was awarded $104 million by the IRS. As serendipity would have it, at the same time Birkenfeld's award was publicly announced, leading Swiss bankers and their consultants were holding a major industry meeting in Geneva, Switzerland. A reporter from *Agence France-Presse* was in attendance and had a bird's-eye view of the reaction leaders of Swiss banking had to Birkenfeld's award.

According to the reporter's firsthand account, the bankers "seethed" at Birkenfeld and attacked his "total lack of morality" for blowing the whistle on them. However, in their very next breath, they also acknowledged that Birkenfeld had "driven the nail into the heart of the once seemingly invincible Swiss bank secrecy" system. A highly respected banking consultant was reported declaring that their U.S. client offshore banking program was finished.

Paying Birkenfeld a historic reward had an immediate impact on the entire Swiss banking system. The day after the Birkenfeld award was announced, the publication *SwissInfo* summarized these reactions as reported in various Swiss newspapers:

> The *Blick* tabloid newspaper said . . . it proves how ruthlessly US officials are pursuing tax evaders and how determined they are to dry up tax havens.
> Zurich's *Tages-Anzeiger* went further, describing it as a "seductive offer for bankers." "This enormous reward show how the US are raising the stakes in their tax fight with Switzerland . . . in promising such high compensation the IRS are hoping that more incriminating material is handed over."
> The French-speaking daily *Le Temps* agreed that Birkenfeld's huge reward could encourage other bank employees to follow his example.

Deterrence was the name of the game. It was clear to these industry leaders that Swiss bankers could make far more money turning in their U.S. clients then they could serving them. For example, after the Birkenfeld case became public, news reports confirmed another massive Swiss bank whistleblower case. The defendant in that case was Switzerland's oldest bank, Wegelin & Co. The bank, founded in 1741, admitted to hiding $1.2 billion for American tax evaders. After pleading guilty to criminal charges,

Wegelin was forced to close and declare bankruptcy, sending new shock waves throughout the international offshore banking community. The fact that Wegelin only had branches in Switzerland did help it escape the long arm of U.S. law enforcement, and some of its executives remain international fugitives.

Like in the Birkenfeld case, press accounts confirmed that Wegelin bank whistleblowers were paid millions in rewards. Following these high-profile whistleblower cases, all (or most all) known illegal U.S. accounts in Switzerland were closed, and *billions upon billions* of dollars in monies formerly held in illegal offshore accounts were repatriated to the U.S. economy. These monies would be taxed forever and become part of the lawful U.S. economy.

The Department of Justice bragged about this revolution in offshore tax compliance. According to Justice, it demanded that every Swiss bank make "a complete disclosure of their cross-border activities," provide DOJ "on an account-by-account basis" information on U.S. taxpayers, pay "appropriate penalties," and agree to close accounts of non-compliant U.S. citizens in order to avoid the fate of Wegelin and UBS. As predicted, Swiss banks agreed to these terms in droves. Almost the entire Swiss banking empire, from large publicly traded banks to small banks with offices only in Switzerland, accepted the DOJ deal. These banks, and the terms of their settlements, are all published on the DOJ website at https://www.justice.gov/tax/swiss-bank-program.

The full impact of successfully using *qui tam* whistleblower laws to trigger compliance was explained by then-chairman of the IRS Advisory Council, University of California–Davis law professor Dr. Dennis Ventry. In a 2014 article in the *Villanova Law Review*, Ventry described how Birkenfeld's whistleblowing changed Swiss bank secrecy forever: "'Collateral impact' hardly does justice to the effect of Birkenfeld's whistleblowing." He not only triggered the "UBS debacle" but also "everything that followed," including "more than 120 criminal indictments of U.S. taxpayers," "additional indictments against foreign bankers, advisors, and lawyers," "closure of prominent Swiss banks—including the oldest private bank," other persons "ratting out banks," and "banks themselves disclosing the names and accounts of [US] clients."

Ventry carefully laid out the benefits derived by the United States from the *qui tam* whistleblower program: The "treasure trove of inside information" that Birkenfeld provided U.S. officials formed "the foundation for the UBS debacle and everything that followed." He further explained:

> [T]he U.S. government (take a deep breath) received: $780 million and the names of 250 high-dollar Americans with secret accounts as part of a deferred prosecution agreement (DPA) with UBS; another 4,450 names and accounts of U.S. citizens provided as part of a joint settlement between the U.S. and Swiss governments; more than 120 criminal indictments of U.S. taxpayers . . . more than $5.5 billion collected from the IRS Offshore Voluntary Disclosure Program (OVDP), with untold tens of billions of dollars still payable . . . banks themselves disclosing the names and accounts of clients who refuse to participate in the program to avoid their own monetary penalties and to defer or avoid criminal prosecution.

Prior to the Birkenfeld case, attempts to crack Swiss bank secrecy had failed. But paying insiders large rewards radically increased the risk of detection, and the notorious Swiss banking system collapsed, at least as it impacted U.S. citizens. The *qui tam* model worked on a global scale.

But the greatest dividend obtained from *qui tam* laws goes toward deterrence of future crimes. Ventry clearly saw this in the context of Swiss banking: "[Whistleblowers] prevent noncompliance from happening in the first place. An effective whistleblower program . . . add[s] significant risk to noncompliance by increasing the probability of detection and the likelihood of potential penalties, the two most important variables in traditional tax deterrence models."

Ventry's conclusion that a successful whistleblower program could have a massive deterrent effect on wrongdoing was fully documented in report No. GAO-13-318, issued by the U.S. Government Accountability Office and available online at https://www.gao.gov/assets/gao-13-318.pdf. The report compared two nearly identical voluntary tax compliance programs. Both targeted illegal Swiss offshore banking. Both offered amnesty and other benefits to tax evaders who voluntarily came forward and reported their secret accounts. The only difference between the two programs was one occurred *before* the Birkenfeld-UBS tax case, when most U.S. account holders did not fear detection. The second was implemented after the Birkenfeld-UBS tax case, with the intent to leverage the increased fear of detection generated by the UBS prosecution and the newly minted IRS whistleblower law that was targeting offshore banking.

The report provided hard data comparing the pre- and post-whistleblower voluntary compliance program. The results confirmed what common sense dictated: Fear of detection is a strong stimulus for deterring crime. Fear of detection can and will dramatically increase voluntary compliance with the law. The GAO numbers speak for themselves:

Pre-Whistleblower 2003 Program

Total amount collected:	*$200 million*
Total number of participants:	*1,321*

Post-Whistleblower 2009 Program

Total amount collected:	*$4.1 billion*
Total number of participants:	*19,337*

The numbers alone demonstrate a nearly 20:1 increase in voluntary compliance after the enactment of the IRS whistleblower law and one extremely successful high-profile case against a major bank. However, these numbers don't tell the entire picture. The IRS was flooded with taxpayers who wanted to turn themselves in. At the time of the GAO report, the government had only closed out 10,439 tax cases of the 19,337 persons who applied for amnesty under the post-Birkenfeld reward program, so the actual amount of compensation returned to the American taxpayers would ultimately be far above the $4.1 billion figure. Everything predicted by the Becker economic model for deterring crime was empirically documented.

Academic studies have further confirmed this deterrent effect. Professor Giancarlo Spagnolo and Theo Nyreröd at the Stockholm School of Economics published a paper concluding that "whistleblowing deters financial misreporting." Professors Philip Berger and Heemin Lee, from the University of Chicago Booth School of Business and the Zicklin School of Business at the City University of New York, respectively, confirmed the "high direct deterrence value of whistleblower cases," and concluded that the "opportunity for a large payout creates incentives for a whistleblower to come forward" and "creates a profit motive for rooting out impropriety." Assistant professor at the Boston University Questrom School of Business, Jetson Leder-Luis put a dollar figure to whistleblower-induced deterrence in the healthcare industry. After looking at cases where the United States recovered $1.9 billion from whistleblower-triggered cases, he developed an economic model that concluded the long-term deterrence effect caused by these cases was "around 6.7 times the settlement value" over a five-year period. Thus, without having to fire a shot, taxpayers were able to save another $18.9 billion in healthcare costs alone.

The U.S. Securities and Exchange Commission is the first government agency to formally acknowledge the deterrent effect that whistleblowing has on crime. In 2022 the commission cited to the numerous academic studies supporting these findings to significantly strengthen its whistleblower program, in part to increase deterrence:

> Whistleblower programs, and the SEC's whistleblower program in particular, have been studied by economists who report findings consistent with award programs being effective at contributing to the discovery of violations. For example, a recent publication reports that, among other benefits, "[w]histleblower involvement [in the enforcement process] is associated with higher monetary penalties for targeted firms and employees." In addition, current working papers report that the SEC's whistleblower program deters aggressive (i.e., potentially misleading) financial reporting and insider trading.

Wall Street lobbyists and their Big Business allies continue to oppose strengthening whistleblower laws. But the fact remains, whistleblowing works. Its success at reducing white-collar crime is objectively documented, as is its utility in holding the largest fraudsters accountable and ensuring fair competition. Since the False Claims Act was amended, no less than $100 billion has been collected from white-collar criminals, money launderers, bribe-payers, and drug companies that bilked Medicare and Medicaid. The deterrent effect of these successful prosecutions can be estimated to be within the range of $1 to $2 trillion dollars. The key to this growth in successfully holding the most powerful special interests accountable, and establishing true equal justice under the law, is the willingness of all three branches of government to support a developing partnership between whistleblowers and law enforcement.

The Vindication of Sutherland and Becker

Starting in the 1930s Professors Sutherland and Becker developed a theoretical framework for combating white-collar crimes. But until the False Claims Act was amended in 1986, these theories were largely untested. Once whistleblowers were empowered, the predicted explosion in successful prosecutions and corresponding deterrence occurred. The modernized reward laws solve the detection dilemma that, for years, had undermined enforcement of anti-corruption laws. Only then was it clear that Sutherland and Becker's understanding of how to fight white-collar crime were vindicated. Today modern whistleblowing has changed the historical dynamic where whistleblowers were always on the losing side of the equation. The new laws create a realistic path forward for fighting corporate crime. When whistleblowers win, the public is well served.

PART V:

Checklists

Author's Note: To help readers understand their rights and defend themselves in court, I have created an online law library where readers can access, free of charge, the laws and major court opinions cited in the Rules. The law library also links to important legal updates. By linking the key cases and laws online these maerials can be updated so the reader can easily access the best information needed to prevail in a whistleblower case. The law library is located at www.kkc.com/law-library.

Always remember that the Rules and authorities discussed herein are not a substitute for obtaining independent advice from an attorney.

CHECKLIST 1

Whistleblower Reward Laws (*Qui Tam*)

Federal Qui Tam *Laws*

Anti-Money Laundering (AML) Act	31 U.S.C. § 5323
Act to Prevent Pollution from Ships (APPS)	33 U.S.C. § 1908(a)
Commodity Exchange Act	7 U.S.C. § 26 17 C.F.R. Part 165
Endangered Species Act	16 U.S.C. § 1540(d)
False Claims Act	31 U.S.C. § 3729–3732
Financial Institutions Reform, Recovery, and Enforcement Act (FIRREA)	12 U.S.C. §§ 4201–10
Fish and Wildlife Improvement Act	16 U.S.C. § 742l(k)
Foreign Corrupt Practices Act	15 U.S.C. §§ 78m, 78dd, 78ff Filing procedures for FCPA cases are identical to the SEC and CFTC procedures published at 17 C.F.R. Parts 240 (SEC) and Part 165 (CFTC)
Internal Revenue Code	26 U.S.C. § 7623
Lacey Act	716 U.S.C. § 3375(d)
Major Frauds Act	18 U.S.C. § 1031(h)

Motor Vehicle Safety Act	49 U.S.C. § 30172
Securities Exchange Act	15 U.S.C. § 78u-6
	17 C.F.R. § 240

State and Municipal False Claims Acts

Alaska (City of Anchorage)	City of Anchorage FCA AO No. 2016-48.
California	California False Claims Act § 12650, et seq.
Colorado	Colorado False Claims Act, C.R.S. § 25.5-304, et seq.
Connecticut	Connecticut False Claims Act § 17b-301a.
Delaware	Delaware False Claims and Reporting Act § 1201, et seq.
District of Columbia	District of Columbia False Claims Act § 2-381.01, et seq.
Florida	Florida False Claims Act § 68.081–68.093.
	Miami Dade County False Claims Ordinance (Ord. No. 99-152, § 1, 11-2-99) § 21-256-266.
Georgia	State False Medicaid Claims Act § 49-4-168–§ 49-4-168.8, et seq.
Hawaii	False Claims to the State § 661-21–§ 661-29, et seq.
	Qui Tam Actions or Recovery of False Claims to the Counties § 46-171–§ 46-179, et seq.
Illinois	Illinois Whistleblower Reward and Protection Act § 175-1–§175-8, et seq.
Indiana	Indiana False Claims and Whistleblower Protection IC 5-11-5.5–IC 5-11-5.5-18.
Iowa	Iowa False Claims Act, Title XV, Subtitle 5, Ch. 685.
Louisiana	Louisiana False Claims Act § 46:437.1–46:437.14, 438.1–438.8, 439.1–439.2, 439.3–439.4, 440.1–440.3.
Maryland	Maryland False Claims Act § 2-601–2-611.
Massachusetts	Massachusetts False Claims Act Ch 12 § 5A-12 § 5O, et seq.
Michigan	The Medicaid False Claims Act MCL 400.611.
Minnesota	Minnesota False Claims Act Minn. Stat. § 15C.01, et seq.
Montana	Montana False Claims Act § 17-8-401–§ 17-8-403, et seq.
Nevada	Nevada Submission of False Claims to State or Local Government § 357.010–§ 357.250, et seq.
New Hampshire	Medicaid Fraud and False Claims § 167:61-b–§ 167:61-e, et seq.
New Jersey	N.J.S.A. 2A:32C-1.
New Mexico	Medicaid False Claims Act § 27-14-1, et seq.
	Fraud Against Taxpayers Act § 44-9-1–§ 44-9-14, et seq.

New York	New York State False Claims Act § 187–§ 194, et seq.
	New York City False Claims Act § 7-801–§ 7-810.
	Rule Governing the Protocol for Processing Proposed Civil Complaints Pursuant to the New York City False Claims Act § 3-01–§3-03, et seq.
North Carolina	North Carolina False Claims Act § 1-605–§ 108A-63.
Oklahoma	Oklahoma Medicaid False Claims Act Title 63 § 5053, et seq.
Rhode Island	Rhode Island False Claims Act § 9-1.1-1–§ 9-1.1-8.
Tennessee	Tennessee Medical False Claims Act § 71-5-181–§ 71-5-186.
Texas	Texas False Claims Act § 32.039.
	Medicaid Fraud Prevention § 36.001–36.008, § 36.051–§36.055, § 36.101–§ 36.117, § 36.131–§ 36.132.
	Health and Human Services Commission § 531.101–§ 531.108, § 531.1061–§ 531.1062, et seq.
Vermont	Vermont False Claims Act, 32 V.S.A. §§ 630-642.
Virginia	Virginia Fraud Against Taxpayers Act § 8.01-216.1–§ 8.01-216.19, et seq.
Washington	Washington False Claims Act, Title 74, ch.74.66, et seq.
Deficit Reduction Act of 2005	42 U.S.C. § 1396(h)
	Provides extra financial incentives for states to enact False Claims Acts.

CHECKLIST 2

Whistleblower Protections under Federal Law

Laws that have been effectively used to protect whistleblowers are marked with an *.

A. Constitutional Protection: First Amendment "Freedom of Speech"

*U.S. Constitution First Amendment (Also see discussion below on 42 U.S.C. § 1983, which applied the First Amendment to state and local government employees.)	Protection for public employees who blow the whistle on matters of public concern.
*Civil Rights Act of 1871, 42 U.S.C. § 1983 [Applying First Amendment Protection to State and Municipal Employees]	Statutory protection for state and local government employee whistleblowers whose speech is protected under First Amendment. Law permits federal court lawsuit for damages and other relief. Compensatory and punitive damages permitted. Cases heard by jury trial.
Civil Rights Attorney Fee Awards Act, 42 U.S.C. § 1988(b) and (c)	Provision in law permitting award of statutory attorney fees in employment discrimination and retaliation cases filed under Title VII of the Civil Rights Act and the Civil Rights Act of 1871, 42 U.S.C. §§ 1983 and 1985.

B. Consumer Product Safety Whistleblower Protections

*Consumer Product Safety Act of 2008	Protection for employees who blow the whistle on covered consumer safety hazards and violations.
15 U.S.C. § 2087	Claims filed with U.S. Department of Labor/OSHA within 180 days of adverse action. Claims can be removed to federal
29 C.F.R. § 1983	court for jury trial.

C. Corporate Whistleblower Protection

*Dodd-Frank Wall Street Reform and Consumer Protection Act of 2010 Public Law No. 111-203	The Dodd-Frank Act of 2010 contained three new whistleblower protection provisions and amended the Sarbanes-Oxley Act and False Claims Act whistleblower laws.
	Section 748 (created rewards and anti-retaliation provisions for reporting violations of the Commodity Exchange Act), 7 U.S.C. § 26.
	Section 922 (created rewards and anti-retaliation provisions for reporting violations of the Securities Exchange Act, including violations of the Foreign Corrupt Practices Act), 15 U.S.C. § 78u-6.
	Section 1057 (whistleblower anti-retaliation protections for disclosures to the Bureau of Consumer Financial Protection), 12 U.S.C. § 5567.
Criminal Antitrust Anti-Retaliation Act (15 U.S.C. § 7a-c)	Anti-retaliation law modeled on Department of Labor whistleblower statutes. 180-day statute of limitations. Claims filed with DOL.

Sarbanes-Oxley Act of 2002, 18 U.S.C. § 1514A	Protection for employees who blow the whistle on fraud against shareholders and violations of securities laws.
Department of Labor Rules at 29 C.F.R. Part 1980.	Complaint filed with U.S. Department of Labor within 180 days of adverse action. Reinstatement, back pay, special damages, and attorney fees permitted.
Sarbanes-Oxley Act Audit Committee 15 U.S.C. § 78j-1(m)(4)	Requirement that publicly traded corporations have independent audit committee that can accept employee concerns on a confidential basis.
Sarbanes-Oxley Act Rules of Professional Responsibility for Attorneys 15 U.S.C. § 7245	Requirement that attorneys disclose wrongdoing and limitations on attorney-client privilege. SEC Rules implementing law: 17 C.F.R. 205.1, et seq.
*Banking Industry 12 U.S.C. § 1790b (Credit Unions) 12 U.S.C. § 1831j (FDIC Insured Institutions)	Federal court remedies for employees in banking industry, including the Federal Reserve, any "insured depository institution," and other private and federal financial institutions. Two-year statute of limitations.
Protection for Whistleblowers Who Disclose Trade Secrets Defend Trade Secrets Act 18 U.S.C. § 1833(b)	Whistleblowers can disclose trade secrets when they confidentially report suspected violations of law to federal or state law enforcement authorities. Disclosures can also be filed confidentially in court cases concerning whistleblower retaliation. The Defend Trade Secrets Act sets forth specific procedures for disclosing trade secrets and requires employers to notify employees concerning their rights under this law.

D. Criminal Prohibition Against Retaliation

Obstruction of Justice, Retaliation Against Whistleblowers 18 U.S.C. § 1513(e)	Federal felony to harm an employee's livelihood in retaliation for providing truthful information about potential crimes to federal law enforcement. Passed as part of the Sarbanes-Oxley Act of 2002.
Racketeer Influenced and Corrupt Organizations Act 18 U.S.C. § 1961, 1962 and 1964	*DeGuelle v. Camilli*, 664 F.3d 192 (7th Cir. 2011) (permitting whistleblower to file a Civil RICO case based on violations of § 1513e); the post-SOX federal obstruction of justice statute).

E. Environmental Protection, Ocean Pollution, and Wildlife Trafficking

*Environmental Whistleblower Protections 42 U.S.C. § 7622 (Clean Air Act) 42 U.S.C. § 300j-9(i) (Safe Drinking Water) 42 U.S.C. § 6971 (Solid Waste Disposal) 42 U.S.C. § 9610 (Superfund) 15 U.S.C. § 2622 (Toxic Substances) 33 U.S.C. § 1367 (Water Pollution)	Broad coverage for environmental whistleblowers, but law has short statute of limitations (thirty days) and must be filed with the Department of Labor. Remedies include reinstatement, back pay, compensatory damages, and attorney fees. Safe Drinking Water and Toxic Substances also permit exemplary damages. 29 C.F.R. Parts 18 and 24 (DOL rules implementing the environmental whistleblower protection provisions).
*Pipeline Safety Improvement Act 49 U.S.C. § 60129	Similar protections and rules as contained under the Atomic Energy Act and Sarbanes-Oxley Act. Department of Labor rules implementing the act are codified at 29 C.F.R. Parts 18 and 1981. There is a 90-day statute of limitations for filing a complaint with the DOL.
Surface Mining Act 30 U.S.C. § 1293	Legal protections similar to other environmental statutes, but administered by the Department of the Interior, not the Department of Labor. Department of the Interior rules codified at 30 C.F.R. § 865.
Act to Prevent Pollution from Ships (APPS) 33 U.S.C. § 1908(a)	Court can award whistleblowers up to 50 percent of monies obtained from criminal and civil penalties collected for violations of the APPS.
Endangered Species Act (ESA) 16 U.S.C. § 1540(d)	Secretaries of Commerce, Interior, and Treasury (and for plants, Agriculture) can pay rewards based on monies obtained from fines and penalties in ESA cases.
Fish and Wildlife Improvement Act 16 U.S.C. § 742l(k)(2)	The U.S. Fish and Wildlife Service and the National Marine Fisheries Service can pay rewards under all wildlife protection laws (plants, fish, and animals) administered by these two agencies to whistleblowers who report violations, even if no final enforcement action is undertaken.
Lacey Act 16 U.S.C. § 3375(d)	Secretaries of Commerce, Interior, and Treasury (and for plants, Agriculture) can pay rewards based on monies obtained from fines and penalties in Lacey Act cases.

F. Federal Contractor Fraud

*Department of Defense Contractor Fraud Anti-retaliation 10 U.S.C. § 4701	Misuse of Department of Defense (DOD) monies by a contractor. Complaints filed with the DOD (or NASA) inspector general. After exhausting administrative remedy, employee can file a claim in federal court and request a trial by jury. Compensatory damages available. This statute is substantially identical to the Enhancement of Whistleblower Protection for Contractor and Grantee Employees Act, codified at 41 U.S.C. § 4712.
Federal Acquisition Regulations; Contractor Business Ethics Compliance and Contractor Whistleblower Protection Rules 48 C.F.R. Ch. 148 C.F.R. Subpart 3.900 73 *Federal Register* 67064	Regulations mandating that federal contractors not retaliate against whistleblowers and establish ethics/compliance programs. Employees suffering retaliation by a federal contractor may file a complaint with the inspector general from the agency that awarded the grant. Federal contractors are prohibited from using confidentiality agreements to restrict an employee's right to report "waste, fraud, or abuse" to an appropriate law enforcement officer. See 48 C.F.R. § 3.909.
*False Claims Act, Whistleblower Anti-retaliation 31 U.S.C. § 3730(h)	Strong protections for employees who disclose violations of the False Claims Act (fraud in federal contracts). Claims filed in federal court, employees entitled to reinstatement, double back pay, special damages, and attorney fees. Cases under this subsection are often filed as part of a *qui tam* lawsuit under the FCA in order to obtain a financial reward pursuant to 31 U.S.C. §§ 3729–32.
Major Frauds Act, Whistleblower Anti-retaliation Provision 18 U.S.C. § 1031(h)	Similar remedy as contained under the False Claims Act, 30 U.S.C. § 3730(h).
Public Contracts—Procurement Provisions, Contractor Employees: Protection from Reprisal for Disclosure of Certain Information 41 U.S.C. § 265	Note: Employees who state a claim under this law may also have a claim under the False Claims Act, 31 U.S.C. § 3729-32.
Enhancement of Whistleblower Protection for Contractor and Grantee Employees 41 U.S.C. § 4712	Protected disclosures include information evidencing the "gross mismanagement of a Federal contract or grant, a gross waste of Federal funds, an abuse of authority relating to a Federal contract or grant, a substantial and specific danger to the public health or safety, or a violation of law, rule, or regulation related to a Federal contract or grant." Initial complaints must be filed with the Office of Inspector General of the agency involved with the contract or grant within three years of any adverse action. Contractors who work on projects related to the U.S. intelligence community are exempt from this law.

H. Federal Court Witness Protection

*Civil Rights Act of 1871 42 U.S.C. § 1985(2)	Conspiracy to interfere with the administration of justice in U.S. courts by retaliating against witnesses in federal court proceedings. *Haddle v. Garrison*, 525 U.S. 121 (1998) ("at-will" employees fired for obeying a grand jury subpoena stated claim).

I. Federal Employee Whistleblower Protections

Restrictions on Federal Nondisclosure Agreements P.L. 112-199 § 115, 5 U.S.C. § 2302 note and 5 U.S.C. §§ 2302(a)(2)(A)(xi) and 2302(b)(12)	Amendment to Appropriations Act that prevents the Executive Branch from utilizing overly broad nondisclosure agreements that prevent federal employees from reporting violations of law. As part of the Whistleblower Protection Enhancement Act of 2012, this anti-gag provision was incorporated into the federal civil service laws. Nondisclosure agreements used by the U.S. government must inform employees and government contractors of their right to provide information about serious misconduct to Congress, inspectors general, and other appropriate law enforcement agencies.
Civil Service Reform Act, Whistleblower Protection Act 5 U.S.C. § 2302 5 U.S.C. § 1211-1215, 1218-1219, 1221-1222	Major law protecting most federal employee whistleblowers. Employees can file retaliation complaints with Office of Special Counsel and appeals with the Merit Systems Protection Board.
Principles of Ethical Conduct for Government Officers and Employees Executive Order 12731, §101(k) 5 C.F.R. § 2635.101 57 *Federal Register* 35006	Requires federal employees to report waste, fraud, abuse, and corruption to appropriate authorities.
Inspector General Act 5 U.S.C. Appendix, §§ 3 and 7	Inspectors general can receive allegations of misconduct and investigate retaliation.
Lloyd-LaFollette Act, Employees' Right to Petition Congress 5 U.S.C. § 7211	Federal employees permitted to contact members of Congress.
No Fear Act 5 U.S.C. § 2301 (Note) P.L 107-174	Requires federal agencies to notify and train federal employees concerning their rights under whistleblower protection and antidiscrimination laws.
Congressional Accountability Act 2 U.S.C. § 1301, et seq.	Protections for congressional offices under traditional employment discrimination laws, such as Title VII and OSHA. Law establishes special office and procedures for employees.

J. Food Safety Whistleblower Protections

Food Safety Modernization Act of 2010 21 U.S.C. § 399d	Covers all employers "engaged in the manufacture, processing, packing, transportation, distribution, reception, holding or importation of food." § 1012(a).

K. Healthcare Whistleblower Protections

Patient Protection and Affordable Care Act § 1558 of Public Law No. 111-148 29 U.S.C. 218C	Employees who disclose violations of Title I of the Patient Protection and Affordable Care Act or section 2706 of the Public Health Service Act obtain protections modeled on those contained in the Consumer Product Safety Act of 2008, 15 U.S.C. § 2087. These provisions relate to the "affordability and accountability" sections of the act.

L. IRS: Taxation of Attorney Fees

Taxation of Attorney Fees 26 U.S.C. § 62(a)(20)-(21)	Provisions of the tax code that prevent the double taxation of attorney fees. Clients do not have to pay taxes on fees paid to attorneys under employment and whistleblower retaliation laws, False Claims, Securities Exchange, and Commodity Exchange Acts, and the IRS reward laws.

M. Military Whistleblower Protection, Department of Defense Components (Including Military Departments, Combatant Commands, Secretary of Defense, and All Other Department of Defense Agencies)

Coast Guard Whistleblower Protection 33 C.F.R. Part 53 56 *Federal Register* 13404 (April 2, 1991)	This regulation implements the statutory protections afforded to members of the armed services, codified in 10 U.S.C. § 1034 for members of the Coast Guard. This is a DOL case with similar procedures and law as found under the Energy Reorganization and Sarbanes-Oxley Acts.
Department of Defense Employees of Non-appropriated Fund Instrumentalities 10 U.S.C. § 1587	Department of Defense Directive No. 1401.03 (June 13, 2015, amended May 7, 2021).
Department of Defense Office of Inspector General Rules and Procedures Governing Department of Defense Component and Contractor Complaints	Department of Defense Directive No. 7050.6 (July 23, 2007). Defense Hotline Program, Department of Defense Directive No. 7050.01 (December 17, 2007).
Armed Forces/Prohibition Against Retaliation (Reemployment Rights) 38 U.S.C. § 4311 38 U.S.C. § 4322–24 (procedures)	Cause of action to challenge retaliation for invoking reemployment rights.

Armed Forces/Prohibition Against Retaliation (Active Duty Military) 10 U.S.C. § 1034	Permits members of the armed services to contact members of Congress, the Office of Inspector General, DOD auditors, and other military officials designated to receive complaints.

N. National Security Whistleblower Protection

CIA Employee Disclosures to Inspector General 50 U.S.C. 403q	CIA Inspector General Act authorized to accept complaints and investigate retaliation against employees of the agency.
Homeland Security Act of 2002 6 U.S.C. § 463	Provides protection for Homeland Security employees pursuant to the Civil Service Reform Act, 5 U.S.C. § 2302(b)(1) and § 2303 (b)(8) and (b)(9).
Department of Defense Intelligence Agencies (National Security Agency, Defense Intelligence Agency, and other Department of Defense Intelligence-Related Components) 96 Stat. 751 § 8	DOD inspector general authorized to accept complaints from DOD intelligence-related components, including those excluded from coverage under the Civil Service Reform Act.
Title VII Whistleblower Protection for Intelligence Community; Employees Reporting Urgent Concerns to Congress 4 U.S.C.A. App. Sec. 3 § 8H note: Public Law 105-277, Title VII, § 701(b)	Procedures for national security/intelligence agency employees to obtain protection for contacting Congress concerning classified matters.
Federal Bureau of Investigation Whistleblower Protection Act 5 U.S.C.A. § 2303 28 C.F.R. Part 27 (implementing regulations)	Retaliation claims for FBI employees filed with Department of Justice Office of Inspector General.
Inspector General of the Intelligence Community Whistleblower Protection Act Public Law § 405, 111-259, 50 U.S.C. § 403-3h.	Prohibits reprisals against intelligence community employees who disclose waste, fraud, or abuse to the intelligence community inspector general. The act also provides a procedure for intelligence community employees to report serious abuses to Congress.
Presidential Policy Directive/PPD-19 (October 10, 2012)	The Presidential Directive requires that intelligence agencies, including the Central Intelligence Agency, the National Security Agency, and the Defense Intelligence Agency, establish procedures to protect employees who make disclosures covered under the directive. The rights under the directive cannot be enforced in court, and the ultimate decision-making authority under the directive is vested with the head of the agency for which the employee works.

O. Nuclear Safety Whistleblower Protection

*Atomic Energy Act/Energy Reorganization Act 42 U.S.C. § 5851	Broad protection for employees who disclose safety and regulatory violations at civilian nuclear facilities and nuclear weapons facilities. Complaints must be filed with Department of Labor within 180 days. 29 C.F.R. Parts 18 and 24 (Department of Labor rules implementing nuclear safety protections). The Nuclear Regulatory Commission also has rules prohibiting retaliation against employees who raise safety concerns. 10 C.F.R. § 50.7.
Department of Energy, Defense Activities, Whistleblower Protection Program 50 U.S.C. § 2702	This law is weak and the Atomic Energy Act, 42 U.S.C. § 5851 should be used, if possible.

P. Occupational Health and Safety

Asbestos School Hazard Detection and Control, Employee Protection Provision, 15 U.S.C. § 2651	Claims filed with Department of Labor within ninety days of adverse action. The DOL conducts review and litigation under the Occupational Safety and Health Administration law, 29 U.S.C. § 660(c).
*Mine Health and Safety Act, Nonretaliation Act 30 U.S.C. § 815(c)	Retaliation complaints must be filed with the U.S. Department of Labor's Mine Safety and Health Administration within sixty days of an adverse action. Employees are entitled to preliminary reinstatement if an initial review determines that the complaint was not "frivolously brought." Damages include reinstatement, back pay, and attorney fees.
Occupational Safety and Health Act (OSHA), Nonretaliation Provision 29 U.S.C. § 660(c)	Claims must be filed with the Department of Labor within thirty days of an adverse action. There is no private right of action under the federal law. It is up to the DOL to file a suit against the employer on the employee's behalf. If the DOL does not litigate the case on behalf of the employee, the case is closed. Because of the weaknesses in this federal law, many employees have utilized state laws that prohibit retaliation against employees who blow the whistle on unsafe or unhealthy working conditions.

Q. Privacy Act

*Privacy Act 5 U.S.C. § 552a	Prevents federal government from leaking confidential information; permits persons to obtain copies of their government records and request a correction of record to ensure they are accurate. Damages available from the U.S. government for willful violations of the act. However, these damages are limited to actual economic harm caused by the leaks.

R. Transportation Whistleblower Protection

*Airline Safety 49 U.S.C § 42121	Department of Labor rules implementing the act are codified at 29 C.F.R. Parts 18 and 1979. There is a ninety-day statute of limitations under this law. This is a DOL case with similar procedures and law as found under the Energy Reorganization and Sarbanes-Oxley Acts.
Automobile Safety 49 U.S.C. § 30171 (anti-retaliation)	Employees working for automobile manufacturers, part suppliers, and dealerships are protected if they raise safety concerns with their employers or the Department of Transportation. Complaints must be filed with the DOL within 180 days of an adverse action. Procedures are consistent with those contained in the Food Safety Act and the Consumer Product Safety Act.
49 U.S.C. § § 30172 (rewards)	The Motor Vehicle Safety Whistleblower Act authorizes the secretary of transportation to pay rewards to employees who disclose safety violations in accordance with the procedures set forth in the act and regulations issued by the Department of Transportation.
*Public Transportation (National Transit Systems Security Act) 6 U.S.C. § 1142	Protections for public transportation workers are substantially identical to those contained in the Surface Transportation Act, 49 U.S.C. § 31105.
*Truck Safety 49 U.S.C. § 31101 49 U.S.C. § 31105	Protection for employees who file complaints concerning commercial motor vehicle safety or who refuse to operate the vehicle due to safety or security concerns. An employee can file a claim in federal court and request a trial by jury.
*Railroad Safety Act 49 U.S.C. § 20109	Protections for railroad workers are substantially identical to those contained in the Surface Transportation Act, 49 U.S.C. § 31105.
Safe Containers for International Cargo Act, Employee Protection Provision 46 U.S.C. § 80507	Complaints filed with Department of Labor within sixty days of adverse action. DOL must file claim in court on behalf of employee. There are no reported cases of the DOL ever seeking to protect an employee under this law.
Seamen Whistleblower Protection 46 U.S.C. § 2114	Department of Labor and Federal Court jurisdiction over complaints filed by seamen alleging retaliation for raising concerns with the Coast Guard. Back pay, attorney fees, and compensatory and punitive damages available.

S. Workplace Discrimination: EEO Retaliation

Age Discrimination in Employment Act, 29 U.S.C. § 623(d)	See Title VII—similar rights and procedures.
Americans with Disabilities Act 42 U.S.C. § 12203	See Title VII—similar rights and procedures.
Civil Rights Act of 1964, Title VII 42 U.S.C. 2000e-3(a)	Title VII contains a broad anti-retaliation provision protecting from retaliation employees who oppose discriminatory practices or who participate in Title VII proceedings.

Civil Rights Act of 1871, Conspiracy to interfere with civil rights 42 U.S.C. 1985(3)	Claims filed in U.S. District Court. Remedies similar to 42 U.S.C. § 1983. [Note: Both § 1983 and § 1985 are part of the original Civil Rights Act of 1871.]
Reporting discrimination in sale or lease of property 42 U.S.C. 1982	*Sullivan v. Little Hunting Park*, 396 U.S. 229 (1969) (implied cause of action prohibiting retaliation).
Family and Medical Leave Act 29 U.S.C. 2615(a)&(b)	See Title VII—similar rights and procedures.
Reporting/opposing discrimination in contracts 42 U.S.C. 1981(a)	*CBOCS West, Inc. v. Humphries*, 553 U.S. 442 (2008) (implied cause of action prohibiting retaliation).
Reporting/opposing discrimination under Title IX (women's athletic programs) 20 U.S.C. 1681, et. seq.	*Jackson v. Birmingham Bd. of Ed.*, 544 U.S. 167 (2005) (implied cause of action prohibiting retaliation).

T. Workplace Discrimination: Labor Rights

Employee Polygraph Protection 29 U.S.C. § 2002 (defining protected activity) 29 U.S.C. § 2005 (enforcement procedures)	Anti-retaliation provision protecting employees who object to illegal polygraph examinations. Claims filed in federal court.
*Fair Labor Standards Act (FLSA)/Equal Pay Act, Nonretaliation Provisions 29 U.S.C. § 215(a)(3) 29 U.S.C. § 216 (penalties and damages) 29 U.S.C. § 255 (statute of limitations)	Employees who suffer retaliation for filing FLSA complaints may file claims either in federal court or with the Department of Labor within two years of an adverse action.
Longshore and Harbor Workers' Compensation Act 33 U.S.C. § 948a	Anti-retaliation law under maritime workers' compensation law (protecting employees who testify in proceedings or file claims). Complaints filed with the U.S. Department of Labor. 20 C.F.R. §§ 702.271–274.
Migrant and Seasonal Agricultural Workers Protection Act, Nonretaliation Provision 29 U.S.C. § 1855	*Centeno-Bernuy v. Perry*, 302 F. Supp.2d 128 (W.D.N.Y. 2003) (injunctive relief).
National Labor Relations Act (NLRA), Nonretaliation Provision, Unfair Labor Practices 29 U.S.C. § 158(a)(4)	*NLRB v. Scrivener*, 405 U.S. 117 (1972) and *John Hancock v. NLRB*, 191 F.2d 483 (D.C. Cir. 1951) (broad interpretation to scope of protected activity).

Employment Retirement Income Security Act (ERISA) 29 U.S.C. § 1140 29 U.S.C. § 1132 29 C.F.R. § 2560	Prohibition against retaliation for participating in an ERISA retirement plan or blowing the whistle on ERISA violations.

CHECKLIST 3

Proof of Retaliation

Facts Used to Demonstrate Pretext and Causation

A. Allegation of Disloyalty/Vague and Subjective Personality Issues

Statement by decision maker that employee was not loyal.	*Decaire v. Mukasey*, 530 F.3d 1 (1st Cir. 2008) (protesting illegalities "cannot be a basis for a loyalty test") ("As a matter of law, the filing of an EEO complaint cannot be an act of disloyalty . . . which would justify taking adverse action.").
	Mandell v. County of Suffolk, 316 F.3d 368 (2nd Cir. 2003) (viewing protected activities as a "betrayal of the department").
Statement that person providing information to investigators was a rat.	*Raniola v. Police Commissioner*, 243 F.3d 610 (2nd Cir. 2001) ("There is an investigation going on in the precinct and there is a rat here . . . so everyone watch what you are doing").
Vague and subjective personality issues.	*Bobreski v. J. Givoo Consultants*, 2008-ERA-3 (DOL ARB, June 24, 2011) (citing cases).

B. Antagonistic or Derogatory Remarks Concerning Protected Activity

"Antagonistic statements concerning the protected activity provide circumstantial evidence of a retaliatory motive."	*Douglas v. Skywest Airlines*, 2006-AIR-14 (DOL ALJ, Airline Safety Whistleblower Case) (October 3, 2007).
Derogatory comments by decision makers.	*Santiago-Ramos v. Centennial P.R. Wireless Corp.*, 217 F.3d 46 (1st Cir. 2000) (comments made by key decision maker to employee and coworkers).
Discriminatory comments made by decision maker.	*Ashe v. Aronov Homes, Inc.*, 354 F. Supp. 2d. 1251 (M.D. Ala. 2004) ("comments or remarks that suggest discriminatory animus can be sufficient circumstantial evidence to establish pretext").
Referring to protected activity as "baggage."	*Mandell v. County of Suffolk*, 316 F.3d 368 (2nd Cir. 2003) (referring to past protected activity as "baggage" that could harm career).
Employer "irritated" by protected activities.	*Fasold v. Justice*, 409 F.3d 178 (3rd Cir. 2005) (statement that employee's complaint "irritated" the supervisor).
Statement by supervisor to employee critical of employee's protected activity.	*Fierros v. Texas Dept. of Health*, 274 F.3d 187 (5th Cir. 2001) (statement by manager to employee admitting to retaliatory motive).
Threat to fire employee for "stirring up" regulatory concern.	*Simas v. First Citizen*, 170 F.3d 37 (1st Cir. 1999) (stating whistleblower should be fired for "stirring up" regulatory issue).
Manager "upset" with allegation he was "stealing."	*Dunn v. ELCO Enterprises*, 2006 U.S. Dist. LEXIS 26169 (E.D. Mich. 2006).
Supervisor "frustrated" over safety concerns.	*Testa v. Consolidated Edison*, 2007-STA-27 (DOL ALJ decision) (December 4, 2007), affirmed Administrative Review Board (March 19, 2010).

Supervisor statement that employee could not "keep his mouth shut."	*Cecil v. Flour Hanford*, 2004-ERA-11 (Labor Department Judge) (August 16, 2006) (manager's statement that employee laid off "because he did not 'keep his mouth shut'" constituted "direct evidence of discrimination").
Manager pointing to fact that employee had filed an "unsubstantiated" complaint as evidence employee was a "problem employee."	*Fabela v. Socorro Independent School District*, 329 F.3d 409 (5th Cir. 2003) (statement constituted direct evidence of causation).

C. Change in Conduct after Protected Disclosures

Long record of positive performance, bad performance findings after engaging in protected activity.	*Fierros v. Texas Dept. of Health*, 274 F.3d 187 (5th Cir. 2001); *Thomas v. Texas Dept. of Criminal Justice*, 220 F.3d 389, 394 (5th Cir. 2000) (evidence that employee had eighteen-year record of no prior complaints, but disciplined after filing EEO complaint).
Change in demeanor.	*Abramson v. William Paterson College*, 260 F.3d 265 (3rd Cir. 2001) ("change in demeanor" after employee made protected disclosure).
Change in behavior toward employee after protected activity.	*Che v. Massachusetts Bay Transportation Authority*, 342 F.3d 31 (1st Cir. 2003) ("evidence of a pattern of antagonism following protected conduct"). *Hite v. Vermeer*, 446 F.3d 858 (8th Cir. 2006) ("escalating adverse and retaliatory action" after protected disclosures). *Brammer-Hoelter v. Twin Peaks*, 492 F.3d 1192 (10th Cir. 2007) (obtaining "poor performance evaluations" that "differed materially" from prior evaluations "during the period in which they exercised their First Amendment rights") ("very positive" opinion of employee prior to protected activity).
Making unfounded allegations against plaintiffs after they engaged in protected activity.	*Centeno-Bernuy v. Perry*, 302 F. Supp. 2d 128 (W.D. N.Y. 2003).
Satisfactory performance/no criticism for year before protected activity/fired shortly after blowing whistle.	*Fleeman v. Nebraska Pork*, 2008-STA-15 (DOL judge) (February 9, 2009), affirmed Administrative Review Board (May 28, 2010) (truck-safety case).

D. Conflicting Reasons/Shifting Explanations

"An employer's shifting explanations for its adverse action may be considered evidence of pretext, that is, a false cover for a discriminatory reason."	*Douglas v. Skywest Airlines*, 2006-AIR-14 (DOL ARB Airline Safety Whistleblower Case) (September 30, 2009) (citing other cases); *Clemmons v. Ameristar*, 2004-AIR-11 (DOL ARB 2010).
Shifting explanations evidence of motive and pretext.	*Wallace v. DTG Operations*, 442 F.3d 1112 (8th Cir. 2006) ("shifting explanations" for adverse action evidence of pretext) timing part of overall record justifying finding of retaliation.

Conflicting reasons as to why disciplinary actions were administered.	*Waddel v. Small Tube*, 799 F.2d 69, 73 (3rd Cir. 1986) (inconsistent reasons for discharge).
	Bechtel Construction v. SOL, 50 F.3d 926, 935 (11th Cir. 1995) ("pretextual nature" of termination "demonstrated" by employer's "shifting explanations for its actions").
Conflicting justifications evidence of post hoc rationalizations.	*Gaffney v. Riverboat Services*, 451 F.3d 424 (7th Cir. 2006).

E. Deviation from Procedure

Failure to follow disciplinary procedures.	*Smith v. Xerox*, 584 F. Supp. 2d 905 (N.D. Tex 2008).
Disregarding termination procedures in manual.	*Florek v. Eastern Air Central*, 2006-AIR-9 (DOL ARB) (May 21, 2009).
Deviation from policy or practice evidence of pretext.	*Hite v. Vermeer*, 446 F.3d 858 (8th Cir. 2006) ("employee can prove pretext by showing that the employer varied from its normal policy or procedure to address the employee's situation"). *Dietz v. Cypress Semiconductor*, 2014-SOX-2 (DOL ARB) (March 30, 2016) (failure to follow "Global Whistleblower Policy").
Conducting "superficial investigation."	*Lawson v. United Airlines*, 2002-AIR-6 (DOL judge) (December 20, 2002).
Swift use of "progressive disciplinary procedures."	*Pierce v. U.S. Enrichment Corp.*, 2004-ERA-1 (Department of Labor Administrative Review Board) (August 29, 2008).
Failure to seek input from employee's immediate supervisor.	*Diaz-Robainas v. FP&L*, 92-ERA-10 (January 19, 1996); *Donovan v. Peter Zimmer America, Inc.*, 557 F. Supp. 642 (D. S.C. 1982) (employee's immediate foreman did not want employee fired).
Failure to provide employees an opportunity to explain their version of the events.	*Donovan v. Peter Zimmer America, Inc.*, 557 F. Supp. 642 (D.S.C. 1982).
No oral or written warnings before termination.	*Clean Harbors v. Herman*, 146 F.3d 12 (1st Cir. 1998).

F. Direct Evidence/Charges of Disloyalty

Supervisor upset over employee's protected activity.	*Bechtel Construction v. SOL*, 50 F.3d 926, 935 (11th Cir. 1995) (supervisor "admitted that he was 'a little upset'" when employee raised safety issue).
Protected activity described as "disruptive."	*Donahue v. Exelon*, 2008-PSI-1, DOL (ALJ order under Pipeline Safety Act) (December 4, 2008).
Reference to employee as troublemaker.	*Stone & Webster v. Herman*, 115 F.3d 1568 at 1574 (11th Cir. 1997).
Anger, antagonism, or hostility toward complainant's protected activity.	*Lewis Grocer Co. v. Holloway*, 874 F.2d 1008 (5th Cir. 1989).

G. Disparate Treatment

"Disparate treatment of similarly situated employees may also provide evidence of pretext. 'Similarly situated' employees are those involved in or accused of the same or similar conduct but disciplined in different ways."	*Douglas v. Skywest Airlines*, 2006-AIR-14 (DOL ARB Airline Safety Whistleblower Case) (September 30, 2009). *Kowaleski v. New York State Dept. of Correctional Services*, 942 N.E.2d 291, 295 (N.Y. 2010) ("whistleblower protections . . . must shield employees from being retaliated against by an employer's selective application of theoretically neutral rules."
Disciplinary rules applied against whistleblower in uneven or selective manner.	M& S Steel Co., 148 NLRB 789, 795 (1964), enforced, 353 F.2d 80 (5th Cir. 1965). *Vieques Air v. DOL*, 437 F.3d 102 (1st Cir. 2006) ("less severe sanction imposed" on nonprotected employee). *EEOC v. Thomas Dodge Corp.*, 2009 U.S. Dist. LEXIS 24838 (E.D.N.Y.) (other employee with low sales figures not fired) (not obligated to show disparate treatment regarding "identically situated employees"). *Miller v. Fairchild Industries*, 885 F.2d 498 (9th Cir. 1989) (laying off protected employee, while offering other employees opportunity to transfer to other department). *Donovan v. Zimmer America, Inc.*, 557 F. Supp. 642, 652 (D.S.C. 1982) (no prior enforcement of rule) (actions taken against employees were "selective and unevenly applied"). *Donovan on Behalf of Chacon v. Phelps Dodge Corp.*, 709 F.2d 86, 93 (D.C. Cir. 1983). *NLRB v. Heck's Inc.*, 386 F.2d 317, 320 (4th Cir. 1967). *Che v. Massachusetts Bay Transportation Authority*, 342 F.3d 31 (1st Cir. 2003) (discrimination demonstrated when employer did not punish other employees who engaged in the same actions). *Reich v. Hoy Shoe*, 32 F.3d 361 (8th Cir. 1994) (employees with "equivalent or worse records" were "not discharged").
Disciplinary response clearly does not fit with the type of infraction at issue.	*Conley v. Yellow Freight*, 521 F.Supp. 2d 713 (E.D. Tenn. 2007) ("no employee" other than whistleblower had "ever been terminated" for violating policy; no training in policy).
Substantially disproportionate discipline is evidence of retaliation.	*Pogue v. U.S. DOL*, 940 F.2d 1287, 1291 (9th Cir. 1991). *Borel Restaurant Corp. v. NLRB*, 676 F.2d 190, 192-193 (6th Cir. 1982).
Anger, antagonism, or hostility toward complainant's protected conduct.	*NLRB v. Faulkner*, 691 F.2d 51, 56 (1st Cir. 1982). *Lewis Grocer Co. v. Holloway*, 874 F.2d 1008 (5th Cir. 1989).
Disparate treatment of hiring process.	*Dartey v. Zack Co.*, 82-ERA-2, D&O of SOL, at 10 (April 25, 1983).

H. Evidence of Violations/Antagonism Regarding Protected Activity or Safety

Antagonism toward protected activity.	*Timmons v. Mattingly Testing Services*, 95-ERA-40, D&O of Remand by ARB, at 12, 14-15 (June 21, 1996) ("antagonism toward activity that is protected . . . may manifest itself in many ways, e.g., ridicule, openly hostile action, or threatening statements, or in the case of a whistleblower who contacts the NRC, simply questioning why the whistleblower did not pursue corrective action through the usual internal channels").
Making employees perform work "at expense" of safety.	*Bechtel Construction v. SOL*, 50 F.3d 926, 935 (11th Cir. 1995) (supervisor was "preoccupied with getting work started quickly at the expense of proper safety procedures").
Hiding evidence of wrongdoing from whistleblower.	*Jayaraj v. Pro-Pharmaceuticals*, 2003-SOX-32 (DOL ALJ Order under Sarbanes-Oxley Act) (February 11, 2005) (managers "hid the existence" of suspect contract from vice president of investor relations).
Ignoring employee's safety concerns.	*Evans v. Miami Valley Hospital*, 2006-AIR-22 (DOL ARB) (June 30, 2009).
Instructing employee not to file safety concern/backdating response to safety filing.	*Lawson v. United Airlines*, 2002-AIR-6 (DOL judge) (December 20, 2002).
Pressure on employee to work in unsafe conditions.	*Ferguson v. New Prime*, 2009-STA-47 (DOL judge) (March 15, 2010) (pressure to operate truck in unsafe conditions).
Whistleblower allegations of wrongdoing found to be correct.	*Seater v. Southern California Edison*, 95-ERA 13 (DOL ARB) (September 27, 1996). *Dilback v. General Electric Company*, 2008 WL 4372901 (W.D. Ky. Sept. 22, 2008 ("existence of false claims . . . may be probative of the Defendant's motivation.")
Evidence that the company permitted safety violations.	*Khandelwal v. Southern California Edison*, 97-ERA-6 (DOL ARB) (March 31, 1998).
Statements of decision maker.	*Patane v. Clark*, 508 F.3d 106, 117 (2nd Cir. 2007) (overhearing conversation between supervisors to "drive" employee "out of her job"). *Doe v. C.A.R.S. Protection Plus, Inc.*, 527 F.3d 358 (3rd Cir. 2008) ("stray remarks" demonstrating hostility toward protected conduct). *Santiago-Ramos v. Centennial P.R. Wireless Corp.*, 217 F.3d 46 (1st Cir. 2000) (comments made by key decision maker or those in position to influence decision). *Bess v. J.D. Hunt Transport*, 2007-STA-34 (decision of DOL judge) (January 7, 2008) (manager's statement that if he believed employee's concern was legitimate, he would not have fired him). *Carter v. Marten Transport*, 2005-STA-63 (DOL ARB) (June 30, 2008) (statement by deciding official that employee raised "excessive complaints").

Evidence that company violated rules/ failed to discipline employees who violated rules.	*Assistant Secretary v. R&B Transportation*, 2006-STA-12 (DOL ARB) (June 26, 2009) (government report demonstrating that company was "cited for violations" was introduced into evidence).

I. Knowledge of Protected Activity

Employer knowledge required to demonstrate retaliation.	*Staub v. Proctor Hospital*, 131 S.Ct. 1186 (2011) (upholding "cat's paw" theory of liability) ("if supervisor performs an act" that is "motivated by animus" that is part of the "proximate cause" for an adverse action, the company is liable, even if the final decision maker was unaware of the protected activity).
	Bobreski v. J. Givoo Consultants, 2008-ERA-3 (DOL ARB, June 24, 2011) (citing cases) (rubber stamp approval of discharge by "neutral" decision maker can be tainted with bias).
	Gordon v. New York City Board of Education, 232 F.3d 111 (2nd Cir. 2000) (general corporate knowledge of complaints satisfied this requirement) (jury can find knowledge of retaliation even if company agent denies knowing that employee filed a complaint).
	Patane v. Clark, 508 F.3d 106, 115 (2nd Cir. 2007) (general corporate knowledge sufficient/complaint to company employee whose job required investigation into discrimination sufficient).
	Stegall v. Citadel Broadcasting Company, 350 F.3d 1061 (9th Cir. 2003) (employer denial of knowledge of protected activity found not credible).
	Donovan v. Peter Zimmer America, Inc., 557 F. Supp. 642 (D.S.C. 1982) (firing "innocent" employees merely suspected of contacting government is retaliatory).
	Reich v. Hoy Shoe Co., 32 F.3d 361 (8th Cir. 1994) (termination of employee "suspected" of blowing whistle constituted retaliatory action).

J. Outside Chain of Command/Failure to Follow Chain of Command

"An employer may not, with impunity, discipline an employee for failing to follow the chain of command, failing to conform to established channels, or circumventing a superior, when the employee raises a health or safety issue."	*Talbert v. WPPSS*, 93-ERA-35 (Labor Department Administrative Review Board) (September 27, 1996) (nuclear safety case). *Leveille v. New York Air National Guard*, 94-TSC-3/4 (Secretary of Labor) (December 11, 1995) (environmental whistleblower case). *Anthoine v. North Central Counties*, 605 F.3d 740 (9th Cir. 2010) ("low-level employee" "jumping chain of command" to report directly to the governing board).
Upset that employee filed complaint to manager above employee's immediate supervisor.	*Wallace v. DTG Operations*, 442 F.3d 1112 (8th Cir. 2006) ("displeased" that employee "had gone over" supervisor's head).
Policy mandating "chain of command" reporting.	*Robinson v. York*, 566 F.3d 817 (9th Cir. 2009) ("An employer's written policy requiring speech to occur through specific 'channels' cannot serve as pretext for stifling legitimate speech.") *Brockell v. Norton*, 732 F.2d 664 (8th Cir. 1984) (chain of command requirements in local police department).
Increasing restrictions against "outside" speech.	*Brammer-Hoelter v. Twin Peaks*, 492 F.3d 1192 (10th Cir. 2007) (imposing "strict prohibitions on speaking outside of school as a result of plaintiff's speech").
Direct evidence of pretext.	*Anderson v. All Flex*, 2003-WPC-6 (Decision of Labor Department Administrative Law Judge) (March 3, 2004).

K. Pretextual Justification for Termination/Adverse Action

Unworthy credence of proposed reason.	*Smith v. Xerox Corp.*, 584 F. Supp. 2d 905 (N.D. Texas 2008); *Clemmons v. Ameristar*, 2004-AIR-11 (DOL Airline Whistleblower Case, 2010).
Proof that reason given for adverse action is "unworthy of credence" is evidence of discrimination.	*Reeves v. Sanderson Plumbing Products, Inc.*, 530 U.S. 133 (2000) ("trier of fact can reasonably infer from falsity of the explanation that the employer is dissembling to cover up a discriminatory purpose . . . factfinder is entitled to consider a party's dishonesty about a material fact as 'affirmative evidence of guilt.'"). *Desert Palace v. Costa*, 539 U.S. 90 (2003) ("evidence that a defendant's explanation for an employment practice is unworthy of credence is one form of circumstantial evidence that is probative of intentional discrimination"). *Handzlik v. U.S.*, 2004 U.S. App. LEXIS 2493 (5th Cir.) ("trier of fact may infer retaliation . . . from the falsity of the employer's explanation"). *Richardson v. Monitronics*, 434 F.3d 327 (5th Cir. 2005); *Smith v. Xerox Corp.*, 584 F. Supp. 2d 905 (N.D. Tex. 2008). (Desert Palace analysis applies to retaliation cases).

Discrepancies in justification.	*Gordon v. New York City Bd. of Edu.*, 232 F.3d 111 (2nd Cir. 2000) (employee not required to demonstrate pretext to prove retaliation). *Abramson v. William Paterson College*, 260 F.3d 265 (3rd Cir. 2001) ("revealing discrepancies in the proffered reasons can also constitute evidence of the causal link").
A lie is evidence of consciousness of guilt.	*AKA v. Washington Hospital Center*, 156 F.3d 1284, 1293 (D.C. Cir. 1998); *Salazar v. WMATA*, 401 F.3d 504 (D.C. Cir. 2005) ("jury can conclude that an employer who fabricates a false explanation has something to hide; that 'something' may well be discriminatory intent").
Evidence of pretext also can be used as evidence of causation.	*Wells v. Colorado Dept. of Trans.*, 325 F.3d 1205 (10th Cir. 2003) ("evidence of pretext can be useful in multiple stages" of a "retaliation claim").
Unfounded claims against plaintiff.	*Centeno-Bernuy v. Perry*, 302 F. Supp. 2d 128 (W.D. N.Y. 2003).
Unfavorable attitude toward employees who reported violations first to the government rather than discussing them with company personnel.	*Housing Works, Inc. v. City of New York*, 72 F. Supp. 2d 402, 422, (S.D.N.Y. 1999).
Reference to employee as troublemaker.	*Stone & Webster v. Herman*, 115 F.3d 1568 at 1574 (11th Cir. 1997).
Determination that the employee was not guilty of violating the work rule under which she was charged.	*Lewis Grocer Co. v. Holloway*, 874 F.2d 1008 (5th Cir. 1989).
"After-the-fact justifications" for the adverse action.	*Santiago-Ramos v. Centennial P.R. Wireless Corp.*, 217 F.3d 46 (1st Cir. 2000) (memo justifying termination prepared after company learned employee was filing legal challenge).

L. Temporal Proximity

Timing between a protected disclosure and an adverse action evidence of improper motive.	*Clark County v. Breeden*, 532 U.S. 268, 273–74 (2001) (temporal proximity must be "very close" in time if used, standing alone, to demonstrate causation).
	Marra v. Phila. Housing Authority, 497 F.3d 286, 301 (3rd Cir. 2007).
	Mariani-Colon v. Department of Homeland Sec., 511 F.3d 216, 224 (1st Cir. 2007) (timing sufficient to establish prima facie burden).
	Yartzoff v. Thomas, 809 F.2d 1371 (9th Cir. 1987) (years of good performance ratings until employee engaged in protected activity, then bad ratings).
	Dohner v. Clearfield County, 2009 U.S. Dist. LEXIS 77121 (W.D. Pa. 2009) (termination within one month of protected disclosure evidence of causation).
	Stegall v. Citadel Broadcasting Company, 350 F.3d 1061 (9th Cir. 2003) ("timing of adverse action can provide strong evidence of retaliation").
	Lindsay v. Yates, 578 F.3d 407 (6th Cir. 2009) (close temporal proximity circumstantial evidence of causation).
	Wallace v. DTG Operations, 442 F.3d 1112 (8th Cir. 2006) (timing part of overall record justifying finding of retaliation).
	Bechtel Construction v. SOL, 50 F.3d 926, 934 (11th Cir. 1995) (employee "terminated shortly after he complained" raised an "inference of causation").
	Housing Works, Inc. v. City of New York, 72 F. Supp. 2d 402, 422 (S.D.N.Y. 1999).
	Ellis Fischel State Cancer Hosp. v. Marshall, 629 F.2d 563 (8th Cir. 1980).
	Moon v. Transportation Drivers, Inc., 836 F.2d 226, 229 (6th Cir. 1987) (adverse action shortly after the employee engaged in protected activity).
	Jim Causley Pontiac v. NLRB, 620 F.2d 122, 125 (6th Cir. 1980).
	Dietz v. Cypress Semiconductor, 2014-SOX-2 (DOL ARB) (actions taken by employer after protected disclosures).
Temporal proximity meets "contributing factor" test.	*Collins v. Beazer Homes*, 334 F. Supp. 2d 1365 (N.D. Ga. 2004) (contributing factor test); *Vieques Air Link v. DOL*, 437 F.3d 102 (1st Cir. 2006) (contributing factor test); *Fato v. Vartan National Bank*, 2009 U.S. Dist. LEXIS 620 (M.D. Pa).

Lack of temporal proximity.	*Farrell v. Planters Lifesavers*, 206 F.3d 271 (3rd Cir. 2000) ("when temporal proximity between protected activity and allegedly retaliatory conduct is missing, courts may look to the intervening period for other evidence of retaliatory animus"). *Mandell v. County of Suffolk*, 316 F.3d 368 (2nd Cir. 2003) (long lapse of time between protected disclosures and denial of promotion not, per se, grounds to dismiss plaintiff's case). *Riess v. Nucor Corp.*, 2008-STA-11 (DOL ARB, Nov. 30, 2010) (the closer the temporal proximity, stronger the inference). *Pardo-Kronemann v. Jackson*, 541 F.Supp.2d 210 (D.D.C. 2008); *Porter v. Cal. Dept.*, 419 F.3d 885 (9th Cir. 2005) (causal connection found based on "first opportunity" to retaliate).

M. Unfounded Allegations/Lawsuits Against Employees/References Disclosing Protected Activity

Making "baseless allegations" against employees. Accusing employees of being terrorists. Reporting employees to INS to try to have them deported.	*Centeno-Bernuy v. Perry*, 302 F. Supp. 2d 128 (W.D.N.Y. 2003). *Sure-Tan v. NLRB*, 467 U.S. 883 (1984) (reporting employees to INS for deportation in retaliation for asserting workplace rights constitutes an unfair labor practice).
Filing baseless lawsuit against employees in response to protected activities.	*Bill Johnson's Restaurants, Inc. v NLRB*, 461 U.S. 731 (1983); *Martin v. Gingerbread House*, 977 F.2d 1405 (10th Cir. 1992); *EEOC v. Outback Steakhouse*, 75 F. Supp. 2d 756 (N.D. Ohio 1999).
References that inform new employers that employee engaged in protected activity.	*Johnston v. Davis Security*, 217 F. Supp. 2d 1224 (D. Utah 2002) ("calling and telling her new employer that she was suing"). *Gaballa v. Atlantic Group*, 94-ERA-9 (Secretary of Labor, January 18, 1996) (nuclear whistleblower case). *Earwood v. Dart Container*, 93-STA-16 (Secretary of Labor, December 7, 1994) (surface transportation whistleblower case).

N. Warning or Prohibition Against Blowing the Whistle

Warning not to "push" complaints.	*EEOC v. Thomas Dodge Corp.*, 2009 U.S. Dist. LEXIS 24838 (E.D.N.Y.) (warning by direct supervisor "not to push" complaints).
Warning to "keep mouth shut."	*Mandell v. County of Suffolk*, 316 F.3d 368 (2nd Cir. 2003) (supervisor telling plaintiff to "keep his mouth shut").
Warning not to make "unsubstantiated charges" against company.	*Simas v. First Citizen*, 170 F.3d 37 (1st Cir. 1999) (warning not to make "unsubstantiated charges" against company direct evidence of animus).
Requiring employee to sign waiver of rights to sue employers for blacklisting under the ERA as a condition of employment constituted discrimination.	*Rudd v. Westinghouse Hanford Co.*, 88-ERA-33, D&O of Remand by ARB, at 8 (November 10, 1997).

Restrictions that interfere with an employee's right to engage in protected activity violate the whistleblower laws.	*CL&P v. DOL*, 85 F.3d 89 (2nd Cir. 1996).
Interrogation of employees regarding protected activity.	*Fasold v. Justice*, 409 F.3d 178 (3rd Cir. 2005) (questioning employee about his complaint).

CHECKLIST 4

Discovery

Obtaining the Evidence Needed to Win a Case Against an Employer

Copies of model discovery requests can be accessed at the free online whistleblower law library located at www.kkc.com/law-library.

A. Whistleblowers Have a Right to Broad Discovery in Their Retaliation Cases

Broad right to discovery.	*McDonnell Douglas v. Green*, 411 U.S. 792, 804–05 (1973) (recognizing importance of pretrial discovery to prove pretext in employment cases).
	Hollander v. American Cyanamid Co., 895 F.2d 80, 85 (2nd Cir. 1990) (broad discovery in employment cases).
	Morrison v. City and County of Denver, 80 F.R.D. 289, 292 (D. Col. 1978) ("very broad scope of discovery" because "plaintiffs must rely on circumstantial evidence" to prove case).
	Jones et al. v. Forrest City Grocery Inc., 2007 U.S. Dist. LEXIS 19482 (E.D. Ark. 2007) (scope of discovery broad, not limited to admissible evidence, issues raised in the pleadings or the merits of a case).
	Williams v. The Art Institute of Atlanta, 2006 U.S. Dist. LEXIS 62585 (N.D. Ga. 2006) (permitting discovery into company's affirmative defenses).
	Sallis v. Univ. of Mich., 408 F.3d 470, 478 (8th Cir. 2005) ("the Supreme Court has acknowledged . . . liberal civil discovery rules give plaintiffs broad access to document their claims.").
Basic rules of discovery set forth in Federal Rules of Civil Procedure (FRCP).	General Scope of Discovery, Obtaining Protective Orders and Mandatory Disclosure Rules. FRCP 26.
	Rule permitting employees to obtain documents from employers and other witnesses. FRCP 34.
	Rule permitting employees to depose (question under oath) witnesses. FRCP 30.
	Rules permitting employees to file written questions or requests for admission from their employer. FRCP 33 and 36.
	Rule concerning disclosure of expert witness discovery. FRCP 26(a)(2).
Conducting depositions as an important discovery tool in whistleblower cases.	*Naftchi v. N.Y.U.*, 172 F.R.D. 130 (S.D.N.Y. 1997) ("exceedingly difficult" to justify blocking deposition of witness).
	Alexander v. FBI, 186 F.R.D. 113, 121 (D.D.C. 1998) (depositions "rank high in the hierarchy of pretrial, truth-finding mechanisms").
	Daniels v. AMTRAK, 110 F.R.D. 160 (S.D.N.Y.) (discovery materials may be withheld until after deposition is conducted to preserve the opportunity to impeach witness).

Private confidentiality agreements do not limit discovery.	*Zoom Imaging v. St. Luke's Hospital*, 513 F. Supp. 2d 411 (E.D. Pa. 2007). *U.S. v. Davis*, 702 F.2d 418, 422 (2nd Cir. 1983).
Broad right to obtain computer-related discovery.	*In re: Yasmin*, 2010 U.S. Dist. LEXIS 14092 (S.D. Ill.) (definition of "documents" included "electronically stored information on hard drives, USB or thumb drives, databases, computers, handheld devices, floppy disks, CD-ROM, magnetic tape, optical disks, or other devices for digital data storage or transmittal" and "e-mail, removable computer storage media, document image files, Web pages" and "digital records").
Sanctions against employers for hiding documents requested in discovery.	*Roadway Express v. DOL*, 495 F.3d 477 (7th Cir. 2007); *Dann v. Bechtel*, 2005-SDW-4/5/6 (DOL ALJ Aug. 26, 2005); *Beliveau v. Naval Undersea Warfare Center*, 97-SDW-1 (DOJ ALJ June 29, 2000).

B. Ten Key Areas of Discovery

1. Disparate Treatment: Comparison between How Whistleblower Treated/Disciplined Compared to Other Employees

Employee disciplinary records.	*Morrison v. Philadelphia Housing Authority*, 203 F.R.D. 195, 197 (E.D. Pa. 2001) (disciplinary records of other employees). *Northern v. City of Phil.*, 2000 U.S. Dist. LEXIS 4278 (E.D. Pa.) (disciplinary records of employees accused of violating same rule as plaintiff).
Employee performance records.	*Ellison v. Patterson-UTI*, 2009 U.S. Dist. LEXIS 88313 (S.D. Tex. 2009) (upholding request for "any and all documents evaluating the work of plaintiff or comparing his job and work performance to other employees of defendants").
Proof of pretext.	*Onwuka v. Federal Express*, 178 F.R.D. 508 (D. Minn. 1997) ("wide discovery of personnel files" to "demonstrate pretext"). *Coughlin v. Lee*, 946 F.2d 1152, 1159 (5th Cir. 1991) (discovery of personnel files of other employees to demonstrate pretext).
Statistical evidence.	*Lovoi v. Apple One Employment Services*, 2000 U.S. Dist. LEXIS 18811 (E.D. La. 2000); (discovery of list of previous employees).
Documents showing egregious acts of similarly situated employees who were not disciplined.	*Northern v. City of Philadelphia*, 2000 U.S. Dist. LEXIS 4278 (E.D. Pa. 2000) (personnel files of "similarly situated" employees). *Graham v. Long Island Rail Road*, 230 F.3d 34, 39 (2nd Cir. 2000) (records of other employees relevant in case).
Company practices.	*Schreiber v. State of Nebraska and the Nebraska State Patrol*, 2006 U.S. Dist. LEXIS 78211 (D. Neb. 2006). *Williams v. The Art Institute of Atlanta*, 2006 U.S. Dist. LEXIS 62585 (N.D. Ga. 2006) (company handbooks and documents governing corporate policy). *Gutierrez v. Johnson and Johnson, Inc.*, 2002 U.S. Dist. LEXIS 15418 (D. N.J. 2002) (only sought parent's headquarters practices and were therefore not overly broad). *EEOC v. Lockheed*, 2007 U.S. Dist. LEXIS 39342 (D. Haw. 2007) (documents produced for all entities plaintiff worked).

Personnel files.	*Beasley v. First American Real Estate Information Services, Inc.*, 2005 U.S. Dist. LEXIS 34030 (N.D. Tex. 2005) (files containing ratings of employees are discoverable except for Social Security information).
	Morrison v. Philadelphia Housing Authority, 203 F.R.D. 195, 197 (E.D. Pa. 2001) (disciplinary records are clearly relevant to evidence in a disparate treatment claim).
	MacIntosh v. Building Owners, 231 F.R.D. 106, 108–09 (D.D.C. 2005).
	Ellison v. Patterson-UTI, 2009 U.S. Dist. LEXIS 88313 (S.D. Tex. 2009) (upholding document request for personnel files of employees who replaced discharged plaintiff) (upholding interrogatory question to iden tify other employees, including names, addresses, dates of hire, dates of separation, and job position).
	Duke v. University of Texas, 729 F.2d 994 (5th Cir. 1984) (company-wide discovery on information concerning employees).
Past practice of employer in similar situations.	*Timmons v. Mattingly Testing*, 95 ERA-40 (DOL ARB, June 21, 1996) (past practices "relevant to determining . . . disparate treatment, which may provide highly probative evidence of retaliatory intent").
Time frame.	*Briddel v. Saint Gobain*, 233 F.R.D. 57, 60 (D. Mass. 2005) (employee files discoverable for time periods ranging from three to ten years).

2. Use Discovery to Obtain Information on Investigations

Investigative reports.	*St. Paul Fire and Marine Ins. Co. v. SSA Gulf Terminals, Inc.*, 2002 U.S. Dist. LEXIS 11776 (E.D. La. 2002) (in-house insurance documents are not protected by the work product privilege).
	Fernandez v. Navistar International Corp. et al., 2009 SOX-43 (DOL ALJ, October 16, 2009) (reports from investigation conducted by a law firm and distributed to third party).
Self-critical analysis (discovery into internal corporate reviews of employee concerns or internal peer reviews).	*Univ. of Pa. v. EEOC*, 493 U.S. 182 (1990) (declining to permit a company's assertion of a so-called "self-critical analysis privilege" to block discovery). *Zoom Imaging, L.P. v. St. Luke's Hospital and Health Network*, 513 F. Supp. 2d 411, 413 (E.D. Pa. 2007).
Attorney-client documents provided to the FBI during investigation ordered produced.	*Beliveau v. Naval Warfare Center*, 1997-SDW-6 (DOL ALJ, May 31, 2000.) *U.S. v. Quest Diagnostics*, 734 F.3d 154 (2nd Cir. 2013) (restrictions on attorney whistleblowers using privileged information).
Work product doctrine not applicable.	*St. Paul Fire v. SSA Gulf Terminals*, 2002 LEXIS 11776 (E.D. La.) (work product doctrine not applicable to in-house investigative report).
Hotline reports discoverable.	*McDougal-Wilson v. Goodyear*, 232 F.R.D. 246 (E.D.N.C. 2005) (compelling production of "reports on concerns" made on the company hotline).
Corporate communications with government regulators.	*Winstanley v. Royal Consumer Information*, 2006 U.S. Dist. LEXIS 44702 (D. Ariz).

3. Try to Obtain Access to Information on Investigations Conducted by Corporate Attorneys

Investigative report prepared by attorney.	*Walker v. County of Contra Costa, et al.*, 227 F.R.D. 529, 534 (N.D. Cal. 2005) (discoverable when company asserted affirmative defense based on internal investigative findings). *Matter of the Application of Vincenzo Nieri, for subpoenas pursuant to 28 USC 1782*, 2000 U.S. Dist. LEXIS 540 (S.D.N.Y. 2000) (attorney-client privilege did not per se protect in-house investigative reports). But see *In re KBR*, 796 F.3d 137 (D.C. Cir. 2015) (prohibiting disclosure of investigatory reports prepared for an attorney).
Memoranda of interviews conducted by attorney for city employees.	*Reitz v. Mt. Juliet*, 680 F.Supp.2d 888 (M.D. Tenn. 2010) (use of attorney report to justify defense results in waiver of "work product" privilege).
Correspondence to general counsel.	*Ovesen v. Mitsubishi Heavy Industries of America Inc.*, 2009 U.S. Dist. LEXIS 9762 (S.D. N.Y. 2009) (the general counsel served as vice president of the defendant's predecessor company as well). *Sokol v. Wyeth, Inc.*, 2008 U.S. Dist. LEXIS 60976 (S.D. N.Y. 2008) (communications between attorney and third parties not represented by counsel).
Information compiled for federal investigators or pursuant to law.	*Georgia Power Co. v. EEOC*, 412 F.2d 462, 468 (5th Cir. 1969).

4. Obtain Discovery from Government Regulators

Correspondence between agencies/with agencies.	*Winstanley v. Royal Consumer Information Products, Inc., et al.*, 2006 U.S. Dist. LEXIS 44702 (D. Ariz. 2006). *Winstanley v. Royal Consumer*, 2006 U.S. Dist. LEXIS 44702 (D.C. Ariz. 2006).
Copies of complaints filed by employees with state or federal regulatory agency.	*Owens v. Sprint/United Management Company*, 221 F.R.D. 649, 653 (D. Kan. 2004) (other employee complaints filed with state or federal regulatory bodies).
Statements of employees gathered by government agency.	*Chao v. General Interior System, Inc.*, 2009 U.S. Dist. LEXIS 90066 (N.D. N.Y. 2009) (rejecting informant's privilege).
Compelling testimony of public officials.	*United States v. Lake County Board of Commissioners*, 233 F.R.D. 523, 528 (N.D. Ind. 2005). *Chaplaincy of Full Gospel Churches v. Johnson*, 217 F.R.D. 250, 256 (D.D.C. 2003).

Discovery into government's decision-making process.	*Jones v. the City of College Park, Georgia*, 237 F.R.D. 517, 520-521 (N.D. Ga. 2006) (the government's interest in protecting these communications is outweighed by the plaintiff's interest in disclosure). *Tri-State Hospital Supply Corporation v. United States of America*, 226 F.R.D. 118, 130 (D.D.C. 2005). *Anderson v. Cornejo*, 2001 U.S. Dist. LEXIS 10312 (N.D. Ill. 2001).
Government's deliberative process privilege waived if evidence of misconduct.	*Alexander v. FBI*, 186 F.R.D. 154, 164 (D.D.C. 1999). *In re Sealed Case*, 121 F.3d 729, 746 (D.C. Cir. 1997).
Deliberative process privilege waived if government's intent at issue.	*Tri-State Hosp. v. U.S.*, 226 F.R.D. 118, 134-35 (D.D.C. 2005); *U.S. v Lake County*, 233 F.R.D. 523 (N.D. Ind. 2005). *Jones v. City of College Park*, 237 F.R.D. 517 (N.D. Ga. 2006).
Law enforcement privilege may be waived.	*Tri-State Hosp. v. U.S.*, 226 F.R.D. 118 (D.D.C. 2005) (citing the Rizzo factors).
Government employee interview statements.	*Reitz v. City of Mt. Juliet*, 680 F.Supp.2d 888 (M.D. Tenn. 2010).
Information may be obtained from federal government agencies under Freedom of Information Act.	Freedom of Information Act, 5 U.S.C. 552.
Government agencies must produce records on individuals maintained in a "system of records."	Privacy Act, 5 U.S.C. 552a.

5. Use Discovery to Prove That the Employer Engaged in Misconduct or Disregarded the Law

Discovery into company wrongdoing.	*In the Matter of the Application of Vincenzo Nieri, for subpoenas pursuant to 28 USC 1782*, 2000 U.S. Dist. LEXIS 540 (S.D.N.Y. 2000) ("the extent and circumstances of any wrongdoing . . . might help to explain why the company fired [the whistleblower]").
Hostility toward regulations/ deliberate violations of law or safety rules.	*Timmons v. Mattingly Testing Services*, 95-ERA-40 (DOL ARB, June 21, 1996) (opportunity for broad discovery critical for achieving the safety purposes behind the nuclear whistleblower law) (evidence of "deliberate violations" of government regulations relevant). *Khandelwal v. Southern California Edison*, 97-ERA-6 (DOL ARB) (March 31, 1998) ("discovery in a whistleblower proceeding may well uncover questionable employment practices and nuclear safety deficiencies about which the government should know"). *Tipton v. Indiana Michigan Power Co.*, 2002-ERA-30 (ALJ June 29, 2004). *McNeil v. Crane Nuclear, Inc.*, 2001-ERA-3 (ALJ Oct. 4, 2001). *James v. Pritts McEnany Roofing, Inc.*, 96-ERA-5 (ALJ Aug. 22, 1996).
Manager failed to follow findings of government investigation.	*Northern v. City of Philadelphia*, 2000 U.S. Dist. LEXIS 4278 (E.D. Pa. 2000).

6. Get Every Document the Company Has about the Whistleblower

Court upheld this document request filed by employee: "Any and all documents evaluating the work of plaintiff or comparing his job and work performance to other employees of defendants."	*Ellison v. Patterson-UTI*, 2009 U.S. Dist. LEXIS 88313 (S.D. Tex. 2009).
Information on employee's pay and benefits.	*McDougal-Wilson v. Goodyear*, 232 F.R.D. 246 (E.D. N.C. 2005).
Employee's own personnel file.	*Milner v. National School*, 73 F.R.D. 628, 633 (E.D. Pa. 1977).

7. Learn about Witnesses and Obtain the Personnel Files on Supervisors Who Engaged in Retaliation

Personnel files on managers and employee's supervisor.	*Williams v. The Art Institute of Atlanta*, 2006 U.S. Dist. LEXIS 62585 (N.D. Ga. 2006) (supervisor's file); *Owens v. Sprint*, 221 F.R.D. 649 (D. Kan. 2004) (supervisor's file); *Phillips v. Berlex Laboratories, Inc.*, 2006 U.S. Dist. LEXIS 27389 (D. Conn.) (supervisor's file). *Cardenas v. The Prudential Insurance Co. of America*, 2003 U.S. Dist. LEXIS 1825 (D. Minn. 2003) (personnel files of company CEO and other top managers).
Deposition of high-ranking executives.	*Blanton v. Biogen IDEC, Inc.*, 2006-SOX-4 (DOL ALJ, April 18, 2006) (allowed because inquiry might lead to admissible evidence, despite the executive seemingly had no "superior and unique" knowledge).
Personnel files on employees who engaged in harassment.	*Cason v. Builders*, 159 F. Supp. 2d 242, 247 (W.D.N.C. 2001) (personnel files of "harassers" discoverable).
Information on conduct and character of witness.	*Phillips v. Berlex Laboratories, Inc.*, 2006 U.S. Dist. LEXIS 27389 (D. Conn. 2006) (evidence of the conduct or character of witness that suggests testimony may be untruthful).
Home addresses and phone numbers of witnesses.	*Phillips v. Berlex Laboratories, Inc.*, 2006 U.S. Dist. LEXIS 27389 (D. Conn. 2006).
The "thoughts" and "mental impressions" of decision makers are discoverable.	*U.S. v. Lake County*, 233 F.R.D. 523 (N.D. Ind. 2005); *RECAP v. Middletown*, 294 F.3d 35, 49–53 (2nd Cir. 2002).

8. Obtain Documents on the Prior Discrimination Complaints Filed Against the Company

Evidence that company or manager discriminated or retaliated against other similarly situated employees.	*Sprint v. Mendelson*, 552 U.S. 379 (2008) (standard for discovery regarding discrimination or retaliation against other employees).
	Cardenas, Muldoon, Struzyk v. The Prudential Insurance Co. of America, 2003 U.S. Dist. LEXIS 1825 (D. Minn. 2003) (company-wide information concerning past history of employees is relevant to discrimination cases and is therefore discoverable). *Williams v. The Art Institute of Atlanta*, 2006 U.S. Dist. LEXIS 62585 (N.D. Ga. 2006). *Jones et al. v. Forrest City Grocery Inc.*, 2007 U.S. Dist. LEXIS 19482 (E.D. Ark. 2007).
	Equal Employment Opportunity Commission v. Lockheed Martin, 2007 U.S. Dist. LEXIS 39342 (D. Haw. 2007) (documents are relevant to case and had to be produced despite the burden of producing such large amounts of documents, discovery limited to a reasonable number of years prior to discrimination).

9. Beware of Employer's Efforts to Abuse Discovery or Obtain Damaging Information on Whistleblower

Limits on employer's use of discovery to obtain psychological or medical information on employee.	*Fox v. Gates Corp.*, 179 F.R.D. 303, 307 (D. Col. 1998) (setting forth conditions in which an employee would not be required to submit to an independent medical examination conducted by doctor for employer) (majority rule).
	Vanderbilt v. Town of Chilmark, 174 F.R.D. 225 (D. Mass. 1997) (narrow view of waiver; rejecting discovery and finding no waiver of patient privilege simply for seeking emotional distress damages).
	Jackson v. Chubb Corporation, 193 F.R.D. 216, 225 (D. N.J. 2000) (records not privileged because plaintiff placed her current medical condition at issue) (rejecting holding in *Vanderbilt*).
	Williams v. The Art Institute of Atlanta, 2006 U.S. Dist. LEXIS 62585 (N.D. Ga. 2006) (medical records discoverable, provided proper protective order issued).
Blocking discovery against journalist who obtained information from whistleblower.	*Management Information Technologies v. Alyeska Pipeline*, 151 F.R.D. 478 (D.D.C. 1993).
Denying request for protective order shielding information produced in discovery from public access.	*Avirgan v. Hull*, 154 F.R.D. 252 (D.D.C. 1987); *Alexander v. FBI*, 186 F.R.D. 60, 65–66 (D.D.C. 1998).
Shielding whistleblowers from identifying their confidential sources that are employed by the company.	*Management Information Technologies v. Alyeska Pipeline*, 151 F.R.D. 478 (D.D.C. 1993).

10. Beware of Employers Using Discovery to Try to Obtain Evidence that the Whistleblower Engaged in Misconduct Such as Lying on a Résumé or Stealing Company Documents

	McKennon v. Nashville Banner, 513 U.S. 352 (1995) (no fishing expeditions into employee misconduct under the "after acquired evidence" doctrine permitted).
	Nesselrotte v. Allegheny Energy, Inc., 2007 U.S. Dist. LEXIS 79147 (W.D. Pa. 2007) (plaintiff's removal of documents from work could give rise to an employer defense).

CHECKLIST 5

Violations Actionable under Dodd-Frank

A. Commodity Exchange Act (CEA)	
Violations of the CEA identified in the Commodity Futures Trading Commission (CFTC)'s "Whistleblower Alerts" CFTC, "Whistleblower Alerts," www.whistleblower.gov/whistleblower-alerts	Actions that seek to improperly influence foreign officials with personal payments or rewards—commonly thought of as bribes
	Any scheme designed to cause price of commodity to artificially move
	Bank Secrecy Act violations committed by futures commission merchants or introducing brokers
	Bribes employed to secure business
	Commodity pool fraud
	Corrupt practices (including bribes and kickbacks)
	Corrupt practices that alter the prices in commodity markets that drive U.S. derivatives prices
	Corrupt practices used to manipulate benchmarks
	Corrupt practices that impact the prices in commodity markets or manipulate benchmarks.
	Corrupt payments used to secure business. Corrupt practices used to misappropriate material nonpublic information that traders would want to know.
	Failure to comply with Bank Secrecy Act regulations, including those on money laundering, filing currency transaction reports, and suspicious activity reports
	Failure to file suspicious activity reports
	Failure to protect customers and the markets from fraud and corruption
	Foreign currency trading fraud
	Foreign Corrupt Practices Act violations
	Fraudulently soliciting investments in virtual currencies
	Improper enforcement of trading limits assigned by regulators
	Improper supervision and records violations
	Insider trading in Material Nonpublic Information (MNP)
	Manual and automated trading schemes
	Misrepresentation of supply or demand in order to induce other traders to act in a way beneficial to the spoofer
	Multiple orders of the same size repeatedly and simultaneously being placed and canceled
	Precious metals fraud
	Price manipulation
	Pump-and-dump schemes
	Spoofing (when a trader places an order in a futures market with the intention to cancel the order prior to execution)
	Virtual currency fraud
	Virtual currency futures or option contracts or swaps traded on an unregistered domestic platforms

B. Securities Exchange Act	• Abusive naked short selling
	• Accounting and auditing violations
Example of violations iden-	• Advance fee frauds
tified on Securities and	• Affinity fraud
Exchange Commission web-	• Binary options fraud
site, www.sec.gov	• Books, records, and internal control violations
	• False statements
	• Bribery of, or improper payments to, foreign officials
	• Broker-dealer compliance with money laundering requirements
	• Broker dealer frauds
	• Delinquent filings
	• Digital asset frauds
	• ESG disclosure violations
	• False or misleading disclosures regarding environment or climate
	• False or misleading reports submitted to SEC
	• False or misleading statements about a company
	• False or misleading statements about a company's cybersecurity
	• False or misleading statements regarding a company's corporate governance
	• Foreign Corrupt Practices Act violations
	• Fraudulent conduct associated with municipal securities transactions
	• Fraudulent conduct associated with public pension plans
	• Fraudulent conduct involving securities
	• Fraudulent investment schemes
	• Fraudulent or unregistered securities offering
	• General trading practices or pricing issues
	• High-yield investment scheme
	• Initial coin offerings and cryptocurrencies
	• Insider trading
	• Investment advisor frauds
	• Issuer reporting violations
	• Manipulation of a security
	• Manipulation of a security's price or volume
	• Market manipulation
	• Material misstatement or omission in a company's public filings or financial statements
	• Microcap fraud
	• Municipal securities transactions or public pension plans
	• Nondisclosure agreements prohibiting reporting to SEC
	• Ponzi schemes
	• Pre-IPA investment schemes
	• Prime bank investment scams
	• Promissory note schemes
	• Public finance abuse
	• Pump-and-dump schemes
	• Pyramid schemes
	• Registered investment company compliance with AML rules
	• Special Purpose Acquisition Company (SPAC) frauds
	• Theft or misappropriation of funds or securities
	• Unregistered digital asset exchanges
	• Unregistered securities offering
	• Violation of rules governing internal controls

Annotated Chapter Sources

Author's note: To help readers understand their rights and defend themselves in court, I have created an online law library where readers can access, free of charge, the laws and major court opinions cited in the Rules. The law library also links to important legal updates. The law library is located at www.kkc.com/law-library.

Introduction: The Revolutionary Roots of Modern Whistleblowing

America's First Whistleblowers

Letters of Delegates to Congress, 1774-1789, Paul H. Smith, editor (Washington, DC: Library of Congress/Government Printing Office, 1976-2000): Examination of John Grannis by subcommittee of the Marine Committee (Mar. 25, 1777); Letter from Congress to Marven and Shaw (July 31, 1778) (transmitting resolution from Congress); Letter dated September 19, 1785, from Samuel Adams to Shaw discussing payment of attorney fees and costs, *The New York Public Library Digital Collections*. 1785.

Journals of the Continental Congress (Washington, DC: Government Printing Office, 1908): Vol. VII, p. 202 (report from Marine Committee after examination of Grannis), p. 204 (suspension of Hopkins); Vol. X, p. 13 (dismissal of Hopkins); Vol. XI, pp. 713 and 732 (first resolution of the United States declaring "duty of all persons" to disclose "earliest information" of "misconduct" to "proper authority," pp. 732-33 (vote to pay *Warren* whistleblowers' "reasonable expenses" and to release documents concerning Hopkins to the whistleblowers); Vol. XIV, p. 627 (approved payment of "fourteen hundred and eighteen dollars and 9/90" for the defense of whistleblowers Shaw and Marven). Congress directed that the fee be paid to Samuel Adams for his services, and Adams was required to pay attorney William Channing).

The *Warren* sailors originally approached, Robert Treat Paine, a member of the Continental Congress, a signer of the Declaration of Independence, and a delegate from Taunton, Massachusetts. Paine was a well-known attorney who had led the prosecution of the British soldiers who had killed colonists during the Boston Massacre. Paine advised the whistleblowers to file their concerns directly with Congress and apparently recommended that the whistleblowers work with Samuel Adams. See *Grannis to Paine* (Feb. 11, 1777). See *Letters of Delegates to Congress*, explanatory note to *Letter from Grannis to Marine Committee* dated March 25, 1777.

The recognition by the Founders of the United States that courage stood behind those willing to report wrongdoing and exercise their freedom of speech is highlighted in the landmark concurring opinion of Justice Brandeis in *Whitney v. California*, 274 U.S. 357 (1927).

Information on Esek Hopkins

John G. Coyle, "The Suspension of Esek Hopkins, Commander of the Revolutionary Navy, XXI," *Journal of the American Irish Historical Society* 193 (1922) (reprints original petition from the *Warren* sailors and the individual statements each of the sailors had delivered to Congress).

Edward Field, *Esek Hopkins, Commander-in-chief of the Continental Navy during the American Revolution, 1775–1778, Master Mariner, Politician, Brigadier-General, Naval Officer and Philanthropist* (Preston & Rounds: Providence, 1898).

Hopkins' role as the commander of the notorious slave ship *Sally* is fully discussed in the Brown University report on the role of the university in the slave trade. Aboard the *Sally* conditions were abysmal and the enslaved passengers rose in rebellion. As Hopkins reported: "Slaves Rose on us Was obliged fire on them and Destroyed 8 and Several more wounded badly." Thereafter, conditions on board continued to deteriorate, and Hopkins discussed the death of his human cargo: "Some Drowned themselves, Some Starved and other Sickened and Dyed." All told, 109 people died aboard the *Sally*. James Campbell's "Navigating the Past: Brown University and the Voyage of the Slave Ship Sally, 1764–65."

Qui Tam Laws Passed by the First Congress

A full list of the *qui tam* reward laws enacted by the First Congress of the United States are listed in the Testimony of Stephen M. Kohn before the House of Representatives Committee on Oversight and Government Reform in the hearing on "Restoring the Power of the Purse: Legislative Options" (Dec. 1, 2016), available at https://oversight .house.gov/wp-content/uploads/2016-12-01-NWC-Kohn-Testimony.pdf. These early laws were cited by Supreme Court Justice Antonin Scalia in his decision upholding the constitutionality of the False Claims Act's *qui tam* whistleblower reward law. See *Vermont Agency of Natural Resources v. U.S. ex rel. Stevens,* 529 U.S. 765 (2000).

National Whistleblower Appreciation Day

Since the history of America's first whistleblowers was uncovered and recounted in the first edition of *The Whistleblower's Handbook* (Lyons Press, 2011), the U.S. Congress and numerous executive agencies, scholars, and public interest organizations have recognized the importance of the Continental Congress' first whistleblower law and the courage of the ten sailors and marines who stepped forward. NWAD website: https:// kkc.com/national-whistleblower-day/.

Every year since 2013 the U.S. Senate has unanimously passed a resolution recognizing July 30 as National Whistleblower Appreciation Day. See Senate Resolution 324 (117th Congress), online at https://www.congress.gov/bill/117th-congress/ senate-resolution/324.

Numerous executive agencies such as the Securities and Exchange Commission, Department of Labor, Environmental Protection Agency, Department of Homeland Security, and the Director of National Intelligence have all recognized National Whistleblower Appreciation Day with public events and online statements of support.

See, e.g., Office of Personnel and Management Statement (2022), online at https://www.opm.gov/news/releases/2022/07/joint-message-on-national-whistleblower-appreciation-day-issued-by-the-opm-director-and-opm-inspector-general/; Summary of agencies that recognized National Whistleblower Appreciation Day in 2022, online at https://whistleblowersblog.org/national-whistleblower-day/federal-agencies-celebrate-national-whistleblower-day-2022.

Part 1: The New Rules for Whistleblowers

Rule 1: In with the New—Out with the Old!

The old whistleblowing: *English v. General Electric Company*, 85-ERA-2, Decision and Order of Administrative Law Judge (Aug. 1, 1985), *reversed* by Final Decision and Order of the Under Secretary of Labor (Jan. 13, 1987); Ernesto Reuben and Matthew Stephenson, "Nobody likes a rat: On the willingness to report lies and the consequences thereof," 93 *Journal of Economic Behavior & Organization* 384 (Sept. 2013). Statistics confirming the difficulty of winning a traditional retaliation case are published annually by the U.S. Department of Labor, OSHA division, at https://www.whistleblowers.gov/factsheets_page/statistics.

The success of the new whistleblower laws has been fully documented by the government officials who enforce these laws and by objective academic studies published by internationally respected economists. For example, the SEC's Office of the Whistleblower's 2022 Annual Report described the Dodd-Frank whistleblower law's impact:

Since the beginning of the program, the SEC has paid more than $1.3 billion in 328 awards to individuals for providing information that led to the success of SEC and other agencies' enforcement actions.

Whistleblowers have played a critical role in the SEC's enforcement efforts in protecting investors and the marketplace. Enforcement actions brought using information from meritorious whistleblowers have resulted in orders for more than $6.3 billion in total monetary sanctions, including more than $4.0 billion in disgorgement of ill-gotten gains and interest, of which more than $1.5 billion has been, or is scheduled to be, returned to harmed investors.

"SEC Whistleblower Office Announces Results for 2022," *SEC* (Nov. 15, 2022), https://www.sec.gov/files/2022_ow_ar.pdf.

The 2022 ACFE report explained the importance of whistleblower tips in identifying corporate fraud: "Despite the increasing number of advanced fraud detection techniques available to organizations, tips were still the most common way occupational frauds were discovered in our study by a wide margin, as they have been in every one of our previous reports. As shown in Figure 10, 42% of cases in our study were uncovered by tips, which is nearly three times as many cases as the next most common detection method." Report to Nations, p. 21.

Additional information on the success of the modern whistleblower laws is set forth in the conclusion.

Major Whistleblower Reward and Protection Laws

The most important "new" whistleblower laws have mandatory rewards, prohibit retaliation, and provide for partial or complete confidentiality.

Dodd-Frank Act (Commodities Frauds and Foreign Corruption), 7 U.S.C. § 26

Dodd-Frank Act (Securities Fraud and Foreign Corruption), 15 U.S.C. 78u-6

Motor Vehicle Safety Act, 49 U.S.C. § 30172

False Claims Act, 31 U.S.C. § 3729-32

Tax Evasion and Underpayments (IRS), 26 U.S.C. § 7623

Older or Discretionary Reward Laws

Act to Prevent Pollution from Ships (APPS), 33 U.S.C. § 1908(a)

Antarctic Conservation Act, 16 U.S.C. §§ 2409 and 2439

Anti-Money Laundering Act, 31 U.S.C. § 5323

Endangered Species Act, 16 U.S.C. § 1540(d)

Financial Institutions Reform, Recovery and Enforcement Act, 12 U.S.C. §§ 4201–23

Fish and Wildlife Improvement Act, 16 U.S.C. § 742l(c)(3)

Lacey Act, 16 U.S.C. § 3375(d)

Major Frauds Act, 18 U.S.C. § 1031

Rhinoceros and Tiger Conservation Act, 16 U.S.C. § 5305a(f)

Wild Bird Conservation Act, 16 U.S.C. §§ 4912(c) and 4913(b)

Rule 2: Be Confidential

See Rules 17–25 discussing different levels of confidentiality under various reward laws.

Dodd-Frank Confidentiality
The rule for proceeding confidentially and anonymously under the Commodity Exchange Act is located at 17 C.F.R. 165.4; the rule for proceeding confidentially and

anonymously under the Securities Exchange Act (and also the Foreign Corrupt Practices Act) is located at 17 C.F.R. § 240.21F-7.

IRS Confidentiality

The confidentiality rules at the IRS Office of the Whistleblower are located at 29 C.F.R. § 301.6103(h)(4)-1(e). The IRS Whistleblower Office is required to protect the confidentiality of whistleblowers to the "fullest extent permitted by the law." *Internal Revenue Manual* § 25.2.2.10. In *Montgomery v. IRS*, 40 F.4th 702 (D.C. Cir. 2022), the U.S Court of Appeals for the District of Columbia Circuit recognized that "the IRS is in fact required by Treasury Regulations to use its best efforts to protect the identity of whistleblowers," citing to IRS rule 26 C.F.R. § 301.7623-1(e).

Confidentiality under the Freedom of Information Act (FOIA)

Federal agencies should withhold information that could identify a whistleblower under the exemptions to the FOIA and under the Privacy Act, 5 U.S.C. 552a. The applicable FOIA exemptions include: 5 U.S.C. § 552(b)(3) (disclosure prohibited by statute) and § 552(b)(6) (invasion of personal privacy). The most applicable exemption is the law enforcement privilege. Pursuant to exemption § 552(b)(7), agencies should withhold information that "could reasonably be expected to interfere with enforcement proceedings," "could reasonably be expected to constitute an unwarranted invasion of personal privacy," "could reasonably be expected to disclose the identity of a confidential source," or "could reasonably be expected to endanger the life or physical safety of any individual."

In *Montgomery v. IRS*, 40 F.4th 702 (D.C. Cir. 2022), the U.S Court of Appeals upheld the broad authority of federal agencies to protect the identity of whistleblowers under the FOIA. The court affirmed the IRS' use of the so-called "Glomar Response" to hide whether or not whistleblowers were involved in an investigation. The court explained the meaning of a Glomer Response as "Named after a ship in a long-ago CIA secrets case, . . . [a] Glomar Response refers to an agency's refusal to either confirm or deny the existence of the records requested." Thus, telling a requester that an agency was withholding documents could confirm that an agency was working in a confidential manner.

Under this precedent not only did the IRS refuse to confirm or deny the existence of any documents that could imply that a whistleblower had provided information in an investigation, the IRS' invocation of a Glomer Response was upheld. The court approved the practice of the IRS to refuse to confirm or deny the existence of a whistleblower in *all cases* where a whistleblower *could* have been involved, whether or not there was a whistleblower. The court recognized that "revenge-seeking" requesters should not be permitted to use FOIA to figure out whether or not a whistleblower was involved in a case, as the "pool of potential whistleblowers" at a job site may be "very small" and the way an FOIA request was answered could be harmful to a whistleblower. Thus, a blanket refusal to confirm or deny the existence of any such records was endorsed. The Department of Justice's FOIA web page has a full explanation of the Glomar rule. See https://www.justice.gov/oip/blog/foia-update-oip-guidance-privacy-glomarization.

Auto Safety and Money Laundering

Both the Motor Vehicle Safety and Money Laundering whistleblower laws permit anonymous and confidential filings in a manner identical to the SEC and CFTC. See 31 U.S.C. § 5323(g)(4) (money laundering) and 49 U.S.C. § 30172(f) (auto safety). However, the agencies responsible for implementing these laws, i.e., the Department of Transportation (auto safety) and Department of Treasury (money laundering), have not published procedures for making anonymous filings. Thus, when using these laws, whistleblowers should explicitly request anonymity and ask for instructions as to the procedures to use to ensure full confidentiality and anonymity.

Referrals to Other Agencies

Under Dodd-Frank if the responsible agency refers information about the whistle-blower's claims to a sister federal agency (or in limited circumstances a foreign law enforcement agency) that sister agency must also guarantee confidentiality. Thus, if the Securities and Exchange Commission (Dodd-Frank/FCPA), Commodity Exchange Commission (Dodd-Frank), Department of Transportation (auto safety), and/or the Department of Treasury (money laundering) refer a whistleblower's claim to another federal agency, those agencies are required to honor the confidentiality and anonymity requirements mandated under Dodd-Frank But these types of referrals, for a variety of reasons, often do not occur. Regardless, whistleblowers should request that referrals made to sister law enforcement or regulatory agencies be transferred pursuant to the confidentiality requirements set forth in the law.

Because there is no uniform federal law protecting the identity of a whistleblower, whis-tleblowers need to exercise due care in securing the highest level of protection available under law or within the discretion of the agencies. The best method to maintain strict confidentiality is to have one of the four agencies identified above refer the whistle-blower's information to a federal agency under the strict confidentiality rules mandated under Dodd-Frank, the AML, and the auto safety laws.

False Claims, Inspector General, and Whistleblower Protection Acts

Other whistleblower laws also have varying levels of protection. The False Claims Act requires that complaints be filed under seal and the defendants not be informed that there is a whistleblower or that a complaint was filed. See 31 U.S.C. § 3730(b)(2). This affords a whistleblower confidentiality during the investigation of their case, but after the investigation is concluded, the seal is lifted and the identity of the whistleblower can be revealed. The Inspector General Act, located at Public Law 95-452 (as amended), requires that the IGs protect the confidentiality of federal employees. Similarly, the U.S. Office of Special Counsel has strict confidentiality rules protecting sources pursuant to the Whistleblower Protection Act, 5 U.S.C. § 1213.

Confidential Informant Status

A whistleblower should also consider requesting confidential informant status whenever they are providing any information to law enforcement. The Attorney General's guide-lines for CI status are linked at: https://irp.fas.org/agency/doj/fbi/dojguidelines.pdf.

Limits on Confidentiality

Under the U.S. Constitution a defendant in a criminal case has the right to learn the identity of all the government witnesses and to access information that may impeach the truthfulness of a witness. Thus, if a case is actually going to court, the Justice Department or other federal agencies may be required to turn over information related to the whistleblower, including the whistleblower's identity and the fact that the whistleblower could obtain a financial reward. This option is rarely used, as the government usually structures cases so as to limit the risk that the whistleblower will be needed as a witness. Additionally, most of the civil or regulatory cases triggered by a whistleblower disclosure settle out of court.

Problems Faced by Whistleblowers If Their Identity Is Revealed

Cases discussing the problems encountered by employees who are not confidential: *Management Information Technologies v. Alyeska Pipeline*, 151 F.R.D. 478 (D.D.C. 1993); *Halliburton v. ARB*, 771 F.3d 254 (5th Cir. 2014) (explaining adverse consequences that follow an employee being outed as a whistleblower).

Rule 3: Don't Leave Money on the Table

See Rules 1, 16–25 that detail how the major reward laws work, the types of frauds covered under the laws, and the procedures necessary to quality for a reward. Sources cited in the conclusion discuss the importance and success of the whistleblower reward laws. Checklist 1 also lists the major reward laws.

The amount of money annually paid to whistleblowers is published in the Annual Reports of the IRS, SEC, and CFTC whistleblower offices. Additionally, the Justice Department annually publishes online statistics on False Claims Act recoveries.

Rule 4: "It Takes a Rogue to Catch a Rogue"

The original legislative history of the False Claims Act with Senator Howard's remarks was published in the *Congressional Globe* on February 14, 1863, p. 956. In these statements he confirms a core law enforcement principle underlying all effective reward laws: It can take a "rogue to catch a rogue."

The SEC discussed participant eligibility for rewards at 76 *Federal Register* 34300, 34549-50 and n. 389 (June 13, 2011). The SEC rule covers both securities fraud and reports concerning the Foreign Corrupt Practices Act. The CFTC discussed participant eligibility for rewards at 76 *Federal Register* 53172 at 53191-92 (Aug. 25, 2011). Both of these agencies permit participants in the underlying frauds to qualify for a reward.

Although people who participated in fraud schemes can qualify for a reward, whenever a whistleblower admits to having engaged in the criminal act care must be taken to convince the government not to prosecute. The best defense is a good offense: complete confidentiality, confidential informant status, and full cooperation. Sometimes whistleblowers are offered a nonprosecution agreement, whose terms must be meticulously followed. There is also the concept of a proffer, also known as being a "queen for the day." Under this rule a whistleblower cannot be prosecuted for the information they directly provide, but can still be prosecuted if the government learns of their criminal conduct from other sources.

Regardless, never lie about your past misconduct, and do not hide facts from the government. They will find out, they will be angry, and you may find yourself in trouble. Lying to a government investigator is a criminal offense under 18 U.S.C. § 1001.

When providing information to the U.S. Department of Justice, you are far more vulnerable to criminal charges than when you provide information to other agencies. Why? Unlike the SEC, IRS, and CFTC, the DOJ does not have a Whistleblower Office, is not required to grant whistleblowers confidentiality, and has no provision for accepting anonymous claims. However, because the DOJ is responsible for the criminal investigations triggered by whistleblower disclosures, they are often involved in all the big whistleblower cases. This creates an obvious tension between the right of a participant in a fraud to qualify as a whistleblower and the potential risk that the whistleblower may be prosecuted based on the information they voluntarily provide to the government.

The Justice Department has a variety of tools at its disposal to resolve this tension. However, even if a whistleblower is granted immunity, enters into a non-prosecution agreement, or reaches another understanding with Justice concerning their potential criminal liability, the failure to strictly adhere to any of these agreements can result in prosecution.

Reward laws that permit participants to obtain compensation are: 17 (False Claims Act); 18 (Tax); 19 (Dodd-Frank); 20 (FCPA); 21 (AML); and 22 (Auto Safety).

Links to the Congressional and regulatory history behind the "participant coverage rule," along with updates concerning relevant changes in the laws, are available at the free online law library created by the author, located at www.kkc.com/law-library.

Rule 5: Avoid the Traps

TRAP #1: DOING THE "RIGHT THING" IS NOT ENOUGH

The hardships and emotional distress facing whistleblowers, even those who prevailed and obtained large monetary recoveries, are described in a "Special Report" published by the *New England Journal of Medicine*: Aaron Kesselheim et al., "Whistle-Blowers' Experiences in Fraud Litigation against Pharmaceutical Companies," *N. Engl. J. Med.* 362:19 (May 13, 2010). But many whistleblowers escape the horrors often highlighted in the news media. The Harvard Business School conducted a comprehensive study of whistleblowing under the False Claims Act. That law has strong anti-retaliation provisions (double back pay and federal court access), permits whistleblowers to file initial cases under seal, and provides for mandatory rewards, Under the FCA many whistleblowers land on their feet. Professors Aiyesha Dey, Jonas Heese, and Gerardo

Pérez Cavazos, "Cash-for-information whistleblower programs: Effects on whistleblowing and consequences for whistleblowers," 59 *Journal of Accounting Research* (December 2021), pp. 1689–1740.

The loopholes that face many employees were well stated in *Bricker v. Rockwell*, 1991 U.S. Dist. LEXIS 18965 (E.D. Wash.), where it was noted that a "gap in coverage" had "caught" a well-deserving whistleblower in "limbo." After highlighting the credibility of the whistleblower and his "compelling evidence of health and safety problems," the court found that the "system" "failed him miserably." The whistleblower's case was thrown out of court.

Additionally, whistleblowers have been criminally prosecuted when they tried to alert the public to serious wrongdoing by the government, including national security whistleblowers Reality Winner, Tom Drake, and Daniel Ellsberg (see Rule 30) and tax whistleblower Bradley Birkenfeld (see Rule 18). In each of these cases, although the whistleblower tried to do the right thing, they were not immunized from prosecution. The Justice Department can be very shortsighted when it comes to whistleblowers, even when it is obvious that the whistleblowers have served the public interest.

TRAP #2: THINKING WHISTLEBLOWING IS AN EMPLOYMENT DISPUTE

The new whistleblower laws place an emphasis on providing the government with actional evidence of serious crimes and frauds. All of these non-employment laws are set forth in Checklist 1. Under these laws whether or not the whistleblower has been fired is irrelevant. The issue is whether the company committed the crime, not whether the whistleblower was a good employee.

The Success of the Whistleblower Reward Laws in Comparison to Employment Laws

The success of these non-employment related whistleblower laws are extensively discussed in the annual reports issued by the SEC, CFTC and IRS. See Annual Reports, CFTC Office of the Whistleblower, available online at https://www.whistleblower.gov; Annual Reports, IRS Office of the Whistleblower, available online at https://www.irs.gov/compliance/whistleblower-office; Annual Reports, SEC Office of the Whistleblower, available online at https://www.sec.gov/whistleblower. The web pages of the IRS, SEC, and CFTC Whistleblower Offices also explain in great detail the success of these non-employment-related whistleblower laws and how they should be used. The websites for these offices are listed at the end of the book, under Resources. The annual reports can be compared with the statistics published by OSHA, which paint a dark picture regarding the outcome of retaliation cases: https://www.osha.gov/sites/default/files/Data-and-Statistics-for-FY16-to-FY21.pdf.

The statistics published by OSHA highlight the difficulty of prevailing in a whistleblower employment case. See https://www.osha.gov/sites/default/files/Data-and-Statistics-for-FY16-to-FY21.pdf. For example, 3,156 cases were filed in 2021 under twenty separate whistleblower laws, ranging from Dodd-Frank to the environmental statutes. OSHA issued a merits decision in favor of a whistleblower in only thirty-nine of these cases. However, settlements were reached in 776 cases, so all was not lost.

Information on the success of the modern whistleblower laws is set forth in the conclusion.

TRAP #3: IGNORING POWERFUL TOOLS

See Rules 16–25. The most important "new" whistleblower laws are:

False Claims Act, 31 U.S.C. § 3729-32.

Tax Evasion and Underpayments (IRS), 26 U.S.C. § 7623.

Dodd-Frank Act (Commodities Frauds), 15 U.S.C. 78u-6.

Dodd-Frank Act (Securities and Foreign Corruption), 7 U.S.C. § 26.

Motor Vehicle Safety Act, 49 U.S.C. § 30172.

Anti-Money Laundering Act, 31 U.S.C. § 5323.

The tremendous success of these laws are discussed in Rules 1, 2, 6, and in the conclusion.

TRAP #4: DELAY

English v. General Electric Company, 85-ERA-2, Decision and Order of Administrative Law Judge (Aug. 1, 1985), *reversed* by Final Decision and Order of the Under Secretary of Labor (Jan. 13, 1987).

Cases discussing how to calculate statute of limitations include *Delaware State College v. Ricks*, 449 U.S. 250 (1980); *Chardon v. Fernandez*, 454 U.S. 6 (1981) (key Supreme Court cases discussing how to calculate running of the statute of limitations); *National Railroad v. Morgan*, 536 U.S. 101 (2002) (continuing violation theory).

The doctrines of "equitable tolling" and "equitable estoppel" may provide grounds for an employee to enlarge the filing deadlines based on the actions or statements of an employer: "Equitable tolling focuses on the plaintiff's excusable ignorance of the employer's discriminatory act. Equitable estoppel, in contrast, examines the defendant's conduct and the extent to which the plaintiff has been induced to refrain from exercising his rights." *Rhodes v. Guiberson Oil Tools Div.*, 927 F.2d 876, 878 (5th Cir. 1991), quoting *Felty v. Graves-Humphreys*, 785 F.2d 516, 519 (4th Cir. 1986). See also *Zipes v. Transworld Airlines*, 455 U.S. 385 (1982); *Bonham v. Dresser Industries*, 569 F.2d 187 (3rd Cir. 1977); *School District of Allentown v. Marshall*, 657 F.2d 16 (3rd 1981); *Carlile v. South Routt School Dist.*, 652 F.2d 981 (10th Cir. 1981).

All whistleblower reward programs encourage employees to quickly file allegations of fraud with the appropriate authorities. They all have a version of a "first to file" rule that can result in the disqualification of whistleblowers who delay filing a rewards claim, if another whistleblower files a similar or identical claim first. See Rules 16–22

The statute of limitations for filing a False Claims Act reward case is six years after the date of the violation *or* within three years of the date for which an official of the United States should have been reasonably aware the violation occurred (but in no event greater than ten years from the initial violation), 31 U.S.C. § 3731(b). A wrongful discharge case under the FCA must be filed within three years, 31 U.S.C. § 3740(h)(3).

The United States has a catch-all statute of limitations for cases for which a civil fine, penalty, or forfeiture may be imposed. See 28 U.S.C. § 2462. Under this law, if a statute does not impose a specific statute of limitations, civil cases that can result in a fine or penalty being imposed must be filed within five years of the violation.

TRAP #5: DENIAL
See cases and authorities discussed in Rules 10–12.

Once you are identified as a whistleblower, retaliation often follows. Myron and Penina Glazer, *The Whistleblowers: Exposing Corruption in Government and Industry* (New York: Basic Books, 1989); Aaron Kesselheim et al., "Whistle-Blowers' Experiences in Fraud Litigation against Pharmaceutical Companies," *N. Engl. J. Med.* 362.19 (May 13, 2010) (documenting the severe emotional distress and hardships suffered by whistleblowers, even when they prevail in a major case); *Greenberg v. Kmetko*, 840 F.2d 467, 477 (7th Cir. 1988) (*en banc*) (dissenting opinion of Judge Cudahy) ("Dissenters and whistleblowers rarely win popularity contests or Dale Carnegie awards. They are frequently irritating and unsettling. These qualities, however, do not necessarily make their views wrong or unhelpful . . .").

The Institute of Internal Auditors survey of auditors is known as the Global Internal Audit Common Body of Knowledge. The survey's results were analyzed in *The Politics of Internal Auditing* by Patricia Miller and Larry Rittenberg, published by the IIA Research Foundation, Altamonte Springs, Florida (2015). See also Larry Rittenberg, *Ethics and Pressure: Balancing the Internal Audit Profession* (The IIA Research Foundation, 2016). These surveys explain in gory detail how auditors are subject to retaliation and pressure to cover up wrongdoing simply by not doing their job too well. Auditors and compliance officials are not immune from retaliation, even when they are paid by the company to investigate fraud. Persons in these positions must be on alert to the early signs of retaliation and should not think that their position within the company gives them sanctuary.

The Senate Judiciary Committee, "The Corporate and Criminal Fraud Accountability Act of 2002," S. Rep. No. 107-146 (May 6, 2002), pp. 4–5, 10, 20 (discussing Enron attorneys' advice regarding firing Sherron Watkins after she blew the whistle internally to her management). Also see Mimi Swartz and Sherron Watkins, *Power Failure: The Inside Story of the Collapse of ENRON* (New York: Doubleday, 2003).

Supreme Court decisions finding internal whistleblowing not protected under the Dodd-Frank Act and First Amendment: *Digital Realty Trust v. Somers*, 138 S.Ct. 767 (2018), and *Garcetti v. Ceballos*, 547 U.S. 410 (2006). However, a wealth of cases decided before *Digital* and *Garcetti* explained the fact that whistleblowers often used internal reporting processes and should deserve protection. See *Phillips v. Interior Board*, 500 F.2d 722 (D.C. Cir. 1974) and Rule 32.

Rule 6: Think Globally

Rule 20 discusses the Foreign Corrupt Practices Act whistleblower provisions. Also see Rules 17–25, all of which can provide rewards for non-U.S. citizens if international jurisdiction can be established.

INTERNATIONAL CONVENTIONS

The United States and more than 140 other nations have approved the United Nations Convention against Corruption, which contains two mandates for the protection of whistleblowers. Article 32 prohibits retaliation against witnesses. Article 33 urges nations to enact domestic legislation to provide protection against "unjust treatment" for any person who reports evidence of corruption to competent authorities. The convention is available at www.unodc.org/unodc/en/treaties/CAC/index.html.

Council of Europe, Civil Law Convention on Corruption. Article 9 requires European countries to protect whistleblowers.

On July 27, 2000, the U.S. Senate ratified the Inter-American Convention against Corruption. Article III (8) of that convention stipulates that the United States, and other countries that ratified the agreement, create "Systems for protecting public servants and private citizens who, in good faith, report acts of corruption, including protection of their identities, in accordance with their Constitutions and the basic principles of their domestic legal systems" (www.oas.org).

European Union Whistleblower Directive

The European Union approved a directive requiring all member states to implement domestic whistleblower laws as of December 2021. However, most EU nations failed to meet the deadline, and others that have implemented laws that fall short of the mandatory requirements of the directive. The EU Whistleblower Directive is available online at https://eur-lex.europa.eu/legal-content/EN/TXT/PDF/?uri=CELEX:32019L1937. Criticism of the EU's implementation of the directive can be found at "Will Europe Fail to Protect Whistleblowers?" available online at www.jdsupra.com; Theo Nyeröd et al., "Chapter 5: Whistleblowing in the EU: The enforcement perspective," Selected Papers from the International Whistleblowing Research Network Conference at Maynooth University (Sept. 2021).

Whistleblowers in EU nations need to review their country's specific law implementing the directive and should also review the directive itself for legislative history concerning its numerous requirements.

The United Kingdom and former Commonwealth States

Information on the Canadian offshore tax reward program is published online by the Canadian Revenue Agency, at www.cra-arc.gc.ca/gncy/cmplnc/otip-pdife/menu-eng.html.

Information on the Ontario Securities Commission's whistleblower program is located online at www.osc.gov.on.ca/en/whistleblower.htm.

A critique of the United Kingdom's whistleblower law: Simon Wolfe and Mark Worth, *Not Measuring Up: PIDA Now Rates Poorly against International Standard* (Thompson Reuters Foundation, 2016).

A critique of whistleblower status in Australia: "America Pays Millions to Whistleblower at BHP; We Hound Them from Their Jobs," *Sydney Morning Herald* (Aug. 29, 2016). The article describes problems facing Australian whistleblowers.

Information on the murder of South African whistleblower Jimmy Mohlala is available at www.dailymail.co.uk/news/article-3121989/Widow-murdered-2010-South-Africa-Fifa-World-Cup-whistle-blower-Jimmy-Mohlala-says-husband-alive-today-hadn-t-exposed-multimillion-dollar-stadium-fraud.html#ixzz4MK4PIoyh.

Secondary Sources on International Protections

Transparency International's recommendation for whistleblower protections is posted at www.transparency.org/files/content/activity/2009_PrinciplesForWhistleblowing Legislation_EN.pdf.

The Centre for Media Pluralism and Media Freedom publishes an online overview of whistleblower protections in all European Union countries at http://journalism.cmpf .eui.eu/maps/whistleblowing.

The Organization for Economic Co-Operation and Development (OECD) published "Whistleblower Protection: Encouraging Reporting," an overview of international whistleblower laws in its publication *CleanGovBiz* (July 2012). The article is available at www.oecd.org/cleangovbiz/toolkit/50042935.pdf.

Various articles discussing the status of international whistleblower protections are available at https://euobserver.com/justice/121873 (European Union rejects whistleblower protections); http://knowledgeofindia.com/list-of-whistleblowers-in-india/ (whistleblower from India killed); http://mg.co.za/article/2009-01-05-anc-whistleblower-killed (South African whistleblower killed); www.ifex.org/philippines/2005/03/30/whistleblower_murdered/ (whistleblower in Philippines killed).

UNITED STATES

Public Law 112-208 (Dec. 14, 2012) is a U.S. law imposing sanctions on Russia due to the death of whistleblower Sergei Leonidovich Magnitsky.

The following cases hold that international whistleblowers *cannot* obtain on-the-job protection under U.S. whistleblower laws: *Carnero v. Boston Scientific Corp.*, 433 F.3d 1 (1st Cir. 2006) (international employee not covered under Sarbanes-Oxley Act wrongful discharge law); *Liu Meng-Lin v. Siemens AG*, 763 F.3d 175 (2nd Cir. 2014) (international employee not covered under Dodd-Frank Act anti-retaliation law).

Commodity Exchange Act/International Market Manipulation

CFTC Whistleblower Alert: Blow the Whistle on Foreign Corrupt Practices in the Commodities and Derivatives Markets (May 2019), https://www.whistleblower.gov/ whistlebloweralerts/FCP_WBO_Alert.htm; CFTC Press Release Number 8326-20, CFTC Orders Vitol Inc. to Pay $95.7 Million for Corruption-Based Fraud and Attempted Manipulation (Dec. 3, 2020), https://www.cftc.gov/PressRoom/PressReleases/8326-20; Dept. of Justice, Press Release, Vitol Inc. Agrees to Pay over $135 Million to Resolve Foreign Bribery Case (Dec. 3, 2020), https://www.justice.gov/opa/pr/vitol-inc-agrees-pay -over-135-millionresolve-foreign-bribery-case; CFTC Enforcement Advisory: Advisory on

Self-Reporting and Cooperation for CEA Violations Involving Foreign Corrupt Practices (Mar. 6, 2019); CFTC Press Release Number 7884-19, CFTC Division of Enforcement Issues Advisory on Violations of the Commodity Exchange Act Involving Foreign Corrupt Practices (Mar. 6, 2019), www.cftc.gov/PressRoom/PressReleases/7884-19; Remarks of CFTC Director of Enforcement James M. McDonald at the American Bar Association's National Institute on White Collar Crime (Mar. 6, 2019), https://www.cftc.gov/PressRoom/SpeechesTestimony/opamcdonald2.

Securities Exchange Act/Foreign Corrupt Practices Act
The Foreign Corrupt Practices Act, 15 U.S.C. § 78m and § 78dd-1, et seq.

The Department of Justice resource page on the FCPA is located at www.justice.gov/criminal-fraud/foreign-corrupt-practices-act.

The legislative history of the FCPA is published by the DOJ at www.justice.gov/criminal-fraud/legislative-history.

The best source of information explaining the requirements of the FCPA is the *Resource Guide to the U.S. Foreign Corrupt Practices Act*, published by the Criminal Division of the DOJ and the Enforcement Division of the Securities and Exchange Commission.

The FCPA statute is translated into fifty languages at www.justice.gov/criminal-fraud/statutes-regulations.

The SEC publishes a list of FCPA prosecutions at www.sec.gov/spotlight/fcpa/fcpa-cases.shtml.

The following articles provide additional information and perspectives on FCPA. Bryan Cave, "Alert: The Implications for FCPA Enforcement of the SEC's New Whistleblower Rules" (June 22, 2011), available at www.bryancave.com; Philip M. Nichols, "The Neomercantilist Fallacy and the Contextual Reality of the Foreign Corrupt Practices Act," 53 *Harvard Journal on Legislation* 203 (Winter 2016) (broad scope of FCPA); Daniel Grimm, "Traversing the Minefield: Joint Ventures and the Foreign Corrupt Practices Act," 9 *Virginia Law and Business Review* 91 (2014) (broad reach of FCPA).

The SEC has a web page, "FCPA Spotlight," located at www.sec.gov/spotlight/fcpa.shtml. The SEC's website also contains a list of every foreign company that sells stocks to Americans under the American Depository Receipt program.

An FCPA violation also implicates the following laws, which can give rise to additional penalties: Sarbanes-Oxley Act, Section 302 (15 U.S.C. § 7241) (accuracy of financial reports), Section 404 (15 U.S.C. § 7262) (internal controls over financial reporting), Travel Act (18 U.S.C. § 1952), as well as laws covering money laundering, mail and wire fraud, false certifications, and violations of the Internal Revenue Code.

International Banking
See Rules 18 (IRS) and 21 (money laundering).

John A. Koskinen, Commissioner, Internal Revenue Service, Remarks at the U.S. Council for International Business–OECD International Tax Conference (June 3, 2014), available at https://www.irs.gov/pub/newsroom/Commissioner%20Koskinen's%20Remarks%20at%20US%20CIB%20and%20OECD%20Int%20Tax%20Conf%20June%202014.pdf; Matthew Allen, "Swiss-U.S. Tax Evasion Saga: Where Are We Now?" (Jan. 2016), www.swissinfo.ch/eng/business/unfinished-business_swiss-us-tax-evasion-saga--where-are-we-now-/41924910.

IRS Press Release, "Offshore Compliance Programs Generate $8 Billion."

Documentation regarding the impact of Bradley Birkenfeld's whistleblowing is set forth in Stephen Kohn's article "$13.769 Billion Reasons to Thank Whistleblowers on Tax Day" (Apr. 18, 2016), www.whistleblowersblog.org/2016/04/articles/news/13-769-billion-reasons-to-thank-whistleblowers-on-tax-day.

Act to Prevent Pollution from Ships
See Rule 23. The APPS whistleblower reward provision is codified at 33 U.S.C. § 1908(a).

The International Convention for the Prevention of Pollution from Ships (MARPOL 73/78) is available at http://library.arcticportal.org/1699/1/marpol.pdf.

A practical guide to the MARPOL convention is available at https://maddenmaritime.files.wordpress.com/2015/08/marpol-practical-guide.pdf.

U.S. DOJ, Environment and Natural Resources Division. A motion requesting 50 percent whistleblower reward in *U.S. v. Overseas Shipholding Group, Inc.*, 06-CR-10408 (D. Mass, March 15, 2007).

Michael G. Chalos and Wayne Parker, "The Criminalization of MARPOL Violations and Maritime Accidents in the United States," 23 *University of San Francisco Maritime Law Journal* 206 (Fall 2011). Although anti-whistleblower in tone and content, this article sets forth the various laws and legal standards applicable to APPS prosecutions.

"Avoiding the APPS Magic Pipe Trap," Officer of the Watch website (Nov. 14, 2012), offers another anti-whistleblower position, https://officerofthewatch.com/2012/11/14/avoiding-the-apps-magic-pipe-trap.

A detailed listing of APPS cases for which rewards were paid (including copies of the indictments, plea agreements, and whistleblower reward filings) is posted at https://www.kkc.com/law-library.com.

The Marine Defenders organization publishes information on APPS whistleblower rules and also has a handbook designed to help seamen involved in government investigations.

U.S. v. Efploia Shipping Co. S.A., Case 1:11-cr-00652-MJG, Bench Decision *Re: Whistleblower Award* (D. Maryland) (2016). The court discussed congressional intent behind the APPS whistleblower provision and the fact that most, if not all, APPS prosecutions come from evidence provided by whistleblowers.

Political Asylum in the United States
The first case to recognize whistleblowing as a potential justification for political asylum was *Grava v. INS*, 205 F.3d 1177 (9th Cir. 2000). *Antonyan v. Holder*, 642 F.3d 1250

(9th Cir. 2011) broadened the scope of the *Grava* holding. Since 2000 the *Grava* case has been followed in other federal court jurisdictions that considered this issue. See, for example, *Bu v. Gonzales*, 490 F.3d 424 (6th Cir. 2007); *Cao v. Attorney General*, 407 F.3d 146 (3rd. Cir. 2005); *Rodas Castro v. Holder*, 597 F.3d 93 (2nd Cir. 2010); *Haxhiu v. Mukasey*, 519 F.3d 685 (7th Cir. 2008); *Hayrapetyan v. Mukasey*, 534F.3d 1330 (10th Cir. 2008); *Zhu v. Mukasey*, 537 F.3d 1034 (9th Cir. 2008).

Aimee L. Mayer-Salins, "Asylum and Withholding of Removal Claims Involving Corruption and Whistleblowing," published in DOJ newsletter "Immigration Law Advisor," available at www.justice.gov/sites/default/files/eoir/pages/attachments/2015/02/26/vol9no2ed.pdf.

Part II: Tactics You Need to Know

The quote from "Deep Throat" comes from Carl Bernstein and Bob Woodward, *All the President's Men* (New York: Simon and Schuster, 1974), pp. 268–69.

Rule 7: Protect Yourself

Argyropoulos v. City of Alton, 539 F.3d 724 (7th Cir. 2008) (warning that anti-retaliation laws do not grant employees the right to engage in "dubious self-help tactics").

Jefferies v. Harris County Community Action, 615 F.2d 1025 (5th Cir. 1980) (setting forth the "reasonableness test" for self-help tactics). See also *Hochstadt v. Worcester Foundation*, 545 F.2d 222 (1st Cir. 1976); *Wrighten v. Metropolitan Hospital*, 726 F.2d 1346 (9th Cir. 1984) (setting forth "balancing test").

The court in *Smith v. Chi Transit Auth.*, 2016 U.S. App. LEXIS 11553 (7th Cir. 2016) described what a court should consider when evaluating whether an employee was reasonable in disclosing confidential e-mails: "Reasonableness depends on how [the employee] obtained the e-mails, whom he shared them with, the type of confidences revealed, their relevancy to the discrimination charge, whether [the employee] had a good-faith belief in their relevancy, the scope of the [employer's] confidentiality policy, and whether [the employee] could have sought the evidence in a way that would not have violated the policy."

Privacy Rights Clearinghouse, "Fact Sheet 7: Workplace Privacy and Employee Monitoring" (online publication) (information on management's rights to monitor employees at work).

Government employees have had some success in challenging e-mail monitoring. On June 20, 2012, the Executive Office of Management and Budget issued a government-wide "Memorandum for Chief Information Officers and General Counsels" warning that warrantless searching of public employee e-mails could violate whistleblower disclosure laws.

McKennon v. Nashville Banner Publishing, 513 U.S. 352 (1995) ("after-acquired evidence" standards).

Deltek v. Department of Labor, No. 14-2415 (4th Cir. 2016) (reasonableness of taping and document removal upheld).

Rule 8: Document, Document, Document

The six-factor test for removing documents in an employment case is explained in *Niswander v. Cincinnati*, 529 F.3d 714 (6th Cir. 2008); *Jefferies v. Harris County Cmty. Action Ass'n*, 615 F.2d 1025, 1036 (5th Cir. 1980); *O'Day v. McDonnell Douglas*, 79 F.3d 756 (9th Cir. 1996) (rejecting the removal of documents and warning against "rummaging through" the "supervisor's office").

Employment cases permitting document removal: *Deltek v. Department of Labor*, No. 14-2415 (4th Cir. 2015) (affirming DOL decision permitting removal of documents); *Kempcke v. Monsanto Company*, 132 F.3d 442 (8th Cir. 1998) (innocent removal of confidential documents permitted); *Westlake Surgical v. Turner*, 2009 Tex. App. LEXIS 6132 (removal of confidential documents permitted); *Erhart v. BOFI Holding, Inc.*, Case No. 15-cv-02287-BAS-NLS (S.D. Cal. Feb. 14, 2017).

Permitting document removal in False Claims Act cases: *Ruhe v. Masimo Corp.*, 929 F. Supp. 2d 1033, 1038-39 (C.D. Cal. 2012); *Siebert v. Gene Sec. Network, Inc.*, No. 11-CV-01987-JST, 2013 WL 5645309 (N.D. Cal. Oct. 16, 2013).

Cases permitting the government to use information illegally obtained by a private citizen: *Bacon v. United States*, 97 F. 35, 40 (8th Cir. 1899); *Barnes v. United States*, 373 F.2d 517, 518 (5th Cir. 1967); *McLindon v. United States*, 329 F.2d 238 (D.C. Cir. 1964); *United States v. Jacobsen*, 466 U.S. 109, 104 S. Ct. 1652 (1984); *United States v. Gianatasio*, 578 F. Supp. 3d 105 (D. Mass. 2021); *Watson v. United States*, 391 F.2d 927 (5th Cir. 1968); *United States v. Wilson*, 13 F.4th 961 (9th Cir. 2021); *Carson v. N.J. State Prison*, Civil Action No. 17-6537(RMB), 2019 U.S. Dist. LEXIS 119411 (D.N.J. July 18, 2019) ("Evidence obtained as a result of an unlawful search by the government is inadmissible at trial. . . . This protection only extends, however, to unreasonable searches that are a result of governmental action. . . . Evidence that obtained by a private citizen, even wrongfully, is not barred from evidence at trial, so long as it was without participation by the government.").

JDS Uniphase Corp. v. Jennings, 473 F.Supp.2d 697 (E.D. Vir. 2007) strongly rejected an employee's justifications for removing documents from work.

Richard Moberly, "Confidentiality and Whistleblowing," 96 *North Carolina Law Review* 751 (2018).

Kempcke v. Monsanto Company, 132 F.3d 442 (8th Cir. 1998) (innocent removal of confidential documents permitted); *Westlake Surgical v. Turner*, 2009 Tex. App. LEXIS 6132 (removal of confidential documents permitted).

Don't destroy evidence. Whistleblowers have been sanctioned when they destroyed documents related to their case. See, *Leon v. IDX Systems Corp.*, 2:03-cv-01158-MJP (W.D. Wash. 2004) (sanctions for wiping out computer hard-drive); *Burris v. JPMorgan Chase*

& Co., No. 18-cv-03012 (D. Az. Oct. 7, 2021) (default judgment against employee for destroying electronic files).

Employers also have been sanctioned for destroying documents relevant to a whistle-blower case. See *Webb v. Government for the District of Columbia*, 175 F.R.D. 128 (D.D.C. 1997) (default judgment against employer for destroying documents). Under New Jersey state law, an employer that destroys evidence not only can have an adverse inference drawn against it, but can also be liable for the tort of fraudulent concealment. *Tartaglia v. UBS PaineWebber*, 961 A.2d 1167 (N.J. 2008).

Rule 9: Should You Tape?

Under federal law and in most states, one-party taping is permitted. This means that only one of the parties to a conversation has to consent to the recording, while other parties may not have any idea it is happening. An excellent summary of the federal and state laws government one-party taping of conversations was published by Alma Rosina, "Call Recording Laws by State—Everything You Need to Know," Firefiles.ai blog (Feb. 14, 2022), https://fireflies.ai/blog/call-recording-laws-in-50-states-3/.

Court Cases on One-Party Taping: *Lopez v. U.S.*, 373 U.S. 427 (1963) (Supreme Court permits one-party taping); Omnibus Crime Control Act, 18 U.S.C. § 2511(2)(d) (federal law permitting one-party taping); Reporters Committee for Freedom of the Press (online publication) (state-by-state review of one-party taping laws); *Heller v. Champion International*, 891 F.2d 432 (2nd Cir. 1989) (one-party taping permitted for gathering evidence of discrimination).

Cases finding one-party taping not only legal, but also a potentially protected activity: *Haney v. North American Car*, 81-SWDA-1 (ALJ Order, Aug. 10, 1981), affirmed by the secretary of labor (June 30, 1982); *Mosbaugh v. Georgia Power Co.*, 91-ERA-1/11 (Order of Secretary of Labor) (Nov. 20, 1995); *Melendez v. Exxon*, 93-ERA-6 (DOL ARB, July 14, 2000) (one-party taping protected activity); *Deltek v. Department of Labor*, No. 14-2415 (4th Cir. 2015) (affirming DOL decision permitting taping).

Rule 10: Know the Limits of "Hotlines"

The Goldstein-SAFETEAM cases are published by the U.S. Department of Labor: *Goldstein v. EBASCO Contractors, Inc.*, 86-ERA-36, Labor Department rulings dated Mar. 3, 1988 (Administrative Law Judge ruling), Apr. 7, 1997 (Secretary of Labor ruling), Aug. 16, 1993 (Secretary of Labor ruling), *reversed*, 986 F.2d 1419 (5th Cir. 1993).

Whether auditors, compliance officials or employees whose duties require them to perform compliance functions are protected against retaliation remains a controversial topic. Two decisions issued by the Supreme Court demonstrate that without specific statutory coverage, internal disclosures by these classes of employees may be unprotected. See Supreme Court decisions finding internal whistleblowing not protected under the Dodd-Frank Act and First Amendment: *Digital Realty Trust v. Somers*, 138 S.Ct.

767 (2018); *Garcetti v. Ceballos*, 547 U.S. 410 (2006). Numerous cases decided before *Digital* and *Garcetti* upheld the principle that whistleblowers who use internal reporting processes deserve protection: *Phillips v. Interior Board of Mine Op.*, 500 F.2d 772 (D.C. Cir. 1974); *Mackowiak v. University Nuclear Systems*, 735 F.2d 1159 (9th Cir. 1984); *Kansas Gas & Electric v. Brock*, 780 F.2d 1505 (10th Cir. 1985); *Passaic Valley Sewerage Commissioners v. DOL*, 992 F.2d 474 (3rd Cir. 1993); *U.S. ex rel. Yesudian v. Howard University*, 153 F.3d 731 (D.C. Cir. 1998); *Bechtel v. DOL*, 50 F.3d 926 (11th Cir. 1995); *Poulos v. Ambassador Fuel Oil Co.*, 86-Clean Air Act Case No. 1 (Apr. 27, 1987).

Statutes that explicitly protect internal whistleblowing to supervisors include: Atomic Energy Act, 42 U.S.C. § 5851; Sarbanes-Oxley Act, 18 U.S.C. § 1514A; Consumer Product Safety Act, 15 U.S.C. § 2051; Aviation Investment and Reform Act, 49 U.S.C. § 42121; National Transit Systems Security Act, 6 U.S.C. § 1142; Railroad Safety Act, 49 U.S.C. § 20109; Surface Transportation Act, 49 U.S.C. §31105; Mine Health and Safety Act, 30 U.S.C. § 815(c); American Recovery Reinvestment Act, Public Law No. 111-5, §1553; Pipeline Safety Improvement Act, 42 U.S.C. § 60129; Dodd-Frank Act (Consumer Protection Bureau), 12 U.S.C. §5567; Taxpayer First Act, 26 U.S.C. § 7623(d); and the AML Whistleblower Act, 31 U.S.C. § 5323(g)..

After *Garcetti* some courts interpreted state and whistleblower statutes narrowly to exclude coverage for internal whistleblowers. See *Skare v. Extendicare Health Services*, 515 F.3d 836 (8th Cir. 2008); *Talhelm v. ABF Freight Systems*, 2010 U.S. App. LEXIS 1663 (6th Cir. 2010). However, the U.S. Congress strongly repudiated the *Garcetti* line of cases when it enacted the Whistleblower Protection Enhancement Act and explicitly reversed court rulings that were consistent with *Garcetti*. In Public Law 112-199, §§ 101 and 102, Congress used words such as "undermine," "wrongly focused," and "contrary to congressional intent" in describing court cases that failed to fully protect whistleblowers who raised concerns with their supervisors. See Committee on Homeland Security and Governmental Affairs, U.S. Senate, "Whistleblower Protection Enhancement Act of 2012," pp. 4–5 (S. Rep.112-155, Apr. 19, 2012).

Corporate-sponsored think tanks have carefully evaluated the deficiencies in internal compliance programs and have strong recommendations for improving the current systems. See Michael D. Greenberg, *Perspectives of Chief Ethics and Compliance Officers on Detection and Prevention of Corporate Misdeeds: What the Policy Community Should Know* (Rand Center for Corporate Ethics and Governance, 2009). A 2010 report by the corporate-sponsored Ethics Resource Center titled "Too Big to Regulate? Preventing Misconduct in the Private Sector" (ERC 2010) quoted leading complaints that programs were simply "paper tigers" and were plagued by a "lack of action and seriousness."

The Sarbanes-Oxley law requiring publicly traded companies to establish independent employee concerns programs is codified at 15 U.S.C. § 78j-1(m)(4). SOX protects internal employee disclosures pursuant to its statutory terms.

The Federal Sentencing Guidelines provide for sentence reductions for corporations engaged in criminal activities that have instituted an internal compliance program. U.S. Sentencing Commission Guidelines Manual, Section 8B2.1. These guidelines do not provide specific protections for employees. Also see David Hess et al., "The 2004

Amendments to the Federal Sentencing Guidelines and Their Implicit Call for a Symbiotic Integration of Business Ethics," XI *Fordham Journal of Corporate and Financial Law* 725 (2006).

The Close the Contractors Fraud Loophole Act, Public Law 110-252, Title VI, Chapter 1, mandates stronger controls over compliance departments in companies working under government contracts. It is implemented by Federal Acquisition Regulations, Contractor Business Ethics, Compliance Program and Disclosure Requirements, Final Rule, 73 *Federal Register* 67064 (Nov. 12, 2008).

The protection of internal whistleblowing under state law is a confusing mess. For example, some courts have determined that internal complaints, which would cover complaints to compliance departments, are not protected. See *Skare v. Extendicare Health Services*, 515 F.3d 836 (8th Cir. 2008); *Talhelm v. ABF Freight Systems*, 2010 U.S. App. LEXIS 1663 (6th Cir.). Other statutes, like the New Jersey whistleblower law, require most whistleblowers to report internally before they report to the government. Beyond employment law, employers that create compliance programs may be subject to breach of contract lawsuits if they violate their promises to employees. Richard Moberly, "Protecting Whistleblowers by Contract," 79 *University of Colorado Law Review* 975 (Fall 2008). But contract lawsuits tend to have very low payouts and do not cover attorney fees.

On June 13, 2011, the Securities and Exchange Commission published final rules implementing the Dodd-Frank whistleblower reward program. SEC Commentary and Final Rule, 76 *Federal Register* 34300 (June 13, 2011). These rules created strong incentives for corporations to develop independent and ethical compliance programs. Id., pp. 34317–19 (circumstances in which compliance officials can file reward claims with the SEC); pp. 34322–27 (employee can qualify for rewards based on information they provided to internal compliance programs). However, pursuant to the Supreme Court's precedent in *Digital*, Dodd-Frank does not protect internal whistleblowers from retaliation.

The False Claims Act should be interpreted as protecting internal disclosures. See *U.S. ex rel. Schweizer v. Oce N.V.*, 677 F.3d 1228 (D.C. Cir. 2012).

The Foreign Corrupt Practices Act prohibits a range of conduct not directly tied to the payment of bribes to foreign officials. The most important of these concerns the obligation of publicly traded companies or "issuers" to maintain quality internal controls and record-keeping systems. 5 U.S.C. § 78m(b)(2). See Jones Day Newsletter, "The Legal Obligation to Maintain Accurate Books and Records in U.S. and Non-U.S. Operations" (Mar. 2006) ("The Foreign Corrupt Practices Act is usually associated with its prohibitions against foreign bribery. The provisions of the Act relating to bookkeeping and internal controls receive less publicity but are much more likely to form the basis of a government proceeding against companies subject to the Act."). But for obvious reasons non-U.S. citizens who report violations of the FCPA in foreign countries have not obtained protection under U.S. employment laws.

Rule 11: Don't Let the Lawyers Throw You under the Bus

The U.S. Supreme Court is clear: Company lawyers owe no loyalty to employees. Company lawyers represent the company, not the employees who seek advice from them or report concerns to in-house counsel. See *Upjohn v. U.S.*, 449 U.S. 383 (1981). Worse still, the company lawyers can act nice to you, while behind your back building a case against you to have you fired or blame you for the underlying frauds. In a similar vein, communications with company lawyers may not constitute a protected disclosure unless a specific law protects internal whistleblowing. See Rule 5, Trap #5 and Rule 10.

Under the code of ethics company lawyers are supposed to make employees aware that they represent the company and not the employee, but this often does not happen, especially in the context of corporate compliance programs managed by lawyers. See, Jeffrey Eglash et al., "Avoiding the Perils and Pitfalls of Internal Corporate Investigations: Proper Use of *Upjohn* Warnings," ABA Section of Litigation Corporate Counsel CLE Seminar (ethical rules governing attorneys who work on or manage corporate compliance investigations); Ethics Opinion 269: "Obligation of Lawyer for Corporation to Clarify Role in Internal Corporate Investigation" (DC Bar, January 1997). Available at www.dcbar.org/bar-resources/legal-ethics/opinions/opinion269.cfm.

Bar rules relevant to the ethical obligations corporate lawyers owe to employees include: ABA Model Rule 4.2: "Communication with Person Represented by Counsel" and ABA Model Rule 4.3: "Dealing with Unrepresented Person." The ABA Model Rules of Professional Conduct are available at www.americanbar.org/groups/professional_responsibility/publications/model_rules_of_professional_conduct/model_rules_of_professional_conduct_table_of_contents.html.

Donna Boehme, a highly respected expert who managed BP's compliance program, warned against having corporate attorneys manage compliance programs. See "DOJ Tells HSBC and Corporate America: Reform Your Compliance Departments," *Corporate Counsel* (Dec. 20, 2012); "Making the CCO an Independent Voice in the C-Suite," *Corporate Counsel*, www.law.com/corporatecounsel/PubArticleCC.jsp?id=1202592518804&Making_the_CCO_an_Independent_Voice_in_the_CSuite. *From Enron to Madoff: Why Many Corporate Compliance and Ethics Programs Are Positioned for Failure*, Rand Center for Corporate Ethics and Governance (2009).

Michael D. Greenberg has published extensively on the issue of lawyers running compliance programs: *Transforming Compliance: Emerging Paradigms for Boards, Management, Compliance Officers, and Government*, Rand Center for Corporate Ethics and Governance (2012); *Culture, Compliance, and the C-Suite: How Executives, Boards, and Policymakers Can Better Safeguard against Misconduct at the Top*, Rand Center for Corporate Ethics and Governance (2013); *For Whom the Whistle Blows: Advancing Corporate Compliance and Integrity Efforts in the Era of Dodd-Frank*, Rand Center for Corporate Ethics and Governance (2011); *Directors as Guardians of Compliance and Ethics within the Corporate Citadel: What the Policy Community Should Know*, Rand Center for Corporate Ethics and Governance (2010).

Jacelyn Jaeger, "The Importance of Splitting Legal and Compliance," *Compliance Week* (Dec. 2011).

Society for Corporate Compliance and Ethics and Health Care Compliance Association. "Compliance Professionals Overwhelmingly Reject General Counsel Reporting Structure," *P.R. Newswire* (Mar. 11, 2013), www.prnewswire.com/news-releases/compliance-professionals-overwhelmingly-reject-general-counsel-reporting-structure -196884911.html (survey of compliance professionals finding that 88.5 percent oppose general counsel serving as chief compliance officer).

Michael Volkov, "Redefining the Relationship of the General Counsel and Chief Compliance Officer," p. 8, Rand Center for Corporate Ethics and Governance (May 28, 2014) (comprehensive article supporting a narrow interpretation of the privilege in compliance investigations).

The chairman of the Senate Judiciary Committee provided strong testimony opposing efforts to require employees to communicate with corporate compliance programs, and pointed out the conflicts of interest in these proposals: "Statement for the Record by Senator Chuck Grassley of Iowa, Chairman, Senate Judiciary Committee at a House Judiciary Subcommittee on the Constitution and Civil Justice Hearing on 'Oversight of the False Claims Act,' April 28, 2016."

Whistleblower as Confidential Informant

If a whistleblower is acting in the capacity of a confidential informant, are they allowed to attend attorney-client meetings held by the company? The short answer is yes, but there are restrictions. See David R. Lurie, "Sixth Amendment Implications of Informant Participation in Defense Meetings," *58 Fordham L. Rev.* 795 (1990). Available at: https://ir.lawnet.fordham.edu/flr/vol58/iss4/9. The leading Supreme Court case on the issue is *Weatherford v. Bursey*, 429 U.S. 545 (1977). In *Weatherford* the Supreme Court explained that a confidential informant would be put in a position of unmasking themselves by refusing to participate in a meeting with attorneys if asked to do so by the target of the investigation. According to the Court, prohibiting informants from participating in such meetings "would require the informant to . . ., for all practical purposes, to unmask himself."

Rule 12: Don't Tip Off the Crooks

As explained in Rule 5, Trap #5 and Rules 10–11, reporting fraud or misconduct internally can be very risky. Protections for those who report fraud or misconduct to supervisors, corporate attorneys, or compliance programs are scattered or, under many laws, simply do not exist. Further, reporting concerns internally often triggers retaliation, as no boss wants to hear that they may be breaking the law.

Whistleblowers should always weigh the benefits of being strictly confidential. There are numerous options available. See, FAQs discussing confidentiality: "Should I be anonymous," https://kkc.com/frequently-asked-questions/should-i-be-an-anonymous-or -confidential-whistleblower/; "How to report anonymously as an SEC whistleblower," https://kkc.com/frequently-asked-questions/reporting-anonymously-as-an-sec -whistleblower/; "How to report anonymously as a CFTC whistleblower," https://kkc .com/frequently-asked-questions/reporting-anonymously-as-a-cftc-whistleblower/.

Confidentiality for federal employees: "Federal employee's rights to file confidential complaints," https://kkc.com/frequently-asked-questions/can-federal-employees-blow-the-whistle-confidentially/; the law protecting the confidentiality of federal employees under the Whistleblower Protection Act is located at 5 U.S.C. § 1213.

Rule 13: Special Rules for Directors, Partners, or Auditors

The problems faced by auditors and compliance officials are well documented. See, Institute of Internal Auditors, "Political Pressure Intense on Internal Audit: IIA Research Report Reveals Pervasive Efforts to Influence Internal Audit Findings," press release (Mar. 10, 2015). The Institute of Internal Auditors survey of auditors is known as the Global Internal Audit Common Body of Knowledge. The survey's results were analyzed in *The Politics of Internal Auditing* by Patricia Miller and Larry Rittenberg, published by the IIA Research Foundation, Altamonte Springs, Florida (2015). See also Larry Rittenberg, *Ethics and Pressure: Balancing the Internal Audit Profession* (The IIA Research Foundation, 2016).

Compliance officials can qualify for rewards. SEC decisions granting awards to compliance officials: SEC Press Release 2014-180 (Aug. 29, 2014) (first compliance official obtains monetary reward), SEC Press Release 2015-73 (Apr. 22, 2015) (compliance official awarded $1.5 million), www.sec.gov/news/pressrelease/2015-73.html.

Requirement that publicly traded companies have a program to accept confidential employee concerns regarding questionable accounting and auditing practices is codified at 15 U.S.C. § 78j-1(m); 17 C.F.R. § 2400.10A-3.

The development of the SEC's rule on director, partner, attorney, and compliance official coverage is discussed at "Speech by Chairman Mary L. Schapiro," U.S. Securities and Exchange Commission, Washington, DC (May 25, 2011), www.sec.gov/news/speech/2011/spch052511mls-item2.htm (SEC whistleblower program); Stephen Kohn, "The SEC's Final Whistleblower Rules and Their Impact on Internal Compliance," West Law Publishing (Oct. 2011) (rights of compliance officials to blow the whistle).

Whether auditors, compliance officials, or employees whose duties require them to perform compliance functions are protected against retaliation remains a controversial topic. However, the two decisions issued by the Supreme Court demonstrate that without specific statutory coverage, internal disclosures by these classes of employees may be unprotected. See Supreme Court decisions finding internal whistleblowing not protected under the Dodd-Frank Act and First Amendment: *Digital Realty Trust v. Somers*, 138 S.Ct. 767 (2018); *Garcetti v. Ceballos*, 547 U.S. 410 (2006). A wealth of cases decided before *Digital* and *Garcetti* explained the fact that whistleblowers often used internal reporting processes and should deserve protection: *Phillips v. Interior Board of Mine Op.*, 500 F.2d 772 (D.C. Cir. 1974); *Mackowiak v. University Nuclear Systems*, 735 F.2d 1159 (9th Cir. 1984); *Kansas Gas & Electric v. Brock*, 780 F.2d 1505 (10th Cir. 1985); *Passaic Valley Sewerage Commissioners v. DOL*, 992 F.2d 474 (3rd Cir. 1993); *U.S. ex rel. Yesudian v. Howard University*, 153 F.3d 731 (D.C. Cir. 1998); *Bechtel v. DOL*, 50 F.3d 926 (11th Cir. 1995); *Poulos v. Ambassador Fuel Oil Co.*, 86-Clean Air Act Case No. 1 (Apr. 27, 1987).

Pre-*Digital* cases discussing whether compliance officials/auditors/attorneys are covered under anti-retaliation laws: *Brown & Root v. Donovan*, 747 F2d 1029 (5th Cir. 1984) (auditor not protected), but the case was reversed in *Willy v. ARB*, 423 F.3d 483 (5th Cir.) (an attorney protected in *Willy*); *Kansas Gas & Elec. v. Brock*, 780 F.2d 1505 (10th Cir. 1985) (quality assurance inspector protected); *Mackowiak v. University Nuclear*, 735 F.2d 1159 (9th Cir. 1984) (inspector protected); *Van Asdale v. International Game Tech.*, 577 F.3d 989 (9th Cir.) (attorney protected).

The AML and sanctions whistleblower law's exclusion concerning whistleblowers whose normal course of job duties includes policing AML or sanctions rules is located at 31U.S.C. § 5323(c)(2)(A)(ii).

Rule 14: Don't Fear NDAs

The case record for *Macktal* is docketed at the U.S. Department of Labor Office of Administrative Law Judges, Case Number 86-ERA-26. The appeals court case is *Macktal v. Secretary of Labor*, 923 F.2d 1150 (5th Cir. 1991). The hearings on *Macktal* were published by the U.S. Senate Subcommittee on Nuclear Regulation, *Hearings on Secret Settlement Agreements Restricting Testimony at Comanche Peak Nuclear Power Plant*, Senate Hearing No. 101-90 (May 4, 1989).

Retaliation against whistleblowers who contact federal law enforcement about possible criminal activity violates the federal Obstruction of Justice statute: 18 U.S.C. § 1513(e).

The SEC and CFTC have enacted rules prohibiting nondisclosure agreements that restrict communications with the SEC or other federal agencies: 17 C.F.R. § 240.21F-17 (SEC) and 17 C.F.R. § 165.19 (CFTC). Pursuant to these rules the Securities and Exchange Commission has enforced strict rules prohibiting restrictions on employee whistleblowing. See Office of Compliance Inspections and Examinations, "Examining Whistleblower Rule Compliance, VI *National Examination Risk Alert* 1 (Oct. 24, 2016) (explaining commission decisions on restrictive agreements and warning companies of various improper contractual methods being employed to prevent or intimidate employees from contacting SEC or applying for rewards), posted at www. sec.gov/ ocie/announcement/ocie-2016-risk-alert-examining-whistleblower-rule-compliance. pdf. Cases sanctioning companies for illegal NDAs include: *In the Matter of The Brink's Company*, File No. 3-20904 (June 22, 2022); *In the Matter of David Hansen*, File No. 3-20820 (Apr. 12, 2022); *In the Matter of Guggenheim Securities, LLC*, File No. 3-20370 (June 23, 2021); *SEC v. GPB Capital Holdings, LLC, et al.*, 21-cv-00583 (E.D.N.Y., filed Feb. 4, 2021); *SEC v. Leon Vaccarelli et al.*, 17-cv-01471 (D. Conn., filed Aug. 31, 2017); *SEC v. Collector's Coffee, Inc.*, 19-cv-04355 (Nov. 4, 2019); *SEC v. Kenneth W. Crumbley*,16-cv-00172 (N.D. Tex.)(Sept. 13, 2018); *In the Matter of Homestreet, Inc. and Darrell Van Amen*, File No. 3-17801 (Jan. 19, 2017); *In the Matter of BlackRock, Inc.*, File No. 3-17786 (Jan. 17, 2017); *In the Matter of SandRidge Energy, Inc.*, File No. 3-17739 (Dec. 20, 2016); *In the Matter of Anheuser-Busch InBev SA/NV*, File No. 3-17586 (Sept. 28, 2016); *In the Matter of Health Net, Inc.*, File No. 3-17396 (Aug. 16, 2016); *In the Matter of BlueLinx Holdings Inc.*, File No. 3-17371 (Aug. 10, 2016); *In the Matter of Merrill Lynch, Pierce, Fenner & Smith Incorporated and Merrill Lynch Professional Clearing Corp.*, File No. 3-17312 (June 23, 2016); *In the Matter of KBR, Inc.*, SEC File No. 3-16466 (Apr. 1, 2015); *In the Matter of NeuStar*, SEC File No. 3-17736 (Dec. 19, 2016).

Defend Trade Secrets Act: 18 U.S.C. § 1833(b) (setting forth how employees can blow the whistle on matters a corporation classifies as a trade secret).

Connecticut Light & Power v. Secretary of Labor, 85 F.3d 89 (2nd Cir. 1996) (upholding cause of action based on illegal hush money settlement).

Jon Bauer, "Buying Witness Silence: Evidence-Suppressing Settlements and Lawyers' Ethics," 87 *Oregon Law Review* 481, 493 (2008) (listing examples of restrictive settlements that interfered with the public's ability to learn about serious safety issues).

Town of Newton v. Rumery, 480 U.S. 386 (1987) (Supreme Court case on public policy under contract law).

EEOC v. Astra USA, 94 F.3d 738 (1st Cir. 1996); *EEOC v. Cosmair*, 821 F.2d 1085 (5th Cir. 1987) (enjoining corporation from using settlement agreements to prevent employees from disclosing information to the EEOC); *In re JDS Uniphase Corp. Securities Litigation*, 238 F.Supp.2d 1127 (N.D. Calif. 2002) (enjoining use of "confidentiality agreements to chill former employees from voluntarily participating in legitimate investigations into alleged wrongdoing"); *U.S. ex rel. Longhi v. Lithium Power*, 575 F.3d 458 (5th Cir. 2009) (refusing to enforce employee release of FCA claims); *U.S. v. Purdue Pharma*, 600 F.3d 319 (4th Cir. 2010) (upholding release of FCA claims when government had prior knowledge of the frauds disclosed by employee).

Rule 15: Talking to the Press

Retaliation: Cases upholding the right of public employees to lawfully report concerns to the news media: *Pickering v. Board of Education*, 391 U.S. 563 (1968), and *Andrew v. Clark*, 561 F.3d 261 (4th Cir. 2009) (First Amendment); *Dept. of Homeland Sec. v. MacLean*, 574 U.S. 383 (2015) (contacting news media protected under Whistleblower Protection Act); *Huffman v. Office of Personnel Management*, 263 F.3d 1341, 1351 (Fed. Cir. 2001) (citing *Horton*, 66 F.3d at 282, holding that media disclosures are an indirect way of disclosing information of wrongdoing to a person in a position to provide a remedy) (Whistleblower Protection Act case).

But federal employees working for national security and intelligence agencies need to comply with agency prepublication review requirements before publishing information in the news media or writing books or articles. *Snepp v. U.S.*, 444 U.S. 507 (1980); *U.S. v. Marchetti*, 466 F.2d 1309 (4th Cir. 1972) (obligation to submit to prepublication review for FBI employees and employees working in national security or intelligence agencies).

Cases discussing news media disclosures under private sector whistleblower laws (administered by Department of Labor or EEOC): *Donovan v. R.D. Anderson*, 552 F.Supp. 249 (D. Kan. 1982) (contacting news media protected under OSHA); *Chambers v. Dept. of Interior*, 602 F.3d 1370, 1379 (Fed. Cir. 2010) (media contacts protected under Whistleblower Protection Act); *Haney v. North American Car Corp.*, 81-SWDA-1,

Recommended Decision and Order of Labor Department Administrative Law Judge (Aug. 10, 1981), *affirmed*, Secretary of Labor (June 30, 1982) (under environmental whistleblower laws); *Diaz-Robainas v. Florida Power & Light Co.*, 92-ERA-10, Order of Secretary of Labor (Jan. 10, 1996) (Atomic Energy Act); *Wrighten v. Metropolitan Hosp., Inc.*, 726 F.2d 1346, 1355 (9th Cir. 1984) (holding a press conference is protected under Title VII).

In a 2011 decision, a three-judge panel of the U.S. Court of Appeals for the Ninth Circuit broke with most precedent and found that employee contacts with the press were not protected under 18 U.S.C. section 1514A(a)(1) of the Sarbanes-Oxley Act. However, the court left open the issue as to whether contacts with the press were protected under another clause of the act, section 1514A(a)(2): *Tides v. Boeing*, 644F.3d 809 (9th Cir. 2011).

Even if a contact with the news media is protected under federal law, whistleblowers who use a state law as the basis for a complaint risk losing their case: *Pacheco v. Waldrop*, 84 F.3d 606 (W.D. Ky. 2015) (media disclosure not protected under state whistleblower statute).

Rewards: There are very few cases discussing the application of original information provisions permitting whistleblowers to initially alert the government to violations via a disclosure to the news media. However, under all of these laws a whistleblower would have to prove (a) that they were the source of the information to the news media, and (b) that the government relied on the media disclosure in sanctioning the company. Furthermore, all of the other technical filing requirements would have to be met. The statutory provisions that permit whistleblowers to obtain rewards if they initially alert the press to the violations are:

> False Claims Act: 31 U.S.C. § 3730(e)(4)(A).
>
> Securities and Exchange Act/Foreign Corrupt Practices Act: 15 U.S.C. § 78u-6(a)(3).
>
> IRS whistleblower reward law: 26 U.S.C. § 7623(b)(2)(B).
>
> Commodity Exchange Act: 7 U.S.C. § 26(a)(4).
>
> Motor Vehicle Safety Act: 49 U.S.C. § 30172(a)(3).
>
> Anti-Money Laundering Act: 31 U.S.C.§ 5323(a)(3).

How whistleblower disclosures to the news media serve the public interest is well documented in U.S. history. See Carl Bernstein and Bob Woodward, *All the President's Men* (New York: Simon & Schuster, 1974).

Part III: Rewards—The Laws

Rule 16: Follow the Money

Checklist 1 lists the major state and federal *qui tam* or rewards-based whistleblower laws. Links to the significant laws, cases, and updates are available at www.kkc.com/law-library/.

The legislative history of the FCA is set forth in three critically important Senate Reports. The first explains in detail the history of the FCA and the impact of the 1986 amendments that revived the law. See S. Rep. 99-345, 99th Cong., 2nd Sess. (1986). This Senate Report remains the most authoritative source for interpreting the FCA.

A second major source of information is the legislative history of the False Claims Act Correction Act of 2008. See S. Rep. 99-345, 99th Cong., 2nd Sess. (1986); S. Rep. 110-507, 110th Cong., 2nd Sess. (2008). Although this law did not pass, many of its provisions were approved (either in whole, in part, or in a modified form) by Congress in three separate laws. See the Fraud Enforcement and Recovery Act, Public Law No. 111-21, § 4 (May 20, 2009); the Patient Protection and Affordable Care Act, Public Law No. 111-148, § 10104(j)(2) (Mar. 23, 2010); and the Dodd-Frank Act, Public Law No. 111-203, § 1079A (July 21, 2010).

The third report explains the meaning of the FCA amendments included in the Fraud Enforcement and Recovery Act of 2009. See S. Rep. 111-10, 111th Cong., 1st Sess. (2009).

U.S. Department of Justice, Civil Division, *Fraud Statistics—Overview: Oct. 1, 1987–Sept. 30, 2020*. These statistics are updated annually. Published at www.doj.gov/civil/frauds (FCA statistics).

The early legislative history of the FCA can be found at Cong. Globe, 37th Cong., 3rd Sess., pp. 952–58 (1863); "Report of the House Committee on Government Contracts," March 3, 1863; H. R. Rep. No. 2, 37th Cong., 2nd Sess., pt. ii—a, pp. xxxviii–ix (1862). President Lincoln signed the original FCA into law on March 2, 1863. See Statutes at Large, 37th Cong., Sess. II, Chapter LXVII (Mar. 2, 1863).

On April 1, 1943, the House voted to repeal the FCA. The repeal would have been readily approved but for a prolonged filibuster by Senator William Langer (Rep., N. Dak.). During the filibuster Senator Langer put into the *Congressional Record* information on the legislative purposes and cases pending under the FCA. See Volume 89 of the *Congressional Record*, Senate debates between July 8 and December 17, 1943. Langer's central arguments in opposition to repealing or gutting the FCA are set forth in his "Minority Views" to Senate Report 291, Part 2, 78th Cong., 1st Sess. (June 25, 1943) and in the *Congressional Record* on pp. 7437–45 (July 8, 1943), pp. 7576–79 (Sept. 15, 1943), pp. 7601-7 (Sept. 17, 1943). Senator James Murray (Montana) also spoke out against the repeal; *Congressional Record* pp. 7575–76 (Sept. 15, 1943), pp. 7609–10 (Sept. 17, 1943). Senator Joel Bennett Clark (Missouri) also condemned the repeal; see *Congressional Record* pp. 7611–14 (Sept. 17, 1943). In the House of Representatives, Congressmen Vito Marcantonio (New York) and Louis Miller (Missouri) opposed the repeal; see *Congressional Record* pp. 10846–49 (Dec. 17, 1943).

Based on Langer's actions the FCA was not repealed, but instead severely weakened. The amendments gutting the law were approved by Congress and signed into law by President Roosevelt on December 23, 1943; see 57 Stat. 608.

The Bradley Birkenfeld story has been widely reported in the international press. See Michael Bronner, "Telling Swiss Secrets: A Banker's Betrayal," *Global Post* (Aug. 5, 2010); Juan Gonzales, "UBS Whistleblower Bradley Birkenfeld Deserves a Statue on Wall Street, Not Prison Sentence," *New York Daily News* (Jan. 6, 2010); David Hilzenrath, "Beware the Whistle: A Swiss Banker's Saga Offers a Cautionary Tale," *Washington Post* (May 16, 2010). The exchange between the court and the federal prosecutor is contained in the Sentencing Transcript, *U.S. v. Birkenfeld*, 08-60099-CR-Zloch (U.S. Dist. Court, S.D. Florida) (Aug. 21, 2009). Bradley Birkenfeld, "Lucifer's Banker UNCENSORED: The Untold Story of How I Destroyed Swiss Bank Secrecy," https://lucifersbanker.com.

Rule 17: The False Claims Act Reborn—With a Vengeance

The False Claims Act (FCA), 31 U.S.C. §§ 3729–32. The legislative history of the FCA is set forth in Rule 16. Also see Extension Remarks by Congressman Berman, *Congressional Record*, pp, E1296–97 (June 3, 2009).

Decisions interpreting the original intent of the FCA: *U.S. ex rel. Marcus v. Hess*, 317 U.S. 537 (1943); *United States v. Griswold*, 24 F. 361 (D. Ore. 1885).

Decisions interpreting the 1986 amendments: *Vermont Agency of Natural Resources v. U.S. ex rel. Stevens*, 529 U.S. 765 (2000) (FCA is constitutional); *Rockwell International Corp. v. U.S. ex rel. Stone*, 549 U.S. 457 (2007) (limiting recoveries by relators; partially reversed by 2010 amendment to FCA); *Cook County v. U.S. ex rel. Chandler*, 538 U.S. 119 (2003) (municipal corporations covered under FCA); *KBR v. U.S. ex rel. Carter*, 135 S.Ct. 1970 (2015) (clarifying statute of limitations and original source standards); *Universal Health Services v. U.S. ex rel. Escobar*, 136 S.Ct. 1989 (2016); *State Farm v. U.S. ex rel. Rigsby*, 137 S.Ct. 436 (2016) (sanctions for violating seal).

The broad coverage of employers and contractors under the FCA's anti-retaliation provision was explained in *U.S. ex rel. Bias*, 816 F.3d 315 (5th Cir. 2016).

Articles explaining the FCA and *qui tam*: Note, "The History and Development of Qui Tam," *Wash. U. L. Q.* 81 (1972); Claire Sylvia, "The False Claims Act: Fraud against the Government," *Thomson/West* (Danvers, MA, 2004); Joel Hesch, "Understanding the 'Original Source Exception' to the False Claims Act's 'Public Disclosure Bar' in Light of the Supreme Court's Ruling in *Rockwell v. United States*," 7 *DePaul Bus. & Com. Law Journal* 1 (Fall 2008).

Elleta Callahan and Terry Dworkin, "Do Good and Get Rich: Financial Incentives for Whistleblowing and the False Claims Act," 37 *Vill. L. Rev.* 273 (1992); Thomas Harris, "Alternative Remedies & The False Claims Act: Protecting *Qui Tam* Relators in Light of Government Intervention and Criminal Prosecution Decisions," 94 *Cornell Law Review* 1293 (2009).

The U.S. Department of Justice discloses information on FCA recoveries on the web page for the Civil Division, Commercial Litigation Branch, Civil Frauds site. See DOJ Civil Fraud press releases regarding FCA settlements and judgments at http://www .justice.gov/civil/frauds/Civil%20Fraud.htm. The Civil Frauds web page also has statistics on FCA recoveries and a "primer" outlining basic tenets of the FCA.

Sources documenting the success of the reward laws are cited in the conclusion.

Rule 18: Tax Evasion and Underpayments: Report to the IRS

The IRS reward law is codified at 26 U.S.C. § 7623. IRS Notice 2008-4, 2008-1 C.B. sets forth procedures for submitting claims to the IRS Whistleblower Office. See also *Internal Revenue Manual*, Part 25.2.2 (updated June 18, 2010). The IRS is in the process of publishing final rules for its whistleblower program at 26 C.F.R. § 301. The IRS Whistleblower Office website is https://www.irs.gov/compliance/whistleblower-office.

Although the IRS law does not provide for anonymous or confidential filings, the IRS regulations require strict confidentiality, the IRS regulations do require the service to "use its best efforts to protect the identity of whistleblowers." 26 C.F.R. § 301.7623-1(e). The IRS will also protect whistleblowers from the release of data about their identities or filings under the Freedom of Information Act, *Montgomery v. IRS*, 40 F.4th 702 (D.C. Cir. 2022).

Whistleblowers can appeal award decisions to Tax Court. The rules for these appeals are at U.S. Tax Court, Title XXXIII, "Whistleblower Actions," Rules 340–344.

Tax Court decisions on whistleblower cases: *Cooper v. Commissioner*, 2010 Tax Court LEXIS 20, 135 T.C. No. 4 (July 8, 2010) (court can hear appeals filed by whistleblowers that challenge both the amount of an award or the denial of an award); *Whistleblower 21276-13W v. Commissioner of IRS*, 147 Tax Court 4 (Aug. 3, 2016) (Tax Court expands scope of "alternative remedy" provision). (Note: The commission does not approve of this ruling.); *Whistleblower 21276-13W v. Commissioner of IRS*, 144 Tax Court 290 (2015) (Form 211 need not be filed before whistleblower provides information to other parts of the IRS).

Articles and reports on tax whistleblower law: Department of the Treasury Inspector General for Tax Administration, "Deficiencies Exist in the Control and Timely Resolution of Whistleblower Claims" (Aug. 20, 2009); Dennis Ventry Jr., "Whistleblowers and *Qui Tam* for Tax," 61 *Tax Lawyer* 357 (2007); Karie Davis-Nozemack et al., "Lost Opportunities: The Underuse of Tax Whistleblowers," 67 *Administrative Law Review* 321 (2015); Government Accountability Office, *IRS Whistleblower Program: Billions Collected, but Timeliness and Communication Concerns May Discourage Whistleblowers*, GAO-16-20 (Oct. 2015).

Government Accountability Office, *Offshore Tax Evasion: IRS has Collected Billions of Dollars, but May be Missing Continued Evasion*, GAO-13-318 (Mar. 2013); Stephen Ohlemacher, "Tips on tax cheats skyrocket with bigger rewards," Associated Press (Oct. 1, 2009); Barry Shlachter, "Tax Whistleblowers Stand to Reap Bigger IRS Rewards," Star-Telegram.com

(Apr. 14, 2010); John Koskinen, Commissioner, IRS, Prepared Remarks Before the U.S. Council for International Business-OECD, International Tax Conference (Washington, DC, June 3, 2014).

Bradley Birkenfeld, the most famous tax whistleblower, told his story in his book *Lucifer's Banker: The Untold Story of How I Destroyed Swiss Bank Secrecy* (Austin TX: Greenleaf Book Group Press, 2016).

Sources documenting the success of the IRS reward law are cited in the conclusion.

Rule 19: Dodd-Frank (Securities and Commodities): Report to the SEC/CFTC

The two main whistleblower reward laws in Dodd-Frank are codified at 7 U.S.C. § 26 (commodities) and 15 U.S.C. § 78u-6 (securities). The SEC and CFTC also have jurisdiction to investigate and pay rewards related to foreign corruption cases. See Rules 6 and 20. The Dodd-Frank whistleblower laws are now the most popular whistleblower laws, given their broad reach and the ability to file confidential and anonymous claims. As of 2023 over 70,000 whistleblowers had filed claims with the two commissions, and over $1.5 billion in rewards were paid. See SEC and CFTC Whistleblower Office websites at: https://www.sec.gov/whistleblower and https://www.whistleblower.gov/ (CFTC Office).

The SEC's program was praised by the commission in its 2022 Annual Report:

> *Whistleblowers have played a critical role in the SEC's enforcement efforts in protecting investors and the marketplace. Enforcement actions brought using information from meritorious whistleblowers have resulted in orders for more than $6.3 billion in total monetary sanctions, including more than $4.0 billion in disgorgement of ill-gotten gains and interest, of which more than $1.5 billion has been, or is scheduled to be, returned to harmed investors. The Commission also received a record high number of whistleblower tips alleging wrongdoing. In FY 2022, the Commission received over 12,300 whistleblower tips—the largest number of whistleblower tips received in a fiscal year. (https://www.sec .gov/files/2022_ow_ar.pdf)*

The SEC and CFTC published rules governing the whistleblower rewards provisions of Dodd-Frank. The SEC's rules are codified at 17 C.F.R. Parts 240 and 249. The CFTC rules are codified at 17 C.F.R. Part 165. *Reward claims must be filed as mandated under the rules of the SEC or CFTC. The failure to follow these procedures can result in the denial of a reward.* These rules apply to both U.S. violations and violations related to foreign corruption.

Detailed explanations of the original rules were published by the two commissions. See 76 *Federal Register* 34300 (SEC) and 76 *Federal Register* 53172 (CFTC). The rules have subsequently been amended. On September 23, 2020, the SEC completed a second major rule making concerning its whistleblower program, which was published at 85 *Federal Register* 70898 (Nov. 5, 2020). The CFTC also amended its initial whistleblower rules. See 82 *Federal Register* 24487 (May 30, 2017). On August 26, 2022, the SEC again amended its rules. See 87 *Federal Register* 54140 (Sept. 2, 2022), https://www.sec.gov/rules/final/2022/34-95620.pdf. These new rules clarified how whistleblowers can obtain "related action" awards and prohibited the commission from reducing rewards in large cases. The Dodd-Frank rules are subject to future amendments.

Both the SEC and CFTC publish all of the reward decisions on their respective websites. These decisions should be carefully reviewed, as they set forth the administrative precedents and case law explaining the basis relied upon by the two commissions when adjudicating award decisions. The websites also have extremely valuable information about the investigative priorities of agencies and links to the governing statutes, regulations, press releases, and annual reports discussing details of the award cases.

The Dodd-Frank Act, Public Law No. 111-203, 124 Statutes at Large 1376 (July 21, 2010), also included a number of enhancements for whistleblower protections in addition to the reward laws. The following sections of Dodd-Frank enhanced whistleblower rights: § 748 created a new section 23 of the Commodity Exchange Act that not only provided for mandatory whistleblower rewards, but also prohibited retaliation; § 922 creates a new 21F of the Securities Exchange Act that provides for mandatory whistleblower rewards, but also included a section that prohibited retaliation; §§ 922 and 929A contained the provisions that amended and improved the Sarbanes-Oxley whistleblower protections; § 924 required the SEC to establish a special whistleblower office and enact regulations enforcing whistleblower rules; § 1507 established new whistleblower protections for employees who make protected disclosures related to the enforcement of the Bureau of Consumer Financial Protection; § 1079B(c) amended the False Claims Act anti-retaliation law to provide for a universal national three-year statute of limitations to file wrongful discharge/retaliation claims under the FCA.

The legislative history of Dodd-Frank: U.S. Senate Committee on Banking, Housing, and Urban Affairs, "The Restoring American Financial Stability Act of 2010," Senate Report No. 111-176, 111th Cong., 2nd Sess. (Apr. 30, 2010) (the final Senate Report containing the legislative history/analysis of the Dodd-Frank Act). Also see U.S. Senate Committee on Banking, Housing, and Urban Affairs, "Dodd-Frank Wall Street Reform and Consumer Protection Act: Conference Report," Senate Report No. 111-517, 111th Cong., 2nd Sess. (June 29, 2010) (containing the final text of the Dodd-Frank Act).

Prior to the passage of the Dodd-Frank Act, the inspector general for the SEC concluded that the existing voluntary bounty program was gravely deficient. Securities and Exchange Commission, Office of Inspector General, Office of Audit, "Assessment of the SEC's Bounty Program," Report No. 474 (Mar. 29, 2010). The Office of Inspector General was also very critical of the SEC's handling of the Madoff scandal and the whistleblower who had stepped forward, but was ignored. See SEC, Office of Inspector General, Office of Investigations, "Investigation of Failure of the SEC to Uncover Bernard Madoff's Ponzi Scheme," OIG Report No. OIG-509 (Aug. 31, 2009). This scandal fueled efforts to enact effective whistleblower protections for Wall Street employees.

Sources documenting the success of the Dodd-Frank reward laws are cited in the conclusion.

Rule 20: Foreign Corruption and Bribery: Report to the SEC/CFTC

See Rule 6 for information on the Foreign Corrupt Practices Act and the jurisdiction of the SEC and CFTC to police international corruption. The Department of Justice and SEC co-publish a comprehensive manual on the FCPA. See "A Resource Guide to the FCPA" published at https://www.justice.gov/criminal-fraud/file/1292051/download. The FCPA is codified at 15 U.S.C. §§ 78dd-1, 78dd-2, 78dd-3, 78m, 78ff. The maximum penalty per/bribe is $2 million, the maximum penalty for a books and records violation is $25 million. Under other provisions of law companies can be sanctioned up to two times the value of the profits obtained from the bribes paid.

The original legislative history behind the FCPA is located at H. R. Rep. No. 95-640, available at https://www.justice. gov/sites/default/files/criminal-fraud/legacy/2010/04/11/houseprt-95-640.pdf. and S. Rep. No. 95-114 (1977). The history behind the 1988 amendments is located at H.R. Rep. No. 100-576, at 916-24 (1988). Also see S. Rep. No. 105-277, at 2 (1998) (discussing efforts by U.S. government to encourage U.S. trading partners to enact legislation similar to FCPA following 1988 amendments) [hereinafter S. Rep. No. 105-277]; International Anti-Bribery and Fair Competition Act of 1998, Pub. L. 105-366, 112 Stat. 3302 (1998).

Information on the OECD's Anti-Bribery Convention and its implementation is available at OECD, Country Reports on the Implementation of the OECD Anti-Bribery Convention, available at http://www.oecd.org/document/24/0,3746,en_2649_34859 _1933144_1_1_1_1,00.html.

Rule 21: Money Laundering and Sanctions-Busting: Report to FinCEN/Treasury

The AML whistleblower law is codified at 31 U.S.C. § 5323 and administered by the Financial Crimes Enforcement Network, better known as FinCEN. The AML Whistleblower Improvement Act was signed into law on December 29, 2022, by President Biden.

The legislative history of the AML Improvement Act is located at House Report No, 117-423 (July 20, 2022), online at https://www.congress.gov/congressional -report/117th-congress/house-report/423/1?overview=closed.

The statutes under which whistleblowers can make protected disclosures include: the Bank Secrecy Act, 31 USC 5311 et seq.; Chapter 35 of Title 31; 50 USC §§ 4305 and 4312 and the Foreign Narcotics Kingpin Designation Act, 21 U.S.C. 1901 et seq., and for conspiracies to violate any of these laws.

Information on the Danske Bank case and whistleblower Howard Wilkinson:

Department of Justice Press Release on Danske Bank Prosecution: https://www.justice. gov/opa/pr/danske-bank-pleads-guilty-fraud-us-banks-multi-billion-dollar-scheme-access-us-financial; SEC Press Release on Danske Bank sanctions (Dec. 13, 2022), https://www.sec.gov/news/press-release/2022-220; Howard Wilkinson biography web page, https://kkc.com/whistleblower-case-archive/howard-wilkinson/; Bruun and Hjejle. *Report on the Non-Resident Portfolio at Danske Bank's Estonian branch.* (2018).

The campaign to enact the AML Whistleblower Improvement Act is explained at https://kkc.com/pro-bono/aml-whistleblower-improvement-act/. See "Big Banks get a Big Break on Pending Whistleblower Law," *The Hill* (Dec. 7, 2020), https://thehill .com/blogs/congress-blog/politics/528995-big-banks-get-a-big-break-on-pending -whistleblower-law/; "Congress Needs to Pass Money Laundering and Sanctions Busting Whistleblower Protections," *The Hill* (Aug. 11, 2022), https://thehill.com/opinion/ congress-blog/3597582-congress-needs-to-pass-money-laundering-and-sanctions -busting-whistleblower-protections/; "The House Must Act on Whistleblower Bill to Protect Insiders who Report Russian Money Laundering," *The Hill* (Dec. 12, 2022), https://thehill.com/opinion/congress-blog/3772481-house-must-act-on-whistleblower -bill-to-protect-insiders-who-report-russian-money-laundering/; "Loopholes Doom Money Laundering Anti-Retaliation law, *JD Supra* (Feb. 4, 2021), https://www.jdsupra.com/ legalnews/loopholes-doom-money-laundering-anti-7495814.

FinCEN has numerous regulations implementing the Bank Secrecy Act, including 31 C.F.R. Chapter X (formerly 31 C.F.R. Part 103). FinCEN cases issue civil money penalties violations under 31 C.F.R §1010.415, for failing to file a currency transaction report (CTR) in violation of 31 C.F.R. §1010.311, a suspicious activity report (SAR) in violation of 31 C.F.R. § 1021.320, or a report of foreign bank and financial accounts (FBAR) in violation of 31 C.F.R §1010.350. FinCEN can take enforcement actions against money services businesses for failure to register with FinCEN in violation of 31 C.F.R §1022.380.

FinCEN's enforcement actions, which spell out the legal basis for violations, is located online at: https://www.fincen.gov/news-room/enforcement-actions.

The IRS whistleblower law that covers crimes investigated by the IRS criminal division is located at 26 U.S.C. § 7623(c)(2). Money laundering violations are also covered under the SEC and CFTC Dodd-Frank Act programs.

For links to statutes and regulations, and for updates on the Departments of Justice and Treasury and FinCEN's implementation of this law, see kkc.com/law-library/.

Rule 22: Auto Safety: Report to the DOT

Reward law: 49 U.S.C. § 30172.

Legislative history of the reward statute: Senate Report 114-13, "Motor Vehicle Safety Whistleblower Act, Report of the Committee on Commerce, Science, and Transportation on S. 304" (Apr. 13, 2015); Office of John Thune press statement on reward law: "Thune, Nelson Introduce Legislation to Help Prevent Auto Injuries, Deaths from Faulty Parts by Incentivizing Whistleblowers" (Nov. 20, 2014), www.thune.senate.gov/public/index.cfm/2014/11/thune-nelson-introduce-legislation-to-help-prevent-auto-injuries-deaths-from-faulty-parts-by-incentivizing-whistleblowers.

The anti-retaliation law: 49 U.S.C. § 30171. The Department of Labor regulations implementing the anti-retaliation law: 29 C.F.R. § 1988.

Information on the Sheridan case: "Examining S. 3302, The Motor Vehicle Safety Act of 2010," hearing before the Committee on Commerce, Science, and Transportation, U.S. Senate (Senate Hearing 111-991) (May 19, 2010); Statement of Senator Jay Rockefeller IV, press release (May 4, 2010); *ABC Prime Time Live*, "Mini Van Danger" (May 3, 2008); Bill Vlasic, "Fired Employee Battles Chrysler in Courtroom," *Detroit News* (July 2003); *Chrysler Corp. v. Sheridan*, No. 227757 (Mich. Court of Appeals, 2003) (unpublished) (dismissing whistleblower's lawsuit).

Rule 23: Whistleblowing on the High Seas: Report to the Coast Guard

The APPS whistleblower reward provision is codified at 33 U.S.C. § 1908(a). An index of major APPS cases, including links to the indictments, plea agreements, and decisions on whistleblower rewards, is available at: https://kkc.com/laws-statutes-and-regulations-2/cases-under-the-act-to-prevent-pollution-from-ships-apps/. Also see information on the APPS published by the National Whistleblower Center at https://www.whistleblowers.org/stop-shipping-pollution/.

Rule 24: Wildlife Trafficking, IUU Fishing, and Deforestation: Report to FWS

The main wildlife whistleblower reward laws are codified as follows: Lacey Act, 16 U.S.C. § 3375(d); Endangered Species Act, 16 U.S.C. § 1540(d); Rhinoceros and Tiger Conservation Act, 16 U.S.C. § 5305a(f); Antarctic Conservation Act, 16 U.S.C. §§ 2409 and 2439; Fish and Wildlife Improvement Act, 16 U.S.C. § 742l(c)(3); and Wild Bird Conservation Act, 16 U.S.C. §§ 4912(c) and 4913(b). All of these laws are substantially identical.

The sweeping authority granted the Fish and Wildlife Service and the National Marine Fisheries Service to award whistleblowers under any wildlife protection laws administered by these agencies for reporting violations was enacted as part of the Fish and Wildlife Improvement Act, 16 U.S.C. § 742l(k)(2).

The congressional history behind the original 1981 amendments to the Lacey Act, which included the whistleblower reward laws, is located in House Report No. 97-276 (Oct. 19, 1981).

The legislative history of the 1982 Fish and Wildlife Improvement Act, which empowered the Fish and Wildlife Service and the National Marine Fisheries Service to pay rewards under all wildlife laws administered by these agencies, is set forth in 128 Cong. Rec. H10207 and H31972 (Dec. 17, 1982).

For a complete understanding of the wildlife whistleblower laws and the scope of their coverage see Kohn, "Monetary Rewards for Wildlife Whistleblowers: A Game-Changer in Wildlife Trafficking Detection and Deterrence," 46 *Environmental Law Reporter* 10054 (Jan. 2016), and the report issued by the National Whistleblower Center, "Special Report: The Critical Role of Whistleblowers in Enforcing Wildlife Protection Laws" (Sept. 14, 2019), published at https://kkc.com/wp-content/uploads/2020/08/Wildlife _Report-Sept-2019.pdf.

The testimony of Assistant Attorney General John Cruden was submitted to the House Committee on Foreign Affairs, Subcommittee on Terrorism, Nonproliferation and Trade (Apr. 22, 2015), www.justice.gov/opa/speech/poaching-terrorism-national -security-challenge-statement-assistant-attorney-general.

The Convention on International Trade in Endangered Species of Wild Fauna and Flora (CITES), 27 UST 1087; TIAS 8249; 993 UNTS 243; see https://www.cites.org/ eng. CITES is the international convention signed by over 150 countries, including the United States, prohibiting trafficking in protected plants, fish, and animals. The Lacey Act implements this treaty.

Articles on the IUCN resolutions supporting whistleblowers are linked at https://whistle blowersblog.org/environmental-whistleblowers/motion-39-passes-at-iucn-marseilles -conference-2021 to-be-a-groundbreaking-year-for-environmental-defenders-and -whistleblowers/ and https://whistleblowersblog.org/government-whistleblowers/iucn -motions-essential-in-guiding-new-international-whistleblower-law-environmental -whistleblower-policy-expert-explains/.

Rule 25: Don't Think Small

Related action payments are available under most whistleblower reward laws. See Rules 16–25.

The SEC discussed related actions at 76 *Federal Register* 34300 (June 13, 2011). The SEC rule covers both securities frauds and reports concerning the Foreign Corrupt Practices Act.

The CFTC discussed related actions at 76 *Federal Register* 53172 at 53179-80 (Aug. 25, 2011). On August 26, 2022, the SEC approved new rules governing related action claims and payments. See 87 *Federal Register* 54140 (Sept. 2, 2022), https://www.sec.gov/rules/ final/2022/34-95620.pdf.

Dodd-Frank permits the SEC and CFTC to pay rewards based on sanctions obtained by other government agencies. But the related action provisions also permit rewards to be paid on sanctions or fines issued by approved private sector entities known as self-regulatory organizations or SROs. Thus, whistleblowers who provide information to SROs can obtain a reward for fines or sanctions issued by the SROs, if the SEC also sanctions the company over $1 million.

The SEC defines covered SROs as: "(1) any national securities exchange, (2) registered securities association, (3) registered clearing agency, (4) the Municipal Securities Rulemaking Board, and (5) any other organizations that may be defined as self-regulatory organizations under Section 3(a)(26) of the Exchange Act (15 U.S.C. 78c(a)(26))."

SEC-covered SROs include national securities exchanges such as the BOX Exchange LLC; Cboe BYX Exchange, Inc.; Cboe Exchange, Inc.; Investors Exchange LLC; Long-Term Stock Exchange, Inc.: MEMX, LLC; Miami International Securities Exchange; MIAX Emerald LLC: MIAX PEARL, LLC; Nasdaq BX, Inc.; The Nasdaq Stock Market; New York Stock Exchange LLC; NYSE Arca, Inc.; NYSE Chicago, Inc.: NYSE American LLC and the NYSE National, Inc.; CBOE Futures Exchange, LLC: Chicago Board of Trade; One Chicago, LLC and the Financial Industry Regulatory Authority (FINRA). The following registered clearing agencies are also included within the definition of an SRO: the Depository Trust Company (DTC), National Securities Clearing Corporation (NSCC), Fixed Income Clearing Corporation (FICC), Options Clearing Corporation (OCC), ICE Clear Credit LLC (ICC), ICE Clear Europe Limited (ICEEU), and the LCH SA. The Municipal Securities Rulemaking Board is also classified as a covered SRO.

The CFTC also will grant rewards in related actions issued by SROs approved by the commission. These include the SROs covered by the SEC, along with international commodities regulators.

A list of agencies covered under the related action rule, including the numerous SROs covered by either the SEC or CFTC, is located at the online law library, kkc.com/law-library.

Part IV: Retaliation—Fighting Back

Rule 26: Find the Federal Law That Works

Caution: Congress periodically amends these laws, and the most recent version of the law should always be checked. Furthermore, courts are continuously interpreting statutes, and the most recent judicial interpretations must also always be checked. Lower courts often disagree over the interpretation of a law, and it is also important to check the specific judicial rulings relevant in the judicial district or court for which you may file a claim. Links to these authorities, along with updates concerning relevant changes in the laws, are available at the free online law library created by the author, located at www.kkc.com/law-library.

DEPARTMENT OF LABOR AUTHORITIES

The U.S. Department of Labor has an extensive law library and detailed regulations governing the various laws administered by the DOL. The Labor Department also has detailed regulations governing the hearing procedures in DOL cases.

DOL sources applicable to *all* Labor Department cases:

OSHA whistleblower website, located at https://www.whistleblowers.gov.

Procedural rules for hearings before DOL Administrative Law Judges: 29 C.F.R. Part 18.

The U.S. Department of Labor Office of Administrative Law Judges comprehensive listing of whistleblower decisions and practice guides covering all DOL-administrated laws is at www.oalj.dol.gov.

MAJOR FEDERAL ANTI-RETALIATION LAWS

Below is an outline of the major federal whistleblower laws. Other laws are cited or discussed in Checklists 1 and 2.

Airline Safety

Aviation Investment and Reform Act, 49 U.S.C. § 42121. Department of Labor rules implementing this law are codified at 29 C.F.R. Part 1979. "Memorandum of Understanding between the Department of Labor and the FAA," 67 *Federal Register* 55883 (2002). The rules governing administrative hearings are located at 29 C.F.R. Part 18.

Clemmons v. Ameristar, 2004-AIR-11 (Dept. of Labor Administrative Review Board, May 26, 2010); *Evans v. Miami Valley Hospital*, 2006-AIR-22 (Dept. of Labor Administrative Review Board, June 30, 2009) (cases setting forth elements of an airline whistleblower case).

Anti-Money Laundering (AML) Whistleblower Protection Act

See Money Laundering.

Anti-Trust Whistleblower Law

The Criminal Antitrust Anti-Retaliation Act is codified at 15 U.S.C. § 7a-3. Cases must be filed with the U.S. Department of Labor, and the procedures used by the DOL are those that are applicable to the airline whistleblower law, 49 U.S.C. § 42121(b). Claims must be filed with the OSHA division of the DOL within 180 days of an adverse action.

Banking and Financial Institutions

Three laws explicitly cover employees in the banking sector: 12 U.S.C. § 1790b (credit unions), 12 U.S.C. 1831j (FDIC), and 31 U.S.C. § 5323 (money laundering). The Financial Institutions Reform, Recovery and Enforcement Act (FIRREA), another old and outdated law, also covers employees in the banking section. All of these older laws lack key protections now available under modern corporate whistleblower laws. Better alternatives, if you can obtain coverage under these laws, are the Dodd-Frank Act (DFA), the IRS whistleblower law, the AML whistleblower law, and the Sarbanes-Oxley Act. The AML, DFA, and IRS laws also have reward provisions.

Commodity Exchange Act

See Rules 6, 19–20.

Consumer Financial Protection Act

The whistleblower protection provision for employees who make protected disclosures to the Bureau of Consumer Financial Protection or concerning matters within the jurisdiction of the bureau, are set forth in Section 1057 of the Dodd-Frank Act, codified at 12 U.S.C. § 5567.

Consumer Product Safety

The statute is located at 15 U.S.C. § 2051. The Department of Labor rules implementing this law are published at 29 C.F.R. Part 1983.

Contractor Protection Enhancement Act

This law is codified at 47 U.S.C. § 4712. Also see False Claims Act, which covers much of the same areas.

Criminal Obstruction of Justice/RICO

The criminal obstruction of justice law specifically applicable to whistleblowers was enacted as part of the Sarbanes-Oxley Act and is codified at 18 U.S.C. § 1513(e).

The Justice Department has responsibility for filing criminal obstruction cases on behalf of whistleblowers. See *U.S. v. Edwards*, 291 F.Supp.3d 828 (S.D. Ohio 2017) is one of the first cases prosecuted under this law. The case was affirmed at *U.S. v. Edwards*, 2019 West Law 3853573, Case No. 18-3541 (6th Cir. 2019).

The obstruction of justice act has also been used by whistleblowers to justify civil RICO claims. 18 U.S.C. § 1961–62 and 64. See *DeGuelle v. Camilli*, 664 F.3d 192 (7th Cir. 2011) where the court permitted a whistleblower to file a civil RICO case based on violations of § 1513(e).

Discrimination Laws

All the major antidiscrimination laws (i.e., laws that prohibit discrimination based on race, sex, religion, age, disability, national origin, labor union activities, minimum wage violations, etc.) contain anti-retaliation provisions that protect employees who blow the whistle on discriminatory practices, testify in discrimination cases, or file complaints protected under law. Citations to the anti-retaliation provisions of these laws are set forth in Checklist 2. Because of the large number of cases filed under these laws, courts often rely on case precedent decided under laws such as Title VII of the Civil Rights Act or the National Labor Relations Act for authority in whistleblower cases.

Dodd-Frank Wall Street Reform and Consumer Protection Act

See Rules 6, 19–20.

Public Law No. 111-203 (2010) is the entire Dodd-Frank Act, including all whistleblower protection and enhanced antifraud provisions. The legislative history of Dodd-Frank is set forth in S. Rep. 111-176, 111th Cong., 2nd Sess. (2010). The securities whistleblower provisions are codified at 15 U.S.C. § 78u-6. The commodities whistleblower provisions are codified at 7 U.S.C. § 26. The SEC's rules on filing securities *qui tam* claims are codified at 17 C.F.R. Parts 240 and 249.

The SEC has sanctioned companies for retaliating against whistleblowers or requiring employees to sign nondisclosure agreements that interfere with an employee's right to communicate with government investigators. See *In the Matter of BlackRock, Inc.*, SEC Administrative Filing 3-17786 (Jan. 17, 2017) ($340,000 sanction for restrictive language in severance agreements); *In the Matter of SandRidge Energy*, Administrative Proceeding No. 3-17739 (Dec. 20, 2016) ($1.4 million penalty for retaliating against whistleblower); *In the Matter of KBR*, Administrative File No. 3-16466 (Apr. 1, 2015) ($130,000 sanction for requiring employees to sign restrictive nondisclosure agreements as part of the company's compliance program). SEC actions taken against corporations that have engaged in retaliation are described on the website of the SEC Office of the Whistleblower.

Employment Contracts/Union Grievance Procedures

Wright v. Universal Maritime Service, 525 U.S. 70 (1998), and *Lingle v. Norge Division of Magic Chef*, 486 U.S. 399 (arbitration of claims covered under a union contract).

The National Labor Relations Board and the Department of Labor's OSHA division entered into a Memorandum of Understanding concerning retaliation cases for employees who raise workplace safety concerns on January 12, 2017.

Environmental Laws

Clean Air Act, 42 U.S.C. § 7622.

Comprehensive Environmental Response (Superfund), 42 U.S.C. § 9610.

Pipeline Safety Improvement Act, 49 U.S.C. § 60129.

Safe Drinking Water Act, 42 U.S.C. 300j-9(i).

Solid Waste Disposal Act, 42 U.S.C. § 6971.

Surface Mining Act, 30 U.S.C. § 1293.

Toxic Substances Control Act, 15 U.S.C. § 2622.

Water Pollution Control Act, 33 U.S.C. § 1367.

The environmental whistleblower laws are all administered by the Department of Labor. Except for the Pipeline Safety Improvement Act, all of these laws have a thirty-day statute of limitations. The pipeline law has a 180-day statute of limitations.

The Department of Labor rules implementing these laws are codified at 29 C.F.R. Part 24 (environmental); 29 C.F.R. Part 1981 (pipeline). The rules governing Department of Labor adjudications are codified at 29 C.F.R. Part 18. The Interior Department has jurisdiction over the Surface Mining Act, 30 C.F.R. § 86515.

Collins v. Village of Lynchburg, 2006-SDW-3 (Dept. of Labor Administrative Review Board, Mar. 30, 2009) (elements of proof Safe Drinking Water case); *Hamilton v. PBS*

Environmental, 2009-CER-3 (Dept. of Labor Administrative Review Board, Oct. 19, 2010) (elements of proof Superfund case).

False Claims Act

See Rules 4 and 16–17. The False Claims Act is codified at 31 U.S.C. § 3729-32, and the Major Frauds Act is codified at 18 U.S.C. § 1031. The FCA's anti-retaliation provision is codified at 31 U.S.C. § 3730(h).

First Amendment Protections for Public Employees

In the landmark case of *Pickering v. Board of Education*, 391 U.S. 563 (1968), the U.S. Supreme Court held that state and local public employee whistleblower disclosures made on matters of public concern are protected under the First Amendment. Causes of action under the First Amendment are filed under the Civil Rights Act of 1871, 42 U.S.C. § 1983. Attorney fees are available under 42 U.S.C. § 1988.

Most states have also enacted specific laws protecting state and local government employees, and some states include government workers under their Whistleblower Protection Act statutes. State legal protections for government workers should always be considered as an alternative or supplement to a government whistleblower claim, especially after the U.S. Supreme Court's decision in *Garcetti v. Ceballos*, 547 U.S. 410 (2006) (a 5–4 ruling that limited the scope of protected activity in First Amendment employment cases).

First Amendment—Disclosures to the News Media

First Amendment: *Pickering v. Board of Education* 391 U.S. 563 (1968) (landmark case protecting the right of government employees to blow the whistle to the press).

A federal employee's right to blow the whistle to the news media was recognized in *Dept. of Homeland Sec. v. MacLean*, 574 U.S. 383 (2015).

Department of Labor decisions protecting disclosures to the media: *Diaz-Robainas v. Florida Power & Light Co.*, 92-ERA-10, Order of Secretary of Labor, 1996 DOL Sec. Labor LEXIS 6 (Jan. 10, 1996); *Donovan v. R.D. Andersen Constr. Co.*, 552 F. Supp. 249 (D. Kan. 1982).

Title VII decision protecting disclosures to the news media: *Wrighten v. Metro. Hosps., Inc.*, 726 F.2d 1346 (9th Cir. 1984).

Financial Institutions Reform, Recovery and Enforcement Act (FIRREA)

The FIRREA whistleblower provision is codified at 12 U.S.C. §§ 4201-23. Due to weaknesses in this law, whistleblowers should consider filing claims under other whistleblower laws, including the Dodd-Frank Act, the IRS reward law, and the anti-money laundering whistleblower law.

Major federal lawsuits under FIRREA: *United States of America vs. The Bank of New York Mellon Corporation*, 941 F. Supp. 2d 438, 451 (S.D.N.Y. 2013); *United States ex rel. O'Donnell v. Bank of America*, No. 12-01422 (S.D.N.Y. filed Oct. 24, 2012); *United States v. Wells Fargo*, No. 12-7527 (S.D.N.Y. filed Oct. 9, 2012).

Nan S. Ellis et al., "Use of FIRREA to Impose Liability in the Wake of the Global Financial Crisis: A New Weapon in the Arsenal to Prevent Financial Fraud," 18 *University of Pennsylvania Journal of Business Law* 119 (2016).

Food Safety

Congress passed the Food Safety Modernization Act during the last days of the lame duck session in December 2010. After more than twenty years of missed opportunities, employees who blew the whistle on food safety violations on FDA-regulated foods finally obtained protection. See Renee Johnson, *Food Safety in the 111th Congress: H.R. 2749 and S.510*, Congressional Research Service (Oct. 7, 2010). The official bill, H.R. 2751, passed on December 21, 2010, and is codified at 21 U.S.C. § 399d.

The FDA Food Safety Modernization Act contains a strong whistleblower anti-retaliation provision modeled on the Sarbanes-Oxley and Airline Safety whistleblower laws. See H.R. 2751. The whistleblower provision is codified at 21 U.S.C. § 399d.

Legislative history: Committee on Energy and Commerce, "Food Safety Enhancement Act of 2009," House Report No. 111-234 (July 29, 2009).

Regulations implementing the food safety whistleblower law are published by the Department of Labor at 29 C.F.R. Part 1987.

The FDA and Department of Labor entered into a Memorandum of Understanding to implement the law on June 20, 2011.

The food safety whistleblower law was passed after a peanut butter contamination scandal. See Hearings before the U.S. House of Representatives, Committee on Energy and Commerce, Subcommittee on Oversight and Investigations, "The Salmonella Outbreak: The Continued Failure to Protect the Food Supply" (Feb. 11, 2009). The hearing record includes extensive testimony and documentation regarding the Peanut Corporation of America's handling of the contaminated peanut butter scandal.

News articles on the peanut butter contamination scandal: *ABC News*, "Former Manager Says Peanut Plant Complaints Ignored" (Feb. 17, 2009), abcnews.go.com; Michael Moss, "Peanut Case Shows Holes in Safety Net," *New York Times* (Feb. 9, 2009); Darren Perron, WCAX-TV, "Vt. Family Sues Over Salmonella" (Feb. 9, 2009); Corky Siemaszko, "Peanut Corporation Whistleblower: Rats, Cockroaches Roasted with Peanut Butter," *New York Daily News* (Feb. 9, 2009); Around the Nation, "Peanut Recall Prompts FEMA to Replace Meals," *Washington Post* (Feb. 7, 2009); Associated Press, "FDA: Georgia Plant Knowingly Sold Peanut Butter Tainted with Salmonella" (Feb. 6, 2009); Times Wire Services, "Schools, Disaster Victims May Have Gotten Tainted Peanut Butter," *Los Angeles Times* (Feb. 5, 2009); AFP, "U.S. Launches Criminal Probe in Peanut Better Health Scandal" (Jan. 30, 2009).

Foreign Corrupt Practices Act

See Rules 2, 4, 6, and 20. The FCPA whistleblower provision is part of the Dodd-Frank Act administered by the Securities and Exchange Commission. Additionally, the Commodity Futures Trading Commission will investigate and sanction companies that pay bribes impacting the international commodities markets. The Justice Department also has jurisdiction over FCPA violations, but it is important to file with the SEC and CFTC before filing with the DOJ to maximize the ability to obtain sanctions.

Fraud against Shareholders
See Rule 2, 4, and 19 (Dodd-Frank Act).

Two major laws cover fraud against shareholders: the Dodd-Frank and Sarbanes-Oxley Acts. The DFA has both a financial reward provision and anti-retaliation provisions covering the Securities Exchange Act and the Commodity Exchange Act. The Sarbanes-Oxley Act is codified at 18 U.S.C. § 1514A (anti-retaliation); 15 U.S.C. § 78j-1-4 (confidential employee concerns program); 15 U.S.C. § 7245 (attorney whistleblower rules); 29 C.F.R. Part 1980 (DOL regulations implementing SOX whistleblower law). Two critically important Department of Labor decisions interpreting the scope of protected activity, employer coverage, and the requirements needed for filing a complaint are *Sylvester v. Parexel International*, 2007-SOX-39/42 (DOL ARB 2011), and *Johnson v. Siemens*, 2005-SOX-15 (DOL ARB 2011). Both cases provide broad protections for employees. Also see *Funke v. Federal Express Corp.*, 2007-SOX-43 (DOL ARB, July 8, 2011) (broad definition of protected activity covering third party fraud) (disclosures to local law enforcement protected).

The U.S. Supreme Court broadly interpreted the scope of employers covered under SOX. See *Lawson v. FMR LLC*, 134 S.Ct. 1158 (2014) (independent contractors working for mutual funds are protected under SOX).

Kohn et al., "Whistleblower Law: A Guide to Legal Protections for Corporate Employees" (Westport, CT: Praeger, 2004) (comprehensive guide to the Sarbanes-Oxley Act's whistleblower protections prior to Dodd-Frank amendments).

S. Rep. No. 107-146, 107th Cong., 2nd Sess. (2002) (legislative history of SOX whistleblower law prior to the Dodd-Frank amendments).

Healthcare Entitlement
Affordable Care Act, Public Law 111-148, §1558, codified at 29 U.S.C. § 218C (reporting violations of the Public Health Service Act). When blowing the whistle on abusive patient care, whistleblowers should also review applicable state laws for potential coverage.

The Affordable Care Act's whistleblower provision primarily covers employers who may seek to retaliate against employees for asserting their rights under the act or for reporting infractions of the law's accountability provisions. The law follows the standard Department of Labor procedures.

IRS Whistleblower Rewards and Anti-Retaliation
The IRS whistleblower reward and anti-retaliation statute is located at 26 U.S.C. § 7623. The *Internal Revenue Manual*, available on the IRS's website, contains the relevant regulations covering IRS enforcement investigations and the rules governing the whistleblower program.

The anti-retaliation law, known as the Taxpayer First Act, is administered by the OSHA division of the Department of Labor, and claims must be filed with OSHA within

180 days of an adverse action. The rules implementing that law are located on the Department of Labor/OSHA website.

Military/Armed Services

Protected Communications, 10 U.S.C. § 1034(a) ("No person may restrict a member of the armed forces in communicating with a member of Congress or an Inspector General"). In addition to permitting members of the armed forces to communicate with Congress and an inspector general, the statute also permits members of the armed services to blow the whistle to their supervisors, DOD, auditors, or law enforcement officers and other persons designated by rule or regulation. The inspector general regulation implementing this law is set forth in DOD Directive 7050.06 (July 23, 2007).

A comprehensive paper on the armed services whistleblower law was published online at http://thomasjfiscus.net/files/Whistleblower_Paper_JM.pdf. The paper is titled "Whistleblowers and the Law; An Analysis of 10 U.S.C. § 1034: The Military Whistleblower Protection Act," and is dated April 30, 2005. No author is listed.

Additional laws and regulations provide protection for members of the Coast Guard (33 C.F.R. Part 53), employees of DOD "non-appropriated fund instrumentalities" (10 U.S.C. § 1587), and former members of the armed services who file complaints concerning the failure of an employer to comply with reemployment rights (38 U.S.C. §§ 4311, 4322–24).

Mine Health and Safety

Mine Health and Safety Act (anti-retaliation), 30 U.S.C. § 815(c).

James A. Broderick and Daniel Minaham, "Employment Discrimination under the Federal Mine Safety and Health Act," 84 *West Virginia Law Review* 1023 (1982).

Money Laundering

AML Whistleblower Protection Act, 31 U.S.C. § 5323, has a discretionary reward law and an anti-retaliation provision that covers only a small segment of the banking community. It follows the standard Department of Labor procedures.

The IRS whistleblower law also covers money laundering crimes that are investigated by the IRS criminal division. Whistleblowers may also be covered under the banking whistleblower provisions, corporate whistleblower laws (such as the Sarbanes-Oxley Act), and the Dodd-Frank Act. The complex nature of laws that cover money laundering are further explained at www.kkc.com/Rules.

Nuclear Safety

The nuclear safety whistleblower law is codified as Section 211 of the Energy Reorganization Act, 42 U.S.C. § 5851. It follows the standard DOL administrative procedures covered under 29 C.F.R. Part 24 and 29 C.F.R. Part 18.

Silkwood v. Kerr-McGee Corp., 667 F.2d 908 (10th Cir. 1981), *reversed at* 464 U.S. 238 (1984).

The Nuclear Regulatory Commission considers the harassment and intimidation of whistleblowers as a serious safety matter and has implemented regulations that sanction companies that engage in retaliation. 10 C.F.R. § 50.7. See *In re Five Star Products*, 38 NRC 169 (1993); "Freedom of Employees in the Nuclear Industry to Raise Concerns without Fear of Retaliation"; Policy Statement, 61 *Federal Register* 24336 (1996); "Memorandum of Understanding between NRC and Department of Labor, Employee Protection," 47 *Federal Register* 54585 (1982).

Vinnett v. Mitsubishi, 2006-ERA-29 (Dept. of Labor ARB, July 27, 2010), and *Speegle v. Stone & Webster*, 2005-ERA-6 (Dept. of Labor ARB, Sept. 24, 2009) (cases setting forth elements of nuclear safety claims and proof of discrimination).

OSHA/Workplace Safety

OSHA section 11(c) is codified at 29 U.S.C. § 660(c). The Labor Department regulations are located at 29 C.F.R. Part 1977.

Government Accountability Office, *Whistleblower Protection Program: Better Data and Improved Oversight Would Help Ensure Program Quality and Consistency*, GAO 09-106 (Jan. 2009).

Reich v. Cambridgeport Air Systems, 26 F.3d 1187 (1st Cir. 1994) (permitting compensatory and punitive damages to be awarded under OSHA).

The problems with OSHA are well documented. See U.S. House of Representatives, Hearing Before the Subcommittee on Workforce Protections (Apr. 28, 2010) (Testimony of Lynn Rhinehart, general counsel, AFL-CIO); *Wood v. Department of Labor*, 275 F.3d 107 (D.C. Cir. 2001). During the April 28, 2010, hearing before the House Subcommittee, Neal Jorgensen testified about a similar incident in Preston, Idaho, in which he was fired by Plastics Industries. Again, the OSHA investigators determined that he was illegally fired, but the OSHA attorneys decided that they would not file a lawsuit in court. See Statement of Neal Jorgensen.

Court decisions protecting OSHA whistleblowers under state law: *Kinzel v. Discovery Drilling*, 93 P.3d 427 (Alaska 2004); *Boston v. Penny Lane Centers*, 170 Cal. App. 4th 936 (2009); *Fragassi v. Neiburger*, 646 N.E.2d 315 (Ill. App. 1995); *George v. D.W. Zinser Co.*, 762 N.W.2d 865 (Iowa 2009); *Hysten v. Burlington Northern*, 108 P.3d 437 (Kan. 2004); *Abraham v. County of Hennepin*, 639 N.W. 342 (Minn. 2002); *Cerracchio v. Alden Leeds, Inc.*, 538 A.2d 1292 (N.J. Superior 1988); *Gutierrez v. Sundance*, 868 P.2d 1266 (N.Mex. App. 1993); *D'Angelo v. Gardner*, 819 P2d 206 (Nev. 1991); *Jenkins v. Central Transport*, 2010 U.S. Dist. LEXIS 7739 (N.D. Ohio); *Vasek v. Board of County*, 186 P.3d 928 (Okla. 2008); *Walters v. Boll'n Oilfield*, 2008 U.S. Dist. LEXIS 12931 (D. Oreg. 2008). *Contra.*, *Burham v. Karl and Geld*, 745 A.2d 178 (Conn. 2000). See also Maine Whistleblower Protection Act, 26 M.R.S. §§ 831–833.

Pipeline Safety Act

Pipeline Safety Improvement Act, 49 U.S.C. § 60129, implemented by the U.S. Department of Labor under 29 C.F.R. Part 1981. The rules governing administrative hearings are codified at 29 C.F.R. Part 18.

Public Health/COVID-19

There is no single federal law that covers public health and safety violations.

Employees forced to work in unsafe conditions are protected under OSHA. If state or federal funds are involved, a whistleblower may be covered under the False Claims Act. Most federal employees are covered under the Whistleblower Protection Act, and employees of the Public Health Service Commissioned Corp are covered under 10 U.S.C. 1034. See Commissioned Corps Directive CCD 121.06 (Jan. 11, 2017).

Most states cover public health and safety disclosures under state common law (public policy exception) or by statute.

See Kohn, "Whistleblowing and the Coronavirus Crisis," *National Law Review* (Mar. 16, 2020), and "Can OSHA Protect Coronavirus Whistleblowers?" *National Law Review* (Apr. 21, 2020).

Sarbanes-Oxley Act (SOX)

See Fraud Against Shareholders section and Rule 19.

The Sarbanes-Oxley Act is codified at 18 U.S.C. § 1514A, and complaints must be filed with the Department of Labor within 180 days of an adverse action. The law is administered by the DOL in accordance with regulations published at 29 C.F.R. Part 1980. See sources listed under the Fraud Against Shareholders section and cases referenced in Checklist 2.

Seaman Whistleblower Protection

Protection of Seaman against Discrimination, 42 U.S.C. § 2114. The law follows the standard Department of Labor procedures. The DOL regulations covering this law are located at 29 C.F.R. § 1986.

Securities Exchange Act

See Rules 2, 4, 19–20.

Trade Secrets

Defend Trade Secrets Act, 18 U.S.C. § 1833(b), provides a safe avenue for whistleblowers to disclose information to law enforcement authorities even if the company considers the information a confidential trade secret.

Senate Committee on the Judiciary, *Defend Trade Secrets Act of 2016*, Report No. 114-220 (Mar. 7, 2016).

Transportation (Trucking, Railroads, and Public Transportation)

National Transit Systems Security Act, 6 U.S.C. § 1142.

Railway Safety Labor Act, 49 U.S.C. § 20109.

Surface Transportation Act, 49 U.S.C. §§ 31101 and 31105.

All three laws follow the standard Department of Labor procedures. The DOL rules implementing the transportation whistleblower laws are 29 C.F.R. Part 1978 (surface transportation) and 29 C.F.R. Part 1982 (national transit and railroad safety). The rules governing the administrative hearings are located at 29 C.F.R. Part 18.

Department of Labor cases setting forth elements of railroad and trucking safety laws, damages, and how to calculate statute of limitations: *Anderson v. Amtrak*, 2009-FRS-3 (Dept. of Labor ALJ, Aug. 26, 2010), and *Canter v. Maverick Transportation*, 2009-STA-54 (Dept. of Labor ALJ, Oct. 28, 2010).

Witnesses in Federal Court Proceedings

Civil Rights Act of 1871, 42 U.S.C. § 1985.

The Supreme Court upheld federal claims under this Reconstruction-era statute in *Haddle v. Garrison*, 525 U.S. 121 (1998). Unlike most employment laws, this law was enacted in 1871 when the current employee-employer relationships did not exist. Instead of prohibiting wrongful discharge, this statute prohibits "conspiracies" to interfere with witnesses at federal court proceedings. Victims of such conspiracies can obtain full tort remedies, including damages for economic harm, compensatory damages, and punitive damages. An issue critical to the future effectiveness of this law is known as the "intracorporate conspiracy doctrine." Under this doctrine persons employed within one corporation cannot conspire with each other. If the courts accept this rule, retaliation cases based on the *Haddle* precedent would be nearly impossible to establish in the modern work environment.

However, a number of courts have rejected this doctrine and permitted *Haddle*-based claims to go forward. See *McAndrew v. Lockheed Martin*, 206 F.3d 1031 (11th Cir. 2000) (*en banc*).

Rule 27: Don't Forget State Laws

State public policy common law and statutory remedies for whistleblowers, along with citations to major cases and a state-by-state analysis of the public policy exemption case law, are posted online at www.kkc.com/law-library.

Lawrence Blades, "Employment at Will v. Individual Freedom: On Limiting the Abusive Exercise of Employer Power," 67 *Columbia Law Review* 1404 (Dec. 1967). In the early days of the development of the "public policy exception," this groundbreaking law journal article was relied on in numerous court decisions as providing a legal justification for changing the "at-will" doctrine.

First case upholding state cause of action for a whistleblower: *Petermann v. International Brotherhood of Teamsters*, 344 P.2d 25 (Cal. App. 1959).

For detailed state-by-state analysis, see Stephen Kohn, "Concepts and Procedures in Whistleblower Law," Quorum Press 2000 (Chapter 2) (setting forth state-by-state analysis), and Robert G. Vaughn, "State Whistleblower Statutes and the Future of Whistleblower Protection," 51 *Administrative Law Review* 581 (1999).

Wendeln v. Beatrice Manor, 712 N.W.2d 226 (Neb. 2006) (discussing difference in damages available to whistleblower under tort versus contract theories of recovery under state law).

Federal preemption cases: *English v. General Electric*, 496 U.S. 72 (1990) (state common law not preempted despite existence of federal safety-related whistleblower law); *Gervasio v. Continental Airlines*, 2008 U.S. Dist. LEXIS 58767 (N.J. 2008) (no federal preemption under Airline Deregulation Act); *Hawaiian Airlines v. Norris*, 512 U.S. 246 (1994) (no preemption under federal Railroad Safety Act); *Lingle v. Norge Division*, 486 U.S. 399 (1988) (state retaliatory discharge law not preempted by collective bargaining agreement). In addition, many whistleblower statutes, including those in the Dodd-Frank Act and the Sarbanes-Oxley Act, contain an explicit "savings clause" that preserves an employee's right to file state lawsuits based on the same underlying facts as those set forth in the federal lawsuit. See, for example, 18 U.S.C. § 1514A(d) (SOX).

Rule 28: Government Retaliation: Use the First Amendment

Pickering v. Board of Education, 391 U.S. 563 (1968) (government employee speech on matters of public concern protected under the First Amendment) (holding applies to all employees who work in the public sector).

Civil Rights Act of 1871, 42 U.S.C. § 1983 (federal civil rights law that permits state and local employees to file *Pickering* claims in whistleblower retaliation cases). When seeking damages under § 1983, it is advisable to always name the government employees and managers responsible for the retaliation in the lawsuit, as there are strict limits on the ability to directly sue a state or municipality under that law. See *Monell v. New York City*, 436 U.S. 658 (1978) (setting forth rule on suing municipalities); *Will v. Michigan*, 491 U.S. 58 (1989) (states and state employees acting in an official capacity immune from lawsuits under § 1983); *Harlow v. Fitzgerald*, 457 U.S. 800 (1982) (setting forth standards necessary to sue individual government managers and supervisors in their "personal capacity" under the "qualified immunity" standard).

Legal standards governing *Pickering* causes of action: *Mt. Healthy v. Doyle*, 429 U.S. 274 (1977) (standard of proof); *Givhan v. Western Line*, 439 U.S. 410 (1979) (complaints raised internally may still be protected, even if no public disclosure); *Connick v. Myers*, 461 U.S. 138 (1983) (First Amendment protections only apply on issues of public concern, private workplace grievances not covered under *Pickering*); *Rankin v. McPherson*, 483 U.S. 378 (1987) (broad definition of protected activity); *Bush v. Lucas*, 462 U.S. 367 (1983) (when seeking damages, federal employees must exhaust administrative remedies); *U.S. v. NTEU*, 513 U.S. 454 (1995), and *Sanjour v. EPA*, 56 F.3d 85 (DC Cir. 1995) (*en banc*) (injunctive relief available to prevent chilling effect on First Amendment); *Swartzwelder v. McNeilly*, 297 F.3d 228 (3rd. Cir. 2002) (Circuit Judge now Supreme Court Justice— Samuel Alito upholding preliminary injunction concerning police department rule that limited employee rights to make protected disclosures).

The scope of First Amendment protection afforded state and local employees was severely limited in the case of *Garcetti v. Ceballos*, 547 U.S. 410 (2006). That case narrowed the definition of protected activity to exclude most internal disclosures made pursuant to official duties.

In *Borough of Duryea v. Guarnieri*, 131 S.Ct. 2488 (2011), the Supreme Court held that petitions to government bodies filed by public employees (including lawsuits filed in court) are protected under the First Amendment if they address matters of public concern.

Rule 29: Federal Employees Are Special

The major law covering federal employee whistleblowers is the Civil Service Reform Act, 5 U.S.C. § 2302, and the Whistleblower Protection Act of 1989, *as amended*, 5 U.S.C. §§ 1211–15, 1218–19, and 1221–22. See Passman and Kaplan, P.C., *Federal Employees Legal Survival Guide* (Cincinnati, OH: National Employee Rights Institute, 1999); Robert Vaughn, *Merit Systems Protection Board: Rights and Remedies* (New York: Law Journal Press, 1984); and Peter Broida, *A Guide to Merit Systems Protection Board Law and Practice* (Dewey Publications, 1998).

The U.S. Merit Systems Protection Board published a case law guide for the Whistleblower Protection Act. The guidebook was published before the law was amended in 2012 and is out of date on various issues. See MSPB, *Whistleblower Protections for Federal Employees* (Sept. 2010); published at www.mspb.gov.

The MSPB also publishes a Q&A on filing whistleblower cases: www.mspb.gov/appeals/whistleblower.htm.

An excellent decision outlining the proof employees need to prevail in a WPA action is *Chambers v. Department of Interior*, 2011, MSPB 7 (Jan. 11, 2011) (ordering the chief of U.S. Park Police reinstated to her position). This decision was issued before the 2012 amendments that significantly strengthened the WPA.

On November 27, 2012, President Obama signed the Whistleblower Protection Enhancement Act (Public Law 112-199) into law. The act improved the legal protections afforded federal workers under the WPA. The legislative history of the Enhancement Act is contained in Senate Report 112-155, published by the U.S. Senate Committee on Homeland Security and Government Affairs, "Whistleblower Protection Enhancement Act of 2012") (Apr. 19, 2012).

The Whistleblower Protection Enhancement Act of 2012 prohibited government agencies from using restrictive nondisclosure forms that would prohibit an employee's ability to file complaints with various government agencies, including the Office of Special Counsel, or to communicate with Congress. See Public Law 112-199 § 115(a). Additionally, Congress uses the Appropriations Act process to prohibit the use of any government funds to pay the salary of any government employee who is responsible for having employees execute nondisclosure forms that restrict an employee's ability to file complaints or blow the whistle to Congress. See Consolidated Appropriations Act of 2016, Public Law 114-113 § 713.

Executive Order 12731, § 101(k) (Oct. 17, 1990), mandates that all federal employees "shall disclose waste, fraud, abuse, and corruption to appropriate authorities." The Office of Government Ethics interpreted this mandate broadly and intended that the executive order encourage the "over reporting" of potential abuses. Office of Government Ethics, "Standards of Ethical Conduct for Employees of the Executive Branch, Final Rule," 57 *Federal Register* 35006 (Aug. 7, 1992).

Federal employees have a right to report violations or disclose information to Congress. In January 2019 the House of Representatives created the Office of the Whistleblower Ombuds. See H. Res. 6, Sec 104(e). House Rules Package, 116 Congress (January 9, 2019). Its website is found at https://whistleblower.house.gov/about/leadership and provides extensive information on whistleblowing in general and communications with Congress in particular. Because the office was created by a House Rule, its existence is subject to continued support for this rule in each Congress.

Mixed Cases: If an employee alleges retaliation based on both discrimination (i.e., a sex or race discrimination claim) and whistleblowing, the two cases can be joined and litigated in U.S. District Court: 5 U.S.C. § 7702; *Ikossi v. Navy*, 516 F.3d 1037 (D.C. Cir. 2008); *Bonds v. Leavitt*, 629 F.3d 369 (4th Cir. 2011).

Major cases and laws establishing the right of government employees to engage in outside speaking, writing, and teaching critical of their employing agency include: *United States v. Treasury Employees*, 513 U. S. 454 (1995) (applying Pickering to federal employees); *Department of Homeland Security v. MacLean*, 135 S.Ct. 913 (2015) (permitted disclosures to the press); and *Sanjour v. Environmental Protection Agency*, 56 F.3d 85 (1995) (*en banc*)(viewpoint-based restrictions on employee speech made on their own time is unconstitutional). The provisions of the Whistleblower Protection Act that permit whistleblowing outside of the federal government include: 5 U.S.C. §2302(a)(2)(D), (b) (8) and (9), and (f).

Federal employees are also protected under some specific federal laws that govern limited areas of the government. For example, a number of the environmental whistleblower laws also cover federal employees. In *Erickson v. U.S. EPA*, 1999-CAA-2 (consolidated case; ARB, May 31, 2006) (available online at http://www.oalj.dol.gov/PUBLIC/ARB/DECISIONS/ARB_DECISIONS/CAA/03_002A.CAAP.PDF.), the Department of Labor, after briefings from the solicitor of labor, held that federal employees were protected under the Clean Air Act, 42 U.S.C. § 7622, and the Solid Waste Disposal Act, 42 U.S.C. § 6971. The solicitor of labor argued that federal employees were also covered under the Comprehensive Environmental Response (Superfund), 42 U.S.C. § 9610, and the Safe Drinking Water Act, 42 U.S.C. § 300j-9(i). The DOL indicated that it would follow that guidance, but did not formally decide the issue.

The case law under the federal environmental whistleblower statutes, which provide protection for federal employees, is located at http://www.oalj.dol.gov/LIBWHIST.HTM.

Employees of the Federal Reserve, the Federal Housing Finance Board, the Comptroller of the Currency, and the Office of Thrift Supervision are covered under the Depository Institution Employee Protection law, 12 U.S.C. § 1831j. Under the Credit Union Act, 12

U.S.C. § 1790b, federal employees of the National Credit Union Administration have whistleblower protections independent of the weaker WPA.

The Privacy Act is codified at 5 U.S.C. § 552a. This law covers all persons, including federal employees.

Federal employees who suffer adverse employment actions based on an unconstitutional law cannot challenge that law directly in federal court. They must first exhaust their administrative remedies before the MSPB before being able to raise a challenge in federal court. Moreover, that challenge may have to be raised as part of the appeal of a final decision of the MSPB, which presumably (as a federal administrative agency) will have to uphold the constitutionality of the challenged statute (*Elgin v. Department of Treasury*, 132 S.Ct. 2126 [2012]). However, pre-enforcement challenges to rules, policies, or practices of federal agencies that violate the First Amendment may be directly challenged in federal court (*Weaver v. USIA*, 87 F.3d 1429 [D.C. Cir. 1996]).

The administrative processes open to federal employees under the Whistleblower Protection Act, and the exclusion of federal employees who perform work for intelligence agencies from protection under the law, have been severely criticized: Senate Committee on Homeland Security and Government Affairs, "The Federal Employee Protection of Disclosures Act: Amendment to the Whistleblower Protection Act," hearing (Nov. 12, 2003); House Committee on Oversight and Government Reform, "Protecting the Public from Waste, Fraud, and Abuse: H.R. 1507, The Whistleblower Enhancement Act," hearing (May 14, 2009).

Rule 30: The Danger Zone: National Security Whistleblowing

National Security and Intelligence Agency Whistleblowers, 50 U.S.C. § 3234. The full public law enacting protections for intelligence agency whistleblowers is located at Public Law 113–126, title VI, § 604, July 7, 2014, 128 Stat. 1421.

Rodney Perry, *Intelligence Whistleblower Protection: In Brief*, Congressional Research Service (Oct. 23, 2014), is an excellent overview of the laws covering intelligence agency whistleblowers.

Office of the Director of National Intelligence web pages explaining the Intelligence Community Whistleblower Protection Act are located at www.dni.gov/files/documents/ICD/ICD%20120.pdf.

U.S. Department of Defense Office of Inspector General, *Guide to Investigating Military Whistleblower Reprisal and Restriction Complaints*, www.dodig.mil/Programs/Whistleblower/ioguide.html.

Presidential Policy Directive 19 (PPD-19) (Oct. 10, 2012), *Protecting Whistleblowers with Access to Classified Information*, provides some protection for intelligence community employees against retaliation for lawfully blowing the whistle. In addition, employees and contractors are protected from reprisals in the security clearance adjudication process. PPD-19 requires that the inspector general review whistleblower reprisal allegations in violation of PPD-19. See www.whitehouse.gov/sites/default/files/image/ppd-19.pdf.

The Intelligence Community Whistleblower Protection Act is an early law that sets forth procedures for intelligence agency employees to report information to Congress. It is limited to reporting "urgent concerns." The act may protect employees from criminal prosecution, but it does not prohibit retaliation and is therefore deficient. See Public Law 105-272.

Dan Meyer and David Berenbaum, "The WASP's Nest: Intelligence Community Whistleblowing and Source Protection," 8 *Journal of National Security Law and Policy* (May 8, 2015).

New York Times Co. v. United States, 403 U.S. 713 (1971) (Pentagon Papers case).

Snepp v. U.S., 444 U.S. 507 (1980); *U.S. v. Marchetti*, 466 F.2d 1309 (4th Cir. 1972) (cases discussing the prepublication review process).

The FBI Whistleblower Protection Act is codified at 5 U.S.C. § 2303. Regulations implementing the law are located at 28 C.F.R. Part 27.

In 2015–16 the FBI whistleblower program was studied by both Congress and the Government Accountability Office (GAO). See U.S. Government Accountability Office, *Whistleblower Protection: Additional Actions Needed to Improve DOJ's Handling of FBI Retaliation Complaints* (GAO-15-112, Jan. 2015); and Senate Judiciary Committee, "FBI Whistleblower Protection Enhancement Act of 2016," Senate Report No. 114-261 (May 25, 2016), located at https://www.congress.gov/114/crpt/srpt261/CRPT-114srpt261.pdf.

Rule 31: Winning a Case

The basic law setting forth an employee's prima facie case necessary to withstand an employer motion to dismiss or for summary judgment is set forth in Kohn, *Concepts and Procedures in Whistleblower Law* (Quorum Books: Westport, CT 2001), pp. 238–79.

Cases setting forth a standard prima facie case in whistleblower or retaliation cases: *Aka v. Washington*, 156 F.3d 1284 (D.C. Cir. 1998); *Housing Works v. City of New York*, 73 F.Supp.2d 402 (S.D.N.Y. 1999); *DeFord v. Secretary of Labor*, 700 F.2d 281 (6th Cir. 1983). The Supreme Court uses a similar evaluation process in discrimination cases: *McDonnell Douglas v. Green*, 411 U.S. 792 (1973).

Curl v. Leroy Reavis and Iredell County, 740 F.2d 1323 (4th Cir. 1984) (example of a court review to determine whether the plaintiff qualified as an employee under the statute prior to proceeding to review other issues).

NLRB v. Scrivener, 405 U.S. 117 (1972); *Pettway v. American Cast Iron Pipe Co.*, 441 F.2d 998 (5th Cir. 1969) (determination of whether employee engaged in protected activity as a threshold legal issue).

Frazier v. MSPB, 672 F.2d 150 (D.C. Cir. 1982) (key case defining proof necessary to demonstrate "knowledge").

Passaic Valley Sewerage Commissioners v. DOL, 992 F.2d 474 (3rd Cir. 1993) (Clean Water Act case on "good faith" whistleblowing referenced in SOX legislative history).

Burlington Northern v. White, 548 U.S. 53 (2006) (landmark case on defining adverse action).

Desert Palace, Inc. v. Costa, 539 U.S. 90 (2003) (key case regarding evidence needed to demonstrate discriminatory motive necessary to survive a motion for summary judgment).

In *Staub v. Proctor Hospital*, 131 S.Ct. 1186 (2011), the Court held that an employer cannot hide behind a layered decision-making process to escape liability for illegally firing an employee by claiming that the final decision maker was unaware of the protected activity or did not have discriminatory animus.

The exhaustion of administrative remedies doctrine was explained in *Brown v. GSA*, 425 U.S. 820 (1976). The doctrine was applied in Sarbanes-Oxley whistleblower cases in *Portes v. Wyeth*, 06-cv-2689 (S.D. N.Y. 2007); *Williams v. Boston Scientific*, 08-cv-01437 (N.D. Calif. 2008); and *Curtis v. Century Surety*, 08-16236 (9th Cir. 2009). Under this doctrine, although an employee can eventually have a jury trial, they must utilize various administrative remedies in order to file a case in court.

Cases discussing the statute of limitations are located at Rule 5, Trap #4.

Although this rule is titled "Getting to the Jury," a large number of whistleblower laws provide employees with an option of having their case heard before a jury or an administrative judge, specifically, numerous whistleblower laws as administered by the U.S. Department of Labor. The decision as to whether or not to have a case heard before a judge or jury, or whether to have it tried within the Department of Labor before an Administrative Law Judge is a tactical decision based on numerous factors, including costs, the reputation of the respective judges, and the evidence that will be presented in any given case. The bottom line is to pick the forum that will hear your case with ease, whether that is a state court, a federal court, or an administrative agency.

Rule 32: Your Disclosures Must Be Protected under Law

James Madison's floor speech introducing the Bill of Rights in Congress is found in *The Annals of Congress*, 1st Cong., 1st Sess. (June 8, 1789), p. 451, and is posted on the Library of Congress website at http://memory.loc.gov/ammem/amlaw/lwac.html.

The following list is a non-exhaustive summary of cases that define the scope of protected activity under various state and federal laws. The whistleblower protection laws themselves also contain explicit statutory provisions defining various protected disclosures. Always double-check the specific law to ensure that your whistleblower disclosures are protected. Not all federal laws protect the same activities. Each state has its own definition of a protected disclosure.

It is important to keep in mind that under the anti-retaliation laws a whistleblower's report need not be proven. However, there must be a reasonably objective factual basis for making the report. See *Passaic Valley Sewerage v. Department of Labor*, 992 F.2d 474, 478-79 (3rd. Cir. 1993); *DeKalb County v. Department of Labor*, 813 F.3d 1015 (11th Cir. 2016).

Also, even if a protected disclosure "engender[s] disruption, controversy and adverse publicity," this is not grounds to deny protection to an otherwise lawful report: *Curl v. Reavis and Iredell County*, 740 F.2d 1323 (4th Cir. 1984).

EXAMPLES UNDER STATE LAW

Under the public policy exception most (if not all) state courts protect the disclosure of a "statutory violation for the public's benefit": *Gantt v. Sentry*, 824 P.2d 680 (Calif. 1992) (cases interpreting state public policy exception); or an employee's exercise of a statutory or constitutional right: *Gantt v. Sentry*, 824 P.2d 680 (Calif. 1992); *Thompson v. St. Regis Paper Co.*, 685 P.2d 1081 (Wash. 1984) (cases interpreting state public policy exception).

Most (if not all) states that recognize the public policy exception also protect disclosures that are required under law (such as giving truthful testimony in court). See *Petermann v. International Brotherhood of Teamsters*, 344 P.2d 25 (Calif. App. 1959) (refusal to commit perjury); *D'Agostino v. Johnson & Johnson*, 628 A.2d 305 (N.J. 1993) (refusal to commit an act in violation of clear mandate of public policy); and *Thompson v. St. Regis Paper Co.*, 685 P.2d 1081 (Wash. 1984) (refusal to violate a law).

Court decisions that provide a good explanation of the various interpretations of the meaning of public policy include: *Tameny v. Atlantic Richfield*, 610 P.2d 1330 (Calif. 1980); *Carl v. Children's Hospital*, 702 A.2d 159 (D.C. App. 1997) (*en banc*) (see analysis contained in various concurring and dissenting opinions); *Kelsay v. Motorola, Inc.*, 384 N.E.2d 353 (Ill. 1978); *Pierce v. Ortho Pharmaceutical Corp.*, 417 A.2d 505 (N.J. 1980); *Payne v. Rozendaal*, 520 A.2d 586 (Vt. 1986) (cases interpreting state tort laws).

Internal complaints: Most state courts protect internal complaints to management. However, caution must be exercised when making internal disclosures, as under federal law these types of disclosures most likely will not be protected unless specifically covered under federal law. See *Digital Realty Trust v. Somers*, 138 S.Ct. 767 (2018) (interpreting federal Dodd-Frank Act), and *Garcetti v. Ceballos*, 547 U.S. 410 (2006) (interpreting First Amendment).

Some state laws require, under some circumstances, that an employee make an initial complaint to their management: *Tartaglia v. UBS PaineWebber*, 961 A.2d 1167 (N.J. 2008). Other states protect internal disclosures, even if not covered under federal law: *Darrow v. Integris Health, Inc.*, 176 P.3d 1204 (Okla. 2008) (complaint about patient safety).

Other types of conduct protected under the public policy exception have included: Report to government agency: *Wendeln v. The Beatrice Manor, Inc.*, 712 N.W.2d 226 (Neb. 2006);

Testimony before city council: *Carl v. Children's Hospital*, 702 A.2d 159 (D.C. App. 1997) (*en banc*); *Williams v. Johnson*, 597 F.Supp.2d 107 (D.D.C. 2009);

Threat to make protected disclosure: *Shallal v. Catholic Social Services*, 566 N.W.2d 571 (Mich. 1997); *Tartaglia v. UBS PaineWebber*, 961 A.2d 1167 (N.J. 2008);

Unsafe employer practices: *Palmateer v. International Harvester*, 421 N.E.2d 876 (Ill. 1981); *Wheeler v. Caterpillar Tractor*, 485 N.E.2d 2d 372 (Ill. 1985) (cases interpreting state public policy exception);

Violation of criminal laws: *Palmateer v. International Harvester*, 421 N.E.2d 876 (Ill. 1981); *Hodges v. Gibson Products*, 811 P.2d 151 (Utah 1991); *Thompson v. St. Regis Paper Co.*, 685 P.2d 1081 (Wash. 1984).

EXAMPLES UNDER FEDERAL LAW

Broad interpretation of scope of protected activity under federal laws: *NLRB v. Scrivener*, 405 U.S. 117 (1972) (National Labor Relations Act); *Clean Harbors v. Herman*, 146 F.3d 12 (1st Cir. 1998) (Surface Transportation Act); *U.S. ex rel. Yesudian v. Howard University*, 153 F.3d 731 (D.C. Cir. 1998) (False Claims Act). See also definition of protected activity in the EEOC Compliance Manual, § 8-II(B)(2).

Congress: *Richards v. Mileski*, 662 F.2d 65 (D.C. Cir. 1981); *Tremblay v. Marsh*, 750 F.2d 3 (1st Cir. 1984); *Robinson v. Southeastern Pennsylvania Transp.*, 982 F.2d 892 (3rd Cir. 1993); *Chambers v. Department of Interior*, 515 F.3d 1362, 136768 (Fed. Cir. 2008) (claim under Whistleblower Protection Act). The Lloyd-LaFollette Act of 1912 provides that "the right of employees" to "petition Congress or a Member of Congress" and to "furnish information" to Congress "may not be interfered with": H. Rep. 388, 62nd Cong., 2nd Sess. (1912). The congressional debates on this early whistleblower law are at 48 *Congressional Record* 671–77, 4513, 4654, 10728–10733, 10792–10804, and 10676 (1912). Congress also enacted anti-gag rules as part of the appropriations process (i.e., prohibiting federal agencies from spending any money on gag orders that restrict employee communications with Congress). See The Consolidated Appropriations Act of 2023, Section 743, Public Law 117-328.

Direct contact with federal law enforcement or regulatory authorities: Most whistleblower statutes explicitly protect these contacts. The federal obstruction of justice statute makes it a criminal offense to harm any person in their livelihood who provides truthful information to federal law enforcement: 18 U.S.C. § 1512(e); *DeFord v. Secretary of Labor*, 700 F.2d 281 (6th Cir. 1983).

Disclosing allegations though an attorney: *Eng v. Cooley*, 552 F.3d 1062, 1073 (9th Cir. 2009).

Failure to raise concerns through the chain of command or by using mandatory procedures: *Fabricius v. Town of Braintree*, 97-CAA-14, Decision and Order of Department of Labor Administrative Review Board (Feb. 9, 1999) (Clean Air Act case); *Pogue v. DOL*, 940 F.2d 1287 (9th Cir. 1991) (environmental laws); *Dutkiewicz v. Clean Harbors Environmental Services*, 95-STA-4, Decision of Department of Labor Administrative Review Board (Aug. 8, 1997), *affirmed* 146 F.3d 12 (1st Cir. 1998) (Surface Transportation Act).

Internal reports "before plaintiff puts together all the pieces of the puzzle": *Young v. CHS Middle East, LLC*, 2015 U.S. App. LEXIS 8732 (4th Cir. 2015).

Internal complaints to supervisors: The most important cases on this issue come from the Supreme Court, which cautions employees that if a statute does not explicitly protect internal disclosures, most likely they will not be protected. In *Digital Realty Trust v. Somers*, 138 S.Ct. 767 (2018), the High Court found that only contacts with the SEC were protected. In *Garcetti v. Ceballos*, 547 U.S. 410 (2006), the High Court held that internal complaints were not protected in employment cases under the First Amendment.

A number of well-reasoned older cases take a more expansive view of internal protected disclosures, including *Munsey v. Morton*, 507 F.2d 1202 (D.C. Cir. 1974); *Phillips v. Board of Mine Operations Appeals*, 500 F.2d 772 (D.C. Cir. 1974) (Mine Health and Safety Act); *Passaic Valley Sewerage Commissioners v. DOL*, 992 F.2d 474 (3rd Cir. 1993) (Clean Water Act); *Haley v. Retsinas*, 138 F.3d 1245 (8th Cir. 1998) (banking whistleblower laws); *Givhan v. Western Line Consolidated*, 439 U.S. 410 (1979) (First Amendment).

News media: *Pickering v. Board of Education*, 391 U.S. 563 (1968), and *Andrew v. Clark*, 561 F.3d 261 (4th Cir. 2009) (First Amendment); *Dept. of Homeland Sec. v. MacLean*, 574 U.S. 383 (contacting news media protected under Whistleblower Protection Act); *Donovan v. R.D. Anderson*, 552 F.Supp. 249 (D. Kan. 1982) (contacting news media protected under OSHA); *Chambers v. Dept. of Interior*, 602 F.3d 1370, 1379 (Fed. Cir. 2010) (media contacts protected under Whistleblower Protection Act); *Haney v. North American Car Corp.*, 81-SWDA-1, Recommended Decision and Order of Labor Department Administrative Law Judge (Aug. 10, 1981), *affirmed*, Secretary of Labor (June 30, 1982) (under environmental whistleblower laws); *Diaz-Robainas v. Florida Power & Light Co.*, 92-ERA-10, Order of Secretary of Labor (Jan. 10, 1996) (Atomic Energy Act); *Wrighten v. Metropolitan Hosp., Inc.*, 726 F.2d 1346, 1355 (9th Cir. 1984) (holding a press conference is protected under Title VII); *Huffman v. Office of Personnel Management*, 263 F.3d 1341, 1351 (Fed. Cir. 2001) (citing *Horton*, 66 F.3d at 282, holding that media disclosures are an indirect way of disclosing information of wrongdoing to a person in a position to provide a remedy) (Whistleblower Protection Act case).

In a 2011 decision, a three-judge panel of the U.S. Court of Appeals for the Ninth Circuit, *Tides v. Boeing*, 644F.3d 809 (9th Cir. 2011, broke with precedent and found that employee contacts with the press were not protected under 18 U.S.C. section 1514A(a)(1) of the Sarbanes-Oxley Act. However, the court left open the issue as to whether contacts with the press were protected under another clause of the act, section 1514A(a)(2). Even if a contact with the news media is protected under federal law, whistleblowers who use a state law as the basis for a complaint risk losing their case: *Pacheco v. Waldrop*, 84 F.3d 606 (W.D. Ky. 2015) (media disclosure not protected under state whistleblower statute).

The significant impact of whistleblower disclosures to the news media is well documented in U.S. history. See Carl Bernstein and Bob Woodward, *All the President's Men* (New York: Simon & Schuster, 1974).

Opposing conduct made illegal under federal law: *Learned v. City of Bellevue*, 860 F.2d 928 (9th Cir. 1988) (Title VII).

Oral complaints: *Kasten v. Saint-Gobain,* 131 S.Ct. 1325 (2011) (oral complaints covered).

Participating in legal or administrative proceedings: *Pettway v. American Cast Iron,* 411 F.2d 998 (5th Cir. 1969) (Title VII); *Merritt v. Dillard Paper Co.,* 120 F.3d 1181 (11th Cir. 1999) (Title VII).

Public interest organization: *Nunn v. Duke Power Co.,* 84-ERA-27, Decision and Order of Deputy Undersecretary of Labor (July 30, 1987) (Atomic Energy Act).

Quality control inspectors or compliance officials reporting violations: *Mackowiak v. University Nuclear Systems,* 735 F.2d 1159 (9th Cir. 1984); *Kansas Gas & Electric v. Brock,* 780 F.2d 1505 (10th Cir. 1985) (Atomic Energy Act); *White v. Osage Tribal,* 1995-SDW-1 (DOL ARB, 1997); *Warren v. Custom Organics,* 2009-STA-30 (DOL ARB, 2012).

Refusing to accept a hush money settlement agreement: *CL&P v. Secretary of Labor,* 85 F.3d 89 (2nd Cir. 1996).

Refusing to perform dangerous work: *Whirlpool Corp. v. Marshall,* 445 U.S. 1 (1980) (OSHA); *NLRB v. Washington Aluminum Co.,* 370 U.S. 9 (1962) (NLRA); *Gateway Coal Co. v. United Mine Workers,* 414 U.S. 368 (1974).

Statements made to employer during internal investigation: *Crawford v. Metropolitan Government of Nashville,* 129 S.Ct. 846 (2009).

Taping: Under Department of Labor precedent, one-party taping for the purpose of gathering evidence of retaliation or violations of law (if permitted under state law). See *Benjamin v. Citationshares Management,* 2010-AIR-1 (DOL Administrative Review Board, Nov. 5, 2013), and *Mosbaugh v. Georgia Power Co.,* 91-ERA-1/11 (Secretary of Labor, Nov. 20, 1995).

Testimony in court or deposition: *Merritt v. Dillard Paper Co.,* 120 F.3d 1181 (11th Cir. 1997) (protected under Title VII's anti-retaliation provision); *Karl v. City of Mountlake,* 678 F.3d 1062 (9th Cir. 2012); *Alpha Energy Savers Inc. v. Hansen,* 381 F.3d 917 (9th Cir. 2004); *Haddle v. Garrison,* 525 U.S. 121 (1998) (under 42 U.S.C. § 1985).

Threat to make protected disclosure: *Macktal v. DOL,* 171 F.3d 323 (5th Cir. 1999) (Atomic Energy Act); *Thomas v. City of Blanchard,* 548 F.3d 1317 (10th Cir. 2008) (First Amendment).

Union safety committee: *Cotter v. Consolidated Edison,* 81-ERA-6 (Department of Labor, July 7, 1987), *affirmed, Consolidated Edison v. Donovan,* 673 F.2d 61 (2nd Cir. 1982).

ATTORNEY DISCLOSURES
Attorneys can file retaliation suits under federal law: *Van Asdale v. Int'l Game Tech.,* 577 F.3d 989 (9th Cir. 2009); *Willy v. ARB,* 423 F.3d 483 (5th Cir. 2005); *Kachmar v. SunGard,* 109 F.3d (3rd Cir. 1997).

17 Code of Federal Regulations Part 205 (SEC rules on attorney reporting).

Lawrence West, "Can Attorneys be Award-Seeking SEC Whistleblowers," *Harvard Law School Forum on Corporate Governance and Financial Regulation* (2013); https://corpgov.law.harvard.edu/2013/06/17/can-attorneys-be-award-seeking-sec-whistleblowers/.

INSUBORDINATE CONDUCT/ILLEGAL DISCLOSURES

Protected disclosures can lose their protection and become an independent justification for disciplining an employee if the activities are illegal, insubordinate, or unjustifiable: *Dunham v. Brock*, 794 F.2d 1037 (5th Cir. 1986) ("abusive or profane language coupled with defiant conduct" stripped employee of protection, even though disclosure was safety related); *Pettway v. American Cast Iron*, 411 F.2d 998 (5th Cir. 1969) (libelous complaint filed with EEOC may be protected); *Linn v. United Plant Guard*, 383 U.S. 53 (1966) (applying *New York Times v. Sullivan* standard in evaluating protected speech under NLRA); *O'Day v. McDonnell Douglas*, 79 F.3d 756 (9th Cir. 1996) (engaging in protected activity "is not" a "license to flaunt company rules").

However, courts have recognized that employees filing a protected complaint "may well engender disruption, controversy, and adverse publicity" but "nevertheless" are fully protected because "Congress has elected to protect employees who file such charges from retaliation . . . allegations of disruption and injury to close working relationships become irrelevant": *Curl v. Leroy Reavis and Iredell County*, 740 F.2d 1323 (4th Cir. 1984).

Rule 33: Make Discovery Your Best Friend

Checklist 5 identifies the major cases and precedents applicable to discovery in employment retaliation and whistleblower cases. The discovery rules for DOL cases are found in 29 C.F.R. Part 18; the rules for federal employee cases before the MSPB are found at 5 C.F.R. Part 1201. Rules for discovery in federal court are located in the Federal Rules of Civil Procedure, starting with Rule 26, which is the overview rule. Destroying documents that may be relevant to your case may result in sanctions or the dismissal of a whistleblower's case: *Burris v. JPMorgan Chase & Co.*, No. 18-cv-03012 (D. Az. Oct. 7, 2021) (Order).

Model discovery forms for employment cases are linked at www.kkc.com/law-library/model-discovery.

Rule 34: Prove Motive and Pretext

Checklist 4 identifies numerous court precedents regarding the types of proof necessary for an employee to demonstrate improper motive or pretext in a retaliation case.

Links to authorities demonstrating the evidence needed to prove discriminatory motive, pretext, or a contributing factor, along with updates concerning relevant changes in the laws, are available at the free online law library created by the author, located at www.kkc.com/law-library.

Rule 35: Truth Is Power

The case record for the Jane Turner case is found at *Turner v. Gonzales*, 421 F.3d 688 (8th Cir. 2005) and the case file in the U.S. District Court for the District of Minnesota (Minneapolis Division). Dan Browning, "Ex-Agent Wins Lawsuit Against FBI," *Minneapolis Star Tribune* (Feb. 5, 2007); Tad Vezner, "Former FBI Agent Wins Suit," *Pioneer Press* (Feb. 6, 2007).

Rule 36: The Boss Must Make You Whole

DAMAGES FOR EMPLOYEES

All state and federal laws contain their own rules governing the types of damages permitted under whistleblower protection laws. The following list spotlights some of the major categories of damages permitted under various laws:

General damages available under whistleblower laws: *Reich v. Cambridgeport Air Systems*, 26 F.3d 1187 (1st Cir. 1994); *Nord v. U.S. Steel*, 758 F.2d 1462 (11th Cir. 1985). *Hobby v. Georgia Power Co.*, 90-ERA-30 (ALJ, Sept. 17, 1998), affirmed DOL Administrative Review Board (Feb. 9, 2001) and U.S. Court of Appeals for the 11th Circuit (Sept. 30, 2002), carefully reviewed the full range of damages available to employees under Department of Labor–administered whistleblower laws. In *Wooten v. BNSF Railway Co.*, No. 16-cv-00139 (D. Mont. Apr. 23, 2019), the court extensively reviewed damage award standards and upheld awards of $1.4 million in front pay, $500,000 for emotional distress, $650,000 in attorney fees, and $233,000 in expert witness fees.

"Affirmative relief," equitable or preliminary relief: *NLRB v. Gissel Packing*, 395 U.S. 575 (1969); *Florida Steel Corp. v. NLRB*, 620 F.2d 79 (5th Cir. 1980); *Donovan v. Freeway Constr. Co.*, 551 F.Supp. 869 (D.R.I. 1982); *U.S. v. Montgomery*, 744 F.Supp. 1074 (M.D. Ala. 1989).

Back pay: *NLRB v. J.H. Rutter-Rex*, 396 U.S. 258 (1969).

Compensatory damages: *Walters v. City of Atlanta*, 803 F.2d 1135 (11th Cir. 1986); *Neal v. Honeywell*, 995 F.Supp. 889 (N.D. Ill. 1998); *Smith v. Atlas Off-Shore Boat Service*, 653 F.2d 1057 (5th Cir. 1981); *Heaton v. Weitz Co.*, 534 F.3d 882 (8th Cir. 2008).

Front pay: *McNight v. General Motors*, 908 F.2d 104 (7th Cir. 1990); *U.S. v. Burke*, 504 U.S. 229, footnote 9 (1992).

Interest: *Parexel International v. Feliciano*, 2008 U.S. Dist. LEXIS 99348 (E.D. Pa. 2008); *Donovan v. Freeway Constr.*, 551 F.Supp. 869 (D.R.I. 1982); *Clinchfield Coal v. Federal Mine Safety and Health Comm.*, 895 F.2d 773 (D.C. Cir. 1990).

Lost overtime pay: *Blackburn v. Martin*, 982 F.2d 125 (4th Cir. 1992).

"Make whole" remedy: Most laws mandate that an employee who prevails in a retaliation case be made fully whole. Under this remedy, "compensation shall be equal to the injury" and the "injured party is to be placed, as near as may be, in the situation he would have occupied if the wrong had not been committed." *Albemarle Paper Co. v. Moody*, 422 U.S. 405, 418–19 (1975), quoting from *Wicker v. Hoppock*, 6 Wall. 94 (1867).

Promotions: *Edwards v. Hodel*, 738 F.Supp. 426 (D. Col. 1990).

Punitive damages: *Smith v. Wade*, 461 U.S. 30 (1983); *BMW v. Gore*, 517 U.S. 559 (1996) (explaining constitutional standards for calculating); *Parexel International v. Feliciano*, 2008 U.S. Dist. LEXIS 98195 (E.D. Pa. 2008); *Weidler v. Big J. Enterprises*, 953 P2d 1089 (N.M. App. 1997); *Howard v. Zack*, 637 N.E.2d 1183 (Ill. App. 1994); *Anderson v. Amtrak*, 2009-FRS-3 (DOL ALJ, Aug. 26, 2010).

Reinstatement: *Reeves v. Claiborne County*, 828 F.2d 1096 (5th Cir. 1987).

Restoration of pension: *Blum v. Witco Chemical Corp.*, 829 F.2d 367 (3rd Cir. 1987).

Restoration of seniority: *Sands v. Runyon*, 28 F.3d 1323 (2nd Cir. 1994).

Special damages: *Neal v. Honeywell*, 191 F.3d 827 (7th Cir. 1999).

Stock options: *Hobby v. Georgia Power Co.*, Civil Action No. 1:01-cv-1407 (N.D. Georgia, Feb. 15, 2006).

Tort liability for First Amendment claims filed under 42 U.S.C. § 1983: *Carey v. Piphus*, 435 U.S. 247 (1978).

MITIGATION AND REDUCTION OF DAMAGES

Damages can be reduced if an employee fails to mitigate the harm caused by the retaliatory discharge. For example, courts have reduced awards where an employee failed to seek other comparable employment after being fired. Similarly, an unconditional offer of reinstatement can act to cut off back-pay liability. If an employee obtains a new job after being fired, wages from that new job can be deducted from a back-pay award. *Phelps Dodge Corp. v. NLRB*, 313 U.S. 177 (1941); *Tubari Ltd. v. NLRB*, 959 F.2d 451 (3rd Cir. 1992) (explaining the mitigation rule); *Grocer Co. v. Holloway*, 874 F.2d 1008 (5th Cir. 1989); *Donovan v. Commercial Sewing, Inc.*, 562 F.Supp. 548 (D. Conn. 1982) (offers of reinstatement).

TAX ISSUES

Under current law back pay, punitive damages, and compensatory damages are subject to taxation. The Attorney Fee Civil Rights Act exempts employees from being taxed on the attorney fees awarded to their counsel: 26 U.S.C. § 62(a) (20), (21), and (e). These provisions include both employment laws and rewards under the federal False Claims Act. Congress also passed special laws exempting whistleblowers from having to pay federal taxes on attorney fees paid in cases where rewards are obtained under state False Claims Acts, the Dodd-Frank Act, and IRS reward cases.

As part of the settlement process, employees can have their companies establish tax-deferred compensation or annuity plans that help reduce the amount of tax. These plans were approved in the Tax Court case of *Childs v. Commissioner of Internal Revenue*, 103 T.C. 634 (1994).

Rule 37: How to Afford a Lawyer

The major cases interpreting the statutory fee provisions contained in most whistle-blower protection laws are set forth in the practice tips cited at the end of Rule 37. The best single source of information on how to prepare a fee petition to ensure that attorneys are paid at a fair market value and compensated for all reasonable time is set forth in the numerous rulings decided under the Civil Rights Attorney Fee Awards Act, 42 U.S.C. § 1988. Precedents decided under this act are regularly applied to other civil rights, employment, and whistleblower laws that contain statutory fee provisions: *Perdue v. Kenny*, 130 S.Ct. 1662 (2010) ("virtually identical language appears in many fee shifting statutes"). Attorney fees are generally not available under state common law remedies. If filing a claim under a statute, review the specific language and ensure that there is a fee provision.

Attorney fee awards can be substantial and may be even larger than the damages awarded a plaintiff. In *Murray v. UBS Securities, LLC*, No. 14-cv-927 (S.D. N.Y. Dec. 16, 2020), the district court reviewed the law on attorney fees in a SOX whistleblower case. The court made significant reductions in the fees, but still awarded the plaintiff's counsel over $1.6 million.

CONCLUSION: Can Whistleblowers Drive a Spike through the Heart of Corruption?

White-Collar Crime

Sutherland, Edwin H., *Principles of Criminology* (United States Armed Forces Institute, 1939).

——. *White Collar Crime* (New York: Holt, Rinehart & Winston, 1949).

——. 5 *American Sociological Review* 1 (Feb. 1940).

Becker, Gary, "Crime and Punishment: An Economic Approach," *Journal of Political Economy* 76 (1968), 169–217.

——. *Essays in the economics of crime and punishment (Human behavior and social institutions)* (New York: National Bureau of Economic Research, distributed by Columbia University Press, 1974).

Becker, Gary, and Guity Nashat Becker, "The Economics of Life: From Baseball to Affirmative Action to Immigration, How Real-World Issues Affect Our Everyday Life" (McGraw-Hill, 1997).

The Detection Conundrum

U.S. House of Representatives, Committee on the Judiciary, Subcommittee on Crime, "Hearings: White-Collar Crime" (June 21, July 12 and 19, and Dec. 1, 1978).

Congress Wakes Up

U.S. Senate, Committee on the Judiciary, "The False Claims Act of 1985," S. Rep. 99-345, 99th Cong., 2nd Sess. (1986).

Senator Charles Grassley, *Congressional Record* (Aug. 1, 1985) (statement introducing False Claims Act amendments).

Senate Committee on the Judiciary, "The False Claims Act Correction Act," Senate Rep. No. 110-507 (Sept. 25, 2008).

Whistleblowing Works

Whistleblowing and the effectiveness of whistleblower reward laws are well documented.

Academic Studies
Studies that document the importance of whistleblowing in the detection of fraud and misconduct: Harvard Business School professors Aiyesha Dey, Jonas Heese, and Gerardo Pérez Cavazos, 59 *Journal of Accounting Research* (Dec. 2021), pp. 1689–1740; Alexander Dyck et al., "Who Blows the Whistle on Corporate Fraud," *The Initiative on Global Market's Working Paper No. 3*, University of Chicago Booth School of Business (Oct. 2008); Jeffrey Vincent Butler, Danila Serra, and Giancarlo Spagnolo, "Motivating Whistleblowers" (Oct. 23, 2017), *CEIS Working Paper No. 419*, available at SSRN: *https://ssrn.com/abstract=3086671*; Andrew C. Call et al., "Whistleblowers and Outcomes of Financial Misrepresentation Enforcement Actions," papers.ssrn.com (last revised Jan. 24, 2017); Stephen Kohn, "Does Whistleblowing Work," *Pro Market*, a publication of the Stigler Center at the University of Chicago Booth School of Business; Asher Schechter, "Experts: Financial Rewards and Protections are the Best Way to Incentivize Whistleblowers," *Pro Market*; Geoffrey Rapp, "Beyond Protection: Invigorating Incentives for Sarbanes-Oxley Corporate and Securities Fraud Whistleblowers, 87 *Boston University Law Review* 91 (2007); Ernesto Reuben and Matthew Stephenson, "Nobody likes a rat: On the willingness to report lies and the consequences thereof," 93 *Journal of Economic Behavior & Organization* 384 (Sept. 2013).

Butler, Jeffrey Vincent and Serra, Danila and Spagnolo, Giancarlo, "Motivating Whistleblowers" (October 23, 2017). *CEIS Working Paper No. 419*, Available at SSRN: https://ssrn.com/abstract=3086671.

See Jeffrey Vincent Butler, Danila Serra, and Giancarlo Spagnolo, Motivating Whistleblowers (Oct. 23, 2017), CEIS Working Paper No. 419, available at SSRN: https://ssrn.com/abstract=3086671 or http://dx.doi.org/10.2139/ssrn.3086671, which concluded: "Law-breaking activities within an organization benefiting the firm at the expense of the general public are widespread but difficult to uncover, making whistleblowing by employees desirable. We employ a novel laboratory experiment to investigate if and how monetary incentives and expectations of social approval or disapproval, and their interactions, affect the decision to blow the whistle. Experimental results show that: i) financial rewards significantly increase the likelihood of whistleblowing."

Act to Prevent Pollution from Ships
U.S. DOJ, Environment and Natural Resources Division. A motion requesting 50 percent whistleblower reward in *U.S. v. Overseas Shipholding Group, Inc.*, 06-CR-10408 (D. Mass, Mar. 15, 2007); *United States v. Sun Ace Shipping Company*, 2:06-cr-00705, "Motion and Memorandum in Support of Award" (D. N.J. Nov. 15, 2006)(motion by U.S. Attorney Christopher Christie); *U.S. v. Efploia Shipping Co. S.A.*, Case 1:11-cr-00652-MJG, Bench Decision *Re: Whistleblower Award* (D. Maryland) (2016).

Corporate/Trade Association Reports
Association of Certified Fraud Examiners, "Report to the Nations on Occupational Fraud and Abuse: Global Fraud Study" (published annually), (available online at https://legacy.acfe.com/report-to-the-nations/2022/); Ethics Resource Center, *Blowing the Whistle on Workplace Misconduct* (Dec. 2010); Corporate Crime Reporter, "Twenty Things You Should Know about Corporate Crime," *Corporate Crime Reporter* (June 12, 2007); Ethics Resource Center, "The Ethics Resource Center's 2011 National Government Ethics Survey: Workplace Ethics in Transition"; Julie Goldberg, "Compliance Officers Take Their Own Path," *New York Law Journal* (Apr. 19, 2007); PricewaterhouseCoopers, Investigations and Forensic Services, "Economic Crime: People, Culture, and Controls; *Winters v. Houston Chronicle*, 795 S.W.2d 723, 727–33 (Tex. 1990) (concurring opinion of Justice Lloyd Doggett); Charles S. Clarke, "Whistleblowers," 7 *The CQ Researcher* 1059 (Congressional Quarterly, Inc. 1997); Transparency International, "Whistleblowing: An Effective Tool in the Fight against Corruption," *Policy Position # 01/2010* (Berlin 2010) (available online at www.transparency.org).

Dodd-Frank Reward Law
Annual Reports, SEC Office of the Whistleblower, available online at https://www.sec.gov/whistleblower; https://www.sec.gov/files/2022_ow_ar.pdf.; Annual Reports, CFTC Office of the Whistleblower, available online at https://www.whistleblower.gov.

Statements from SEC officials: SEC Chairman Jay Clayton (Sept. 2020), "Strengthening Our Whistleblower Program"; SEC Director of Enforcement Stephanie Avakian (Sept. 2020), "Protecting Everyday Investors and Preserving Market Integrity: The SEC's Division of Enforcement"; SEC Commissioner Allison Herren Lee (Sept. 2020), "June Bug vs. Hurricane: Whistleblowers Fight Tremendous Odds and Deserve Better"; Mary Jo White, "Remarks at the Securities Forum" (Oct. 9, 2013), located at https://www.sec.gov/News/Speech/Detail/Speech/1370539872100; Chair White, "The SEC as the Whistleblower's Advocate," published at https://www.sec.gov/news/speech/chair-white-remarks-garrett-institute; SEC Chair Gary Gensler statement on the whistleblower program published on *YouTube*, https://www.youtube.com/watch?v=kgwqO5GrDZY; Chair Gensler's speech praising the SEC program during the 2021 Whistleblower Day, published online at: https://www.sec.gov/news/speech/gensler-whistleblower-celebration.

False Claims Act
Statistics documenting the successful monetary recoveries obtained by the United States under the False Claims Act are available online at U.S. Department of Justice, Civil Division, Commercial Litigation Branch, Civil Fraud Division: *Fraud Statistics—Overview*, published annual at https://www.justice.gov/civil/fraud-section. The 1986-2021 statistics are available at: https://www.justice.gov/opa/press-release/file/1467811/download. The Department of Justice publishes its press releases, which extensively document the amount of money the United States recovers as a result of whistleblower disclosures under the False Claims Act. The recoveries cited in this section are derived from these releases. See U.S. Department of Justice, Civil Division, Commercial Litigation Branch, *Press Releases.*

Statements of DOJ officials: Attorney General on the False Claims Act: Eric Holder, U.S. Department of Justice, "Attorney General Eric Holder Speaks at the 25th Anniversary of the False Claims Act Amendments of 1986" (Jan. 31, 2012); Statement of the Assistant Attorney General on the False Claims Act: Assistant Attorney General, U.S. Department of Justice, "Remarks at American Bar Association's 10th National Institute on the Civil False Claims Act and *Qui Tam* Enforcement" (June 5, 2014).

Internal Revenue Service
Annual Reports, IRS Office of the Whistleblower, available online at https://www.irs.gov/compliance/whistleblower-office.

John A. Koskinen, commissioner, Internal Revenue Service, Remarks at the U.S. Council for International Business–OECD International Tax Conference (June 3, 2014).

Dennis J. Ventry Jr., "Not Just Whistling Dixie: The Case for Tax Whistleblowers in the States," *Villanova Law Review* 59, no. 3 (Aug. 2015); Matthew Allen, "Swiss-U.S. Tax Evasion Saga: Where Are We Now?" (Jan. 2016), www.swissinfo.ch/eng/business/unfinished-business_swiss-us-tax-evasion-saga--where-are-we-now-/41924910; IRS Press Release, "Offshore Compliance Programs Generate $8 Billion."

Documentation regarding the impact of Bradley Birkenfeld's whistleblowing is set forth in Stephen Kohn's article "$13.769 Billion Reasons to Thank Whistleblowers on Tax Day" (Apr. 18, 2016), www.whistleblowersblog.org/2016/04/articles/news/13-769-billion-reasons-to-thank-whistleblowers-on-tax-day.

International
The Organization for Economic Cooperation and Development (OECD) has fully documented the importance of whistleblowers and whistleblower reward laws in detecting foreign corruption. See OECD Phase IV Follow-up Report on U.S.A., documenting that whistleblowers were the number one source of information on foreign bribery, https://www.oecd.org/daf/anti-bribery/united-states-phase-4-follow-up-report.pdf. The OECD's initial Phase IV report was also highly supportive of the Dodd-Frank whistleblower law. https://www.oecd.org/corruption/anti-bribery/United-States-Phase-4-Report-ENG.pdf.

OECD Phase IV Follow-Up Report (2022), https://www.oecd.org/daf/anti-bribery/united-states-phase-4-follow-up-report.pdf; National Whistleblower Center, "FCPA Report," https://www.whistleblowers.org/wp-content/uploads/2018/12/nwc-fcpa-report.pdf; "Whistleblower Reward Programs: An International Framework for the Detection of Corruption and Fraud" (2015); "Bank of England Rebuttal report," https://www.whistleblowers.org/wp-content/uploads/2018/11/boe-report.pdf.

Theo Nyreod and Giancarlo Spagnold, "A Fresh Look at Whistleblower Rewards," published online at: https://papers.ssrn.com/sol3/papers.cfm?abstract_id=3871748; "Myths and Numbers on Whistleblower Rewards," https://onlinelibrary.wiley.com/doi/abs/10.1111/rego.12267; "Rewarding Whistleblowers to Fight Corruption?" online at https://papers.ssrn.com/sol3/papers.cfm?abstract_id=3871748.

Whistleblowing Research Network, "Selected Papers," Chapter 5, "Whistleblowing in the E.U.: The Enforcement Perspective (Sept. 2021).

World Wildlife Federation, Topic Brief, "Whistleblower Protection," published at: https://www.worldwildlife.org/pages/tnrc-topic-brief-whistleblower-protection-an-essential-tool-for-addressing-corruption-that-threatens-the-world-s-forests-fisheries-and-wildlife.

Public Officials
Numerous public officials and members of Congress have made public statements strongly supporting whistleblowers and whistleblower reward laws. Many of these presentations are published on the YouTube channel of the National Whistleblower Center, online at: https://www.youtube.com/@NationalWhistleblowerCenterDC/videos. Video speakers include Senators Charles Grassley, Ron Wyden, Tammy Baldwin, James Lankford, Tammy Duckworth, and Ron Johnson; Representatives John Garamendi, Kathleen Rice, Jackie Speier, and Elijah Cummings; the inspector general of the Department of Justice, the secretary of labor, the director of the Federal Bureau of Investigation, U.S. special counsel, director of the IRS Whistleblower Office, chairman of the SEC. The testimony of the Senate Judiciary chair in support of the False Claims Act: "Statement for the Record by Senator Chuck Grassley of Iowa, Chairman, Senate Judiciary Committee at a House Judiciary Subcommittee on the constitution and Civil Justice Hearing on 'Oversight of the False Claims Act,' Apr. 28, 2016; Testimony of Stephen Kohn before the House Committee on Government Oversight and Reform": https://oversight.house.gov/hearing/restoring-power-purse-legislative-options.

Wildlife Whistleblower Laws
See special report published by the National Whistleblower Center that extensively cites to the award decisions issued by the U.S. Fish and Wildlife Service confirming the key contributions of whistleblowers, published at https://www.whistleblowers.org/wp-content/uploads/2019/09/Wildlife_Report-Sept-2019.pdf.

Academic studies and articles that document the deterrent effect of whistleblower reward laws include:
Professor Dennis J. Ventry, "Not Just Whistling Dixie: The Case for Tax Whistleblowers in the States," 59 *Vill. L. Rev.* 425 (Aug. 2015).

Niels Johannesen and Tim Stolper, "The Deterrence Effect of Whistleblowing: Evidence from Offshore Banking" (2017).

Christine I. Wiedman and Chunmei Zhu, "Do the SEC Whistleblower Provisions of Dodd-Frank Deter Aggressive Financial Reporting?" (2017).

Jaron H. Wilde, "The Deterrent Effect of Employee Whistleblowing on Firms' Financial Misreporting and Tax Aggressiveness" (2017).

Professors Philip Berger and Heemin Lee, "Do Corporate Whistleblower Laws Deter Accounting Fraud?" (2019).

Professor Jetson Leder-Luis, "Whistleblowers, the False Claims Act, and the Behavior of Healthcare Providers" (2019).

Professor Giancarlo Spagnolo and Theo Nyreröd, "SITE Working Paper, No. 44: Myths and Numbers on Whistleblower Rewards," Stockholm Institute of Transition Economics, Stockholm School of Economics (2018).

Ben Johnson, Minnesota House Research Department, "Do Criminal Laws Deter Crime? Deterrence Theory in Criminal Justice Policy: A Primer," available at https://www.leg.mn.gov/docs/2019/other/190398.pdf.

The Swiss banking leaders' response to the Birkenfeld whistleblower reward was documented in an *Agence France-Presse* article, reprinted at https://www.swissinfo.ch/eng/whistleblower-payoff_birkenfeld-reward-may-temptother-bankers/33500198.

Contacts for Whistleblowers

Commodity Futures Trading Commission
Three Lafayette Centre
1155 21st St. NW
Washington, DC 20581
www.whistleblower.gov (website for Office of the Whistleblower)

Department of Defense
Office of Inspector General
Defense Hotline Compliance Complaints
www.dodig.mil/HOTLINE

Equal Employment Opportunity Commission (EEOC)
1801 L St. NW
Washington, DC 20507
www.eeoc.gov

Inspectors General
Ignet/Federal Inspectors General web page
www.ignet.gov

Internal Revenue Service
Whistleblower Office
SE: WO 1111
Constitution Ave. NW
Washington, DC 20224
http://irs.gov/compliance
www.irs.gov/uac/whistleblower-informant-award (Office of the Whistleblower web page)

Merit Systems Protection Board (MSPB)
1615 M Street NW
Washington, DC 20419
(202) 653-7200
(202) 653-7130 (fax)
www.mspb.gov
mspb@mspb.gov

National Whistleblower Center
3238 P St. NW
Washington, DC 20007-2756
(202) 342-1902
www.whistleblowers.org

U.S. Department of Justice
Freedom of Information Act Homepage (FOIA)
www.usdoj.gov/04foia

U.S. Department of Labor
Occupational Safety and Health Administration (OSHA)
200 Connecticut Ave. NW
Washington, DC 20210
www.osha.gov
www.whistleblowers.gov (OSHA whistleblower programs web page)

U.S. Department of Labor
Office of Administrative Law Judges (OALJ)
800 K St. NW, Ste. 400N
Washington, DC 20210
www.oalj.dol.gov

U.S. Office of Special Counsel (OSC)
1730 M St. NW, Ste. 201
Washington, DC 20036-4505
www.osc.gov

U.S. Securities and Exchange Commission
SEC Office of the Whistleblower
100 F St. NE
Mail Stop 5971
Washington, DC 20549
(703) 813-9322 (fax)
www.sec.gov/whistleblower

Index

Abbott Labs, 285
Act to Prevent Pollution from Ships (APPS), 41, 47, 183–187, 185*fig*, 186*fig*
Administrative Procedure Act, 149, 181
administrative remedies/procedures, 245
admissibility, 52
admissions, requests for, 256–257
adverse actions, 242–243
adverse-interest script, 73–74
Affordable Care Act, 202, 262
after-acquired evidence, 54
Age Discrimination Act, 204
Agence France-Presse, 127, 288
Airline Safety Act, 202, 244*fig*, 262
Alcalel-Lucent, 47, 159
Alito, Samuel, 223, 273
Alternative Fines Act, 163
American Association of Port Authorities, 187
American Banker, The, 168
American Bar Association, 117
American Depository Receipts (ADRs), 41, 138, 160, 162
American Health Care Association, 115
American Jobs Creation Act, 275
Americans with Disabilities Act, 204
Amerigroup Insurance, 283
amnesty, 149
Anaconda Wire & Cable Company, 106
Anderle, Renee, 267
Andrew, Michael, 98
anonymity, 4, 7, 27, 75, 81, 132, 139, 140, 144–145, 173
Anonymity-Enhanced Cryptocurrencies (AECs), 169
anti-dumping duties, 46
anti-fraud laws, 16
Anti-Money Laundering Act (AML)
    anonymity and, 7, 9, 77
    confidentiality and, 241
    disclosures and, 250
    importance of, 32
    mandatory filing procedures and, 248
    press and, 98
    retaliation cases and, 202
    top executives and, 81, 84
    wildlife trafficking and, 191
anti-money laundering (AML) requirements, 45, 170
Anti-Money Laundering (AML) Whistleblower Act, 87, 262
Anti-Money Laundering (AML) Whistleblower Enhancement Act, 205
Anti-Money Laundering (AML) Whistleblower Improvement Act, 41, 163, 169
Anti-Money Laundering Improvement Act, 112, 157, 169, 171–173, 175, 195, 196, 205
appeals, 148–149, 181
appropriated funds, awards from, 190
Aquarosa, 184
arbitration agreements, 148
Archdiocese of New Orleans, 283
armed services, 207
Armor Holdings, Inc., 283
Association of Certified Fraud Examiners (ACFE), 30, 37–38
Atkinson, Michael, 237

Atomic Energy and Energy Reorganization Act, 202
attorneys
    affording, 273–276
    attorney-client privilege, 71–72, 81, 251–252
    for corporations/companies, 68, 71–75
    disclosures by, 251–252
    fees for, 74, 124, 274, 275
at-will doctrine, 215
auditors, special rules for, 81–87
Auto Safety Act, 202
auto safety whistleblower law, 7, 97, 110, 177–181
awards. *see* rewards/reward law

B. Braun Melsungen AG, 46
back pay with benefits, 269
Bacon v. United States, 59
BAE Systems, 159
Baer, Bill, 117
balancing test, 51, 58–59
Baltimore Police Department, 98
Baltimore Sun, 98
Banco Central del Uruguay, 43, 164
bank fraud, 42, 45, 205, 244*fig*
Bank Leumin, 45
Bank of America, 167, 283, 285
bank secrecy, 44
Bank Secrecy Act, 7, 43, 112, 169–171, 172, 173, 175, 205
Barko, Harry, 71, 73
Barrday, 46
Bayer Corporation, 285
Bear Stearns, 32–33
Becker, Gary, 278–279, 282, 291
Behnam, Rostin, 151, 164
benchmark manipulation, 43, 153
Benton barracks, 106
Berger, Philip, 290–291
Berman, Howard, 108, 114
Bermuda Monetary Authority, 43, 164
Beverly Enterprises, Inc., 283
Biden, Hunter, 237
Biden, Joe, 169, 237, 288
Bill of Rights, 95, 247
Birkenfeld, Bradley, 45, 110–112, 127, 134, 288
BitMEX, 171, 172, 174
Bittrex, Inc., 169, 171–172, 175
Blanchard v. Bergeron, 276
Blum v. Stenson, 276
BNP Paribas, 47
Board for Correction of Military Records, 207
Boehme, Donna, 67
Boeing, 285
Boese, John T., 117
Bonds v. Leavitt, 230
Bonham v. Dresser Indus., 246
books and records provision, 156–157, 161–162
BP/Amoco, 217, 285
Brazilian Securities Market Commission, 43
Breaux, John, 90, 191
bribery, 41*fig*, 155–165
Bristol-Myers Squibb, 283
Brown & Root, 89–90
burden of proof, 228, 262

Burlington Northern & Santa Fe Railway Co. v. White, 242, 245
Bush, George W., 66, 275
business purpose test, 161

California State Assembly, 215
Cambridge Analytica, 96
Capitol One Bank, 172
Carey v. Piphus, 223
Carnegie-Illinois Steel Corporation, 106
Carnival Corporation, 187
Carter, Jimmy, 235
causation
   evidence of, 243
   proving, 259–263
cell phones, monitoring of, 52
Centers for Disease Control, 212
Central Intelligence Agency (CIA), 234, 235
Ceresney, Andrew, 158
chain of command, bypassing, 251, 259
Challenger disaster, 108
Chevron Corp., 159, 285
Chrysler Corporation, 177
Cicso Systems, 283
Ciena Capital, LLC, 283
Citigroup, 283
City of Ontario v. Quon, 52, 56
City of Riverside v. Rivera, 276
Civil Rights Act, 98, 100, 204, 205, 213, 222, 245, 250, 270, 273
Civil Rights Attorney Fee Awards Act, 273, 276
Civil Rights Tax Relief Act, 275
Civil Service Reform Act, 225, 235, 236
Civiletti, Benjamin, 279–280
CL&P v. SOL, 93
classified information, 99, 233–234
Clauson's Inn, 61
Clayton, Jay, 137, 288
Clean Air Act, 202, 213, 230, 244*fig*, 245
Clean Water Act, 64, 244*fig*
Clinton, Bill, 61, 225, 236
Close the Contractor Fraud Loophole Act, 69
CMAI, 46
Coast Guard, 183–187
coconspirators, 21–23
Code of Professional Conduct, 74
Code of Professional Responsibility, 74
collateral benefits, 15
Comanche Peak nuclear power plant, 89
Comissão de Valores Mobiliários, 164
commodities and futures, *qui tam* laws and, 110
Commodity Exchange Act (CEA)
   anti-retaliation provisions in, 146
   appeals and, 148–149
   arbitration agreements and, 148
   attorneys' fees and, 275
   bank fraud and, 205
   description of, 163–165
   disclosures and, 249, 250
   Dodd-Frank and, 138
   importance of, 155
   international applications of, 150–151
   mandatory filing procedures and, 248
   press and, 98

retaliation and, 199, 204
statute of limitations and, 244*fig*
success of, 150–152
third-party disclosures and, 142
transnational application of, 41, 42, 43, 164
waiver of rights and, 147
Commodity Futures Trading Commission (CFTC)
anonymity and, 8, 9, 11, 140, 144–145
appeals and, 148–149
awards from, 150–151, 152*fig*
banks sanctioned by, 44*fig*
BitMEX and, 174
compliance programs and, 69
disclosures and, 249
FCPA and, 157
filing claim with, 140–149
internal reports and, 77–79
non-U.S. citizens and, 40, 41, 44–45, 165
qui tam laws and, 112
reporting to, 137, 155–165
reports from, 15
reward law and, 14, 140–149
sanctions collected by, 286–287, 287*fig*
scope of authority of, 43
timing and, 33
tips received by, 153*fig*
top executives and, 81, 84–86, 87
transnational application of, 42–45
Whistleblower Office of, 150–152
common law protections, 217
communications
discovery process and, 258
monitoring of, 52–53, 61–64
restrictive agreements barring, 150
compensatory damages, 269–270
compliance departments, 65–69
compliance programs, 71–74, 179–180, 250
Comprehensive Environmental Response, Compensation and Liability Act, 202
computers, monitoring of, 52–53
confidential informants, 7, 15, 27–28, 59, 74, 132, 145, 181, 208
confidentiality, 7–11, 27, 68, 75, 81, 96, 119, 120–121, 131, 147, 180–181
confidentiality agreements, 150
Congress
contacting, 228–229
protections established by, 3–4
reports to, 249
see also individual committees; individual members
Conoco Phillips, 283, 285
Consumer Financial Fraud, 244*fig*
Consumer Financial Protection Act, 202, 262
Consumer Product Safety Act, 202, 244*fig*, 262
Contractor and Grantee Whistleblower Protection Act, 204
Contractor Whistleblower Act, 262
contributing factor threshold, 228, 262
Convention on International Trade in Endangered Species of Wild Flora and Fauna (CITES), 46, 190
corporate integrity agreements, 117
corporations, fraud detection and, 30–31
corporations/companies
attorneys for, 68, 71–75
destruction of evidence and, 53
monitoring by, 52–53

preemption and preclusion and, 218–219
    see also individual entities
corrupt intent, 161
counterclaims, retaliation cases and, 201
court testimony, protection of, 250
COVID-19, 210–212
C.R. Laurence Co., 283
Credit Suisse bank, 45
"Crime and Punishment: An Economic Approach" (Becker), 278
crime as rational economic activity, 278–279, 280
Criminal Anti-Trust Act, 202
Cruden, John, 189
cryptocurrencies, 43, 153, 169, 170–171
Currency Transaction Reports, 175
CVS Corporation, 284
cyber currency, 44

damages, 269–271
Danske Bank, 42, 87, 167–168, 173, 174
Danske Bank Estonia, 167–168
Davis, Roger S., 61–62
deadlines, 243
debentures, 138
"Deep Throat," 95, 225
defective products, 46
Defend Trade Secrets Act, 93, 213
defense contracts, 47
deforestation, 189–192
DeGuelle, Michael J., 208
DeGuelle v. Camilli, 209
Delaware State College v. Ricks, 246
delay, trap of, 32–33
Delery, Stuart, 120
Deltek, Inc., 54–56
Deltek v. Department of Labor, 56, 59
denial, trap of, 34–35
Denson, Jessica, 92
Denson v. Donald J. Trump for President, Inc., 93
Department of Agriculture, 189, 190
Department of Commerce, 190
Department of Defense, 108
Department of Energy, 95
Department of Homeland Security (DHS), 99
Department of Homeland Security v. MacLean, 99, 101
Department of Justice (DOJ)
    amounts recovered by, 29*fig*
    Aquarosa case and, 184
    on bookkeeping requirements, 162
    Danske Bank and, 42, 167–168
    on definition of bribe, 160–161
    Environment and Natural Resources Division, 186, 189
    False Claims Act (FCA) and, 109, 110
    FBI Whistleblower Protection Act and, 236
    FCA recovery statistics and, 282–283
    FCPA and, 157
    on importance of whistleblowers, 159
    on interstate commerce, 160
    offshore banking and, 289
    related action provision and, 195
    reports from, 15
    Ross case and, 32–33
    Vitol, Inc. and, 164

Department of Justice (DOJ) Tax Division, 134
Department of Labor (DOL)
    Administrative Law Judge (ALJ), 200
    Administrative Review Board (ARB), 200
    environmental whistleblower laws and, 230
    Goldstein case and, 66
    Macktal case and, 89, 90
    MAP-21 and, 178
    mine safety and, 207
    press and, 101
    retaliation and, 199–203
    Wensil case, 95
    Whistleblower Protection Program, 90
Department of the Interior, 190, 213
Department of the Treasury, 45, 87, 167–175, 190
Department of Transportation, 47, 177–181
depositions, 256
derivative, futures and options trading, 43, 152
Desert Palace, Inc. v. Costa, 263
destruction of evidence, 57
detection
    comparison of methods of, 30*fig*
    conundrum pertaining to, 279–281
    necessity of, 278–279
deterrent effect, 15, 288–291
Deutsche Bank, 284
Diaz-Robainas v. Florida Power & Light Co., 101
Dickens, Mashima, 267
Digital Realty Trust v. Somers, 35, 69, 249, 250, 253
Director of National Intelligence (DNI), 236–237
directors, special rules for, 81–87
discharge logs, 183–184, 186
"disclosure" statements, 8
disclosure statements, 120, 121–122
discovery process, 227–228, 255–258
discrimination law, 204
discriminatory animus, 243
disgorgement/disgorgement penalties, 139, 141, 163
disparate treatment, 257–258, 260–261
disqualification, 145–146
document requests, 256
documentation
    attorneys' fees and, 274
    discovery process and, 255–258
    internal disclosures and, 68
    IRS and, 131
    see also evidence
documents, removing, 54–56, 57–59
Dodd-Frank Wall Street Reform and Consumer Protection Act
    anonymity and, 7, 8–9, 10, 77, 81, 139
    anti-retaliation provisions in, 146
    complaints received under, 10
    confidentiality and, 241
    constitutional protections and, 9
    culpable persons and, 22–23
    disclosures and, 249
    FCPA and, 157–158
    foreign corruption and, 155
    importance of, 31
    increase in reports after, 16
    internal compliance programs and, 69
    internal disclosures and, 77–78

international applications of, 155–165
NDAs and, 91, 93
non-U.S. citizens and, 158
press and, 97
protections established by, 4
qui tam laws and, 112
related action provision and, 193–196
removing documents and, 58
reporting under, 137–153
retaliation cases and, 203, 204
reward law in, 138–139
success of, 286
top executives and, 81, 84–86
transnational application of, 37, 39–40, 42
wildlife trafficking and, 191
domestic concerns, definition of, 160
Donovan v. R.D. Andersen Constr. Co., 101
Douglas, William, 233
Douglass, Frederick, 103, 247
Drake, Thomas, 234
drug companies, 46, 47, 110
Duke University, 284
Dyck, Alexander, 32

Eastern Ohio Regional Wastewater Authority, 64
EBASCO Constructors, Inc., 65–67
Edelhertz, Herbert, 280
Eli Lilly and Company, 123, 284
Ellsberg, Daniel, 95, 233–234, 281
e-mail, monitoring of, 52–53
Employee Polygraph Protection Act, 204
Employee Retirement Income Security Act, 204
employment cases, 16, 57–58
employment disputes, 27–28
Endangered Species Act, 41, 46, 189–191
endangered species, protection of, 46
English, Vera, 3, 218
enhanced compliance programs, 15
ENI, 159
Enron, 29, 34, 57
Environmental Protection Agency (EPA), 194–195, 223, 229, 230
environmental whistleblower laws, 99, 230, 244*fig*
Equal Opportunity Employment Commission (EEOC), 199, 231
Erhart v. BOFI Holding, Inc., 58, 59
Erickson v. EPA, 230
Espionage Act, 234
European Union, whistleblower protections and, 37
evidence
    after-acquired, 54
    of causation, 243
    circumstantial, 240–241, 260–261
    destruction of, 53, 57
    disclosure statements and, 120
    discovery process and, 255–258
    illegally obtained, 52, 58–59, 131
    preservation of, 53, 63, 256
    retaliation cases and, 201
    see also documentation
exemplary damages, 270
exemptions, 149
exhaustion doctrine, 245

Facebook, 96, 208
Fair Labor Standards Act, 204
False Claims Act (FCA)
    anonymity and, 77
    attorneys' fees and, 275
    bank fraud and, 205
    Barko case and, 71
    cases involving, 125
    confidentiality and, 8, 241
    culpable persons and, 23
    current status of, 113–118
    damages and, 271
    destruction of evidence and, 53
    disclosures and, 250
    effectiveness of, 17
    examples of violations of, 114–115
    expansion of scope of, 114–115
    filing claim under, 118–124
    first to file concept/rule and, 243
    Harvard study on, 31
    health care fraud and, 206–207
    history of, 106–112
    internal disclosures and, 78
    mandatory filing procedures and, 248
    modernization of, 28–29, 281–282, 285, 291
    NDAs and, 92
    online services and, 100
    original, 21, 22, 134, 281–282
    press and, 96–98, 118–119
    protected disclosures and, 249
    protections under, 113
    public health and, 211
    recoveries under, 110*fig*, 116*fig*, 286*fig*
    related action provision and, 195, 196
    removing documents and, 58
    retaliation cases and, 204
    reward law and, 13–14
    reward statistics and, 282–283
    rewards paid under, 116
    state versions of, 216–217, 218
    statute of limitations and, 244*fig*
    timing and, 32–33
    top executives and, 81, 84
    transnational application of, 41, 46
    wildlife trafficking and, 191
False Claims Reform Act, 108, 109
false reporting, 153
Family and Medical Leave Act, 204
FBI Whistleblower Protection Act, 236, 237
Federal Acquisitions Regulations (FAR), 68, 69
Federal Bureau of Investigation (FBI), 234, 236, 265–267
federal employees, 99, 225–231
Federal Obstruction of Justice statute, 93
Federal Railway Safety Act, 249
Federal Rules of Civil Procedure, 200, 219
federal wiretapping law, 62–63
Fifth Amendment, 100
Financial Institutions Reform, Recovery, and Enforcement Act (FIRREA), 205
FinCEN (Financial Crimes Enforcement Network), 167–175
FINRA (Financial Industry Regulatory Authority), 141
First Amendment, 98, 199, 205, 211, 244*fig*, 247, 249, 270, 273
first to file concept/rule, 32–33, 119–120, 121–122, 144, 243

Fish and Wildlife Improvement Act, 46, 190, 192
fixed price contracts, 47
food safety, 244*fig*
Food Safety Act, 202
Fordham v. Fannie Mae, 263
Foreign Bank and Financial Accounts (FBAR) requirements, 129
Foreign Corrupt Practices Act (FCPA)
    anonymity and, 8, 77
    attorney fees and, 74
    awards from, 158
    bribery cases and, 41
    confidentiality and, 241
    description of, 156–158
    Dodd-Frank and, 138, 155–156
    international applications of, 158–160
    jurisdiction of, 160–163
    mandatory filing procedures and, 248
    non-U.S. citizens and, 37
    press and, 98
    qui tam laws and, 110
    related action provision and, 195
    retaliation cases and, 204
    reward law and, 14
    top penalties under, 159*fig*
    transnational application of, 39–42, 159–160
foreign corruption, 153, 155–165
foreign currency, 43, 153, 169
foreign exchange, 44
forex trading, 153
Form 211, 10, 131, 132, 199
Form TCR, 9, 140, 141, 142, 143–144, 146, 148
Fourteenth Amendment, 21
Fraizer v. MSPB, 245
fraud, removing documents and, 58
fraud detection, science of, 30–31
Freedom Mortgage Corp., 284
Freedom of Information Act, 10, 147, 189
front pay, 269

Gacki, Andrea, 171
gag rules, 228
Garcetti v. Ceballos, 222, 223
General Account Office, 116
General Electric Co., 3, 285
General Motors, 178
Genovese organized crime family, 172
Gensler, Gary, 13, 43, 152, 288
Georgia Power Company, 61
Gibson and Dunn, 43, 44, 163–164
Ginsburg, Ruth Bader, 77
GlaxoSmithKline, 284
Glazer, Myron, 26
Glazer, Penina, 26
Glencore International A.G., 43, 151, 164
Goldman Sachs Group, 87
Goldstein, Ronald J., 65, 66–67, 69
Goldstein v. EBASCO, 69
good faith standard, 241–242
government contractors, 29, 106–107, 115. *see also* False Claims Act (FCA)
Grassley, Chuck, 73, 107, 113, 128, 129, 281–282
Grassley Amendment, 133–134
Grava, Dionesio, 205–206

Great Recession (2008), 137
Grimm, Daniel, 160
Guardian, The, 95–96
Gunther, Dinah, 54–56
Gunther v. Deltek, Inc., 54–56

Haddle v. Garrison, 213
Hague, Frank, 106–107
Hague Machine, 106–107
Halliburton v. ARB, 69, 246
Halliburton/Brown & Root, 89
Harlan, John, 61
Harvard School of Business, 31
Harvard University, 285
health care fraud, 206–207
Heck v. Humphrey, 223
heightened pleading standard, 121
Heller v. Champion International, 64
Hensley v. Eckerhart, 276
Hercules, Inc., 285
Hesco Bastion Limited, 47
Hexcel Corporation, 283
Hobby v. Georgia Power Co., 271
Holder, Eric, 111
Hong Kong Securities and Futures Commission, 43, 164
Hospital Corporation of America, 284
hotlines, 65–69
Houston Lighting and Power Co., 65–67
Howard, Jacob M., 21, 23, 106
Huffman v. Office of Personnel Management, 101
Hyundai, 47, 177

illegal logging, 46, 190–191
Immigration and Naturalization Service (INS), 206
immigration law, 205–206
immunity, 23
implied certification, 115
In re Grand Jury, 75
In re KBR, 75, 150
In re Quarles and Butler, 197
In the Matter of KBR, Inc., 93
Infosys Technologies, 46
Ingersoll-Rand, 285
insider trading, 43, 153
"insiders," 21–23
Institute of Internal Auditors, 81, 83
insubordination, 252
Intelligence Authorization Act, 235
intelligence community. *see* national security; *individual agencies*
Intercept, The, 100
internal compliance programs, 71–74, 179–180, 250
internal controls, lack of, 69
internal disclosures, 67–69, 77–79
internal reporting programs, 65–69
Internal Revenue Act
    anonymity and, 77
    top executives and, 81
    transnational application of, 41
Internal Revenue Code
    disclosures and, 250
    mandatory filing procedures and, 248

Internal Revenue Service (IRS)
    anonymity and, 10, 11
    attorneys' fees and, 275
    bank fraud and, 205
    confidentiality and, 7, 241
    contributing factor test and, 262
    filing claim with, 130–135
    internal disclosures and, 78
    money laundering and, 174–175
    press and, 97
    qui tam laws and, 110–112
    related action provision and, 195, 196
    reporting tax fraud to, 127–135
    reports from, 15
    reward law and, 13–14, 129–130, 133–134
    top executives and, 84
    transnational enforcement and, 45
    Whistleblower Office of, 129, 132–134
international application of whistleblower laws, 37–48, 38*fig*, 39*fig*, 42*fig*, 44*fig*
International Convention for the Prevention of Pollution from Ships, 47, 183–187
international corruption, fight against, 38–40
International Monetary Fund, 161
international treaty against foreign bribery, 39–40
International Union for the Conservation of Nature (IUCN), 191–192
interrogatories, 256–257
interstate commerce, 160
IRS Offshore Voluntary Disclosure Program (OVDP), 289
Itochu, 46
IUU fishing, 189–192

Johnson Atoll Chemical Agent Disposal System, 209–210
Joint Committee on Reconstruction, 21
joint ventures, 160
Journalist's Guide to Taping Phone Calls and In-Person Conversations in the 50 States and D.C., A, 62–63
JPMorgan Chase, 167
Julius Baer Group Ltd., 45
jury trials, retaliation cases and, 201

Kavanaugh, Brett, 72
KBR v. U.S. ex rel. Carter, 125, 246
Kellogg Brown & Root et al. v. U.S. ex rel Carter, 33
Kellogg Brown & Root (KBR), 71–73, 91, 150, 159
Kesselheim, Aaron, 26
Khandelwal v. Southern Cal. Ed., 268
Kia, 47, 177
Kirkland & Ellis, 71
"know your customer" (KYC) requirements, 170, 172
knowledge requirement, 162–163, 240–241
Koskinen, John, 127–135
Kropf, Sara, 75
Laboratory Corp. of America, 216
Lacey Act, 41, 46, 189–191
Lane v. Franks, 223
Langer, William, 107
Latham & Watkins, 252
lawyers. *see* attorneys
Lay, Kenneth, 34
Leahy, Patrick, 51, 56
Leder-Luis, Jetson, 291
Lee, Heemin, 290–291
Lewinsky, Monica, 61
Lincoln, Abraham, 21, 106, 107, 108, 134, 281
Lincoln Fabrics, 46

Lloyd-LaFollette Act, 228
local government employees, 222
Lockheed Martin, 284
lodestar calculation, 274
logging, illegal, 46, 190–191
Lopez, German, 61
Lopez, Salvador, 184
Lopez v. United States, 61–62, 63
Los Angeles Department of Water and Power, 284
Louis Dreyfus Group, 46
Luxembourg Commission de Surveillance du Secteur Financier, 43, 164

Macktal, Joseph J., Jr., 89–90
MacLean, Robert J., 99
Madison, James, 95, 247
Madoff, Bernard, 137
Maine Whistleblower Protection Act, 210
make whole remedy, 13, 269–271
Management Information Technologies v. Alyeska Pipeline, 11
mandatory requirements checklist, 239
Manning, Chelsea, 100
Marine Defenders handbook, 187
market manipulation, 43
MARPOL Protocol, 47, 183–187
Marshall, Thurgood, 221
Martin, Lynn, 66–67
materiality, definition of, 115–116
McAuliffe, Christa, 108
MCI/WorldCom, 285
McKennon v. Nashville Banner Publishing, 54, 56
Medicaid, 46, 110, 110*fig*, 115, 122, 123, 206–207, 211, 218, 291
Medicare, 13, 46, 110, 110*fig*, 123, 206–207, 211, 291
Mellon Bank, 285
Merck, 284
Merit Systems Protection Board (MSPB), 225–226, 227*fig*, 230, 231
Mexico Comisión Nacional Bancaria y de Valores, 43, 164
Migrant and Seasonal Agricultural Workers Act, 204
Military Whistleblower Protection Act, 207
Mine Health and Safety Act, 207, 245
Mine Health and Safety Commission, 207
mine safety, 207
misconduct, removing documents and, 58
Missouri v. Jenkins, 276
mixed cases, 230
"Monetary Rewards for Wildlife Whistleblowers" (Kohn), 192
money, following, 105
money laundering, 14, 43, 44, 45, 81, 97, 110, 167–175. *see also* Anti-Money Laundering Act (AML)
money services businesses (MSBs), 169, 175
money transmission, 169
Montgomery v. IRS, 11, 135
Morton-Thiokol, 108
Mosbaugh, Allen, 61
Mosbaugh v. Georgia Power Co., 64
motive, proving, 259–263
motor vehicle safety, 47
Motor Vehicle Safety Act, 32, 248, 250
Motor Vehicle Safety Whistleblower Act, 14, 98, 241, 262
Moving Ahead for Progress in the 21st Century Act (MAP-21), 177–178

NASA (National Aeronautics Space Administration), 108
NASDAQ, 138
National Highway Transportation Safety Administration (NHTSA), 177, 178, 181

National Labor Relations Act, 204
National Nurses Union (NNU), 212
National Nursing Home Initiative, 211
National Oceanic and Atmospheric Administration (NOAA), 189
national security, 233–237
National Security Agency (NSA), 235
National Transit Security Act, 202
National Whistleblower Appreciation Day, 237
National Whistleblower Center (NWC), 91, 207
Nat'l R.R. Passenger Corp. v. Morgan, 246
NetCracker Technology Corp., 284
Neustar, Inc., 150
New Deal, 106
New York State Bar Association Committee on Professional Ethics, 73–74, 75
New York Stock Exchange, 138, 141
New York Times, 95–96, 233
New York Times v. Sullivan, 223
news media, 95–101, 118–119, 173, 201, 229
Nichols, Philip M., 157
Niswander v. Cincinnati, 59
Nixon, Richard, 49, 95, 225, 233
NLRB v. Scrivener, 245
nondisclosure agreements (NDAs), 58, 89–93, 147
non-prosecution agreement, 149
Northrop Grumman, 284
Nuclear Regulatory Commission (NRC), 3, 89–90
nuclear safety laws, 61, 245*fig*
nuclear whistleblower laws, 66–67, 99
Nyreröd, Theo, 290

obstruction of justice, 208, 248
Occupational Safety and Health Act (OSHA), 99, 209–210, 245*fig*
Occupational Safety and Health Administration (OSHA), 90–91, 178, 200, 209–210
oceans, pollution of, 47, 183–187
O'Connor, Sandra Day, 260
O'Day v. McDonnell Douglas, 59
Office Depot, 285
Office of Foreign Assets Control (OFAC), 170–171, 172
Office of Professional Responsibility, 236
OfficeMax, 285
offshore banking, 45
off-the-books accounting, 156, 161
oil drilling, 46
one-party taping, 61–63
online services, 100–101
Opinion 650, 73–74
Oracle, 284
Organization for Economic Co-operation and Development (OECD), 39–40, 48, 155–156
Organization of American States, 161
Organon International, 46
original information, 142
"original source," 118–119
outside speaking/writing rules, 223, 229–230
Owens v. Okure, 244*fig*

Pacheco v. Waldrop, 101
partners, special rules for, 81–87
Passaic Valley Sewerage Commissioners v. U.S. Dept. of Labor, 245
pendant jurisdiction, 219
Pentagon Papers, 233
Perdue v. Kenny, 273–274, 276
perjury, 100, 215

Petermann, Peter, 215
Pfizer, Inc., 284
Phillips, Franklin, 105
Phillips v. Interior Bd. Mine Op., 35
Pickering, Marvin, 221
Pickering v. Board of Education, 101, 221, 222, 223, 229
Pipeline Safety Act, 202
Pipeline Safety Improvement Act, 262
pleading requirements, 121
political asylum, 205–206
Politics of Internal Auditing, 83
Power of Attorney, 135
Pratt & Whitney, 284
preclusion, 218–219
preemption, 218–219
Prendergast, Tom, 107
prepublication clearance policies, 230, 234
press, 95–101, 118–119, 173, 201, 229
pretext, proving, 258, 259–263
Princeton Review, 285
Principles of Criminology (Sutherland), 277–278
Privacy Rights Clearinghouse, 52
prosecution, risk of, 23
protected activity, 201, 241–242
protected disclosures, 240, 247–253
protected disclosures under, concept of, 15
Protection of Intelligence Community Whistleblowers Act, 231, 235–236, 237
psychological records, 257
public disclosure, 118–119, 142
public employees, 98
Public Health Service (PHS) Commissioned Corps, 212
public health/public health service, 210–212
public policy exception, 218
public policy tort, 215–216
publicly traded companies, FCPA and, 156–157, 162
Pucillo, Domenick, 172
punitive damages, 270
Purdue Frederick Co., 284
Putin, Vladimir, 167

Quest Diagnostics, 216
Quest Diagnostics case, 252
qui tam laws
    civil cases and, 124
    damages and, 271
    Dodd-Frank and, 137–139
    False Claims Act (FCA) and, 106–107, 109, 110, 281–282
    FCA and, 28–29
    Harvard study on, 31
    Howard and, 21
    IRS and, 135
    NDAs and, 92
    press and, 96–97
    state laws and, 216, 218
    success of, 289–290
    tax fraud and, 129

Racketeer Influenced and Corrupt Organizations Act (RICO), 208–209
Railroad Safety Act, 262
Railway Safety Act, 202
Ranbaxy Laboratories, 47
Rand Corporation, 233

Reagan, Ronald, 282
recruitment-in-place (RIP), 27–28
refusing to violate law, 250
Reich, Robert, 61
reinstatement, 269
related action provision, 173, 193–196
removing documents, 54–56, 57–59
Reporters Committee for Freedom of the Press, 62–63
retaliation
    employment cases and, 16
    False Claims Act (FCA) and, 123
    federal employees and, 225–231
    federal laws governing, 199–214
    First Amendment and, 199, 221 223
    gag provisions and, 90
    protection from, 15
    removing documents and, 58
    SEA and CEA on, 146
    state laws governing, 215–219
    tax fraud and, 129
    top executives and, 83–84
    Whistleblower Protection Act (WPA) and, 226–227
    winning cases involving, 239–246
Reuben, Ernesto, 25, 26
rewards/reward law
    admissibility and, 52
    anonymity and, 8, 9–10
    Anti-Money Laundering Improvement Act and, 173, 174
    APPS and, 184–185
    attorneys' fees and, 275
    CFTC and, 140–149, 287fig
    culpable persons and, 22–23
    disclosures to Congress and, 249
    disqualification and, 145–146
    Dodd-Frank and, 138–139
    dos and don'ts regarding, 18
    effectiveness of, 16–17, 30–31
    employment cases versus, 16
    FCA and, 113, 116, 285–286, 286fig
    filing deadlines and, 243
    internal disclosures and, 77–78
    MAP-21 and, 178–179
    overview of, 13–20
    press and, 96–97
    protected disclosures and, 248
    qui tam laws and, 111–112
    scope of, 193–196
    SEC and, 14fig, 140–149
    size of awards and, 18–20
    statistics on, 282–283
    tax fraud and, 129–130, 133–134
    top executives and, 84–86
    transnational application of, 40–48
    for violations not covered by law, 193–196
    wildlife trafficking and, 190
Reyl, Francois, 127
Reyl & Co, 127
right to privacy, 59, 62
Rivera, Yarushka, 115
Roberts, John, 99
Roche Biomedical Laboratories, 285
Rockwell International, 285

Rockwell International case, 122
Roosevelt, Theodore, 228
Rosenbaum, James, 267
Ross, Eugene, 32–33
Royal Dutch Shell, 46
Ruhe v. Masimo Corp., 58, 59
Rule 11, 201
Rules of Civil Procedure, 121, 256

Safe Drinking Water Act, 202, 230, 244*fig*
SAFETEAM, 66–67
sanctions, retaliation cases and, 201
sanctions whistleblower laws, 81
sanctions-busting, 167–175
Sandell, Thomas, 216
SandRidge Energy, 146
Sanjour v. EPA, 101, 223, 229
Sarbanes-Oxley Act (SOX)
    anonymity and, 77
    anti-retaliation provisions in, 146
    arbitration agreements and, 148
    confidentiality and, 68, 69
    contributing factor test and, 262
    corporate code of silence and, 89
    disclosures and, 249
    evidence and, 53, 55
    internal disclosures and, 252
    Leahy on, 51
    press and, 100, 101
    retaliation cases and, 202, 203
    statute of limitations and, 245*fig*
    waiver of rights and, 147
Savannah River Site nuclear weapons complex, 95
S.C. Johnson & Son, Inc., 208
Schering Plough, 284
Science Applications International Corporation, 285
Scooter Store, The, 285
Seaman's Protection Act, 202
Seamen Whistleblower Protection Act, 262
Seater v. Southern Cal. Ed., 268
Securitas GmbH Werkschutz, 47
Securities and Exchange Commission (SEC)
    anonymity and, 7, 9, 11, 140, 144–145
    appeals and, 148–149
    attorney conduct and, 252
    awards from, 14*fig*, 149–150, 150*fig*
    on bookkeeping requirements, 162
    complaints received by, 10, 16
    compliance programs and, 69
    culpable persons and, 22
    Danske Bank and, 167
    on definition of bribe, 160–161
    deterrent effect and, 291
    disclosures and, 249
    exemptions and, 149
    FCPA and, 157
    filing claim with, 140–149
    freedom of the press and, 96
    on importance of whistleblowers, 159
    internal reports and, 77–79
    international rewards and, 42
    on interstate commerce, 160

Macktal case and, 91–92
nondisclosure agreements and, 58
non-U.S. citizens and, 40, 165
press and, 98
qui tam laws and, 112
reporting to, 137–153, 155–165
reports from, 15
reward law and, 14–15, 140–149, 193–195
Ross case and, 32–33
success of whistleblower program of, 287–288
timing and, 33
tips received by, 17*fig*, 156*fig*
top executives and, 81, 84–86, 87
Whistleblower Office of, 148
Securities Exchange Act (SEA)
anti-retaliation provisions in, 146
appeals and, 148–149
arbitration agreements and, 148
attorneys' fees and, 275
bank fraud and, 205
damages and, 271
Danske Bank and, 174
disclosures and, 249, 250
Dodd-Frank and, 138
mandatory filing procedures and, 248
retaliation cases and, 204
rewards/reward law and, 193
statute of limitations and, 244*fig*
third-party disclosures and, 143
transnational application of, 41
waiver of rights and, 147
securities fraud, 110
security clearances, 231
self-help tactics, 51–56
self-regulatory organizations (SROs), 141
Senate Judiciary Committee, 17
Senate Report on the Civil Rights Attorney Fee Awards Act, 273
Serono, 46
Shell Oil Company, 285
Sheridan, Paul, 177–178
Siemens, 159, 216
Silkwood, Karen, 207
Simon, Joshua B., 71, 75
Simpson, Alan K., 90
Smithkline Beecham Clinical Laboratories, 285
Snepp, Frank W., III,, 234
Snepp v. United States, 234
Snowden, Edward, 96, 234, 235
Solid Waste Disposal Act, 203, 230
Song, John, 71, 75
South Texas Project, 65–67
Spagnolo, Giancarlo, 290
S.p.A./Snamprogetti Netherlands, 159
special damages, 269–270
spoofing, 43, 152
Sprint, 123, 216
state employees, 222
State Farm v. U.S. ex rel. Rigsby, 125
state funds, False Claims Act (FCA) and, 122–123
state laws, 215–219
State of California, 285
statute of limitations, 32, 203, 218, 227, 243–245, 244–245*fig*

statutory fee provisions, 273
Stephenson, Matthew, 25, 26
stock exchanges, 138, 156, 160
Streep, Meryl, 207
Superfund Act, 230, 244*fig*
suppression efforts, 82*fig*, 83*fig*
Supreme Foodservice FZE, 46
Surface Mining Act, 213
Surface Transportation Act, 202, 262
suspicious activity reports (SARs), 170, 172, 175
Sutherland, Edwin H., 277–278, 282, 291
swaps, 43, 152
SwissInfo, 288

Taft, William, 228
Takata air bags, 178
taping conversations, 54–56, 61–64, 201
tariff obligations, 46
Tax Court, 129, 133, 195
Tax Evasion and Underpayments, 31
tax fraud, 45, 110–112, 127–135, 208
tax whistleblower laws, 81, 110–112
Taxpayer First Act, 202, 249
TCR complaint process, 9
Teamsters Union, 215
Tenet Healthcare, 285
testing certificates, 47
Texaco Oil, 285
text messages, monitoring of, 52
third-party disclosures, 142–143
third-party liability, 162–163
third-party subpoenas, 201, 257
Thomas, Clarence, 260
Thune, John, 178
Tides v. Boeing, 101
Title VII, 100, 101, 204, 245, 273
Toxic Substances Control Act, 203
Toyo, Inc., 46
Toyobo Co. of Japan, 285
trade secrets, 213
Transparency International, 155
transportation safety laws, 245*fig*
traps, 25–35
Tripp, Linda, 61, 96, 225
Trump, Donald, 92, 225, 237, 288
Turner, Jane, 265–267
Tuttle, Elbert, 7

UBS bank fraud, 45, 110–112, 127, 288, 289
UK Financial Conduct Authority, 43, 164
Ukraine, war in, 112
"Ukraine whistleblower," 237
union grievance procedures, 204
United Kingdom's Serious Fraud Office, 43, 164
United National Environment Program, 189
United Nations Convention against Corruption, 37
United States Strategy on Countering Corruption, 48, 155, 167
United States v. Efploia, 37
United States v. Gianatasio, 59
United States v. Jacobsen, 59
United States v. National Treasury Employees Union, 229
United Technologies, 285

Universal Health Services, Inc., 115
Universal Health Services v. U.S. ex rel. Escobar, 211
University of Chicago, 32
University of Chicago Booth School of Business, 30–31
University of Pennsylvania, 285
University of Phoenix, 285
University of Toronto, 30–31
Upjohn Co. v. United States, 75
U.S. attorneys general, disclosures to, 249–250
U.S. Chamber of Commerce, 72, 84, 115
U.S. Chamber of Commerce Institute for Legal Reform, 17
U.S. Coast Guard National Response Center, 187
U.S. Constitution, anonymity and, 9
U.S. ex rel. Barko v. Halliburton Co., 75
U.S. ex rel. Escobar v. Universal Health Services, 125
U.S. ex rel. Polansky v. Executive Health, 125
U.S. ex rel. Schutte v. SuperValu, 125
U.S. Fish and Wildlife Service (FWS), 189–192
U.S. House of Representatives Committee on the Judiciary, Subcommittee on Crime, 279
U.S. Office of Legal Counsel, 230
U.S. Office of Special Counsel (OSC), 226–227, 231
U.S. Patriot Act, 100
U.S. Senate Banking Committee, 137
U.S. Senate Finance Committee, 129
U.S. Senate Judiciary Committee, 105, 108
U.S. Senate Subcommittee on Nuclear Regulation, 89–90
U.S. v. Edwards, 208
U.S. v. Efploia Shipping Co. S.A., 187
U.S. v. New York Times, 233
U.S. v. Odfjell, 184
U.S. v. Purdue Pharma, 93
U.S. v. Sun Ace Shipping, 17
USA v. Noble Drilling, 183
USA v. Omni Corporation, 185
USA v. Overseas Shipholding Group, 185
USAA Federal Savings Bank, 172

Valeant Pharmaceuticals, 46
Van Asdale, Lena, 252
Van Asdale, Shawn, 252
Ventry, Dennis, 289–290
venue requirements, 120
Veterans Administration, 46
Vietnam War, 233
virtual currency exchanges, 171, 172
visa violations, 46
Vitol, Inc., 43, 151, 163–164
voluntary requirement, 32–33, 141–142, 179

Walder v. Bio-Rad Laboratories, Inc., 219
Walgreens, 216, 285
Walter, Frances, 107
Warren, Earl, 62
Washington Post, 95, 233
Water Pollution Control Act, 202
Watergate, 49, 233
Watkins, Sherron, 34
WB-APP, 143–144, 148
Webb v. Government for the District of Columbia, 56
websites/Wikileaks, 100–101
Wegelin & Co., 45, 288–289
Wensil, Roger, 95

Whistleblower 13412-12W v. Commissioner, 135
Whistleblower 14106-10W v. Commissioner, 11, 135
Whistleblower 21276-13W v. Commissioner, 135
Whistleblower Award Proceeding No. 2021-91, 196
Whistleblower Protection Act (WPA), 99, 212, 217, 225–231, 262
Whistleblower Protection Enhancement Act, 225, 253
Whistleblowers, The (Glazer and Glazer), 26
White, Mary Jo, 1, 28, 138, 146, 287
white-collar crime, problems with detection of, 277–281
Whitehurst, Frederic, 234, 236
"Who Blows the Whistle on Corporate Fraud?" (Dyck), 30–31, 32, 281
Wikileaks, 100–101
wildlife trafficking, 46, 189–192
Wilkey, Malcolm, 105
Wilkinson, Howard, 167
Wilkinson, J. Harvie, 98
Will v. Michigan, 223
willful blindness standard, 162–163
Winner, Reality, 96, 100, 234
Wirtz v. Continental, 7
Wisdom, John Minor, 90
witness protection, 213
Wood, Roger, 209–210
Woodward, Bob, 49, 95
workplace safety, 209–210
work-product privilege, 72, 81
World Bank, 161
WorldCom, 29
Wrighten v. Metro. Hosps., Inc., 101
Wylie, Christopher, 95–96

Youssef, Bassem, 234

Zoladz Construction Co., 285